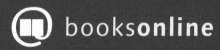 **booksonline**

Read this book online today:

With SAP PRESS BooksOnline we offer you online access to knowledge from
the leading SAP experts. Whether you use it as a beneficial supplement or as
an alternative to the printed book, with SAP PRESS BooksOnline you can:

- Access your book anywhere, at any time. All you need is an Internet connection.
- Perform full text searches on your book and on the entire SAP PRESS library.
- Build your own personalized SAP library.

The SAP PRESS customer advantage:

Register this book today at *www.sap-press.com* and obtain exclusive free trial
access to its online version. If you like it (and we think you will), you can choose to
purchase permanent, unrestricted access to the online edition at a very special price!

Here's how to get started:

1. Visit *www.sap-press.com*.
2. Click on the link for SAP PRESS BooksOnline and login (or create an account).
3. Enter your free trial license key, shown below in the corner of the page.
4. Try out your online book with full, unrestricted access for a limited time!

Your personal free trial **license key**
for this online book is:

eb4u-5rsc-tq9g-hxyf

Applying Real-World BPM in an SAP® Environment

 **PRESS**

SAP PRESS is a joint initiative of SAP and Galileo Press. The know-how offered by SAP specialists combined with the expertise of the Galileo Press publishing house offers the reader expert books in the field. SAP PRESS features first-hand information and expert advice, and provides useful skills for professional decision-making.

SAP PRESS offers a variety of books on technical and business related topics for the SAP user. For further information, please visit our website: *www.sap-press.com*.

Snabe, Rosenberg, Møller, Scavillo
Business Process Management — the SAP Roadmap
2009, 411 pp., hardcover
ISBN 978-1-59229-231-8

Carsten Ziegler, Thomas Albrecht
BRFplus–Business Rule Management
for ABAP Applications
2010, approx. 350 pp., hardcover
ISBN 978-1-59229-293-6

Jan Rauscher, Volker Stiehl
The Developer's Guide to the
SAP NetWeaver Composition Environment
2008, 365 pp., hardcover, with DVD
ISBN 978-1-59229-171-7

Stefan Hack, Markus A. Lindemann
Enterprise SOA Roadmap
2008, 417 pp., hardcover
ISBN 978-1-59229-162-5

Ann Rosenberg, Greg Chase, Rukhshaan Omar,
James Taylor, and Mark von Rosing

Applying Real-World BPM in an SAP® Environment

Galileo Press

Bonn · Boston

Galileo Press is named after the Italian physicist, mathematician and philosopher Galileo Galilei (1564–1642). He is known as one of the founders of modern science and an advocate of our contemporary, heliocentric worldview. His words *Eppur si muove* (And yet it moves) have become legendary. The Galileo Press logo depicts Jupiter orbited by the four Galilean moons, which were discovered by Galileo in 1610.

Editor Florian Zimniak
Developmental Editor Laura Korslund
Copyeditor Ruth Saavedra
Cover Design Silke Braun and Graham Geary
Photo Credit iStockphoto/66North/5275255
Layout Design Vera Brauner
Production Manager Kelly O'Callaghan
Assistant Production Editor Graham Geary
Typesetting Publishers' Design and Production Services, Inc.
Printed and bound in Canada

ISBN 978-1-59229-343-8
© 2011 by Galileo Press Inc., Boston (MA)
1st Edition 2011

Library of Congress Cataloging-in-Publication Data
Applying real-world BPM in an SAP environment / Ann Rosenberg ... [et al.]. — 1st ed.
  p. cm.
Includes bibliographical references and index.
ISBN-13: 978-1-59229-343-8
ISBN-10: 1-59229-343-3
1. Automation. 2. Industrial management—Data processing. 3. Performance technology. 4. Management information systems. 5. SAP ERP. I. Rosenberg, Ann.
 HD45.2.A67 2011
 658.4'01—dc22
 2010042699

Contents at a Glance

PART I   Business Process Transformation 21

1   The Importance of a Business Model 23
2   Business Model Transformation Toward the Service-Oriented
     Enterprise 55
3   Practical Example: How to Develop Performance and
     Value Drivers 85
4   The Holistic Approach: Combining BPM with Value and
     Performance Management, Enterprise Architecture,
     Governance, and SOA 105
5   Conclusion 121

PART II   BPM Case Studies from the Real World 123

6   Observing How SAP Customers Approach BPM: The Gap
     between Business and IT in BPM Projects 125
7   First Applications: Enterprise Information Management 135
8   Industry-Specific Processes 161
9   BPM, Business Transformation, and Continuous Process
     Improvement 197
10   Good Ideas for BPM 217
11   Planning for BPM Transformation 235
12   Conclusion 295

PART III   BPM Anatomy for Implementations 297

13   Methodology and Governance 299
14   BPM Tools — From Modeling to Execution 413
15   Process-Based Implementation Content 553
16   Enablement and Communities 565
17   Conclusion 607

PART IV   Future Outlook 613

18   Future Trends for BPM 615

Appendices 637

A   IT Performance and Value Management Research 639
B   Value Driver Processes Sorted After Strategic, Tactical, and Operational
     Levels 641
C   Bibliography 657
D   The Authors 673

Dear Reader,

Since the publication of SAP PRESS's first book on Business Process Management in early 2009, *Business Process Management — the SAP Roadmap*, BPM has proven to be one of the most dynamic areas in the entire SAP arena: In an impressive manner, SAP has managed to grow both the functionality of their technology products related to BPM, as well as the awareness of and commitment to BPM in their customer base.

This book's contents and its developmental history greatly illustrate the dynamics and breadth of the topic: Covering background, project approach, technology, and customer use-cases, it describes SAP's BPM approach comprehensively and from many different perspectives. Having been involved in all of the conceptual discussions around this book, I know how much time, work, and passion the five authors have invested in interviewing customers, motivating contributors, and editing the material towards the creation of a consistent publication. I am sure that this book will help you, the reader, to get started with your BPM project.

We appreciate your business, and welcome your feedback. Your comments and suggestions are the most useful tools to help us improve our books for you, the reader. We encourage you to visit our website at *www.sap-press.com* and share your feedback about this work.

Thank you for purchasing a book from SAP PRESS!

Florian Zimniak
Publishing Director, SAP PRESS

Galileo Press
Boston, MA

florian.zimniak@galileo-press.com
www.sap-press.com

Contents

Foreword 17

Introduction 19

PART I Business Process Transformation **21**

1 The Importance of a Business Model **23**

1.1   Explaining the Difference in Overall Output Performance 23
1.2   Revisit the Enterprise Model During Economic Turmoil 27
1.3   Core Competitive and Core Differentiated Positioning 29
1.4   A Historic View of Business Models 31
     1.4.1   The Development of Business Model Concepts 35
     1.4.2   Business Model Component Development 36
1.5   New Form of the Business Model Concept 40
     1.5.1   Resources 43
     1.5.2   Capabilities and Abilities 44
1.6   The Logic of a Business Model Framework Based on
        Competencies 46
     1.6.1   Flexible and Free Connection of the Competencies 48
     1.6.2   Consistency and Union of the Competencies 49
1.7   Organizing Business Competencies 49
1.8   Summary and Conclusion 52

**2 Business Model Transformation Toward the Service-Oriented
Enterprise** **55**

2.1   Adaptation of the Service-Oriented Enterprise 56
     2.1.1   Adaptation Driver: Increased Service Orientation 58
     2.1.2   Adaptation Driver: Networked Business 58
     2.1.3   Adaptation Driver: Power-Shift from Supply- to
                Demand-Side 59
     2.1.4   Service-Oriented Enterprise as Goal – Transformation
                as Journey 59
2.2   Business Transformation Change Levers 60
     2.2.1   Change Lever: Customer Offering 61

2.2.2   Change Lever: Business Model 62

2.2.3   Change Lever: Value Creation Coordination 63

2.3   Business Transformation Case Studies 64

2.3.1   Case Study: Rolls Royce Total Care 64

2.3.2   Case Study: Arvato Lead Logistics Services 65

2.3.3   Case Study: Hewlett Packard Managed
Printing Solutions 66

2.3.4   Lessons Learned from the Cases 67

2.4   Information Technology as Dynamic Capability of Business
Enablement 69

2.5   Process-Centric IT Lifecycle Management 73

2.5.1   Closing the Loop of Business Process Management 73

2.5.2   Accelerating the Process Lifecycle 75

2.6   Reaping the Promised Value of Reusing Information and
Services 77

2.7   Summary and Recommendations 79

3   Practical Example: How to Develop Performance and Value Drivers 85

3.1   The Need for Performance and Value Creation 86

3.2   Performance and Value Drivers 88

3.2.1   Value Planning and Identification 92

3.2.2   Value Creation 94

3.3   Dimensions of PPI Measurement 101

3.4   Summary and Conclusions 102

4   The Holistic Approach: Combining BPM with Value and Performance Management, Enterprise Architecture, Governance, and SOA 105

4.1   Applying the Different Approaches 106

4.2   Innovate Your EA Framework with BPM and Value and
Performance Management Principles 107

4.3   Solution Transformation – Harmonizing Enterprise
Architecture, BPM, and SOA 114

4.4   Summary and Conclusions 117

5 Conclusion **121**

PART II   BPM Case Studies from the Real World **123**

6   Observing How SAP Customers Approach BPM: The Gap between Business and IT in BPM Projects **125**

6.1   BPM Usage Clusters in Industry and Application Use Cases 127
    6.1.1   Most Common Industries Adopting BPM 127
    6.1.2   Most Common Applications for BPM 128
6.2   Typical Business Requirements Satisfied by BPM 129
    6.2.1   Articulating and Prioritizing Business Goals and Problems 129
    6.2.2   Qualifying Questions to Instate BPM Projects 130
    6.2.3   Orchestrating Dependent Actions in a Sequence 130
    6.2.4   Orchestrating Actions that Bridge Multiple Systems 131
    6.2.5   Orchestrating Actions Between Organizations 132
    6.2.6   Architecting Processes for Change 132
    6.2.7   Process-Specific User Interfaces 133
    6.2.8   Measuring and Monitoring Business Processes 134

7   First Applications: Enterprise Information Management **135**

7.1   INVISTA: Enabling Cross-System Master Data Management 136
    7.1.1   Background 137
    7.1.2   BPM Solution 138
7.2   Ericsson: Using Business Rules to Enable Globalization of Supplier Master Data Governance 141
    7.2.1   Background 142
    7.2.2   BPM Solution 143
7.3   SAP IT: Accelerating Postmerger Data Enrichment and Migration 150
    7.3.1   Background 150
    7.3.2   BPM Solution 154

8 Industry-Specific Processes 161

8.1   Patrimonio Hipotecaria: Supporting Unique Mortgage Processes
       Attached to SAP for Banking 163
       8.1.1   Background 164
       8.1.2   BPM Solution 166
8.2   Coca-Cola Erfrischungsgetränke AG: Promotion Material
       Planning and Procurement as an Extension of SAP Trade
       Promotion Management 171
       8.2.1   Background 171
       8.2.2   BPM Solution 174
8.3   GISA: Increased Competition in Utilities Demands Efficient
       Customer Service Connections 179
       8.3.1   Background 179
       8.3.2   BPM Solution 181
8.4   Siemens IT Solutions and Services: Balancing Standardization
       and Customizability in a New Solution 184
       8.4.1   Background 184
       8.4.2   BPM Solution 186
8.5   RS Components: Automating Supply Chain Collaboration for
       Inventory Planning and Supplier Performance Management 189
       8.5.1   Background 190
       8.5.2   BPM Solution 191

9 BPM, Business Transformation, and Continuous Process Improvement 197

9.1   KAESER KOMPRESSOREN: Transforming from a Products
       Company to a Service Company 197
       9.1.1   Background 198
       9.1.2   BPM Solution 199
9.2   Braskem S. A.: Realizing the Value of Efficiency and Visibility in
       Supplier Processes 205
       9.2.1   Background 206
       9.2.2   BPM Solution 209

10 Good Ideas for BPM 217

10.1 Public Sector: Potholes and Green Area Maintenance –
Taxpayers Get More for Their Buck 217
    10.1.1 Background 218
    10.1.2 BPM Solution 221
10.2 Airline: Streamlining the Maintenance Process for the
Transportation Industry with BPM 227
    10.2.1 Background 228
    10.2.2 BPM Solution 231

11 Planning for BPM Transformation 235

11.1 Hospira: Integrating Architecture to Become Process-Centric 235
    11.1.1 Company Profile 236
    11.1.2 Need for Business Process Management Discipline 237
    11.1.3 Architecture Practice and BPM 238
    11.1.4 BPM Solution 241
    11.1.5 BPM Center of Excellence (CoE) 246
    11.1.6 Building a BPM Community of Practice 249
    11.1.7 Lessons Learned 249
    11.1.8 What's Ahead? 250
11.2 Danish Defense: Value Drivers in Corporate Businesses 251
    11.2.1 The Importance of Having the Right Business
Model in Place 253
    11.2.2 The Need to Describe the Business Model 255
    11.2.3 The Need for Business Governance 257
    11.2.4 Implementing BPM in the Danish Defense 268
    11.2.5 BPM and Core Business 282
    11.2.6 Danish Armed Forces BPM and Technology Delivery 284
    11.2.7 Terminology and Conventions 287
    11.2.8 Technology Delivery 290
    11.2.9 Implementation of Change 291
    11.2.10 Conclusion 293

12 Conclusion 295

PART III BPM Anatomy for Implementations 297

13 Methodology and Governance 299

13.1 SOA Survey 300
    13.1.1 Feedback Survey for the Methodology 300
    13.1.2 Key Observations and Trends in SOA Projects 301
    13.1.3 Summary 308
13.2 How to Combine Business Modeling and Process Modeling 308
    13.2.1 Business Model Innovation and Optimization 309
    13.2.2 How To Create Value in Connecting the Business
         Model and Processes 309
    13.2.3 The Limitation of Having Only a Process Focus 311
    13.2.4 The Holistic Approach – Creating Value by Connecting
         the Business Model to the Processes 315
    13.2.5 Business Model Approach to Connecting Strategy to
         Business Model and Business Model to Operational
         Model (Processes) 316
    13.2.6 Process Identification and Harmonization on the
         Strategic Level 324
    13.2.7 Process Identification and Harmonization on the
         Tactical Level 325
    13.2.8 Harmonization through a Simple Pattern Using the
         ICASIO Approach 327
    13.2.9 Definition and Validation of Process Step Variants
         Using the RACI Model Approach 329
    13.2.10 Process Identification and Harmonization on the
         Operational Level 332
    13.2.11 Conclusion 337
13.3 ASAP Methodology 7 Core 339
    13.3.1 Project Preparation 342
    13.3.2 Business Blueprint 353
    13.3.3 Realization 363
    13.3.4 Final Preparation, Go-Live Support, and Run 377
13.4 Business Add-Ons to ASAP 387
    13.4.1 Business Add-Ons to ASAP – a New Flavored Approach ... 388
    13.4.2 Tools for Applying Business Add-Ons to ASAP 393

13.4.3 Business Add-Ons to ASAP Methodology, Governance Frameworks, and Implementation Technology Content: Part I 398

13.4.4 Business Add-Ons that Deliver Methodology, Governance Frameworks, and Implementation Content: Part II 408

14 BPM Tools — From Modeling to Execution 413

14.1 Composite Development Architecture Guidelines 414
  14.1.1 Value Proposition of SAP NetWeaver CE 414
  14.1.2 Platform Overview 414
  14.1.3 Structure of Composites 419
  14.1.4 Separation of Functionality 443
  14.1.5 SOA Pattern 463
  14.1.6 Conclusion 474
14.2 Highlights of the Innovation Provided by SAP NetWeaver BPM and BRM 475
  14.2.1 Business Analyst Experience 475
  14.2.2 Process Developer Experience 476
  14.2.3 Improved Business Insight 478
  14.2.4 Interoperability with SAP Applications 478
  14.2.5 Interoperability with Other Task User Interfaces 479
14.3 Handling Decisions and Business Rules in a BPM Approach 480
  14.3.1 The Power of Decisioning 481
  14.3.2 Identifying Operational Decisions 486
  14.3.3 Implementing Decisions with Business Rules 492
  14.3.4 Best Practices in Decision Management 499
  14.3.5 Governance 508
  14.3.6 Managing the Organizational Implications 511
14.4 Business Rules Management from SAP 513
  14.4.1 Roots of Business Rule Framework Plus 513
  14.4.2 Roots of SAP NetWeaver BRM 513
  14.4.3 Business Rule Framework Plus 513
  14.4.4 SAP NetWeaver Business Rules Management 529
  14.4.5 Usage Recommendations 541
14.5 Simple Sample Application for Enterprise Service Consumption ... 545

15 Process-Based Implementation Content 553

15.1 Business Add-Ons to ASAP that Deliver Implementation
      Content 554
      15.1.1 Business Add-On to ASAP Delivering Point of Sales
              Implementation Content 555
      15.1.2 Business Add-Ons to ASAP that Deliver Small SOA/
              BPM-Based Implementation Content Packages 559
15.2 SAP Rapid Deployment Solutions 563

16 Enablement and Communities 565

16.1 Enablement: People as Key Success Factor 566
      16.1.1 The Link Between IT and Business 567
      16.1.2 Role-Based Education for Organizational Performance 568
      16.1.3 Roles and Required Skills 571
      16.1.4 Summary 574
16.2 Enablement: SAP University Alliances BPM Curriculum 574
16.3 Enablement: Starter Kit for Business Process Management, an
      Add-On to ASAP 576
      16.3.1 Benefits and Target Audience 576
      16.3.2 Navigating Through the Starter Kit for BPM, an
              Add-On to ASAP 577
16.4 Enablement: SOA KIT, an Add-On to ASAP 579
16.5 Enablement: SOA CIO Guide — Abstract 582
      16.5.1 Solution Space and Key Capabilities 582
      16.5.2 Reference Architectures and Maturity Model 584
      16.5.3 SAP Product Implementation Guidance 596
      16.5.4 Trends and Roadmap 597
      16.5.5 Conclusion 597
16.6 Enablement: Value Prototyping 598
16.7 Enablement: SAP Value Partnership 600
16.8 Enablement: Composite in a Day Workshop 600
16.9 Enablement: Communities 604

17 Conclusion **607**

PART IV Future Outlook **613**

18 Future Trends for BPM **615**

18.1 BPM Future Outlook: Six Ideas 615
18.1.1 Supporting the Knowledge Worker 616
18.1.2 Fostering Collaboration 616
18.1.3 Responding to Rapidly Changing Situations 617
18.1.4 Working Any Time, Anywhere 617
18.1.5 Developing Process Skills 618
18.1.6 Giving Control to the Business 618
18.1.7 Summary 619
18.2 BPM for Knowledge Workers 619
18.2.1 What Is a Business Process? 619
18.2.2 What Is a Business Practice? 622
18.2.3 Business Practice Example: Part Replacement 625
18.2.4 SAP ASAP Methodology 627
18.2.5 Summary 629
18.3 Exploring Additional Future BPM and SOA Trends 629
18.3.1 "Business Process Management and Semantic
        Interoperability" by Alexander Dreiling 630
18.3.2 "SOA for Business Networks – Service Delivery
        Framework" by Alistair Barros 631
18.3.3 "A Requirements Framework for Semantic Business
        Process Modeling" by Alistair Barros and Ingo M.
        Weber 632
18.3.4 "Process-Centric Decision Support" by Mathias
        Fritzsche, Wasif Gilani, and Michael Picht 633
18.3.5 "Semantic Technologies: An Enabler of Intelligent
        Business Processes" by Ivan Markovic 634
18.3.6 "Customer and Partner Views on the Future of BPM:
        A View from Two SAP Mentors" by Twan van den
        Broek and Richard Hirsch 635

Appendices 637

A   IT Performance and Value Management Research 639
B   Value Driver Processes Sorted After Strategic, Tactical, and
    Operational Levels 641
C   Bibliography 657
D   The Authors 673

Index 687

Foreword

Over the past decade, we've seen our planet grow smaller as companies, their customers, and the world's economies become more interconnected. The rise of these business networks has dramatically increased the pace of business and thus the need to quickly respond to challenges and opportunities.

No recent event illustrates this more than when the world's economy literally went into freefall in the autumn of 2008, and companies suddenly found themselves and their customers without credit or liquidity. As the world works through these economic challenges, we are faced with a new uncertainty. Now, more than ever, corporate leaders need the capacity to adapt to change not only defensively, but to realize opportunities for growth and capture market share while their competitors lag behind.

For nearly 40 years, over 100,000 global companies have relied on SAP for the software that runs their core operations, enabling them to optimally run through business processes based on best practices. Building upon that foundation, SAP now strives to help its customers manage processes across their complete business network, breaking the boundaries of individual organizations.

Business Process Management (BPM) directly improves business performance by orchestrating the work of people and software systems in a way that can be understood and managed from a business perspective. BPM is a key pillar of SAP's strategy to help our customers become more agile. This approach and associated methodologies, pre-packaged process-based implementation content, tools, and technologies provide the basis for our customers to quickly deploy new people-centric business applications in support of business process improvement, business network optimization, and business model transformation.

I'm proud to present to you our second book about SAP's BPM approach, a comprehensive reference to the application of real-world BPM in an SAP environment, with insights from SAP's customers who have taken the process transformation journey with SAP.

By following the approach outlined in this book, as illustrated by the experiences of others, we hope that you will find your own opportunities for transformation, an inspiration to aspire to excellence, and a clear path to achievement.

With best regards,
Jim Hagemann Snabe
Co-CEO, SAP AG

Introduction

Business process management is reaching a state of mainstream acceptance and is a key discipline within SAP-centric business IT environments today. The first book from SAP PRESS on the topic, *Business Process Management—the SAP Roadmap* by Jim Hagemann Snabe, Ann Rosenberg, Charles Møller, and Mark Scavillo (SAP PRESS 2009), helped readers prepare their company and their teams for the venture of starting a BPM initiative. It helped to answer such questions as: What are the strategic prerequisites? Which goals should we set for BPM within our organization? What would be a good set-up for a BPM Governance Framework? Is it possible to break this huge transformation down to digestable pieces for the people involved? What does SAP offer to support such an initiative?

What we see today is an increasing number of companies that are now ready to actually start the project of revamping their processes and their systems. This new book is therefore mainly focused on how to apply BPM within SAP implementation projects. It explains how BPM and standard software work together, how to prepare your company for the project, and how to put BPM technology, methodology, governance, and the philosophy behind it in action. Extensive use cases from well-known SAP customers, which include technical and process details, make this book a true real-world experience.

The book is structured into four parts:

In Part I, we introduce business process management as an approach for driving innovation and value creation. We advance this topic by exploring vital aspects missing from many BPM projects today: The concepts of value identification, creation and realization, and how to identify the essential processes and activities that provide competitive differentiation. With this foundation, we then suggest a method for innovating business models and business processes to achieve further business value. Part I closes by exploring business drivers for BPM, the importance of connecting the value lifecycle with the process lifecycle, and how to define process and value drivers.

Part II presents real-world examples from SAP customers, which explains how each company has used BPM to improve its business. These stories provide in-depth insight into their business challenges, BPM-enabled solutions, the lessons they learned, and the benefits that were realized. We also explore the commonalities across BPM implementations and present you with a practical approach for identifying and qualifying potential BPM projects.

Part III provides essential guidance to help you in applying BPM in all its aspects in your SAP-centric business IT environments. It explains how to prepare your company for the process-based implementation; and how to apply SAPs new implementation methodology, implementation technology, pre-packaged process-based implementation content, governance frameworks, skills, and the philosophy behind BPM in action.

In Part IV we present topics of interest from SAP researchers and other thought leaders, which explore potential future trends related to BPM. You will explore the six ideas that can be the heart of BPM's future, and you will be able to explore the in-depth details through a number of BPM articles. These articles are bonus material, and are available on this book's catalog pages on *www.sap-press.com* or *www.sap-press.de*.

While this book can certainly be read cover to cover, depending on where you are in your BPM journey, you may wish to choose a different path. If your company is ready to begin a BPM project, or has already begun its journey, start with Part I to learn about some important but often neglected components of a holistic BPM approach. If you are looking for inspiration, we recommend starting with Part II, where you will discover the motivations and results of other companies that have gone on the BPM journey. Finally, when you begin planning a BPM program or process-based implementation that includes your SAP practice, Part III will provide you with all the guidelines you need.

Part IV provides a future outlook for everyone who would like to explore the glimpse of BPM's future beyond the realm of the structured processes that we have today.

Ann Rosenberg, Greg Chase, Rukhshaan Omar, James Taylor, and **Mark von Rosing**

PART I
Business Process
Transformation

If there is one constant in the market, it is that things are always changing faster and are more dynamic. The pressures on organizations and enterprises around the world to keep up with these changes are increasing. Markets are crowded; margins are squeezed. New challenges pop up seemingly overnight on all fronts. All of this is nothing new, but the question remains: How can companies tackle multiple business changes in globalization, productivity, innovation, compliance, information overload, and the changing nature of people and work, plus not forget the golden rule of business: customers first?

Most companies see process effectiveness, efficiency, and innovation to align to their business model and strategy as one of the essential answers to creating long-term competitive advantage. The need for value creation and realization is certainly not new, especially with any topics related to process modeling, process optimization, and process innovation. But companies are struggling to adapt their business models at this accelerating pace to identify where and how to create the needed value. Everything around them seems to be changing faster than they are able to keep pace. In such changing times, many things are important to consider when you want to create superior value. And the internal change alignment (active and reactive) can be initiated from many areas to create the needed value within an organization.

This explains why business process management (BPM) is growing from a hype-cycle into a mature concept, where according to many market analysts, BPM is the fastest growing initiative in today's IT market. The level of interest and the concomitant around BPM has reached a crescendo, where BPM is announced by Gartner Group to "win the 'Triple Crown' of saving money, saving time, and adding value." The real questions are how this promise can be fulfilled and how the potential to deliver significant value can be realized, because BPM is neither a technology nor an updated version of business process reengineering (BPR), Six Sigma, or Lean. It is an IT-enabled management discipline, because the relationship between business value creation and how a company can manage their processes is symbiotic. For each part of the value the enterprise delivers to a customer, employee, or shareholder, they have to manage the processes that support their business model.

We will therefore elaborate in Part I on the important need for companies to adapt their business model (Chapter 1) and how BPM and service-oriented architecture (SOA) need to go hand in hand to enable the needed business innovation and transformation (Chapter 2), the important connection of the value lifecycle with the process lifecycle and the application lifecycle in defining performance and value drivers (Chapter 3), and the important need to combine BPM with enterprise architecture, value management, SOA, and governance (Chapter 4). In this manner, these chapters will cover the vital steps, approaches, and thought processes that are missing in too many project engagements today.

"The whitest swan will still throw a dark shadow."
– Johann Helge Benthin, Artist

1   The Importance of a Business Model

Henrik von Scheel, Ann Rosenberg, Mark von Rosing

A central question in both theory and practice is: What explains the difference of overall output performance among organizations? Many different and practical theories and methods have been proposed and argued in different management theories, many of which surprisingly are aligned with one of two views, which we will focus on in this chapter.

The first view is the *industry view*. It suggests that industry factors, such as market size and barriers to entry, form the most important explanation for performance heterogeneity. Industrial organization in economics and industry analysis in the strategy field are examples of this view [e.g., Porter, 1980].

The second is the *firm view*, which argues that organizations' endowments and competencies/capabilities, and the difficulty of replicating these, are why organizations exhibit different output in terms of performance. The resource-based perspective is one example of this view.

A lot of literature is based on arguing and testing which of these two views better explains differences in firm output in terms of overall performance. In this chapter, we will elaborate on how overall output and performance are connected to the business model of the company.

1.1   Explaining the Difference in Overall Output Performance

The industry view of performance heterogeneity among organizations is usually associated with industrial organization (IOs). Porter [1980] develops the early IO structure-conduct-performance framework into a foundation for competitive advantage. In this view, firm performance is primarily determined by industry-level factors such as market share, entry barriers into the industry, and relative cost positions. Schmalensee and Rumelt provide surveys of the industry view.

The firm view offers a different explanation of performance heterogeneity. It has many variants, of which an important one is the resource-based view [Amit et al., 1993]. Organizations can produce sustained superior performance if they have valuable, scarce, inimitable, non substitutable factor access or competencies/capabilities. Other variants include dynamic theories consistent with the firm view, such as those on organizational population and evolutionary economics by Hannan and Nelson, and the dynamic competencies/capabilities perspective by Teece. The empirical literature focuses on disentangling the industry and firm explanations of performance heterogeneity. Schmalensee [1985], using data on lines of businesses, reports that the industry view explains 20% of return on assets (ROA) heterogeneity, whereas the firm view — using market share as a proxy — has negligible explanatory power. However, his study leaves 80% of performance variance unexplained.

Partly driven by the large unexplained variance, Rumelt [Bowman et al., 2001] uses four years of Federal Trade Commission (FTC) data and a composite measure of firm effects. Unlike Schmalensee, he reports that firm (business unit) effects account for 34 to 46% of explained ROA heterogeneity, whereas industry effects account for only 8 to 18%, of which about half is transient, as measured by the interaction of industry effects with year effects. Rumelt also includes a corporate-parent effect and finds that it is negligible. This is interpreted as consistent with the firm view: Corporate strategy that structures industry and positions a firm within that industry does not matter [Carroll, 1993; Ghemawat et al., 1993]. Rumelt's paper leads to a stream of others that focus on the robustness of his findings [e.g., Bowman et al., 2001]. Recent papers agree that firm effects dominate industry effects [Amit et al., 2001; Lubatkin et al., 2001; McNamara et al., 2003; Vilmos et al., 2006], but see some differing opinions [Hawawini et al., 2005]. There is also an important branch of the empirical literature that argues that it is persistence that is important, and on this measure, industry effects dominate [e.g., Denrell, 2004; McGahan et al., 1999; McGahan et al., 2009].

It can be concluded that both industry factors and organizations competencies matter, because it is the organizations' competencies that are positioned in the market, and thereby they compete against the competencies of their competitors in their industry. We will elaborate on this subject and see the connection to an organization's business model, especially because Thomas W. Malone at MIT finds that some business models indeed performed better than others in a dataset consisting of the largest U.S. organizations from 1998 through 2002.

Many studies from IDC, Gartner Group, Forrester, Accenture, and IBM have confirmed this. The latest of these studies is the IBM CEO research study, which analyzed a unique data set from over 2,000 organizations that were publicly listed on American, European, and Asian stock exchanges. As a part of this global research, 1,765 CEOs and 2,936 business leaders representing all major countries across public and private sectors took part. As part of this research, over a five-year period information was sought about the differences between the responses of financial outperformers and those of underperformers. For companies with publicly available financial information, the researchers compared revenue and profit track records with the averages for those in the same industry.

Companies that performed above-average on the particular financial benchmark were tagged as outperformers, and those below the average were labeled as underperformers (see Figure 1.1).

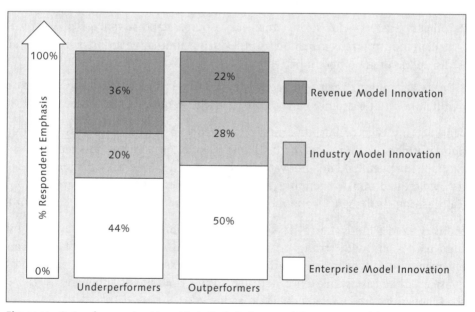

Figure 1.1 Outperformers Are More Likely To Be Industry and Enterprise Model Innovators.

Here are the current types of business model innovation and transformation:

▶ **Revenue model innovation**
Innovate how the company makes money by changing the value proposition (product/service/value mix) and the pricing model.

▶ **Industry model innovation**
Redefine an existing industry, move into a new industry, or create an entirely new one.

▶ **Enterprise business model innovation**
Innovate the way the organization operates, rethinking the organizational boundaries of what is done in-house and what is done through collaboration and partnering.

Successful companies take advantage of emerging opportunities in the new economic environment by innovating their business model in three ways:

1. Many organizations revisit their enterprise business model during a downturn to reduce costs through new collaboration and partnership models and by reconfiguring their asset mix.

2. Industry leaders with strong financial resources take advantage of unprecedented industry transformation by introducing alternative industry models and disrupting their competitors.

3. Many also rethink their revenue model and value propositions to respond to a different set of customer behaviors and market requirements.

Whereas any type of business model innovation can lead to success, financial outperformers are more likely to be industry and enterprise business model innovators than revenue model innovators (see Figure 1.1). Enterprise business model innovation and transformation is the most prominent type of innovation, especially during challenging economic times.

Industry model innovation is less frequent but is more likely to be pursued by industry leaders with strong financial means and industry positions that can leverage bold moves to expand their leadership. Revenue model innovation is considered the easiest but tends not to yield the same financial benefits, because the innovations are less defendable or lasting.

1.2   Revisit the Enterprise Model During Economic Turmoil

Enterprise model innovation is especially prominent during economic downturns as companies seek new ways to gain cost and flexibility advantages (see Figure 1.2). Enterprise model innovators focus on those areas of the business where they have an advantage and deliver value, and they partner extensively for other areas of their business.

Although many of the cases portrayed in Figure 1.2 occurred in earlier economic cycles, they illustrate how organizations exploit enterprise model innovation to reduce costs and increase flexibility during a downturn. We see this playing out again in the economic climate at the time we wrote this book.

Large multinational companies are increasingly interested in outsourcing non-core activities and IT functions to countries with low labor costs. Local governments are also using outsourcing and technology transformation to radically lower their cost bases. Increased collaboration and partnering are prominent in industries such as pharmaceuticals and biotechnology, in which reduced access to capital and resources is driving the need for new funding and partnerships.

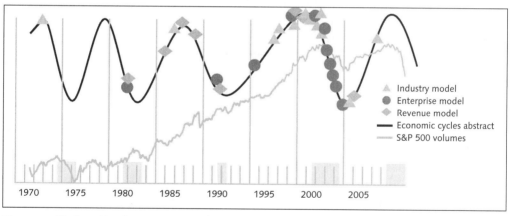

Figure 1.2   Timing of Leading Business Model Innovators Implementing a New Model [Source: Bureau of Economic Analysis USA Today, S&P 500, 2010]

Industry Transformation Drives the Need for Business Model Innovation

During periods of relative stability in the industry landscape, companies can make incremental adjustments to their business model over extended periods of time. They can continue to realize the economic benefits of their existing business model.

During periods of extensive industry change, however, companies must choose to either shake up their industries — harness disruptive technologies, go after new customer segments, dislodge competitors — or face their own demise. Throughout the analyses, information was gathered and conclusions were made based on these top- and bottom-half groupings. The analysis results show that business models matter to the performance of all companies. The research, however, clearly shows the difference in how the outperformers and underperformers focused on their service/product, operations, and business model (see Figure 1.1, Figure 1.2, and Figure 1.3).

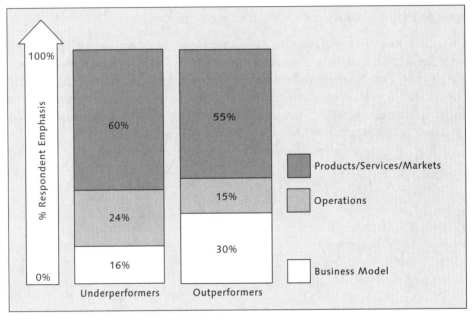

Figure 1.3   Research on Underperformers vs. Outperformers

The underperformers' business model innovation and transformation mostly focused around:

▶ Product/service asset value proposition

▶ Product/service innovation

▶ Operations innovation

▶ Cost reduction

Although the outperformers' business model innovation and transformation also focused on product/service asset value propositions, the focus on business model alignment was the main focus of competitive advantage.

While 96% of all CEOs clearly stated that they know their business model must change and adapt to be more focused, flexible, responsive, and robust, the underperformers tackled it very differently than the outperformers. This emphasized that whereas the business model mattered for all, the underperformers' believed innovation means developing new products and services, and the outperformers clearly understood that the business model, with its core competitive and core differentiated competencies, matters. The challenge of understanding one's business model and knowing what should be used to define the model is the goal of this chapter.

1.3   Core Competitive and Core Differentiated Positioning

Organizations aspire to achieving strategic competitiveness and differentiation within industries' *competitive forces*, which is a term often used by executives to refer to a firm's core competitive and core differentiated competencies to be responsive to its external environment [Hamel and Prahalad, 1994; Sull, 2009]. Strategic competitiveness and differentiation has been defined in the literature as an organization's ability to identify major changes in the external environment, to quickly commit resources and capabilities to new courses of action, and to act promptly when it is time to halt or reverse such capability and resource commitments [Shimizu and Hitt, 2004]. In Figure 1.4 we have summarized the different competitive forces impacting the internal and external environment of an organization [von Rosing, 2010].

Organizations in every industry face the competitive forces shown in Figure 1.4, which are exerted by suppliers, customers, rivals, potential new entrants, complementors, and substitute products. The stronger these competitive forces are, the less profitable the industry's organizations are likely to be [Afuah, 2003].

Where the competitive forces on industry organizations are low, allowing these organizations to be, on average, more profitable than organizations in other industries, as is the case with pharmaceuticals, the industry is said to be an attractive industry — but only if you have the core competitive competencies that can compete and the core differentiated competencies that can differentiate. If, however, these forces are high, as in the case of airlines, they lower the average profitability of the industry's organizations, and therefore, the industry is said to be an unattractive industry. In any case, any firm that formulates and executes a business model should pay attention to its competitive environment as it decides on the set of activities that it will perform to create and offer value to its customers and as it strategizes to profit from the value.

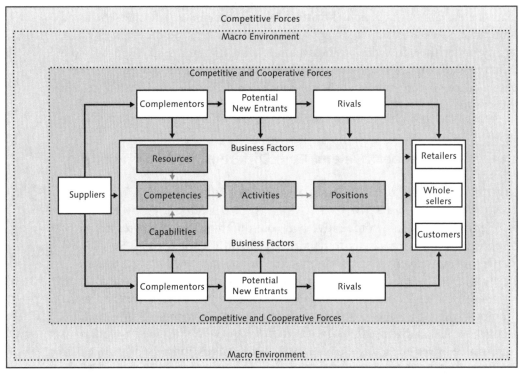

Figure 1.4 Competitive Forces Model (von Rosing and von Scheel, 2010. "How to Identify, Plan, Create and Realize Value")

Suppliers, customers, and complementors are not always adversarial; nor are all rivals. Alliances with customers can allow organizations to offer these customers better value, and cooperation with rivals, where legal, can lower organizations' costs.

The competitive environment in any region or country is also influenced by the region's or country's culture, government policies, fiscal and monetary policies, judicial and legal systems, and technological change.

In almost every industry, there are certain factors that have or are most likely to have a significant impact on competitiveness and/or differentiation. We will call these factors critical core competencies (CCCs) because they have a large impact on the activities that create value and that an organization offers its customers. A firm's positions within an industry consist of:

- The value that the firm offers its customers
- The market segments to which it offers its value
- The sources of revenues within each market segment
- The firm's relative positioning vis-à-vis its suppliers, customers, rivals, potential new entrants, substitute products, and complementors
- The prices it charges its customers

It is an organization's focused, flexible, responsive, and robust CCCs that enable it to outperform its rivals. Organizations can achieve competency focus, flexibility, responsiveness, and robustness through renewal of their core competitive and core differentiated competencies and structural business model innovation and transformation change [Burgelman, 1983].

Practice-oriented literature has expressed enthusiasm for business model innovation as a mechanism for increasing strategic flexibility with extraordinary results [Markides, 2008; Osterwalder et al., 2005]. For instance, 11 of the 27 companies that were created in the last quarter century and grew their way into the *Fortune* 500 in the past 10 years did so through business model innovation [Johnson et al., 2008]. Although managers instinctively understand their business models, academic research refers to business models as the design of organizational structures to enact a commercial opportunity [George and Bock, 2010; Teece, 2010; Amit and Zott, 2001].

1.4   A Historic View of Business Models

Two key points emerge from the above discussion of the determinants of profitability that will help us in our exploration of business models. The first is that a firm's profitability is determined by both industry factors and firm-specific competencies (positions, activities/capabilities, and resources). Thus, because business models are about making money, a business model must also depend on the factors that determine a firm's profitability. That is, a firm's business model is a function of its positions, CCCs, and non-core competencies (NCCs) and the attached main and supporting processes and the industry's factors. As mentioned, a business model is about competencies, which when combined together, build a framework for making money. It is to use the competencies in a set of activities *that* a firm performs, *how* it performs them, and *when* it performs them to offer its customers benefits they want and to earn a profit. Because business models are about applying competencies to make money, let's explore the definition of a business model.

From a historical perspective, the oldest and most basic business model was developed long before people settled down and began to make buildings for commerce. Business was conducted by nomadic peoples who met in camps and exchanged goods, either through barter or using media of exchange such as food and stones and then metals, gold, or rare seashells. In New Zealand, there were no shops prior to Europeans arriving and no money in the European sense, yet business was conducted and business models can be shown to have been operative. The word for money was *utu*. The word for revenge was *utu*. *Utu* meant something similar to "balance." (Think about the scales used in commerce and the scales used in justice.) The business word *utu* would then be equivalent to "exchange value."

Business models include barter, which can be defined as the use of a product and/or service that is exchanged with money or another medium of exchange. They should address both wealth creation and wealth conversion. For example, nomads converted solar energy to human wealth: The sun caused grass to grow. They captured and domesticated sheep, cattle, horses, and other grass-eating animals, thus creating wealth based on "chattel." Wealth conversion occured when other nomads figured out that if they rode on horses with weapons, they could steal chattel. From this came gangs, then armies, then nation-states based in fortified towns. The farmer who grows crops creates wealth (using sun, rain, and soil). The soldier who comes by from one of the fortified towns and says "If you give me some of your food, I will protect you from that other soldier from that other town who wants to steal your food," is a wealth converter. He does not actually generate wealth.

The business model of the East India Company was a shift in technology, where they used ships instead of caravans, thus avoiding having to pay fortified towns along the route home. To protect these ships from pirates and other nation-states, the British Navy became a world power, and the business model of the East India Company included setting up colonies and installing governors. Although the East India Company is defunct, the families who ran it are still some of the most powerful in the world. They just changed their business model from one corporation to many. But it is important to remember that their wealth came from a monopoly given by Queen Elizabeth I on December 1, 1600. Monopoly is a major business model (patents give one a "royalty" for a number of years, so the price is what the market will bear). In the case of the East India Company, most profits came from opium and caffeine (tea), tobacco, alcohol, firearms, and slaves and slavery-based industries, which is an interesting commentary on its business model based on cravings and control.

From the exchange of goods to the traveling salesman, over the years, business models have become much more sophisticated. The bait and hook business model (also referred to as the "razor and blades business model" or the "tied products business model") was introduced in the early 20th century. This involves offering a basic product at a very low cost, often at a loss (the bait) and then charging compensatory recurring amounts for refills or associated products or services (the hook). Examples include: razors (bait) and blades (hook), cell phones (bait) and air time (hook), computer printers (bait) and ink cartridge refills (hook), and cameras (bait) and prints (hook). An interesting variant of this model is a software developer that gives away its word processor reader free of charge but charges several hundred dollars for its word processor writer.

Over the years, business has become much more sophisticated, and this has affected in many ways the very essence, design, innovation, and transformation of the organization. In the 1950s, new business models came from McDonald's and Toyota. In the 1960s, the innovators were Walmart and other hypermarkets. The 1970s saw new business models from FedEx and Toys R Us; the 1980s from Blockbuster, Home Depot, Intel, and Dell Computer; the 1990s from Southwest Airlines, Netflix, eBay, Amazon.com, and Starbucks.

The term *business model* itself is a recent addition to the management literature and is largely a product of the dot com era. Because poorly thought out business models were a problem with many dot-coms, the term is entirely absent from all of the most influential books on organizational design, business strategy, business economics, and business theory through to the mid- to late 1990s. It is, however, mentioned in many books and articles on e-commerce. Scholars such as Hamel [Hamel, 2000], Linder and Cantrell [Linder and Cantrell, 2000], Peterovic and Kittl [Peterovic and Kittl, 2001], Weill and Vitale [Weill and Vitale, 2001], Gordijn [Gordijn, 2002], Afuah and Tucci [Afuah and Tucci, 2004], Fetscherin and Knolmayer [Fetscherin and Knolmayer, 2004], and Osterwalder, Pigneur, and Smith [Osterwalder, 2004] and then again with Y. Pigneur and A. Smith in 2009 [Osterwalder, Pigneur and Smith in 2009], have focused on business model innovation. As Hawkins states, "As the [dot com] bubble grew, the market filled up with books and articles about business models, ranging from the vaguely analytic to the quasi instructional — how to construct viable business models and how to avoid lemons. The business model seemed to fill a niche even if no one could explain exactly what it was" [Hawkins, 2004, p. 65]. At the most fundamental level, a business model is a study of how a firm will make money and sustain its profit stream over time [Stewart and Zao, 2000].

Other approaches are value proposition and value generation architecture. The business model is the organization's core logic for creating value [Linder and Cantrell, 2000]. "Business model describes the logic of a business system for creating value that lies behind the actual processes" according to Petrovic [Petrovic et al., 2001]. In 2002, Magretta [Magretta, 2002] defined business models as stories that explain how enterprises work; business models describe, as a system, how the pieces of a business fit together, but they don't factor in one critical dimension of performance: competition. She argues that a business model is not the same as a strategy, even though many people use the terms interchangeably today, and in a way, how could a company split their business model from what they want to achieve. However, it is to be noted that they are interlinked but not the same.

Today, the understanding that the business model is interlinked with strategy and that they are the basis for competition and differentiation is commonly offered to explain why some organizations do better than others [e.g., Kaplan et al., 2004; [Slywotzky et al., 1997; Timmers, 1998; Tapscott et al., 2000]. Both in theory and practice, the success of organizations such as eBay, Dell, Google, IBM, and WalMart is attributed, not only to their industry or to their firm-specific competencies, but to their unique business models. And among executives, "innovation in products, services, and business models" is the single factor contributing the most to the accelerating pace of change in the global business environment, outranking other factors related to information and the Internet, talent, trade barriers, greater access to cheaper labor, and capital [McKinsey, 2009].

When IBM CEO Louis Gerstner gave his 2001 annual analyst address about the company's new strategic initiatives and changes they need to undergo, he concluded that the new strategic direction "makes more sense given the current business environment and IBM's *business model*" [2001]. This reference to a business model is not unique to IBM. It is understood very well in these sources:

▶ As an alleged source of success in 2001, "Dell's *business model* stands head and shoulders above its competitors" [Gurley, 2001]. And the root of failures for the other business models in the industry was that "HP's, COMPAQ's, IBM's PC division 'had a *business model* problem'" [Spooner, 2002].

▸ Among both information technology and industrial organizations, Bair [Bair, 2003] reports that "along with creating a new airplane (the new Boeing 7E7), we're creating a new *business model* for their industry."

▸ In big-business annual reports — the "GE *Business Model*" [Welch, 2003] — was seen as leading in the way they involve suppliers among analysts, venture capitalists, and consultants.

1.4.1 The Development of Business Model Concepts

While business models developed, so did the concepts and definitions in the existing literature by specifying business models' primary elements and their interrelations. A characteristic, well-known definition is that a business model stands for the architecture of the product, service, and information flows, including a description of the various business actors and their roles, the potential benefits for these actors, and the sources of revenues [Timmers, 1998]. According to Timmers' definition, the business model includes competition and stakeholders. Similarly, other researchers [Weill and Vitale, 2001] define a business model as a description of the roles and relationships among a firm's consumers, customers, allies, and suppliers that identifies major flows of product, information, and money and the major benefits to participants.

Furthermore, business innovation models, named business webs are inventing new value propositions, transforming the rules of competition, and mobilizing people and resources to unprecedented levels of performance. However, all of these approaches and definitions converge toward and agree on the fact and approach that the business model is related to strategy and several managerial concepts that develop the business competencies of the organization. It captures key competencies of a business plan, but a business plan deals with several strategic, tactical, and on some level operational issues that transcend the model. It is not a strategy but incorporates the strategy and includes a number of strategy elements. Similarly, it is not an activity set, although activity sets support each element of a model. These different approaches and methods furthermore agree that a business model can be defined as a business blueprint, or a story, of how an interrelated set of enterprise variables, in the areas of strategy, business competencies, business operations architecture, and economics, are addressed and fit together as a working system. In this sense the discipline of business model management represents the framework for conceptualizing the working description that includes the general details about the strategy and operations of a business.

1.4.2 Business Model Component Development

The latest literature emphasizes the importance of defining the components of a business model. An early pioneer in business models, Horowitz [Horowitz, 1996] argued that a business model should be built based on the strategy, main competencies, and components of a business model. The components Horowitz suggested were price, product, distribution, organizational characteristics, and technology. According to Staehler [Staehler, 2001], a business model consists of three major components: the value proposition, the value architecture, and the revenue model. Alt and Zimmerman increase the number of suggested components to six: mission, structure, processes, revenues, technology, and legal issues. Afuah and Tucci [Afuah et al., 2001] adopt a wider approach to the business model by defining eight competencies: customer, value, scope, pricing, revenue source, connected activities, implementation, capabilities, and sustainability. Timmers' classification is very different: e-shop, e-mail, information services provider, e-auction, value-chain services provider, virtual community, third-party marketplace, and value-chain integrator [Timmer, 1999]. An interesting argument [Chesbrough et al., 2000] is that the business model mediates between the technical and economic domains and specifies business model components through their definition of the six principal functions that a business model has to address:

1. Articulate the value proposition; that is, the value created for users by the offering based on the technology.

2. Identify the market segment; that is, the users to whom the technology is useful and for what purpose.

3. Define the structure of the value chain within the firm required to create and distribute the offering.

4. Estimate the cost structure and profit potential of producing the offering, given the value proposition and value chain structure chosen.

5. Describe the position of a firm within the value network linking suppliers and customers, including identification of potential complementors and competitors.

6. Formulate the competitive strategy by which the innovating firm will gain and hold an advantage over rivals.

Many writers followed this approach and developed different or additional components. One writer, who had quite some success, was Alexander Osterwalder

[Osterwalder, 2004], with his nine building blocks approach that is in four main areas:

1. **Infrastructure**

   ▶ Core resource/capabilities: The resource/capabilities and therefore the competencies necessary to execute a company's business model.

   ▶ Partner network: The business alliances that complement other aspects of the business model.

   ▶ Value configuration: The arrangement of activities and resources that are necessary to create value for the customer.

2. **Offering**

   ▶ Value proposition: The products and services a business offers. Quoting Osterwalder [2004], a value proposition "is an overall view of ... products and services that together represent value for a specific customer segment. It describes the way a firm differentiates itself from its competitors and is the reason why customers buy from a certain firm and not from another."

3. **Customers**

   ▶ Target customer: The target audience for a business' products and services.

   ▶ Distribution channel: The means by which a company delivers products and services to customers. This includes the company's marketing and distribution strategy.

   ▶ Customer relationship: The links a company establishes between itself and its customer segments. The process of managing customer relationships is referred to as customer relationship management.

4. **Finances**

   ▶ Cost structure: The monetary consequences of the means employed in the business model; a company's DOC.

   ▶ Revenue: The way a company makes money through a variety of revenue flows; a company's income.

In 2009 this approach was slightly altered and split into four main areas: value architecture, value proposition, revenue model, and culture/values (Figure 1.5) [Osterwalder et al., 2009].

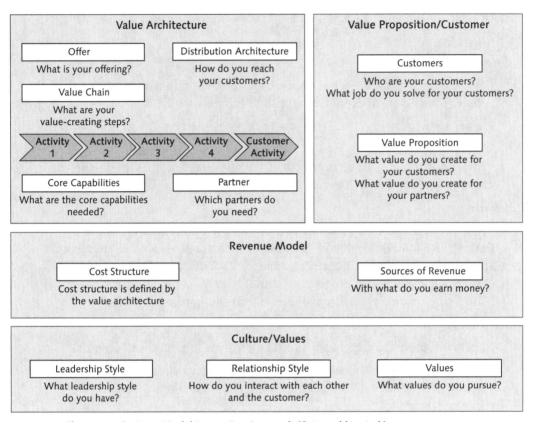

Figure 1.5 Business Model Innovation Approach (Osterwalder et al.)

Even though Osterwalder, Pigneur, and Smith's business model approach can be used to innovate parts of the business model or product, it demonstrates these weaknesses:

▶ The approach is mostly built on the work of the other writers of competency development of the business model and balanced scorecard from Kaplan and Norton [Kaplan and Norton, 2007]. This theory can't be applied to a full business model framework.

▶ It doesn't consider business model design or business model transformation (the approach focuses mostly on business model innovation).

▶ It doesn't include a business model improvement and development methodology.

- ▶ It doesn't include corporate structure and responsibility, which a business model should include.

- ▶ It doesn't include a representation of the main business goals, for example, strategic business objectives, critical success factors, and key performance indicators, which a holistic business model approach should include.

- ▶ It doesn't include a representation of the main business issues/pain points and thereby corporate weakness, which a holistic business model approach should include because these factors represent the threat to the company's business model.

- ▶ It is based on the theory that between the activities that generate cost and the activities that generate revenue is the value proposition. That view is too simplistic because you can't build a business model based on visible figures of cost and revenue alone, even though cost and revenue should be a part of a business model.

- ▶ The linkages among competences, measurements, and results are not explicit.

- ▶ It doesn't have clear cause-and-effect linkages between the competencies, desired outcomes, and measurements. Therefore the business model can help with possible strategic decisions.

- ▶ It doesn't consider the issue of performance measurements, which is vital for business modeling.

- ▶ It doesn't consider the important issue of goal setting, which is critical for developing the business model.

- ▶ It doesn't place enough emphasis on business model management and thereby misses a continuous improvement and governance approach to the business model.

- ▶ It doesn't include a representation of core differentiated and core competitive competencies (only those linked to value propositions), which is a basis for building a business model because they represent some of the most important sources of uniqueness. These are the things that a company can do uniquely well and that no-one else can copy quickly enough to affect competition.

It can be concluded that whereas Osterwalder, Pigneur, and Smith's business model approach can be used to innovate parts of the business model or product, it is not a holistic business model approach. In fact, their model cannot be seen as a business model approach, but rather a business model innovation approach.

1.5 New Form of the Business Model Concept

With the components development, *logic* and *value* became key words in the literature on business models. In recent years IBM Global Services and the IBV (IBM Center for Business Value) have developed an innovative business model approach that includes business model design, business model innovation, and business model transformation. The IBM business model approach is called the Component Business Model (CBM). This was the first time somebody not only used a general method to identify core competencies (resources and capabilities), partner networks, value proposition, customer segments, and relationships, and thereby cost and revenue, but used a logical representation and technique to map the enterprise on a single page. This CBM approach can be used to analyze the alignment of enterprise strategy with the organization's capabilities and investments, identify redundant or overlapping business competencies/capabilities, analyze sourcing options for the different components (buy or build), prioritize transformation options, and create a unified roadmap after mergers or acquisitions. The model is organized as business components along columns and "operational levels" along rows. Business components are defined as large business areas with characteristic skills, resources, processes, and competencies.

The three operational levels (depending on industry) are planning, monitoring, and execution. They separate strategic decisions (planning), management checks (monitoring), and business actions (execution) on business components. This new approach to business modeling took the concept of the business model to a higher and more strategic level. A split began to form between business model approaches, where many of the business modeling approaches continue to focus on functional component requirements without paying sufficient attention to the other nonfunctional issues. The result is a final product that is unsatisfactory and fails to comply with the strategic business objectives of its users. Therefore, the perspective of business model innovation and transformation is not jointly unified.

The other development approaches focused on resources (assets), capabilities, and thereby competencies, which are combined competencies, which a company needs to plan, create, and realize value, in both an effective and efficient way (see Figure 1.6).

In order to plan, create, and realize value in an effective and efficient way, a company should identify the key value drivers of innovation (see Chapter 3), which should yield rewards rather than extra cost in building such competencies. Understanding which processes and initiatives it takes to design, innovate, and transform one's business competencies to match the vision and strategy that is needed should not only help a company gain cost improvement, but differentiate advantage as well.

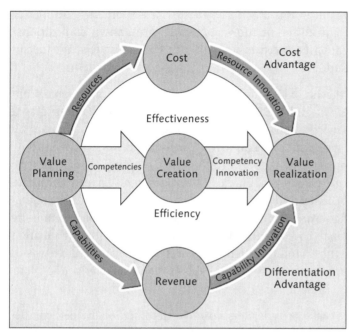

Figure 1.6 Competency – Value Model (von Rosing, 2009. "Business Value Management")

To gain a differentiated advantage, one or more competitive strategies should be chosen. Becoming a leading-edge company occurs by taking offensive or defensive action to create pioneering competencies, and therefore the prime position in an industry or the market, in order to cope successfully with the competitive forces and choices the peers in the industry, have chosen and consequently generate a superior return on investment. When the principles of competitive advantage strategies (from Porter [Porter, 1998]) are applied, there are two basics types of competitive advantage:

▶ Cost leadership (low cost)

▶ Differentiation

Both can be more broadly approached or narrowed to be more specific, which results in the third viable competitive strategy: focus.

A competitive advantage exists when the firm is able to deliver the same competencies and benefits as its competitors, but at a lower cost (cost advantage), or deliver competencies that exceed those of a competing organization (differentiation advantage). Thus, a competitive advantage enables the organization to create superior competencies, and in this manner value, for its customers and superior profits for itself. Cost and differentiation advantages are known as positional advantages since they describe the firm's position in the industry as a leader in either cost or differentiation.

However, contrary to the rationalization of Porter, contemporary research from Kim Chang in 1997, 1998, and 1999 has shown evidence of firms practicing a successful mixture of low cost and differentiation strategy. Research literature by Prajogo [Pajogo, 2007] state that firms employing the hybrid business strategy (low cost and differentiation strategy) outperform the ones adopting a single generic strategy. Sharing the same view point, Charles Hill argues in his paper, "Corporate strategy and Firm Performance," that a successful combination of these two strategies will result in a long-term competitive advantage. As an example, combining these two strategies in one's competencies is successful, when combining a market segmentation strategy with a product differentiation strategy is an effective way of matching your firm's product strategy (supply side) to the characteristics of your target market segments (demand side).

However, combinations such as cost leadership and differentiation in one's competencies are hard (but not impossible) to implement, due to the potential for conflict between cost minimization and the additional cost of value-added differentiation. To achieve a competitive advantage, the firm must perform one or more value-creating competency activities in a way that creates more overall value than do competitors. Superior value is created and realized through lower costs or superior benefits to the consumer (differentiation). In this case a company needs to define on a high level how competitive advantage is created. After the strategies of cost and differentiation leadership are chosen, many writers [Robert M. Dibrell; C. Clay; Kim, Eonsoo Nam; Daeil, Allen; R. Helms, M. Takeda; M. White C.; Stimpert, J.L.] argue that specific and multiple business strategies need to be specified and applied in order for companies to carry out the chosen strategies. According to the resource-based view [Wernerfelt, B., Hoopes, D.G.; Madsen, T.L.; Walker, G], in order to develop different underlying competitive advantage strategies that supports cost advantage and differentiation advantage, the firm must apply the strategies to the resources and capabilities, and in doing so the competencies of the company. As illustrated in Figure 1.6, both resources (assets) and capabilities, which are combined competencies, need to be innovated in order to create and realize value, both in an effective and efficient way. Without applying a cost and/or differentiation approach to one's competencies, the competitors simply could replicate what the organization is doing and any advantage could quickly disappear.

Let's go into the details of each of the capability/resource innovation elements in the competency – value model. We will start with resources.

1.5.1 Resources

Resources (also called assets) can be categorized as tangible, intangible, and human. Tangible assets can be physical, such as plants and equipment, or financial, such as cash. These are the types of assets that are usually identified and accounted for in financial statements under the category "assets." Intangible assets are nonphysical and nonfinancial assets such as patents, brands, copyrights, trade secrets, market research findings, relationships with customers, knowledge in databases, and relationships with vendors. They are usually not identified in financial statements but can be excellent sources of profits. For example, a patent or trade secret that gives a firm exclusive access to a product or process may allow the firm to be the only one producing a product with certain characteristics, thereby making the product highly differentiated and profitable. For a while, the copyright for Intel's microcode allowed the firm to offer differentiated microprocessors to makers of personal computers. Human assets are the skills and knowledge that employees carry with them [Afuah, 2003]. As shown in Figure 1.6, for the most part resources are associated with cost, and therefore resource innovation leads to cost advantage. Resources are the organization-specific assets that are useful for creating a cost advantage; however, certain resource/assets can be applied to differentiation advantage as well, all which few competitors can copy or acquire easily. Resources are inputs into a firm's process, such as capital, equipment, and the skills of individual employees, patents, finance, and talented managers. With increasing effectiveness, the set of resources available to the firm tends to become larger. Individual resources may not yield to a competitive advantage. It is through the synergistic combination and integration of sets of resources that competitive advantages are formed. The following are some examples of such resources:

- Patents and trademarks
- Proprietary know-how
- Employee relations and commitment
- Employee morale

- ▸ Installed customer base
- ▸ Reputation of the firm
- ▸ Brand equity

1.5.2 Capabilities and Abilities

As important as resources/assets are, it usually takes more than resources and assets to offer value to customers. One such additional value is a firm's capabilities.

Capabilities

Capabilities refer to the firm's ability to utilize its resources efficiently. A capability is the capacity for a set of resources to interactively perform a stretch task or an activity. Through continued use, capabilities become stronger and more difficult for competitors to understand and imitate. As a source of competitive advantage, a capability should be neither so simple that it is highly imitable, nor so complex that it defies internal steering and control [Schoemaker and Amit, 1994]. As shown in Figure 1.6, capabilities are associated with revenue potential for the most part; therefore capability innovation should lead to any form of differentiation that would give the company a differentiated advantage.

An example of a capability is the ability to bring a sustainable product to market faster than competitors. Such capabilities are embedded in the processes and activities of the organization, and should be documented from main processes group to sub processes, and thus are difficult for competitors to replicate. The firm's resources and capabilities together form its distinctive competencies. The competencies are mapped on business model level, as described in Part III, Chapter 13. In order to develop one's competencies (resources and capabilities) actively, a firm must:

- ▸ Analyze as-is and to-be competencies
- ▸ Define process value drivers
- ▸ Implement process measurement
- ▸ Define continuous improvement of processes
- ▸ Develop process performance metrics
- ▸ Innovate processes
- ▸ Initiate a process governance model

The active planning, creation, and realization of such competencies strengthens the firm's brand, reputation, enables innovation, meets customer sustainability needs, builds employee relations, productivity, efficiency, quality, all of which can be leveraged to create a cost advantage or a differentiation advantage.

We can conclude that since the goal of a business model is to make money, a task that must interest an organization is the pursuit of a business model. Therefore, the firm's attention must focus on the types of capabilities and resource/assets that are most likely to develop the critical core competencies the organization needs to create and realize the planned value, in order to ensure that the business model is profitable. Furthermore, a firm must acknowledge which capabilities and resource/assets are non-core competencies that most likely to ensure low cost, e.g. standardization and automation, which the organization's business model needs in order to be competitive and profitable.

Abilities

A firm needs to have the ability to convert its resources and assets into competencies that create value (internal and external). Customers will not scramble to a firm's doors simply because the firm has modern resources and assets such as plants, geniuses, and patents. The firm has to use the plants, the geniuses, and the knowledge embodied in the patents to offer customers something they value. Patients do not buy patents or skilled scientists from pharmaceutical companies; they buy medicines that have been developed by skilled scientists using knowledge embodied in patents. Assets must be converted into something that customers want. A firm's ability or capacity to turn its resources into customer value and profits is usually called a competence or competencies. Competences usually involve the use or integration of an organization's capabilities and resources/assets. Logic's ability to quickly turn its "cores" into products that customers want is a competence, which can be either core or non-core competencies. Intel's ability to develop microprocessors that exploit its copyrighted mircrocode and that are compatible with its installed base of microprocessors is a core differentiating competence. So is Coca-Cola's ability to turn its secret formula and brand into a product that many customers perceive as being preferable to its rivals' products [Afuah, 2003.].

Because the goal of a business model is to make money, a question that must interest an organization is: What types of capabilities and resource/assets are most likely to develop the critical core competencies the organization needs to create and realize the planned value and to ensure that the business model is profitable?

1.6   The Logic of a Business Model Framework Based on Competencies

As we have discussed, business models are vital for business design, innovation, and transformation. But putting business innovation and transformation into practice with the right operating model requires executives to think differently, not only about the construct of the organization but also about the interrelationships of the assets they rely on to provide value to their customers. Business models offer a proven approach to driving a critical core competencies focus, both internally and externally. Internally, competencies help organizations rethink the leverage they can achieve with the assets and capabilities they own. Externally, competencies help organizations source specialized abilities they cannot feasibly create themselves.

Combining these types of business innovation and transformation allows organizations to redefine their competitive positions in the face of the sweeping changes in their industries while simultaneously achieving the competing benefits of scale, flexibility, and efficiency. In Figure 1.7 we see an example of a general business model with its business competencies, which are the modular building blocks that make up a business model.

Business Administration				Business Operations			
General Administration	Human Resource Management	Information Technology	Operations Support	Business Development	Operations	Distribution	Marketing, Sales, and Service
Strategic Planning	Organizational Planning	IT Planning	Operations Support Planning	R&D Planning	Operations Planning	Distribution Planning	Segmentation Planning
Legal & Regulatory Affairs	Recruitment	Deployment	Assets	Product Design	Component Manufacture	Scheduling	Selling
Information Analysis	Administration	IT Business Management	Quality	Research	Operations Procurement	Order Fulfillment	Market Analysis
Project Management	Benefits	Risk & Compliance	Environment & Health	Production Setup	Product Manufacture	Transportation	Channels
Finance	Performance Evaluation	Information Management	Sourcing & Procurement	Intellectual Property	Inbound Inventory	Import & Export	Brand Management
Facility Management	Compensation	Service Delivery	Safety & Security	Product Deployment	Product Assembly	Distribution	Customer Account
Accounting	Education	Development	Equipment & Plant	Content	Refining	Finished Goods Inventory	Customer Acquisition
Travel Management	Payroll	Support & Relationship	Data Management	Product Maintenance	Packaging	Costing	Servicing

Figure 1.7   General Business Model Combining Business Competencies (von Rosing, 2009. "Business Value Management")

Each competency of the business model encompasses seven dimensions (see Figure 1.8):

1. The competency purpose and service — the logical reason for the competency's existence within the organization, as defined by the service, and thereby value it provides to other competencies.

2. Each competency conducts a mutually exclusive set of activities to achieve its business purpose and thereby create value. This is where processes are interconnected.

3. To create value, competencies require resources — the people, knowledge, and assets that support their activities and processes.

4. Each competency consists of capabilities that use different resources, and therefore company assets.

5. Each competency is managed as an independent entity, based on its own governance model to ensure performance and value realization.

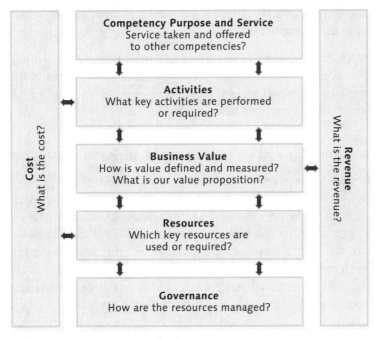

Figure 1.8 Seven Dimensions of a Competency

6. The different competencies each have a cost that can be either measured, optimized, or developed, depending on whether it is a core or non-core competency. A ground rule here is that cost reduction should for the most part only be done within non-core competencies.

7. The revenue a competency generates can be measured, developed, and innovated depending on whether it is a core or non-core competency.

It is important that when determining the boundaries of the competencies, you consider the various dimensions, not just one or two, even though one or two might be the drivers, for cost cutting, value creation, and/or governance. All of the competencies are highly collaborative, working with other competencies both inside and outside the company. Collaboration is accomplished through the exchange of services, activities, and inputs and outputs for all competencies. When a competency requires an input to complete a particular activity, it procures it as a service from another competency. That way it can access the full range of inputs it requires. This competency will in turn provide an output that other competencies can use as their input. Predefined service-level agreements — covering such aspects as formatting, timing, quantity, quality, payment, and provisioning — set the standards for all of these transactions.

Business competencies derive much of their advantage from two related but distinct traits: The loose coupling of links between competencies provides flexibility, adaptability, and responsiveness, whereas the cohesion of activities within each competency provides efficiency and enhanced quality.

1.6.1 Flexible and Free Connection of the Competencies

Interaction and connection between competencies is characterized by flexible, loose, and free coupling. Instead of "hardwired" inflexible links based on proprietary or customized connections, competencies interface through clearly defined service boundaries, forming and breaking connections as they initiate and respond to service requests to each other. Flexible coupling also relies on a common sharing principle, so that even incompatible underlying systems can be joined based on competency value-added communication. This aspect of competency sharing and thereby development gives organizations much more scalability in the services they provide and use among each other and more flexibility in deciding whether to source a competency within the firm or outside it. In either case, the competency requesting an input in terms of service is indifferent to how that service is implemented. Please note that we are not talking about SOA services, but how competencies give value-added services to each other.

From the process perspective this would be competency activities that are illustrated in a process model as value-added chain diagrams. Value-added chain diagrams are used to illustrate and identify those competency activities within the company that are directly involved in the creation of a company's added value. These functions can be interlinked by creating a competency and function sequence and thus a value-added chain. Such a value-added chain diagram not only enables you to express a subordination of competency activities; it can also display the competency functions' links to the business model and thereby the organizational units and information objects. From the outside a competency is a "black box" whose inner workings are irrelevant. The possibilities of developing business competencies and building on the value-added services they can share with each other is a great potential for value creation and realization within an organization (refer to Chapter 2).

1.6.2 Consistency and Union of the Competencies

Internally, competencies deliver scale and efficiency gains through consistency, the union of similar competency activities from across the organization into a business competency group. To achieve cohesion, each competency activity must belong uniquely within one competency group, with no duplication within or between competencies (because they should share these competencies as described in Section 1.6.1). An added benefit of bringing these competency activities together in a business model competency group is to expose the relative performance discrepancies between competency activities and others that are not performing and thereby create high costs for executing the competency. In this area there are great possibilities for developing, optimizing, and innovating competency activities for cost cutting and value creation and realization within an organization (see Part III, Chapter 14, for more information).

1.7 Organizing Business Competencies

Business modeling provides a framework for organizing competencies by accountability level. By employing such a framework, executives can begin to envision how current business activities might function as an interlocking set of modules.

Categorizing activities by business competency yields a high-level view of competencies according to the type of value they provide to the enterprise. Different firms in different industries model their competencies differently, but in every case, each activity should line up under a particular competency.

Examples of competencies are HR, operations, distribution, business development (see Figure 1.6 and Figure 1.7).

Assigning each activity to one of three accountability levels — strategic, tactical, and operational — can also help executives begin to flesh out the business competency development vision/roadmap (see Figure 1.9). The level of a given competency should be intuitive, although exceptions exist. The three accountability levels are defined as follows:

1. **Strategic**

   Competencies at this level provide strategic direction, planning, and corporate policy to other competencies. They also facilitate collaboration with other competencies. These strategic competencies provide the business actions that drive value planning in the enterprise.

2. **Tactical**

   These mid-tier competencies serve as control, monitoring, checks, and balances between the strategic and operational levels. They monitor performance, manage exceptions, and act as gatekeepers of assets and information. These tactical competencies provide the business actions that drive value planning, monitoring, and governance in the enterprise.

3. **Operational**

   These low-level competencies provide the business actions that drive value identification and creation in the enterprise. They process assets and information for use by other competencies or the customer.

The three accountability levels imply different priorities. At the operational level, for example, the emphasis is on keeping people fully occupied and productive. From a technology standpoint speed of data entry and real-time availability are important. Contrast this with activities related to the strategic tier, where such high-level activities as planning and launching new products are handled. This level houses a small number of people who have a very large impact on shareholder value.

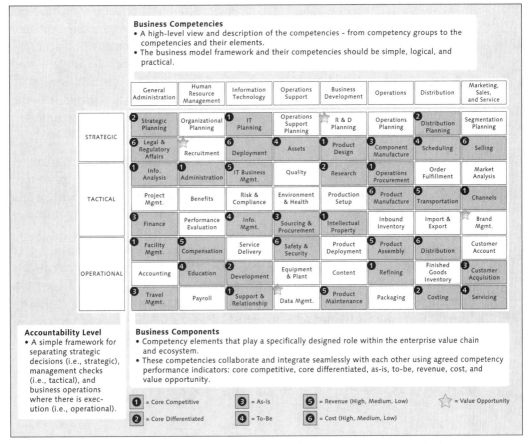

Business Competencies
- A high-level view and description of the competencies - from competency groups to the competencies and their elements.
- The business model framework and their competencies should be simple, logical, and practical.

	General Administration	Human Resource Management	Information Technology	Operations Support	Business Development	Operations	Distribution	Marketing, Sales, and Service
STRATEGIC	② Strategic Planning	Organizational Planning	① IT Planning	Operations Support Planning	☆ R & D Planning	Operations Planning	② Distribution Planning	Segmentation Planning
	⑥ Legal & Regulatory Affairs	☆ Recruitment	⑥ Deployment	④ Assets	① Product Design	③ Component Manufacture	④ Scheduling	⑥ Selling
TACTICAL	① Info. Analysis	① Administration	⑤ IT Business Mgmt.	Quality	② Research	① Operations Procurement	Order Fulfillment	Market Analysis
	Project Mgmt.	Benefits	Risk & Compliance	Environment & Health	Production Setup	⑥ Product Manufacture	⑤ Transportation	① Channels
	③ Finance	Performance Evaluation	④ Info. Mgmt.	Sourcing & Procurement	① Intellectual Property	Inbound Inventory	Import & Export	① Brand Mgmt.
OPERATIONAL	① Facility Mgmt.	⑤ Compensation	Service Delivery	⑥ Safety & Security	Product Deployment	⑤ Product Assembly	⑥ Distribution	Customer Account
	Accounting	④ Education	② Development	Equipment & Plant	Content	① Refining	Finished Goods Inventory	③ Customer Acquisition
	③ Travel Mgmt.	Payroll	① Support & Relationship	☆ Data Mgmt.	⑤ Product Maintenance	Packaging	② Costing	④ Servicing

Accountability Level
- A simple framework for separating strategic decisions (i.e., strategic), management checks (i.e., tactical), and business operations where there is execution (i.e., operational).

Business Components
- Competency elements that play a specifically designed role within the enterprise value chain and ecosystem.
- These competencies collaborate and integrate seamlessly with each other using agreed competency performance indicators: core competitive, core differentiated, as-is, to-be, revenue, cost, and value opportunity.

① = Core Competitive   ③ = As-Is   ⑤ = Revenue (High, Medium, Low)   ☆ = Value Opportunity

② = Core Differentiated   ④ = To-Be   ⑥ = Cost (High, Medium, Low)

Figure 1.9   Business Model with the Three Accountability Levels (von Rosing and von Scheel, 2010. "How to Identify, Plan, Create and Realize Value")

Launching a new product requires collaboration among several elements, including marketing, risk, finance, regulations, and credit. Input from all of these stakeholders is needed to make the launch a success, so workflow is a key requirement. From a technology standpoint, activities typically require people (resources) and capabilities to discern patterns and trends from rich, multidimensional data, usually stored in a data warehouse. Systems at the strategic level are not designed for speed of data entry, but rather for ease, breadth, and depth of analysis. Real-time interfaces are not needed, because data is often months old and processed in batches.

To drive as much revenue, value creation, and realization as possible from business model competency development, only core competitive and core differentiated competencies across the firm are aggregated. It is an organization's CCCs that enable an organization to outperform its rivals. These competencies with the attached seven dimensions should, when automated and supported with an IT system, be treated as own practice. Far too often such competencies are automated with the IT system's Best Practices, and therefore their uniqueness and differentiation can potentially be destroyed.

Whereas the IT system Best Practices are vital to cut costs, for example, fast implementation, fewer mistakes, standardization, and less risk, because it is proven to work, this can't be applied in the area of CCCs that enable core competitive and core differentiated competencies. However, even if a firm offers the right customer value to the right market segments and does so better than its rivals, it is still possible that the firm might not be profitable. That is, superior relative customer value offered to the right customer segments, although necessary, is not always a sufficient condition for profitability. Therefore, the cost of making money is a vital ingredient for succeeding. Offering the right value to the right customer segments and being positioned advantageously vis-à-vis suppliers, customers, rivals, potential new entrants, and substitute products may still not be enough for a firm to capture the revenues that its positions suggest it should. To keep the cost low a company should standardize its NCCs and thereby apply IT system Best Practices to all NCCs and the attached main and supporting processes.

1.8   Summary and Conclusion

We have discussed the important fact that a business model is not a strategy. The separation of model from strategy is the strength and weakness of the business model concept. Because the business model is the product of the strategy, a business model can only be as strong as you're your strategic business objectives (SBOs), critical success factors (CSFs), and key performance indicators (KPIs). If a company wants business-IT alignment, it needs to align the strategy to the business model, the business model to the process model, and the process model to its systems — and all of this with the right architecture and governance framework.

The primacy of how the strategy does and should interlink with the business model is apparent in Michael Porter's influential strategic framework and value chain framework. See the mention of Porter [1994] in the Bibliography for his own synthesis of the evolution of his thinking on competitive strategy, which aims at fusing what he describes as the two main and contrasting views of strategy, one that emphasizes organizational differentiation via what is now termed core competitive and core differentiated competencies and one where "competitive advantage was defined by a single variable: cost." Porter's own conclusion is that strategy "must begin by declaring a clear goal for the enterprise: in our view, this should be superior, long-term return on investment" [Porter, 2004, p. 251]. Out of this perception came his five forces of industry model, followed by the value chain. One of Porter's most central tenets hints at one reason for the emergence of business model conceptualization: "The fundamental unit of analysis for developing strategy is the industry" [Porter, 1994, p. 290].

The industry is in effect the input to one's business model and how it should compete. The business model is simply a working description that includes the general details about the operations of a business. As part of the business model, there is a need to address internal factors that relate to the ongoing operation of the company. The competencies that are contained within the business model address functions, purpose, offerings, and services, including such factors as:

▶ Corporate structure, infrastructure, responsibilities

▶ The main business goals, for example, strategic business objectives, critical success factors, and key performance indicators

▶ Business issues, pain points, and weakness clusters

▶ Core and non-core competencies

▶ Value planning, identification, creation, and realization

▶ Financial indicators: revenues and costs

Working with one business model helps a company maintain focus on core competitiveness and core differentiation while keeping a comparative advantage with the non-core competencies. Periodic reviews and updates help keep the business model relevant to current competition, market changes, economic conditions, and consumer demands. Generally, the most that has to do with the strategic decisions and operation of the corporation can be said to be part of the business model.

Every organization needs to review carefully whether the time is right to revisit its business model, either to pursue new opportunities in its industry or to respond to competitive or technology threats posed to their existing model. The possibilities for developing, optimizing, and innovating your competencies for both cost cutting and value creation and realization are tremendous for an organization. See also Part III, Chapter 14, where we have developed a structured approach to help you make the journey.

> **More Information**
>
> For more information or questions about business modeling, business model examples, and a business model template, please visit *www.openroundtable.org*.

"Try not to talk about change, but rather to enable it."
– Thorkil Lund, Danish Bank, Director, 1989 (attributed)

2   Business Model Transformation Toward the Service-Oriented Enterprise

Carsten Linz, Patrik Fiegl, Mark von Rosing

As we discussed in the introduction to Part I, business model innovation and transformation is one of the most vital parts of a company's competitive advantage. But putting business innovation and transformation into practice requires executives to think differently, not only about the construct of the organization but also about the interrelationships and services of the competencies they rely on to create and realize value. Whereas pressure to control costs and maintain operational efficiency is still a priority for businesses of every size and across every industry, most are reporting a renewed emphasis on top-line growth. Globalization and technology advances are giving rise to an unprecedented level of competition while creating extraordinary opportunities to differentiate.

For many companies, growth — perhaps even survival — depends on innovation and transformation of their business model. Business model innovation and transformation is an important widely recognized concept. As already discussed, the majority of CEOs today consider business model innovation and transformation to be an answer to intense business competition, increased customer expectations, and globalization. Enterprise service orientation enables a flexible IT infrastructure and plays a significant role in enabling business model innovation and transformation. This chapter clarifies the role of service-oriented architecture (SOA) in reinventing and transforming business models while we focus on the business perspective.

In this chapter, we start by discussing three selected trends that drive adaptation toward a service-oriented enterprise and thereby enable business innovation and transformation. This chapter also discusses both the business and the IT perspective of companies actively transforming themselves into a service-oriented enterprise. From the business viewpoint, we will discuss, first, trends and thus market forces driving such a transformation. Second, we will elaborate on the parameters of change in more detail to better understand the deltas between a function-oriented enterprise and a service-oriented enterprise. Third, transformation case studies exemplify the transformation toward a service-oriented enterprise.

We will then adopt an IT perspective and discuss how the service-oriented enterprise can become a reality supported by the use of proper methods and tools of service and process enablement and information technology. First, we will address the question of which methods help us capture business ambitions and intentions so that IT can understand them. Second, we will look into the content elements that flow through these methods. Third, we will address what new capabilities IT needs to use the thus captured content to effectively innovate and transform businesses toward service-oriented enterprises.

2.1   Adaptation of the Service-Oriented Enterprise

Innovating, developing, and optimizing your competencies and thereby transforming your business models has historically been considered a slow and arduous process, but a combination of business process management-specific expertise and the enabling technology of service–oriented architecture is reducing the time barriers to change. Business model innovation and transformation is defined as innovation in the structure and/or financial model of the business, and then being able to execute the innovation a transformational way. The focus of business model innovation and transformation is often in one of three areas:

1. **Customer-focused business competency innovation and transformation**
   New collaborative solutions across partners, customer, and suppliers.

2. **Core business competency innovation and transformation**
   Better customer service and more efficient use of resources through new and innovative approaches to internal business processes.

3. **Supplier-focused business competency innovation and transformation**
   New levels of cost efficiency and best-of-breed solution delivery through global services assembly lines and advanced planning and optimization through the value chain.

Generally, business model innovation and transformation can be viewed as transforming various competencies of the extended value chain. The SOA and BPM paradigms can be applied to the business/IT relationship in a twofold way:

1. Using SOA as a paradigm for the design and management of enterprises. Value chains are understood as arrays of recomposable "services" (combining people, processes, and technology to deliver products and services to the business network).

2. Using SOA as a techno-architectural concept based on notions of functional componentization, provider and consumer contracts, and reuse (allowing design technology to take place in a modular way).

This chapter goes on to show that increasing competition is leading to the rise of service-oriented business models and that a purely architectural SOA (focused on smart design of technology) is not enough.

In this context, SOA-enabled business services form the building blocks of a new category of loosely coupled, network-centric business applications. Business services networks help businesses forge robust, loosely coupled connections among competencies that include people, processes, and systems — within an enterprise or across enterprises. SOA enables an incremental, risk-mitigated approach for IT to deliver value to business. This approach is different from the "big bang" approach described in the book *Business Process Management — the SAP Roadmap* [Snabe et al., 2008]. The approach suggested and described in this book uses more of a process-by-process and/or a project-by-project approach. SOA projects focus on the reuse of existing services and the creation of new services that are available to the business for use in new and creative ways to build the next generation of loosely coupled business processes and applications. As a result, companies can derive successively higher value from SOA with subsequent projects. We refer to this as the *value multiplier* of enterprise-wide business services.

Today, leading organizations are providers of end-to-end processes optimized around service and efficiently servicing stakeholders. Also, through the services duality, comprised of both business services and information technology (IT) services, the services become a pivotal binding and connecting element. This holds true between the provider and the customer and between the provider and suppliers and partners in the business network for solution creation. In this perspective SOA enables companies to conceptualize and define (business perspective) and to implement and adapt (techno-architectural perspective) business processes with unprecedented speed and ease, as well as to break down processes into smaller process steps for reusable enterprise services that can easily be adapted to changing business needs.

2.1.1 Adaptation Driver: Increased Service Orientation

You face challenges that are unique to your industry. You need to overcome the rigid, static nature of inflexible IT methods traditionally used to support business goals, and you need to do so in a way that lets you change rapidly and seamlessly as market forces shift. Service is the new product. For decades we have known that "all industries are, effectively, service industries; some industries merely have greater service components than others" [Levitt, 1972]. Yet today we witness a significant increase in services globally and a shift from services around products toward products around services. So-called hybrids, which are characterized by a tight and effective interplay of product and services, have become the de facto standard in solutions. Due to the duality of services, the rise of business services on the one side is not only mirrored but also accelerated by the diffusion of technical services such IT-based Web services and enterprise services on the other side. As the service complexity increases, we are shifting away from services supporting and differentiating products via services enabling products toward services finally being the product. These factors accelerate the importance of services and ultimately lead to the evolution of an own market for easily consumable services.

2.1.2 Adaptation Driver: Networked Business

Networks, with their market coordination, are increasingly replacing hierarchical coordination mechanisms. Companies are focusing on few but differentiating core competences and, due to diseconomies of scale or scope, they are breaking up their value chain into sub elements, handled by separate companies. Traditional industry boundaries are blurring because — in this networked economy — a customer solution can be aggregated across company and industry borders from many providers. The evolving business networks can be characterized as follows: Relationship is an asset, risk is shared, and innovation is driven collaboratively — often based on open architectures.

As a result of the network paradigm, the following questions become central: What do I stand for as a provider? And what is my superior value contribution to the network as a whole? This is applicable to both consumer markets and business-to-business markets. Take Twitter and Facebook, for example, where your attractiveness to others can be directly measured in terms of your number of "followers" or "friends," respectively. Business-to-business markets are all about interaction with business partners to extend and innovate on business processes across company borders. In a networked economy, constellations can arise where companies must cooperate in one step of the value creation and compete in another, which is referred to as *co-opetition* [Brandenburger and Nalebuff, 1996]. The fundamental idea of a network-based business model is not to grow your own market share only, but to grow the entire market for the business network via network externalities. Hence, in a networked economy, business is no longer a zero-sum game [Neumann and Morgenstern, 1928]. The end result is that companies are required to capitalize on relationships to maximize customer value brought together from different contributors across business networks.

2.1.3   Adaptation Driver: Power-Shift from Supply- to Demand-Side

Customers in networked markets recognize that they can easily connect to share information, collaborate, and join forces for increasing brain or bargain power. We witness a shift in power from the supply- to the demand-side [Cluetrain, 2000] as represented in the power of the customer. Driven by the power of Internet-enabled networked markets with informed buyers supplied by communities, today's customers' standard for a good-enough solution has significantly increased. Consumers seek tight interaction with their providers, and customers can become co-innovators and co-creators. Increasingly, customers are even willing to take over part of the provider's value chain to create the last mile of the solution customer-individually, what is termed *prosumerism* [Toffler, 1980].

2.1.4   Service-Oriented Enterprise as Goal – Transformation as Journey

As companies seek strategic advantage, today's enterprises thrive in a highly networked world, where only the smartest — not necessarily today's largest — companies will survive. Accelerated by the three adaptation drivers outline above, we witness business shifting from top-down, hierarchical ways of working and managing to distributed, agile, collaborative forms of doing business. There is increasing evidence that enterprises are changing gears toward an end-result-orientated solution paradigm, which is centered on the consumption of services from distributed providers in customer-centric networks.

A service-oriented enterprise is characterized by "its ability to reliably deliver new or enhanced services in order to maximize new business opportunities ... Service-driven enterprises are optimized around service, around efficiently servicing customers, employees, partners, all the stakeholders; responding rapidly to their needs, and adapting rapidly to new requirements, to changes in the industry, to changes in the market" [Gold-Bernstein, 2009]. In this setup, services — in the form of a business and/or technical service (duality of service) — become a pivotal binding element and connector between the provider and the customer, as well as between the provider and suppliers and partners in the business network for solution creation. In addition, providers are bound to comply with service-level agreements (SLAs) that they have agreed upon with their clients and subsequently establish SLAs with their suppliers and partners also. These service-oriented enterprises can act as the orchestrators of networked solutions.

Energized by this ambition, an increasing number of companies are setting themselves the ambitious goal of transforming into a service-oriented enterprise and becoming a provider of networked solutions. Because this signifies a substantial shift in terms of business model and related business processes, such a transformation will not happen overnight; it is, rather, about leading a journey of change.

2.2   Business Transformation Change Levers

Successfully transforming a company into a service-oriented enterprise requires solid knowledge of the most relevant change levers and how to manage them effectively. Figure 2.1 contrasts the key characteristics of a function-oriented enterprise with a service-oriented enterprise.

On the left-hand side, the function-oriented enterprise is primarily optimized for singular products and characterized by its focus on excellence per function, for example development, purchasing, procurement, production, marketing, sales, and service. This functional orientation is also organizationally reflected via a hierarchical coordination of vertically focused entities along the activity steps of the enterprise's value chain. Revenue is linked to transactions; profitability depends heavily on efficient production and economies of scale.

On the right-hand side, the service-oriented enterprise provides (networked) solutions, which are often consumed as a service by the customer (SLA) and orchestrated from distributed contributors. These various solution contributions can stem from both own functions and divisions and can be externally sourced from other suppliers, partners, and third-party providers, all again linked by service levels in a business network. When done right, the higher service portion of the solution offering and consumption-based pricing mechanisms can lead to predictable recurring revenues and service-driven profitability.

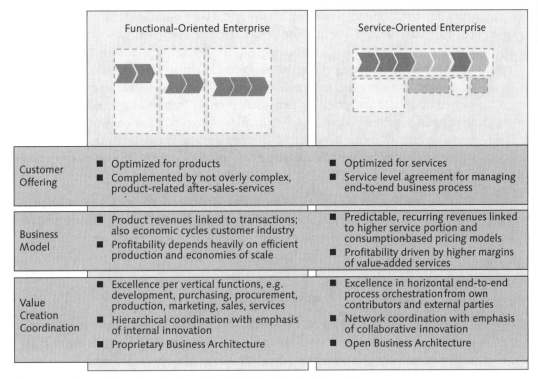

Figure 2.1 Change Levers for a Service-Oriented Enterprise Transformation

After this brief overview, we will discuss three change levers in more detail in the following sections (Section 2.2.1, Section 2.2.2, and Section 2.2.3).

2.2.1 Change Lever: Customer Offering

In a function-oriented enterprise the offering portfolio — to solve a customer problem — often has a certain product focus typically complemented by not overly complex, product-related after-sales services such as guarantee, inspection, maintenance, and spare parts. Because the targeted market is anonymous and standardized, we witness a primarily transaction-based low-touch customer engagement aiming for high volume. Differentiation relies on new and unique features and functions and their combination.

In a service-oriented enterprise the provider can design and manage an end-to-end business process on behalf of their customer and often commits its delivery against a specific service-level agreement. With the holistic solution in focus, the provider aims for the end result of the "job to be done" [Johnson et al., 2008] or, in other words, the root cause of the customer problem to be resolved. Both the integrated view of tightly integrated services and products in the form of a hybrid and the lifecycle perspective are pivotal to meeting the total solution value or *problem coverage* expected by the consumer. In this context, service excellence can be understood as offering high-value services from plan to run, which make up a unique selling proposition for the provider. Leading service-oriented enterprises invest where they can excel in more advanced solution dimensions such as consumability, adoption experience, and lifecycle cost (total cost of ownership [TCO]).

When transforming from a function-oriented enterprise into a service-oriented enterprise, direct customer access with tight provider-consumer collaboration and even co-creation, differentiating service capabilities, and leading project management skills for customer-individual business problem resolution are required.

2.2.2   Change Lever: Business Model

In a function-oriented enterprise the product-driven revenues are transaction-based and rather volatile because they are somehow linked to the economic cycles of the served customer industry. The profitability ceiling can be reached when economies of scale are fully exploited in standardized production because the service profitability is rather low due to its product-support and commodity character. Because mass products are sold to an anonymous market in a low-touch transaction fashion, the prevailing huge marketing investments with their bottom-line impact can be explained.

Following the paradigm of a service-oriented enterprise, an increase in the provider's profitability is linked to differentiating by better satisfying the end-to-end business process requirements of a specific customer with the provided solution. Service-driven revenue flows prevail, which are recurring and thus predictable. Pricing is increasingly linked to the effective consumption of a service level (pay as you go). Besides the impact on the top line, a stronger margin position is achievable, driven by unique high-value-added services and their higher profitability. Based on the SLA, the customer now finds a supplier, which is strategically aligned with their own goals. This can entail a strategic relationship with recurring engagements based on a joint roadmap and a multiyear contract framework, in which the provider ultimately can become the customer's trusted advisor.

When transforming from a functional-oriented enterprise into a service-oriented enterprise, appropriately managing the balance between scope and scale — solution individualization and reuse/standardization — becomes pivotal. This is also referred to *mass customization* [Pine, 1992]. This also holds true regarding professional services. Optimizing the whole and avoiding sub-optimization is the strategic imperative in a service-oriented enterprise.

2.2.3   Change Lever: Value Creation Coordination

In a function-oriented enterprise, vertically integrated value chains prevail. Separate functions and often also processes for development, production, sales, and support are optimized per area and therefore require top-down hierarchical coordination to optimize for the overarching strategic intent of the enterprise. Despite partnerships, the business architecture tends to be closed, assets are self-owned, and physical assets such as production sites play a major role — also in terms of indicators of firm-internal importance.

In the service-oriented enterprise, keeping the SLA commitment requires orchestrating an end-to-end business process on behalf of their customers across their own functions and divisions and across suppliers, partners, and third-party providers within a business network. The required horizontal organizational layer for end-to-end process orchestration is the result of an open business architecture — and thus rather network-based and best-described as loosely coupled with the provider's incumbent organization. Every provider from the network delivers directly or indirectly against the common goal of the SLA, which ultimately ties the various solution contributions together. A portion of the providers are expected to be "virtual," (*cloud-based*) because they provide highly automated and specialized solution contributions without being an enterprise in the traditional sense. Generally, innovation is driven in a more distributed or even open manner relying on the talents of contributors from outside corporate boundaries [Chesbrough, 2003; Surowiecki, 2004; Hippel, 2006]. Ultimately, relationship assets dominate over owned assets, and the management of the service-oriented enterprise's ecosystem becomes a major source of competitive advantage.

When transforming from a function-oriented enterprise into a service-oriented enterprise, the provider requires a profound understanding of all relevant building blocks to deliver an optimally orchestrated solution to the customer, whether these building blocks stem from their own functions and divisions or those from third-party providers or even competitors. As a consequence, integration competencies are pivotal in a solution business to secure interoperability. To achieve this goal, the solution architecture becomes central because it is the company's reusable blueprint of how all required building blocks fit together for a specific customer solution. Due to the heterogeneity of today's customer landscape, the demand for open standards and architectures increases.

2.3   Business Transformation Case Studies

So far, we have studied the drivers of the adaptation of the service-oriented enterprise and how to manage the change levers effectively. To make a transformation toward the service-oriented enterprise more tangible, in the following sections three business-to-business case studies — Rolls Royce Total Care, Arvato Lead Logistics Services, and Hewlett Packard Managed Printing Solutions — outline how they have proactively driven such a business model transformation.

2.3.1   Case Study: Rolls Royce Total Care

With Rolls Royce's Total Care offering, an airline can buy "operating aircraft miles" as holistic solution instead of purchasing engine products, paying maintenance fees, and investing in infrastructure [Rolls Royce, 2010; Linz, 2009c]. The airline orchestrates the customer problem resolution process end-to-end across functions, divisions, partners, and so on to deliver against a service-level agreement with their customer/consumer. To achieve this, Rolls Royce has transformed itself from a product company with loosely coupled functional silos into a services-driven, SLA-oriented provider for total solutions and integrated firms (see the transformation in Table 2.1).

	Function-Oriented Enterprise	**Service-Oriented Enterprise**
Customer offering	▶ Product-oriented with engine, aftermarket spare parts, and support	▶ Solution/SLA-centered via operating aircraft miles ("power-by-the-hour")
	▶ Independence from effective usage, product purchase and recurring support costs occur, and investment in support infrastructure is required	▶ Price linked to effective consumption of service level (pay as you go) leads to more manageable expense stream

Table 2.1   Rolls Royce Function-Oriented vs. Service-Oriented Enterprise

	Function-Oriented Enterprise	**Service-Oriented Enterprise**
Business model	Volatile top line because product revenues are directly linked to economic cycles of airline industry	Predictable revenue flows and a stronger top line and margin position due to higher service profitability
Value creation coordination	▸ Hierarchy with loosely coupled functional silos ▸ Maintenance's job was to maintain, support's job to support, manufacturing's job to build, and so on	▸ Integrated firm orchestrating a business network for end-to-end process performance ▸ Measurement and analytic capabilities to monitor and proactively respond to changes that could affect their SLA

Table 2.1 Rolls Royce Function-Oriented vs. Service-Oriented Enterprise (Cont.)

2.3.2   Case Study: Arvato Lead Logistics Services

Arvato Logistics Services is a subsidiary of Arvato AG, the international media service provider of the Bertelsmann Group. As a lead logistics provider (also a fourth-party logistics provider), they design, orchestrate, and manage significant portions of the outsourced supply chain on behalf of their customers [Arvato, 2010; ARC, 2005].

The goal was to benefit from blurring the borders between the out-sourcing manufacturer, in-sourcing logistics service providers, and their partner/supplier ecosystem and move into more sophisticated, more complex, higher-margin logistics services (refer to Table 2.2).

Arvato Logistics Services was founded in 1964 as Bertelsmann Distribution. They have transformed their business model and now act as a global supply chain manager. Their service offering comprises end-to-end supply chain solutions including customer service, sourcing, production, procurement, warehousing, order-entry, distribution, after-sales services, and financial services. Their core competency is the orchestration of various logistics offerings (transportation, warehousing, value-added services) from several specialized providers without necessarily owning the related assets. Customer value is created through end-to-end process visibility and orchestration.

	Function-Oriented Enterprise	Service-Oriented Enterprise
Customer offering	▸ Regional offering specialized in one category of basic services (e.g., transportation, warehousing); partly extended into more complex services (e.g., fulfillment, global trade, value-added services) ▸ Short-term, tactical focus on transaction costs	▸ Global end-to-end supply chain solution (one-stop shop) ▸ Arvato Logistics coordinates various logistics and information-intensive services including product development, sourcing, financing, and logistics ▸ Deep relationships with their customers and long-term contract based over multiple years
Business model	▸ Transaction-driven revenue portions ▸ Commodity services with low margin due to both high price pressure and asset and people intensity	▸ Predictable revenue flows and a stronger margin position due to higher profitability driven by supply chain design and management and related value-add services ▸ Created new business models and revenue sources through increased flexibility
Value creation coordination	Specialized logistics provider with typically vertically integrated value chain delivered via own people and assets	Arvato Logistics manages a worldwide business network (ecosystem) of partners and suppliers along the value chain to accomplish end-to-end supply chain processes for a specific customer

Table 2.2 Arvato Function-Oriented vs. Service-Oriented Enterprise

2.3.3 Case Study: Hewlett Packard Managed Printing Solutions

Hewlett Packard, as a provider for managed printing services today, runs on behalf of their customers complete office solutions over a one- or multi-year contract period out-of-one hand [HP, 2006, 2010; IDC, 2010]. This entails the management of fleets of printers, scanners, copiers, and facsimile machines and includes value-added services — beyond simple break-fix and ink/toner supplies replenishment —such as installation services, lifecycle management, device usage monitoring/reporting, help desk support, and consulting/implementation services.

Hewlett Packard has transformed itself from a vertically integrated producer and seller of primarily hardware devices into a solution provider that integrates workflow knowledge and technical competencies for holistic and customer-individual office printing solutions (see Table 2.3).

	Function-Oriented Enterprise	Service-Oriented Enterprise
Customer offering	▶ Device-oriented with (personal) printers and peripherals including device guarantee ▶ Installation and maintenance of infrastructure not in scope but locally managed by customer organization	▶ Printing solution/workflow-centered including value-added services and on-site personnel ▶ With Printing Payback Guarantee, HP commits against projected efficiency increase
Business model	Blade-and-razor-type business model with recurring cash streams from (relatively expensive) genuine spare parts and expendable items	▶ Predictable revenue flows and a stronger margin position due to higher profitability, especially of value-add services ▶ Plannable one- or multi-year contract for the outsourced management
Value creation coordination	▶ Product-focused organizational entities optimized for economies of scale ▶ Different sales and go-to-market organizations address large enterprise customer with their printing and imaging offerings	Integrated business unit enterprise printing and imaging solutions since 2006, which orchestrates customers' end-to-end business process requirements across specialist centers in technology, services, and workflows and vertical applications and HP capabilities

Table 2.3 HP Function-Oriented vs. Service-Oriented Enterprise

2.3.4 Lessons Learned from the Cases

Rolls Royce Total Care, Arvato Logistics Services, and Hewlett Packard Managed Printing Solutions have provided three case studies, in which these companies have transformed themselves into service-oriented enterprises. Despite the fact that all of these cases stem from different industries and vary slightly in terms of the business model, they all rely on the same pattern: management of end-to-end processes by SLA is at the core of the service-oriented enterprise. Now the question remains: How can such a transformation be enabled? What role does IT play, and do the typical business characteristics of the service-oriented enterprise, such as service orientation, horizontal network orchestration, and open architecture, also apply on the IT-side?

From these cases we can extrapolate that service and process automation enables businesses to bring the strategic context as well as the organizational processes and technology context together for cost optimization and agility:

► Strategic context: Extends the value of your previous asset investments.
  ► Reduces unnecessary redundancy and complexity.
  ► Removes inefficiencies.
  ► Optimizes costs.
  ► Ensures compliance.
  ► Boosts productivity.

► Organizational context: Enables efficiency through interaction and collaboration.
  ► Connects with fixed and mobile people and systems beyond the traditional organizational perimeter.
  ► Pulls out reusable business functions from your application portfolio.

► Technology context: Enables access to complex, heterogeneous data sources.
  ► Enables information.
  ► Enables flexible, no boundary, any-to-any connectivity.
  ► Builds IT capabilities to match changing business needs using shared information and application investments.

► Process context: offers tools and services to help streamline business process management.
  ► Through processes, the different services are choreographed across disparate applications, people, and systems.
  ► Process automation provides complete flexibility including ad hoc tasks, ability to handle complexities of human workflow, and enforcement of workplace management policies.

- ▸ Continuous improvement context:
  - ▸ Links people, processes, and information for your business in creating new untapped business performance and value.
  - ▸ Enables various business competencies, critical for competitive advantage and differentiation, to share information and services and thereby create a new form of continuous improvement and competitive advantage.

This list provides the means to dramatically increase the alignment and value of IT to the business. Service orientation changes the way we approach and meet the changing needs of the business — providing the basis for working smarter in relation to IT, business processes, and overall business model.

2.4 Information Technology as Dynamic Capability of Business Enablement

As we have seen so far, the management of end-to-end processes by SLA is at the core of the service-oriented enterprise. Speculating on such a vision is one thing; effectively implementing it in a company, however, is another. So let's look at the ambition of the service-oriented enterprise from the perspective of how it can be enabled technologically. Let's start with managing the process by SLA. Doing so requires that we define the right kinds of service levels and then associate them with every level of the process landscape. Business service levels, in turn, need to be translated into IT service levels that can be used to control IT assets throughout the entire lifecycle, from design to operations to improvement, for example, the selection of applications, the availability of information services, their performance during execution, and so on.

The translation of business service levels to IT terms is, however, not a simple forward-mapping exercise: First, we need a common language between the two, which we will call the *translation framework*. The translation framework allows us to represent the business reality including goals, needed enterprise capabilities, business services and their SLAs, and so on at all levels of the company. Second, we want the capabilities of IT, in particular the information services provided by applications, to be exposed in that framework so that the business can "see them" and choose them according to its needs. This bottom-up projection from IT to business terms will help make the top-down mapping from business demands to IT solutions easy. Third, the IT solutions identified by this business-to-IT translation process have to be viable (it must be possible to realize them) from planning via implementing to operating and continually improving — within the given business constraints on time and costs.

The idea of translating business needs to IT based on business concepts, such as goals and metrics, is not new per se. In fact, enterprise resource planning (ERP) was launched as a means to address the business problems by providing off-the-shelf business solutions to the enterprise that were expected to run the business. The translation was sought by reframing the use of IT in functional business terms: Applications were named after functional areas of the enterprise, and the aspiration was to make each of them run better as a whole: logistics, accounting, and so forth.

The challenge of this concept for the service-oriented enterprise is that ERP was designed based on the assumption that once you implement it, the enterprise never stops using it — which is right because its needs are now carved in stone; however, the assumption that this can or will never change is wrong. Today, change is the only constant in business. But change is costly to digest for ERP: By being encompassing and integrated, it was relatively hard to customize at granular levels, so rather than being a friend of change, ERP has in some cases become a resistance factor. As an out-of-the-box solution to bring about change for the better, it turned against later, incremental change.

Fast-forward to the days of the service-oriented enterprise: pressure on IT is mounting as the speed of change is incessantly increasing. Change is, in particular, not confined to the single enterprise anymore, and therefore dealing with change is not a matter of choice but of need. Today's business processes are not confined to single companies; they have been blown to bits by the pervasive presence of the Internet in the business world and now stretch across multiple companies and even time zones and continents. These days, the typical value chain comprises more than a dozen companies. Thus, the limitations of ERP have become contagious beyond the value chain of the enterprise to the whole value web spanning our business networks.

As a consequence, today's challenge for IT is that it needs to sort out how to map business to IT while dealing with the change of business models and the scalability of the business partner network or, put differently, how to make value, material, and information flow through living multipartner supply and demand networks.

To live up to such expectations, IT needs to reinvent itself. The remainder of this chapter will show us the way to this goal.

Requirements for a New, Process-Centric IT Paradigm

Let's start by looking more closely at the two key requirements for a successful business-to-IT-translation process: accurate communication and fast translation.

IT and business need to be learn how to accurately communicate. The still pervasively practiced methods for requirement gathering and translation — involving expert interactions and the creation of written specifications — get lost in an ocean of stakeholders and iterative translations. In that process, the business reality represented losses to make business sense and becomes unduly "technified." IT needs to ensure that business objectives drive the communication end to end for the service-oriented enterprise.

Beyond accurate communication, we need fast translation. Expect that the demands on the responsiveness of IT to changing business conditions will be no less than exorbitant. For example, consider WYSIWYG-type business modeling and the processing of what-if alterations in real time. This requires that the translation framework be algorithmic; that is, it can be processed automatically, possibly even without human intervention.

Both outlined requirements can be addressed by realizing a translation framework that shows how the business perspective and the IT perspective can be mutually mapped. The ideal vehicle for mapping the two perspectives onto one another is the layer of business processes: it is in the process landscape where business strategy meets execution. If we are to improve the execution of the strategy, we should improve the value contribution and effectiveness of its execution through supporting processes. This holds true independent of whether a given process is executed manually or in an automated way, with a supporting IT solution. In the latter case, and taking our translating framework perspective, the supported processes become the linchpin between the business strategy and IT sustaining its execution: It is at the level of processes where our preferred translation framework understands where and how IT should be employed for the support and execution of the business strategy.

This leaves us with the question of how we represent this business-to-IT linchpin in the translation framework. We must go back to our requirement for a fast translation framework; we will represent process models in a formal way, using a formal language with established modeling conventions suited to describing processes such that they can be processed by machine.

In summary, the translation framework at the heart of the new IT therefore has to be implemented in a modeling language with process definitions in its center (see Table 2.4).

Real Entity	Modeled Aspects	Example
Business goals	Objectives and measures	External drivers
Business competencies	Service levels to customers	Service performance
Business Process	**Internal and External Structures**	**Activities, Events, Actors, Inputs, Outputs**
Supporting IT capabilities	Service levels	Service availability
Technical landscape	Elementary IT components	Existing applications

Table 2.4 Levels of the Business-to-IT Translation Framework

Providing a translation framework with the above modeling elements in order to represent the essential layers of business and IT, and ensuring that the models can be read and processed by machine is not enough. As we said, we need the framework to be business-fluent such that it can capture requirements *intuitively*. This requires that all aspects of business reality (goals, capabilities, and processes) are captured at the right level of our framework. But just representing them is not sufficient; they also need to be connected in the right way. Let's break down this linkage from the top.

As elaborated in Chapter 1, when you analyze business models, you find that they contain information on future revenue, gross margin, working capital, investment, and so on. Consider these types of information as stated business ambitions. Each of those ambitions corresponds to a set of business *capabilities* that define what the enterprise needs to be capable of doing in order to fulfill them.

For our purpose, it is crucial to understand which competencies are the essential ones to have in place. Beyond listing and classifying enterprise competencies, you must identify which CCCs are crucial to realizing the strategy and separate them out from those that only support NCCs. By identifying the CCCs and NCCs and understanding what's essential versus supporting the list of business competencies, we establish a top-level criterion for qualifying how the enterprise should operate (selection and execution of processes) in light of what it should be doing to support its business model (fulfilling its strategy).

To break down this criterion to lower levels from business model to business execution, described in Part III, Chapter 14, and in Chapter 3 on value drivers, one would introduce a value-driven model that aligns metrics across the entire business lifecycle of planning the strategy, aligning the organization, aligning operations, executing processes and initiatives, monitoring them, improving them, and finally kicking off the next iteration of the overall strategy management lifecycle. With this value-driver-based coupling of strategy to operational plans and processes, and the linking of operational metrics to strategic metrics, we have made the translation framework truly business-fluent. With the systematic association of value and process that we have described on the business side, the service-oriented enterprise can manage its SLAs from the process level, up.

Finally, going from the process level down into IT, we need to equally link business-service-level requirements (e.g., to execute a given automated activity within a defined process) to the functions and competencies that IT provides (e.g., an on-demand information service).

That mapping of business competencies into IT capabilities is the scope of BPM and enterprise architecture: To define a consistent projection of the requirements of the business that have been pinned down in process definitions (selected following business criteria to provide business SLAs as described above), IT capabilities, and their enabling technical components.

2.5   Process-Centric IT Lifecycle Management

Let's briefly recap what we have discussed so far: In an effort to enable optimal IT support for the execution of business strategy, we have described the traits of a translation framework that establishes top-down alignment in principle. At the core of this framework, process models are the gateway for the connection of metrics for strategy to those for execution, including execution enabled by IT.

Our translation framework is complete; it has the power to truly put the process in the center of a tool-based lifecycle that embeds metrics and execution models, with a consistent, bidirectional mapping from the business strategy, via process definitions to execution in IT. Let's now look at how IT needs to manage the content provided by our framework.

2.5.1   Closing the Loop of Business Process Management

Going back to our comments on the increasing impact of change on the modern enterprise, the question is: For how long did we solve the problem? How do we sustain the alignment that the translation framework has so nicely provided for us? All alignment, once established, will be challenged by business change, entailing a possible disconnection of strategy and execution and a break in value contribution. We still need to equip IT with the capacity for ongoing realignment to strategy. Without this dynamic capability, the ideation and adoption of new business models could easily become pointless because enterprises would risk operational paralysis.

With the framework as "plumbing" in place and content (metrics) flowing through it, we only achieve top-down mapping and alignment. The role for IT in this mapping process is to support the effective creation and maintenance of models that describe the enterprise (people, process, technology). Now, what about the execution of the modeled process? What about the monitoring?

The capabilities to analyze the modeled reality, create formal models, adjust and refine them, deploy and run them, and monitor them in execution are, taken individually, gambling table stakes for contemporary IT. Rather than creating process descriptions in a modeling environment that is solely used to capture and maintain them and then moving on to implement the processes by configuring and enhancing business applications, for the business-IT alignment to be sustainable, as we are now considering, we need IT to act not as an array of tools but as a one entity, as a type of flexible skeleton of the translation framework, enabling not only tool-based business modeling but also model-based execution including all analytics.

This requires taking the defined business process and natively representing it in IT terms such that it can run the content. Here is where IT needs to evolve from present business process management, where IT receives the information from the business and then separates out the modeling from the execution of information functions. Due to this separation, what should be a closed-loop cycle revolving around a business perspective ends up being broken into pieces that show the factual limitations of IT tooling and applications in use. Such process management only occurs in sections limited to only those part of the cycle that the specific applications and IT services can actually support.

The transformation framework that we have described here allows us to go past the present state of affairs and truly put the process in the center of a tool-based lifecycle that embeds metrics and execution models.

Providing models for execution that can also be edited and changed is not something new. However, we are aiming for a framework that provides a template of the enterprise that can be easily adjusted to changing needs, one that does not require restarting the top-down requirements translation but is sufficiently prepared to be modified in the area that requires the change.

Again, such delta-modeling can now be achieved thanks to the business representation that includes performance goals (SLAs) at all levels and is mapped into pertaining IT elements at all levels (including the most granular IT services). Handling change here becomes a matter of testing and adopting a variant of an already existing model. A "what-if" simulation can be achieved by altering a parameter (business metric) of the already established model. In both cases, through the aligned content, an organization benefits from an automatic identification of affected and required IT elements and chooses what to do with them. With a content-rich framework, you can close the gaps in business process management that separate modeling and simulation from implementation and performance measurement and achieve true closed loop behavior, where processes iterate through analysis, design, implementation, and running/monitoring.

2.5.2 Accelerating the Process Lifecycle

Closed-loop business process management will still not happen unless it has acceptable parameters of cost, speed, and quality for the entire effort needed to improve the process lifecycle. We still need to understand how the new IT of the service-oriented enterprise can manage the application landscape process on faster cycles and at lower costs for change without compromising on the quality of the solution.

To answer that, let's us look at where IT can go from here. First, what are the alternatives to the existing ERP paradigm to address the cost/time challenge? One direction is to give up on the ambition of being holistic and integrated and instead focus on providing point solutions for pain areas. Adding to the idea of reducing granularity, a company should add loose coupling of solutions and obtain an on-demand cloud architecture for point solutions that would give them the "ability to use components from different cloud resources and mix and match the solutions they are seeking" [Linthicum, 2009]. Using easily consumable services of various dedicated solutions, be they on-demand or on-premise, could indeed signify a dramatic improvement in the focus areas considered.

There are two things to consider: First, the grindstone of unpredictable business change will end up challenging the selection of the problem (pain spot) and therefore the usefulness of the solution. New business requirements may render the point solution equally useless and outdated. Even if a point solution is cost-effective when looked at in isolation, having to change it will drive up the costs of integration and cause operational problems of huge dimensions. Nimble IT like this alone won't do. It is still fundamental that the deployment speed achieved be balanced with the ability to achieve overall consistency. Point solutions lack the ability to integrate into that flux of top-down metrics-managed strategy to execution alignment, the life stream of closed-loop process management that spans the enterprise. To give a negative example, the proliferation of point solutions results in adoption of minimum standards for data exchange with other applications and, over time gives rise to *dirty data* that spreads across the application landscape and reduces the reliability and thus usability of IT.

Second, static and siloed systems that can't expose their competencies to the network of solutions will not be able to be part of the process orchestration and rapidly become a repository of legacy functionality in maintenance mode. An overarching portfolio of business content holds the key to entering into this process orchestration. Applications consistently exposed as executable models possess the right modularity to be rearranged as business and process models change.

Therefore, an IT approach needed for the service-oriented enterprise fuses the best insights from the tradition of ERP (business fluency and integration) and the still-maturing era of modularity and virtualization (service orientation, loose coupling, cloud computing). The solution is for the service-oriented enterprise to *combine* the two elements to achieve end-to-end business fluency in a network of solutions that leaves room for rapid and economical change and introduction of point solutions in a cloud that are the missing piece of the puzzle. See Table 2.5 for an example evolution of IT for the service-oriented enterprise.

	Function-Oriented Enterprise	Process-Oriented Enterprise	Service-Oriented Enterprise
Main goal	Productivity	Excellence and agility	Excellence, agility, collaboration
Value chain	▸ Monolithic structure of domains ▸ Static domains integration	Value webs spanning multiple enterprises with described interfaces	Value webs spanning multiple enterprises; loosely coupled and dynamic
Managerial focus on BPM	Business process engineering and management	Business process innovation	Business model innovation

Table 2.5 Evolution Toward IT for the Service-Oriented Enterprise

	Function-Oriented Enterprise	Process-Oriented Enterprise	Service-Oriented Enterprise
Process landscape	Defined processes; hard to change	Defined processes; managed for change	Situational business processes
IT buyer	IT as buying center	IT as buying center	LOB as buying center
IT paradigm	System integration	Service-oriented architecture	The cloud
IT components managed	Systems and applications	Layers of applications	Pluggable process elements and user interfaces

Table 2.5 Evolution Toward IT for the Service-Oriented Enterprise (Cont.)

If IT has largely been about productivity, it is now about innovation through collaboration, based on an overarching information base supporting the management of business service levels: the wisdom of crowds, social networking, and cloud-sourcing. Companies must now learn how to survive and thrive in a world transformed by social technologies that are outside any one company's firewall. With such an IT department, the service-oriented enterprise can become a bold reality, clearly offsetting it from its predecessors.

2.6 Reaping the Promised Value of Reusing Information and Services

To wrap up the possible benefit/value discussion we will show how process- and value-centric IT lifecycle management enables us to take full advantage of one of the central tenets of SOA: reuse.

When designing IT services for a service-oriented enterprise, it makes sense to break functionality down into smaller pieces, provided that the pieces or building blocks can be reassembled, rearranged, and reused easily. This often means that more time is spent up front in designing for reuse. However, a bigger payback awaits downstream as time and budget are freed to focus on innovation, differentiation, and the overall return on investment (ROI). However, traditional development paradigms might tempt programmers to code process variation and complexity into the service itself. In doing so, the programmers make it less and less reusable over time and more and more costly to maintain, putting your development team right back where they started. With process service enablement, business rules connections, and policies, complexity can be abstracted from the process and the services, maximizing reuse. Figure 2.2 shows how reuse and ROI build over time with an SOA approach to design.

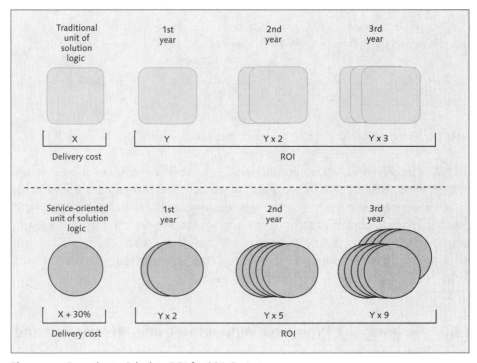

Figure 2.2 Formulas to Calculate ROI for SOA Projects

Duplicate functionality and duplicate processes tend to exist almost everywhere in the average enterprise. As processes are improved by using a service-oriented approach to IT, expensive and inconsistent duplicate functionality can be diagnosed and replaced with a single reusable service. To support such an analysis for reuse in terms of tools, service registries and repositories, which are used to manage and govern service reuse, can be queried to determine whether an existing service is an appropriate candidate for saving time and money and speeding up implementation. Business process and SOA teams are perfectly positioned to guide this as they work on their improvement and design projects. As a consequence, business process logic will no longer be deeply embedded in application code, where it is locked away and expensive to change. Instead, process logic will exist in the form of high-value business services that are reusable. Processes that use these services will be much more flexible and cheaper to maintain over time. They will allow businesses to achieve significantly better results in responsiveness, cost effectiveness, and profitability, as the following list of benefits shows:

▶ Reuse common functions to encourage repeatable business behavior and reduce the chance of errors in process execution or data capture.

▶ Reduce the amount of new code that must be created for business initiatives.

▶ Lower maintenance costs by eliminating redundant systems.

▶ Expedite the roll-out of new business functions by creating shareable composite services and functions from within your applications.

▶ Integrate tasks performed by your legacy applications into broader business functions to establish a simple and effective means to enhance the usefulness of backend-based information and provide the capability across more of the business.

▶ Identify already existing functions such as CRM access in existing applications and processes.

▶ Extend green-screen applications to the Web or to an SOA to realize immediate payback in reduced end-user training and improved staff productivity.

▶ Resolution through faster, simple responsiveness challenges such as technology obsolescence, skills scarcity, or significant business events including merger or acquisition.

▶ Enhance business flexibility and provide a return on investment by maximizing the reuse of services.

2.7   Summary and Recommendations

In times of accelerated change and increased uncertainty, a growing number of companies are increasing the service portion in their offerings, running pay-as-you-go and consumption-based business models, and creating value in customer-centric business networks together with contributing stakeholders. In other words, more and more, companies are adopting ingredients of the service-oriented enterprise paradigm.

The service-oriented enterprise needs to be supported by an IT department that is explicitly and consistently aligned to the services of the business at all levels. That is accomplished through the adoption of an end-to-end translation framework that allows you to define enterprise goals, processes, and metrics and derive supporting business information services. Therefore, the IT organization needs to learn to execute the outputs of business process management in a native environment. If this business-IT alignment is given process management and SOA through the combination of business model, greater overall benefits can be achieved in a shorter period of time with an increased focus on projects that produce clear and measurable business results such as:

▸ Proven problem-solving tools and techniques speed analysis and technical requirements definition.

▸ Process simulation allows alternatives to be more thoroughly evaluated and tested with limited risk and without more costly real-world experiments.

▸ Reusable process and service components become business focused and, as a result, reuse increases over time, further accelerating improvements and innovation.

▸ New improvement options such as business policies, rules, workflow, and process monitoring result in more innovative and flexible improvement and design alternatives and solutions.

▸ Process measures are more predictive, results are focused, and included escalations and alerts are designed to head off problems before they grow.

With the reuse of services and the connection to processes, proposed improvements and process models can be published and shared with process workers by using a browser with embedded discussion capability. By using this discussion capability, feedback can be gathered, even remotely, prior to coding and piloting, which reduces risk and cost and facilitates buy-in and change management.

The set up for the improvement solution should include a business model, a business process linked to services, a definition of attached business rules, automated workflows with built-in escalations and alerts, and integration that automatically passes data from one participating application to another, eliminating rekeying and the associated errors. It might also include user-maintainable business rules that automate decisions and approvals and value and performance drivers. Such value and performance drivers would, as described in Chapter 3, include key performance indicators (KPIs), dashboards that link to critical success factors (CSFs), and strategic business objectives (SBOs).

Furthermore, the improvement solution should provide visibility into individual transactions that make it easier to manage running processes and guaranties greater flexibility, which can be built into the improved process, enabling it to respond to changing conditions either automatically or manually by allowing the process owner to modify business policies or rules through a browser interface. To incorporate this flexibility in an improved or new process, process variation (which is within different business competencies and their service needs) is identified. In addition, business rules are defined in the process model. Rules and policies are expressed in business terms that are easy to understand and change with little or no IT involvement. Table 2.6 shows the as-is process and the to-be process when it is improved by using BPM and SOA technologies.

Current State Process	Future State Process
▶ Bottlenecks and constraints	▶ Streamlined with automated workflow
▶ Rework, errors, and exceptions	▶ Exception-based, including alerts and escalation (out-of-bounds conditions and time-triggered)
▶ Missing, incomplete information	
▶ Fragmented processes that are held together through spreadsheets, rekeying, and informal workarounds	▶ Improved access to accurate information through integration
▶ Numerous approvals and audits	▶ Rules-driven approval and routing
▶ Sequential activities that create delays	▶ Use of managed parallel activities
▶ Paper-based processes	▶ Dashboard monitoring and decision-making based on real-time KPIs linked to CSFs and SBOs
▶ Lack of measures and performance indicators (decisions based on feelings vs. facts)	
	▶ Improved ability to respond to and implement required regulatory controls
▶ Lack of documentation	▶ Reusable business services
▶ Processes that are too slow and costly to be competitive	

Table 2.6 BPM- and SOA-enabled Process Improvement

Reusable services are added to the future-state model from the service repository (service reuse accelerates implementation while reducing risk and cost). Technical attributes can be added to the process model by making it immediately usable by the applications. The model serves as a requirements contract. It is imported directly into the application development environment, creating clarity and speeding deployment of a limited-scope pilot project and eventually production implementation. PPIs, KPIs, and measures dashboards are integrated into the solution user interface, allowing all process components (applications, workflows, measures, alerts, and email) to be accessed from a single window or interface.

As illustrated in Figure 2.3, knowing which processes are the sources of differentiation and how they fit into the business architecture is critical to remaining competitive. Therefore, it is necessary to view the business competencies as a value-producing whole and to recognize where organizational structure either gets in the way or adds unnecessary costs. Look closely at the business model and the connected processes in a view of process architecture, as they cross organizational boundaries, and use simulation to test for the impact of improvements upstream and downstream. Connect PPIs and KPIs that measure the result of the defined CSFs and SBOs of the organization (versus the department or function alone). Deploy dashboards early on to provide needed information visibility and alert process owners to changing conditions and problems. Using an approach that aligns the business model, the business process linked to services, the definition of attached business rules, automated workflows, and value and performance drivers, you can establish the service-oriented enterprise and reach a cohesive yet agile alignment of business and IT (see Figure 2.3).

As shown in Figure 2.3, business model innovation and transformation, and the service-oriented enterprise, needs to be supported by IT that is aligned to the services of the business. There are specific tasks that must be completed by the business before successful implementation:

- Define business competency service needs, as described in Chapter 1, Section 1.7.

- Identify services that will add value to your business competencies.

- Define value drivers when cascading your SBOs and CSFs to measurable performance drivers that define operational and financial KPIs that should be measured through PPIs such as efficiency, volume, cost, time, and quality.

- Map existing service technologies to business processes.

- Link processes with their respective architectures:

  - Business architecture

  - Information architecture

  - Data architecture

- Develop and apply governance principles.

- Set implementation priorities and assess the impact of the new SOA environment on legacy systems.

- Provide an efficient, reliable repository for process artifacts.

▶ Support real-time continuous improvement.

▶ Translate design into execution.

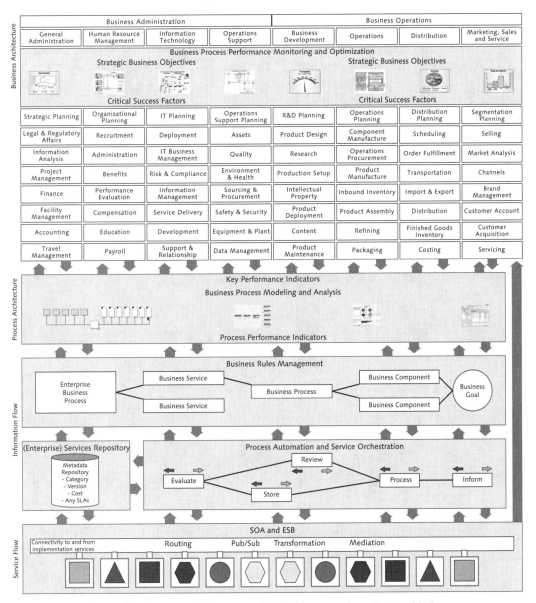

Figure 2.3 Framework for Alignment of Business and IT (Kuhlmann and von Rosing, 2010. "Applying BPM Principles to SAP EAF")

We can conclude that enabling business competencies with services built on SOA-based processes and backed by process-centric IT lifecycle management can dramatically increase the rate of operational improvement while freeing time and resources to focus on new opportunities, business innovation, and growth. In the end, service-oriented enterprises are not just rewarded with affordable and reusable technology; they achieve the process flexibility needed to quickly serve new customers and launch new lines of business.

"What a company doesn't monitor, measure, and control they most likely won't see happening."
– Johan Troels Benthin, CWT, Chief Operations (attributed)

3 Practical Example: How to Develop Performance and Value Drivers

Mark von Rosing, Ann Rosenberg, Ferry Bogaards

Value creation and realization are probably some of the most common dilemmas and challenges confronted by companies today, regardless of factors such as size, revenue, industry, region, or business model. The decision to make large-scale investments in IT-enabled processes, as well as the complex challenges in ensuring that these investments are effective end efficiently transformed into the different competencies to realize concrete business value, need to be managed. In far too many cases, this business value simply is not realized. In recent years, survey after survey has revealed that from 30 to 70 percent of large-scale investments in (for example, IT-enabled change) is wasted, challenged, or fails to bring a return to the company. In fact, one survey on measuring costs and value found that in many enterprises, less than 8 percent of the IT budget is actually spent on initiatives that bring value to the company [Butler Group, 2005]. Another survey from Deloitte [Deloitte, 2004] reported that 124 financial executives claimed that almost 80 percent of IT projects did not actively encourage value creation and thereby realization in their enterprise. A 2009 IBM survey of Fortune 1000 CIOs found that, on average, CIOs believe that 40 percent of all IT spending brought no return to their organizations [IBM, 2009]. A 2007 study conducted by The Standish Group found that only 35 percent of all IT projects succeeded while the remainder (65 percent) were either challenged or failed [Cook, 2007].

However, this lack of value creation and realization is not an issue only specific to IT investments, for very few companies actively manage their value. Research carried out by the Cranfield School of Management suggests that less than 30 percent of the largest companies actually have a formal value management process [Peppard,

Ward, 2003]. They don't have a formal value planning, value creation and value realization formulation, identification, monitoring, or measurement process in place.

Due to these issues, many organizations ask themselves what it takes to get value right. For most companies, the issues of creating performance and real value are not new, which include stiffer cost competition, commoditization of products, and slower growth in their traditional markets. The economic and business environment of 2009 and 2010 makes addressing these issues increasingly urgent. Agile companies, however, will persevere and, in the end, use this economic cycle to their advantage. Behind rising expectations of dazzling efficiency, effectiveness, and stellar business performance is a flood of information that has created an entirely new set of assets just waiting to be applied.

Nourished by real-time information streams, organizations soak up information as avidly as tap roots seek water. Business leaders need to know, for example, the precise whereabouts of critical supplies. They want deeper insights on the buying behaviors of their customers. They seek better understanding of their operations and the financial health of their partners, as well as the economic and environmental consequences of both immediate and distant events. The right information moves organizations forward, instead of holding them back. Analytics describe the use of information in a process to find patterns; identify new possibilities, create new flows, processes, and scenarios; make predictions, and prescribe actions. But the decisions resulting from those insights bear fruit only when the entire organization gets behind them and makes the changes required to "make the break." Of course, this transformation doesn't happen all at once.

3.1   The Need for Performance and Value Creation

In performance and management literature, various reasons are mentioned why companies would manage on economic value. First, it is recognized that traditional accounting measures have shortcomings, such as alternative accounting methods that may be used, risk is excluded, investment requirements are excluded, and the time value of money is ignored. Second, three developments fueled the need to manage a business: shareholder activism, capital activism, and manager activism. Third, the absence of a share price (for firms not listed) or competition was reason to create a benchmark based on economic value, in addition to regulatory requirements.

Even though performance and value management has been discussed in practice and theory over the past 30 years (see Appendix A), the disclosure of information on strategies, business models, critical success factors, value drivers, and performance drivers in general has gained more importance in recent years then it had before, and both theories and methods have developed to incorporate this change.

Value creation is consistent with the value maximizing objective of a firm and the objectives of managers. It facilitates better resource allocation and prevents mere growth without profitability. It provides a good base for executive compensation, which further aligns owner-manager goals [Rappaport, 2008]. When aligned right, it can be used as a strategy for firms and individual business units [Salter and Zwirlein, 2009]. However, you need to consider the full value lifecycle, which means understanding that value that is not planned is difficult to identify. And if you haven't identified where or how to create it, how can it be created? Furthermore, you can only realize value equal to the value you have created. In our discussions of core differentiated competencies in Chapter 1, we illustrated that value that is created through best practices is less than when one tries to compete with best practice: One realizes less value than when one tries to compete with differentiation (see Figure 3.1).

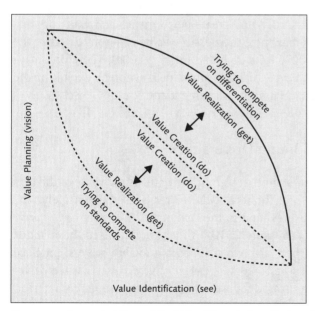

Figure 3.1 Connected Flow of the Value Lifecycle (von Rosing, 2009. "Business Value Management")

Before we move on with our value driver discussion, we would like to note that any value work should follow the value lifecycle phases:

1. Value planning
2. Value identification
3. Value creation
4. Value realization

The supply of information on firms' value lifecycle processes, and thereby performance and value drivers, has been increasing in various reporting media such as annual reports [Williams, 2009], IPO prospectuses [Bukh et al., 2008], and analysts' reports [Meca et al., 2010]. Furthermore, some firms have started developing intellectual capital (IC) benchmarks that compare their own performance with that of their peers in the industry and IC reports that communicate how knowledge resources are managed in the firms within a strategic framework [Mouritsen et al., 2010; Bukh, 2003], and new models for reporting on stakeholder value creation are gradually emerging [GRI, 2002; Elkington, 2007]. But an explicit recognition of performance and value drivers for value planning, identification, creation, and realization as a central part of a business model is generally lacking in practice and the literature. However, because we see this as a vital area for BPM, value management, enterprise architecture, and new implementation projects, we have developed a method to plan, identify, and create performance and value drivers. The goal of any company is to maximize the possible value creation to realize the most created value [Pitman, 2003; Sundaram and Inkpen, 2004]. Therefore, management should focus on the lifecycle that leads to value creation by exploiting the firm's value drivers in the value planning and value identification phases.

3.2   Performance and Value Drivers

A value driver is any important factor that significantly affects the value of the firm [Amit and Zott, 2001]. Therefore, the term *value driver* is used extensively. The term is popular both in the business and in the IT domain. The term *performance* or *value driver* refers to those economic variables that are critical to the revenue and cost functions of a firm. There are two main sorts of value drivers: financial and nonfinancial, which are also termed *managerial value drivers*. A value driver should not be confused with return on investment (ROI), because ROI is a performance measure used to evaluate the efficiency of an investment or to compare the efficiency of a number of different investments. It can only be used to calculate possible return, and because the benefit (return) of an investment is divided by the cost of the investment, the result is expressed as a percentage or a ratio. Therefore, ROI only considers financial indications that can be measured. Value drivers are measurable operational variables that, when changed, can have an impact on one or more assessable values. Such variables can include cost savings, time savings, staffing adjustments, or service improvements. If ROI is a key goal when you embark on an IT project, then value drivers are what will help you get there. This makes value drivers one of the most important topics to help companies create and realize the value they want.

As already mentioned, a value driver is any important factor that significantly affects the value of the firm [Amit and Zott, 2001; von Rosing, 2009]. Researchers disagree about the number of these value drivers: five [Ruhl and Cowen, 1990], six [Moskowitz, 1988], and seven [Rappaport, 1998; Mills and Print, 1995; Mills, et al., 1992]. Turner [1998] has identified eight value drivers. The framework we suggest combines many of the existing methods and approaches; however, it is more tailored to linking strategic business objectives (SBOs) to critical success factors (CSFs) and key performance indicators (KPIs), and process performance indicators (PPIs).

One of the single most important factors is a clear understanding of the drivers, business factors, and the breakdown of the economic business value the investment can and should deliver. Introducing or improving real value-management practices in an organization is not an easy task, and will take time. It may require significant change in terms of value thinking and action around decision-making, value management, performance management, and accountability. Organizations should formalize the breakdown, as illustrated in Figure 3.2, cascading the strategic business objectives (SBOs) and its attached business performance indicators (BPIs), to the critical success factors (CSFs) with the associated key performance indicators (KPIs) and the attached process performance indicators (PPIs) in order to get the right identification and monitoring, or measurement process, in place [von Rosing, 2009].

An illustrative example could look like this:

▸ SBO = Accelerate profitable growth
▸ BPI = Growth +17% market share profit +9%

- ▸ CSF = Increase new customer acquisition rate
- ▸ KPI = 50 new customers per month
- ▸ PPI = Business transition rate = 60%

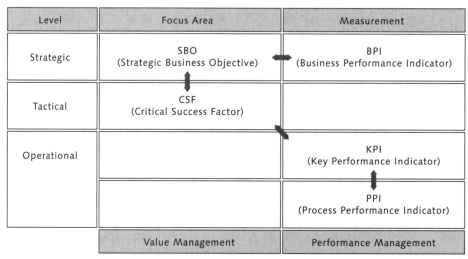

Figure 3.2 Breakdown of Organizational Value Drivers (von Rosing, 2009. "Business Value Management")

Defining performance and value drivers as illustrated in Figure 3.2 with the needed strategic link to operational levels is a challenging job, and that may be one of the reasons most organizations have difficulty putting this into operation, where they would combine the value drivers with the needed activities (process lifecycle) and then with the attached applications/solutions. In addition to combining the three lifecycles (value, process, and application), you need to incorporate the organization, the roles, and thereby the competencies they work with to ensure links to the business model as shown in the performance and value driver approach, illustrated in Figure 3.3.

As we can see from Figure 3.3, there are different levels of performance and value drivers that require different approaches to ensure that value drivers are planned, identified, created, and realized.

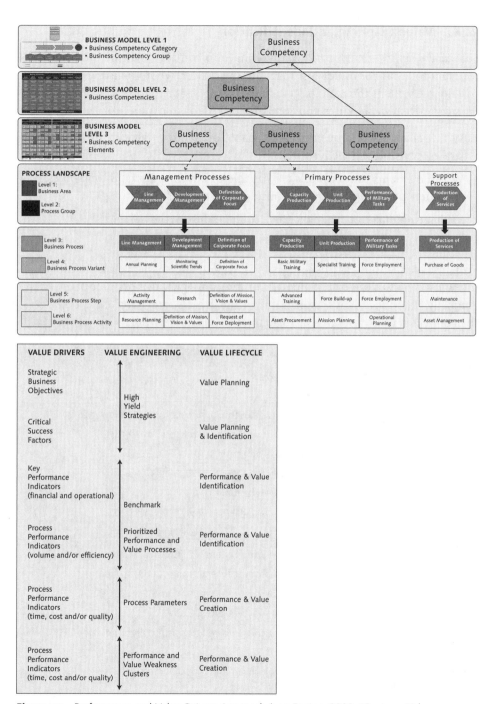

Figure 3.3 Performance and Value Drivers Approach (von Rosing, 2009. "Business Value Management")

3.2.1 Value Planning and Identification

For *value planning and identification,* you have to consider that the business environment today is about not just reaction, but action, where focusing on creating sustainable value is the main target. Therefore, it is vital to identify the main business competency categories and competency groups to explore:

▶ Which elements of a business are capable of creating value in supporting the strategic business objectives?

▶ Which elements of a business are capable of optimization and thereby cutting costs in supporting the strategic business objectives?

▶ Which elements of a business are capable of destroying value?

▶ Who would be the business owners of these value drivers?

Proper value planning at this level is the key element in uncovering and identifying what creates and drives value within the strategic business objectives of the company. Table 3.1 shows an example of the main strategic business objectives, the connected critical success factors, and the business owners.

Strategic Objectives	Critical Success Factors
Increase shareholder value – CEO	▶ Increase revenue through volume optimization – CFO, CMO ▶ Increase revenue through price optimization – CFO, CMO ▶ Reduce sales and administration costs – CFO, COO ▶ Reduce cost of goods sold – CFO, COO ▶ Reduce income taxes – CFO ▶ Capital optimization – CFO
Improve competitiveness – CEO	▶ Strengthen innovation – CMO, CRDO ▶ Speed up time-to-market – CMO, CRDO ▶ Improve responsiveness – CFO, CMO ▶ Improve customer interaction – COO, CMO ▶ Improve customer satisfaction and Loyalty – COO, CMO ▶ Improve brand awareness – CMO ▶ Improve partner and relationship collaboration – CFO, COO

Table 3.1 Examples of Strategic Business Objectives and Critical Success Factors (von Rosing, 2010. "Building New Levels of Excellence")

Strategic Objectives	Critical Success Factors
Lower risk – CEO	▶ Optimize intelligence – CFO, COO
	▶ Optimize regulation compliance – CFO
	▶ Improve risk planning – CFO, CRSO
	▶ Improve risk management – CFO, CRSO
	▶ Improve business recovery - CRSO, CIO
Improve operational efficiency – CEO	▶ Improve development and production – COO
	▶ Improve logistics, material, and services – COO
	▶ Improve corporate services – CFO, COO
	▶ Improve human capital management – CHRO
	▶ Improve capital management – CFO
	▶ Improve data management – CFO, CIO

Table 3.1 Examples of Strategic Business Objectives and Critical Success Factors (von Rosing, 2010. "Building New Levels of Excellence") (Cont.)

The value identification phase can be done by a focused review and analysis of the organization's business model from four different approaches:

▶ **Approach 1**
Interview or conduct a workshop with the management team, key personnel, customers, suppliers, or other business partners to gain an understanding of the strategic business objectives and critical success factors and business issues and pain points of those responsible for the different business model competencies, for example, CFO, COO, CMO, CHRO, and so on.

▶ **Approach 2**
Review financial and management reports and statements and conduct executive analysis to identify potential value gaps and thereby drivers such as high inventory levels or a decrease in revenues.

▶ **Approach 3**
Compare the premises and benchmarking competencies or end-to-end processes against similar organizations to identify potential value drivers. The value creation potential of improving each of the current and prospective performance benchmarks of the organization is evaluated.

▶ **Approach 4**
This is the process review approach, where the organizational competencies and/or end-to-end processes are systematically examined to find relevant value drivers. These functions can include the business strategy; marketing, sales, and

business development; human resources management; information systems; finance; research and development; quality; operations, logistics, and procurement; cost accounting; organizational structure; risk management; customer service and support; and project management.

Whereas approaches 1 and 2 are more top-down focused approaches, thereby being more value management focused, approaches 3 and 4 illustrate a more a bottom-up approach, focusing on performance management. However, in all of these approaches the goal is to identify not only value drivers, but also value gaps. The core weakness identification approach, which we know as the new ASAP methodology framework (see details in Part III, Chapter 14, Section 14.3), focuses on weakness cluster identification and mapping. Such a weakness cluster mapping is based on the current pain point situation (PPS) and any weaknesses within the processes. A current weakness cluster view with a pain/gain impact estimation (P/G-IE) is used to map and then analyze the PPS with the resulting pain point effects (PPEs) or undesirable effects (UDEs) in terms of results and the possible root problems of the organization and thereby determine the impact to the business model. A PPE or UDE is any major issue that prevents the organization from achieving its goal and is therefore a great source of value potential, as shown in Table 3.2.

As Table 3.2 illustrates, many of the PPEs and UDEs include problems and thereby weakness cluster symptoms that were revealed by the other approaches, as well as detailed or new UDEs. The distinction between situation, problems, and symptoms is crucial, because the real value creation potential lies in solving the core problems, not the situation or the symptoms.

3.2.2 Value Creation

We realize that for many readers the value drivers we illustrate in Table 3.2 might seem very high level. However all in all, value planning should incorporate strategic direction and thereby the challenges of the different C-level executives (e.g CEO, CFO, COO, CMO, CIO), indicating a significant need for restructuring, streamlining, and innovating processes and supporting the fields of the other executive officers whose strategic directions and challenges are possibly interlinked, pointing to possible shared business issues, pain points, and weakness clusters.

Pain/Gain Impact Estimation

Critical Success Factors	Pain Point Situation (PPS)	Pain Point Effects (PPEs) or Undesirable Effects (UDE)	Value Potential	Best Case in %
Reduce Sales and Administration Costs	Nine ERP systems that cover financial reporting	No corporate standard, double work of financial department leading to inefficiency and quality mistakes	Strengthen enterprise-wide financial reporting standards	▲ 4% less volume ▲ 3% efficiency gain ▲ 7% cost cutting ▲ 35% time improvement ▲ 13% Quality improvement

Best case and worst case would have to be rated in % gained within either volume and/or efficiency and then in either cost, time, or quality indicators

Worst Case in %	Estimated Likelihood that it Can Happen in %	Business Owner	Process Owner
▲ 2% Less Volume ▲ 2% Efficiency Gain ▲ 5% Cost Cutting ▲ 25% Time Improvement ▲ 7% Quality Improvement	▲ Less Volume = 80% ▲ Efficiency Gain = 85% ▲ Cost Cutting = 90% ▲ Time Improvement = 65% ▲ Quality Improvement = 90%	▲ Keren Happuk ▲ Keren Happuk ▲ Hans Peter ▲ Keren Happuk ▲ Keren Happuk	▲ Bjørn Storch ▲ Sven Thorleif ▲ Keren Happuk ▲ Sven Thorleif ▲ Bjørn Storch

Table 3.2 Example of a Pain/Gain Impact Estimation

As the challenges of the stakeholders implies, the scope of the challenges are quite extensive and in many cases most likely interlinked. Therefore, the value lifecycle and the process lifecycle should not be separated. The executive strategies we identified ranged from supporting growth, capital optimization, cost cutting, improving competitiveness, lowering risk, and operational efficiency topics, which all involve developing performance and value drivers on the operational level. This means rethinking many aspects of how business processes are done in the organization to create value. However, many BPM initiatives have fallen dramatically short of their possible value creation potential. The main cause for this is that most organizations take the as-is process and refine it to an improved design of the to-be process definition. This is similar to the way in which many organizations implement their systems (far too many still do it this way today). The reason why this approach is so limited is that in general the philosophical approach for these types of techniques accepts the basic process shape (the as-is) as valid, seeking to optimize and refine the process shape within the current constrained model of the process.

Michael Hammer, the father of business process reengineering (BPR) identified this issue and said that BPR only applies to optimization and refinement of the process within the current constrained model; for new process development or process innovation, you should apply business process engineering (BPE) principles. Although it's not common knowledge, most enterprises don't really understand the depth and breadth of their business processes if they haven't made a recent business modeling effort. This is based on the fact that most common processes that were designed years ago have been adapted for volume changes, exceptions, managerial regime changes, and additional regional activities. Processes tend to become costly and burdensome as a result of process entropy (what nonengineering types call decay). During economic downturns, the modeling of processes shows opportunities for cost savings that enterprises thirst for during tough times. This is an ongoing opportunity, but enterprises tend to forget this when new opportunities burgeon in an up economy.

In the previous section we discussed the need to link the value lifecycle to the process lifecycle and thereby bridge the gap between value planning, value identification, and value creation. The degree of value creation and the benefits the customer can get by implementing complex systems depends on how well the organization can align their processes, ranging from increased efficiency to greater business awareness. It is therefore important not to settle for the obvious easily achievable benefits of BPM, but to aim for the full level of value drivers. Figure 3.4 shows a process flow example of how such a value driver approach is executed.

The purpose of such an approach is to determine value drivers and thereby define key process changes for an implementation project. In order to not only plan the value drivers, but also create and realize these values, an organization should utilize the competencies (e.g. resources and capabilities) in the described approach (see Figure 3.4), which ensures that the organizational value drivers are implemented in the right processes as well as solutions and/or services. This approach establishes a shared understanding in the organization regarding which values should be achieved by which role, the needed information, transactions, and activities. Such a value management and performance management approach, as related to the important activities/processes of the organization in the context of its resources and capabilities, are vital to achieve the wished results.

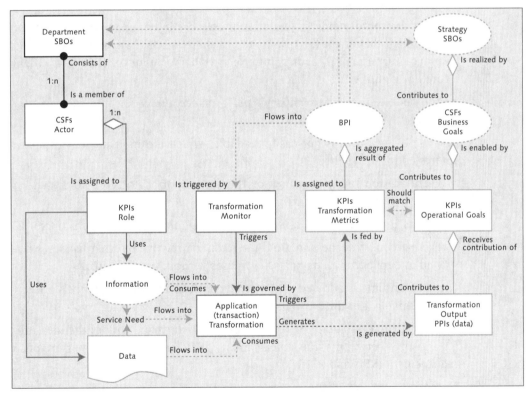

Figure 3.4 Process Flow and Steps in Defining Performance and Value Drivers

The following bullets highlight some of the reasons why so many such value driver approaches and other performance approaches fail to deliver the desired value and performance.

97

- The value definitions and performance measures are not credible with intended data users (roles) because:
  - The measures are based on unreliable, sparse, or old data.
  - The measures are being collected, complied, and/or reported by people who are not trained or held accountable for doing so.
  - The meaning of the measures is not clear (e.g. only performance measurements, for example PPIs, are done), which is not interlinked to the overall wished results.
  - The measures are not thought to be valuable or are out of date.
  - The people whose performance is needed for results are not aware of the measured results.
  - There are confounding factors other than those intended to be stimulated or controlled that affect the results; the cause relationship is unclear (e.g. pain point situation (PPS), pain point effects (PPEs) or undesirable effects (UDE) are not identified).
  - The actions needed to improve performance under the measure are not clear.
- The use of measures is not easily readable, which means management is not interested in the results:
  - There are too many measures or they are reported too frequently, which overwhelms data compilers and users.
  - Results are reported too infrequently to keep the organization on course.
  - There are too few measures and their context relative to other factors is not well understood e.g., having sales figures without profit figures.
- Not enough time is allowed for corrective actions to take effect; goals are too short-term (e.g. not linked SBOs and CSFs).
- There is no accountability or recognition for performance under the measure, e.g. no link between value management (SBOs and CSFs) and performance management (KPIs and PPIs).
- Goal targets are unrealistic.
- The goals drive the wrong performance.
- The results are not reported clearly or with sufficient detail and explanation.
- The end results are not used to make business decisions, which means there is no feedback loop and therefore no continuous improvement approach in place.

Approaching value drivers in the right way is a key for success; therefore, some practical experience of what to do and what not to do is shared and suggested in the next pages.

Value Driver Implementation

Ideally, value drivers, and therefore value identification, is done before the project begins or as a "lite" version during project preparation. At the latest, this should be done at the beginning of the blueprint phase. A strategy or business case, if one exists, is the starting point for value planning. Based on the input of business stakeholders and/or process owners, a pain-point analysis weakness list is made and key process changes are determined. Thus, key process changes drive the value of the project. The value tree, sometimes called the value map, associates strategic business objectives, critical success factors, and the operational key performance indicators as well as pain points, key process changes, and process performance indicators to measure success. The defined value drivers, therefore, are the central deliverable for value identification and value creation. Depending on the defined scope of the implementation, value identification and thereby determination is executed in a lite version or comprehensive manner. The deliverables of the new ASAP core methodology focus on the lite version of value determination. Therefore, it is vital to know that the results from ASAP value determination are, as needed, mapped to the process and solution design. A link is maintained through value maps, where KPIs and PPIs are defined, thereby developing operational value drivers.

It is the key process changes that will be identified in the value creation phase and that determine the value realization of the running system. The value drivers correlate to pain points, key process changes, and performance indicators and are thus the central deliverable for value creation and therefore for realization — the new ASAP core methodology includes the entire value lifecycle (value planning, value identification, value creation, and value realization). For more details about the new ASAP core methodology, please see Part III, Chapter 13, Section 13.3. Thus, you can conclude that the depth of value identification that was illustrated earlier defines the possibility for value creation, where the value lifecycle and process lifecycle meet with the application lifecycle. The results are value drivers that are mapped to the process and solution design, which is maintained through the connection of the value drivers described in Table 3.1 and the process illustrated in Figure 3.4, namely strategic business objectives and critical success factors with operational value drivers (KPIs and PPIs). At the business process area and process group level, operational and financial KPIs that are interlinked with PPIs come into play, and at the process level, PPIs are the link to the value drivers that now have become performance drivers.

In an implementation project, an optional as-is analysis can catalog existing process documentation, supporting to-be process modeling as reference material. As-is process models are mostly *not* created or updated at this point. Optionally, a solution transformation roadmap or landscape can also be created to illustrate how the overall solution is sequenced in implementation cycles. BPM principles can be applied to identify over- and underperformers using process volume and efficiency indicators. In a value driver process model, these indicators can be used for benchmarking with similar (internal or external) processes. Furthermore, they are used as the main source for the financial and operational KPIs. On the business process and business process variant level the process information is used to control the processes. Aggregated information on resource consumption (costs), exception handling (quality), and throughput (time) helps managers gain control over their processes and helps improve planning and sourcing activities.

In the business process step and business process activity, real-time or near-time process data can be used to guide the execution of processes, avoiding bottlenecks and unnecessary delays to ensure value realization. It is important that if a company wants to measure the performance in addition to the value, they need to know the activities related to this process on the operational level. The outcomes of these activities provide a lot of information about the effectiveness, efficiency, time, volume, and cost of the processes. Through connecting the value lifecycle with the process lifecycle, a company can achieve leverage to control the organization on an operational, tactical, and even strategic level.

The key to value creation is the linkage of strategic business objectives with critical success factors (CSFs, key performance indicators (KPIs), and process performance indicators (PPIs). The implementation of PPIs on a strategic, tactical, and operational level in the process landscape lays the foundation for closing the continuous improvement loop to value planning, value identification, and value creation through process performance. Appendix B illustrates how processes can and should be sorted after strategic, tactical, and operational activities and then at all levels linked to the key performance indicators , critical success factors, and strategic business objectives — including the business owner that would receive the value. Please note that as already stated in the new ASAP 7 methodology framework, which we will introduce in detail in Part III, Chapter 15, Section 15.3, the value lifecycle inputs for such value drivers are statement of work, scope determination, business case, initiative roadmap as applicable, to-be solution design as it exists, and as-is analysis.

However, the actual value creation and performance improvement start by identifying the process characteristics and resources that are used in business process steps and activities. When these parameters are identified, the basis for the process performance indicators on time, costs, and/or quality is available.

As mentioned in Chapter 1, there is a direct link between strategy, business model, and thereby value management between strategic business objectives, critical success factors, key performance indicators, and PPIs. Therefore, on a strategic (process) level, only PPIs that are relevant to the implementation of the business competencies are used. Managers on the strategic process level use benchmarking, process analytics, and simulation of the process parameters to determine the direction and the required course of action for the improvement of the processes.

The view of the process data changes from an actionable perspective (cost, time, quality) to a strategic one, where the data is aggregated to an analytical perspective (volume, efficiency). This is required because the data is used to support key decision-making and strategic decisions regarding the implemented business competencies defined as KPIs in the business models. Weight factors will be used to determine the contribution of the PPIs to the financial and operational KPIs.

3.3   Dimensions of PPI Measurement

Measurement needs to be made on an operational level and within two dimensions. The first dimension is the administration of the activities of the process flow. This gives the process participants important information about the status of activities within the process step. Depending on the processing of the activity, the outcome can be either expected or unexpected. An expected outcome has the expected output. Keep in mind that this tells you nothing about the quality of this output. If the activity is wrong, it will still generate the expected output. An unexpected outcome can be an escalation result (no resources to handle the activity correctly on time) or an exception result (human cancellation or failure by handling the activity) during the activity. Therefore, an activity always has three outcomes to handle. The expected outcome goes directly to the next function. An unexpected outcome is handled by an alternative activity or process step or even stops the flow. For continuous improvement, it is very important to measure all three outcomes; otherwise we would not be able to improve the process to create the goal value.

The second dimension is the summarized administration data of the process flows within a time frame. This gives the process owner important information about the activity and the complete process based on volume, average cycle times, involved participants, and quality based on time-outs, cancellations, and failures. Efficiency, effectiveness, and costs cannot be measured directly, but can be calculated based on the information we can measure. The quality of the expected output of an activity can also not be measured directly, but must be based on analysis.

From the two dimensions you can see that measurement, calculations, and analysis can become very complex, so you must ask yourself if measuring PPIs is worth the effort. The answer is very simple: Yes. It gives you the ability to relate value drivers, business processes, process steps, and activities on an operational level directly to the strategic business objectives of the strategic level. You can build business cases aligned with your strategy to improve your operation by simulating changes and analyzing the outcomes before implementing them. Furthermore, it helps middle management monitor and manage the activity effort within an organization by calculating a forecast based on historical data.

3.4 Summary and Conclusions

As illustrated in this chapter, you can unlock new possibilities by interlinking value drivers with your processes. By applying value drivers to your processes, you can get in-depth information about the process and have improved process control ability by measuring the true PPIs linked to the core competencies of your business model and to the KPIs, CSFs, and SBOs of your organization. By measurement and simulation, an organization can simplify its processes and create the needed value output defined by the strategic business objectives (SBOs). As defined are there two very different ways to go about this:

1. The first way is a bottom-up approach, which could incorporate:
   ▶ Analyzing inefficient processes (very difficult and costly)
   ▶ Analyzing the external and internal process changes
   ▶ Analyzing ineffective processes (a bit easier, but still very costly)
   ▶ Analyzing process weakness clusters
   ▶ Prioritizing process improvement and applying the changes either for the entire organization (big bang) and process by process or project by project

2. The second way is the top-down approach, which could include:
   ▶ Agreeing on the business model level

- ▸ Identifying executive strategic business objectives

- ▸ Business issues, challenges, and pain point situations (PPSs) as well as pain point effects (PPEs) and the undesired effect (UDE)

- ▸ Determining which core competitive and core differentiated competencies need to be adjusted

- ▸ Determining which competencies should be as cost-effective and efficient as possible and applying the changes either for the entire organization (big bang) and process by process or project by project

Today, the first approach is the most commonly applied, and it has multiple challenge and disadvantages. Some of these are links to executive business issues; challenges and point points are very low to nonexistent; the link with strategy is not very strong, even though it's very time-consuming; the link with the business model is very low and therefore the needed business model innovation and transformation often don't occur; the operational approach is very complex and therefore is a very difficult to control and very costly approach because it tackles operation-level processes, and unless input and output are measured on operational processes, it is difficult for executives to monitor and measure the value creation and realization that is happening and very complex to build a continuous improvement feedback loop from the reactions of the company to the changes needed.

We are not saying that defining value drivers is easy, but it is worth the effort, and we hope these examples have given some motivation in the right direction.

> **More Information**
>
> For more information or questions about performance management, performance, and/or value drivers and value management, please visit *www.openroundtable.org*.

"The first future you can really see is the future you can get."
– His Holiness, the 14th Dalai Lama

4 The Holistic Approach: Combining BPM with Value and Performance Management, Enterprise Architecture, Governance, and SOA

Robert Eijpe, Caspar Laar, Ann Rosenberg, Sascha Kuhlmann, Mark von Rosing

Over the past few years, many initiatives have come to life for SAP customers: Initiatives from service-oriented architecture (SOA), business process management (BPM), value management (VM), enterprise architecture (EA), and with this not only the technology architecture and information architecture, but also the business architecture. In addition to this, SAP's new ASAP Methodology for Implementation has been totally remodeled for the release ASAP 7. For additional information please see Part III, Chapter 15, Section 15.3.

This is a lot to handle, and more than one customer has become confused by the sheer numbers of methods and approaches. They start wondering how all of the pieces fit together and are concerned that all of them require governance to be in place. Seeing the potential of cost cutting and value creation with the business processes based on developing competencies and operational excellence, customers are nonetheless willing to invest in these products and embark on a journey to restructure and streamline their business. However, customers struggle with a lot questions. Some of the most common questions run along the lines of: Are these frameworks, methods, and approaches complementary to each other? Are they overlapping or contradicting? Can I do the one without paying attention to the other? And most of all: Where do I start?

4.1   Applying the Different Approaches

First, there is no defined answer to what comes first or where a customer should start. However, every customer should have a clear and accurate understanding of the business strategy, business model, and business architecture. All methods focus on the linkage between strategy, the organization, the processes, and how to integrate it all into technology to create performance and value. They focus on improving the way business activities are organized or executed and have cyclic methods for improving the efficiency and effectiveness of the implementation of the operational model. BPM, enterprise architecture, value management, and service-oriented architecture address similar topics, but from a different perspective, and enable different forms of performance and value creation (see Figure 4.1):

- *Enterprise architecture* (EA) focuses on setting the framework for the business design and sets in place standards, guidelines, policies, and procedures for ensuring the design, integrity, and, if identified and planned, performance, value creation, and realization for the business as a whole.

- *Business process management* (BPM) focuses on the management of the business process lifecycle, outlining the way the organization can and will execute its competencies. True performance happens at the activity level, and therefore most form of value creation happens at this level. One of the real benefits of introducing BPM principles to your processes is that you can add the principle of continuous improvement to the process lifecycle.

- *Value management* (VM) adds the concept of the value lifecycle form of value planning, value identification, value creation, and value realization, and benchmarks on the operational and strategic level and thereby identification of cost-cutting and improvement potential. Doing this improves the process lifecycle and EA setup. It also materializes the concept of operational excellence by adding characteristics and metrics used for setting up performance measurement.

- *Service-oriented architecture* (SOA) focuses on providing the design principles for an application architecture based on reusable components (services) and a flexible orchestration layer, which are applied when performing the solution transformation from business process requirements to the supporting IT solution.

- *Governance* focuses on continuously applying the principles in a structured and managed fashion. Governance is applied on all levels of the enterprise, and harmonization should be achieved between business, process, and IT governance.

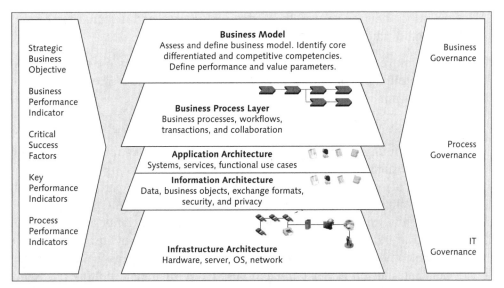

Figure 4.1 Applying Governance Principles to the Business Model, Business Process, Value and Performance Management, and Governance (Kuhlmann and von Rosing, 2010. "Applying BPM Principles to SAP EAF")

The different perspectives overlap on topic but not on content (see Figure 4.1). They support each other, and by harmonizing the governance of these perspectives, they will add value to one another and improve the quality of the individual improvement cycles. The same governance principles should be applied to the business model, business process, value and performance management, and realization in the IT domain. Furthermore, harmonization of these perspectives aligns business and IT initiatives because they are based on common standards, policies, and procedures and a shared orientation on the business processes. So business governance is one of the principles that can add tremendous value to the various business areas from the business model, EA, BPM, and value management disciplines, because it combines the different business areas.

4.2   Innovate Your EA Framework with BPM and Value and Performance Management Principles

The year 2007 marked the 20-year anniversary of enterprise architecture. In that time, several enterprise-architectural methodologies have come and gone. Today, four methodologies dominate the field: The Zachman Framework for Enterprise Architectures, The Open Group Architecture Framework (TOGAF), which SAP customers are advised to use, the Federal Enterprise Architecture Framework (FEAF), and Gartner (formerly the Meta Framework).

You could ask yourself if you should care about a field that is more than 20 years old. A good and right consulting answer would be: "It depends." The field of enterprise architecture was inaugurated to address two major problems in IT that were already becoming apparent by then. The first problem was managing the increasing complexity of information technology systems. The second problem was the increasing difficulty in aligning business with IT in delivering real business value with those systems. Sadly, most enterprise architects today only concentrate on the first part of the EA vision, neglecting the important second part, which focuses more on IT alignment. A good example of this is that most enterprise architects know hardly anything about business models, business operation models, value maps, value trees, and value drivers, which are all disciplines of business architecture. Developments in the business domain in the past few years have, however, put new demands on IT flexibility and business-IT alignment, putting this topic right back into the spotlight.

The more complex a system is, the less likely it is that it will deliver maximum business value without the linkage to business model and strategy. The better an organization can manage complexity, the more the organization improves the chances of delivering real business value. So should an organization care about fields of EA, BPM, governance, SOA, and business modeling? It depends on how an organization feels about value identification, creation, and realization and thereby positively affecting the bottom line. If managing system complexity and delivering business value are key priorities for the organization, they should care about these subjects.

Value Management

The key that combines the discussed material is that principles, policies, and standards from the enterprise architecture are applied throughout the enterprise continuum to the processes and the definitions of performance and value needs. This helps organizations harmonize the business model, business process, application, information, and infrastructure domains that are all part of the enterprise architecture. Understanding the business architecture is the first step in any enterprise architecture and the key to harmonization of the different perspectives on the same architecture domains. The business architecture is the discipline that combines and incorporates the business strategy and thereby the direction of the organization, its business model, and its operational model. Core (competitive and differentiated) and non-core competencies are identified and business activities are prioritized based on their importance to the performance and value creation of the organization. The business architecture thereby not only leads the definition and implementation of the business model and operational business model, but also sets up the objectives and indicators required to measure performance on both the business (strategic and tactical) and operational levels. This makes business architecture one of the most important disciplines to define the business model, performance, and value needs (see Figure 4.2 [Kuhlmann and von Rosing, 2010]).

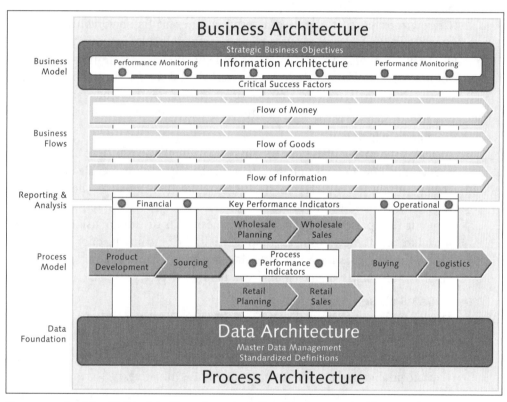

Figure 4.2 Applying EA Principles Throughout the Business Architecture (Kuhlmann and von Rosing, 2010. "Applying BPM Principles to SAP EAF")

Because the organization of the business and process models is aligned with the measurement and reporting of organizational performance, enterprises can adequately manage the organization. Applying the same set of principles, policies, and standards throughout the organization therefore becomes a value driver for operational excellence. We do, however, often see that the principles are not applied enough.

One of the major benefits of combining BPM with EA is that it can add value to both. BPM lacks the architectural principles, policies, and standards that emerge and develop during the architecture lifecycle. On the other hand, the BPM principles and disciplines can add a lot of value to the enterprise architecture framework of any company. Here are some examples [Kuhlmann and von Rosing, 2010] of the missing parts of enterprise architecture. Although the maturity of the enterprise architecture framework has been developed over the years, they are still lacking.

▶ **Standard deliverables**
These are proposed to be used across the different frameworks (similar to a project plan that is part of every project methodology): common "translators" or adoption guides for actual architectural content such as business capability/competency models, value trees, process models, data models, and so on. Today everyone is leveraging best practice or out-of-the box content from organizations such as APQC, but this is not the best way to do this.

▶ **Change management**
Although we have a phase in EA frameworks like the architecture change management in TOGAF, these phases are not robust enough to handle any kind of change. If you run a successful business architecture initiative, the developed requirements for the enterprise can result in a massive change request not only for your IT department, but also for business units or even divisions (e.g., the introduction of a new business competency or the outsourcing of one). Depending on the impact to the enterprise, these projects require a more or less heavy emphasis on change management even before the project starts.

▶ **TOGAF B phase**
The business architecture that is the TOGAF B phase is missing vital parts to develop a business architecture as defined above:

   ▶ The link to the business model is missing, and this results in the lack of strategic alignment, a presumption of any EA initiative.

   ▶ The link between the business model and the process landscape (process levels) is missing, which results in a missing alignment between the strategic level and the operational level, something that any EA initiative needs.

▶ **EA domains**
EA domains from business architecture, information architecture, and technology architecture are all missing a formal value management and performance management approach, which identifies, plans, creates, and realizes value. If these principles are applied, they are defined and developed individually. Hav-

ing every enterprise architect repeatedly develop the same needed approach and method is very costly and totally inefficient and ineffective.

Enterprise architecture frameworks and methods today have a project approach. This by itself is acceptable, especially when an organization is just implementing an enterprise architecture initiative. However, if an organization has already implemented enterprise architecture initiatives, this is not good enough anymore, because organizations need a continuous improvement and governance approach around their EA initiatives — not only an EA project approach. If EA initiatives are handled on a project-by-project basis, the whole concept of continuous improvement and governance is lost.

The good news is that when you're applying BPM (process lifecycle) principles to the architecture lifecycle, the missing areas identified above can be added to an organization's enterprise architecture initiative and/or framework. Figure 4.3 [Kuhlmann and von Rosing, 2010] illustrates how the value principles (value identification, value planning, value creation, and value realization) and continuous improvement and governance are added to the TOGAF approach.

This is how to apply the process lifecycle to Enterprise Architecture: The basic principle is that each pass through of the architectural lifecycle has a fixed set of EA project goals and thereby principles that apply throughout the iteration/phases (A to H). Within the iteration of the architecture lifecycle phases, the planning, identification, creation, realization, and governance of the value management principles are being applied. For the realization of the business value, individual iterations of the process lifecycle are initiated. When we enter such an iteration, governance and project approaches such as the process management lifecycle (PML) come into play. This continuous improvement process of business performance is guided by the business governance. It is important that at the end of every cycle, lessons learned, insight gained, and applied or developed standards are adopted in the principles, policies, and standards of the enterprise architecture so they will be available for the next cycle. SAP develops these approaches to go from the business innovation to the business transformation (business model, business value, and business performance) to the operational model and support the required solution transformation for IT solutions.

One of the key principles that helps organizations level the playing field is the *metamodel* that comes with TOGAF. As with all TOGAF content, the metamodel should be adjusted to the specific requirements of the enterprise to maximize the harmonization between architecture domains. The metamodel can be used as a basis for the definition of a common data model and for the creation of process modeling conventions and filters. In applying the above value principles to the metamodel, you can use the metamodel for the assignment of value and performance management principles to the individual entities.

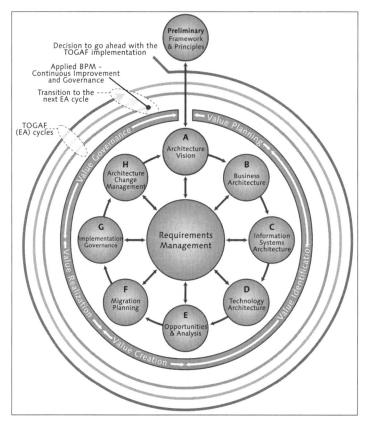

Figure 4.3 Applying the Process Lifecycle to Enterprise Architecture (Kuhlmann and von Rosing, 2010. "Applying BPM Principles to SAP EAF")

As illustrated in Figure 4.4, the EA metamodel can add tremendous value to BPM initiatives as well because the metamodel plays a key role in the definition of a common information and thereby application and data model for the business domain. Based on the organization's specific requirements, the services and process modeling extensions can be adopted, and the data modeling extensions can be extended to allow modeling of the data representations in the business process model. This adds a lot of information to the process models and is key to the alignment of business process requirements and IT solutions during the solution transformation phase of projects.

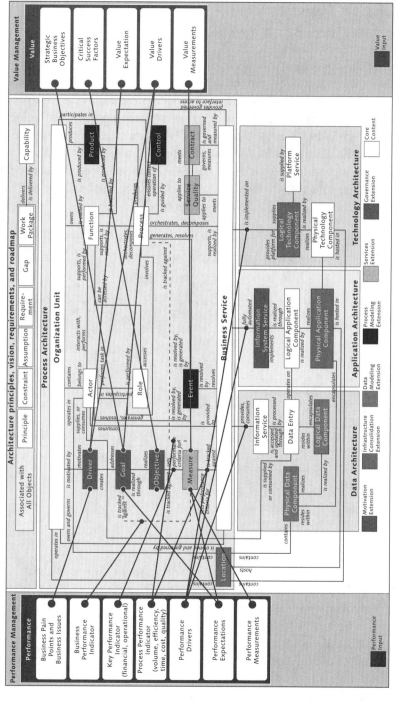

Figure 4-4 Applying the Performance Management and Value Management Principles to the TOGAF Metamodel B Process Architecture (Kuhlmann and von Rosing, 2010. "Applying BPM Principles to SAP EAF")

4.3 Solution Transformation – Harmonizing Enterprise Architecture, BPM, and SOA

To ensure that the operational organization of processes and IT solutions stays in line with the business strategy, model, and value proposition, solution transformation should be directly linked to the business architecture. In the new ASAP 7 methodology and governance approach, this link is guaranteed by assimilating the BPM process lifecycle in the project approach. Taking the business processes and process steps as the starting point for the transformation design, the IT solutions at least have a process-oriented basis. Adding SOA in the solution transformation phase even further enhances the link of the IT solution to the business processes and provides better-suited and flexible IT solutions.

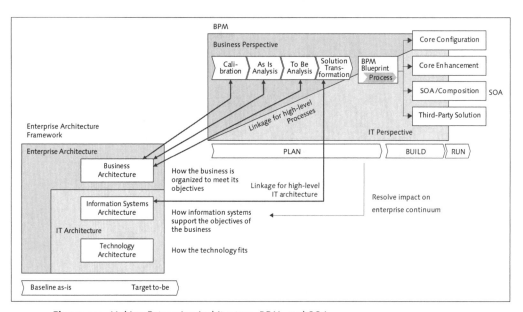

Figure 4.5 Linking Enterprise Architecture, BPM, and SOA

As illustrated in Figure 4.5, the transition process should therefore always start with a clear understanding of the business requirements. BPM helps identify these requirements through the ASAP methodology approach of calibration, as-is analysis, and to-be analysis phases (for more details please see Part III, Chapter 14, Sections 14.3 and 14.4.3). Sources for these analyses are always the business strategy and model provided in the enterprise architecture and the objectives and indicators from the value management perspective. This linkage between EA and the BPM method guarantees a consistent top-down approach throughout all of your projects and increases the reuse of existing information. Applying the BPM method and approach to EA, you can add SOA capabilities in a new way and even define their value during the phases, as shown in Figure 4.6.

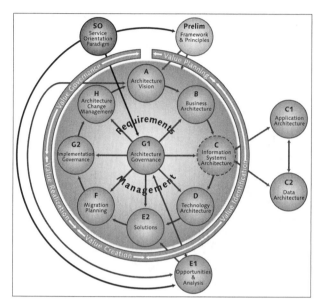

Figure 4.6 Linking TOGAF to BPM, and Therefore Value Principles and SOA (Kuhlmann and von Rosing, 2010. "Applying BPM Principles to SAP EAF")

Going through the analysis and design of the business processes gradually adds details and information about business activities. In the business blueprint phase, BPM work streams of the new ASAP 7 core approach the process step variants are broken down into activities, and SAP and non-SAP solutions are plotted against them. Here, Business Process Modeling Notation (BPMN) modeling enriches the solution design by describing the process activity flows and the required data flows and by identifying the automated and human tasks involved in the activity.

From an SOA perspective, on this level the primary identification and modeling of the involved business objects and domain services can be executed. Once there is agreement on the designed solution, further detailing of the solution on the implementation level is required. Here the individual core, non-core and service-oriented components are identified; service definitions, customizing, and enhancements are designed; and evaluation of existing solutions is performed. The result is complete documentation of the required solution known in ASAP 7 core as the business blueprint document that incorporates the organization's process and service needs (see Figure 4.7).

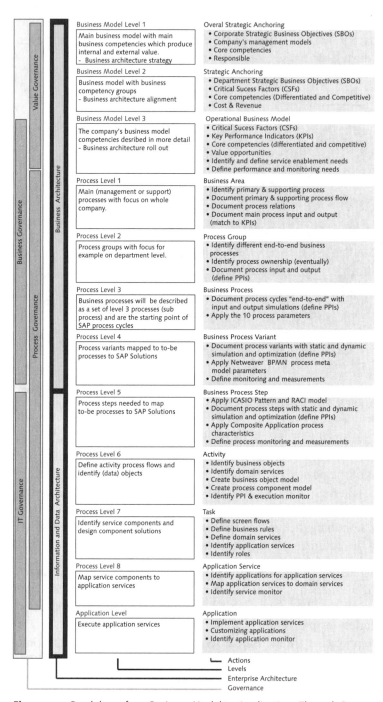

Figure 4.7 Breakdown from Business Model to Applications Through Process Levels

Linking the relevant outputs back to the enterprise architecture is essential to guarantee consistency and to evaluate the impact of a BPM project on the overall business architecture.

4.4   Summary and Conclusions

Planning for process alignment, value creation, continuous improvement, architectural principles, standards, rules, and governance is a necessity for most modern organizations, yet plans that are never executed because of missing approaches of how to do so have very high planning costs and very little operational value. The sections in this chapter are aligned and derived from the proper coordination between planning and execution of the overlapping principles in the approaches. This in turn requires a firm understanding of the lifecycles of the enterprise and the establishment of appropriate collaboration and governance approaches to ensure interlinking of the described approaches.

Whereas value management, business process management, service-oriented architecture, enterprise architecture, and business governance each have value on their own, we have described how they are naturally synergetic and work best when used together for better business performance and value outcomes and strategic alignment of business and IT. When these approaches are used together, value engineering (VE) provides the benchmarks and high impact strategies and thereby possible improvement areas. BPM provides the business context that outlines where to change the input-output model and provides an understanding of where to create the value and how and where to measure performance. SOA provides the design principles for solution transformation, and EA provides the discipline for translating business vision and strategy into architectural change. Although governance principles can apply the needed standards and rules, all are required for sustainable continuous improvement, optimization, and innovation.

It is important to realize the value of direct collaboration across the described boundaries. Only when supported by appropriate collaboration and governance processes can BPM, SOA, and EA roles work effectively together toward the common goals of the enterprise. The key to business-IT alignment and what glues it all together is the processes and activities. The notion of having business process optimization and integration of approaches has been around even longer than VE, SOA, EA, and governance. Yet around the same time that EA and governance became a mainstream topic in the context of business and IT alignment, the focus in many process optimization communities shifted subtly to BPM to go beyond an optimization approach. The key distinction for BPM as a discipline is added focus on flexible and dynamic process design and process orchestration and automation through IT enablement. In addition to reduced costs through continued improvement and automation, BPM also provides the foundation for converged and agile business and IT responsiveness and is the key to applying the principles discussed in this chapter. Figure 4.8 shows these principles from the process management lifecycle perspective in integrating business modeling, process modeling, governance, ownership, business value, and business performance.

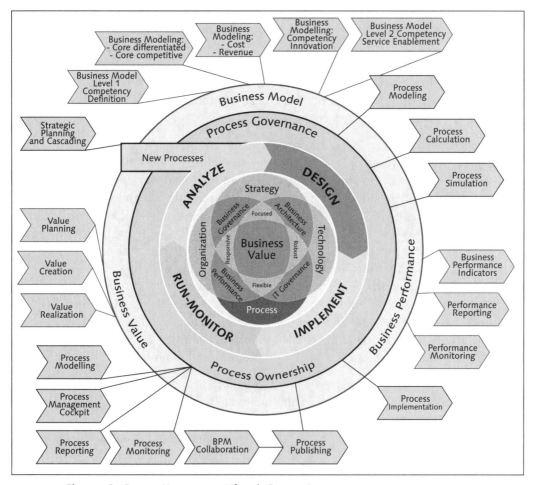

Figure 4.8 Process Management Lifecycle Perspective

Whereas each discipline has value on its own, Figure 4.8 illustrates how the disciplines are naturally synergetic. When combined, they provide better business outcomes in terms of performance, value creation, business architecture, and governance, which all are about strategic alignment of business and IT. To that end, the new ASAP methodology and governance framework (which will be described in Chapter 13, Sections 13.3 and 13.4.3) are a good starting point. ASAP 7 core combines the application lifecycle, the process lifecycle, the project lifecycle, and the value lifecycle; and the Business Add-Ons to ASAP provide governance frameworks for BPM, SOA, EA, Value Management, etc.

> **More Information**
>
> For more information or questions about how to use business modeling, process modeling, enterprise architecture, governance, ownership, business value, and business performance, please visit *www.openroundtable.org*.

"A man is saved no faster than he gets knowledge."
– Joseph Smith, 1843

5   Conclusion

In the last four chapters we have covered vital knowledge, approaches, and methods that are missing in too many project engagements today. Among the knowledge we have covered is how value identification, creation, and realization matters — and how business models should be the prime targets for innovation and transformation of an organization's core competitive and differentiated competencies. We have discussed the important fact that a business model is not a strategy. The separation of model from strategy is the strength and weakness of the business model concept. Because the business model is the product of the strategy, a business model can only be as strong as your strategic business objectives (SBOs), critical success factors (CSFs), and key performance indicators (KPIs). If a company wants business-IT alignment, they need to align the strategy to business model, the business model to the process model, and the process model to their systems — and all of this with the right architecture and governance framework. Given the potential impact of business model innovation and transformation, we have discussed how critical it is to take a close look at your competencies to identify the few essential processes and activities that set you apart — and find innovative ways to create and realize value.

In addition, we have explored the important missing links of how to link C-level needs and wants (drivers) into an organization's BPM project and then develop performance and value drivers.

All opportunities that SAP supports within the process (value, project, and process and application lifecycles) will be illustrated and demonstrated in the use cases in Part II. In addition, you will be introduced to various SAP methods, frameworks, BPM tools, process-based pre-packaged implementation content, enablements, and approaches in Part III of this book, where you will find the guide to enable you to apply BPM in all of its aspects for your SAP-centric business and IT environment.

We will now move into Part II, where we will explore a collection of BPM use cases from different corners of the world. This section aims to share already collected experiences/knowledge and the value drivers and lessons learned from BPM initiatives executed by SAP customers. You will be able to gain an insight into how to approach BPM from both the management and the technology perspectives.

PART II
BPM Case Studies
from the Real World

In Part I of this book we discussed the business drivers of BPM and central topics, such as business models, business model transformation, service orientation and how BPM can combine the important approaches of enterprise architecture (EA), service-oriented architecture (SOA), governance, performance, and value management. In this part we present a compilation of real-world BPM use cases from SAP customers that share experiences and lessons learned in different industries. You will obtain the necessary insight needed to approach BPM from either a management or a technology perspective. These use cases will give you inspiration for possible starting-point ideas for your projects, hurdles and challenges to watch out for, and possible benefits.

Before we look at the different ways in which SAP customers have approached business process management and applied it in specific use cases, it's helpful to take a broader look at the commonalities of BPM implementation between customers and partners to understand the pros and cons of each scenario. For instance, reading our description of a function or shortcut within a program may not help you understand the potential nuances or difficulties involved when implementing this program in a specific enterprise. How can you foresee a lack of experience or maturity, missing prerequisites, a need for expediency, or extenuating factors that require adjusting a methodology to fit? In this section, we try to bypass the difficulty of understanding a conceptual theory without real-life examples by showing you some qualitative observations of how BPM adoption occurred among the early SAP customer base.

"Experience without theory is blind, but theory without experience is mere intellectual play."
– Immanuel Kant

6 Observing How SAP Customers Approach BPM: The Gap between Business and IT in BPM Projects

Greg Chase, Rukhshaan Omar, James Taylor, Mark von Rosing, Gregor Müller

Many SAP customers have been experimenting with or using BPM tools from non-SAP vendors for several years. Market surveys of SAP customers done in 2009 and 2010 showed that at least 50% had some sort of business process management initiative in progress. In some cases, these customers had even deployed projects based on BPM in their company, but these projects very rarely related to or integrated with their SAP core applications. Based on our observations, these experiments have nearly always been proofs of concept to test the BPM technology and have generally not led to the establishment of a BPM competency within the customer's organization — at least not one that has worked with the core SAP processes and supporting SAP IT SAP Basis teams. In contrast, BPM is very new to the vast majority of SAP-based teams. At the time of this book's development, SAP had been talking about BPM as an approach with its forthcoming toolset, SAP NetWeaver BPM, for several years — the first version of this component becoming generally available to the market in June 2009. Despite this publicized announcement, the core IT teams and service integrators supporting SAP installations remained blissfully unconcerned about this forthcoming change.

So when SAP released SAP NetWeaver Business Process Management, SAP was suddenly on the list of BPM vendors that IT departments had to consider when a business asked them to support BPM initiatives. SAP Basis teams found themselves scrambling to establish a new IT procurement cycle to find the best possible BPM process modeling tools. And when the IT procurement team was asked what business problem or business goals this new BPM initiative was going to address, they typically answered, "We don't know," or "We were asked to start doing BPM."

Many of these customers failed to retain this process-oriented competency in-house and thus have found that their process maps have become out-of-date. Also, the process maps have tended to focus on the scope of the SAP applications, not the end-to-end process that involves all of a customer's employees, suppliers, and customers.

In nearly all of the instances above, an SAP or competitor product was selected as a solution for the company. However, either the purchase did not actually happen, or the purchased product has been gathering dust on the shelf, still looking for a business problem to solve. And because no consideration was given to the business side of the problem, in these cases the IT team is running a risk that significant gaps will remain between the acquired tool and the solution designed to solve the problem.

The "tools-first" tendency of undisciplined IT teams is symptomatic of an aimless BPM program without a business method. Because the program and teams are not clearly oriented toward achieving prioritized business goals as measured by mapped key performance indicators (KPIs) or metrics, the program runs the risk of failing to achieve any rapid returns for the business.

On the other hand, an IT focus on "composition" leads to good development results, but not to continuous improvement. A forward-thinking set of SAP NetWeaver competency teams within SAP customers and partners worked hard to refine a development methodology for composition. They developed custom applications that typically bridged multiple SAP and non-SAP systems by calling service-oriented architecture (SOA) functions and then provided a pleasing interface for business users.

In addition, developers supporting SAP landscapes typically leveraged toolsets such as SAP NetWeaver CE and agile development methods such as Scrum. The results of these projects typically included higher acceptance by the business and generally faster time to completion.

However, these projects were rarely updated and maintained within a company. It proved hard for IT to demonstrate return on investment or measurable improvement toward business goals when implementing these tools. There was no clear orientation to the business goal, mapping toward metrics or measurement, or a commitment to review and assess business value. In other words, the business sense was missing from this process methodology. Today, this business sense has been incorporated into the new ASAP methodology, which will be introduced in Part III, Chapter 14, Section 14.3.

6.1 BPM Usage Clusters in Industry and Application Use Cases

The benefit of the BPM program is that it provides a better approach for processes that tend to experience more frequent changes in requirements compared to more classic IT implementation techniques. However, despite being industry and application agnostic, BPM adoption among SAP customers is definitely showing up in clusters. We will now introduce some of the most common industries adopting BPM.

6.1.1 Most Common Industries Adopting BPM

Adoption of BPM is occurring in industry sectors that are also among the most rapidly growing for SAP products in general. These industries include:

▶ Utilities

▶ Consumer packaged goods

▶ Banking and insurance

Also represented are customers in SAP's more traditional sectors:

▶ Manufacturing

▶ Wholesale and distribution

Conditions in SAP's faster growing industry sectors that favor adoption of BPM include:

▶ Deregulation, leading to rapid innovation and adaptation of business models

▶ Rapid fluctuation of commodity costs, requiring rapid adaptation of business models

▶ Rapid growth and globalization of previously regional companies through new lines of business and strategic acquisitions

▶ Consolidation and modernization of archaic IT landscapes

These conditions have much to do with why SAP is finding these sectors to be fast-growing and why BPM appeals to these customers. The BPM approach is applicable to business problems within any industry, but these fast-growing industries are the ones with the business drivers who are begging for solutions that are best provided by BPM methods and tools. In Chapter 8 we will introduce BPM use case stories from Patrimonio Hipotecaria, Coca-Cola, GISA, and Siemens IT Solutions and Services that reflect this.

BPM is also applicable to SAP's more traditional sectors. These sectors are the most established and financially stable and are thus not necessarily driven to meet needs that are adequately served by the existing SAP systems that they have been running for years. To illustrate the application of BPM in these sectors we introduce BPM use case stories from RS Components (Chapter 8), and Braskem and KAESER KOMPRESSOREN (Chapter 9).

6.1.2 Most Common Applications for BPM

BPM as an approach and toolset is also application agnostic. That being said, we are definitely seeing clusters of BPM in these areas:

▶ Managing business processes for enterprise information management (EIM)— especially master data governance (see description in Chapter 7)

▶ Supplier collaboration and payment (see description in Chapter 9)

These application areas are especially ripe with requirements that are perfectly suited to a BPM implementation. In addition, two factors favor the clustering of applications in these categories:

▶ SAP NetWeaver Master Data Management (MDM)'s most recent release is engineered to work with BPM with features generated from custom user experiences and Web service functions. Example use cases include the following from Chapter 7:

  ▶ INVISTA

  ▶ Ericsson

  ▶ SAP

▶ Enabling closer relationships with suppliers and customers is a business goal for many companies. Whether related to demand planning, faster payment, or service, BPM helps companies add flexibility to their relationships. Example use cases include:

  ▶ RS Components

  ▶ Braskem

  ▶ KAESER KOMPRESSOREN

6.2 Typical Business Requirements Satisfied by BPM

Whereas all business problems will benefit from a BPM-style approach, only some require implementation with BPM tools. It is fine to address many typical problems with standard Best Practices and technologies, unless there are unmet needs related to the uniqueness of your particular case.

6.2.1 Articulating and Prioritizing Business Goals and Problems

To determine if a business issue might qualify as a potential use case for BPM, you must first clearly articulate your business goals. Ask any line-of-business leader, and they'll usually have no trouble stating their top three business problems. Typically these will be statements geared toward improving or reducing business conditions related to:

▶ Speed/process cycle time

▶ Scale

▶ Quality of operations

▶ Liability or compliance

▶ Revenue opportunity or loss

Another important consideration is determining the relative priority of a business issue. Sometimes this is easy, because the company's senior management has already named it a strategic imperative. Other times, you can determine a gross measure of a process's importance by considering the "size" of a particular process occurrence or cycle in terms of revenue, cost, or number of employees involved, multiplied by the number of occurrences in a year. This means processes with relatively few occurrences but relating to a lot of revenue will be important, as are those costs with relatively little cost per occurrence but that involve several thousand requests per year. This rule of thumb does not replace a formal value-engineering study that should be conducted as part of the business case consideration once a BPM project is selected.

6.2.2 Qualifying Questions to Instate BPM Projects

After analyzing the business problem and determining the requirements, these questions can be used to help qualify whether a project might be a good fit for BPM:

1. Is the activity a series of dependent actions?

2. Do these actions bridge multiple systems?

3. Do these actions bridge multiple organizations or business partners?

4. Do I need to account for frequent differences or changes to process cycles?

5. Do I need to engage different kinds of users into the process steps?

6. How important is measurement and monitoring of process cycles?

The first question requires a "Yes" answer. If you don't have a process, then BPM doesn't apply. The more of the remaining questions you answer "Yes" to, the better the fit with the BPM approach and tools. The following questions relate to the main categories of requirements that SAP customers are addressing with BPM:

- Orchestrating dependent actions in a sequence
- Orchestrating actions that bridge multiple systems
- Orchestrating actions between organizations
- Architecting processes for change
- Process-specific user interfaces
- Measuring and monitoring business processes

6.2.3 Orchestrating Dependent Actions in a Sequence

Business process management is about viewing, addressing, and optimizing business actions in sequences. But when dependencies exist between sequence steps without a way to coordinate them, users and employees within the business observe these kinds of symptoms:

- Ineffective task handover across functional teams
- Duplication of work

- No timely detection of problems

- Bottlenecks in workload (overload or underload)

These kinds of problems are caused by related teams working in silos with no explicit definition of how to work together. And because there is no global coordination or governance of the process, there are unnecessary local variations of how these teams work.

A BPM approach helps coordinate dependent actions in a process by providing an explicit map of everything that should happen. This map provides the opportunity to rationalize and optimize the process, a medium for automating flow between process steps, and visibility of the status of each occurrence within the process. An example of a common use case that exhibits this requirement is the need to manage workflows for entry and approval, such as master data governance. The case study from INVISTA, a global producer of polymers and fibers (Chapter 7), is an excellent example of vendor and materials master data governance.

6.2.4 Orchestrating Actions that Bridge Multiple Systems

BPM is about coordinating end-to-end processes, especially those that bridge heterogeneous systems — requiring data to be pulled from multiple sources, transformed or acted upon by some human action, and then syndicated to systems downstream. When these processes are not adequately addressed, customers see these types of symptoms:

- Users must log into multiple systems to execute a process task or decision.

- Information captured in systems used earlier in the process is lost or must be reentered into downstream systems.

These kinds of problems exist when data that is important to the process must be pulled from multiple nonintegrated, unrelated systems, and then the results of human decision-making are syndicated to one or more downstream systems. A BPM approach allows for automated consolidation of data from multiple systems for display in process, step-specific user interfaces, a context for remembering the data related to the process occurrence, and orchestrated syndication of this data to downstream systems.

A great example is RS Components' customer discount manager. This system pulls data from older versions of SAP Customer Relationship Management (CRM), SAP ERP, and business intelligence systems to administer customer discounts (profiled in Chapter 8). Another example is KAESER KOMPRESSOREN's creation of a customer service process. Their program pulls information from multiple systems to create a single screen, which makes the jobs of telephone support agents and field service engineers much easier when responding to customer support requests (profiled in Chapter 9).

6.2.5 Orchestrating Actions Between Organizations

Typical BPM use cases often call for coordination of dependent actions between departments within a company or suppliers, vendors, and customers. Without this coordination, there is a lack of a means to receive proactive notifications and a lack of transparency into process occurrences (both status and measurement). The separation between organizations exacerbates the need for orchestration, causing symptoms such as:

- Constant status checking through phone calls and email
- Problems discovered too late for mitigation
- Poor performance by business partners, which creates unexpected liabilities

A BPM approach helps orchestrate actions between organizations by allowing explicit definition of steps and responsibilities through the process model, tracking of the process status for each occurrence through BPM tools, providing proactive notification for process participants through work lists and other communication, and allowing measurement of process performance for enforcement of service-level agreements.

An example can be found in the use case of Braskem S.A. (in Chapter 9), which involves orchestrating invoicing and payment between suppliers, an outsourced service provider, multiple campuses of Braskem, and a global shared services center.

6.2.6 Architecting Processes for Change

BPM is especially useful for processes that need to account for frequent changes in decision-making or variations between occurrences. Indicators that processes need to manage change more efficiently include:

- Response time for IT to roll out supporting automation is too slow.
- Changing of backend systems results in extensive retraining for users.
- Decision-making remains a human step, because policies change too frequently.

These symptoms are a result of depending on core enterprise systems that often require extensive testing cycles or custom coding to be modified, and they signify that user interfaces are too tightly coupled to these systems.

A BPM approach provides the ability to architect a process to handle frequent changes through tools that support process modeling and simultaneously generate execution flow. These tools make it easy for the business to describe changes to processes quickly and for IT to roll out the new automation quickly. Embedding business rules into BPM processes also allows for simplifying and consolidating processes by automating decision-making. Automating decision-making with embedded business rules provides a means for the business to rapidly change rules whenever new policy changes roll out without needing to be serviced by IT.

Ericsson's master data governance implementation best demonstrates this architecture. The program consolidated master data creation into a single global process via application intelligence that assisted users with entering country-specific tax information for new suppliers. For more details please see the Ericsson case study profiled in Chapter 7.

6.2.7 Process-Specific User Interfaces

BPM-based orchestration provides the opportunity to simplify user experiences for each human step in a business process flow. Symptoms that user experiences are too complicated include:

▶ Unwillingness of business users to adopt applications

▶ Reliance on power users to enter all process-related data into systems

▶ Changing of backed systems, which requires time-consuming retraining of users because of changes to user experiences

▶ Increased error rates and users' support/training needs

Through BPM's orchestration of a process, it is possible to know the role, task, and context in which the user is working. This allows simplified user interfaces that are focused specifically on the action to be created, along with all available information that is specific to the process context. This makes it easier for casual users to engage with automation related to the process, making it possible to extend business processes out of core applications to actual participants. BPM business processes are also decoupled from system tasks. If decoupled user interfaces are used as well, it is possible to create a process user experience that is separate from backend systems. In such a case, if backend systems are changed, it's possible to keep the process and its related user experience the same.

The BPM use case of postmerger data migration business processes by SAP IT (profiled in Chapter 7) is a great example of this — where the user experience of an otherwise complex process is simplified to make data stewards productive and involve business managers in data governance.

6.2.8 Measuring and Monitoring Business Processes

Without a cohesive framework, it is extremely difficult to take explicit measurements. A BPM implementation provides the opportunity to see a process occurrence's status within the process flow and the ability to measure its progress in relation to KPIs mapped to business goals. Symptoms of processes that lack this kind of visibility and measurement include:

▶ The need for manual checking with participants about their progress or status

▶ A lack of clear prioritization of tasks

▶ No indication of missed deadlines or missing dependencies

▶ A lack of data about the business value received by an IT implementation

These symptoms are a result of the lack of a cohesive framework for managing process occurrences within an orchestration and the lack of any explicit measurement being built into the process execution so you can track metrics and KPIs.

BPM implementation tools provide the inherent ability to track the progress of process occurrences through the process model, including the status of current processors at any step. Additionally, the system is able to generate notification when steps take too long for completion, when resources are overtaxed or unavailable, and when there are missing dependencies. Simple process measurements such as step and process cycle times are generally easy to implement. The process context can also provide the opportunity for implementation of more sophisticated measurements such as the number and ratios of exceptions versus standard process runs.

The use case from Braskem S.A. (Chapter 9) that tracks the KPI of "payment assertiveness" (how often a payment is made within the targeted payment date of an invoice) is a great example of this.

7 First Applications: Enterprise Information Management

Greg Chase, Rukhshaan Omar, Darwin Deano, Jan Hvass, Stacey Drinan,
James Taylor, Oktavian Wagner, Wayne Morris

Companies that first start to implement BPM typically begin with optimizing operational business processes within the IT department, or certain foundational subprocesses such as data governance. Completing these projects can provide immediate business value (unlike a proof of concept) while at the same time having a relatively low risk to the business in case of failure.

Streamlining the MDM governance process is a good first project, because these projects tend to be scoped to limit the number of users. Hence, this is one of the most common use cases, where SAP's BPM technology is applied within SAP environments (i.e., creating explicit processes to manage and govern master data). The goals is to decrease the amount of incomplete and poor-quality master data entered into the system while simultaneously increasing the speed in which master data becomes available in the system. These projects provide immediate business value, because poor-quality master data severely hampers any process improvement initiative. The lack of an accurate global repository for materials, vendors, and customer master data impacts the time to market for introducing a new product, creates issues in the supply chain, and leads to inefficient interactions with customer.

So why do so many companies have issues related to master data quality? Many companies have either grown organically or have complex business operations (e.g., operate in multiple geographies), work with international partners, or offer a range of diverse products. This makes describing and maintaining enterprise information more complex.

What follows are three examples in which SAP customers have created processes to govern their master data using a BPM approach together with SAP NetWeaver BPM tools. A fundamental shift in customers' approach has been putting the governance of master data back in the hands of business users — both the definition and operations — rather than IT owning it.

In the first case, INVISTA, a global producer, embarked on a procurement excellence process improvement initiative. The company quickly identified the effective master governance process as a critical first step in this initiative. They deployed BPM methods and tools to orchestrate the required activity to ensure effective governance of common global vendor and material master records.

The second case involves Ericsson, a world-leading provider of telecommunications equipment and related services. This company faced the dual challenge of streamlining the process and finding a way to manage their country-specific requirements. In addition to using BPM for orchestrating the dependent actions, they leveraged business rules management to ensure that the process could enforce the country-specific policies associated with supply tax and registration numbers.

In the third case, SAP itself demonstrates how the combination of SAP NetWeaver BPM, SAP NetWeaver Business Rules Management (BRM), and SAP BusinessObjects Data Services was applied to implement an end-to-end postmerger data migration process, thus allowing SAP to migrate master data for multiple acquisitions faster in parallel with increased data quality.

7.1   INVISTA: Enabling Cross-System Master Data Management

BPM enabled the implementation of a standard master data request process for vendors and materials across multiple SAP systems with varying versions, languages, and configurations. This resulted in fewer data errors, reduction of duplicates, and efficiency gains due to the process automation.
– Cynthia Bailey Grunewald, PEP Project Lead, INVISTA

INVISTA, a global producer of polymers and fibers, launched a Procurement Excellence Project (PEP) with the objective of enabling a world-class procurement organization to provide a global competitive advantage. One of the key work streams was master data management to standardize data governance across multiple SAP systems and reduce data errors and duplicates to support procurement operations. INVISTA utilized BPM in conjunction with MDM to standardize and streamline the management of vendor and material master records across multiple versions and configurations of SAP ERP.

7.1.1 Background

INVISTA is one of the world's largest integrated producers of polymers and fibers, primarily nylon, spandex, and polyester applications. INVISTA operates in more than 20 countries across North America, South America, Europe, and the Asia-Pacific region.

In the last quarter of 2007, INVISTA embarked on the Procurement Excellence Project, with the ultimate objective of creating a world-class procurement organization that provides global competitive advantage by leveraging a global sourcing methodology, technology-enabled strategic sourcing, and the sourcing professional's knowledge and experience.

Business Case

As a subset of the Procurement Excellence Project, INVISTA wanted to streamline master data management processes across multiple SAP ERP systems to standardize procedures, enforce consistency, and improve the quality of vendor and material master records across the entire INVISTA organization. This activity was deemed critical to deliver the full business benefit of the Procurement Excellence Project (PEP). INVISTA understood that to obtain and sustain the full benefit of streamlined procurement processes, effective data governance processes must be defined, implemented, and continuously improved.

As-Is Process

Before the PEP project, INVISTA had various business processes for maintaining vendor and material master data across the four SAP systems in their organization. There were approximately 50,000 active vendor master records out of more than 366,000 vendor records on file. Furthermore, there were more than 1.1 million material master records, of which approximately 600,000 were active. Duplicate records and master data inconsistencies were a huge problem due to the difficulty of consolidating reports across the four SAP systems. Finally, each of the four systems was configured differently to support the various site-specific and regional requirements. Table 7.1 describes the as-is processes:

Characteristic	As-Is Condition
Business process management tool	Multiple varied processes – mostly manual with some sites using Lotus Notes
Business process	Multiple varied processes; each site had its own process and approval levels
Standardization of global fields	Inconsistent governance

Table 7.1 INVISTA's As-Is Process

7.1.2 BPM Solution

To achieve the PEP business objectives, INVISTA asked Deloitte (Deloitte Consulting LLP, a subsidiary of Deloitte LLP) to help them in their efforts to leverage SAP's BPM and MDM capabilities. The goal was to define a solution that streamlines business process execution, manage the global common data, and standardize the process for maintenance of local data for vendor and material master records. The solution required analysis of all major business processes across all major regions of the INVISTA organization.

Implementing the Solution

One of the biggest challenges INVISTA's IT team faced was to overcome the tendency to approach this effort from a technical/tool perspective, as opposed to a business transformation project to improve master data. The critical first step required to put the BPM methodology in action was to define the future business process based on the business requirements set out by the PEP initiative. INVISTA leveraged Deloitte Consulting's Industry Print tool — a Business Process Modeling Notation (BPMN)-compliant process model used to capture a diagram of the future ideal process (see Figure 7.1).

After designing the process, it was critical to understand the components and layers of the conceptual architecture required to realize the process design (see Table 7.2).

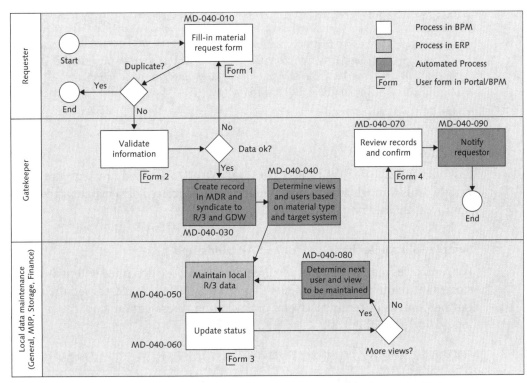

Figure 7.1 Material Request Process Designed in the Deloitte Consulting Industry Print Tool

Layer	Requirement	Approach
Orchestration	Coordinate the end-to-end process across various parties (requestor, approver, local data maintenance)	Utilize business process management to facilitate orchestration
Presentation	Abstract the end user from the complexities of the underlying applications as much as possible	Utilize portals to provide a single, consistent, simple frontend on top of the various applications
Application	Leverage the necessary functionality from SAP ERP and SAP NetWeaver MDM	Utilize MDM and version-neutral ERP functionality

Table 7.2 Process Design

Layer	Requirement	Approach
Integration	Ensure that information flows seamlessly from the user interface to MDM and finally to the multiple ERP environments	Utilize SAP NetWeaver Process Integration to provide the integration functionality

Table 7.2 Process Design (Cont.)

Results of the Project

Less than a year after the project Go Live, INVISTA is already reaping the business benefits through reduction of duplicates, standardized data maintenance, and improved reporting capabilities.

Sample Solution Architecture for an SAP Landscape

For companies that have similar requirements than those described within this case story, the architectural components that can be utilized to address requirements can be thought in terms of layers: orchestration, presentation, application, and integration (see Table 7.3).

Layer	Actual Architecture Component
Orchestration	SAP NetWeaver BPM
Presentation	Portals
Application	SAP ERP and SAP NetWeaver MDM
Integration	SAP NetWeaver Process Integration (PI)

Table 7.3 SAP Components of the Reference Architecture

Figure 7.2 provides a logical view of how to leverage these architectural components to deliver the MDM solution.

A solution featuring SAP components would include SAP NetWeaver BPM for managing orchestration, Web Dynpro for managing presentation to business users, SAP ERP, SAP NetWeaver Master Data Management (MDM) and integration using SAP NetWeaver Process Integration.

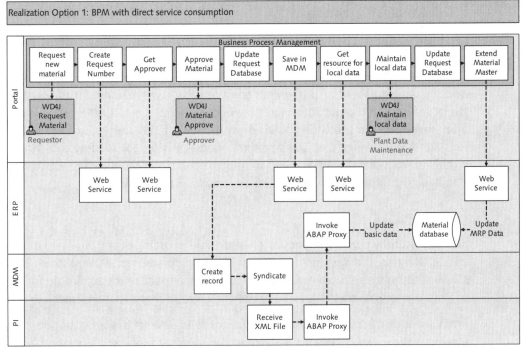

Figure 7.2 Sample Architecture Utilizing SAP NetWeaver BPM Platform

7.2 Ericsson: Using Business Rules to Enable Globalization of Supplier Master Data Governance

The many country-specific requirements make it difficult to consolidate supplier master data governance globally. By leveraging BPM and business rules to guide users through these requirements, the project has delivered a robust and user-friendly solution.
— Stacey Drinan, IT Platform Area Manager, Ericsson AB

Ericsson, a global supplier of telecommunications equipment, has been engaged in a multi-year program of continuous improvement of its master data processes. In its latest project, Ericsson sought to add an additional level of usability to its supplier master data processes. The company incorporated business rules into their process automation to guide correct user input of supplier data, which had specific and individual needs for the countries where the suppliers are located. This project is expected to speed up the master data process by over 50% — and with a high business-user acceptance rate.

7.2.1 Background

Ericsson is a world-leading provider of telecommunications equipment and related global services to mobile and fixed network operators. Over 1,000 networks in more than 175 countries utilize their network equipment, and 40% of all mobile calls are made through Ericsson's systems. Ericsson is one of the few companies worldwide that can offer end-to-end solutions for all major mobile communication standards. For more information please see *www.ericsson.com*.

Business Case

Ericsson is a truly global company and, as such, the sourcing organization is global, with interaction and agreements made with suppliers in over 200 countries. The scope of the agreements varies from global agreements that are applicable for all of Ericsson, to agreements specific to only select local Ericsson operations.

From a strategic perspective, Ericsson was consolidating its business support systems into a few global systems. Related to the sourcing processes, Ericsson had:

▶ Two global SAP systems (that were being merged into one at the time) where all procurement was done

▶ A global SAP business warehouse for follow-up and reporting

▶ A global contract management system

▶ A global tool for strategic sourcing

In this environment, accurate and high-quality supplier master data was key to ensure that the business processes ran smoothly and that accurate reporting could be performed. It was also crucial that suppliers could be identified across the global sourcing systems to ensure this quality in processes and reporting.

Ericsson had worked with master data quality in the global systems for many years. At the time that Ericsson decided to implement BPM, a central global master data management group was responsible for the process of maintaining master data in the global business systems, on request from the business units.

The business case for this project included two goals: first, increasing master data quality to increase efficiency in overall business processes and accuracy of analytics and, second, increasing efficiency in the specific process of creating and maintaining supplier master data. The Global Master Data Management group handled around 3,000 requests monthly for supplier master data updates. The business case calculation was based on a 50% reduction of handling time per request. The solution goal would be to capture the request handling time for each request for easy reporting on this important KPI.

As-Is Process

In the original process, a request for master data changes for supplier master data was made by sending an Excel form to the Global Master Data Management group. Any issues with the request were handled by emailing back and forth between the business user who was requesting the change and the responsible person at the Global Master Data Management group. Once the request was validated, the responsible person at the Global Master Data Management group had to enter the data manually in up to four different systems, depending on the type of request.

In typical business fashion, many of the business rules detailing what information had to be entered into the supplier master data were scattered in different instruction manuals and in the heads of staff members. The business rules state whether data is mandatory or optional, qualifies as default values, requires specific formatting of data, and so on. Many of these business rules dependent on in which country the supplier is located or in which country the supplier is to be used. Global and regional alignment cause these rules and requirements to change frequently. For supplier master data, such business rules are related to the following types of data:

▶ Payment methods

▶ Bank details

▶ Tax numbers

▶ Withholding tax

▶ Business partner roles in SAP

▶ DUNS numbers

▶ Vendor returns

7.2.2 BPM Solution

The vision for the project was to streamline (see Figure 7.3) and automate (see Figure 7.4) the process via the following solutions:

1. **Self-service creation**

   Business users access online request forms in the SAP NetWeaver Portal. The forms guide the users to enter data correctly, depending on the scenario and other key selection criteria (i.e., country).

2. **Intelligent guidance**

   Online forms guide the users to enter data correctly, with business rules adding "intelligence" to the forms to help business users with specific requirements, such as a country's tax information.

3. **Orchestrated request routing**

   The request is routed through a workflow, using SAP NetWeaver BPM, to the Global Master Data Management group for enrichment and validation.

4. **Automated data syndication**

   When the request is approved, the data is automatically posted in SAP NetWeaver Master Data Management (MDM) and automatically syndicated to all relevant consuming systems.

With this solution, data integrity and data quality are ensured with a minimum of manual intervention and without copying and pasting of data at any stage. Also, the solution guides the business users to enter the correct data in their requests from the beginning, which significantly reduces the overall lead time for processing the request and increases business user satisfaction with request handling.

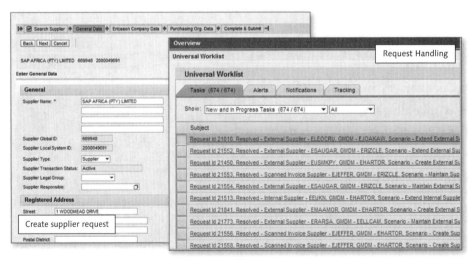

Figure 7.3 Streamlining the Request Process in the Core To-Be Process

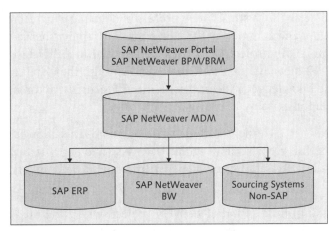

Figure 7.4 Automated Syndication of Data as Part of the To-Be Process

Implementing the Solution

The project ran for about 1.5 years with the following phases:

1. Prestudy/business justification: four months. The business case was developed simultaneously with Ericsson's beta testing of SAP NetWeaver BPM and SAP NetWeaver Business Rules Management (BRM) to evaluate the feasibility of the upcoming project. During the feasibility evaluation, parts of an existing guided procedures–based scenario were ported to BPM to understand how well this would support Ericsson's requirements.

2. Requirement gathering: five months. This stage focused on data model and process aspects. Meanwhile, the IT team was entering the ramp-up program for SAP NetWeaver BPM.

3. Iterative design-prototype-test cycles: six months

4. Final build: one month

5. Final test and go-live preparation: two months

6. Go-live and business rollout: one month

The architecture of SAP NetWeaver BPM and SAP NetWeaver BRM allowed for a very efficient project development model, with a lot of interaction between the lead developers and lead business users in rapid design-prototype-test cycles. This ensured that all key business requirements were captured early in the process and that key business users got an early feeling for the new process and solution.

A lot of effort was put into designing a streamlined process and an engaging user experience to speed up rollout and adoption of the new process. Usability specialists were engaged throughout the project. Additionally, a special usability test week was performed with 12 business users who were familiar with the existing business process but had no knowledge of the new solution. This activity captured critically useful information for usability improvements.

The rollout was done globally in a condensed three-wave schedule. This allowed the project to complete the full global rollout within six weeks. To support the rollout, online training material was produced alongside the final developments in the project.

The project was run as a joint business and IT delivery project, where the business was responsible for requirement gathering, business alignment, testing, and business rollout. The IT delivery team was responsible for the design, build, and deployment of the solution. Experts from SAP Partner Ecenta AG delivered the main design and build work around SAP NetWeaver BPM, SAP NetWeaver BRM, and SAP NetWeaver Master Data Management. This had been part of an overall IT project managed through Ericsson's outsourcing partner, IBM.

Results of the Project

During the assembly of information for this use case, the project had been live for a week and the first batch of live requests had been processed. Experience from the last week in production and the user training and business testing sessions clearly indicated that the business users appreciated the solution as intuitive and easy to use. Business users also appreciated the guided approach and the prompt validation of input data using the business rules. Now, correctly entered data is helping Ericsson reach their "zero errors" vision for their business processes. Measurements of request handling time also indicate that the project goal of reducing the request handling time more than 50% is clearly within reach.

Sample Solution Architecture for an SAP Landscape

The solution was built on the existing enterprise IT architecture at Ericsson that includes the following SAP systems (see also Figure 7.5):

▶ SAP NetWeaver MDM as the single-source-of-truth repository of supplier master data

▶ SAP NetWeaver Portal for all end-user interaction with the solution

▶ SAP NetWeaver Process Integration for integrating the different components of the solution

▶ SAP NetWeaver BPM as the primary workflow and orchestration engine for the new process

▶ SAP NetWeaver BRM for managing and maintaining business rules related to master data

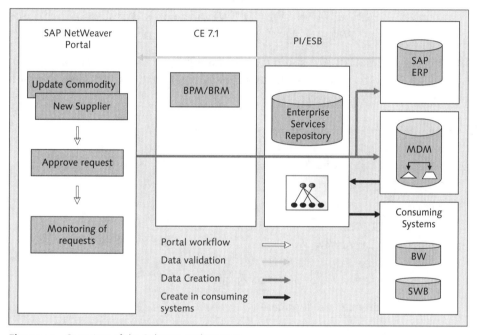

Figure 7.5 Overview of the Solution Architecture

The architecture of the solution consists of four layers with clearly defined responsibilities:

1. The portal layer is used for all end-user interactions with the solution. This layer manages access control to the solution and all screens/workflows, which the end users access through the enterprise portal interface.

2. The CE environment is the host for the SAP NetWeaver BPM and SAP NetWeaver BRM components. SAP NetWeaver BPM is the process engine where the business process logic and workflow are executed, as are the rules engine where the business rules are executed at runtime. The SAP NetWeaver Composition

Environment (CE) also hosts the Java-based enterprise services to manage the interaction between BPM and the MDM/ERP systems.

3. SAP NetWeaver PI is used as the communication middleware for the solution. The enterprise services are registered in the service registry of SAP NetWeaver PI, which manages their runtime execution.

4. Consuming systems are the last level, which consume new and updated master data from the master data management solution. Consuming systems are SAP systems (SAP ERP and SAP NetWeaver BW) and a non-SAP system — the Sourcing Workbench (SWB) — a supplier/procurement management solution.

The process is a request and approval workflow built with SAP NetWeaver BPM (see Figure 7.6). The associated process step implementations included standard and custom-built Web services.

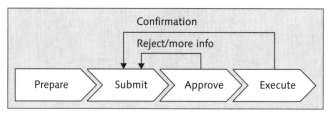

Figure 7.6 Request and Approval Workflow

The process covers various business scenarios:

▶ Create/maintain external supplier

▶ Create/maintain internal supplier

▶ Create/maintain supplier candidate

▶ Maintain payment block

▶ Create "other" request

All business scenarios share the same basic workflow structure and the same superset of available attributes for entry or modification. For each scenario, several other key attributes such as supplier, country, and buying organization/country and several business rules are defined. The business rules state which information and attributes should be captured, whether the information is mandatory or optional, and what default values and validation rules apply. All business rules are centrally defined, maintained, and executed in the SAP NetWeaver BRM component. Permitted value ranges are taken from SAP NetWeaver MDM or from the SAP ERP system. Validation of ERP-related attributes such as payment and shipping details is done by calling services from the SAP ERP system.

Figure 7.7 shows how the business rules are defined in SAP NetWeaver BRM, based on which business scenario is being executed. For a certain scenario (for example, create external supplier), and for a certain attribute (for example, order currency), the rule defines whether the attribute is mandatory, optional, hidden, or read-only (present).

Another of Ericsson's requirements within the program has been to very accurately capture the legal tax and registration numbers for suppliers. The business rules for this information vary by country all over the world. The type of numbers, how many are needed, and format vary by country, but at the same time it is very important to capture this information accurately to ensure a smooth relationship with key suppliers. Ericsson used SAP NetWeaver BRM to define the rules, by country, for which fields should be entered and how they should be validated. Figure 7.7 shows a sample of these rule definitions.

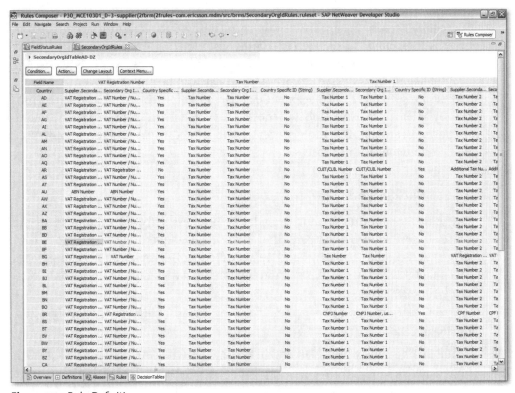

Figure 7.7 Rule Definitions

The rules for capturing tax and registration numbers are expected to change (and improve) frequently. With an integrated tool like SAP NetWeaver BRM, it is anticipated that the master data business experts at the Ericsson Global Master Data Management group will be able to maintain the rules directly, verify them, and then apply the updated rules for the productive application without a big IT project each time.

7.3 SAP IT: Accelerating Postmerger Data Enrichment and Migration

Our goal is to get faster at integrating acquisitions. A key component of this is migrating and enhancing the quality of data of the acquired company to our core systems in a rapid fashion. Using BPM allows us to define and continuously improve a best-practice data migration process and to easily adapt it for a project's unique requirements.
– Oliver Bussman, CIO, SAP AG

Shareholder return on any acquisition correlates with how fast the acquired company is integrated, so SAP AG is continuously looking for ways to improve its methods for postmerger integration. One area for improvement is how fast the acquired company's business processes and data can be migrated over to the core SAP systems. To meet a management mandate for improving the speed of this process by at least 50%, SAP Global IT chose to leverage a BPM approach to streamline its postmerger data migration processes and turned to SAP's value prototyping team to implement this process.

7.3.1 Background

SAP AG is the world's leading provider of business software solutions and the fourth-largest software company in the world. Headquartered in Walldorf, Germany, with regional offices around the world, SAP offers applications and services that enable companies of all sizes and in more than 25 industries to become best-run businesses.

Business Case

While SAP's strategy relies largely on organic growth, SAP also pursues growth opportunities through strategic acquisitions. A key factor in realizing value from a major acquisition is successfully integrating the acquired company as fast as possible with as little disruption as possible for the employees, the customers, and the products. Much of this work is a strategic IT task — supporting, adapting, and integrating business processes in the acquirer's systems, migrating data with high quality, and at the same time, lowering IT operating costs and simplifying IT complexity as quickly as possible.

SAP views the assimilation of acquired companies as a continuously improving competency. This outlook mirrors the philosophy of continuous process improvement that is core to a business process management approach, so it was natural for the SAP Global IT Business Process and Application Migration Team to choose BPM to optimize and continuously improve their business process for postmerger data migration.

SAP maintains a very high standard of quality for data, and historically, the data quality of acquired companies has required remediation to meet SAP's standards. In addition, the acquired company's master and transactional data typically need to be transformed and extended to align with SAP's system and data governance requirements, and any duplicates with existing data in SAP's systems need to be reconciled. Because much of the data carries with it revenue considerations and commitments and obligations to customers, line-of-business managers need to be involved in the acceptance of newly migrated data objects.

After the 2008 acquisition of BusinessObjects, SAP management set a general goal for speeding up postmerger data migration by 50%. Additional goals for process improvement included:

▶ Significantly improving data quality for each migration

▶ Enabling multiple data migration/acquisition projects to run in parallel

▶ Improving user experiences to engage both data stewards and line-of-business managers in automation

▶ Automating the process to remove as much manual effort as possible

▶ Approaching the process of postmerger migration as evolving Best Practices

As-Is Process

Before the acquisition of BusinessObjects by SAP, data migrations were performed with the support of custom and third-party tools that were manual — not fully integrated. This manual process was time-consuming, prone to errors, and did not consistently improve the quality of the data migrated from legacy systems.

The BusinessObjects acquisition was SAP's first experience with a large postmerger data migration project. As a result, the business process for the data migration had to be set up quickly. The process was IT-led. The IT team found that in the original process, the involvement of line-of-business managers in the data acceptance process was handled manually via emailed spreadsheets. Business rules for data survivorship and matching were not defined globally.

SAP's as-is process for improving the data quality of an acquired company before migration is depicted in Figure 7.8. Generally, each progression between steps was a manual effort, requiring human intervention to copy or set up data or to configure tools before running any batch processes. First, the data migration team extracted data from the acquired company's systems and then enriched the data from third-party sources, such as Dun & Bradstreet. The data analysts then set up the enriched data to be evaluated for duplicates and quality. Based on this evaluation, three groups of data were created: unique records, clear duplicates, and "clericals," which are ambiguous and needed human consideration to resolve whether they are unique or partial duplicates. Unique records were kept. Ambiguous records, including potential duplicates or incomplete records, were manually parsed by data analysts for resolution. Recommended resolutions were compiled into spreadsheets and emailed to business managers for their approval; the business rules for survivorship were generally kept within business managers' heads and were sometimes inconsistent between different managers. When business managers returned the changes, the resulting kept data had a structure and standard of quality close to SAP's requirements.

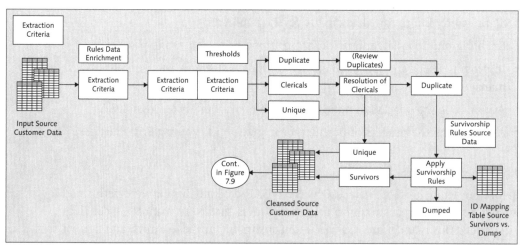

Figure 7.8 As-Is Process for Improving Data Quality of an Acquired Company Before Migration to SAP's Systems

Figure 7.9 shows the subprocess for matching cleansed data from the acquired company with data from SAP. Similar to the data improvement process, the data was matched against existing SAP records. Clear matches were compiled into spreadsheets and emailed to business managers, who would decide which duplicates should survive for upload into SAP's systems or be dumped. Clear and unique entries were passed through to the system. Records that might have matched, but weren't clear duplicates (e.g., different addresses) were reviewed manually and resolved by data analysts. The data analysts compiled their resolutions into spreadsheets, which were emailed to business managers for approval.

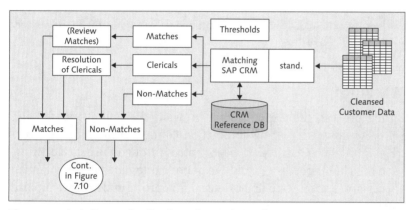

Figure 7.9 As-Is Process for Matching Cleansed Data from an Acquired Company with Existing Records within SAP's Systems

The end of the as-is process consisted of cleansed and transformed unique data being uploaded into SAP's systems (see Figure 7.10). Duplicate data was processed with special treatment and survivorship rules to determine if any changes or additions should be made to existing SAP records based on information from the acquired company's records. Due to the manual nature of the process, especially with regard to business approvals, the approved data sets often were of inconsistent quality, requiring further reworking or remediation at a later time. In addition, the migration process was slow and required a lot of IT personnel time to perform.

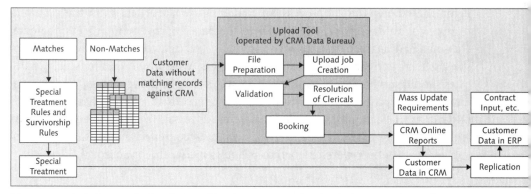

Figure 7.10 As-Is Process for Resolution of Duplicate Data and Upload of Approved Data from an Acquired Company into SAP's Systems

7.3.2 BPM Solution

For the optimized process, the acquisitions team wanted a fully integrated and orchestrated process flow. Supporting automation connected the acquired company's landscape from which data was to be migrated, through the data cleansing, enrichment, and matching process — inclusive of both automated and any human intervention necessary — through to line-of-business approval and finally to upload into SAP's systems.

In addition, the new process would provide baseline evolving best practice for data migration that could be flexibly adapted to different landscape architectures of other future acquired companies. Another major improvement in the process would be the way in which all participants, from data analysts to line-of-business managers, would be orchestrated and engaged to facilitate the specific task for each step of the process. Specific to this process, line-of-business managers, such as sales managers and customer support managers, were involved in the acceptance of data objects, because they had a vested interest in the quality of the migrated data.

Implementing the Solution

The new data migration process leverages SAP NetWeaver BPM to orchestrate the process flow between systems and users, SAP BusinessObjects Data Services to automate much of the data cleansing and improvement steps, and Web Dynpro to facilitate user interaction where needed. The BPM architecture is able to handle multiple occurrences, meaning that multiple data migration projects from multiple acquisitions can be processed in parallel.

The new process (see Figure 7.11) extracts data from an acquired company's systems and transforms the objects to conform to the schema for SAP's systems. Extracted data is then uploaded to a staging database. After an automated validation check that is performed by SAP BusinessObjects Data Services, and a human overview check to ensure that everything within the staging database appears correct, the process then automatically checks the required fields within the extracted data and then performs address lookup and data enrichment using online services, including Dunn & Bradstreet.

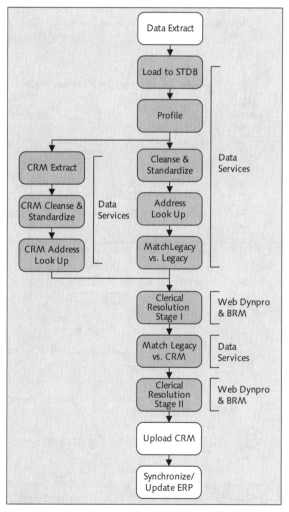

Figure 7.11 New Data Migration Process Orchestrated with BPM, with Automated Steps Leveraging SAP BusinessObjects Data Services

Extracted data is then checked for duplicates within its own data and cleansed. In the new process, this step begins automatically, without any human intervention or setup. Similar to the as-is process, some ambiguous matches need human intervention to resolve. Data analysts are then given the task of resolving ambiguous matches, and appropriate line-of-business managers (according to region) are given the task of approving the proposed resolution by data stewards, as depicted in Figure 7.12.

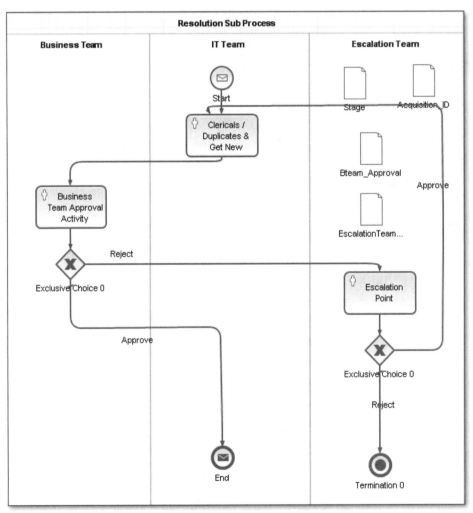

Figure 7.12 BPMN Subprocess for Duplicate Resolution with Human Workflow Steps for Data Analyst Resolution and Business Manager Approval

Manager approval routing is based upon business rules that are related to the location of the customer in question. The BPM flow calls survivorship business rules, which are also used to define protocol in the case of duplicates — which record to keep and which to throw out, based on standards such as quality of data and the number of transactions related to the master data object.

The new process features task-specific Web Dynpro interfaces for each process step, such as the resolution process for data analysts (see Figure 7.13).

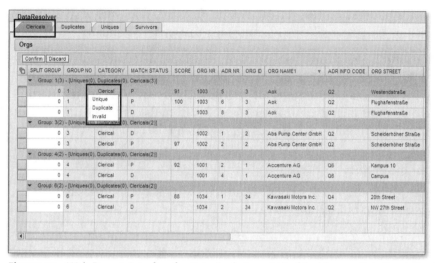

Figure 7.13 Web Dynpro Interface for Data Analysts as Part of Ambiguous Data Resolution Steps

The acquired company's improved data is then matched against existing SAP records to find and eliminate duplicates. Again, this step is automatically orchestrated. Where ambiguous duplicate data exists, such as similar records with different addresses, the data is resolved with human intervention in a subprocess, which is similar to the previous process of leveraging specific user experiences designed for this task. Similar to the previous subprocess, business managers are part of the approval process for the resolved ambiguous duplicates.

Next, the high-quality archetype data is uploaded to the respective SAP Business Suite solution, such as SAP Customer Relationship Management. As a final step, the new customers are attributed as active customers in SAP ERP.

A beneficial feature of the new process is that it supports corporate controls and compliance audits through integrated user security, access control, and logging.

Only the appropriate users are provided access to modify key data such as customers and contracts, and a record of these changes is available in an audit history.

To accelerate development of the process, SAP Global IT engaged SAP's Value Prototyping team, which is a specialist consulting group that uses SAP technology and works with SAP customers and partners to develop proof-of-concept implementations of innovative solutions. Working in partnership with Value Prototyping, the SAP Global IT Business Process and Application Migration team conducted workshops with process participants and managers. During this process, they designed an optimized business process for data migration to meet the goal of speeding up data migration by 50% while maintaining high data quality standards.

The Value Prototyping team then leveraged their rapid development approach to provide a prototype of automation that supported the process, complete with SAP BusinessObjects Data Services integration within six weeks of the project starting. This prototype was then used to garner feedback from the various participants in the process, including line-of-business approvers and data analysts.

Results of the Project

During the compilation of this book, the process was ready to run, awaiting forthcoming acquisition transactions to close.

This new solution will continue to be expanded to incorporate other M&A processes that go beyond data and process integration, such as employee on-boarding, vendor and bank data migration, and transactional data migration.

Sample Solution Architecture for an SAP Landscape

A new solution was created using SAP NetWeaver Composition Environment, SAP NetWeaver BPM, SAP NetWeaver BRM, and SAP BusinessObjects Data Services technologies, allowing SAP to standardize and automate this process (see Figure 7.14). As depicted in Figure 7.14, SAP NetWeaver CE manages the runtime process automation, including the BPM engine, which manages the process orchestration, business rules (which define rules for acceptance of duplicate data), and the Web Dynpro screens, where process participants interact with each other to accomplish their tasks within the process. SAP BusinessObjects Data Services provides the functionality for data quality improvement and duplicate matching batch jobs that are called by BPM orchestration. SAP BusinessObjects Data Services also manages the upload of data to SAP systems as part of the final step. The remaining systems include the acquired company's legacy landscape (not depicted) that is the source of data to be migrated and the SAP core systems that receive the cleansed, de-duped data after it has been accepted by business managers.

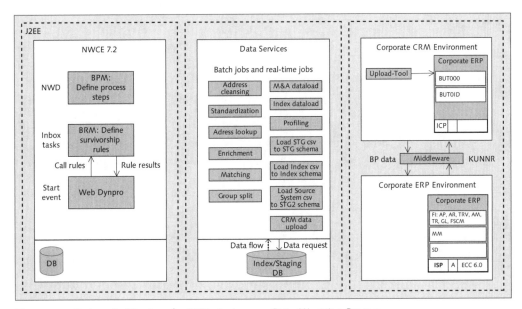

Figure 7.14 System Architecture for SAP's Postmerger Data Migration Process

8   Industry-Specific Processes

Greg Chase, Rukhshaan Omar, Gerardo Morales, Manish Argarwal,
Alexander Grobe, Gregor Müller, Hans Ludwig Reinecke, Christian Heuer,
Fin Jennrich, Owen Pettiford, Graham Wiffen

Today, organizations are benefiting from SAP's deep vertical insight, which is contained within industry-specific SAP Business Suite applications. These applications provide comprehensive, proven, industry-specific, and prepackaged best in-class processes (Best Practices). With SAP NetWeaver BPM, organizations can extend these Best Practices to create differentiating processes (own practices) that orchestrate and extend the business logic within SAP Business Suite applications. Using NetWeaver BPM ensures that organizations do not spend unnecessary energies on the commoditized aspects of a process, but rather focus on innovation for differentiation.

In general, BPM is applicable for all industries. However, early adoption of SAP's BPM offerings are occurring in industry sectors that are also among the most rapidly growing for SAP products in general. All of these industries share intense competition, pricing, and growth pressures. We see a special focus on industries that have to particularly deal with frequently changing business processes and unique requirements, such as industries involved in financial services, consumer products, utilities, and high tech. In addition, all industries that have a high need for regulatory compliance are relevant for BPM. Let's look at the primary drivers and example applications for each of these industries:

▶ **Financial services**
Intense competition, growth, and cost pressures are drivers for streamlining customer-facing processes in the financial services industry. Business process management tools become critical as banks need to streamline their processes to be able to differentiate themselves from the competition in regard to the quality and speed of their service. In an example of loan management, the bank needs to be able to provide the necessary tracking and traceability required to ensure that bottlenecks and issues in the processing of loans are handled quickly and efficiently. Due to this need, we are seeing leaders in banking select

modern SOA-based applications such as the SAP for Banking set of solutions, to provide a solid foundation to build their flexible process with BPM.

Section 8.1 gives an example of Patrimonio Hipotecaria, a Mexico-based mortgage bank that applied BPM to streamline a government-sponsored mortgage loan processing business process. This business area of the bank was growing by double digits every year, making it an excellent first project for BPM. Implementing BPM demonstrated immediate business value by improving operational excellence and customer satisfaction.

▶ **Consumer products**
Escalating costs, the ever-changing consumer, and retailer preferences are trends that are forcing consumer products manufacturers to focus on streamlining processes across departments to increase brand awareness and customer loyalty. We have included an example of the German bottler of Coca-Cola (a separate company from Coca-Cola Enterprises) in Section 8.2, which developed a localized demand planning process by seamlessly integrating activities across marketing, sales, and procurement. This company used BPM tools and methods to effectively implement the bottler-specific localization of global initiatives, including handling language and local legal requirements.

▶ **Utilities**
Traditional utilities are being transformed into a complex ecosystem consisting of generation, transmission, distribution, retail, and meter operation, which increases the complexity of processes across multiple stakeholders. Additionally, volatile energy prices, innovations such smart grids/smart meters, changing demand curves, and active consumers are driving the need for greater efficiency to gain and retain customers. All of this creates the need for utilities to create dynamic collaborative processes across the utility supply chain that cater to the variations across electricity, gas, water supply, and district heating providers. What follows are examples from two SAP partners that use process templates for SAP NetWeaver BPM to effectively meet this industry's requirements:

▶ GISA, an IT-related consulting services provider with customers in utilities, media, and the public sector, has created BPM process templates to streamline their new service connection process (see Section 8.3).

▶ Siemens IT Solutions and Services is part of Siemens, a global powerhouse in electrical engineering and electronics. They have developed an abstract business concept for strategic grid management consisting of processes, key performance indicators (KPIs), and reference data models (see Section 8.4).

▶ **High tech**

Shrinking product lifecycles, pressure to provide complete solutions, and demanding customers are driving high tech companies to initiate process improvement initiatives. Additionally, the trend in high tech is to build innovative multi-tiered business networks to increase the efficiency of manufacturing and distribution processes. Hence, efficient collaboration along the value chain is business critical for high tech companies. Therefore, they are applying BPM tools and methods to streamline the interaction between manufacturers, logistic service providers, distributors, and customers. We have included the example of RS Components, a company that automated supply chain collaboration to optimize stock inventory levels. RS Components is a trading brand of Electrocomponents plc, which is one of the largest global catalog and Web-based distributors of electronic components (see Section 8.5).

8.1 Patrimonio Hipotecaria: Supporting Unique Mortgage Processes Attached to SAP for Banking

In the banking industry, competitive differences are in service speed, quality, and efficiency, because banking services are essentially a commodity. The SAP NetWeaver technology platform is a key enabler of our agility and ability to respond to market demands. A BPM approach and the SOA-based SAP for Banking solutions are helping us rapidly implement collaborative processes to improve business process quality and efficiency in supporting our financial and mortgage lending products.

– Alejandro Marroquin, Chief Information Officer, Patrimonio Hipotecaria

Patrimonio Hipotecaria, a Mexico-based mortgage bank founded in 1995 with 17 regional branches, is recognized by Standard & Poor's for its highly efficient operations, which result from its integrated and flexible core IT systems. To keep pace with its rapid growth, Patrimonio developed a strategy to replace over 20 legacy applications with the SAP IS-Banking and the SAP NetWeaver technology platform. To support their unique end-to-end financial processes that span between SAP for Banking and non-SAP applications, Patrimonio leveraged SAP NetWeaver Business Process Management.

8.1.1 Background

Patrimonio Hipotecaria is one of the leading Mexican mortgage and construction lending companies. They specialize in the housing and real estate development sector, with multiregional coverage servicing loans in different states of Mexico, and are an active servicer of residential mortgages, with total assets under management of US $1.2 billion.

Patrimonio's double-digit annual growth began to overtax the company's complex array of 20-plus homegrown internal applications, threatening to blunt the company's growth and competitive advantage. In 2009, Patrimonio selected SAP for Banking to manage their business and technology requirements. In addition to providing the core banking solution, Patrimonio chose to leverage the SAP technology platform for process automation and cross-application integration for their financial processes. Patrimonio decided to implement this project with the expectation that they would increase their insight into the business, which would enable them to create innovative new product offerings for their customers. Their goal was to accelerate the time to market for these new banking offers.

Business Case

Patrimonio intended to use SAP NetWeaver BPM to automate the processes that supported their financial and banking products, such as loan origination processes for mortgage lending. For the first project, Patrimonio chose to automate their "FOVISSSTE process" — a government-sponsored funding model for housing developments, where the loan origination process was outsourced to Patrimonio. The number of loan applications through the FOVISSSTE process was growing by double digits every year, which made it an excellent first candidate for BPM. The FOVISSSTE process had common characteristics with other, more complex financial processes at Patrimonio:

▶ **Cross-department dependencies**
Business process and physical document exchange spanned local branches and the central office in Mexico City.

▶ **Companywide**
The FOVISSSTE process was deployed to most of the bank branches.

▶ **Long-running process**
The last step to conclude the loan origination was projected to take six months from the point of the loan initiation.

Patrimonio approached the FOVISSSTE process as a first iteration of a broader process improvement program. The organization-wide deployment of this process allowed Patrimonio's employees to become familiar with the user experience, which was planned to become the basis for other processes. This project allowed Patrimonio to develop a competency in the BPM approach by helping to establish:

▸ Process modeling Best Practices

▸ An implementation process and methodology for SAP NetWeaver BPM

▸ Guidelines for monitoring and production support for SAP NetWeaver BPM

▸ Development and backend integration guidelines for process user experiences

▸ SOA and service governance

As-Is Process

Most loan origination processes at Patrimonio had automated workflow support through their Lotus Notes platform — the software with which they began. However, the FOVISSSTE loan origination process was highly manual; it was managed through spreadsheets that had evolved in complexity over the years. When the paperwork files were exchanged between branch offices, their tracking was captured in Excel, as were all open issues and clarifications related to a loan application.

The tracking spreadsheets were not standardized, and the company found that different users had customized them to suit their individual preferences. Exception conditions on loan applications had to be tracked manually. As a result, centralized tracking and visibility across the entire FOVISSSTE process visibility was not possible. The process itself was disconnected from the backend SAP system; the relevant financial transactions related to the loan application had to be manually entered by super-users into the SAP for Banking system, causing an operational bottleneck in the process. Funds receipt and disbursal reconciliation were time-consuming. Operational and managerial reporting data required a lot of manual work and took over a day to compile from the various branches. Table 8.1 illustrates the as-is process parameters.

Key Process Requirements	As-Is Condition
Process planning and modeling	Process sequence maintained in master spreadsheet
Process interaction and documentation	Interaction between participants and exchange of documents managed manually through phone calls and email
Process visibility, status tracking, exception handling	Limited — managed manually through spreadsheets and by directly contacting participants
Integration with backend SAP system	No integration — the activity was handed off to super-users for applications reaching the stage requiring SAP FI transactions; several SAP transactions were executed manually for each loan application
Process flexibility to introduce a new business activity	Lack of centralized process management; poor control over whether local process managers institute changes to their local manual process variants
Process KPI measurements (e.g., number of applications waiting on activity X)	KPI reporting — a highly manual task requiring compilation of data from all branches
Strategic reporting	Due to individually maintained spreadsheets, managerial and strategic reporting not available on-demand

Table 8.1 Patrimonio As-Is Process Parameters

8.1.2 BPM Solution

To develop their BPM-based processes, Patrimonio selected Nagarro, an SAP implementation partner that provides consulting services for SAP Business Suite and SAP NetWeaver. Nagarro is headquartered in San Jose, California, with offices in Mexico, Germany, Sweden, and India. Nagarro recommended a roadmap for migrating existing and future business processes to the SAP NetWeaver platform and conducted the BPM implementation for the initial process. For the realization of Patrimonio's loan origination and future business processes, Nagarro recommended SAP NetWeaver Business Process Management, SAP NetWeaver Business Rules Management, SAP NetWeaver Composition Environment (CE), Web Dynpro, and the SOA services provided by SAP for Banking as core components.

Capturing the current business process and simplifying it to the desired state was a key objective realized during the FOVISSSTE business process modeling. Key process owners were interviewed during the discovery phase to develop the as-is and the to-be business process model. A user interface mockup was developed in SAP NetWeaver CE using Web Dynpro to simulate the end-user experience. The business process provided the capability to handle business exceptions such as collaboration between branch offices to resolve issues related to a specific loan application. Additionally, operational reports were developed to provide process statistics and KPIs such as the number of processes waiting on a business step per branch or region.

In the to-be process (see Figure 8.1), the process participants were branch executives from the 17 branches, the executive responsible for the FOVISSSTE process at headquarters, and the commercial department.

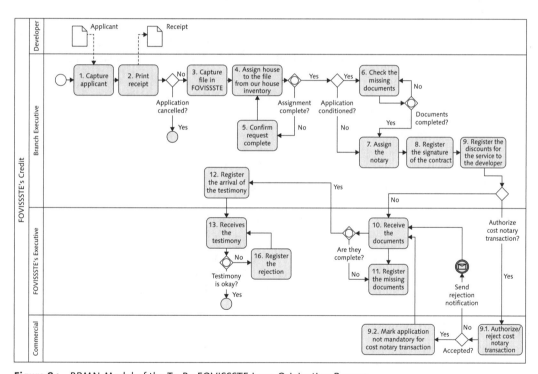

Figure 8.1 BPMN Model of the To-Be FOVISSSTE Loan Origination Process

The branch executive processed the loan application file through its various stages. All files from the various branches were sent to Mexico City to the FOVISSSTE executive, who then registered them into the FOVISSSTE Web portal provided by the Mexican Federal Government. The Commercial department authorized payments to the third-party notary service provider. Upon the receipt of the property title document ("testimony") up to six months later, the FOVISSSTE loan application process was completed.

Establishing the reference architecture for future process implementations was another key objective of this project. Table 8.2 gives a consolidated view of the reference architecture.

Capability	Product/Architecture Principle
Business process modeling and orchestration	SAP NetWeaver BPM: provides the capability for implementing user-centric business processes across roles and user profiles.
UI presentation platform	SAP NetWeaver CE: provides portal capability for secure, consistent, and unified access to backend applications.
UI technology for each business activity	Web Dynpro: the UI for each process step is developed independently, allowing for reuse across other business processes with similar tasks.
Service-oriented architecture	Enterprise-class services were leveraged from SAP for Banking and Microsoft .NET-based legacy applications for implementing process steps.
Custom enterprise services	Where needed, custom enterprise services were modeled in an enterprise services repository, implemented in backend applications, and published in a service registry.
Business rules	SAP NetWeaver BRM will enable automation in enforcing checking for the presence of mandatory loan documents, checking the document validity dates with respect to loan tenure, and checking the status of the house if it has pre-existing loans.

Table 8.2 FOVISSSTE Reference Architecture

Implementing the Solution

Because BPM was a new approach for Patrimonio, the implementation was conducted in phases to achieve specific milestones at the completion of each phase. The SAP NetWeaver CE landscape was installed in the typical three-instance configuration, consisting of development, quality, and production instances.

For each BPM step, the user interface screen was defined in terms of screen elements, information capture logic, business logic, and end-user interaction. The user experience for each step was then implemented in Web Dynpro as mock user-interface screens and associated with the appropriate manual steps in the BPM process flow.

FOVISSSTE process owners were then walked through the screen flow of the process; the BPM model was further refined and simplified based on the feedback they provided. The user-interface mockup captured the handoff between the bank branch and head office, which allowed all process participants to visualize the process choreography. After the key process owners approved the baseline business process, the SAP NetWeaver BPM realization phase was started. Each BPM activity was implemented as an independent Web Dynpro component; the input and output context parameters were kept simple and generic to promote reuse across other similar loan origination business processes. The agile development process ensured that each Web Dynpro component was developed independently, such that the customer could see the final process being assembled in a shorter time frame.

The key process owners were involved in acceptance testing of the developed BPM process. Once testing was completed, the production go-live was conducted as a "soft launch" across a few branches; the process was gradually deployed across all of the bank branches.

Results of the Project

The production rollout of the FOVISSSTE process across Patrimonio provided immediate business value. Process tracking and traceability have vastly improved. Operational reports provide macro indicators on processes through the company and highlight process bottlenecks. The process is integrated with the SAP IS-Banking platform and has eliminated the need for manual entry of loan application information. User adoption has been swift; the "train-the-trainer" approach was used, where the key user in each branch was trained by the core implementation team. The process is being consistently refined with subflows to handle additional scenarios such as management of third-party notary agents, who provide notary services to loan applications.

Patrimonio is now working toward implementing additional business processes to be managed with SAP NetWeaver BPM, such as individual loan origination, loan servicing, and collection management.

Sample Solution Architecture for an SAP Landscape

Figure 8.2 maps the SAP components for implementing business processes similar to the FOVISSSTE process at Patrimonio.

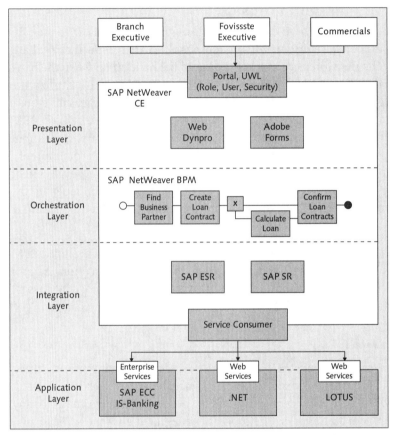

Figure 8.2 Suggested Solution Architecture for BPM-Based Composite Applications Related to SAP for Banking

As depicted in Figure 8.2, the solution architecture can be thought of in terms of a presentation layer for managing user interactions, an orchestration layer for managing the end-to-end business processes, an integration layer for integrating system-to-system process steps, and an application layer where many of the business functions required for automatic process steps reside. The presentation layer consists of the user-interaction capabilities for displaying data, obtaining user input, validating frontend data, and printing data. The SAP components deployed are the SAP NetWeaver Portals, Universal Worklist, Web Dynpro, and Adobe Forms.

In the orchestration layer, SAP NetWeaver BPM provides user-centric workflow capabilities. The workflow allows allocation of activities to different actors through role-based authorizations.

The integration layer handles integration between the SAP NetWeaver CE server and the enterprise systems such as SAP ERP Central Component (SAP ECC). The FOVISSSTE implementation uses SAP enterprise services and Web services through direct consumption. Enterprise Services Repository (ES Repository) and the Services Registry are key components for enabling the SOA-based integration.

Within the application layer reside the enterprise systems such as SAP ECC, Microsoft.NET, and Lotus that participate in the business scenario. Integration options based on the enterprise system capability have to be explored for optimum integration.

8.2 Coca-Cola Erfrischungsgetränke AG: Promotion Material Planning and Procurement as an Extension of SAP Trade Promotion Management

SAP NetWeaver BPM enhances our global standard processes to meet our unique requirements. The optimized demand planning process offers seamless integration of activities across marketing, sales, and procurement.
– Alexander Grobe, Manager Enterprise Architecture and Innovation, CCE AG

Coca-Cola Erfrischungsgetränke AG (CCE AG) needed a cost- and time-efficient approach to localize a global template solution named Coke One. They used BPM tools and methods to effectively implement the bottler-specific language and define legal and local business requirements. Demand determination for promotional material was the first live process CCE AG implemented with SAP NetWeaver BPM. The goal was to optimize marketing budget allocation for promotional materials, and the solution was to create a single environment in which to plan and order promotional material.

8.2.1 Background

CCE AG is the largest German beverage company, selling about 3.4 billion liters per year (2009). Since 2007, CCE AG has been the only franchisee of The Coca-Cola Company (TCCC, Atlanta) in Germany. CCE AG's business is the production (25 facilities) and distribution (70 facilities) of Coca-Cola products to about 95,000 retail customers and 550,000 customers in other trade channels and is supported by a workforce of 11,000 employees. In addition to the classic soft drinks, the product program also consists of water, fruit juices, tea, sports and energy drinks, and cold coffee drinks.

Coca-Cola GmbH (CC GmbH) is a subsidiary of TCCC and is responsible for national consumer marketing and brand management, as well as other central functions such as product and packaging development. Both German entities work closely together to be successful in the highly competitive German market.

Business Case

The SCALE program (System Collaboration Approach Leveraging Excellence) had the goal to deliver a standardized Coca-Cola bottler operating model to the participating bottlers, which is called Coke One. Coke One is a combined offering of best-practice business processes supported by an enhanced SAP Business Suite including SAP partner add-ons and some non-SAP solutions.

Coke One was delivered as a global template solution that must be localized for each bottler prior to go-live. Localization meant implementing the bottler-specific language and legal and unique local business requirements. The promotion planning scenario was the first process to be localized.

Briefly, CCE AG buys the needed concentrate from TCCC, adds water, sugar, and CO_2 and delivers the bottled beverages to its customers. The product margin directly depends on the acquisition price of the concentrate and the selling price of the finished goods. Because CCE AG cannot influence both price points, it has to implement the most efficient business processes possible. Furthermore, growth in sales volume can only be achieved through adding new product offerings and promotions.

As-Is Process

Promotion planning at CCE AG is part of the annual business planning process. The business plan contains planned promotions, which include high-level customer target groups, planned activities, timing, and budgets. It is also the foundation for the annual negotiations with national customers.

When CCE AG decided to implement BPM, the business challenge was to find the best possible allocation for promotional activities, based on a given direct marketing expense budget of the business plan. Because major parts of this budget were the costs involved with buying and delivering promotion material, the demand planning and procurement process of these items was obviously important.

The process originally started top-down with the promotion project manager (PPM) in central marketing. The PPM defined the target groups and the promotional materials and expected volumes planned to be used in the promotion. He then handed this information over to procurement, which would issue a request for a proposal to the promotion material vendors, who would return an initial pricing based on the requested volume. At that point, the PPM might rework the planning, based on the input of the purchasing manager, which would result in another cycle. See Figure 8.3 for the high-level process description.

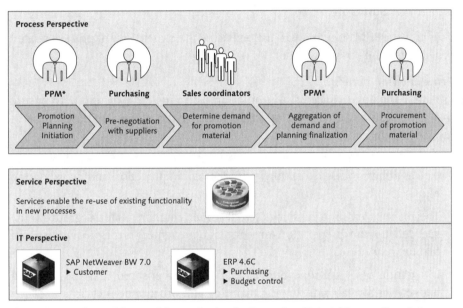

Figure 8.3 High-Level Demand Determination for Promotion Material Process Description

When the promotion was ready from the PPM's viewpoint, the PPM opened the promotion for local planning. Sales coordinators continued the process in the sales centers by adjusting the disaggregated top-down plan in a bottom-up planning step. This included local knowledge of the sales force, for which customer outlets are relevant for the promotion within the selected target group.

Coca-Cola Erfrischungsgetränke AG decided to implement BPM because of several weaknesses within the process that cost time, money, and resources. The old process could not be easily modified to incorporate new business requirements such as integration of an external handling house for the outsourced delivery of promotional materials. During the process execution, the process participants had very limited insight in the process progress and current planning results.

The process was mainly controlled via emails and an intranet site. During the process execution several manual merge, export, and import steps occurred with data losses and inconsistencies. In addition, there was no integration with master data and budget controlling, which resulted in a lot of manual preparation effort.

One of the biggest weaknesses was the lack of integration with procurement. The planning of promotional material for one promotion usually resulted in purchase orders with several hundred line items.

8.2.2   BPM Solution

The case for the BPM solution was justified using the dimensions of process-related improvements and strategic value:

▶ **Process-based benefits**
Timing is the key to successful promotion planning and execution. To ensure that all milestones are met, the participants in the process required process insight and traceability.

  ▶ The PPM required end-to-end responsibility and needed to be able to focus on handling process exceptions with less communication and coordination effort.

  ▶ The reuse of existing master data (customer, vendor, material groups, etc.) speeded up the preparation process and prevented errors resulting from manual procedures.

  ▶ Integration of a real-time budget-check feature ensured that the required budget was available during the planning and procurement cycle.

  ▶ Procurement integration saved a lot of communication and manual entry effort.

  ▶ An external handling house outsourced the delivery of the purchased promotional material to the customer outlets, which saved the sales representatives the time required to drive to CCE AG locations to pick up promotional material.

  ▶ Simplified process and role-specific user interfaces ensured higher productivity and acceptance of the solution.

▶ **Strategic benefits**
Reduced time to value for scenario implementation compared to other approaches for localization of a global template.

▶ Decoupled solution delivery from backend release cycles.

▶ Higher user acceptance resulting from rapid prototyping, based on a common language (BPMN process models and user interface mock-ups).

▶ Nonintrusive localization approach for the Coke One template.

▶ Flexible deployment scenarios with the option to roll in new innovative processes and solutions into the global template.

Implementing the Solution

Not surprisingly, the departments involved in the project specified their requirements, which were based on the old solution and helped the team identify gaps in corresponding documents. Instead of starting the implementation directly, the IT project team exhibited their understandings with rapid prototyping technologies. Process flow and user-interface design were presented to the relevant departments. Misunderstandings could be clarified up front, and a common understanding of the requirements was assured. This led to only a few changes in the later project.

Parallel to the rapid prototyping project, the architecture was prepared: solution architecture reflected the involved systems and corresponding communication protocols. Component architecture described the involved components and their relations. Enterprise Services Repository was used to describe the service interfaces.

Figure 8.4 shows the high-level architecture of the solution. Important building blocks were SAP NetWeaver Business Process Management and the backend systems: SAP NetWeaver Business Warehouse and SAP ERP.

To allow end-user access to the solution, the lightweight portal was used. The BPM process engine executed technically enriched process models and delivered the tasks via the Universal Worklist in the portal. This execution involved choreographing backend services and user interaction with the frontend technology, which was developed using Web Dynpro Java.

As promotion-planning data itself is not relevant to the backend systems, local persistency was used. With Java Persistence API (JPA) technology, only the relevant data structures were kept locally. The result of the planning — the creation of the required purchase orders — was executed via a service in ERP. Services were also used to allow real-time budget checking along with choosing preferred customer target groups.

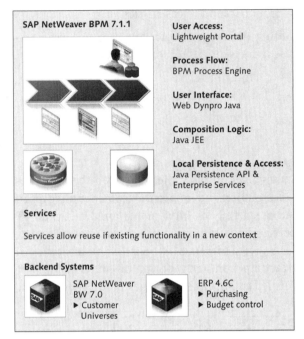

Figure 8.4 High-Level Architecture

With both the functional and technical description finished, the implementation could start. An important key success factor for CCE AG was to enable its own IT team to participate in this BPM project. This was realized with the following elements:

▶ Up-front training measures were conducted.

▶ Solution architecture had to divide the work into small, manageable, and delimited work packages. This allowed CCE AG employees to contribute significantly when combined with training and coaching on the job.

While development was running, test management was initiated. The project team agreed on roles, processes, and tools to conduct intense testing. The testing included having the test cases for module and integration testing ready. In a phased approach, the development team first conducted tests and then handed the results over to functional departments.

Target Process Model: Sample Solution Architecture

Figure 8.5 shows the executable target process model in BPMN. To provide a better understanding, we describe all process steps in more detail in Table 8.3.

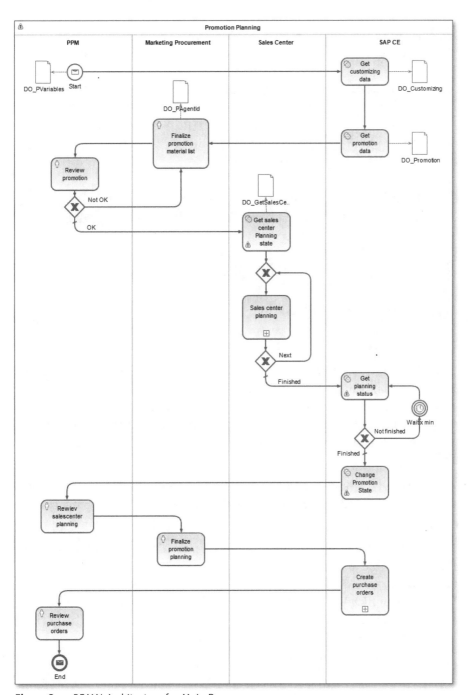

Figure 8.5 BPMN Architecture for Main Process

Roles	Responsible Actions	Responsible Data Set
Promotion project manager	Initiate promotion	Promotion basic data
Procurement manager	Negotiate preliminary prices	Promotion material list and centrally estimated demand
Sales center planner	Detailed planning of the participating customers and material used	Local plan
Sales center manager	Approval of the local plan	Local plan
Sales representative	In-store setup of the promotion material	List of participating customer outlets
Delivery house	Distribution of promotion material to customer outlets	List of participating customer outlets

Table 8.3 Activities of the Main Process

Results of the Project

As a result of this project, the marketing and procurement departments were able to achieve a faster planning process, focusing on exception handling with progress transparency for all involved process participants. The process was streamlined through the automation of formal manual process steps and end-to-end process integration. Less end-user training was needed due to the intuitive user-friendly interface.

The solution was accepted for Coke One localization of SAP Trade Promotion Management (SAP TPM). For this localization, the existing developments were reused.

BPM and composition supported by SAP NetWeaver Composition Environment will be used for the localization of several other scenarios, for example, in master data management (SAP NetWeaver BPM) and the automation of signatory rules (SAP NetWeaver BRM). Midterm, it will replace CCE AG legacy solutions, leading to lower total cost of ownership (TCO). The composition approach will also likely be adopted for Coke One Template development.

8.3   GISA: Increased Competition in Utilities Demands Efficient Customer Service Connections

With BPM and SOA we can deliver process chain flexibility to integrate different market players. That is exactly what enterprises require in the liberalized energy market.
– Hans Ludwig Reinecke, SAP manager, GISA GmbH

GISA GmbH is the largest independent IT, process, and outsourcing supplier in central Germany. GISA has more than 100 customers, with a strong focus on the utilities sector in Germany. As such, GISA was perfectly positioned to leverage their expertise to deliver innovative process templates to enable their utility customers to meet the regulated limits for new service connections. The resultant template streamlined and automated manual, paper-based activity across multiple stakeholders. The process template was developed using SAP NetWeaver BPM and SAP NetWeaver BRM, which are components of SAP NetWeaver Composition Environment, and leverage the service-enabled functionality of SAP Business Suite.

Model-based development of the process ensured that the project was delivered in half the time (compared to traditional programming), and GISA achieved a 20–30% reduction in integration costs by leveraging standard enterprise services. What's more, changes made to these processes to meet customer-specific requirements were achieved through the incorporation of business rules. This enabled GISA customers to make changes to the running process in a third of the time required before. This has led to faster development and reduced costs, and GISA expects to write off their development costs within the next three years.

8.3.1   Background

GISA GmbH offers a wide range of IT-related consulting services with customers in utilities, media, and the public sector. The service provider is based in Germany, employs 430 people, and generated €73 million revenue in 2008. To accelerate its growth while improving support to its customers, GISA GmbH was an early adopter of a future-oriented IT landscape based on SOA.

Business Case

Market liberalization has eliminated guaranteed territorial monopolies. Consumer switching is expected to increase as competition between incumbent energy suppliers and new entrants intensifies. Assuming an average customer base of 1.9 million and an estimated 10% customer volatility, the expected additional workload for utilities is 190,000 inquiries per year that must be manually processed. This is driving utility distributors to automate new service connection inquiries. Additionally, energy production, transportation, and distribution have been unbundled, thereby further increasing the complexity of the process by extending the process across multiple stakeholders (i.e., producers, networks, and energy retailers). Furthermore, the process varies across electricity, gas, water supply, and district heating providers.

GISA addressed this market opportunity by offering BPM-enabled process templates, which enable its customers to automate the new service-connection inquiry process and flexibly connect different market players.

As-Is Process

When a consumer requests an electricity connection, this may require infrastructure enhancement that comprises steps such as checking the feasibility, getting cost estimates and quotes, making an offer, creating service orders, triggering the installation of a new connection, and billing (see Figure 8.6). This process was manual, paper-based, and required interaction with multiple systems such as SAP ERP, SAP Records Management, external systems, geographical information systems (GISs), etc., and was the responsibility of a single supplier. The energy liberalization has introduced complex handoffs across multiple stakeholders and stringent regulated deadlines for new service connections.

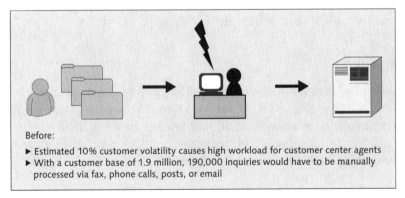

Before:
▶ Estimated 10% customer volatility causes high workload for customer center agents
▶ With a customer base of 1.9 million, 190,000 inquiries would have to be manually processed via fax, phone calls, posts, or email

Figure 8.6 The As-Is Process Using a Call Center

8.3.2   BPM Solution

GISA used SAP NetWeaver BPM to create innovative process templates for meeting utility-specific market requirements. They streamlined the process of managing customer inquiries for new electricity connections by replacing manual paper-based activities with automated workflows and decisions.

The process was divided into three phases:

1. Customer inquiry

2. Offer and requisitioning and building completion

3. Invoicing, start-up, and controlling

The second process phase was performed classically by utilizing the functionality of SAP ECC 6.0 EhP4 and the SAP for Utilities solution portfolio, whereas the first and third phase leveraged enterprise services from the SAP ECC 6.0 EhP4 to compose the process. The service-oriented approach enabled GISA to create a process with maximum flexibility while enabling seamless integration of commercial and technical tasks such as offer generation and technical examination. This process removed the workaround of using manually completed forms (see Figure 8.7). Additionally, it enabled faster integration of changing market players, for example, faster integration during online examination of the network capacity.

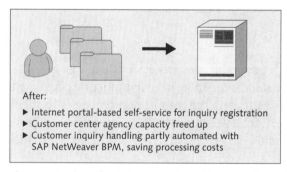

After:

▶ Internet portal-based self-service for inquiry registration
▶ Customer center agency capacity freed up
▶ Customer inquiry handling partly automated with
   SAP NetWeaver BPM, saving processing costs

Figure 8.7   The "After" Process with the Customer Online Portal

Implementing the Solution

GISA implemented the software in the context of a ramp-up project. They developed the solution using SAP NetWeaver Composition Environment by using the components SAP NetWeaver BPM and SAP NetWeaver BRM. The entire process chain was modeled and controlled by rules defined in SAP NetWeaver BPM (see Figure 8.8). For example, the process could be determined from the customer data whether a standard or individual connection was needed, and hence the request was automatically directed to the responsible specialist for processing. This process leveraged the Best Practices provided by service-enabled applications such as the SAP Business Suite.

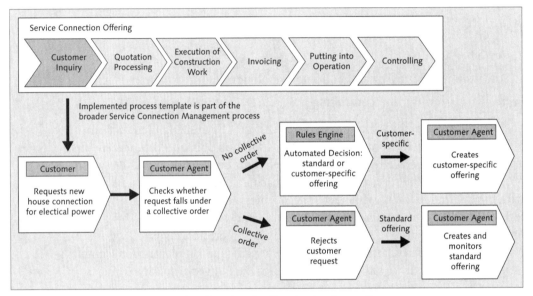

Figure 8.8 Process Template Overview for New Service Connections

Results of the Project

This flexible approach enabled GISA to realize the process twice as fast as using traditional programming tools to extend the service-enabled processes delivered by SAP business applications. What's more, changes to these processes to meet customer-specific requirements were achieved through the incorporation of business rules. This enabled GISA customers to make changes to running processes in a third of the time required before.

The BPM approach has led to faster development at reduced costs, and GISA expects to amortize their development costs within the next three years (see Table 8.4).

SOA and BPM make a flexible approach possible. Next, GISA plans to integrate data from geographical information systems (GIS) so that power suppliers can indicate connections directly on a map. An extension for gas and water suppliers is planned.

KPI	Impact
New service connection process execution time	Reduced
Process transparency and revision security	Increased
Customer satisfaction	Increased
Quotation times for service connection	Reduced
Scalability of process – no customers	Increased
Model-based development of process	Twice as fast as programming
Realizing changes to running processes	Realizable in a third of the time
Reduction in integration costs	20–30% reduction by leveraging standard enterprise services

Table 8.4 GISA's Key Performance Indicators

Sample Solution Architecture for an SAP Landscape

Figure 8.9 depicts the scope of the various phases (packages) for realizing the process steps. It also highlights the enterprise services for each process step.

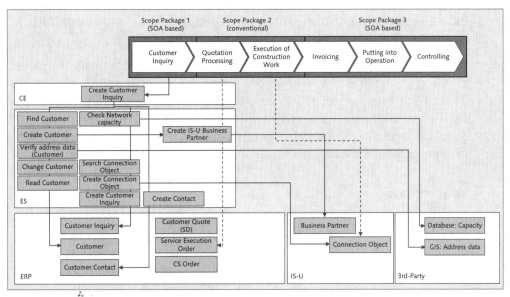

Figure 8.9 House Connection Process Architecture

8.4 Siemens IT Solutions and Services: Balancing Standardization and Customizability in a New Solution

The unique capabilities of business process management and service-oriented architectures enabled us to develop a new business concept and a template implementation as project accelerator for establishing Strategic Grid Management at T&D companies.
– Christian Heuer, Global Head of Smart Grid, Siemens AG, Siemens IT Solutions and Services

SAP does not provide any standard solutions for strategic asset management that leverage the unique characteristics of grid companies. Siemens IT Solutions and Services developed Strategic Grid Management for transmission and distribution (T&D) companies that leverage SOA and BPM capabilities to accelerate customer projects.

8.4.1 Background

Siemens is a global powerhouse in electrical engineering and electronics. The company has 405,000 employees working to develop and manufacture products, design and install complex systems, and originate projects for a wide range of industries. Siemens provides pioneering technologies and comprehensive know-how to benefit customers in over 190 countries.

Siemens IT Solutions and Services is a cross-sector business of Siemens. It provides IT operations services and develops comprehensive, industry-specific IT solutions by connecting specialized, innovative technologies from Siemens and other industry leaders, with core business processes via IT. In fiscal year 2009, Siemens IT Solutions and Services had about 35,000 employees worldwide and a sales volume of approximately €4.7 billion.

Business Case

Deregulation changed the business model for grid operators from operating as cost centers that were only focused on reliable energy delivery, to having to become profit-driven. While many of their existing power infrastructure assets are approaching the ends of their lives, limited budgets force them to use more effective strategies for the maintenance and replacement of grid assets.

Until now there were no standard solutions for strategic asset management on the market that leveraged the unique characteristics of grid companies such as the existence of a topology. One of the reasons for this was that regulation split the limited market into even smaller local markets. Siemens had to find a new balance between standardization and customizability to enable a new offering, Strategic Grid Management for T&D companies.

The recent developments around the SAP NetWeaver technology platform brought new capabilities to control and customize processes and to integrate existing functionalities of already deployed applications to the table. Leveraging the new technology enabled Siemens to define an abstract business concept for Strategic Grid Management consisting of processes, key performance indicators (KPIs), reference data models, and so on. They then used the SAP NetWeaver technology platform to develop a reference implementation of these processes and packaged them as content for the platform.

The SAP NetWeaver technology platform allows Siemens to fully leverage their domain knowledge as an accelerator for customer projects with globally reusable processes and the capability to easily adapt these to local company and regulation requirements. Without business process management (BPM) and service-oriented architectures (SOAs), this kind of solution accelerator would not be competitive.

As-Is Process

The number of companies operating in the energy industry is relatively small compared to other industries such as discrete manufacturing. Hence, the market for strategic asset management solutions is even smaller. Business in this market is additionally complicated by two aspects:

1. Local regulation splits the small market into multiple even smaller submarkets with individual (and in some cases often changing) requirements.

2. Grid operators tend to build their business upon many years of individual experience and therefore often demand individual solutions uniquely designed to fit their needs.

These circumstances are the main reasons for a limitation in business potential for standardized Strategic Grid Management solutions and products for Siemens and other huge competitors. Individual solutions fit better with the circumstances; however, they have the drawback of higher cost and effort. Such custom solutions can cover the individual requirements of grid operators in small, local markets, but they tend to be more expensive because nearly the complete functional scope has to be developed specifically for each customer; practice-sharing can only be leveraged in a limited way. Additionally, these solutions are not easily reusable, which reduces their attractiveness for global solution providers like Siemens.

8.4.2 BPM Solution

Driven by the challenges and to create a new offering for Strategic Grid Management at T&D companies, Siemens had to find a new approach for balancing standardization and customizability.

The necessity of a business concept as a foundation for the new offering was derived from a content perspective. The business concept contained a modular process blueprint, predefined KPIs, required capabilities, business levers, and the conceptual data model for the solution. This would ensure that the content was standardized at an abstract level but would remain open to being customized regarding individual requirements.

On its own, the introduction of the business concept did not allow Siemens to overcome all of the challenges. The missing requirement was a platform that enabled and supported reusable template implementations while providing flexibility for customization. The recent technological advances in SOA and BPM platforms were a very good match. Such platforms provide a variety of features such as modeling, controlling, and customizing of processes and capabilities to easily integrate them with existing functionality from already deployed products and solutions.

Together, the business concept and the platform allowed Siemens to build a reference implementation for Strategic Grid Management. In this manner, the process blueprint was divided into several business packages that were deployable content packages with process templates for an SOA/BPM platform.

Implementing the Solution

Siemens built the Grid Asset Management Suite (GAMS) solution as a reference implementation for Strategic Grid Management.

Leveraging BPM significantly enabled Siemens to adopt the new approach for solution development. While the business concept was being developed, the process mock-up was directly modeled utilizing a modeling tool that was capable of Business Process Modeling Notation (BPMN). Compared to classic process design, this was a major change. The utilization of such a modeler has a significant advantage. Whereas processes previously had to be designed in one place and later implemented somewhere else, with the new approach each process model was directly executable, and disconnects between the abstract and the executable models would be avoided. In addition, this approach also enabled closer cooperation between business experts and developers. The process dimension gave them a common layer both sides could comprehend. This helped prevent classic problems such as misunderstandings between technical and business experts.

In general, there was a strong parallelism in the development of the business concept and the reference implementation. With the use of a rapid prototyping approach, progress relating to the business concept had been transferred directly into the implementation. Experience from the different prototypes and refinements derived from this process found its way back into the business concept through a feedback channel.

Results of the Project

In retrospect, leveraging an SOA and BPM platform as the carrier for modular content packages was a huge step in the right direction for Siemens. This will strongly support the competitiveness of future solution developments.

Today, Siemens can offer customers in different markets an individual solution for Strategic Grid Management based on a reference implementation that functions as a globally reusable solution accelerator. The predefined and implemented process templates allow efficient and cost-effective tailoring of the solution to the customer's needs. At the same time, reuse of the standardized solution core for individual customer projects ensures a competitive way of practice sharing.

Leveraging the SAP NetWeaver technology platform as a foundation and carrier for Siemens' domain knowledge allowed Siemens to overcome a variety of challenges and enabled the balance between standardization and customizability required to realize the Grid Asset Management Suite as reference a implementation for Strategic Grid Management.

In conclusion, GAMS helps Siemens' customers optimally operate their grid as they balance asset reliability with optimized capital expenditures and operating expenditures.

Sample Solution Architecture for an SAP Landscape

An essential requirement for the development of the solution was an explicit process focus, unlike in traditional applications where the process logic is implemented implicitly and therefore hidden from the user. Therefore, there are two dimensions that have to be examined separately from an architectural standpoint.

The first dimension focuses on the process model and its provisioning in a form of separate business packages. The second dimension concerns the platform as a carrier for the content packages. Both are equally relevant for Siemens' solution.

As part of the business concept, the high-level reference process model was defined utilizing the SAP Solution Composer, whereas the detailed process modeling was executed directly in the SAP NetWeaver Developer Studio (NWDS). Besides the process modeling, the different perspectives of the developer studio are also the core component for nearly all development activities, such as the implementation of processes, rules, persistence, Web services, and user interfaces (see Figure 8.10).

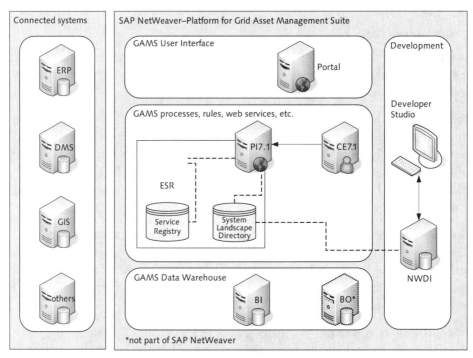

Figure 8.10 GAMS: Reference Processes Bundled into Business Packages

To be able to effectively deploy and use the business packages, a platform capable of storage, presentation, and control is required. Therefore, huge parts of the SAP NetWeaver technology platform are required, including SAP NetWeaver Composition Environment with SAP NetWeaver Business Process Management and SAP NetWeaver Business Rules Management functionalities, the process integration with its enterprise service bus, business intelligence as a central data warehouse, and a portal as a Web-based presentation layer. The landscape is completed by the SAP NetWeaver Development Infrastructure (NWDI), which is responsible for software lifecycle management (see Figure 8.11).

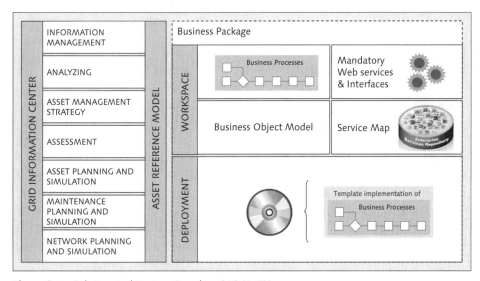

Figure 8.11   Solution Architecture Based on SAP NetWeaver

8.5   RS Components: Automating Supply Chain Collaboration for Inventory Planning and Supplier Performance Management

CompriseIT's BPM approach has allowed us to automate standard supply chain collaboration for product lead times — further improving the accuracy of our stock availability promises and allowing our supply chain teams more time to focus on improving supplier performance.
– Graham Wiffen, SAP Practice Manager, RS Components

RS Components operates in 27 countries and sells hundreds of thousands of products. The supply chain team is constantly looking for ways to increase agility in the supply chain, with the main goals being to drive down inventory costs and increase on-shelf availability.

One key area that impacts performance for RS Components is the accuracy of the suppliers' lead-time, because this has a significant impact on planning optimum stock levels. RS Components worked with CompriseIT to utilize SAP NetWeaver BPM to automate the process that allows suppliers to maintain their own lead times while maintaining control via supplier-specific business rules.

8.5.1 Background

Electrocomponents plc is one of the largest global catalog and Web-based distributors of electronic, electromechanical, and industrial components. Operating under the trading brands of RS Components, Radiospares, Radionics, and Allied Electronics in the U.S., Electrocomponents plc serves nearly 1.6 million customers in over 80 countries worldwide. Through operations in 27 countries and 17 warehouses, RS Components distributes 500,000-plus products from over 2,500 suppliers. RS Components is one of the operating companies within the Electrocomponents group, and it satisfies the small-quantity product needs of customers who are typically electronics or maintenance engineers in businesses. A large number of high-quality goods are stocked, which are dispatched the same day the order is received. The group manages tens of thousands of orders for customers across the world each business day.

Business Case

RS Components is continuously expanding its business by increasing the market share and volume of the components it provides to its customers. They achieve this by optimizing the availability of supply and by carrying a wider range of options from an increasing number of suppliers.

Efficiently managing the ever-increasing supplier base and optimizing the availability of components is very important to maximize sales opportunities. RS Components needed to increase the automation between suppliers and itself to achieve the above goals, because the sheer volume of data made manual processing impractical.

Lead times are a key piece of information shared between RS Components and its suppliers. This information provides critical input to the planning and execution systems as they drive safety stock levels. By keeping these up-to-date, RS Components could have confidence in their supply chain plans and therefore reduce the amount of stock on hand, allowing them to make working capital more readily available.

RS Components' process was identified as a candidate for SAP NetWeaver BPM using the CompriseIT composite application checklist; as shown in Table 8.5, the process scored high across all five dimensions. For more detail and information on composite application, please refer to Part III, Chapter 17, Section 17.8.

Process Requirements	Suitability Ranking for SAP NetWeaver BPM
Process crosses internal or external boundaries	High
Process requires information to be used or created	High
Process required specific steps to be carried out	High
Process crosses systems	High
Process needs a new channel	High

Table 8.5 CompriseIT Composite Application Checklist

As-Is Process

At the time of BMP implementation, all lead time updates were manually input by supply chain personnel into a Standard Attribute Change Request (ACR) form, irrespective of their format. The Content Data team received the ACR form and processed it through several Excel macros, which formatted the data for entry into their preexisting SAP R/3 system. Due to the manual nature of the process, updates from suppliers were often made yearly, which meant that lead times were often not accurate. The delay in supplier feedback had a direct impact on the stock RS Components held and the on-shelf availability of products.

8.5.2   BPM Solution

Suppliers were asked to send a file to RS Components via electronic data interchange (EDI) on a monthly basis, containing lead times for the products they supply. They were also able to send ad hoc changes to RS Components. These files were sent in a supplier-specific format, but the integration layer was used to transform the data into a canonical (common) format.

Once this file was received it was processed through a set of business-maintained rules to determine if the system could be updated automatically, as depicted in Figure 8.12.

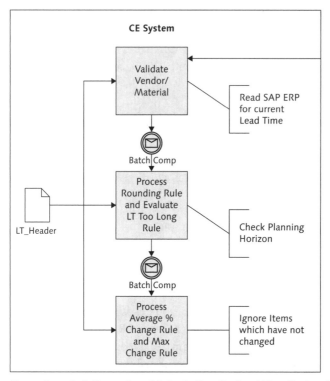

Figure 8.12 Bulk Processing of Rules in Supplier Lead Time Update Process at RS Components

These rules include the questions:

▶ Is the product valid for the supplier?

▶ Has the average lead time changed by x%?

▶ Has a specific product changed by y%?

For most of the rules, if a threshold was reached, an alert was triggered to the planner in charge of that product so he would be warned of a potential impact on the next planning run. Supply planners could then determine whether they needed to communicate with the supplier to negotiate a more favorable lead time. When rules were breached by a larger margin, an exception was raised that postponed the update of the lead time until it had been approved by the product's planner, as depicted in Figure 8.13.

Any technical exceptions were checked, such as if a material was locked in the ERP system, and these issues were routed to technical support for resolution. Figure 8.14 shows these checking and alerting sets.

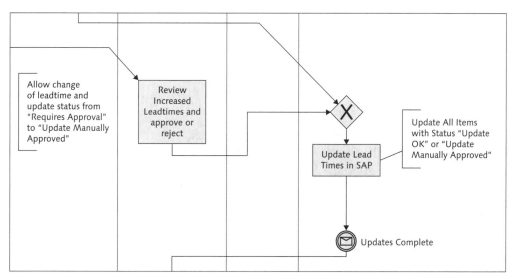

Figure 8.13 Lead Time Exception Requiring Supply Planner Approval in Supplier Lead Time Update Process at RS Components

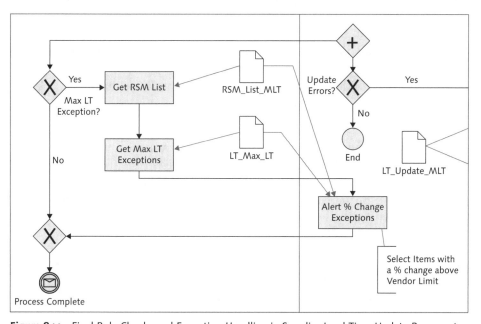

Figure 8.14 Final Rule Checks and Exception Handling in Supplier Lead Time Update Process at RS Components

The status of updates could be reported at each stage in the process. This information could then be used to trend lead time performance of each supplier. This information was collected in SAP NetWeaver Business Warehouse from both SAP ERP and SAP NetWeaver BPM.

Implementing the Solution

At the start of the project, the to-be supplier update process was modeled repeatedly using BPMN over three half-day workshops that included both business process participants and IT. At the end of the first design week, a requirements document was created, which described each step in the process and any business rules associated with the decisions made in a specific process step.

The joint workshops and easy-to-understand to-be process models helped create an aligned understanding of goals between business and IT, which enabled all parties involved (business, RS Components IT, and CompriseIT) to confidently sign off on the requirements.

Following the Scrum agile methodology, these requirements were then divided into two development iterations, with key requirements being developed over a three-week period. Implementing the agile development approach meant that the challenging time line of the project could be achieved (iteration 1) with key features live within weeks. The business was then able to have additional features added to the solution (iteration 2), without having to refactor iteration.

Results of the Project

At the time of this book's development, the solution was nearing the end of the first iteration and was due to go live. Early prototypes of the solution were well received by the business, and the match between "what they imagined they would get" and the solution were very close as they signed off on both BPMN models and SAP NetWeaver Visual Composer screen mock-ups.

Future plans for the solution are the addition of a "small" supplier version, which will enable smaller suppliers to upload files directly over the Web. The files will then be integrated into the same BPMN process used above for the larger suppliers. This situation illustrates a great example of reuse that is driven by SOA.

At the time of writing this use case, other features were planned and will be developed in parallel structure and deployed as they are tested by the business.

Sample Solution Architecture for an SAP Landscape

Figure 8.15 depicts the architecture of the solution. The vendor or supplier sends lead time update files (which can be thousands of records) on a monthly basis via a business-to-business (B2B) hub such as EDI. The file is then picked up by the enterprise application integration (EAI) layer, where the data is transformed into a common format. This data is then passed to the SAP NetWeaver BPM system using a Java Message Service (JMS) queue, where the data is fed into a BPM process. The process executes several rules to check the data and then either processes the update into the SAP system or raises exceptions, which are routed to the responsible product manager for either information or approval.

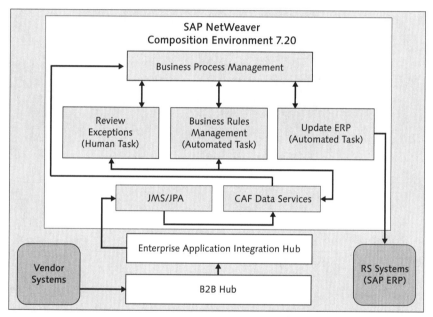

Figure 8.15 Architecture of Supplier Collaboration – BPM-Based Lead Time Update Process

9 BPM, Business Transformation, and Continuous Process Improvement

Greg Chase, Rukhshaan Omar, Jewgeni Kravets, Alberto Carrera, Marcelo Santa Rita

The majority of BPM applications today are achieving quick results by automating manual steps. However, the true long-term value of BPM tools and methods is taking a continuous improvement approach to optimize processes end-to-end and using a value engineering approach to identify which processes should be streamlined. What follows are two examples of companies that have applied BPM to transform their businesses.

The first example is KAESER KOMPRESSOREN, a leader in industrial air compressors. KAESER streamlined the compressed-air-as-a-service delivery process. The company built a highly efficient, responsive service delivery process that involves every department of the company and suppliers and partners around the world.

The second example is Braskem S.A., a leading manufacturer of thermoplastic resins in Latin America. They first built a solid business case for their BPM project and identified 13 key business processes. Braskem successfully deployed BPM to streamline their high-priority accounts payable process.

9.1 KAESER KOMPRESSOREN: Transforming from a Products Company to a Service Company

With BPM, KAESER KOMPRESSOREN rebuilt a highly efficient, responsive service delivery process that involves every department of the company, as well as suppliers and partners around the world.
– Falko Lameter, CIO, KAESER KOMPRESSOREN GmbH

KAESER KOMPRESSOREN, one of the leaders in industrial air compressors and their complementary products, wanted to become a supplier of compressed air as a service. This required streamlining and unifying its disjointed service delivery process and creating a more flexible, modular IT infrastructure. KAESER first established a sound foundation by adopting service-oriented architecture (SOA) and enterprise services from SAP. It then deployed business process management and business rules management technology to automate the process flow. The resultant process is now more efficient (smoother service transfers between participants), which leads to greater efficiency in service delivery. The established software allows the company to resolve issues faster, thus firmly establishing the company's position as the industry's premier supplier of compressed air as a service.

9.1.1 Background

KAESER KOMPRESSOREN GmbH offers products, services, and complete systems for the generation, treatment, and delivery of energy in the form of compressed air. The company was founded in 1919 in Coburg, Germany, and now has approximately 4,000 employees and three manufacturing plants in Germany and France. KAESER operates in more than 80 countries, with 40 subsidiaries and 30 partners throughout the sales regions of Europe, the Middle East, and Africa; the Americas; and Asia and the Pacific.

Business Case

With its commitment to product innovation and quality, KAESER has become one of the largest, most successful companies in the compressed air industry. Its products are used by companies of all sizes in every industry. In recent years, however, heightened competition and shrinking margins led the firm to realize that no matter how innovative their products were, this factor alone was not sufficient to support the company's growth and success goals. KAESER realized that their customers were increasingly looking to purchase compressed air benefits without having to become compressed air product experts. To capitalize on this market opportunity to boost revenues and margins, KAESER decided to sell compressed air as a service. This, however, required KAESER to transform from a product vendor to a service provider. Table 9.1 lists the business goals for the service delivery process.

Business Goal	Process KPIs
Process execution time	Maximum 2 days
Equipment down time	Maximum 1 day
Technician visit	Maximum 1 visit

Table 9.1 Business Goals for the Service Delivery Process

Business Goal	Process KPIs
Increase customer satisfaction	–
No incidents	–

Table 9.1 Business Goals for the Service Delivery Process (Cont.)

As-Is Process

The service delivery value chain at KAESER was complex and involved not only every department within the company, but its suppliers and partners around the world as well. The service delivery consisted of troubleshooting, complaint processing, maintenance, contracting, spare part deliveries, and technical assistance activities. These activities required flexible, efficient behind-the-scenes support for order and logistics planning, service scheduling, and parts and information provisioning. Their existing service delivery was lengthy, disjointed, and fragmented. As such, sometimes emergencies would go temporarily unaddressed.

9.1.2 BPM Solution

The business goal was to improve customer satisfaction by eliminating media breaks and thereby ensuring that all service requests were dealt with within defined service limits. Therefore, KAESER had to raise levels of efficiency, transparency, and quality of service delivery throughout the value chain. They faced the following key challenges:

▸ Coordinating global service and supply chain service planning, logistics, and IT processes

▸ Providing just-in-time provisioning of service materials and information

▸ Unifying and optimizing service fulfillment processes

The business department used a value engineering approach to identify which processes should be streamlined. These models provided a high-level business perspective of the to-be process flow between departments.

KAESER then sourced the expertise of SAP consultants to translate the high-level processes modeled in SAP Enterprise Modeling by IDS Scheer for implementing flexible and responsive service processes. The team used BPM methods and tools, as depicted in Figure 9.1, namely, emergency maintenance, planned maintenance, spare part availability, spare parts logistics, up-front shipment, slot finding for emergency visit, problem classification, economical negotiation, service confirmation, sales handover, and master data creation support.

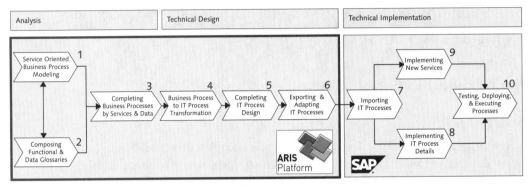

Figure 9.1 10 Steps from Process to Execution

Figure 9.2, Figure 9.3, and Figure 9.4 depict one of the service processes, namely, the emergency maintenance by service technician and the associated critical business factors at a high level.

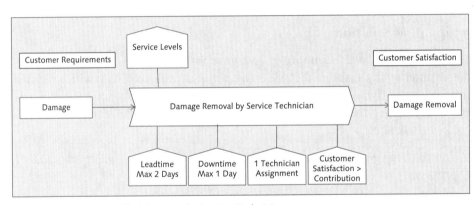

Figure 9.2 Emergency Maintenance by Service Technician

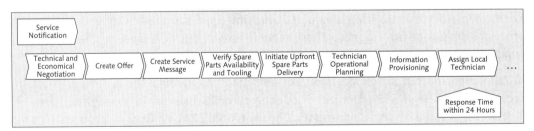

Figure 9.3 Repair by Service Technician Process

Figure 9.4 BRFplus Decision Table

A key decision KAESER KOMPRESSOREN made early in the implementation process was to avoid modification of the SAP standard application due to TCO considerations. Hence, within the solution transformation step, the team identified where the standard SAP-delivered standard functionality could be leveraged as-is in each process and where customer-specific extensions had to be developed using SAP NetWeaver BPM.

For example, a customer who purchased equipment from an alternate supplier calls to make a service request. The standard SAP functionality for the creation of the service message requires that the associated master data (business partner and equipment) exist in the backend application. This means that when using the standard SAP-delivered processes, the call center operator would have to capture the master data for the customer and/or equipment before being able to create the service message.

KAESER's requirement necessitated the creation of a BPM process extension to capture the necessary customer and equipment details for forwarding data to the supervisor to create the master data in the backend and fulfillment. Similarly, the process extension allowed failures (see the BRFplus decision table in Figure 9.4) to be classified using an automated rules-enabled failure catalog using BRFplus that matched symptoms to failures. If during a call the rule does not find a match, the BPM process extension routes the call to a specialist for manual classification. Using rules in BRFplus allows a loose coupling to the process model so that on-the-fly extension of such rules can be made without having to change the underlying business process. When KAESER produces a new compressor type, the business department needs only to add the necessary rules for the new compressor type, test the rules (see Figure 9.5), and deploy them before the call center is allowed to process customer inquiries for the new compressor.

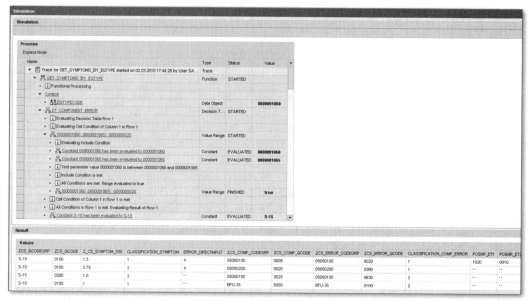

Figure 9.5 BRFplus Simulation Result

Implementing the Solution

The project team began by upgrading to SAP ERP from an earlier version of SAP software. Then it used SAP NetWeaver Business Process Management, SAP NetWeaver Business Rules Management, and SAP NetWeaver Composition Environment as its primary tools. Along with 50 standard enterprise services from SAP, the team built a composite application with several use cases (business services). Instead of users having to be trained in the complexity of navigating several ERP screens, these business services guide users to the relevant screens with relevant data. Concurrently, the team designed processes using SAP NetWeaver BPM that leveraged these business services to replace lengthy manual processes. The resultant process is highly automated with consistent role-based tasks, smooth handoffs, and no interruptions.

The team used value engineering and SAP's ASAP methodology to realize the solution. This consisted of:

► Modeling of to-be processes as the standard event process chain (EPC)

► Identification of requirements for service enabling

- Enhancement of processes with services (service provisioning)
- Identification of missing services and verification of existing services
- Creation of business services that enable sharing of business objects and data among role-based work centers (these can easily be reused to implement the process steps within the BPM process flows)
- Modeling the process extension via SAP NetWeaver BPM using BPMN
- Implementation of the consumption layer

The following factors ensured a successful outcome of the project:

- Having the process landscape in place so that the dependencies and interconnection between the processes can be clearly understood
- Cleansed customer, equipment, and other business master data to provide one source of the truth
- A clear and strong method concerning the solution architecture
- Early prototyping for proving the parts of the architecture (e.g., intersection between BPM and ERP, intersection between BRFplus and BPM)
- Usability design and mock-up preparation, which improved communication with the business department, enabling users to visualize processes from a screen/navigation perspective
- Early adopting of SAP NetWeaver CE 7.1, participation in the ramp-up program, which ensured that product-related issues were resolved by the SAP development team

Results of the Project

Service call center employees can now record every detail of a malfunction during the initial customer contact. They can transfer all required information, including purchase orders and technical data, along the process chain to the next-level participants.

The streamlined, integrated processes have slashed the time it takes KAESER to satisfy service requests. KAESER now responds reliably and immediately to emergencies that before could temporarily go unaddressed due to processing time. Failures are diagnosed correctly the first time and are often fixed on location. After resolution, the customer can sign the service order, which is sent electronically for rapid invoice processing. These dramatic improvements are boosting customer satisfaction and propelling the company into its position as the industry's premier supplier of compressed air as a service.

Table 9.2 illustrates the financial and strategic benefits achieved by the project.

Key Performance Indicator	Impact
Response time to emergency incidents	-33%
Shutdown time per emergency incident	-67%
Service execution speed	+60%
Service order processing time	-60%
Service order errors	Eliminated
Invoice processing time	-87%
Invoicing productivity	+500%
Service orders per technician	+50%

Table 9.2 Financial and Strategic Benefits Achieved by the Project

The solution also improved the following levels of service:

▶ Standardized service incident recording.

▶ Raised levels of efficiency, transparency, and quality throughout the service chain.

▶ Improved flexibility and the ability to react to new business requirements.

▶ Shortened the time frame to expand the collaboration network to embrace new partners.

The resultant solution significantly reduced the total cost of ownership for KAESER, resulting in a larger profit margin:

▶ Cut development costs by 50% through code reuse and reduction in new coding.

▶ Reduced training time by simplifying the user interface.

▶ Used modular architecture for a longer application lifecycle and faster, less costly extensions.

▶ Avoided the need for new office equipment and supplies by revitalizing existing assets.

▶ Using model-driven process tools significantly increased IT's alignment with business and responsiveness to corporate strategy.

Sample Solution Architecture for an SAP Landscape

Figure 9.6 illustrates KAESER's modular architecture. With this service-oriented architecture, KAESER has developed a software infrastructure that is capable of building highly efficient and responsive processes throughout the value chain.

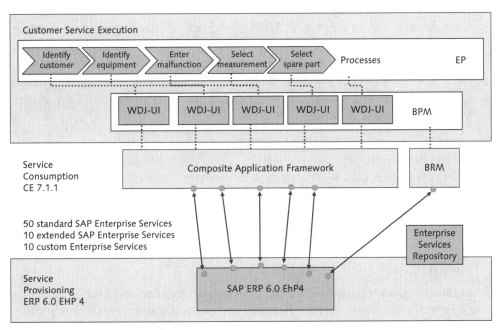

Figure 9.6 Solution Architecture

9.2 Braskem S.A.: Realizing the Value of Efficiency and Visibility in Supplier Processes

The value realization that is part of BPM methodology was what made this approach so compelling to Braskem. We were introduced to this by the SAP Value Academy and leveraged the SAP Value Lifecycle Manager as the value management tool for our BPM Center of Excellence.
– Marcos Antonio Miliani, Processes and Systems Manager, Braskem S.A.

Braskem S.A. is Latin America's leading manufacturer of thermoplastic resins, founded from the merger of several companies. To help support the integration and simplification of their operations, Braskem worked with SAP partner Firsteam to use the BPM methodology from SAP and leveraged the SAP NetWeaver Business

Process Management component to deploy more integrated and transparent business processes. Initial improvements from this large-scale project have already resulted in new operational efficiencies and cost reductions.

9.2.1 Background

Braskem S.A., headquartered in São Paulo, Brazil, is the largest petrochemical company in the Americas by production capacity and the seventh-largest in the world. As Latin America's leader in thermoplastic resins, Braskem understands the transformative power of technology. The plastics made by this innovative Brazilian company are used in thousands of products, from toothbrushes and baby bottles to automotive parts and computer components.

Market leadership, competitiveness, and technological autonomy aligned with the commitment to promote sustainable development are the basis for Braskem's strategy. Braskem uses leading-edge technology in its manufacturing operations and to support its business objectives. As part of this vision, Braskem initiated a company-wide program to simplify, integrate, and energize its business processes through the power of service-oriented architecture.

Business Case

Braskem S.A. was established in 2002 from the merger of several companies as part of a major consolidation of the Brazilian petrochemical industry. Since that time, Braskem has acquired additional companies to expand its product portfolio and area of operations. As a result, a chief concern of Braskem was the integration and simplification of operations and business processes that incorporate the business of the acquired companies.

Braskem's IT group was tasked to develop a programmatic approach for integrating business operations and strengthening the business management model. This would then lay a foundation for further growth and internationalization of Braskem.

First, Braskem needed to establish a means of common communication and goal-setting between business leaders and IT so that IT implementations were aligned with business operational needs with the strategic vision of the company. Additionally, Braskem's IT department needed to learn a methodology for business-value identification and a way to prioritize IT demands.

With a clear method for aligning business and IT in place, Braskem could then focus on integrating and optimizing end-to-end operations. Braskem wanted to be able to proactively identify inefficiencies and opportunities for optimization by enabling measurement and monitoring of process operations. Also, Braskem wanted to simplify employee training and improve user adoption of IT systems by creating consistent user experiences for process automation. With these goals in mind, the company developed a solid business case for the project after attending the SAP Value Academy program and using the value lifecycle manager tool from SAP to identify the specific business benefits. The business case strategy followed the SAP value engineering methodology. With this tactic, they compared development costs using SAP NetWeaver BPM with a more traditional approach of custom development through writing code. For the first project, Braskem estimated the productivity they would gain by automating the first targeted process and centralizing operations within a shared services center.

Braskem decided to set up a business process competency center for process redesign and chose the SAP NetWeaver BPM component to help model and deploy the new process automation.

The company identified 13 key business processes for reengineering and selected the high-priority accounts payable process for services suppliers as a starting point — a logical choice because Braskem had the following business scenario:

▸ Over 3,000 services suppliers spread throughout Brazil

▸ 20,000 *notas fiscais* (Brazil-specific invoices filed with the government) received per month

▸ Approximately 1,200 contract managers

▸ A highly manual process with handling errors that caused rework and losses

▸ Payments that were not being received within required periods

▸ A process without traceability and control

Braskem's vision for the solution was to eliminate unnecessary payment delays and improve their visibility and control over costs and expenses. Specific business goals for this process redesign project included:

▸ Better visibility of spending per vendor and traceability of payments

▸ Improved efficiency when executing the payment process

▸ Improved cost optimization through on-time payment and ability to leverage early payment discounts

▸ Automated compliance with Brazilian requirements for registering legal invoicing documents

▶ Learning and realizing benefits of the BPM approach for continuous process optimization

Metrics chosen to map these goals included:

▶ Measurement of process cycle times

▶ Tracking of on-time payment rate

▶ Average design man-hours for process design

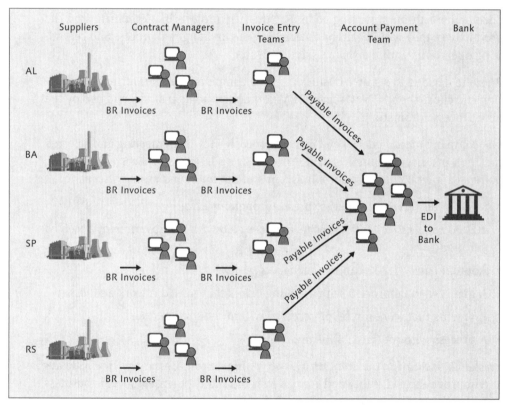

Figure 9.7 Braskem's As-Is Supplier Payment Process

As-Is Process

As depicted in Braskem's as-is supplier payment process in Figure 9.7 (decentralized and manual invoice receipt, acceptance at company plants and regional centers, and centralized accounts payable), Braskem's old payment process was a highly manual process that was spread across many teams and as a result lacked visibility and control. Invoices were received by contract managers at each of Braskem's local plants and sent to one of several regional invoice entry teams to manually enter the invoice into SAP ERP. Checking invoices against data in the SAP systems and the many related tracking spreadsheets for mismatches to contracts, due dates, value, and quantities was a manual process. Every time an error (deviation) was found, the invoice had to be sent back to the contract manager to fix the error. This particular manual exception was the main reason for payment delays.

9.2.2 BPM Solution

As part of the process redesign, Braskem decided to concentrate the handling of invoices in one shared services center as depicted in Figure 9.8. This figure illustrates the to-be process of outsourced digitization of invoices and a shared services center for approving and paying invoices.

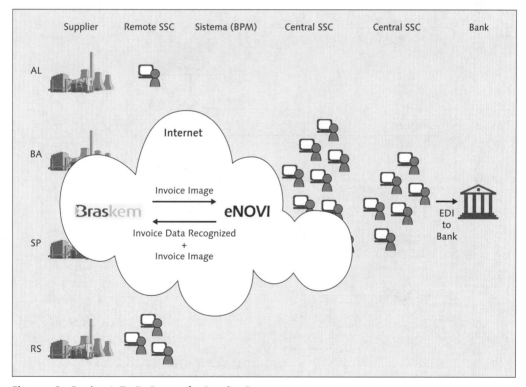

Figure 9.8 Braskem's To-Be Process for Supplier Payment

As depicted in Figure 9.8, *notas fiscais* (invoice) submitted by suppliers to Braskem are scanned and sent to the service provider, eNOVI, who digitizes the invoice and transmits the information electronically to Braskem. Invoices are automatically matched with purchase orders. When a discrepancy is noticed, or a match cannot be made, a contract manager manages the exception and work with the supplier to correct the invoice. When automation shows a match with no discrepancies, and for invoice problems that are resolved by the contract manager, the invoice is then sent to the accounts payable team.

After analysis and optimization, the process for automating validation and approval of invoices was designed in SAP NetWeaver BPM (see Figure 9.9).

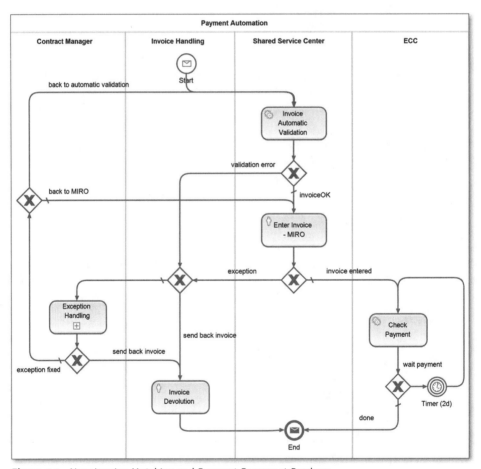

Figure 9.9 New Invoice Matching and Payment Process at Braskem

As designed by the IT team, Braskem's BPM payment process starts via a Web service that receives invoice data. The first step is an automated process step that verifies invoice data against data within Braskem's SAP system. Several validations take place, such as validation of invoice value, entry sheet, due date, and tax value. Validations in this step depend on invoice type and are performed using decision tables that are implemented using business rules within BRM decision tables and custom-developed enterprise services provisioned within the ERP system. If there is any exception during this process, BPM routes the invoice to a contract manager to handle the exception. If the data passes validation, the next step is to enter the invoice using a MIRO transaction.

During the MIRO step, it is now possible to see the invoice image, data entered during the BPM process, and any resolutions made by contract managers. At any time during the process, it is possible to cause BPM to enter a devolution step, where the devolution is registered and process is completed.

Once the invoice has been entered into the system, another automated step checks payment data within ERP to update the process status for KPI tracking and completes the process, keeping a record of the payment execution.

To help Braskem's business managers monitor the status and progress of specific status instances, the dashboard depicted in Figure 9.10 was developed.

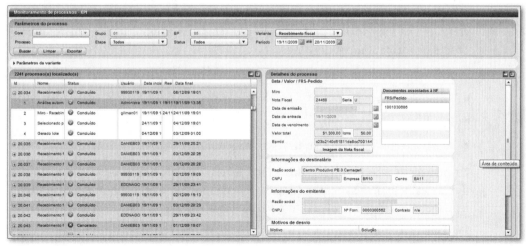

Figure 9.10 Braskem's Dashboard for Viewing Process Status and Context

Implementing the Solution

For the business blueprint, the methodology chosen was the SAP SOA Implementation Roadmap. This was an obvious choice, because the version of ASAP methodology available at the time did not include SOA and BPM accelerators. (Editor's note: the new ASAP methodology 7.0 as described in this book has incorporated the SAP SOA Implementation Roadmap and now supports BPM and SOA implementations.)

One complicating factor was the need for Braskem to upgrade their SAP for Oil and Gas solution portfolio to leverage preexisting functionality to implement their BPM processes and to take advantage of SAP-supported enterprise services. The upgrade cycle for this solution caused the BPM implementation to take longer than it ordinarily would while the enhancement pack was tested, and SAP worked to fix some errors in Brazilian localization.

Another issue solved during the realization phase was the requirement to send a process instance to a different number of approvers depending on the owner of the object. This feature was not available out-of-the-box in the first version of SAP NetWeaver BPM 7.11, so a workaround was developed using a mix of BPM objects and Web Dynpro programming. The workaround developed is depicted in Figure 9.11.

An additional complicating factor was that each contract manager needed to receive a specific task alert if a particular invoice processing exception was related to a contract that the contract person managed. This was complicated by the following process information relationships:

▶ An invoice is related to n entry sheets

▶ Entry sheets are related to a purchase order

▶ Purchase orders are related to a service contract

▶ A service contract has n contract managers

To manage a task involving this many levels, the process needed the ability to dynamically branch synchronous parallel tasks for the variable number of contract managers that may be related to a particular invoice.

The solution subprocess dynamically creates each necessary task with specific information for each manager and controls the execution of the tasks. The subprocess ends only when all processing exceptions are handled and then synchronizes information from multiple steps to send back to the main process.

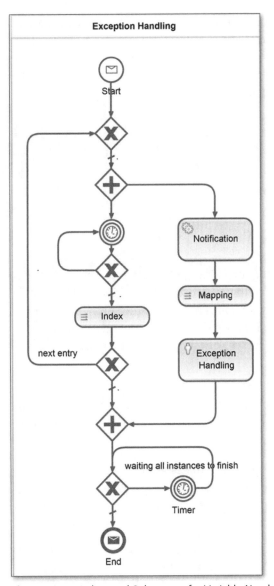

Figure 9.11 Workaround Subprocess for Variable Number of Approvers

Results of the Project

With the initial phase of the project completed, Braskem has deployed an integrated payment process that addresses the complete workflow from invoice receipt and approval through payment processing. As a result, invoice registration and processing costs have dropped 30%, and 95% of supplier payments are now made on schedule, which helps Braskem take advantage of discounts and avoid penalties. The ability to process electronic invoices more efficiently is also making individual transactions easier to track (see Table 9.3).

Key Performance Indicator	Impact
Time needed to redesign processes	-20% to -30%
Training costs	-20%
Invoice registration and processing costs	-30%
On-time payment rate improvement	60% to 95%

Table 9.3 KPI Tracking

Braskem's process transformation program is just getting started. The company is now turning its attention to the remaining 12 processes. Braskem's goals include enhancing traceability in contracting, streamlining sales order entry, and simplifying the company's critical export processes. Such improvements will play an important role in shaping the future success of this growing chemical company.

Sample Solution Architecture for an SAP Landscape

With Braskem's broad SAP software landscape, SAP NetWeaver BPM was a particularly attractive choice, offering native integration and a less costly and complex implementation than alternative technologies.

As shown in Figure 9.12, the payment process initiates with digitalization of Brazilian invoices. The digital invoice image is sent to a service provider who, through an OCR process, recognizes fields from the invoice image and sends it back to Braskem, integrated via an interface with SAP NetWeaver PI.

The service provider sends the invoice picture as a PDF file and the fields recognized from the invoice image as xml data. SAP NetWeaver PI receives this information. The PDF file is then stored in the SAP content server, and the invoice data is sent to a custom Web service that starts the BPM process in SAP NetWeaver CE.

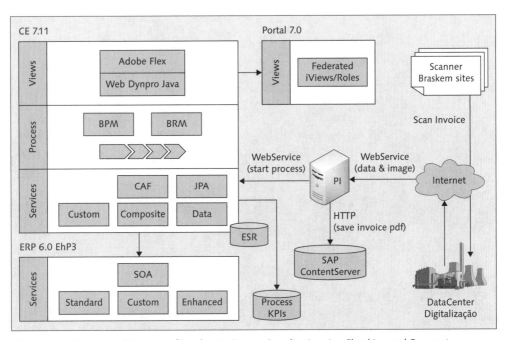

Figure 9.12 System Architecture of Braskem's Service Supplier Invoice Checking and Payment Process

10 Good Ideas for BPM

Greg Chase, Rukhshaan Omar, Andreas Muno, Wayne Morris, Gregor Müller

Whereas BPM adoption tends to cluster in certain applications and industries, the approach and tools are broadly capable of streamlining business processes in many different applications. This section suggests two great applications for BPM in theoretical use cases from SAP experts.

The first example suggests an implementation in the public sector. The main driver of BPM adoption in the public sector is the desire to help governments run more efficiently by reducing paperwork and manual activities. The public sector example explores how BPM tools and techniques can streamline public administration and mission-critical, line-of-business processes to achieve sustainable, long-term public value. The use case demonstrates how BPM can automate and speed up the handling of citizen service requests, while reducing labor and paper-based activities.

The second example, though applicable to several industries, is set within the airline industry. The example demonstrates how to apply BPM to streamline the maintenance process by balancing maintenance capacity and demand across several roles and IT systems. It caters to highly regulated preventative maintenance and random corrective maintenance requirements.

10.1 Public Sector: Potholes and Green Area Maintenance – Taxpayers Get More for Their Buck

Governments are under increasing pressure from constituents to improve visibility and to optimize their operations. BPM is a management discipline with supporting technology available from SAP that provides a great way for governments to transform their operations into continually improving business processes.
– Mike De La Cruz, SVP Public Sector, SAP

Chief maintenance officers can achieve significant savings while increasing citizen satisfaction and delivering a higher quality of service by:

▸ Implementing principles of maintenance excellence

▸ Outsourcing unplanned maintenance with well-established agreements that focus on service levels for quality and timeliness

▸ Improving citizen relations through personal interaction

Putting BPM to work at the heart of this business transformation will allow CMOs to rapidly change strategy and visibly improve operations.

10.1.1 Background

Public services agencies are often reproached for inefficient operations. However, on the local level, where citizens feel the impact of their governments' actions (or inactions) the most, there are many examples of ways governments try to be quite responsive in interacting with their constituents. For example:

▸ Cities have established call centers where citizens only need to know one central number to access all of the services they require, for example, 311.

▸ City websites allow online service requests to be submitted 24/7, expanding the availability to citizens beyond business hours.

▸ Cities increasingly provide their citizens with smart phone apps. Users can download them for free from an app store. There are apps for reporting potholes, blocked sidewalks, pedestrian safety, graffiti and trash removal, etc.

Sometimes online service requests take the form of an email sent to a government agent, but from there the same bureaucratic procedures may be in place, effectively preventing the kind of rapid, top-notch experience customers expect when dealing with great enterprises.

Business Case

We will use a city's department of public works as an example. The concept of maintenance excellence is at the center of our suggestions for a best-run public services maintenance department. In our example, Public Works is responsible for green areas, public parks, playgrounds, tree-lined streets, pothole repair, and for changing light bulbs in street and traffic lights. For too long, maintenance has not been taken seriously enough to warrant its own organization. Even though there is some scheduled maintenance, the quality is often low, so the same problem has to be fixed ad hoc shortly after an initial repair — sometimes over and over again. The work atmosphere is tense, stress levels are high, and over-burdened staff members sometimes avoid answering the phones. Consequently, citizens asking for service are perceived as a nuisance to some staff instead of legitimate customers of the services provided by the maintenance department.

A new approach is needed that allows for sound business processes that closely connect citizens, staff, and external service providers. Maintenance staff should concentrate on scheduled maintenance only, with strong emphasis on quality. Citizens must be treated as customers. They deserve quality service and customer support from real people. Best business practices such as outsourcing unplanned maintenance to external service providers need to be established, rather than constantly sourcing in external providers to deal with emergency repairs.

We recommend optimizing one business process at a time and covering all process steps end-to-end, showing how SAP's BPM tools put the line-of-business manager into the driver's seat, moving toward the goal of maintenance excellence. Developed over decades by practitioners in the field turned researchers, the concept of maintenance excellence comprises aspects of customer satisfaction, service quality, pride in maintenance, productivity, and sound planning into key performance indicators, allowing for sound measures of success.

As-Is Process

Many of the current processes in the example maintenance department are unstructured, paper-based, and lack control, so maintenance costs keep increasing while citizen satisfaction declines. The town's homepage offers a complaint form for citizens, but there is only an email address behind it, so there is no follow-through. It is not an explicit and transparent process.

A first step to handle the issues is to establish measures and indicators that show the actual state of the business based on the reported goals. This is where we introduce the maintenance manager dashboard, which consolidates multiple indicators for maintenance excellence (see Figure 10.1). It also comprises historic data for the past 12 months, showing trends for cost and performance.

With a high and growing ratio of unplanned maintenance, subpar productivity that results in increasing costs, mediocre quality, and dissatisfied customers, the indicator for maintenance excellence remains solidly in the red.

Unplanned maintenance takes resources away from performing scheduled maintenance and may increase the number of overtime hours, incurring higher costs. And when unplanned maintenance is the rule, not the exception, increased stress levels may lead to a higher number of staff sick days. Although it is impossible to avoid unplanned maintenance altogether, a consistent increase in unplanned maintenance indicates consistent management failures in the past.

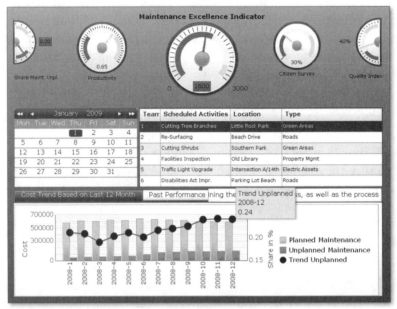

Figure 10.1 Cost Trend Based on Past 12 Months

Figure 10.2 shows the maintenance department's as-is situation at a glance. By implementing BPM tools and processes, it is possible for public sector departments to quickly and efficiently convert to the to-be situation.

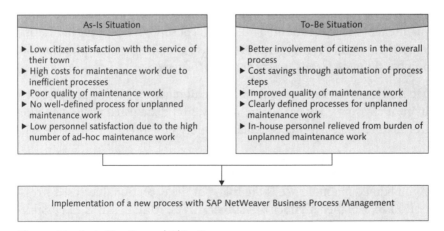

Figure 10.2 As-Is Situation and Objective

10.1.2 BPM Solution

A quick analysis shows that most issues reported by citizens can be processed in similar ways, typically requiring an ad hoc repair job. SAP NetWeaver BPM provides a quick and easy way to visualize common process steps and deviations. Starting with a citizen reporting an issue like a pothole, a flickering street light, or broken playground equipment, the maintenance department personnel would then decide what action to take. They would also estimate the value of the requested service. Above a predefined threshold in the system, the city's funds manager would have to approve the ad hoc maintenance.

Experience has shown that maintenance, when well planned and executed, lowers the total cost of ownership of the asset and keeps staff productive and happy. A quick and effective best-business practice measure to manage unplanned maintenance is outsourcing. In our city maintenance department, we plan to slowly begin outsourcing, starting with unplanned maintenance.

As seen in Figure 10.4, when funding for the maintenance services is approved, the SAP NetWeaver BPM process prompts the SAP ERP system to automatically create a maintenance order (if the service is outsourced, a service order) using SAP enterprise services. When servicing is completed, the internal or external service provider locks in the time needed and the expenditure associated with it, the ceiling being the previous cost estimate. The maintenance department then checks the quality of the service provided and, upon acceptance, notifies the citizen. Based on the purchase order, the service provider can then submit his electronic invoice, which is automatically processed and paid for.

In this type of business process the public administration acts as the manager of public affairs, establishing service-level agreements, ensuring quality, and bringing together citizen requirements and private sector solutions (Figure 10.3).

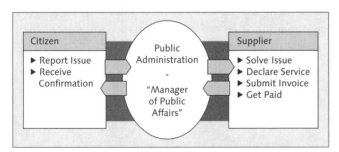

Figure 10.3 Process Flow

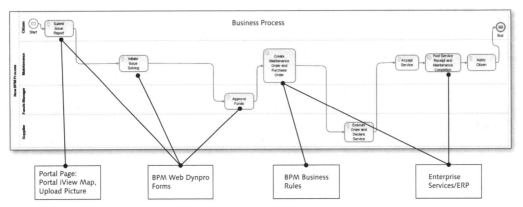

Figure 10.4 Overview of New Process Using BPM

Implementing the Solution

In 2009 SAP introduced its new BPM offering to the market based on SAP NetWeaver CE 7.11. The Public Sector Solution management team was in charge of creating a customer demo in our probate SAP demo landscape, called IDES. Modeling the standard business process and the screens with SAP NetWeaver BPM turned out to be the easiest part of the overall effort.

The most difficult activity in the 2009 project was finding out how to use the enterprise services (ES). Finding them on the SAP Developer Network (SDN) was no problem, but getting to know the different parameters and figuring out which ones are mandatory, what length they have, whether you need leading zeros in product numbers and the like — this was truly painful. When we raised the issue with ES and SDN colleagues at SAP, they came back promising improvement. The recently revamped SDN ES workplace now contains sample data for every ES, making this step of evaluating enterprise services much easier.

We were using five ES: creating maintenance and purchase order (PO) (see Figure 10.5 and Figure 10.6), release maintenance order, maintenance order confirmation, and inbound delivery with reference to PO.

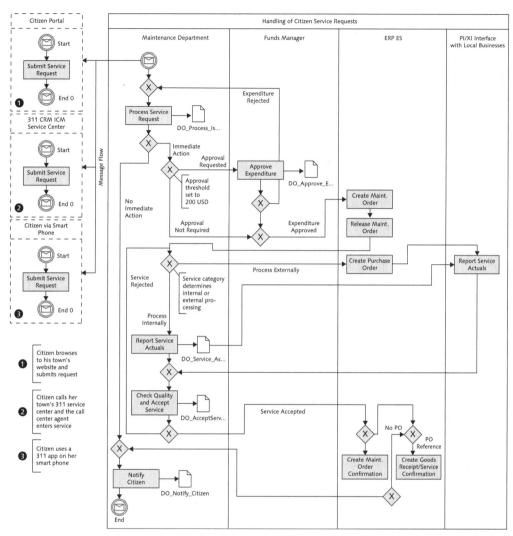

Figure 10.5 BPMN Process Model

Once tested in their native ERP landscape, with only the most necessary customizing in plant maintenance and procurement, the ES worked beautifully in the background.

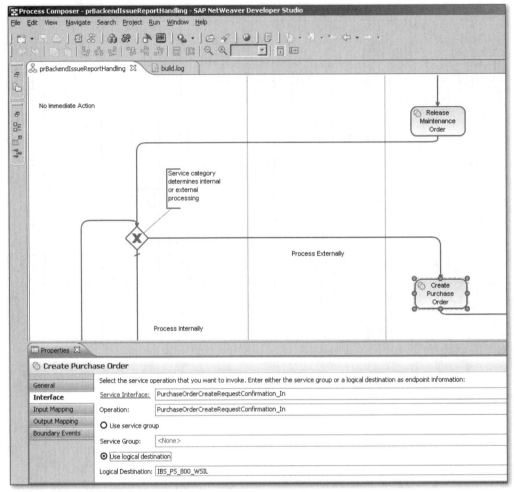

Figure 10.6 ES Create Purchase Order in Process Context

Business rules determine which maintenance activities are provided by local companies and which activities are done in-house (see Figure 10.7).

There are many parameters you can simply fill with defaults; only dynamic parameters are mapped (see Figure 10.8).

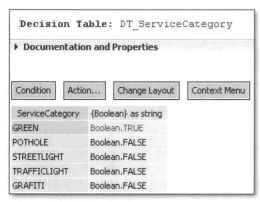

Figure 10.7 Mapping ES to Process Context

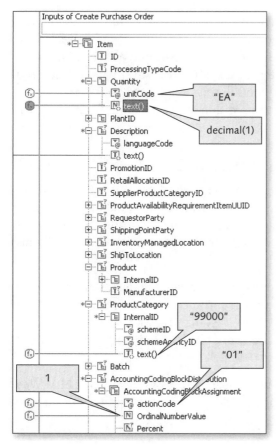

Figure 10.8 Example of Defaults in ES Parameters

When the process gets a bit more complex with rules and gateways, it may take some time and multiple iterations to determine how to put them together correctly. A good understanding of the "language" of BPM, BPMN, helps. It is intuitive enough for line-of-business people to come up with the first process models.

Results of the Project

Streamlined and reduced to the most minimal user interactions, a complete standardized end-to-end process for unplanned maintenance was established, allowing for very short roundtrip times. We included a process step for quality control, incentivizing suppliers and employees to produce only high-quality outcomes, and a step for personal feedback from the citizen, which, together with the short roundtrip times, is intended to increase citizen satisfaction. Outsourcing unplanned maintenance keeps costs predictably low, and the department's employees can concentrate on high-quality scheduled maintenance. This, in turn, reduces their stress; they happily report to work more regularly and are more productive. Simple rules in the business process and the flexibility of SAP NetWeaver BPM allow for similar maintenance processes to be run in similar ways, without the need for further programming. With just two full-time employees on the project, the team was able to establish tangible results within just two months from using SAP NetWeaver BPM.

Sample Solution Architecture for an SAP Landscape

Most local authorities already have public websites allowing citizens to log in issue reports of many kinds. Alternatively, SAP NetWeaver Portal may be used as a citizen-facing website. Issue reporting forms should support the output format Web Services Description Language (WSDL), for example, Adobe Interactive Forms or Web Dynpro.

The data in these reports would be transferred through the town's firewall to the town clerks workplaces, where these issue reports become work items in their Universal Worklists (UWLs), provided by BPM. BPM has its own portal infrastructure, but if there are corporate intranet portal work places already in place, BPM work items may alternately be sent to these UWLs.

The user opens work items from the worklist and processes them facing BPM Web Dynpro screens. These screens are specially designed for the task at hand and very intuitive.

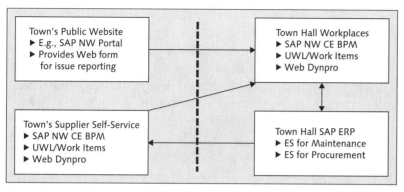

Figure 10.9 Suggested IT Landscape for Scenario

The actual transactions in the town's ERP backend are triggered through BPM, and purchase orders are sent to the supplier. Depending on the supplier's software, he may get the purchase order on paper, as an email, via EDI, as XML, or via a Web service, automatically triggering a sales order in his system. The order contains a link to a supplier self-service website, where he would enter the performed service data. That screen is another Web Dynpro screen. Typically, government agencies place self-service websites outside of their firewall.

Back in the maintenance department, the user receives a work item with the supplier's service data, checks the quality of the service provided, and approves the services. The approval triggers enterprise service postings of maintenance receipt and inbound delivery confirmation in the town's ERP system. The citizen is then notified that the reported issue has been solved.

10.2 Airline: Streamlining the Maintenance Process for the Transportation Industry with BPM

It takes a business network to deliver against a client's operational availability requirements. From parts, skilled labor, to specialized tools and facilities, the necessary maintenance resources must be orchestrated with great efficiency and effectiveness in highly regulated environments. Business process management (BPM) provides the means to establish robust and agile business networks that deliver responsive and flexible maintenance services to the exacting needs of our clients.
– Bob Cowley, Rear Admiral, US Navy (Ret.), SVP – Global Defense & Aerospace Industry Solutions Management

Consider a big airline that is operating hundreds of planes in a tight schedule across the globe. Maintenance demand is generated either by preventive maintenance, which is highly regulated, or by corrective maintenance, which occurs randomly at any given time. The maintenance demand is covered by several depots, which provide the necessary work capacity. The capacity is fixed, and changes have to be planned for the long term, whereas the demand can fluctuate depending on changes in regulations, supplier callbacks, or season. Balancing maintenance capacity and demand is very complex and requires sophisticated processes involving several roles and IT systems. The maintenance team's background is typically mixed, with some employees used to working with sophisticated systems, whereas others are not familiar with information technology at all. One more complication is that the maintenance process also involves other stakeholders and agencies that are part of the business network but may be external to the company.

10.2.1 Background

Airlines' most expensive assets are their aircraft, and running profitably requires that their utilization is maximized. Taking them out of flight operation to perform maintenance is expensive because they always need to balance the revenue from a flight with having extra aircraft available for substitution with passenger safety. That is the simple view. As mentioned above, large airlines have the complexity of managing mandatory preventative maintenance and fault repairs when something is not working as designed. When you begin to factor in all of the other variables such as location, parts availability, employee skills, and different makes and models of aircraft, you soon see that this process could be a scheduler's nightmare. In a perfect world all this would come together seamlessly in a synchronized fashion, but uncertainties often arise that make plans obsolete.

To better understand the problem at hand, let's first focus on applications that play a crucial role in the maintenance process: the maintenance system, which administers service cycles and problems (including their priorities), an ERP system, which maintains stocks of spare parts, and a supplier relationship management (SRM) system, which is responsible for procurement processes. In addition to these applications, a scheduling system determines when maintenance is possible, whereas a human relations (HR) system can determine when resources with specific qualifications are available in a certain depot. And a document management system stores a record for every plane and determines which maintenance measures have been conducted when and by whom, including certificates of the replaced spare parts.

All of the roles and systems fulfill their specific tasks within the maintenance process. The following section will describe one way to optimize the entire process by including all involved roles within a coherent process and reusing the existing functionality of the above-mentioned systems in a new context.

Business Case

Streamlining the maintenance process with BPM can lead to increased productivity of maintenance staff, both in areas of planning and execution. Hence, from the business perspective, several goals are pursued within a maintenance process:

1. Balance workload across different depots.

2. Avoid media breaks between people and IT systems.

3. Enable process insight and traceability.

4. React to unfulfilled deadlines.

5. Enable collaboration and task execution without complex user interfaces.

6. Protect investment of existing IT systems.

First, balancing workload between the various depots is of great value: depots working beyond their capacity will produce delays in maintenance and likely affect the schedule. Overtime hours in busy depots can be avoided, as can idle time in underutilized ones. Furthermore, balanced capacity utilization leads to planning safety in regard to purchasing new airplanes while simultaneously planning the needed maintenance capacity for them. In addition to this, weather could cause a flight delay, which in turn could cause the plane to miss a planned maintenance appointment. People need to be able to use of all the available tools to replan and find an alternate appointment for this aircraft.

Second, media breaks occur if information is passed from one person to another or from one system to another in an unstructured way such as copy and paste, fax, mail, or telephone. Consider an example maintenance planning scenario where the planner has to correlate information from various systems. The maintenance system provides information on what has to be maintained. From this information, resource and spare part needs can be derived. Their availability can be found in the HR and ERP systems, respectively. If the required spare parts are not available, an order must be placed in the SRM system. Using single applications, all of the information has to be copied from one system to the next. But media breaks can also occur between people. For example, the engineer needs the information from previous process steps. That is: What was maintained? Which spare parts were exchanged? His input, such as mileage and clearance for the planes, must be passed to the back office to keep the airplane record up to date.

These media breaks complicate process insight. For people to see the planning for a specific plane or determine if spare parts are available, all systems have to be checked. However, a responsible manager would like to have a clear view of process performance indicators (such as planning time and exceptions to process performance indicators) to better plan and optimize the process. This brings us to the third point. Steady process optimization is key to holding and fostering a competitive advantage. This type of information should be available at the push of a button but can take hours to manually compile if systems are not orchestrated. Furthermore, traceability is a topic of revision safety. Being able to reconstruct the entire process flow (which supplier delivered a specific spare part, who replaced the part, and who checked the clearance) within seconds in a single screen saves a lot of time when auditors need this information.

The fourth goal is to simplify user interfaces and make them widely available to all maintenance staff, regardless of location. User interfaces are often highly sophisticated and require significant training to use efficiently. However, within the maintenance and inspection process, information is often captured on paper at locations where no computer is available and by people who are often not IT-experienced. Consider a maintenance technician recording mileage for a specific part. Why not include him in the process by providing a simplified user interface on a mobile device? Or consider a flight attendant who can report minor problems with an offline solution while flying. This saves media breaks and training.

Last, the airline has invested millions into their IT infrastructure: licenses, customizing and development, support, changes, and so on. The software perfectly fulfills the company's need in terms of different parts of the end-to-end process. These systems should be able to support this maintenance process in a coordinated cross-system fashion, allowing the functionality to be used in a new way without having a negative effect on the existing processes. Services allow reuse of existing functionality in a new context, as provided through a standardized service interface.

As-Is Process

The airline maintains many highly specialized applications that fulfill tasks out of the end-to-end process (see Figure 10.10). Workers currently have to spend time and money finding ways around the media breaks that occur manually. For example, the maintenance planner has to access the maintenance system to find needed maintenance measures and then has to access the scheduling system to find possible maintenance windows. Afterward, he will iterate every possible maintenance window to ensure that needed capacity is available in the corresponding depot. The typical worker uses many applications and copies and pastes information from one application to the next. Being unable to handle this information in a structured way leads to concentration mistakes. These have to be adjusted manually again. Missing data is gathered via telephone or email, which interrupts the flow of work. Instead of finishing one task at a time, the maintenance planner has to swap between many, which costs a lot of adjustment time.

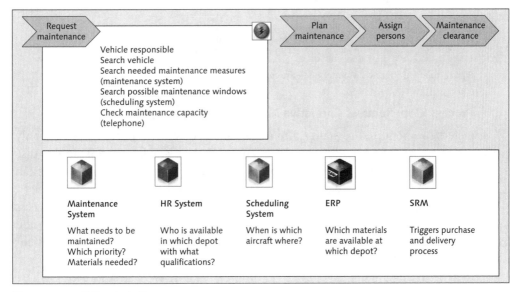

Figure 10.10 Airline As-Is Process

10.2.2 BPM Solution

How can BPM be used to optimize the process while spanning multiple IT systems and empowering the multiple manual roles involved? Figure 10.11 shows the four major steps in the corrective maintenance process. Each of these steps can span different IT systems and involve multiple employees in different roles to work together in an orchestrated fashion. BPM can be used to bridge the process steps across system and organizational boundaries. The process starts with a maintenance planer choosing an aircraft that needs maintenance measures. She must determine the time frame, possible depot, and services needed in one system. With the depot chosen, the next employee in the process is determined and the process continues supported by BPM: The chosen depot staff reviews the maintenance request and checks the availability of a work place, resources with appropriate qualifications, and necessary spare parts. BPM can drive each of these process steps, including the loop back to the scheduler if any of the dependencies are not available. Depending on the availability of all items, the request can be accepted or rejected. Once the airplane arrives at the depot, All subsequent processing steps can also be orchestrated through BPM, including the clearance for the airplane to leave the depot again. This ensures that all of the data is captured at the source with a user interface and tool that meets the needs of the workers, thus preventing media breaks.

Figure 10.11   Corrective Maintenance Process

Process Step: Request Corrective Maintenance

Defects are reported regularly into a maintenance system. Smaller ones are only recorded, whereas high-priority defects prevent the plane from flying. In this case corrective maintenance has to take place immediately. A business rules engine can be used to evaluate small and medium defects and propose planes that will need a maintenance measure in the near future to the maintenance planer. He can access the plane's record, including the defect coming from the maintenance system and planned maintenance measures in the future. The planner has the option to either extend the existing maintenance request or create a new one. Information from the scheduling system is very helpful for creating a new request. Knowing where the aircraft is at any time can aid in proposing maintenance windows in a given timeframe. Merging possible time frames and locations with information about the capacity utilization from the corresponding depot reveals a first proposal about which time frame is preferable, which in turn leads to balancing depot utilization.

In our maintenance scenario, implementing BPM in the maintenance system will allow a business rules engine to quickly pull all relevant information from the system and evaluate it, create a report from the plane's record, submit requests, choose locations, and adjust time frames. In this situation we have the business rules engine evaluating the maintenance need and proposing relevant planes for maintenance. Rules, in contrast to coding, can be changed at runtime without a need for programming, extensive testing, or transport management and therefore can adapt quickly to new external facts. Blending BPM and SOA allows composition of information from various sources on a single user interface by accessing existing functionality from different backend systems and forwarding those to the next person in the process.

Process Step: Planning the Maintenance

Orchestrating all of the requirements for the maintenance service is like conducting an orchestra. The facility (depot) must be available with all of the correct tools and equipment, and all of the variable resources, people, parts, documents, certificates — just like the members of the orchestra — must show up on time. It only takes one missing resources for the entire maintenance task to be postponed.

In the BPM scenario, the depot responsible for a repair receives the maintenance request. This appears as a task that includes all information on a single screen. We composed information out of various backend systems: the maintenance system for planned measures and available workspace, the HR system for available and qualified resources, the ERP system for spare parts availability, and the SRM system to create purchase orders if needed. Furthermore, SOA provides both the option of accessing information from a backend system and the ability of the backend system to raise alerts (such as if the delivery won't be available in time for the repair) and correlate that back into the BPM process.

The next step in the BPM process requires the maintenance employee on shift to check his daily tasks. He needs to check if the workplace assignment is still valid and then assign the people with the required skills to the different maintenance tasks and create the work orders. Furthermore, he will have the needed stock taken from the inventory. The BPM system allows workers to have their task assignments available on mobile devices, which also provide access to blueprints, lessons learned, or regulations for a specific task. After completion, they can register task-related information such as mileage. Also, by confirming the exchange of a specific part they can trigger the transfer of certificates from the document management system into the aircraft record.

To complete the maintenance process, a mobile device provides access to all process-related information such as service measures planned and accomplished and additional information from the airplane record in the document management system. New frontend technologies like SAP Interactive Forms by Adobe are used to generate approval forms that can communicate with the backend systems and at the same time are the documents that have to be signed after printing to fulfill legal directives. This approval will forward the process to the back office that will maintain the airplane record accordingly.

Implementing the Solution

The actual implementation of a BPM process starts with an as-is analysis of the end-to-end process including existing weaknesses, media breaks, and errors. The to-be process is described, focusing on business goals including process performance indicators.

After the functional blueprint is completed, the BPMN process is modeled, and required technical services and user interfaces are identified. User interfaces should be modeled and presented to important stakeholders and iterated as required. At the same time, the technical services are modeled according to SOA design time governance and the provider systems are identified. All of this is the input for implementation to follow.

Sample Solution Architecture for an SAP Landscape

Figure 10.12 shows the sample solution architecture. SAP NetWeaver BPM will be used to execute the process models, which choreograph human interactions via Web-based frontend technologies and enterprise services calls. The Enterprise Services Repository is used to model and design enterprise services according to SOA design time governance. The various backend applications provide their existing functionalities via enterprise services.

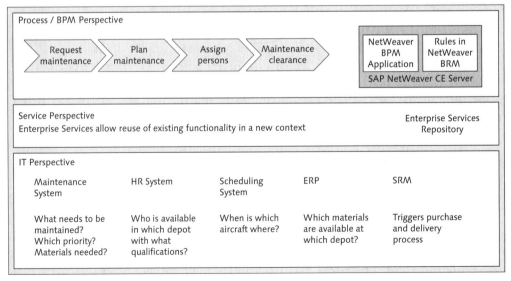

Figure 10.12 Sample Solution Architecture

11　Planning for BPM Transformation

Torben Claus Dahl, Kim Peiter Jørgensen, Jens Theodor Nielsen,
Raghavendra Subbarao, Mark von Rosing

In the previously illustrated BPM use cases, we learned from different real-life examples from a business process management and/or technology perspective. In the next two BPM use-case examples, we will learn from a perspective where BPM is being applied as the central instrument of combining different models in which the interrelationship of management concepts — such as business modeling, enterprise architecture, performance management, value management, business governance, and business architecture — are linked and joined in order to enable the organization for BPM transformation. This process is done with the purpose of interconnecting important disciplines to create value, the approach of business modeling, process modeling, defining value drivers, and aligning the enterprise architecture, which was described in Part I.

11.1　Hospira: Integrating Architecture to Become Process-Centric

We can't solve problems by using the same kind of thinking we used when we created them.
– Albert Einstein

The relationship between enterprise architecture and business process management is symbiotic; whereas business process management provides the context and background for what needs to be architected for the business, enterprise architecture helps business processes be enabled in a sustainable and agile manner. Addressing one without the other leads to partial results, at best. However, if performance and value are to be created, processes need to be enabled and structured in the business model and in the operational process execution. Both automated IT processes and nonautomated processes play a key role in developing the business competencies to create the needed performance and value. The integration of the architectural domains of business architecture and the information architecture are vital. As shown in Figure 11.1, the key to linking these to architectural domains is the process architecture.

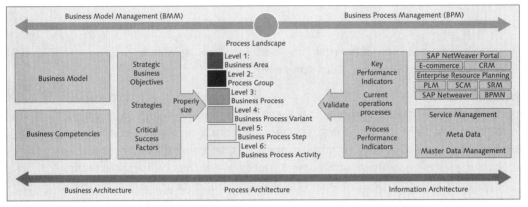

Figure 11.1   Process Architecture (Kuhlmann and von Rosing, 2010. "Applying BPM Principles to SAP EAF")

In the following sections, we will look at the efforts that Hospira is undertaking in integrating its architecture efforts to become a process-centric organization.

In the book *Business Process Management — the SAP Roadmap* (SAP PRESS 2009), the introductory note on the first chapter has a quote by Antoine de Saint Exupery that reads, "If you want to build a ship, don't drum up the men to gather wood, divide the work and give orders. Instead teach them to yearn for the vast and endless sea." That is exactly how Hospira set out to embrace BPM as an organization-wide discipline to successfully drive its enterprise architecture practice.

11.1.1   Company Profile

Hospira is a global specialty pharmaceutical and medication delivery company with headquarters in Lake Forest, IL. Hospira's portfolio includes generic acute-care and oncology injectables and integrated infusion therapy and medication management systems. Hospira's portfolio of products is used by hospitals and alternate site providers such as clinics, home healthcare providers, and long-term care facilities. They understood that the challenge to align their business model and process model could only be achieved through the business architecture. Hospira therefore started their BPM journey realizing that for enterprise architecture to become successful, BPM is a precursor and should flourish first. With all of the energy invested and the support from the leadership team, the Hospira business architecture project is currently on their way to becoming the process champions for the rest of the enterprise.

11.1.2 Need for Business Process Management Discipline

Since the spinoff of Hospira in 2004, followed by a major acquisition of Mayne Pharma in 2006, Hospira Information Technology had been heavily focused on helping the business stabilize itself as an independent, global organization. This, in addition to the regulatory demands and changing business environment, resulted in an IT organization that was heavily focused on technology, with less emphasis on strategic architecture and business processes. The IT portfolio consisted of hundreds of custom applications and thousands of interfaces between the SAP ECC and legacy systems.

Today, a single global instance of SAP ECC acts as the business process platform for Hospira. In addition to SAP ECC, the SAP landscape consists of SAP Solution Manager, SAP Advanced Planning & Optimization, SAP NetWeaver Business Warehouse, SAP NetWeaver Portal, SAP NetWeaver PI, and SAP NetWeaver Composition Environment.

In 2009, Hospira embarked on an organization-wide strategic initiative, which involved optimizing their product portfolio, evaluating nonstrategic assets, streamlining the organizational structure, and so on. On the IT side, this led to co-sourcing of certain IT functions, introduction of new technologies, and so on. Given all of the changes happening across the organization, the leadership team realized that business process was the only element that was 100 percent under management's control, because processes represent the corporate memory of how assets are used and work is done.

Generally, within organizations, one or more individuals have a broad understanding of the IT landscape, the business processes they enable, and the intricacies of their functional groups. Such isolation of information creates *islands of knowledge*, causing stagnation of innovation and a risk to the organization. Also, whereas business excellence can be achieved only by moving away from functional silos, usually, functional groups try to optimize their processes without properly understanding the influences of upstream-downstream processes. This often results in incomplete information and leads to less than desired results.

Probably, the biggest challenge faced by IT organizations (and the business) is to verify that the processes enabled by IT solutions are executed the way they were defined during the blueprinting sessions. Even with thorough blueprint documentation, efficient implementation, and elaborate training, processes tend to be executed by people in several ways. Process owners on the business side require information on how their processes are executed by their groups, and IT organizations struggle to provide this information, even though the processes are enabled by their IT systems.

These are some of the key issues that BPM attempts to solve by aligning the organization to processes (as opposed to functions) and centralizing the knowledge of processes, roles, and systems in a consistent fashion, thereby fostering collaboration.

To better support the business transformation and mitigate risks that occur due to organizational realignment, Craig Baumgardner, director of solutions delivery and integration (SD&I), initiated a program with the goal to mature BPM as a discipline within the organization.

Working with various technology strategy groups within SAP, Hospira realized that SAP is transforming its business suite not only to support end-to-end processes across the enterprise, but also to exchange business processes and information across the value chain by driving standardization and composition.

11.1.3 Architecture Practice and BPM

Without business context, architectural activities within IT simply focus on technology solutions. To illustrate this, we can compare an enterprise to a city with highways, subdivisions, plumbing, electricity, nature preserves, and so on. (In industry-speak, enterprise architecture (EA) and process reference models are generally referred to as the city plan, enterprise models, etc.) Just as a city has dependencies between roads, utilities, construction, sewage, and so on, interdependencies exist between functions, business processes, technology, organizational culture, and so on within an enterprise. (We wouldn't want to dig a foundation where there is a major electric line running, would we?) Whether the functional group is supply chain or IT or finance, it is still a part of the "city" and has interdependencies with other groups. Addressing the needs of just one of the components might negatively impact one or more of the other components. To see the big picture and the interdependencies, architects have to understand the various factors that influence an enterprise, including people, process, customers, technology, and so on. Having visibility across all of these factors helps architects and decision makers better predict the *butterfly effects* (how one infinitesimal action can have a huge effect on the course of a much larger event).

BPM is an integral part of architecture because it allows IT to properly enable business capabilities using the right technologies and to measure performance in the context of the business. By integrating BPM with the architecture practice, organizations can achieve the level of transparency across the enterprise that is required to directly trace IT organizations' value to the business and measure it (see Figure 11.2).

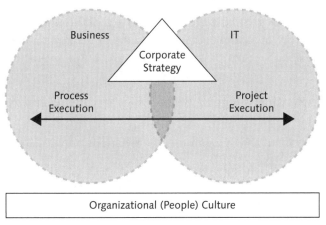

Figure 11.2 Business-IT Alignment Challenges

To ensure business-IT alignment, it is critical that the overall corporate strategy, which represents business goals, is directly tied to various IT initiatives, and the outcome should be monitored and measured in a repeatable, consistent fashion.

Value of Business Architecture Practice for Hospira

With the ever-changing landscape, the Hospira IT organization had to increase their presence within the business, and business architects thereby had the opportunity to be the eyes and ears of IT within the rest of the organization. Business architects thus become liaisons between business and IT by forging a relationship with their business clients. Building trust and a sense of partnership with business increases the chances of IT being involved in the initial planning instead of being tasked to simply execute a project. This helped the Hospira architects understand the challenges faced by their end customers that otherwise don't come up during regular IT project discussions.

Hospira realized that by becoming their partners instead of service providers, business architects helped the business clients realize the challenges that the IT organization faced from a broader perspective. This helped eliminate the frustration caused by IT not delivering on their expectations. In addition, Hospira realized that communicating the challenges of IT within the business is equally critical as for business architects to communicate their findings from the business with the rest of the IT organization. This helped people in downstream functionalities such as infrastructure architects and programmers see the broad challenges that face business clients and understand the big picture.

Business architects set the guidelines for how the rest of the organization is going to address the BPM discipline. As an example, below are some of the key guiding principles that Hospira established for their process designers and business process experts:

▶ Incorporate the 3C principle while designing processes: clear, comprehensive, and consistent.

▶ Only use terms everyone is familiar with, and use abbreviations only if necessary.

▶ Restate the end state of the BPM journey during the beginning of each strategic discussion. Open each blueprinting session with what the end state would look like if practiced properly.

▶ Process models are meant not for the modeler, but for the end user.

BPM and SOA

Service-oriented architecture is becoming the de facto for many of the product offerings from SAP. With the necessity for organizations to share information and processes across the value chain, a mature understanding of business processes, along with comprehensive governance is critical for the successful rollout of enterprise-level SOA.

As illustrated in Figure 11.3, enterprise architecture has its place between business and technology. For illustration purposes, for each N number of business scenarios there can be $N + M$ technologies within an IT portfolio, which in turn might be enabled by $N + M + O$ solutions — services and so on. But strong management of such an end-to-end portfolio (business, architecture, applications, and technology) will ensure alignment between IT and business.

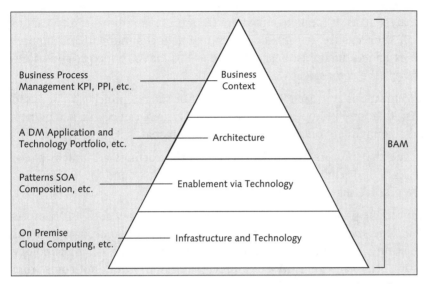

Figure 11.3 BPM – Enterprise Architecture – Process Enablement (Kuhlmann and von Rosing, 2010. "Applying BPM Principles to SAP EAF")

Efficient process management is the precursor to SOA because process awareness leads to service realization. Going back to the objective of enabling traceability from a business context perspective, when building services, there needs to be a clear understanding of the business model, processes, and events that are associated with the service.

To implement true service-oriented architecture, process experts with business acumen should be a part of the stakeholder group and the governance process. This will help the integral components of SOA, such as canonical data models, quality of service, return on investment (ROI) measurement, and so on align with business goals and business competencies.

11.1.4   BPM Solution

The first step in achieving process excellence and architectural maturity is creating process transparency. To build a sustainable BPM and architecture practice, Hospira started BPM as a strategic program, and the first step in this journey was to take a close look at the current state (maturity assessment) and create a roadmap for how and when the BPM practice should be matured. The most common challenges faced by organizations attempting BPM initiatives are:

▶ Maintaining leadership support and commitment on a long-term basis. According to analyst firms, it can take anywhere from eight months to three years to achieve BPM excellence. It's challenging to maintain commitment and support for such extended durations, because it is hard to measure success and value-added during the early stages.

▶ Some organizations approach BPM as a project or silos of projects, as opposed to a transformation-like approach. Because of that, there can be a lack of ownership and accountability once the projects are completed.

▶ At the time that process-oriented organizational structures are put in place, there is a lack of discipline and supporting framework around BPM. This leads to a BPM practice that is unsustainable.

▶ As the quote "Begin with the end in mind" by Steven Covey goes, BPM efforts require an end-state vision and a roadmap to get there. Some organizations tend to view the end state as a repository with all of the process and technology information. The value of BPM and a process repository does not come from storing all of the data in it, but from how that information is applied to improve efficiency.

▶ People factors such as core competency skills, behavioral norms, and culture can make or break the BPM vision. It is critical for the stakeholders to ensure constant organizational buy-in throughout the duration of the BPM journey.

Implementing the Solution

After the initial maturity assessment and peer interviews, Hospira selected ARIS from Software AG (formerly IDS Scheer) as the central global repository for business processes and architectural artifacts, primarily due to its integration abilities with SAP. To ensure successful adoption, Hospira conducted a key influencer analysis, which involved identifying influential people who have credibility within the organization and having them buy in to the initiative, thereby turning them into stakeholders.

The following key artifacts help jumpstart a sustainable BPM practice.

▶ Customized ARIS training materials tailored to various users

- ARIS – SAP Solution Manager integration standards
- SAP Solution Manager change request process changes
- ARIS methods and conventions for process design
- BPM activities within project delivery and system development lifecycle (SDLC) methodologies
- Process governance framework
- Strategic link, for example, business model
- ARIS Release Cycle Management
- Business competency
- Process parameters
- Organizational roles and responsibilities to support BPM
- SAP processes and process framework (e.g. SAP Process Library or APQC) alignment
- Defined value drivers
- Identified performance parameters
- ARIS license management process
- Security and access management standards

The setup and integration of the above points is critical for the success of the project. Some key points and three easy steps to follow are:

1. Define the strategic alignment, including business architecture set-up, business model, business architecture innovation, and transformation need — what to do
2. Translate the chosen path when identifying in which processes and activities you will do this — where to do it
3. Determine who should be doing it and how — the person who is responsible

As shown in Figure 11.4, the alignment and merger prior three points is vital to combine it all into a homogenous and compatible approach.

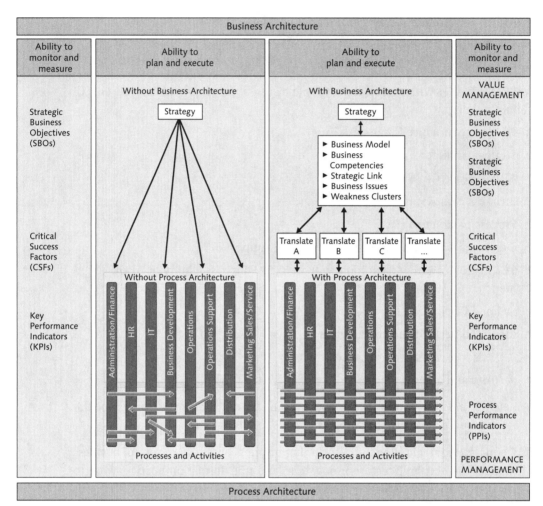

Figure 11.4 Alignment for a Business Architecture Approach (von Rosing, 2009. "Business Value Management")

Achieving business-IT alignment without a business architecture approach is not easy and it would be hard to achieve process and activity alignment in an operational approach. Figure 11.5 shows an example of such an architectural setup that incorporates the ARIS house, the SAP NetWeaver BPM approach, process parameters, value management, and the TOGAF architectural domains (described in more in detail in Part I, Chapter 4).

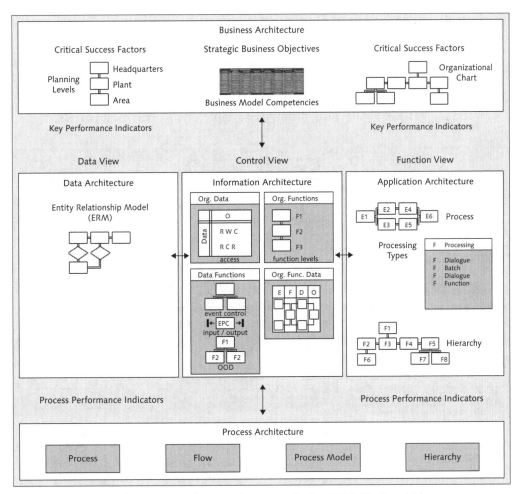

Figure 11.5   Example of a Business Architecture Setup (von Rosing, 2009. "Business Value Management")

To prevent project teams from struggling for direction while in the middle of large transformational projects, communication of the BPM vision, the roadmap, and the framework to all levels within the organization is critical. The Hospira OCM team leveraged several channels such as internal team blogs, lunch and learn road-shows, monthly executive communication, and so on for organization-wide communication.

11.1.5 BPM Center of Excellence (CoE)

To become a true process-centric organization, a strong people framework, comprised of stakeholders from various parts of the organization, is required. Unlike the traditional approach of creating a centralized CoE organization, BPM can thrive under a virtual CoE, as long as all of the stakeholders are aligned with the roadmap and target state. Figure 11.6 illustrates a sample CoE model to support BPM.

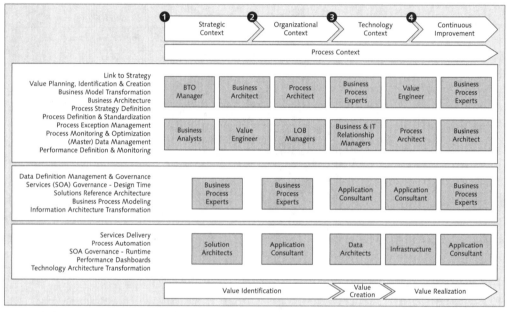

Figure 11.6 BPM Center of Excellence (von Rosing and von Scheel, 2010. "How to Identify, Plan, Create and Realize Value")

BPM requires support from a broad range of people across the enterprise. These individuals (or groups) need to collaborate and function together so that the corporate goals act as direct input to all levels of activities (tactical or strategic) within the rest of the organization. In addition, each tier within the BPM CoE has a comprehensive set of responsibilities that these people are accountable for. Such a CoE model, when those involved act together, becomes the cornerstone of enterprise architecture practice.

As the initial step toward building a BPM CoE, Hospira created a dedicated Business Process Architecture group under the global demand management organization. The responsibility of this group is to foster BPM and work with other strategic groups such architecture and business partners to mature the BPM discipline.

Combining BPM principles with EA principles in a CoE gives the EA approach practical value. One value is that it gives something to EA that is one of the weakest points within any existing EA framework or method. It doesn't matter if you look at a Zachman Framework, the Object Management group, the Gartner EA method, or the TOGAF Framework Enterprise Architecture methods and frameworks; they are missing a continuous improvement perspective and approach in this day and age. This is where the BPM process management lifecycle (PML) can help (see Figure 11.7).

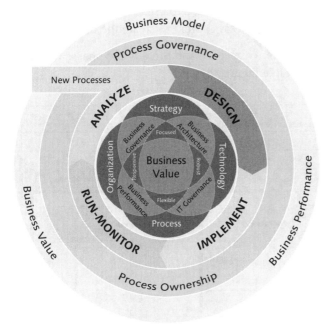

Figure 11.7 Process Management Lifecycle

Combining BPM and EA is for many companies a significant change of approach and mindset. A successful approach requires more than just a proven project methodology. You need to consider several elements, concentrating on the four pillars:

1. Analyze

2. Design

3. Implement

4. Run-Monitor

As described in Chapter 10 of the first SAP BPM book, *Business Process Management — the SAP Roadmap* (SAP PRESS 2009), BPM is a continuous improvement phase all about the principle that process work is not a one-time project initiative but rather is a philosophy that must be embedded in an organization to be successful. A company is ready to start with the continuous improvement phase after one cycle of the transition has been successfully completed and any necessary adjustments to the process approach have been made. In this phase of process governance, ownership goes hand in hand with development of the business model, performance, and value management. Any enterprise architecture setup is adjusted and repeated regularly, ensuring that EA becomes institutionalized to get an alignment of the strategic, organizational, technology, and process context to create the needed value.

Applying the continuous improvement approach and thereby the phases to enterprise architecture CoE could look like Figure 11.8.

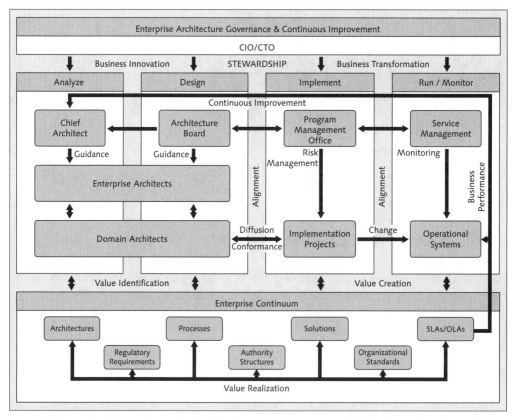

Figure 11.8 Sample Enterprise Architecture (Kuhlmann and von Rosing, 2010. "Applying BPM Principles to SAP EAF")

11.1.6 Building a BPM Community of Practice

The old African proverb, "If you want to go fast, go alone. If you want to go far, go together," applies here. BPM is something that cannot go far without an organization-wide adoption. In addition to support from senior management, employees from across the organization need to buy in to the benefits and adopt it. So Hospira built a BPM "community of practice" that can grow organically. In the book *Cultivating Communities of Practice* by Etienne Wenger (et al.), the structural model of a community of practice consists of three fundamental elements:

▶ **The domain of knowledge**
Creates a common ground and a sense of common identity.

▶ **The community**
Creates a social fabric of learning, by people who care about the domain.

▶ **The practice**
For the community to be effective in that domain. This consists of a set of framework, tools, language, and so on.

The objective was to build a community that does not simply approach BPM as just one more thing to do, but rather is bound by passion, identification, and expertise.

To promote the community, Hospira IT has reward programs to recognize process-oriented thinkers. The outcome is employees voluntarily showing interest in contributing to establishing a centralized repository and maturing the BPM discipline. This opened the door for business process experts to have discussions among themselves and with their clients about how to best orchestrate and optimize the processes.

11.1.7 Lessons Learned

Below are some of the key lessons learned about BPM and enterprise architecture:

▶ Business process management is in the best interest of the business. Ensure that the business owners recognize that and own the discipline. Build a strategy that makes the business the owner of process data. Identify a business owner of record who is accountable for each process.

▶ Architects should foster a culture (discipline) where there is commitment and engagement across the organization. Don't make people feel that this is being pushed on them. Answer the question, "What's in it for me?" for each group.

▶ Raise corporation-wide awareness of the benefits and methodologies of business process management. Demonstrate value quickly and often. Build credibility.

▶ Do not underestimate the "soft side" of BPM. Establish a community of practice. Be prepared to face resistance.

▶ Embed BPM discipline into your organizations' methodologies, including project management methodology. At Hospira, the exit criteria for several stage gates have BPM-related deliverables in them.

▶ Plan ahead to address BPM challenges that the project teams will face. Establish (and publish) the "process" of business process management. It's like building a blueprint for a blueprint.

▶ Actively recruit stakeholders who have a proven record to drive change — ones who have credibility at all levels in the organization.

▶ Socialize and seek buy-in from the business leaders and key influencers before making BPM operational. This will prevent them from thinking BPM is just one additional thing they have to do now.

▶ Establish a BPM center of excellence — even if it has to be a virtual one.

▶ Identify required skill sets for process-centric roles such as business architects, analysts, process owners, and so on. Encourage process-centric thinking (and thinkers) within the organization.

▶ Identify performance parameters and identify value drivers.

11.1.8   What's Ahead?

Hospira's architecture team, in collaboration with the business process architecture group and relationship managers, is planning to further extend the value of BPM by integrating it with various architecture activities.

By establishing a BPM-EA repository as a single source of truth and integrating it with process monitoring and execution platforms such as SAP Solution Manager, SAP NetWeaver, configuration management database (CMDB), and so on, the goal is to:

▶ Accelerate IT efficiency and productivity

▶ Demonstrate IT spending as a percentage of revenue

▶ Demonstrate process automation efficiency and penetration

▶ Spread technology consumption across various business groups

▶ Create service-level agreement metrics from a process context

▶ Identify and create value as described in the introduction of Part I

As the next step in BPM maturity, Hospira plans to bring the right information to the right users' desktops. The objective is to create subscription-based composites, where solutions will allow business users to "subscribe" to events of interest, thereby avoiding having them hunt for information in the SAP and non-SAP systems.

11.2 Danish Defense: Value Drivers in Corporate Businesses

He will win who, prepared himself. Hence the saying: If you know the enemy and know yourself, you need not fear.
– Art of War by SunTzu [SunZi], 500 BC

This section is about how the Danish Defense is using BPM as a management discipline in their organization. The central instrument in the Danish Defense case is a combined approach, as described in Part I, Chapters 1, 3, and 4, which describe the interrelationship of management concepts such as business modeling, performance management, value management, business governance, and highlights the important role and interconnection of BPM.

The work on the model is inspired by the authors' daily business process management work at the Danish Defense Command and their knowledge of the defense industry. However, the model itself has been developed through dialog in external networks, thereby combining best-practice knowledge and principles of different industries and own practice, all necessary to support and enable one of the most complex industries in existence today. A military business must have in some areas the most cost-efficient process possible but in other areas have some of the most innovative and competitive processes.

In some ways it can be argued that competitiveness and, thereby, focus, flexibility, and responsiveness while maintaining robustness is the foundation of a military business. Therefore, the principles of how to identify the right value drivers to align, innovate, change, and transform one's business model is applicable to both profit and non-profit organizations.

The armed forces of the Kingdom of Denmark, known as the Danish Defense (Danish: *Forsvaret*) is charged with the defense of the Kingdom of Denmark.

The chief of defense is the head of the Danish Armed Forces and is head of the Defense Command, which is managed by the Ministry of Defense, which has three purposes and six tasks. Its three primary purposes are to prevent conflicts and war, preserve the sovereignty of Denmark, and secure the continuing existence and integrity of the independent Kingdom of Denmark and further peaceful development in the world with respect to human rights. Its primary tasks are NATO participation in accordance with the strategy of the alliance; detection and repulsion of any sovereignty violation of Danish territory (including Greenland and the Faroe Islands); defense cooperation with non-NATO countries, especially Central and East European countries; international missions in the areas of conflict prevention, crisis-control, humanitarian mission, peacemaking, and peacekeeping; participation in "total defense" in cooperation with civilian resources, and maintenance of a sizable force to execute these tasks at all times.

Writing this case has been challenging, because it tackles one of the most complex industries. In this industry the political, military, and technological landscape puts greater emphasis than ever before on the efficiency, effectiveness, and capability of defense organizations. This requires more than ever a focused, flexible, responsive, and robust business model and an organization that can work in programs and projects, all with fully integrated cost-efficient processes. As if this would not be enough, process management in such an industry also includes full governance control of:

▶ The various information management processes: ensuring that data is secure, credible, useful, and available to the people who need it, when they need it.

▶ A shared services strategy covering technology and infrastructure.

▶ Enterprise and asset management processes: optimizing defense logistics in complex supply chain scenarios.

▶ High-performance computing environments: powering research and development of new defense processes and in combination with services and technologies.

▶ The total cost picture: the current financial situation causes not only a threat to the economy as a whole, but to national defense organizations as well. Even the defense industries are impacted by the economy, and moderation in their business practices is expected on a global basis. Even though a national defense organization is less vulnerable to economic downturns than other industries, defense spending may be diverted to other federal priorities. Over the long term, the financial bailout will most likely redistribute available funds from defense to other needs. A cost focus will more than ever be a part of survival.

The overview on the following pages will describe the lessons learned and the exciting journey of the necessary process-centric transformation. First, we will introduce the parameters and the value drivers for the business model. Next, we will look at tools and approaches for changing a dynamic organization without losing its focus, responsibility, flexibility, and robustness in undergoing such changes. Throughout this section, we will follow the value flows and focus on where in the organization we get the most performance and value for the money.

11.2.1 The Importance of Having the Right Business Model in Place

To enable our armed forces, coalition forces, and civilian organizations to liaise effectively in a global environment, we need to manage our processes efficiently and cost-effectively and ensure their openness to interaction across organizational boundaries. Bringing together previously unconnected processes allows groups and organizations to improve the visibility and availability of vital information. In the early stages of the business process transformation in the Danish Armed Forces, it became clear that if process changes were deployed without the correct business model management in place, the models used could not deliver the required benefits. The nature of the defense industry, and recent broader regulatory legislation such as the Sarbanes-Oxley Act, makes the management of governance, risk, and compliance (GRC) not only important, but mandatory. Government compliance regulations imposed on this industry go far beyond the regulations imposed on most other industries.

International Traffic in Arms Regulations (ITAR); Registration, Evaluation, Authorization of Chemicals (REACH); Export Administration Regulations (EAR); and unique identification (UID) and radio frequency identification (RFID) are just a fraction of the regulations and mandates for which national defense organizations must demonstrate compliance.

As a point of departure for the analysis, we will define business governance as discussed by Mark von Rosing in Part I of this book and according to Carl von Clausewitz as "the center of gravity." This concept has an orientation toward the outside and the inside core of an organization. Clausewitz explains it as follows:

> *Center of gravity is the characteristics, the capabilities, or the locations from which an organization derives its freedom of action, physical strength, or will to fight for the markets and earn money.*

At the strategy level, center of gravity might include the strength of an alliance, a set of critical capabilities or functions, or an organizational strategy. It also presents a need to choose between characteristics, capability, and location, when in reality all three exist simultaneously in mutual dependency.

An organization operating in a given location is ineffective without essential characteristics and capabilities. Moreover, the use of terms such as *foundation of capability, hub of all power,* and *movement* or *dominant characteristics* is ambiguous enough. Worse, they are invariably accompanied by an expansive list of examples that include alliances, communities of interest, public opinion, and international rules for good commerce. What makes business governance in a defense organization challenging is that it includes far more than choices between characteristics, capability, and location. A business governance framework in a defense organization includes the decision-making process, the direct money flow, the primary processes, and the direct and indirect tasks and the outcome in terms of results (see Figure 11.9).

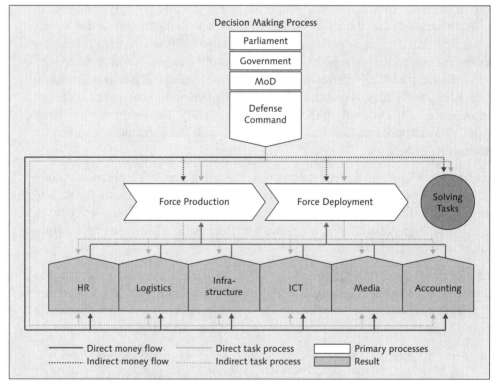

Figure 11.9 Business Governance: Decision-Making Process

11.2.2   The Need to Describe the Business Model

The purpose of a business model is to describe how the core production interacts with the need for competencies and the need for capacity and resources. The business model is seen as a strategy tool to visualize the basic strategy relations in the organization. In the Danish Defense forces the business model has a third purpose: To show how the defense should transfer from a governmental-thinking organization, with money as the driver when creating solutions, to a modern governmental organization, having its focus on the needs of competencies, logistics, weapon platforms, infrastructure, and IT for optimal solutions. The business model development project began in 1994, and the resulting model is still used as a guideline for future development.

Why focus on competencies? Everybody in the organization needs unique knowledge and unique skills for optimized production. Skills and knowledge can be acquired in two ways: you can recruit the right people, or you can educate and develop your employees. Either way, you need resources, capacity, and time to get the right profiles.

In the global world, time is the main parameter. Good business will very soon get competition from other players in the markets, so the more efficient production can be, the higher is the possibly of staying in business, as long as the processes is running effectively. For that you need the right competencies. The same principle applies to the defense industry. Deploying one's force requires collaboration among several competencies. Because there is input from all of the different business units, operational areas are needed to make the force deployment a success, making competency collaboration a key requirement. To drive as much power as possible from the different business model competencies, only the core critical competencies (CCCs) (e.g. core competitive and core differentiated competencies) across the organization are aggregated. The law of competitiveness truly applies to the defense industry, as it is an organization's CCCs that enable that organization to outperform its rivals. An example of such a detailed business model in the defense industry and its core competitive and core differentiated competencies as well as the value opportunities, is shown in Figure 11.10.

Business modeling is not the sole tool for defining and developing one's performance in deploying armed forces, for example, or defining where and how value could or should be created and realized in the different defense business lines.

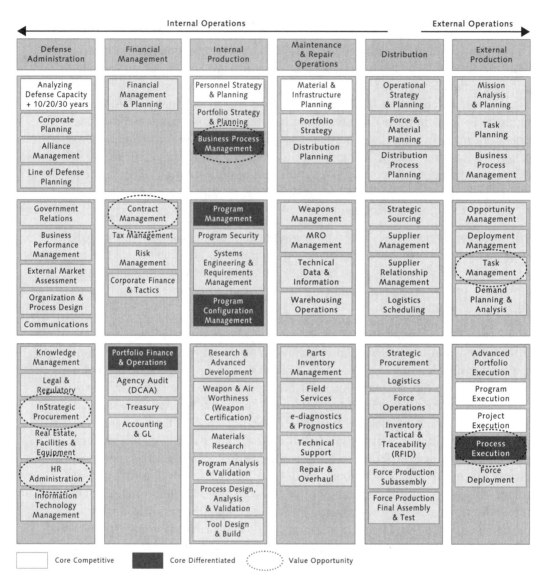

Figure 11.10 Example of a Defense Business Model (von Rosing and von Scheel, 2010. "How to Identify, Plan, Create and Realize Value")

The second main parameter is to align the processes at all times. The focus has to be on how to measure improvement in production capacity and the processes surrounding the production. The measurement or information is a kind of lifeline to business governance, and it creates the value management. The value management creates the need for changes and sometimes new implementations of technology.

11.2.3 The Need for Business Governance

It doesn't matter whether you have a big or a small defense organization in a big or a small country, because in any case ambitious business governance, in addition to effective military command and control, is required to achieve the above-mentioned goals and to ensure the right connection between business model management (BMM) and business process management (BPM) in the organization.

Corporate management and the rest of the management is responsible for ensuring that continuous information is produced on the performance of the organization's core processes. This can be in the form of business intelligence reports or updates about the development of technological capabilities that could possibly support productive and administrative needs.

Business intelligence information could be used to assess, for example, the possibility of replacing manpower with technology within the organization, although attention should be directed toward the unique business needs as the starting point — before any attempts to automate production or administrative activity.

Organizational Leadership and Management

In terms of leadership and management, defense organizations are unique. Military and civilian personnel work together to ensure that the defense force is well managed, well trained, well equipped, and well prepared to protect the country and its national interests, at home and abroad. Strong leadership is central to achieving this goal in both operational and nonoperational environments.

Skills in leadership and management are fundamental to the success of any defense organization and its missions. Defense is committed to developing the leadership and management skills of all personnel, both military and civilian. The interesting thing about a defense organization is that at some point in their careers, everyone in the organization is likely to have leadership responsibilities and must have the capacity to lead and manage effectively from their positions within the organization. Leadership in a defense organization is the process of influencing others to gain willingness to act on orders, without questioning the leader's decisions.

As the foundation for leadership and management activities in a defense organization, the management at the executive level has to establish the necessary line management and focus on tasks in the organization. Senior management also has to look for leadership and efficiency in relation to the processes and the process management. In the toolbox for doing this job, one will find process management, process deployment, and process implementation as tools to move the organization to be more cost focused, effective, and efficient.

The next step is, as described earlier in Chapter 6, to build up a performance and value management system to obtain essential business information. As we already described, value management is probably one of the most common dilemmas and challenges that companies confront today, regardless of factors such as size, revenue, industry, region, and business model. In any organization, but especially in a defense organization, the timing for using information is also essential. As soon as corporate management responds to information and initiates changes through the transition process, the changes in the organization will be simplified and the time spent on change will be shortened.

Organizational and Value Drivers

In a defense organization, values can be understood in multiple ways. For example, the organization's own internal values reflect the long traditions and distinctive identities of the traditional organization and its mission. Some of these specific defense values could be professionalism, loyalty, integrity, courage, innovation, and teamwork.

Such values are established to provide a common and unifying thread for all people working within the defense organization. Developed by the senior defense leadership and typically reaffirmed by a parliamentary defense committee, the defense values are an important component in guiding organizational behavior. In a defense organization, value-based behavior involves individuals at all levels being prepared to accept responsibility and accountability for their missions and to think clearly about the effect of their actions on the mission, project, or tasks. Values are fundamental to good performance.

However, in this section the term *organizational value drivers* is not to be confused with the above internal values of the defense organization. Organizational value drivers are mechanisms that could, for instance, help the Danish Defense optimize the core business of the organization through the dynamic improvement of all subprocesses within the main processes spanning from the management processes over the identified core processes and to the supporting processes. Examples of such value drivers within defense can be seen in typical disciplines such as:

- Traditional cost drivers:
    - Volume optimization
    - Reduced administration costs
    - Reduced cost of operational goods
    - Capital optimization
- Operational value drivers: realization of doctrines
- Competency development:
    - Capacity planning
    - Operational planning
    - Lifecycle planning
    - Technology development: strengthen innovation, speed-up time-to-market, improve responsiveness, improve force interaction, improve partner country collaboration, operational efficiency
- Lower risk:
    - Optimize intelligence
    - Optimize regulation compliance
    - Improve risk planning and management

The decision to make large-scale investments in, for instance, the IT-enabling of business processes, and the complex challenges involved in ensuring that the investments are effective and efficient, need to be managed.

Clear management of these changes will enable the organization to plan the value they want created in the different lines of business and the realization of this value within the context of the organization's overall vision and strategies. Having studied companies' behavior in this field with a scoped approach on the issue from the view of a defense and a public sector organization, we find it interesting that companies spend substantial time trying to realize value, which in itself is quite understandable, but at the same time make that fatal mistake pointed out in Part I,

Chapter 3, which is to not realize the simple and direct connection between value planning, value creation, and value realization.

Value Management

By the term *business value* companies must understand that as defined in Part I, Chapter 3, the value of their investment to stay competitive in today's rapidly changing business world. The gains, process costs, revenue potential, and possible value spots are often hidden and rarely addressed (see Figure 11.11).

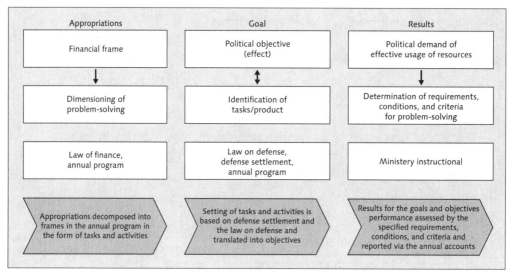

Figure 11.11 Measuring Business Value with Value Management

Also within defense, a prerequisite for value management covering the planning, creation, and realization of value in all lines of business should be seen in a full definition of value drivers for all main process areas in the organization (e.g., management processes, core processes, and supporting processes) and in the subsequent monitoring of these value drivers to be able to react when necessary.

Such an approach to value realization requires the involvement of various roles and responsibilities at different levels of the organization. The interrelationship of roles can be illustrated by the simplified representation of roles in the Danish Defense shown in Figure 11.12.

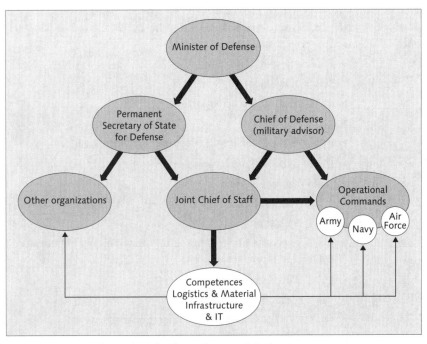

Figure 11.12 Interrelationship of Roles in the Danish Defense

To develop the right value drivers and from the performance drivers in an organization, one needs to incorporate all of the stakeholders that are involved. Table 11.1 illustrates an example of the involvement of the Danish Defense stakeholders and the various roles and responsibilities at different levels of the organization they have in value planning, value creation, and realization, describing how value drivers cascade through the chain of leadership and command.

Role	Value Planning
Minister of Defense	▶ Initiates parliamentary defense commissions
	▶ Sets strategic business objectives (SBOs) and thereby policies and objectives
	▶ Value creation (no activities)
	▶ Value realization
	▶ Evaluates performance

Table 11.1 Danish Defense Value Driver Model

Role	Value Planning
Permanent Secretary of State for Defense	► Sets critical success factors (CSFs) ► Provides legal foundation ► Sets management guidelines ► Value creation (no activities) ► Value realization ► Oversees all of the joint concepts and validates performance
Joint Chief of Staff	► Defines key performance indicators (KPIs) ► Gives planning guidance ► Value creation (no activities) ► Value realization ► Analyzes service budgets to see that activities and initiatives are funded in budget requests
Chiefs of Operational Commands	► Build plans and budgets ► Value creation ► Initiate and conduct ultimate operational activity ► Value realization ► Review plans, budgets, and production
Other	► Build plans and budgets ► Value creation ► Produce support for operational activity ► Value realization ► Review plans, budgets, and production

Table 11.1 Danish Defense Value Driver Model (Cont.)

The value drivers in the model flow from business governance (see Figure 11.13) because business governance is and always will be the central hub of everything that goes on in a complex organization like a national defense organization. The purpose of the Danish Defense value driver model is to explain the way the value drivers normally flow through the organization and to show how the mapping of those drivers can be used to catch business information from the process hierarchy and present it to the senior executives for decision-making.

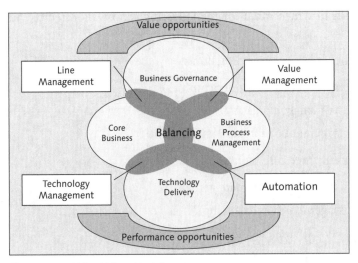

Figure 11.13   Value Driver Model

The value driver model is based on two dimensions: spheres and value driver fields (VDFs):

The spheres are:

▸ Business governance

▸ Core business (organization, tasks, and limitation)

▸ Business process management

▸ Technology delivery

The VDFs are:

▸ Line management

▸ Value management

▸ Technology management

▸ Automation

Balancing the three business management spheres in the model are all known topics on today's business management agenda, but integrating them all in one model together with the delivery of technology and IT and, in particular, putting BPM on the map as an equal partner to corporate governance and line management highlights new interfaces to an organization. The overlapping areas between the spheres constitute fields in which room for maneuvering can be allocated to the value drivers.

The business governance looks in three directions:

▶ Market (via management of business opportunities)

▶ Core business (via line management)

▶ Business process management (via value management)

The core business looks in three directions:

▶ Technology delivery (via technology management)

▶ Business process management (via balancing)

▶ Business governance (via line management)

Business process management looks in three directions:

▶ Technology delivery (via automation)

▶ Core business (via balancing)

▶ Business governance (via value management)

In a defense organization a systematic reading of its value drivers should provide business governance with the best possible performance feedback prior to any decision on changes in the force deployment planning or execution, operation, manufacturing, or logistic activities in the organization. In addition, business governance must ensure that the ongoing programs and projects, just as within force deployment, work to seek new organizational effectiveness and efficiency at the lowest possible price.

All companies have strategies, goals, and some sort of value drivers implied simply by their existence, but very few of them follow value drivers in a way that ensures the most value for the money. One of the main goals of this study project at the Danish Defense Command was determining how to change this. The goals of defining value drivers at the Danish Defense are:

▶ Step 1: to describe the flow of value inside the organization.

▶ Step 2: to analyze how the flow and the processes in the organization could be optimized.

▶ Step 3: to describe how ongoing continuous improvement could be implemented without losing adaptability, efficiency, and flexibility.

One of the outcomes of the study at the Danish Defense Command was a manual for process management that should help introduce common standards and function as a guide to continuous process improvement.

History tells that management at the executive level in a company generally ignores the possibility of aligning the corporate processes and using the big picture to make decisions. BPM could be the tool to do this better, by taking advantage of the feedback coming from all of the spheres illustrated above. Seen from inside a nonprofit organization or a government agency, the need to be "best in class" is to a large extent similar to a private organization. Basically, the requirement to do your job the way it has to be done in the eyes of the customer (in the public sector to produce the kind of services the citizens are willing to pay taxes for) is the same. Changes taking place in politics may appear as quickly as changes in the market, and the need for agility is accepted in both private and public sectors.

However, top management in an organization often makes decisions that are not necessarily in line with the official commitment to effectiveness and efficiency. For instance, numerous examples exist where new IT solutions are purchased without checking the needs in a wider process perspective, and the consequence is often failed implementation with increased costs and less income to follow.

Such examples can also be found in high-profile digitalization initiatives aimed at modernizing business areas. A Danish example could, for instance, be that of a Ministry of Finance initiative to centralize all IT support in the government agencies. A first step was to build up a common learning management system to:

▶ Store all governmental employees' competencies

▶ Provide a platform for E-learning

▶ Provide an IT system for booking

The business case for this system was not based on an analysis of the organizational environment. For example, we in the Danish Armed Forces already operate an integrated system to record all employees' competencies (SAP HR), and in the same system there is good functionality for booking and event management. Platforms for E-learning have existed in the armed forces for over 15 years, but the defense experience from this period was not fully included in the business case.

The vision for the centralization of government IT is to establish a joint enterprise resource planning (ERP) solution. This too will be difficult for the Defense Command because most public services in Denmark use the financial modules of Microsoft Navision, whereas the agencies of the Ministry of Defense use SAP wall-to-wall.

Briefly, the key risk in such a one-size-fits-all approach from the view of the value driver model is that the initiation of IT delivery directly from top governance, ignoring the core business of the various business areas and without having a unified process architecture in place and without a value management driver in place that goes beyond financial bookkeeping, will cause fragmentation in decision-making, management, and practical operations. Basically, in such an approach there is no connection from business governance, IT governance, and process governance to the performance and value governance of automation.

In the following sections we will go through the value driver model developed by Dahl and Nielsen in the Danish Armed Forces, and we will focus on the information needed to achieve value effectiveness and efficiency and value maximizing. To do this we have to look at each of above four spheres, their internal connections, and the way the value drivers turn around in the model.

Core Production

The business governance sphere, through the strategy process, focuses on both external and internal factors (see Figure 11.14). The external view shows the market potential, and the internal view provides a picture of core production. The next step is to align the core production with the organization and the prerequisite needs for capacity and competencies before deciding to build up an organization.

The organization and the available production capacity generally limit production, but other limitations could include governmental rules, environmental rules, and so on. The flow from business governance to core business describes the dimensions of production. Although this does not bring value in itself, it is necessary for understanding the entire process that manages limitations and constraints.

In the dynamic core business sphere, the focus is shaped by the related VDFs. The balancing VDF between the core business and business process management is working in both directions to find a balance. Both spheres need the other sphere to provide feedback and tolerance-level and use the acquired knowledge for optimizing.

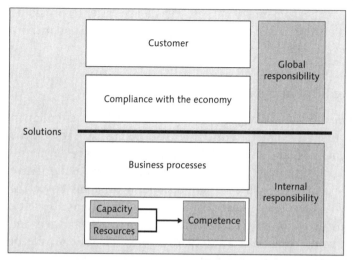

Figure 11.14   Danish Defense Capability and Resource Model

The value driver field (VDF) between the core business and technology delivery (technology management) is not managed consciously in many organizations. Thus, the core business misses an area to be optimized, and the evaluation and running costs between system and core business are consequently unadjusted and off balance.

Lessons Learned from the Industry

Often current operations follow well-known organizational patterns clinging to already known and tried practices for how things are done. The cost is unchanged and follows the price development in the market, the market potential is decreasing, and the executives have three options, or a combination of these:

- ▶ Drop out of the market
- ▶ Use more money for perfection
- ▶ Optimize the processes

The cheapest way is normally to optimize, but with a dynamic core business in place, this has probably already been done. In a defense organization this applies indirectly as well. In such a situation focusing on optimizing the core business through business process management will make the challenge easier by providing the relevant business value drivers and at the same time providing the opportunity to optimize the revenue early in the process.

11.2.4 Implementing BPM in the Danish Defense

Currently, the term *business process management* has gotten substantial attention in various business environments. Numerous discussions are taking place at seminars all over the globe, in journals, and through Web-based media. However, terminology and its perceptions vary from forum to forum and the one authoritative good implementation example to follow is still outstanding. The answer to the most basic question, what BPM really means, is in some organizations also left a little blurred, despite participation in several conferences by both managers and employees. Therefore, some companies and organizations, whether private or governmental, face problems moving from discussion to focused action.

The conclusion we made in the Danish Armed Forces is that BPM simply needs time to mature in an organization, and if the direction seems attractive, then how are the first steps up the maturity ladder taken?

Maturing BPM within the Organization and Top Management

At the Danish Armed Forces we realized very early that support in some form from the top management is necessary for a BPM initiative to succeed. If BPM as a concept is fully integrated with the strategy and the business model, the way ahead can get close to a textbook roadmap, but if top management does not support the need for BPM, even with a well prepared case, BPM will be hard to both sell and implement in its full format.

It is true that processes do sell these days, in particular in large government organizations where many work routines are, due to digital law requirements or cost reduction, IT supported. Typically, even in organizations using ERP systems like SAP ERP, local optimization initiatives within functional areas are likely to be already ongoing. These activities can provide a good platform for BPM because process improvement in such a situation is generally supported and usually also praised when it includes simplification, standardization, building new process relations, optimization, and cutting costs.

Existing process projects, however, also represent serious challenges to the introduction of process management because projects usually are initiated locally and have a functional focus rather than a process focus. Typically, this results in a lack of focus on the concept of value but a heavy focus on financial economics, the result being too many investment instances with limited value for the money spent. Process development projects within narrow functional borders are at risk of losing the cross-organizational perspective, resulting in suboptimization. Sadly, this is typically not recognized—neither by management nor in the organization itself.

A Way Forward with a Prospect of Success

If the ideal starting point with a clear BPM project sponsored by top management is nonexistent, the only real alternative is a slower and more tactical approach to its establishment. If proper BPM is to gain ground in an environment as described above, the logical approach is to work on a show case — basically a BPM initiation project.

The business unit responsible for BPM, the BPM team, should establish or find an already planned business improvement project with a cross-functional project mandate and have the process team work closely with that project team. The project should give priority to a solid analysis of business processes before eventual IT functionality is developed.

The BPM initiation project must also ensure engagement of corporate management to get strategic anchoring and business representatives to understand the defense core processes.

This involvement of Danish Armed Forces top management ensures a top-down approach, which by default is most suitable for highly hierarchical organizations, and the integration with the organizational value drivers.

The Danish Armed Forces BPM team ensured that the process flow was modeled (see Figure 11.15), as well as for internal project purposes for external communication purposes. We learned through previous engagements that graphics often speak louder than words.

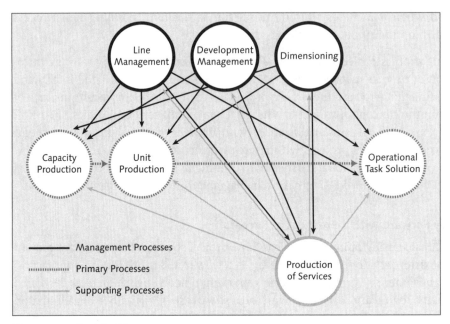

Figure 11.15   Model of Processes

BPM and Facilitating VDFs

BPM is still a new management discipline, and it remains a challenge to explain its real value to managers who believe it is just hype. However, one way to promote BPM would be to explain the value driver model and point out VDFs that exist in the model only due to the existence of BPM. We learned that without awareness of BPM, these fields will not be handled properly.

We will explain the relationship between BPM and the other spheres and the work in the VDFs.

BPM and Business Governance

BPM, as illustrated in the value driver model, constitutes the other two key business spheres. Where the corporate leadership can ensure the delivery of intended outputs in core business through traditional line management, the VDF to be used to ensure that the organization works with as little value drain as possible is value management. Accordingly, BPM is aimed at ensuring that outcomes and products are produced in the preferred and best way throughout the organization.

Within the value management, VDF at an executive level directs activities in the BPM sphere — while the value focus of the BPM activities correspondingly provides the basis for fulfilling value-based management at the very top.

Lessons Learned

To a very large extent, it is hard to convince senior management that the promises of BPM are trustworthy, and management—accordingly and reasonably enough—is reluctant to allocate too much money for the purpose and implement a bigger change. Hence, we realized the need for a showcase demonstrating that the proposed process architecture and the interrelationship between business processes are valid.

Another typical and logical reason for friction is the fact that most armed forces and defense organizations are by nature very command- and structure-driven. Members of senior management hold their authority due to a formal responsibility of a functional line/branch within the organization. Because proper BPM will move the focus toward obtaining results and consequential cross-functional processes and issues, BPM will be perceived as a threat to this established power structure. The perspective of a future role as a process owner might to some degree be of interest, but because the understanding of such a role will be a little blurred in the early stages of BPM, it cannot compete with core business or business as usual. Again, a gradual approach with a breakdown of management, core (primary), and supporting processes seems to be logical.

Measuring and providing data-based information about process performance is also difficult. BPM suites (BPMSs) market themselves as being ready out-of-the-box to provide process intelligence. However, it is unlikely that such a BPMS will be deployed to any large extent if BPM is not already ongoing, and process intelligence is unlikely to convince senior management of the move toward BPM. Value-based management under such conditions is basically not in place.

Value Management VDF

Just as defined in Part I, Chapter 3, corporate management will set strategic business objectives (SBOs), for example, "cut defense budget cost." Furthermore, targets for business performance indicators (BPIs) could in such a case be "to cut the defense budget cost within 6 months by 30 percent." At such a high level this would have to be broken down further into critical success factors (CSFs) to bring it closer to an operational level. Such a breakdown could result in the following:

1. Reduce force operation and administration costs

2. Reduce cost of force deployment

3. Improve capital defense management

4. Capital defense optimization

For an operational understanding, all of the above four areas would have to be broken down into key performance indicators (KPIs). These KPIs are what the organization must seek to achieve. Table 11.2 (von Rosing, Dahl, and Nielsen, 2010. "Business Process Management in the Defense Industry," SAP whitepapers) shows an example of such a cascading from SBOs, to a CSF, and then to KPIs.

SBOs	CSFs	KPIs
Cut Defense Budget Cost	Reduce Force Operation and Administration Costs	Consolidate or outsource defense procurement functions
		Refine vendor strategies
		Consolidate or outsource IT design and development functions
		Consolidate or outsource IT design, development, and deployment services
		Consolidate or outsource IT end-user-support
		Consolidate defense operations and maintenance services
		Consolidate or outsource defense benefits administration functions
		Consolidate or outsource defense learning and development functions
		Consolidate defense recruitment functions
		Improve alignment of defense strategies with corporate armed forces strategies
		Improve alignment of defense structures with defense command strategies
		Consolidate defense payroll functions
		Consolidate or outsource defense property management functions

Table 11.2 Examples of Defense Value Drivers

SBOs	CSFs	KPIs
		Improve alignment of political financial decisions/strategies with corporate defense command strategies
		Analyze enemy targeted markets and segments
		Rationalize deployment portfolio
		Analyze targeted force deployment segments
		Select and enter successful and exit non-successful UN/EU defense projects
		Consolidate defense order fulfillment functions
		Increase focus on enemy insight and forward-looking information
		Minimize recovery costs through "self-healing" recovery capabilities
		Improve focus on higher-value defense capabilities
		Increase use of lower-cost defense capabilities
		Minimize recovery costs
		Better alignment of operations deployment planning, management, and reporting functions
		Minimize costs related to external shocks
		Better alignment of financial accounting and analysis functions
		Consolidate defense real estate/facilities
		Improve alignment of political allowed budgets and program plans with operations priorities
		Increase use of lower-cost activities
		Reduce fixed IT cost by paying for usage, not for availability
		Strengthen defense-wide financial reporting standards
		Design more ease-of-use/self-service operations

Table 11.2 Examples of Defense Value Drivers (Cont.)

SBOs	CSFs	KPIs
		Improve emphasis on design for force deployment packing/shipping efficiency
		Standardize catalogs
		Consolidate defense service and support operations
		Withdraw non-profitable defense projects
		Improve emphasis on project quality and ease of service
		Rationalize and/or refocus service portfolios
		Retarget projects and services and manage project output
		Consolidate billing operations
		Manage procurement for MRO on a national defense basis
		Rationalize/consolidate MRO vendor portfolio
		Consolidate IT, defense Telecom, and force deployment network equipment and facilities
		Implement integrated applications across organizational boundaries
		Rationalize IT application portfolio
		Improve focus on military employee retention
		Improve HR practices

Table 11.2 Examples of Defense Value Drivers (Cont.)

As we discussed in Part I, Chapter 3, defining performance and value drivers with the needed strategic link is a challenging job. It may be one of the reasons why most organizations have difficulty combining the value lifecycle with the process lifecycle, and then with the application lifecycle. In addition to combining the three lifecycles, one needs to incorporate the organization, the roles, and thereby the competencies they work with to ensure a link to business model levels, as shown in the performance and value driver approach as illustrated in Table 11.3 (von Rosing, Dahl, and Nielsen, 2010). ABPM task force or BPM center of expertise (CoE), depending on the process focus and maturity of the company, will be able to break down these KPI targets into process performance indicators (PPIs) and the connected IT application areas to combine value drivers with IT operation.

CSFs	KPIs	BPM Key Focus	Business Model Level	SAP	SAP Level 2
Reduce Force Operation and Administration Costs	Consolidate or outsource defense procurement functions	1. Strategy processes	Strategic	SAP SRM	Strategic Purchasing & Sourcing
	Refine vendor strategies	1. Strategy processes	Strategic	SAP SRM	Strategic Purchasing & Sourcing
	Consolidate or outsource IT design and development functions	1. Strategy processes	Strategic	SAP PLM	Lifecycle Collaboration and Analytics
	Consolidate or outsource IT design, development, and deployment services	1. Strategy processes	Strategic	SAP PLM	Lifecycle Collaboration and Analytics
	Consolidate or outsource IT end-user-support	1. Strategy processes	Operational	SAP ERP	Operations: value generation
	Consolidate defense operations and maintenance services	1. Strategy processes	Operational	SAP ERP	Operations: value generation
	Consolidate or outsource defense benefits administration functions	1. Strategy processes	Operational	SAP ERP	Human capital management

Table 11.3 Examples of Defining Performance and Value Drivers

CSFs	KPIs	BPM Key Focus	Business Model Level	SAP	SAP Level 2
	Consolidate or outsource defense learning and development functions	1. Strategy processes	Operational	SAP ERP	Human capital management
	Consolidate defense recruitment functions	1. Strategy processes	Strategic	SAP ERP	Human capital management
	Improve alignment of defense strategies with corporate armed forces strategies	1. Strategy processes	Strategic	SAP ERP	Analytics, reporting, and operational BI
	Improve alignment of defense structures with defense command strategies	1. Strategy processes	Strategic	SAP ERP	Analytics, reporting, and operational BI
	Consolidate defense payroll functions	1. Strategy processes	Operational	SAP ERP	Human capital management
	Consolidate or outsource defense property management functions	1. Strategy processes	Strategic	SAP ERP	Corporate services

Table 11.3 Examples of Defining Performance and Value Drivers (Cont.)

CSFs	KPIs	BPM Key Focus	Business Model Level	SAP	SAP Level 2
	Improve alignment of political financial decisions/ strategies with corporate defense command strategies	1. Strategy processes	Strategic	SAP ERP	Analytics, reporting, and operational BI
	Analyze enemy targeted markets and segments	6. Force deployment processes	Tactical	SAP CRM	Sales
	Rationalize deployment portfolio	6. Force deployment processes	Operational	SAP CRM	Sales
	Analyze targeted force deployment segments	6. Force deployment processes	Operational	SAP CRM	Sales
	Select and enter successful and exit non-successful UN/EU defense projects	6. Force deployment processes	Operational	SAP CRM	Analytics
	Consolidate defense order fulfillment functions	2. Force production processes	Tactical	SAP ERP	Operations: value generation

Table 11.3 Examples of Defining Performance and Value Drivers (Cont.)

CSFs	KPIs	BPM Key Focus	Business Model Level	SAP	SAP Level 2
	Increase focus on enemy insight and forward-looking information	2. Force deployment processes	Tactical	NetWeaver	Information integration
	Minimize recovery costs through "self-healing" recovery capabilities	2. Force production processes	Operational	NetWeaver	Process enabler and Service repository
	Improve focus on higher-value defense capabilities	2. Force production processes	Operational	SAP CRM	Analytics
	Increase use of lower-cost defense capabilities	2. Force production processes	Operational	SAP CRM	Sales
	Minimize recovery costs	2. Force production processes	Operational	SAP ERP	Analytics, reporting, and operational BI
	Better alignment of operations deployment planning, management, and reporting functions	2. Force production processes	Strategic	SAP ERP	Analytics

Table 11.3 Examples of Defining Performance and Value Drivers (Cont.)

CSFs	KPIs	BPM Key Focus	Business Model Level	SAP	SAP Level 2
	Minimize costs related to external shocks	2. Force production processes	Operational	SAP ERP	Analytics, reporting, and operational BI
	Better alignment of financial accounting and analysis functions	2. Force production processes	Tactical	SAP ERP	Analytics
	Consolidate defense real estate/ facilities	2. Force production processes	Tactical	SAP ERP	Corporate services
	Improve alignment of political allowed budgets and program plans with operations priorities	2. Force production processes	Operational	SAP ERP	Corporate services
	Increase use of lower-cost activities	2. Force production processes	Tactical	SAP ERP	Operations: support
	Reduce fixed IT cost by paying for usage, not for availability	2. Force production processes	Operational	SAP ERP	Analytics, reporting, and operational BI
	Strengthen defense-wide financial reporting standards	2. Force production processes	Operational	SAP ERP	Financials

Table 11.3 Examples of Defining Performance and Value Drivers (Cont.)

CSFs	KPIs	BPM Key Focus	Business Model Level	SAP	SAP Level 2
	Design more ease-of-use/ self-service operations	5. Products & services processes	Strategic	SAP PLM	Lifecycle collaboration and analytics
	Improve emphasis on design for force deployment packing/ shipping efficiency	5. Products & services processes	Operational	SAP PLM	Lifecycle collaboration and analytics
	Standardize catalogs	5. Products & services processes	Strategic	SAP PLM	Lifecycle data management
	Consolidate defense service and support operations	5. Products & services processes	Operational	SAP CRM	Services
	Withdraw non-profitable defense projects	5. Products & services processes	Operational	SAP CRM	Analytics
	Improve emphasis on project quality and ease of service	5. Products & services processes	Tactical	SAP PLM	Quality management
	Rationalize and/or refocus service portfolios	5. Products & services processes	Operational	SAP CRM	Services

Table 11.3 Examples of Defining Performance and Value Drivers (Cont.)

CSFs	KPIs	BPM Key Focus	Business Model Level	SAP	SAP Level 2
	Retarget projects and services and manage project output	5. Products & services processes	Tactical	SAP CRM	Sales
	Consolidate billing operations	5. Products & services processes	Strategic	SAP ERP	Operations: value generation
	Manage procurement for MRO on a national defense basis	7. Supplier processes	Tactical	SAP SRM	Strategic purchasing & sourcing
	Rationalize/ consolidate MRO vendor portfolio	7. Supplier processes	Tactical	SAP SRM	Strategic purchasing & sourcing
	Consolidate IT, defense Telecom, and force deployment network equipment and facilities	3. Technology processes	Operational	SAP NetWeaver	Information integration & application platform
	Implement integrated applications across orga- nizational boundaries	3. Technology processes	Strategic	SAP NetWeaver	Information integration & application platform
	Rationalize IT application portfolio	3. Technology processes	Operational	SAP NetWeaver	Information integration & application platform

Table 11.3 Examples of Defining Performance and Value Drivers (Cont.)

CSFs	KPIs	BPM Key Focus	Business Model Level	SAP	SAP Level 2
	Improve focus on military employee retention	4. Organizational processes	Operational	SAP ERP	Human capital management
	Improve HR practices	4. Organizational processes	Operational	SAP ERP	Human capital management

Table 11.3 Examples of Defining Performance and Value Drivers (Cont.)

A fully operational BPM center of expertise can report on these targets and provide corporate leaders with timely and reliable information on how well, or bad, the organization is performing. Logically, the BPM task force or BPM CoE can also evaluate the process intelligence picture and advise on where to direct management awareness or allocate investments.

The concept of value-based management may be almost as challenging to introduce in an organization as BPM, but it might be possible to assist the introduction of both by explaining the link between them. Thus, both concepts may be easier to sell if the message that management of values and management of processes go hand-in-hand is communicated widely.

11.2.5 BPM and Core Business

The VDF that will facilitate the connection between core business and BPM is usually not given enough attention. It has not really been given a proper name yet. A term like *balancing* has been suggested, for example, ensuring that purpose and performance of intraorganization activities can be managed in a way that makes it possible to deliver the end product to a customer at a price that can compete on the market and delivers as much profit to the organization as possible.

Lessons Learned

As described earlier, process optimization and innovation projects anchored in a functional business area risk losing the cross-organization perspective and may result in suboptimization. We learned that it is hard for BPM promoters to alert the Danish Armed Forces management to these risks because it is hard to change business traditions and convince decision makers of the need for a new approach. In particular, it is hard to sell the need for centrally introduced BPM, with its new terminology and methodology, when all process initiatives so far have been functional and are perceived as successful. If, in addition, the organization is being run on strict budgets allocated only to functional business units, funding for cross-functional projects will also be difficult to achieve.

Another well-known challenge for BPM experts is to eliminate the misconception that BPM is an IT issue. Often the need for process optimization is allocated for the IT division to handle, or maybe the perception that IT resources are limited simply becomes a comfortable excuse for not running optimal processes in the business units. The business foundation proposed repeatedly in this chapter through value drivers is critical for successful implementation of BPM and the underlying processes.

Whereas reluctance in the organization, for the above reasons, may slow down progress in establishing BPM in its own right, the growing awareness of the value of process optimization can be used to get support and funding for the intended first ice-breaking cross-functional BPM initiation project. Those people already involved in process work in the organization, typically persons with some IT tasks in their job descriptions, should be given the opportunity to contribute to the project in some way. They will eventually function as important ambassadors for the process approach in their own units. The dialog facilitated by the first initiation project is vital, because it puts the concept of cross-functional BPM on the map and prepares the grounds for the acceptance of the balancing VDF between BPM and core business.

Balancing VDF

When the appropriate BPM structure has been established in an organization, and the process architecture has been modeled and documented, monitoring of processes can take place. The organization has now moved an important step up its maturity ladder. Transparency of processes and understanding of BPM increases, and as the organization matures, the conflict of interest between core business and BPM fades. Balance of interests slowly develops, and actors in core business realize what's in it for them in relation to BPM.

The crucial next step is to put proper BPM into action and, with very careful timing, to identify process owners. Of course, different kinds of people will be involved in managing a particular process, but only one person should hold the status of a process owner, the most senior person involved in the BPM organization and ideally a management board member. When the process owner and the BPM CoE is in place, real BPM can function.

Balancing indicates, of course, that input is required from both sides of the pivot point. For instance, monitoring KPIs and PPIs and interpreting these should be done in close cooperation. Identification of possible interventions to remedy shortfalls in a process should also be done in a dialog between the BPM CoE and representatives from functional business areas.

When it comes to identifying new process improvement projects, however, decisions on the project mandate should not be decided within this Balancing VDF. The good ideas flowing from joint monitoring and analysis must be presented to the process owners, who raise the issues at the executive level. In the management board, where ideally, all process owners have a seat, the portfolio of development initiatives should be decided. Thus, as a result of the BPM work, new strategic development programs and projects will be launched, and the related continuous improvement will take place with extensive support from the BPM CoE.

If specific needs for process optimization should be identified locally or within functional areas, for instance as a lean initiative, the involvement of the BPM CoE will ensure coordination and will ensure that the focus of the initiative corresponds to the complete process architecture of the organization and that all relevant aspects are communicated to the process owner and other interested parties.

The BPM CoE generally acts as a sort of secretariat for the process owners and provides them with the services their role requires. With senior line managers as process owners and a BPM structure in place, a process-mature organization has a good opportunity to keep the balance.

11.2.6 Danish Armed Forces BPM and Technology Delivery

The VDF between the spheres of BPM and technology delivery is automation. Usually, when talking about processes, that will mean delivery of IT and, in particular, ERP systems.

We also learned that models are good for communicating with upper management and with line managers and, as described in Part I, Chapter 1, that business models are vital in linking strategies and mapping the business competencies.

To ensure the optimal reference model for BPM, an additional business process model and process architecture are needed. This business process model will assist process owners in their work at the top level and at the same time, through the logical breakdown, the operational awareness of processes. Thus, it serves many purposes of process management inside the CoE and in addition, being a visual language, it is the most powerful tool when for the definition and communication of work regulations, the development of end-user manuals, and so on.

The business model and the business process model complement each other, and together they provide a very central reference basis for both management and wider communication. Even for automation of the process architecture, the business model may assist BPM in finding keys to the simplification, standardization, and development of new process flows, and BPM may inspire innovation when it is implemented — innovation understood in the terms of optimal use of resources and capacities and thereby the competencies of the business.

However, for the purpose of establishing the optimal process automation and configuration of an SAP ERP system, it is the business process architecture that does the job.

Lessons Learned

As mentioned earlier, process management has traditionally been closely linked to IT, and this perception is still prevalent outside the BPM sphere. When talking about the automation VDF, the discussion about process management typically triggers an initial power struggle about who is in the lead: BPM or IT (see Figure 11.16).

No doubt, business comes before any IT agendas, but because BPM thinking to a very large extent is the result of the development of ERP and the training of process competencies within IT, the conflict is not difficult to understand.

The solution to this is, throughout the maturity stages, to facilitate careful interaction in the automation VDF and involve competent BPM-interested resources throughout the organization, including IT. When a proper BPM structure is eventually established, the distinct role of technology expertise should be reassessed. Because the usual estimation that only about 20 to 25% of a business process can be automated probably holds true, there is no doubt that further ERP development should be controlled by strategic development programs supported by the BPM CoE.

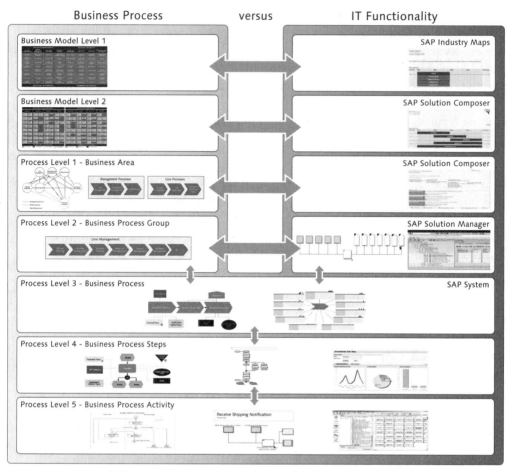

Figure 11.16 Differences Between a Process (Business)-Centric Perspective and an IT-Centric Perspective (von Rosing, 2009. "Business Value Management")

How Others Can Apply the Danish Armed Forces Automation Value Driver Field

The documentation of any IT system should be linked to the business process model with all of the different process levels, systematically broken down to the lowest level. The synchronization of, for example, SAP Solution Manager with a BPMS such as ARIS only makes sense if the modeling is correct. The prospect of achieving generic user instructions or automated testing may be a dream in the earlier BPM stages, but is should not be ignored.

The organization must have a production version of its process model and a setup for process model controlling that can ensure that the integrity of the full process architecture rests with the BPM CoE. The standards for modeling the top three or four levels should be decided in a dialog in the automation VDF, but the requirements of BPM should come first. Meeting the needs of the lower process levels rests with IT only. Logically, the role of a custodian for the BPMS should also rest with IT.

To ensure the continuous maintenance of the process architecture, a sort of permanent modeling board or a BPMS task force is probably needed. This would also ensure IT experts' contribution to business process improvement initiatives and generally facilitate the dialog in the automation VDF.

11.2.7 Terminology and Conventions

Because of the loose interpretation of BPM as a concept, an organization trying to make the move toward BPM will immediately recognize that the establishment of a precise in-house terminology and a coherent methodology is of urgent necessity. How could a business case for BPM possibly be presented in a way that appears sound to not just the convinced enthusiasts, but also to senior managers, if a common language is not in place? The text below suggests how to arrange some of the typical issues.

Danish Armed Forces Process Levels

The most essential terminology to standardize is that of process levels if process models are to be compatible. The term *business process* is very general and is widely used, but at the same time it generates different associations, and the dialog between new BPM advocates and other members of the organization is doomed to be unproductive if the understanding of the granularity and purpose of the various levels are not common.

Different definitions of levels exist, but a typical approach (see Figure 11.17) includes five or six levels, where the main processes of the organization at the top level (level 1) are broken down systematically to the extent that seems reasonable for the particular process.

With reference to the value driver model, such a breakdown makes sense because it supports the logic of the identified business spheres and VDFs. Process level 1, the business area processes, ensures that the reference to the organization's business model remains intact when it is interpreted from a process view.

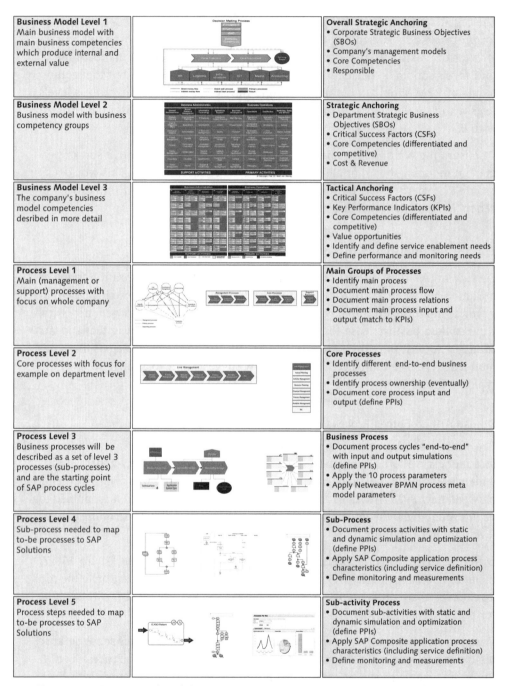

Business Model Level 1 Main business model with main business competencies which produce internal and external value		**Overall Strategic Anchoring** • Corporate Strategic Business Objectives (SBOs) • Company's management models • Core Competencies • Responsible
Business Model Level 2 Business model with business competency groups		**Strategic Anchoring** • Department Strategic Business Objectives (SBOs) • Critical Success Factors (CSFs) • Core Competencies (differentiated and competitive) • Cost & Revenue
Business Model Level 3 The company's business model competencies desribed in more detail		**Tactical Anchoring** • Critical Success Factors (CSFs) • Key Performance Indicators (KPIs) • Core Competencies (differentiated and competitive) • Value opportunities • Identify and define service enablement needs • Define performance and monitoring needs
Process Level 1 Main (management or support) processes with focus on whole company		**Main Groups of Processes** • Identify main process • Document main process flow • Document main process relations • Document main process input and output (match to KPIs)
Process Level 2 Core processes with focus for example on department level		**Core Processes** • Identify different end-to-end business processes • Identify process ownership (eventually) • Document core process input and output (define PPIs)
Process Level 3 Business processes will be described as a set of level 3 processes (sub-processes) and are the starting point of SAP process cycles		**Business Process** • Document process cycles "end-to-end" with input and output simulations (define PPIs) • Apply the 10 process parameters • Apply Netweaver BPMN process meta model parameters
Process Level 4 Sub-process needed to map to-be processes to SAP Solutions		**Sub-Process** • Document process activities with static and dynamic simulation and optimization (define PPIs) • Apply SAP Composite application process characteristics (including service definition) • Define monitoring and measurements
Process Level 5 Process steps needed to map to-be processes to SAP Solutions		**Sub-activity Process** • Document sub-activities with static and dynamic simulation and optimization (define PPIs) • Apply SAP Composite application process characteristics (including service definition) • Define monitoring and measurements

Figure 11.17 Process Levels and the Main Content (von Rosing, 2009. "Business Value Management")

Process level 2, the actual business processes, should be an identification of relevant processes, grouped within management, production, and support processes and given a clear relation to one of the main processes. The number of processes would most likely be 70 to 80, and it will be at this level that process ownership should be identified and overall performance indicators assigned. Business architecture at this level will support the value management VDF.

Process level 3 represents the value chain of subprocesses within the business process, a flow from start to end, with the possibility of assigning all relevant information, including PPIs, as objects in the BPMS. The properly developed flow description, based on consultations between interested parties, becomes the reference for managing, assessing, and reporting on the business processes. At this level, subprocesses all have a reference to a primary level 2 process, but at the same time subprocesses will also reoccur in different process flows. Visualizing these occurrences contributes to breaking up the traditional functional silo approach in the organization and facilitates the balancing VDF.

Process level 4 breaks down a subprocess into an end-to-end activity flow. If the subprocess is to be automated by the SAP functionality, activities in the process flow can be linked to, for example, a transaction code in different SAP applications. The link between business and IT is then created, and the core issue of automation VDF is put in play.

Synchronization of a BPMS and SAP Solution Manager can take place, and documentation at lower levels will also have a clear reference.

Process level 5 is a description of the steps in the activities, and in the SAP system the customization can in theory be documented. Again, this fits into the value driver model's identification of the sphere of technology delivery.

Lessons Learned

Because BPM is new to most people and the terminology is not always agreed upon, process champions should be careful to control the release of new definitions and only use terminology that is required in a certain context and that reflects the maturity of the organization.

The literature often stresses the importance of process owners, but some concern should be raised in relation to timing. Thus, the process ownership should not be allocated before the role can be given any useful practical content. If fancy titles and terminology are being used to excess at an early stage when the organization is immature and the content is purely academic, the terms will be worn out before they have come into practical use. And this will undermine a good case for BPM.

11.2.8 Technology Delivery

Though the technology delivery sphere is wider than mere IT-based deliveries, and making best use of, for example, a new sort of forklift is basically the same issue as the best use of an IT application, the focus will be on IT in this context.

Establishing the Competencies

The need to clarify the roles and set up the right structure for handling the interface with BPM has been covered. In light of the latest developments in SAP and BPMS, the IT department's role in making automation work is bound to be a demanding one. Knowledge of BPMS, IT architecture, customizations in the SAP system, and updated information about future releases of functionality will be in high demand. Building up the necessary competencies will probably be a serious challenge for the business sphere of technology and IT.

To ensure that the required services can be delivered to the BPM CoE or initiated programs and projects, a more focused governance setup in the technology management VDF is likely to be required.

Improving Delivery of Services

The functional IT area in the organization will produce the required IT solutions to the core business and support the day-to-day operation of the systems. In addition to these services, IT should also feed valuable information about state-of-the-art technological options into the rest of the organization. This way, IT contributes to keeping companies on the right track, technologically. While acknowledging its special status as a high-tech business unit, it must be accepted that IT basically remains a supporting service delivering the capacities needed in core business, just like other functional supporting branches.

Lessons Learned

Before establishing BPM and setting up a structure for process optimization in an organization, the ideas for optimization of business processes are typically inspired by the awareness of new IT functionality. Typically, those involved in running and developing the SAP system, whether in the IT department or in core business, will regularly promote ideas of using a specific functionality to optimize processes. As good as these ideas might sound, it also results in narrow project mandates, and projects established on this background will eventually focus on ways to use a tool, for example, the SAP Project System module, rather than improving a proper business process such as resource planning.

Technology Management VDF

An optimized approach to managing IT that reflects the introduction of BPM and observes the ideas of the value driver model could be a well-trimmed business process — the process development of production capacity.

This business process running within the technology management VDF will include stages in the SAP system implementation, lifecycle management, upgrades, training, and so on, but the customization of the SAP system will not be part of it, because this will be dealt with in the automation VDF linking the technology delivery and BPM spheres.

The technology management VDF will adjust the IT management organization accordingly and probably address more attention to the overall IT architecture and upgrade of infrastructure, rather than generate new development projects. This change will complement the work in the BPM sphere and increase the chance that IT will actually end up supporting business processes.

It will not be left for the IT department to be in charge of the complete IT infrastructure autonomously and just feed solutions into to the core business, but IT as a capacity will be developed in cooperation between core business and IT delivery.

11.2.9 Implementation of Change

Implementation of change in the organization includes a number of different perspectives, and they all require careful planning. Field studies have shown that if a large group of employees finds it necessary to conduct changes, then the organization itself will react more proactively during the implementation.

Changes are a way to replace less efficient parts of the production process with more efficient ones. It could be the replacement of a technology solution or the introduction of a more efficient process structure. These changes influence the power relationship between employees. Some will lose, and some will win. The winner will move faster through the transition process to the new structure, whereas the looser may have a negative effect on the work in the new structure. Successful change therefore requires the establishment of a win-win situation for everybody.

Another failure risk arises when core business implements new technology. There are many situations in which the top managers have misunderstood their responsibility for a dynamic change process. Usually, they make a learning program, where employees learn to use the technology, and then business governance expects a fast payback. Normally, they will have to wait quite a long time before the payback, due to the challenges encountered within core business and business process management

The real changes depend on the employees' level of willingness to accept changes.

The challenge in continuous improvement is to:

▶ Make the changes fast

▶ Involve all employees when you start the project

▶ Try to maintain the internal power structure, or you might lose good employees

▶ Build up a win-win situation for the employees

▶ Reallocate employees if it's possible, or try to help them get a new job

Danish Armed Forces Development Management Methodologies

Large development projects like the ones conducted in defense organizations and elsewhere are typically conducted as large IT and SAP projects. Typically, they are just that — IT projects — and not business development projects. Even projects perfectly completed according to methodologies such as PRINCE2 often turn out to have far less effect on business than expected. This reflects the fact that the IT sphere in an organization is simply just another functional silo in the organization, but it also illustrates that all significant modifications to the design or configuration of an SAP system need a strategic rather than a functional anchor.

If BPM is introduced, such a strategic anchor is provided. As illustrated by the value driver model, it becomes clear that IT ultimately serves the corporate management through BPM, making use of the value management and automation VDFs.

This situation also requires new methodological approaches, such as program management and portfolio management. Highly professional project management is not enough.

The experience in the Danish Defense is that the initiative to introduce BPM into the organization would be a good example of a strategic program. The medium-term perspective of a program fits nicely with the organization's need for time to mature the organization and prepare for BPM, and the projects within such a program will contribute to the gradual development of the organization.

11.2.10 Conclusion

In the previous sections of this chapter we have gone through the value drivers seen from the point of view of a defense organization. The value driver model has been promoted as the way to not just understand various business issues, but also to identify the process opportunities for improvement and innovation in an organization.

The value driver model thereby gives an organization a unique approach to identify, create, and realize the goals and results. For the most part, this is in the main area of cost-efficient and effective processes and innovate and competitive process. Once in place, BPM fulfills its purpose through interaction with all of the other business spheres in the value driver model: business governance, core business, and technology delivery.

In a perfect world value drivers will be balanced, BPM can monitor performance, and value-based management can assist executives keep the perspective of the core business wider than just the functional silos. The executives will also, through BPM, be able to ensure that the professionally managed IT capacities result in optimal support of business processes through the automation VDF. The continuous improvement of business processes will, on a smaller scale, be handled by BPM as day-to-day business, whereas larger process changes, like all other business changes, will be handled through development programs within the fields of corporate continuous improvement.

Ultimately, a situation is established in which continuously improved business governance can function, assisted by BPM and probably also by the value driver model.

All together this should help convince corporate management that BPM has a very good business case. In this exciting journey, we have encountered the following benefits from implementing and using BPM:

- ▶ Improved visibility of vital processes and thereby information, enabling enhanced operational effectiveness
- ▶ Establishment of an organization-wide process methodology and a framework to identify the different value drivers, creating the possibility to demonstrate

value planning, creation, and realization of the different defense lines of business

▶ Improved operational effectiveness through the integration of operational processes that facilitate shared situation awareness

▶ Potential savings of millions across the organization, derived from process integration efficiencies

"Action is eloquence."
– William Shakespeare

12 Conclusion

In this part of the book you have seen how some SAP customers are leveraging a BPM approach, including the related BPM tools and methodology frameworks to innovate and transform business processes into seamless end-to-end operations.

This process of interconnecting important disciplines is fundamental to creating performance and value, which we have already mentioned. The aspects of business architecture, with the connected process and value architecture, are one of the most vital parts in today's organizations to ensure business-IT alignment. While defining value drivers are without doubt the answer to the missing value realization that many organizations are looking for, they are also the key to bring the needed strategic link to the process and application lifecycle.

In Part II we have presented numerous examples of industry-specific and cross-industry processes, along with details of the methodology that was followed, the technical implementation that was rolled out, and challenges that the customers dealt with in the implementation. Each of the stories is unique, not only in the business problems they are solving, but also in exemplifying one or more aspects of classic BPM implementation. The stories in Chapter 7 from INVISTA, Ericsson, and SAP IT illustrate how to implement business processes for various information management applications. These are great examples of first projects for a burgeoning BPM competency center to cut its teeth on. The use cases from Chapter 8 provide excellent examples of companies using BPM to implement processes that cover white spaces between a company's enterprise systems. Especially notable in Chapter 8 is the case from Siemens IT solutions, which shows an example of a company providing an ISV solution that is based on BPM tools. Additionally, the RS Components use case shows that you can apply SOA-based BPM implementations against even non-SOA SAP legacy versions.

The latter chapters show more profound transformations using BPM. The case from KAESER KOMPRESSOREN shows the transformation of a company's entire customer service processes, incorporating some of the smaller projects described earlier, such as master data governance. Chapter 10 presents more opportunities that BPM experts at SAP and partners have suggested as great applications for BPM.

Finally, Chapter 11 shows in detail two examples of preparing for a major business innovation and transformation in terms of using one's processes: to build a business architecture at Hospira, and prioritizing value drivers at Danish Defense. Included in the unique knowledge we covered in these two cases is information on how the projects have applied BPM as a part of their strategic, tactical, and operational business initiatives. Initiatives that focus on identifying performance and value potential and then creating them, either with effectiveness, efficiency, and/or innovation process approaches. Our hope is that by exploring the different use cases in Part II, you will find inspiration to start exploring your own opportunities for innovation and transformation. To support this transformation, in Part III you will explore the guide that will enable you to apply BPM in all of its aspects in your SAP-centric business and IT environment. The chapters included in Part III will explain how BPM and standard software work together, how to prepare your company for the project, and how to put implementation methodology, implementation technology, process-based implementation content, governance, skills, and the philosophy behind BPM into action.

PART III
BPM Anatomy for
Implementations

Part III of this book is the guide that will enable you to apply business process management (BPM) in all its aspects in your SAP-centric business and IT environment. The chapters are structured according to the new process-based methodologies and governance frameworks (Chapter 13), the BPM technologies that will support the implementation (Chapter 15), and the new skills and mindset (Chapter 16). Process-based implementation content (Chapter 15) and enablement, including communities where you can get additional information (Chapter 16), are also covered in detail. Figure 1 gives you an overview of Part III's contents.

Skills and Mindset	Process Orchestration by leveraging process based pre-built assets
Methodology and Governance	ASAP 7 provides a proven, comprehensive, repeatable and rich implementation methodology to streamline projects
BPM Tools	Solution Manager, BPM Technology (Business to Model and Modeling to execution)
Process Based Implementation Content	Content Packages: Business add-ons to ASAP, Rapid Deployment Solutions and Content Component: Solution Manager content, Best Practice....
Training	Education: ASA380, TBPM10, TBPM20, SOA200, EA100, VD100, OCM100, TEC001... Associate and Professional Certifications: Project Management, BPX, EA, TEC....
Community	http://www.sdn.sap.com/irj/sdn http://www.sdn.sap.com/irj/bpx http://service.sap.com/asap http://ecohub.sdn.sap.com/ SAP Modeling Handbook External BPM Webinars https://www.sdn.sap.com/irj/bpx/starterkit-for-bpm http://www.sdn.sap.com/irj/sdn/soa-kit

Figure 1 Applying BPM in your SAP-Centric Business and IT Environment

"Anyone who has never made a mistake has never tried anything new."
– Albert Einstein

13 Methodology and Governance

Ann Rosenberg, Jan Musil, Mark von Rosing, Peter Datsichin, Girish Betadpur, Henrik V. Scheel, Robert Eijpe, Caspar Laar, Marco-Antonio Morales, Ingo Pfeiffer, Volker von Gloeden, Rogan Morrison, Sven Roeleven, Alexander Friedrich Holzmann, Klaus Skov Kristensen, Raimar Hoeliner, Jens Broetzmann, Michal Harezlak

In this section of Part III we will introduce in detail the new methodology and governance framework that we recommended you use in your SAP-centric business and IT environment when executing SAP implementations. We will first explore some feedback gathered through a survey (see Section 13.1) that has helped shape the new version of the ASAP methodology, business add-ons to ASAP including the BPM and service-oriented architecture (SOA) kit, an add-on to ASAP from a BPM and SOA perspective. Second, we will introduce in more details the methodology framework for how to connect a strategy to a business model and a business model to operational business processes (see Section 13.2), which was introduced in Part I. This is the starting point for any business process change or creation of new business processes you execute within your operational business process environment. Finally, we will go into the details of the new ASAP 7 methodology framework, which brings together the previous ASAP methodology, Business Intelligence Solution Accelerator (BISA) methodology, value delivery principles, business process management methodology, and service-oriented architecture methodology (see Section 13.3). There are two highly visible components of the new ASAP Methodology for Implementation 7 framework that will be introduced. The first component is the ASAP Roadmap 7 core methodology, which covers four lifecycles: business process, application, project, and value.

The second visible component is the business add-ons to ASAP that extends the ASAP Roadmap with modular business implementation content. The business add-ons provide proven implementation content for implementation of various industries and cross industry solution packages and other related areas such as agile methodology, BPM, SOA, value management, and enterprise architecture (EA) governance and strategy frameworks. In Section 13.4, we will cover the business add-ons to ASAP that deliver methodology and governance, and we will describe the business add-ons to ASAP that deliver implementation content and small BPM- and SOA-based implementation content packages in Section 15.1.

13.1 SOA Survey

The methodology for accelerated transformation to service-oriented architecture (SOA), rolled out by SAP in 2008, addresses the typical activities required to transform an organization's IT landscape to one that is based on enterprise services using the SAP business process platform as a key building block. The methodology was intended to help customers streamline their SOA adoption activities both at an enterprise level where key topics such as strategy, governance and infrastructure were addressed and at the project level where topics related to planning, building, and running a SOA-based composite application are addressed.

The *plan* and *run* phases of the methodology are relevant not just in the context of an SOA transformation but also for all other solutions in general and are independent of the technical implementation option chosen for the solution. The *build* phase of the methodology forms the heart of the SOA methodology and describes the typical activities involved in implementing user-centric composite applications on top of a business process platform.

13.1.1 Feedback Survey for the Methodology

One and a half years after the release of the SOA methodology, a survey was conducted to gain a better understanding of how the accelerated SOA methodology was being used. Although the initial scope of the survey was to gather feedback on the methodology, the scope was later extended to gather general SOA implementation project experiences with an intention to capture any trends in such SOA projects.

The feedback gathered through the survey has helped shaped the new version of the ASAP methodology and business add-ons to ASAP that deliver BPM/SOA prepackaged implementation content packages and agile methodology including the SOA KIT, an add-on to ASAP that we will describe in detail in the following chapters.

The target audience of the survey was SAP consultants who had been involved in one or more SOA related projects since the accelerated SOA methodology was released (2008). The survey included SOA projects from across different continents including Europe, North America, and Australasia.

Because the plan and run phases of the accelerated SOA methodology basically refer to two other generic methodologies, the survey focused on the *build* phase, which is SOA-centric and covers the main aspects of implementing a service-based composite application. The main areas covered by the questions included the following components:

▸ **General information about the project**
This included details such as the motivation behind the project and the budget and time scope for the project.

▸ **Application of the accelerated SOA methodology**
Here, the idea was to understand the extent to which the methodology was being applied in practice.

▸ **Observations and trends in SOA implementation projects**
Using the five subphases of the build phase, various details of a typical SOA implementation project were gathered to analyze the trends currently evolving in SOA projects.

▸ **Suggestions for improving the accelerated SOA methodology**
General feedback on how to improve the methodology so that it can better support SOA implementation projects was captured.

13.1.2   Key Observations and Trends in SOA Projects

The general feedback from the survey highlighted the need for and the importance of a methodology for executing SOA projects. Consultants appreciated the project-management focus of the accelerated SOA methodology and the availability of a list of artifacts that typically need to be produced during the different phases of an implementation project.

A seamless transition across the plan, build, and run phases and the need for more accelerators were highlighted as areas of improvement for the methodology. Both these topics are addressed with the new ASAP methodology, released in the first quarter of 2010, in which the accelerated transformation to SOA methodology and the BPM methodology are integrated. The new ASAP methodology along with its ASAP business add-ons provides more accelerators to ease the implementation of SOA/BPM projects.

Project Management and Cost Estimation

One of the challenges of SOA-based implementation projects is the estimation of the effort involved in developing the composite application. There are three important aspects that set apart an SOA implementation project from a traditional SAP implementation project:

1. **New technology**
   Developing an SOA-based composite application involves deploying and using a new set of tools such as the Enterprise Services Repository (ES Repository), Services Registry, SAP NetWeaver Composition Environment (CE) with BPM/BRM, SAP NetWeaver Administrator, SAP NetWeaver Development Infrastructure (NWDI), Web Dynpro and SAP NetWeaver Visual Composer, which most project managers are not familiar with.

2. **Time constraints**
   In contrast to a standard SAP implementation project that runs for a few months to a couple of years, the time line for implementing composite applications is relatively short. The first SOA projects a customer undertakes are usually pilot projects through which the organization seeks to evaluate the potential of an SOA-based solution.

3. **Configuration vs. development**
   The focus in SOA projects is less on configuration and more on code creation, which involves a completely different set of skills from the project team.

The main metric used in the surveyed projects to arrive at reasonably accurate cost estimates for implementing SOA-based applications is the number of user interface screens and the number of service interfaces that would have to be developed in the project. These two measure the core of a composite application and can be time and resource intensive. Hence, an accurate calculation of these two numbers generally increases the accuracy of the project estimation as a whole.

A key takeaway of this observation is that it is important to put some effort upfront in SOA implementation projects by writing down an architectural blueprint containing detailed specifications of service interfaces and user interface elements.

Tailor-Made Governance

SAP recommends adopting the process integration content (PIC) governance model to ensure a harmonized enterprise model and increase the reusability of enterprise services inside the organization. However, for many organizations it is not clear if they need to adopt the complete PIC process upfront or if they can bypass the governance topic to have a quick start on services.

SAP established the PIC governance process for the creation and definition of enterprise services. In this governance model, a service definition goes through a review process consisting of four phases (PIC-0, PIC-1, GDT-PIC, PIC-3) before the service definition is introduced into the Enterprise Service Repository (ES Repository). The main goals of this governance model are to ensure:

► Reusability of services wherever possible

► Consistency of semantics across solutions

► Identical modeling and documentation rules

► High-quality content for SAP's business process platform

SAP ensures that its enterprise services adhere to a common set of service modeling and implementation guidelines and subjects all service development to the above mentioned specialized review process with its quality gates. Such a rigorous governance process is essential to maintain the consistency of semantics across SAP's business suite and to ensure the reusability of services by thousands of SAP customers.

However, not all organizations develop thousands of services like SAP does, nor do they have the same service-reusability and consistency ambitions as SAP.

The survey revealed that most organizations base their service interface-definition governance model on the reusability of the services. Because organizations usually start off on pilot projects or built services for specialized composite applications, reusability and harmonization are not the main concerns. The focus is on ramping up the IT personnel on the new tools and technologies, integrating the tools with established IT processes and ensuring an early return on SOA related investments.

Nevertheless, these organizations ensure that a certain amount of technical governance is in place before embarking on their SOA journey. This technical governance includes:

► Naming conventions for software components defined in the ES Repository

► Naming conventions for the service interfaces, business objects and data types in accordance with SAP's PIC governance model

► Folder structure within a software component in the ES Repository for the service interface objects

► Namespaces in the ES Repository to suitably partition the services that different departments within the organization may create

This lean governance provides the agility for customers to start off on their SOA journey with minimal bureaucracy and speedily gain an understanding of the new concepts.

Once the SOA concepts are reasonably understood within the organization, the governance model can be extended depending on the requirements for reusability of services and harmonization.

SOA Tool Usage

The accelerated transformation to SOA methodology addresses two aspects of service-oriented architecture:

► **Service provisioning**
Organizations can build their own services in addition to the enterprise services provided by SAP's business process platform

► **Service consumption**
Organizations can build innovative processes by extending the core processes delivered by the business suite and using the services from the business suite. SAP NetWeaver Composition Environment (CE) offers a variety of tools to consume services and build composite applications.

Through the survey, it was observed that most organizations take a fairly similar approach to service provisioning and consumption and closely reflect the recommendations from SAP.

► Services are modeled in SAP's Enterprise Services Repository (ES Repository) which is either installed on an SAP NetWeaver CE server or on an SAP NetWeaver Process Integration (PI) server.

► A single central ES Repository is usually deployed across the entire organization and all services are modeled in this ES Repository independent of whether the services are implemented in Java or ABAP or any other programming language.

► Nevertheless, most organizations typically implement their service interfaces in ABAP on the appropriate backend system. This is nearly unambiguous for customers using one or more SAP solutions.

- Services are generally consumed in Web Dynpro Java-based user interfaces (UIs) that are part of a composite application.

- The main UIs of a composite application are generally built with Web Dynpro Java. SAP NetWeaver Visual Composer is the preferred UI technology for charts through which reporting data is to be presented. A combination of Web Dynpro Java and SAP NetWeaver Visual Composer UIs is normal for many composite applications.

- The adoption of SAP NetWeaver Business Process Management (BPM) has been on the rise and more services are being consumed in processes orchestrated with SAP NetWeaver BPM.

- The usage of Adobe Document Services (ADS) to provide offline form support is also increasing in composite applications.

- Development of composite applications is usually supported through an SAP NetWeaver Development Infrastructure (NWDI). The number of organizations adopting change and transport system (CTS+) for combined transports is increasing.

The above observations can act as a guideline for organizations which are currently in the process of rolling out SOA.

Upskilling the Business and IT Organizations

The previous section reveals the new tools that will probably be making their first appearance in an organization's IT landscape. A reasonable understanding of the composition stack and capabilities provided is essential both for the business and for IT before the organization embarks on its SOA journey.

Business professionals need to understand how best they can leverage on the new tools to deliver on business process innovation. The IT professionals need to have adequate experience with the new tools to easily execute SOA projects.

Most organizations piloting SOA have used SAP's *Enterprise SOA Experience Workshop* to introduce their business/IT personnel to SAP's SOA platform. The experience workshop provides a good overview of the tools and takes the workshop participants through a complete process implementation lifecycle.

It was also observed via the survey that once a basic understanding of the various tools is obtained through the Enterprise SOA Experience Workshop, IT personnel take specialized training (such as courses on Web Dynpro, etc.) to gain additional skills before starting their SOA projects.

In addition, an experienced SOA coach usually supports pilot SOA projects to mitigate the risks involved in trying out a new technology platform.

Agile Development

Many organizations use some form of agile development methodology, such as Scrum, for their SOA implementation projects. The complete application of a standard plan-based methodology is considered unfeasible due to the severe time and budget constraints typical of these SOA projects and the lack of well-defined requirements at the onset of the project. Requirements seem to evolve because the capabilities of the new SOA products are not equally understood by all members of the organization.

SOA implementation projects involve composite applications that are basically extensions to the core business processes. Although business-critical processes can also be realized with the SOA-based composites, early SOA projects tend to address supporting business processes only. One of the main expectations for SOA is the ability to rapidly translate business innovation into an IT solution.

The success of such SOA implementation projects is measured both by the quality of the implementation and by the rapidity with which these process extensions can be realized. Hence, organizations find that an agile methodology like Scrum is better suited for SOA-related implementation projects than a methodology based on the waterfall approach.

The new ASAP methodology takes into account this choice of implementation methodologies by the customers and provides a business add-on to ASAP delivering agile methodology that can be applied to such time- and budget-constrained SOA implementation projects. However, an SAP implementation project should be a combination of both best practices and own practice, where different solution-building techniques such as composition, configuration, and so on are used, which is also why the SOA methodology has been incorporated into the new ASAP methodology core and business add-on to the ASAP framework.

Approaches to Service Definition

The end result of most SOA projects is a composite application that consumes enterprise services from the backend system. Hence, most organizations adhere to a top-down approach to service definition when developing user-centric composite applications. Starting with a business scenario, the data and functionality of the business applications are analyzed to find out the best possible way to bring this to the end users (for example, through user interface components in a work center). This directly leads to the definition of services that are needed from the underlying applications.

In integration scenarios where the service provisioning and consumption take place between two applications (A2A) or between two business units (B2B), service definitions are driven less by specific consumption scenarios and more by the need to keep services as generic as possible to minimize the number of public interfaces. Hence, in these cases, a bottom-up approach in which the services are defined independently of any particular business scenario is considered to be more practical.

IT Organizational Setup

Traditionally, two groups are generally seen in the IT organizations of SAP customers — the *development* group and the *Basis* group. The development group is well versed on the SAP applications and is involved in configuring and customizing the applications. The Basis group is concerned with the SAP application platform and services multiple development groups that may be working on different SAP solutions.

In this traditional setup, development tasks are clearly shared between these two groups, with the development group working on a "development" system in a typical three-system landscape (consisting of development, quality, and production) and the Basis group handling the transport of development artifacts from the development system to the quality and production systems. In scenarios involving data communication between two SAP systems and between an SAP system and an external system, the Basis group is generally responsible for maintaining the necessary technical connections.

With the deployment of a new set of tools in the organization's landscape, questions about responsibilities have to be addressed within the scope of these SOA projects. The survey indicated that the traditional split of responsibilities between the development and the Basis groups can be easily transferred over to the new world of SOA and composite applications.

Developers develop their services and composites on a development NetWeaver CE server. On this development system, it is the responsibility of the development group to configure their service interfaces and composites, for example, configuring the service groups consumed in a composite application.

Once the development is complete, the Basis group transports the service definitions and composites to additional systems along the stream, namely, the quality and production systems. On these systems, the Basis group takes over the responsibility to properly configure the service interfaces and composites based on the security and transport requirements of these systems.

These observations reveal that the scope of a pilot SOA project should not just be to gain an understanding of the SOA concepts and get to know the new tools, but to also address key application lifecycle management aspects such as formalization of organizational responsibilities. This ensures that the IT organization is well prepared to successfully deliver on subsequent SOA projects.

13.1.3 Summary

All of the findings from the SOA survey have been incorporated into the new ASAP methodology core and business add-on to the ASAP framework, the new SOA KIT, an add-on to ASAP and the Business Process Expert (BPX) associate, BPX professional, and associate Project Manager education curriculum, which we will discuss in detail within the following chapters. We will now introduce a methodology framework, which explains how to connect a strategy to a business model and a business model to operational business processes. This is a key link to identify the process improvement or process innovation you would like to execute in your SAP implementation.

13.2 How to Combine Business Modeling and Process Modeling

As defined in the Part I introduction, a simple business model is a framework or, in other words, the design setup for how to make money. A business model without its activities will, however, not perform. It is the connection between the business model and the company's activities, and thereby processes, that is the key to success. To deliver the right value to the right market segments, it is essential for the company to price the product right, focus on the right revenue sources, and position itself well in relation to suppliers, customers, rivals, potential new entrants, and competitors, a firm must perform the activities that underpin these positions. The extent to which a firm can attain and maintain profitable positions is a function of which activities and processes it chooses to perform, how it performs them, and when it performs them. Therefore, in this chapter we will explore how the business model and the processes connect and how you can identify, create, and realize value through this connection.

13.2.1 Business Model Innovation and Optimization

In creating and offering value to its customers to earn a profit, a firm usually has many activities and thereby processes to choose from. Which processes are chosen and how they are executed plays a major role in the positions the firm can attain and maintain. For example, to create and offer value to its customers and earn a profit, a PC manufacturer must choose which activities and processes it can perform. It can conduct extensive research and development (R&D) or none at all, it can manufacture its own products or outsource the activity and its connecting processes, it can target business customers or home users, it can sell its computers through the Internet using a build-to-order strategy or sell them through dealerships and its own retail stores, it can price its computers for outright sale or for lease, it can offer various types of after-sale service or none at all, and it can collect payments from customers well before paying suppliers or collect at about the same time that it pays.

Many PC manufacturers target both business customers and consumers, sell their products through the Internet rather than through dealerships, and usually collect payments before paying its suppliers for the components that go into the computers it has sold. These process choices, in connection with the chosen business model, play an important role in a PC manufacturer's profitability.

This example shows how the chosen business strategy and business model provide direction for the priorities, the attention, and from this, the focus put on the processes that are executed to achieve company performance.

13.2.2 How To Create Value in Connecting the Business Model and Processes

We just discussed how process choices in connection with the business model a company has chosen, play an important role in a company's profitability. The same principle applies to every company in every industry, and is proven by Apple's success in out-competing their industry peers by choosing another business model and applying it to their operational model. Apple Computer's business model of connecting the entire industry network in a new way transformed the entire value chain — and even created fundamentally new markets — by providing companies with access to a wide range of specialized competencies. The example of the Apple iPod, for which they collaborated with external specialists, applied Apple's business model to an operational model in which they took existing, off-the-shelf technologies — such as portable hard drives, liquid crystal displays, and rechargeable batteries — and Apple styling and design savvy and sold the new product as part of an integrated music download service.

In a few short months, the operational specialization of the business model allowed Apple to combine aspects of consumer electronics, media, and information technology to create something truly new. In the process, they showed how the operational specialization of the business model can radically change the ecosystems of entire industries. Today, a wide array of niche companies supply iPod users with ear buds, carrying cases, speakers, remote controls, and attachments for recording voices and transmitting music over radio frequencies. The ability to apply the business model to your operational model and thereby to all of your activities and processes is key for achieving process harmonization and standardization.

Process optimization, harmonization, and standardization reduce coordination costs and transaction hassles in an enterprise and between enterprise networks and market channels. These networks and channels tend to expand, creating new revenue opportunities as enterprises come together in a specialized economy to provide a complete value proposition. Apple had to collaborate with record labels and content owners to make iTunes, the iPod's service component, a reality. The company even had to cooperate with competitors such as Microsoft to support software and music downloads. This sort of collaboration of entire industry value chains is a typical aspect of business model specialization through an operational model. The stellar success of the iPod has shown that achieving such "operational model effects" can be well worth the work to combine your business model with its processes.

The result is a change in the way innovation, efficiency, and effectiveness are applied — not in an operational way as was done in the past. This method involves applying either TQM, BPR, LEAN, or Six Sigma and BPM approaches to process optimization and innovation. Since the 1990s, "business unit-optimized" silos have been steadily broken up as firms opportunistically consolidate their business competencies and processes. These efforts have, as discussed in the first chapter, yielded dramatic operational benefits for many companies:

- ▶ Eliminating non-value-added activities
- ▶ Consolidating duplicate activities to reduce cost, waste, and quality mistakes
- ▶ Automating manual activities to boost speed, volume, and time to market
- ▶ Concentrating activities in service centers to achieve economies of scale

- ▶ Relocating activities to lower-cost centers, geographies, and or partners
- ▶ Outsourcing activities to lower-cost partners or companies
- ▶ Coordinating activities to reduce cycle times

The resulting "process-optimized and managed" business has allowed firms to operate more efficiently and effectively, thereby boosting coordination across the firm. With optimized processes, more people operate in cross-organizational teams, business units share technology costs and risks, and the effectiveness and efficiency of the processes improve.

Yet a business unit, department, or functional silo mentality often remains. Rigid organizational structures limit knowledge sharing and conceal opportunities to generate new return on investment. New SAP implementations are often inflexible, unscalable, and lagging behind the performance and value curve. Even worse, complexity and interconnection costs begin to grow as process designs, optimization, and management must accommodate the idiosyncrasies of different business units. This in a way shows the limits of process optimization/BPM. In realizing this and many other limitations of only taking a process approach, a more holistic and advanced value identification, creation, and realization approach is adapted within the SAP framework. This approach involves moving from only a process focus to a new concept: innovating and optimizing (effectiveness and efficiency) the enterprise on a business-model level and then applying the same approach within the boundaries and focus set by the business model to an operational model.

13.2.3 The Limitation of Having Only a Process Focus

There is no question that business process management principles and thereby process innovation and optimization are necessary and result in a lot of benefits. However, it is not a sufficient means for succeeding in today's marketplace. For all its appeal, a process-focused approach still leaves firms with complex, hard-wired processes. After initial gains, the law of diminishing returns begins to erode improvements in marginal benefits, and the cost of squeezing out remaining inefficiencies within the process office, process center of excellence (CoE), or business transformation office begins to grow. Worse, as processes are optimized internally, the costs of integrating activities across multiple processes may actually increase, a problem that is especially acute in large, complex organizations. Part of the issue is that traditional, process-based optimization can leave firms with the same activity optimized dissimilarly across many different processes. According to a global business study in 2009, the IBM Institute for Business Value revealed that even though process improvements and optimization create interconnections that reach to multiple business units, complexity increases, causing integration costs to rise as the function of a quadratic equation. Thus, as process improvements and optimization mature, this can end up increasing the complexity of the enterprise. The results of some process-based optimization include:

- Higher costs
- Less flexibility
- Slower time-to-market

Most SAP customers already know this and have already studied this, and many researchers argue the same findings that whereas activities across multiple processes increase, thereby being counterproductive and destroying value, all of these conclusions could in many ways be evidence that this occurs due to company size or industry complexity. In their research and publication "Simplify to Succeed," Shanker and Robinson revealed with empirical data that there is very little correlation between the size of a firm and return on equity. Some studies have even found a negative correlation, meaning that larger firms return less value for shareholders. Figure 13.1 illustrates an example of such a negative correlation.

Micro-cap	Small-cap	Mid-cap	Large-cap
12.7%	11.7%	11.3%	10.4%

Figure 13.1 Process Improvement and Maturation

At best, this suggests that the benefits of scale are far more elusive than most executives assume. At worst, it suggests that the traditional process optimization works, and the connection to IT systems of many large organizations has destroyed huge amounts of shareholder value. Either way, process-focused improvement and optimization in this context of SAP implementations falls well short of being a general panacea because it does not have a direct link to strategy, because as shown in Figure 13.2, linking your strategy to your processes is very difficult.

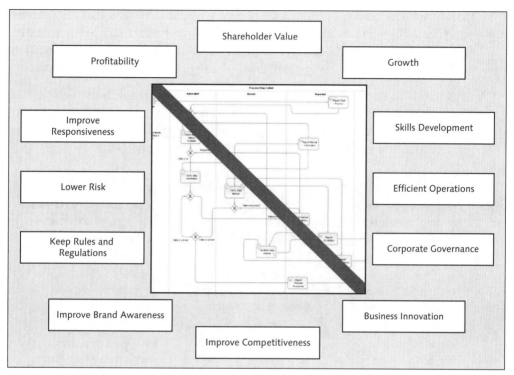

Figure 13.2 The Challenge of Linking Strategy to Processes (von Rosing, 2009. "Business Value Management")

Even if a company succeeded in connecting their strategic business objectives with their processes, the work it required to maintain this link would be very complex and expensive. Just look at the large media and entertainment companies that have worked hard over the past years to improve and optimize their sales and marketing processes with an aim toward selling television, radio, and billboard space more effectively.

While they were occupied, however, advertisers were busy changing the rules of the game. Demand is now growing for complete media packages that target consumers through multiple, coordinated channels for a single price. Ironically, process improvement and optimization has made the task of meeting this unanticipated shift in demand more difficult. These companies should avoid such miscues by taking a different approach. Instead of honing processes based on an established way of doing business, they should have looked at their business model and the action/reaction need to the market. Then they would have seen that they should fundamentally rebuild "customer targeting and reach" as a competency shared across the entire organization. Such business model improvement and optimization makes companies more responsive, flexible, and focused in the face of change.

This points to some of the same difficulties that we explored in the first part of the book related to the status of BPM and the challenges companies encounter. As elaborated in Table 13.1, companies face multiple challenges on all levels of the organization, for example, strategic, tactical, and operational.

Strategic	Tactical	Operational
Missing link between operational efforts and organizational strategy	Missing link between the chosen strategy and the business model competencies	Business competencies are not mapped to processes and activities
Lack of business model transformation and change	Lack of change due to missing link between business model and processes	Lack of tools to link process method and business model method
Lack of innovation on different business levels	Lack of innovation due to missing link between business model core and processes	Weakness in process methodology concerning how to incorporate core business competency innovation
Lack of business governance that incorporates more than business standards, regulations, and monitoring	Lack of business governance that incorporates the needed governance of business model and processes	Lack of BPM continuous improvement initiatives that incorporate business governance
Lack of corporation-wide metrics for business performance	Lack of corporate business performance metrics standards	Lack of BPM tools to support corporation-wide performance metrics
Missing business value realization	Missing method for business value realization	Missing tool to link value realization plans to value creation

Table 13.1 Status of BPM and the Challenges Companies Encounter (Kuhlmann and von Rosing, 2010. "Applying BPM Principles to SAP EAF")

13.2.4 The Holistic Approach – Creating Value by Connecting the Business Model to the Processes

As we have argued, process management by itself is not the "Holy Grail" in accomplishing a company strategic business objective. A process focus by itself can even lead to counterproductive results that do not contribute to the business objectives and strategy. In Part I, Chapters 1, 3, and 5 we argued that a firm's business model is or at least should be a reflection of its realized strategy because there should be a one-to-one mapping from strategy onto business models. Strategy and business models, though related, are nonetheless different concepts. As defined in the first section of this chapter, a business model is the direct result of strategy, but it is not strategy itself. The business model is where the strategy is executed, and it is therefore essential that there is a direct link between a business model and the chosen strategy.

Because business models are concerned with making money, and strategy is concerned with performance and value realization, the two should be highly related and interlinked, always starting from the strategy. The differences between the two start to emerge when you consider the key aspects of strategy. Figure 13.3 outlines the business model approach in three main phases [von Rosing and von Scheel].

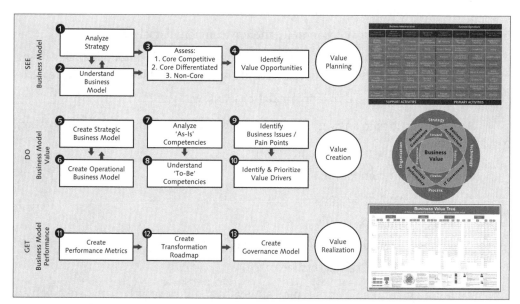

Figure 13.3 Business Model Approach to Connecting Strategy to Business Model and Business Model to Operational Model (Processes) (von Rosing, 2009. "Business Value Management")

1. **Phase 1: see phase**
   Identify core business competencies (value planning).

2. **Phase 2: do phase**
   Create operational model (value creation).

3. **Phase 2: get phase**
   Define transformational roadmap (value realization).

13.2.5 Business Model Approach to Connecting Strategy to Business Model and Business Model to Operational Model (Processes)

Value Planning – Identify Core Business Competencies

Differences have been identified between strategy and operational effectiveness. Strategy involves committing to undertake one set of actions rather than another and, in the process, creating a unique and valuable position that allows the firm to perform better than its competitors. Therefore, the first step in business modeling is to analyze the strategy.

To analyze the strategy, you can use an array of strategy tools such as:

▶ Mission, values, and vision (MVV) statements

▶ External competitive, economic, and environmental analyses

▶ Methodologies such as Michael Porter's five forces and competitive positioning framework, the resource-based view of strategy, and blue ocean strategies

▶ Scenario planning, dynamic simulations, and war-gaming

Six key questions to answer in such an analysis of the organization's strategy are:

▶ What business are we in, and why?

▶ Who are our competitors?

▶ How can we best compete?

▶ What are our chosen strategies?

▶ What are the main issues/challenges we face?

▶ What are the critical success factors?

Table 13.2 gives examples of typical strategies and the executives that are involved in the strategic business objectives (SBOs).

Strategy	Strategic Business Objective
Increase shareholder value – CEO	Increase revenue through volume optimization – CFO, CMO
	Increase revenue through price optimization – CFO, CMO
	Reduce sales and administration costs – CFO, COO
	Reduce cost of goods sold – CFO, COO
	Reduce income taxes – CFO
	Capital optimization – CFO
Improve competitiveness – CEO	Strengthen innovation – CMO, CRDO
	Speed up time-to-market – CMO, CRDO
	Improve responsiveness – CFO, CMO
	Improve customer interaction – COO, CMO
	Improve customer satisfaction and loyalty – COO, CMO
	Improve brand awareness – CMO
	Improve partner and relationship collaboration – CFO, COO
Lower risk – CEO	Optimize intelligence – CFO, COO
	Optimize regulation compliance – CFO
	Improve risk planning – CFO, CRSO
	Improve risk management – CFO, CRSO
	Improve business recovery – CRSO, CIO
Improve operational efficiency – CEO	Improve development and production – COO
	Improve logistics, material, and services – COO
	Improve corporate services – CFO, COO
	Improve human capital management – CHRO
	Improve capital management – CFO
	Improve data management – CFO, CIO

Table 13.2   Examples of SBOs (von Rosing, 2010. "Building New Levels of Excellence")

As the above strategies are ruptured by constant external and internal factors and thereby changes, the adoption of a company's business model to the changes is vital, because the margins of success are increasingly determined by absolute advantage. Focusing on the critical core competencies (CCCs) described in Part I, Chapters 2, 3, and 5, and attached activities become a key to survival. The next steps are therefore related to what the business model is and which competencies and activities to perform. According to Michael Porter, competitive advantage is gained by performing similar activities better, faster, cheaper, and/or differently than rivals perform them. It involves identifying your core competitive and core differentiated business competencies and then determining how to, for example, perform the activities for those competencies faster or with fewer mistakes using operational processes. Many would say that it is about doing the right things right. We, however, think it is about achieving excellence in the right things, which in reality is more about doing the right things better.

The main issue here is that it is not just about doing things right. For this, a company must know which core competitive and core differentiated business competencies it has to perform at its best to create the most value. Because a business model comprises the activities a firm performs, how it performs them, and when it performs them to make a profit, a business model analysis at this stage includes the profit-oriented aspects of value identification (where and how to create the most value). Figure 13.4 illustrates how in the business model approach one identifies CCCs in terms of core competitive or core differentiated competencies and value opportunities/drivers.

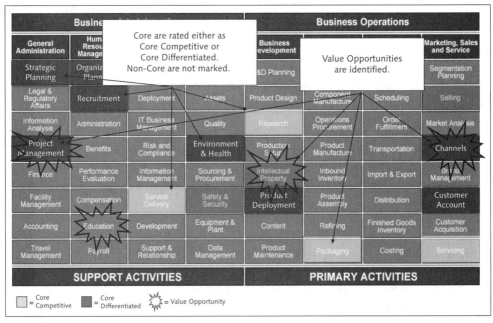

Figure 13.4 Business Model with Core Competitive or Core Differentiated Competencies and Value Opportunities/Drivers (von Rosing, 2009. "Business Value Management")

Identification of value opportunities is not always easy. Here are some practical questions to ask during this process:

▸ Which competencies (CCCs) have the most dramatic impact on their ability to maintain and grow margins?

▸ Which competencies offer significant cost and capital optimization opportunities?

For example, near-term changes that enhance the firm's strategic differentiators are likely to be designated as "value opportunity" areas. Parts of the business that already resemble competencies, such as shared service centers, may also be early priorities. Value quick wins are typically found when disparate and duplicate functions are consolidated into true operational competencies. You can use efficiencies gained in the first round of business modeling to support subsequent business model transformation and change initiatives.

Value Creation – Create Operational Model

After the "see" phase of the business model analysis comes the "do" phase (see Figure 13.3). A well-conceived and executed business model with defined core competitive or core differentiated competencies and value opportunities/drivers can give a firm the competitive advantage and differentiation they are looking for. Recall that a firm has a competitive advantage if it earns a higher rate of profits than its rivals earn in the markets in which it competes or if it has the potential to do so. Here, the firm overlays the value opportunity map onto the existing business. The goal is to identify gaps between the to-be vision of the competencies and the as-is view — a representation of how the organization presently manages its organizational, process, and technology contexts. To capture the full scope of the organization's current competencies and market positioning, this as-is representation must be firmly grounded in empirical data, such as business model, organization charts, operational model, cost drivers, application portfolios, technology investments, key performance metrics, and existing processes.

Those characteristics of a firm's strategic business model that allow it to earn a higher rate of profits than its rivals do are its competitive advantage. A firm's competitive advantage often rests in the operational model and thereby in activities it performs, how and when it performs them, and the possibility to identify their issues/pain points. The degree to which a firm's strategic business model can give the firm a competitive advantage is a function of the extent to which the operational model, and thereby activities the firm performs, how it performs them, and when it performs them, allows the firm to create superior customer value and appropriate it. That is, competitive advantage is a function of the extent to which the operational activities allow the firm to:

▶ Create a strategic business model to attain and maintain the right positions.

▶ Create an operational business model that can compete with the industry's competitive forces.

▶ Better build and exploit its competencies.

▶ Identify business issues and pain points and thereby possible weakness clusters to strengthen the weakest points.

▶ Identify and prioritize value drivers to support whether the firm pursues a best-practice/low-cost with non-core competencies or own practice/differentiation strategy with core competencies.

Value Realization – Define Transformational Roadmap

Finally, in the "get" phase, the firm decides how to close the value realization gaps. This is where a firm formulates and executes its transformation roadmap. It usually has to choose which of the activities of its business system and value system it wants to perform and which ones it does not want to perform. Because creating and appropriating value is achieved through performing the business activities, the related processes are identified. Please note that activities are part of processes (process steps) and are directly related to core and differentiated competencies. However, when we talk about activities at the business model stage, we talk about business activities, for example, a business activity account management versus a process activity create sales order.

The choice of which business activities and processes to perform plays an important role in the firm's profitability. The choice of the right business activities allows a firm not only to offer superior customer value, but also to address the weaknesses of its industry, thereby allowing it to be better positioned to appropriate the value created and realized. In this phase, you should examine:

1. The business activities and process options that are available to a firm within its SAP system and value system.

2. Criteria for choosing business activities and processes that can give a firm a competitive advantage (based on core competitive and core differentiated competencies).

3. Criteria for *not* choosing business activities. In our discussion of item 3 of the business model approach (see Figure 13.3), we will emphasize the fact that the choice of which activities not to perform can be as important as the choice of which activities to perform because the opportunity cost of performing some activities can be very high.

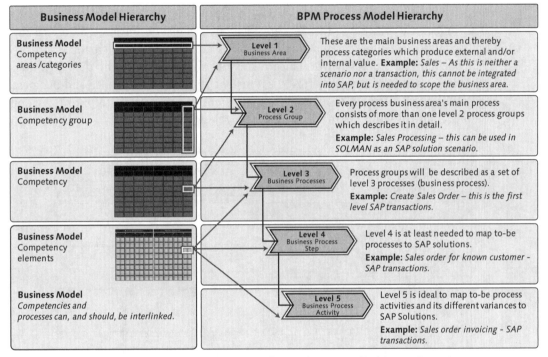

Figure 13.5 Business Model Competency Elements and Primary Processes and Supporting Processes Can/Should Be Interlinked (von Rosing, 2009. "Business Value Management")

To achieve this prioritization of the business processes in relation to the core competencies, the business model hierarchy is related to the process model hierarchy to identify the main and supporting processes (see Figure 13.5). Furthermore, these processes have to be evaluated using a criteria catalog that relates the competencies and processes to the critical success factors (CSFs) and key performance indicators (KPIs) defined in the value planning and value creation steps as defined in Part I, Chapter 3.

Linking the core and non-core competency elements to their respective business process hierarchy is the first step in the evaluation and prioritization of the processes. In the next step, you use a criteria catalog to identify the preferred competency developments and the attached processes per business unit. This catalog relates the critical success factors and key performance indicators that were identified in the value planning and value creation steps to the identified process groups.

In effect, the business processes are related through the business model to the organization's strategy, and a foundation is created for value creation and the evaluation of process performance relative to the creation of the defined value. This provides the company "SAP best insight" (process intelligence and business intelligence). Figure 13.6 shows the main steps to achieve this to prioritize your processes based on the needed competency development.

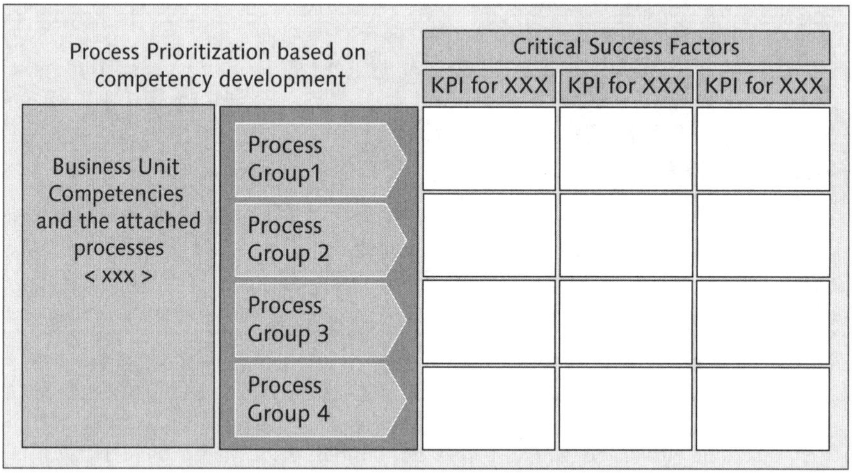

Figure 13.6 Process Prioritization Based on Competency Development

Once the process are prioritized based on your competencies and decisions on the priority of activities have been made, guidance in atomization and standardization discussions can be provided.

SAP implementation projects need to start with a design of the process model and the business blueprint that is linked to the company's business model. We often encounter the view that the blueprint is similar to a business model and so can be specified using process activity diagrams or process models. This is a misunderstanding. The root cause of this misunderstanding is that a business model is not about process but about competencies, and thereby about the value exchanged between roles and their competencies. Failure to make this separation of concerns leads to poor business decision-making and inadequate business requirements, not to mention that the value input-output model is not considered. Process models tend to be relationship- and workflow-oriented: they show the sequence of activities to be performed and the roles (actors) performing them. In addition, they can show branches in a workflow sequence, parallel threads, and synchronizations. Thus, a process model shows *how* a particular SAP solution should be customized.

We do not argue that process models are not useful in an SAP development project. We know they are vital, because a model of the interorganizational business processes is necessary to explain *how* a business model works and results in many requirements for the SAP customization information system to be developed. However, a separation of concerns is needed here, because process models are needed but should not be the starting point for identifying business stakeholder/c-level business drivers, strategic business objectives, business issues, and challenges and thereby needs and wants. We can summarize that business activities related to core competitive and core differentiated competencies are candidates for tailored solutions and should be supported by SAP own practices (e.g., composite applications). Non-core activities, on the other hand, are suitable for standardization and can be supported by SAP best practices.

Unfortunately, you will often experience that most mistakes are made in the above steps. Possible mistakes that can be made in these steps are very vital and long-lasting. If a company chooses the "old" way of implementing IT systems and bases its implementation mostly on best practice, and even does this to their core competencies, then the uniqueness and differentiation a company has might be lost, because they implement industry standard processes and activities in an area where they should differentiate.

This principle is vital, but mostly not understood or applied to processes. Therefore, the operational effectiveness, efficiency, and innovation the company is looking for is often not realized. Worse, the organization's core competitive and differentiated competencies, which are critical to compete, survive, and win, are not identified as such. As a consequence, these competencies are standardized and automated inadequately in the SAP system. In the next few pages we will therefore concentrate on how to combine the above principles to identify own practice (core competencies and attached processes) and best practices (non-core competencies and attached processes) to harmonize and/or standardize them on the strategic, tactical, and operational levels of an organization.

13.2.6 Process Identification and Harmonization on the Strategic Level

The goal and challenge for organizations is to define business processes that represent an appropriate level of commonality across business units, product lines, and regions. Subsequently, the SAP application landscape should be designed to manage an optimal balance of standardization, regional innovations, and flexibility to accommodate both internal and external organizational changes. Because process commonality is a function of the business process and the organizational construct, a one-solution-fits-all strategy does not work. For example, asset management may have a high degree of commonality possible at the enterprise level, whereas planning and scheduling has a low degree of commonality at the enterprise level, but a high degree is possible at the business unit level. Harmonization of process views on different levels is very important to align the strategic, tactical, and operational views on the enterprise.

Strategic level processes are still not very detailed as they are described on business areas and process groups. Furthermore, these processes on the strategic level are modeled as value-added chain diagrams. All of this makes it easier to get agreement faster. On the strategic level, you would usually produce a business model and an enterprise process map where you would split management processes as shown in Figure 13.7, enterprise primary processes, and supporting processes.

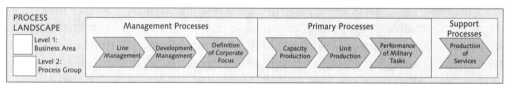

Figure 13.7 Defense Example of Level 1 and Level 2 Management, Primary, and Supporting Processes

These process maps must be described differently from the traditional way of describing core and non-core process, as Michael Porter did in 1996 and as many other companies do it today. As described above, there are many primary/core and supporting/non-core processes within a core competitive or core differentiated competency that is linked to your strategy and that as discussed earlier is the focus of processes in this way in an SAP solution mapping, not in value creating. Figure 13.8 illustrates an example of the connection between business model competencies and the connection to the management, primary, and supporting processes.

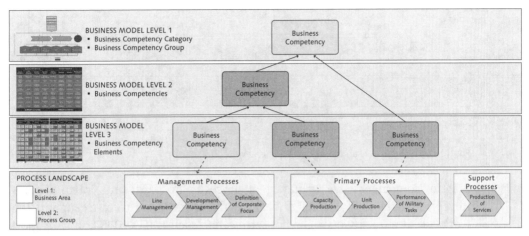

Figure 13.8 Business Model Competencies and the Connection to Management, Primary, and Supporting Processes

The process map only describes processes based on category. Management processes, primary processes, and supporting processes are only described on the business area level (level 1) and process group level (level 2) in the process map, and they are connected with the business model competencies.

13.2.7 Process Identification and Harmonization on the Tactical Level

Alignment of the process views on the tactical and operational levels is more challenging. Processes must be described in more detail, and different potential views are available because enterprises are based on functional classifications and not on process-based organization.

Alignment is even more difficult because alignment on processes is not only needed on the category, the business process level (level 3), but also on the related process characteristics such as process flows, triggers, and resources such as information, people, and systems.

On top of this, conflicting with company performance, people do not always work as described or planned. Because of this, and because the activities that compose the process step might be executed differently, similar business processes could have various underlying process flows.

Those different flows of the same business process comprise the business process variant level (level 4). See examples of levels 3 and 4 in Figure 13.9.

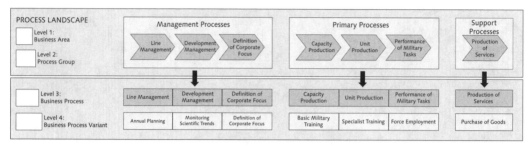

Figure 13.9 Defense Example of Level 3 and Level 4 Processes

A lot of companies have written their processes on paper and drawn pictures to represent them. The main drivers for these initiatives were to support the workforce, for quality management certification such as ISO 90002, or to support implementations of IT systems. Some companies even started to represent their processes in a repository-based tool such as ARIS. With this repository, they can find relations between processes and their resources, which help simplify and standardize these processes.

This is a big advantage, but merely modeling the processes only describes the situation at a certain point in time. Furthermore, it does not guide or support the employees in operating and managing these processes. Making the process executable supports people in the way they work. This also gives many additional advantages such as transparency, insight in processes and resource consumption (including forecasting), and investigation of improvements based on simulations. Organizations can see the advantages but face problems in describing their processes in detail. It becomes even more complex if we also want to execute or outsource these processes, apply (monitoring) dashboards on top of them, and have to choose the right modeling views.

Process levels are mostly described from general category to process execution. Standardization organizations such as APQC (2009) and SCOR (2008) usually describe the top levels and do not go into detailed process characteristics. During business process definition, it is critical to prioritize and focus on common process design and on a relatively smaller number of processes that provide the greatest improvement and impact. Tangible business benefits should be highlighted at the beginning of the definition process and be agreed upon by all key stakeholders to facilitate relatively seamless adoption. Some factors that need be looked into are optimal leverage of the organization's workforce across the value chain, a future strategy of process management/shared services, possible mergers and acquisitions, supplier rationalization, and client experience strategies.

Achieving harmonization throughout the process models does, however, allow for an integrated business process hierarchy that relates to the organization's strategy and aligns with the organization's business model. Furthermore, harmonization of process definitions and conventions allows on an operational level the integration of process execution and monitoring with process modeling. These relations are represented in the new ASAP methodology and governance frameworks and BPM tools (business to model and modeling to execution) (see Figure 13.10), which we will describe in detail in the following chapters.

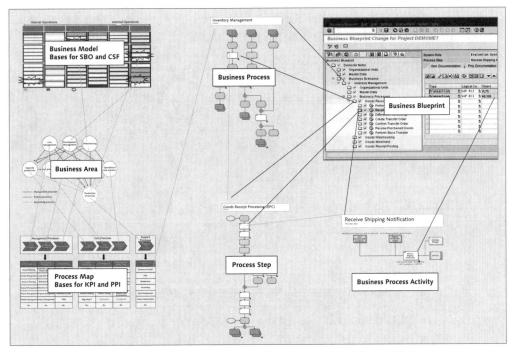

Figure 13.10 The Connection between Business Model, Process Model, Value and Performance Drivers into Solution Manager (Kuhlmann and von Rosing, 2010. "Applying BPM Principles to SAP EAF")

13.2.8 Harmonization through a Simple Pattern Using the ICASIO Approach

In Part I, Chapter 3 we introduced the ICASIO pattern as a process approach around process performance drivers as well as value drivers. In this subsection we will explain how you can use the same ICASIO pattern approach to harmonize processes. For both the successful harmonization of processes and implementation of the transformation roadmap, however, there is a requirement for a standardized approach to modeling, analysis, and detailing of the business processes variants. This is required when we want to go into the process variant details, describe the process (variant) steps, and inventory the related resources and characteristics. To harmonize process modeling and analysis on this level we use a simple pattern of standardized activities.

In a genuine work process, organizations have manual steps to collect and approve data and to inform people about the chains of automated activities. To capture these process step details we developed the ICASIO pattern: input, collect, approve, store, inform, and output (see Figure 13.11). It's a simple pattern that describes on a process step level (level 5) how people work.

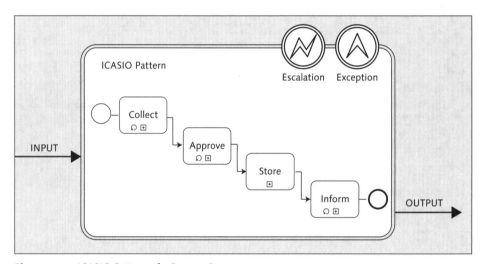

Figure 13.11 ICASIO Pattern of a Process Step

Because enterprises exist that are made up of multiple business units within different countries with different government rules and cultures, enterprises have several implementations of the same process step. We call an implementation of the process step a "process step variant" (level 5.1).

The ICASIO pattern helps enterprises identify the resources and characteristics relevant to the process step and its variants. Using the ICASIO pattern for describing the process step and process step variants gives enterprises a lot of advantages:

▶ Detailed process step descriptions can be used to build business process flows and are the basis for business process harmonization.

▶ A single process step describes the business requirements independent of the implementation. Process step variants describe how people really work and provide detailed information on the flow of tasks. The ICASIO pattern helps identify the relevant variants, activities, and resources.

▶ Identification and definition of the required activities and resources using the ICASIO pattern provides enterprises the opportunity to standardize the description of the process step (variants). This enables the (re)use of process steps as a business service and the writing of service-level agreements in a common way for all process step variants (even outsourced).

▶ The ICASIO pattern helps enterprises standardize the way the process step requirements for resources and performance are described. This enables the enterprises to measure process step variants the same way based on commonly defined performance indicators. This is the basis for continuous improvement.

13.2.9 Definition and Validation of Process Step Variants Using the RACI Model Approach

In process management–related work, the responsibility assignment matrix (RACI) is often used to link roles to processes. RACI describes the participation of various roles in completing tasks or creating deliverables for a project or business process. It is especially useful in clarifying roles and responsibilities in cross-functional and cross-departmental projects and processes.

By defining the roles related to the process data actions that are described using the ICASIO pattern, we created the RACI model for process steps, which helps identify roles, responsibilities, and actors. The key responsibility roles of the RACI model for the ICASIO pattern are:

▶ **Responsible (store)**
Those responsible for persisting (storing) the process data in a backend system

▶ **Accountable (approve)**
Those responsible for approval of the process data and those who will be held accountable for the result of the process step

▶ **Consulted (collect)**
Those who are consulted to check and complement the data of this process step

▶ **Informed (inform)**
Those who must be informed about the result of the process step

Based on these definitions, we can identify the responsibility roles relevant to the execution of the activities of the process step (variant) (see Table 13.3).

	Role 1
Collect	C
Approve	A
Store	R
Inform	I

Table 13.3 RACI Model of a Transactional Pattern

Most software vendors describe a process step by a single transaction, as shown in Table 13.4. The RACI model shows that this is feasible when only one role is involved for all activities required to complete the process step. This happens when the actor of the process step is triggered directly (e.g., by phone), collects all of the information (e.g., by asking questions), and stores the information in the system. By doing this, the actor approves the data implicitly by clicking the SAVE button, and he's informed by the success message that is returned on the screen.

	Role 1	Role 2	Role 3	Role 4	Role 5	Role 6	Role 7
Collect	C	C		C			C
Approve		A	A			A	A
Store		R			R	R	
Inform			I	I			

Table 13.4 RACI Model of a Process Step

However, there are usually multiple roles involved in the completion of a process step. In this case describing the process step by the transaction involved will not be sufficient, and the process step must be described as a flow of activities. Mapping all process step activities identified using the ICASIO pattern against the responsibility roles involved creates the RACI model. This matrix provides information on the simple and complex roles with regard to activities performed in the process step. If a RACI role contains different activities, it must be established if these activities can be combined. Table 13.5 shows activities that can be combined in a single responsibility role.

Combined Activities
Collect + Approve
Collect + Approve + Store
Collect + Approve + Store + Inform (transaction pattern)
Approve + Store
Approve + Store + Inform
Store + Inform

Table 13.5 Valid Combined Activities

Other combinations usually require different actors to be involved in the process step and often lead to the development of additional or changed activity flows. This might be the case when subsequent approval steps are involved or when collection of data is executed by different actors. Applying the RACI model together with the ICASIO pattern thus identifies omissions in the description of the activity flow of the process step and leads to the definition of process step variants. The reasons for the development of these process step variants can be found in localization, regulation, and/or application support. Just keep in mind that a process step variant can have only one "store" activity (single or combined) to be defined correctly.

A good example is the sales order process that can be handled fully automated by the customer (Web shop) or through the company's back office. For the online variant, the customer is responsible for the process (create the order, store the order), and he collects relevant information (product information, address, and payment data). In the backend a real-time inventory check is performed, a sales order is created, and a sales order confirmation is sent out as a generated PDF via email. The implicit approval of the order comes from business rules, and the handling of the payment is the responsibility of the online payment provider. On the other end of the spectrum, the customer might decide to use a more traditional approach and contact his account manager. The account manager now becomes responsible for the sales order process. He collects the required information and checks with the warehouse for the inventory and the customer support desk for the credit check. The company's back office is responsible for entering the data in the sales application, and a line manager has to approve the order before it is executed. Between these two extremes, many variants might exist, with different people involved, and shifting responsibilities emerge from applying the RACI model in combination with the ICASIO pattern.

Using the ICASIO pattern and creating the RACI model for the process step helps identify the differences in activity flows and provides insight to opportunities for harmonization of processes and process steps.

Now that we understand the relationship between RACI and the ICASIO pattern, let's summarize. The ICASIO pattern helps you to identify a process step with its activities in a generic way within a business process. The process step has different variants depending on the flow of its activities. RACI helps you identify the completeness of the process step and its variants. Each role must be part of one or more process step variants, and all activities must have at least one role. RACI and ICASIO together simplify and validate your process work and can be used in workshops to collect the relevant information about processes.

13.2.10 Process Identification and Harmonization on the Operational Level

Now that we know the importance of harmonization of process steps (variants) and have identified the advantages of using the ICASIO pattern and the RACI model for the detailed description of the process step (variants), let's have a closer look at process harmonization on the operational level.

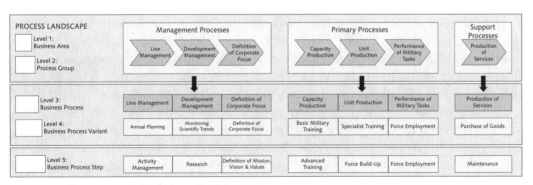

Figure 13.12 Defense Example of Level 5 Processes

To further illustrate the operational level, as shown in Figure 13.12, let's have a closer look at a process step example for creating an order.

Operational Level – Process Steps

At the operational level we have the process steps with variants as described next:

▶ **Variant 1**
If, for example, a call center sales employee gets a call (input), he will ask the customer for his name and required products (collect), check prices and give a discount (approve), complete the sales order (store), and confirm the order to the customer (inform).

▶ **Variant 2**
The SAP system receives an electronic data interchange (EDI) order from a customer (input). The system searches for additional information to create the order in the system (collect). Based on pricing rules, the order is approved automatically or a flag is set for manual approval (approve), the sales order is released (store), and an EDI confirmation is sent to the customer (inform).

▶ **Variant 3**
A customer sends an email with his order (input). A call center employee checks and fulfills the order with the proposed discount (collect). An offline form is sent to the manager for manual approval (approve), the sales order is created and released on the approved form (store), and an email confirmation is sent to the customer (inform).

The results of all three process step variants are similar, but the implementation of activities and the required resources (technology and people) are different. The examples show you the difficulty of describing the processes. Variant 1 describes the way a person works behinds his desk. Variant 2 describes how the system handles the request automatically, and Variant 3 shows how people work together to get the order in the system. Level 5 is the only place where business process requirements and implementation can be decoupled. It is the preferred place to measure process performance and to compare process steps in a generic way.

Operational Level – Process Activities

From a business perspective, process flows are described with events and functions, for example, with an event-driven process chain (EPC) in ARIS. The process step variant has a flow of one or more process activities (level 6). See Figure 13.13 for an example of level 6 processes.

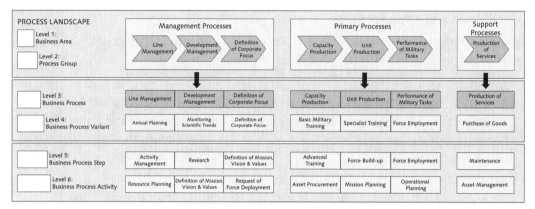

Figure 13.13 Defense Example of Level 6 Processes

The process step variant is described with the following activity types:

▶ **Collect**
Gather data required for fulfilling the activity or task.

▶ **Approve**
Confirm the correctness and completeness of the gathered data.

▶ **Store**
Persist the gathered data in an application.

▶ **Inform**
Provide feedback on the activity to the actors involved in the process step or a combination of those types in one activity.

▶ **Meeting**
Collect and approve with more approvers (people) parallel.

▶ **Transaction**
Collect, approve, store, and inform in a single activity.

Patterns can be found that can be reused in other variants and that make measurement and comparison of process characteristics across the different process activities possible. Figure 13.14 shows an example of the process group to business process step variant and activities.

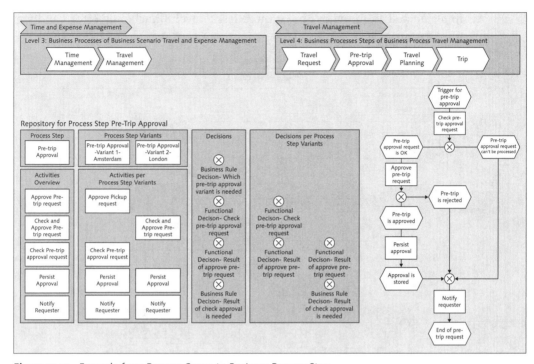

Figure 13.14 Example from Process Group to Business Process Step

Variant and Activities

IT must implement the process activities of the process step flow shown in Figure 13.14. A canonical data model is needed as an overlay over the existing IT landscape. It should describe the business objects and their attributes and methods in a generic way, independent from the underlying IT solution. These generic business objects describe the process data (input/output) of the activity and are used to define the independent definition of business objects for a business domain. This creates the basis for loosely coupled domain services. Business Process Modeling Notation (BPMN) can be used to describe these detailed flows (see Figure 13.15), because it assigns the resources to the activities, handles errors and exceptions, and is eligible for execution.

Operational Level – Process Tasks

The three process step variant examples show us that for executable processes, description of an activity alone is not enough. For translation to the IT requirements, we need to know if the activity is a human task, an automatic task, a decision-making task, or a combination of tasks. The activity within a process step is implemented as a flow of one or more tasks (level 8) including error handling and escalations.

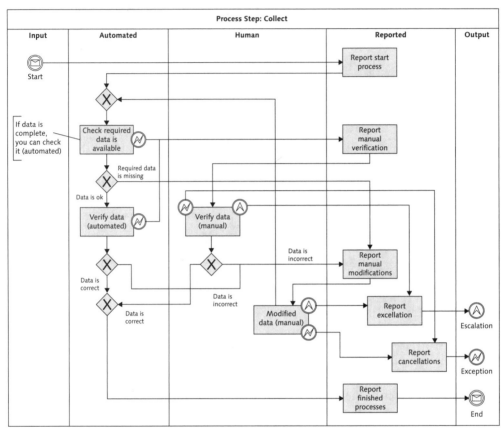

Figure 13.15 Task Flow and Process Performance Indicator (PPI) Measurement within the Collect Activity (BPMN Model)

The tasks are the lowest level discussed between business and IT. The business can describe the requirements of the tasks and must describe the screen flow and the data fields for human tasks if standard solutions will not fit. Also, the decision-making tasks, business rules, and domain services must be described. Domain services are used to read and store data in a standardized way from IT backend systems. The domain services are based on the (domain-specific) canonical data model and implemented in the service layer of the SOA architecture. An enterprise service bus maps the domain services to the application services provided by the IT systems (level 9). Both user interfaces of human tasks and automated tasks use the domain services. This helps the IT solutions to better align with the business processes on the step, activity, and task levels and ensures the implementation of application-agnostic IT solutions.

13.2.11 Conclusion

The connection between the chosen strategy and business model concerns competing successfully, gaining superior performance, establishing a favorable position, carrying out these goals, and establishing a unique and valuable position. In these definitions we can see that the connection between strategy, business model, and operational activities concerns winning, performance, and value realization.

To continuously create value for the organization, it is essential to apply the described approach and interlink the development of strategy, business model, and business process management. In this approach, business modeling and process modeling are combined to define the transformational roadmap. The key to the approach is, as defined, alignment of the strategy and the business model. Using proper analysis, competencies of the organization are classified in core (competitive or differentiated) and non-core competencies. Going through the value planning, value creation, and value realization phases of business model management connects the strategy to the business model and to the operational model where the processes are executed.

The next step in the holistic approach is the harmonization of business processes. This is required for proper alignment of the business processes (on an operational level) to the business model. Only harmonized process definitions and operations can relate the strategy-defined criteria and the value proposition to the actual execution and monitoring of business processes.

Agreement on the definition and conventions on process levels will help your organization harmonize process models from the strategic to the operational level. From top to bottom, each level brings more-detailed information about the process and its required resources (see Table 13.6). Levels 1, 2, 3, and 4 describe the processes and will be monitored. Levels 5 and 6 describe the detailed flow of activities in the process steps and are the basis for translation to process execution. Level 7 connects the resources to the process step (variants), and level 8 connects the application service.

Level	Description
1	Business area
2	Process group
3	Business process
4	Business process variant
5	Process step
5.1	Process step variant
6	Activity
7	Task
7.1	Screen flow (manual task)
7.2	Business rules (automated task)
7.3	Domain service (automated task)
8	Application service

Table 13.6 Process Levels

The value creation ad realization of the process mapping to the SAP solutions and services all rely on the central premise that a company must apply own practice to their core critical competencies (CCCs), best practices to their non-core competencies (NNCs), and best insight with dashboards and reports to ensure the organization's capacity to respond to the complexity of its environment, or as managers say, their business model to be focused, flexible, and responsive while being robust. Most SAP projects should start with the *design* of a business model stating what is offered by who to whom, rather than how these offerings are selected, negotiated, contracted and fulfilled *operationally* — as is explained by a process model.

The implementation of the process as described in the process model supports the cross-company alignment of key and process performance indicators, improving the measurement and monitoring of processes.

This enables enterprises to become more adaptive to changes in their business environments, to continuously improve their existing business models and the processes, and create performance and value more easily. We will now go into the details of the new ASAP framework, which takes this approach into account.

13.3 ASAP Methodology 7 Core

In 2009, behind-the-scenes work was undertaken to harmonize the way we project-manage SAP implementations. The result is the new ASAP Methodology for Implementation 7, which was launched in February 2010. The new ASAP methodology brings together the previous ASAP methodology, Business Intelligence Solution Accelerator (BISA) methodology, value delivery principles, business process management methodology, and service-oriented architecture methodology.

The ASAP implementation methodology is a phased, deliverable-oriented methodology that streamlines implementation projects, minimizes risk, and reduces the total cost of implementation. ASAP takes a disciplined approach to project management, organization change management, solution management, business process management, value management, and other disciplines applied in the implementation of SAP solutions. There are two highly visible components of the new ASAP methodology.

The ASAP Roadmap 7 core, which covers the entire project lifecycle — from evaluation through delivery to postproject solution management and operations — and the value, process, and application lifecycle illustrated in Figure 13.16. The new ASAP Roadmap 7 core has been made leaner, increasing its practicality, and provides transparency of value delivery through consistent business case reflection and ensures efficient guidance for service-oriented architecture (SOA), business process management (BPM), and traditional implementation projects.

More Information

You can view and display the ASAP Roadmap 7 core via different tools. You can download it as an HTML extract via SAP Service Marketplace *http://service.sap.com/asap*, SAP BPX Community *http://www.sdn.sap.com/irj/bpx/asap*, and SAP Solution Manager, where the ASAP Roadmap 7 core can be assigned to your project in project administration, Transaction SOLAR_PROJECT_ADMIN, as illustrated in Figure 13.17 and deployed in Transaction RMMAIN as shown in Figure 13.18.

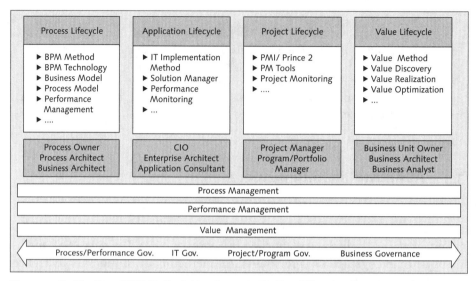

Figure 13.16 The New ASAP Methodology Supports the Four Lifecycles: Process, Application, Project, and Value

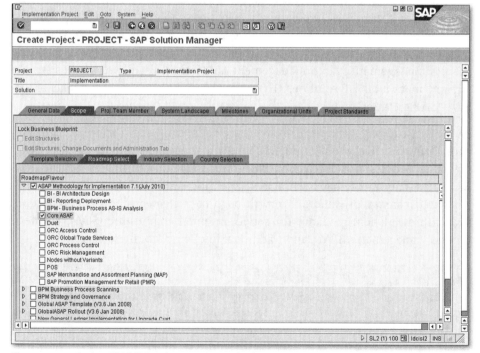

Figure 13.17 Assign ASAP 7 Roadmap in SAP Solution Manager, Project Administration (SOLAR_PROJECT_ADMIN)

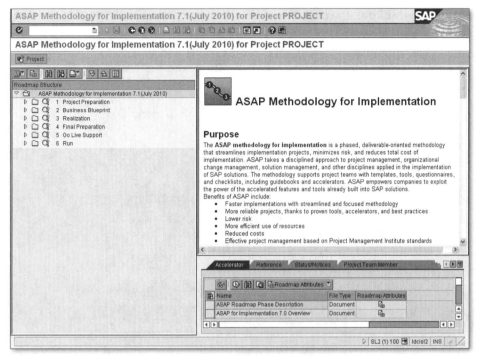

Figure 13.18 ASAP 7 Roadmap in SAP Solution Manager (RMMAIN)

The second set of visible components of the ASAP methodology is the business add-ons to ASAP that extend the ASAP Roadmap with modular business implementation content. The business add-ons provide proven implementation content for implementation of various industry solutions, solutions packages, and other related areas such as agile methodology, BPM, SOA, and enterprise architecture (EA) governance and strategy frameworks. We will describe in detail the business add-ons to ASAP in Section 13.4.

In the following sections we will introduce each of the ASAP phases in the ASAP Roadmap 7 core, as illustrated in Figure 13.19 and describe how value delivery, business process management, and service-oriented architecture are reflected in the new methodology and how to apply it when you implement an SAP solution where you need to take into consideration both enablement of Best Practices and enablement of own practices, also referred to as composite applications. You can build the composite applications on top of SAP Business Suite's Best Practices with the application core processes and on arbitrary backend systems. Composite applications follow the SOA paradigm of "non-intrusiveness," which means these applications are bound to provide modification-free process extensions to the core business applications. This section will also describe which skills enablement are required for the project team members to practice the new ASAP methodology, which now covers the value, process, application, and project lifecycle.

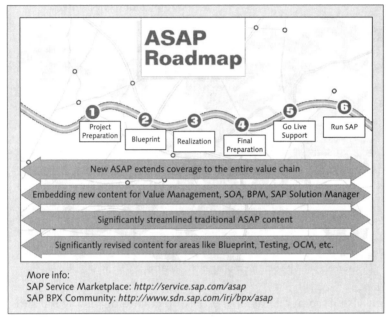

Figure 13.19 ASAP 7 Includes Six Phases

We will start with phase 1, project preparation, and describe how value delivery, business process management, and service-oriented architecture are reflected in this phase, including the skills enablement requirements for the project team members.

13.3.1 Project Preparation

Project preparation is the first phase of the implementation project, where preplanning of all relevant project management disciplines is conducted and documented in the project management plan, for example, procedures for integrated change control, management of issues, scope, time, cost, quality, project staff, communication, risk, and contracted resources and services. Defining these procedures enables structured project execution, monitoring, and controlling in subsequent project phases and contributes to ensuring project success. As shown in Figure 13.20, project preparation includes seven work streams:

▶ 1.1 Project management

▶ 1.2 Organizational change management

▶ 1.3 Training

▶ 1.4 Data management

▶ 1.5 Business process management

▶ 1.6 Technical solution management

▶ 1.7 Integration solution management

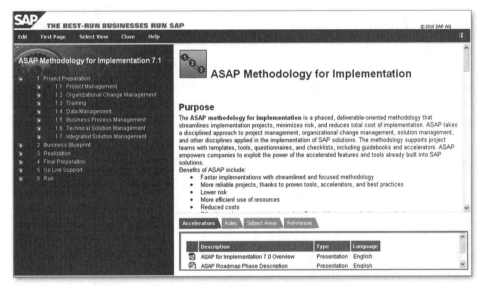

Figure 13.20 Project Preparation – Seven Work Streams

The project management work stream is completely aligned with Project Management Institute (PMI) project management standards as defined in the PMI Project Management Body of Knowledge (PMBOK). Project standards for various activities throughout all phases are defined or start to be defined in this phase:

▶ 1.1.5.1 SAP Solution Manager usage guidelines

▶ 1.1.5.2 Business process modeling standards (new)

▶ 1.1.5.3 Initial development management standards

- ▶ 1.1.5.4 SAP services deployment plan
- ▶ 1.1.5.5 Software system configuration standards
- ▶ 1.1.5.6 Enhancement and modification standards
- ▶ 1.1.5.7 Support package and upgrade standards
- ▶ 1.1.5.8 Change request and transport management standards
- ▶ 1.1.5.9 Test management standards
- ▶ 1.1.5.10 Postimplementation service and support standards
- ▶ 1.1.5.11 Enterprise service design standards (new)
- ▶ 1.1.5.12 Composite application design and development standards (new)

We recommend having these standards in place when implementing an SAP solution. Note that a number of new standards have been added. You can find more details on these standards later in this chapter.

The project preparation phase includes several deliverables, milestones, and key decisions, as illustrated in Table 13.7. For each deliverable, the ASAP Roadmap explains in detail the purpose, inputs, and outputs and where it's applicable and gives further details and information about the expected result.

Purpose	Deliverables	Milestones & Key Decisions
Initial planning and preparation	Project scope defined	Corporate review completed
Define the project goals, scope, and objectives	Implementation plan and rollout strategy	Scope defined
Identify, on-board, and train team members	Detailed scope document	Project team staffed and trained
	Costs and benefits validation	Project team organization, responsibilities and location
	Project standards	Roll-out plan mandates/ constraints
	Project infrastructure	Policies for to be project organization
	Knowledge transfer approach	System retirement objectives/ mandates/ constraints

Table 13.7 Deliverables in Project Preparation

Purpose	Deliverables	Milestones & Key Decisions
	Implementation work plan	Training budget and approach
	Master data design	Key stakeholders for communications identified
	Interface list	Implementation plan in place
	Testing strategy	Corporate review completed
	Data cleansing strategy	

Table 13.7 Deliverables in Project Preparation (Cont.)

After this short intro to the project preparation phase, we will take a closer look at the value delivery considerations in this phase.

Value Delivery Considerations in Project Preparation

Value determination is part of the business process management work stream as shown in Figure 13.21. The purpose of the value determination deliverable is to create a value-based solution design to determine value drivers and key process changes for the implementation project to ensure value delivery.

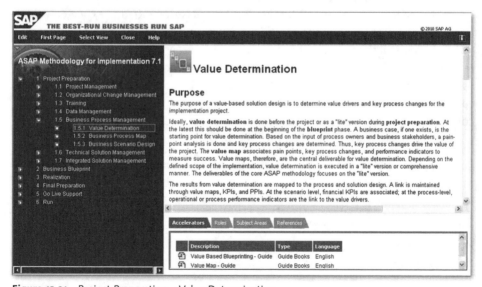

Figure 13.21 Project Preparation – Value Determination

The objective of value delivery is to ensure that the project lives up to the value expectations according to the targets that are stated in the initial business case. This value-based approach serves the following purposes in project preparation phase:

1. Execute the project according to the business case or value map targets.

2. Monitor and track the project value delivery based on the initial business case or value map and report the status of value delivery at an early stage of quality gates (Q-Gates).

Value-based solution design plays a critical role in determining value drivers and key process changes for the implementation project. To realize the intended business value for this initiative, it is essential to address key success factors and establish a clear, shared set of expectations for program value creation; achieve a rapid program launch with effective value-based governance; make the business case actionable and measureable by defining design imperatives, key performance indicators (KPIs) and process performance indicators (PPIs); establish ongoing value management discipline to ensure that the business blueprint phase (following the project preparation phase) and implementation reflect design imperatives.

The inputs required for value determination in project preparation are a value-based opportunity storyline created by clearly identifying the value built into the business case including benefit objectives, relevant processes and key process changes, financial operational KPIs and PPIs for measurement, and expected values and costs. We also recommend establishing project management and value tracking with these methods: including a value expert, integrating a value schedule, and reporting for value delivery. Another recommended activity is to set up a project value framework that includes key inputs such as benefit objectives, relevant processes and key process changes, KPIs, value potentials, and costs. By correctly completing the recommended activities for a value-based approach, the project will gain an overall value-based solution proposal.

Let's now take a closer look at the business process management considerations in the project preparation phase.

Business Process Management Considerations in Project Preparation

Business process management is one of the seven work streams in project preparation. Figure 13.22 shows the BPM work stream.

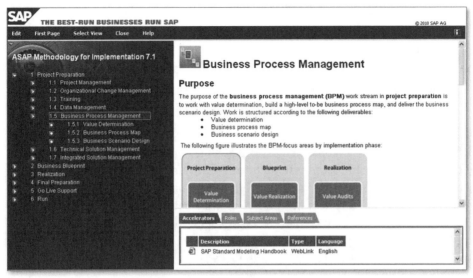

Figure 13.22 Business Process Management Work Stream

The purpose of the business process management work stream in project preparation is to work with value determination, build a high-level to-be business process map, and deliver the business scenario design.

The work-stream deliverables are enhanced to expand on the business case and ensure that the value drivers are incorporated into the solution design. In addition to identifying the value drivers, key process changes are also identified for input into the solution transformation design deliverable that is part of the business blueprint BPM work stream. The creation of business process maps helps the project team verify the agreed upon scope of the project and provide inputs for the business blueprint workshop content. Business process maps provide the framework for business process modeling and therefore help control the scope of the project. Decomposition of the business scenarios during project preparation is the starting point and acts as the foundation for the detailed business process decomposition that takes place during the business blueprint stage. The primary changes for business process management during project preparation therefore involve the new work packages:

▶ **Value determination**
Covered in Section 13.3.1.

► **Business process map**
Builds the foundation for the process hierarchy and process scope of the implementation.

► **Business scenario design**
Provides an understanding of the essential processes at the scenario level and builds the foundation for further process decomposition that will take place in the business blueprint phase.

The inputs required for the business process management work stream are project scope as specified in the statement of work catalog of as-is business process documentation. If the catalog of as-is business process documentation does not exist, we recommend executing an as-is analysis before starting the to-be design. The as-is analysis is not included in ASAP 7 core but can be added via the business add-on to ASAP that delivers business process as-is analysis methodology as illustrated in Figure 13.23, where the add-on to ASAP: Business Process As-Is Analysis is activated.

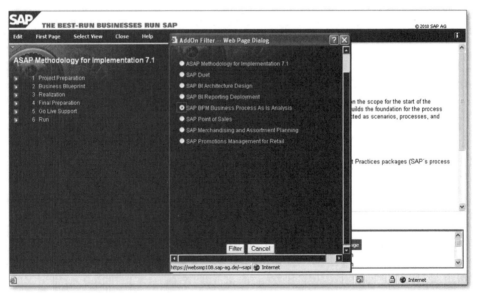

Figure 13.23 Activate Business As-Is Analysis Methodology Add-On

In Figure 13.24 you can see how the additional as-is analysis methodology has been merged into ASAP core.

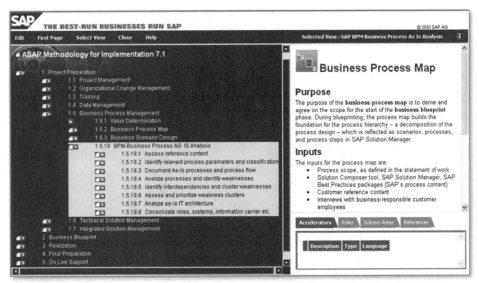

Figure 13.24 Business Add-On that Delivers Business As-Is Analysis Methodology Merged into ASAP Core

You can also get help from the business add-on to ASAP that delivers redocumentation using SAP Solution Manager and SAP Enterprise Modeling by IDS Scheer to identify and analyze your automated as-is business processes. Figure 13.25 illustrates this add-on. For more information please go to SAP EcoHub at *http://ecohub.sdn.sap.com/*.

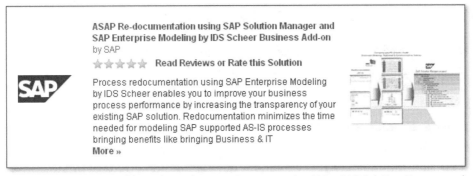

Figure 13.25 Business Add-On that Delivers Re-Documentation Using SAP Solution Manager and SAP Enterprise Modeling

The last input is to define business process modeling standards and business to modeling tools. For this activity we get help from project standards (1.1.5) and business process modeling standards (1.1.5.2).

The purpose of the business process modeling standards is to have a standard approach for executing process modeling. SAP provides a standard modeling handbook that is linked as an accelerator to this deliverable in ASAP.

> **More Information**
>
> The SAP Standard Modeling Handbook is available on the BPX Community as a wiki. For more information please go to *http://wiki.sdn.sap.com/wiki/display/ModHandbook/SAP+Modeling+Handbook+-+Modeling+Standards*.

To support the test management standards (1.1.5.9) and the different test activities during the implementation, the following business add-ons to ASAP are available for delivering content for testing:

- Testing Strategy
- SAP Quality Center by HP
- TAO for SAP
- TDMS
- SAP LoadRunner by HP

> **More Information**
>
> For more information please go to SAP EcoHub at *http://ecohub.sdn.sap.com/*.

Now that we have taken a closer look at value delivery and business process management considerations, we will take a deeper look at the service-oriented architecture considerations in the project preparation phase.

SOA Considerations in Project Preparation

The decision to implement SOA usually represents an important architectural paradigm shift for a company — within both the business and IT organizations. The burden of SOA implementation typically falls most heavily on the organizational side of the enterprise, where new skills and responsibilities have to be introduced along with focused attention to the business requirements including new IT capabilities and to the tighter relationship between IT and business. The ASAP

7 methodology implies key SOA considerations and activities within the following work streams within the project preparation phase:

▶ Work stream: project management (1.1), project management standards (1.1.5). New development standards need to be defined for enterprise service design standards (1.1.5.11) and composite application design and development standards (1.1.5.12).

For more details about composite development architecture guidelines and standards, which is one of the key accelerators, follow the link to composite application design and development standards (1.5.12) (see Section 14.1).

▶ Work stream: technical solution management (1.6). The purpose of the technical solution management work stream is to outline essential technical and infrastructure deliverables that are appropriate to the initial project planning of an SAP implementation project. When defining the technical and infrastructure deliverables, you also need to include the deliverables for a composite application and enterprise services development environment, as illustrated in Figure 13.26.

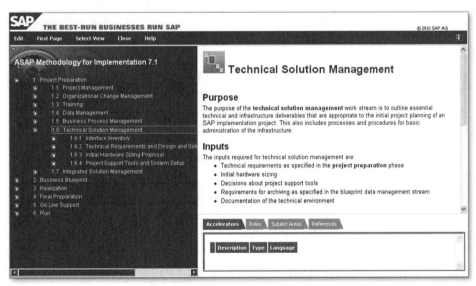

Figure 13.26 Project Preparation – Technical Solution Management

We recommend establishing an enterprise service-oriented architecture strategy and governance to ensure the success of your project. Effective enterprise SOA strategy and governance calls for a holistic management approach that integrates and aligns the corporate business strategy, the IT strategy, and the planning and operational activities associated with enterprise SOA solutions. This approach encompasses people, processes, and technologies. In most companies, some elements of enterprise SOA governance already exist. For instance, you can leverage IT governance as part of the foundation for enterprise SOA governance. But enterprise SOA governance is much more; it involves organizational structures, skills, and procedures aligned with business needs. To establish the enterprise service-oriented architecture strategy and governance you can get help from the business add-on to ASAP that delivers an enterprise service-oriented architecture strategy and governance framework. For more details about this business add-on to ASAP, please go to Section 13.4.3.

Because this is the last part of this section, we will take a look at the skills that project team members need to have to practice the new ASAP methodology.

Consultants, Business Process Experts, Project Managers and Team Leads – Considerations in Project Preparation

Consultants and business process experts who join the project during the project preparation phase play a larger role in the project than before. Not only do they assist the project managers in validating high-level scope, but they have to think in terms of a value- and process-based implementation by assisting in the preparation of to-be process measurement and prepare for value delivery. Team leads are engaged during project preparation to initiate their own work stream. No longer is it sufficient to rely on only the project manager and technical architect to create the deliverables during project preparation. The foundational deliverables in project preparation set the scope, strategy, and value focus for the remainder of the project. In today's global economy and tough economic climate, consultant team leads and project managers need to be business oriented. Meeting the constraints of time, cost, and quality while delivering a project is not enough. Projects must be viewed strategically within the context of the business and provide measureable value. Implementing projects that may not deliver the intended value until a few years down the road is very challenging and will require team leads to gain the knowledge to work with the new paradigm.

We will now go to the next phase — the business blueprint — and describe how value delivery, business process management, and service-oriented architecture are reflected in this phase, including the skills enablement requirements for the project team members.

13.3.2 Business Blueprint

The purpose of this phase is to create the business blueprint, which is a detailed process-oriented and technical documentation of the results gathered during requirements and design workshops. A blueprint consists of multiple documents and is considered to be a body of work that illustrates how the company intends to run its business utilizing SAP solutions. The business blueprint phase includes the same seven work streams as the previous phase.

Projects are based on the assumption that they create value. The business case describes benefits, which can be broken down into value drivers and value enablers. On an operational level, value needs to drive the scope of the implementation. From a blueprinting perspective, value should drive the solution design. This association is performed on process levels, and the project team typically produces a value map of KPIs and PPIs to measure the progress of value delivery.

Blueprinting is an iterative approach to solution design that is organized by processes. The modeling of to-be processes starts at the highest level and moves down the process hierarchy. The SAP process model has five process levels, of which scenarios, processes, process steps, and activities are managed in SAP Solution Manager. Typically, the first two levels of process design are delivered as part of the business process management work stream during project preparation.

We recommend supporting to-be process design with a focused as-is analysis process catalog, applications, and existing data models. As-is documents are intended to serve as a point of reference for the future solution design. The comparison of as-is and to-be processes drives organizational transformation needs.

SAP Solution Manager is intended to serve as the central knowledge repository during the full implementation lifecycle. Blueprinting follows agile principles and leverages best practices, prepackaged implementation content as described in Chapter 15, and techniques such as value prototyping (for details see Section 16.6), show-and-tell, conference room pilots, and sprints to illustrate SAP solution functionality and to visualize the solution design. Characteristics of agile techniques are iterations, time-boxed design, and visualization.

Blueprint content is developed as the result of a series of workshops that are chronologically organized in sequence with the process hierarchy. The business blueprint workshop concept provides detailed information on workshop facilitation and documentation generation. The final outcome of this work stream is a business blueprint, which is typically not a single document but a body of documents that incorporate multiple design elements, such as requirements, models, function solution design, gap analysis, and technical and integration design.

The recommended approach is to manage and create blueprint documents in SAP Solution Manager. However, depending on the implementation scope and the absence of SAP Solution Manager, a document-based or minimalistic approach may be chosen, for which a template is available.

All blueprint variants adhere to the content and blueprinting deliverables as specified in blueprinting work streams. The business blueprint phase includes several deliverables, milestones, and key decisions as shown in Table 13.8.

Purpose	Deliverables	Milestones & Key Decisions
Align business requirements to the SAP business model	Complete and documented business design: ▸ Project plan update ▸ Subprocess definition document ▸ Subprocess flows ▸ Business activity scripts ▸ Key functional specs ▸ Business process master list	Complete design
Identify additional functionality requirements	Assessment of organization and business process changes	Phase quality assessment
Identify data input Requirements	Inventory of reports and conversions	Communication plan
Business process documentation	Confirmation of implementation date	
Obtain business sign-off on requirements		

Table 13.8 Business Blueprint Phase – Deliverables

After this short intro to the business blueprint phase, we will take a closer look at the value delivery considerations in this phase.

Value Delivery Considerations of Business Blueprints

The purpose of a value-based solution design is to determine value drivers and key process changes for the implementation project. Figure 13.27 shows value deliverables in white and process management and technical solution design deliverables in grey.

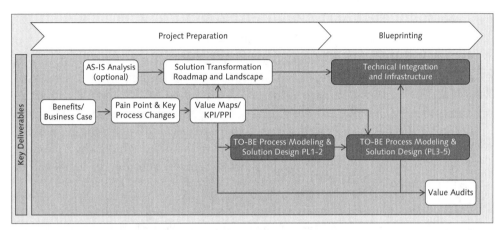

Figure 13.27 Business Blueprint Phase – Value Delivery Considerations

The inputs for value realization are based on outputs from value determination during project preparation. A business case, if available, is the starting point for value determination. Based on the input of process owners and business stakeholders, a pain point analysis is undertaken, and key process changes are determined. A key process change drives the value of a project. The value map correlates pain points, key process changes, and performance indicators and is thus the central deliverable for value determination. The depth of value determination in a project depends on the defined scope of the implementation. The deliverables of the ASAP methodology focus on a less extensive version of value determination.

The results of value determination are mapped to the process and solution design. A link is maintained through value maps, key performance indicators (KPIs), and process performance indicators (PPIs). At the scenario level, financial KPIs come into play, and at the process level, PPIs are the link to the value drivers.

Value realization enhances the ability of the project team to:

▶ Determine priorities for the solution design and manage scope

▶ Determine development needs to ensure that every solution enhancement maps to a value driver

▸ Drive key decisions for the solution design

▸ Track the progress of key process changes

▸ Help tie process performance indicators (PPIs) to the business process hierarchy

Let's now take a closer look at the business process management considerations in the business blueprint phase.

BPM Considerations for Business Blueprints

Blueprinting describes the solution design that entails the technical and process components. The objective of business process management is to describe the solution from a business perspective. Process models serve as central communication tools to describe the design. Project preparation focuses on defining and decomposing business process levels 1 to 2 scenarios. Blueprinting refines the process hierarchy and associates value drivers to the process hierarchies down to process levels 3 to 5, which correspond to the process and process-step levels in SAP Solution Manager.

The business blueprint documents the solution design and therefore serves as the foundation of the solution built during realization. Process models are a central communication tool for the project team. Modeling helps define requirements, responsibilities, and dependencies. The primary changes for business process management during blueprinting are included in five deliverables as illustrated in Figure 13.28.

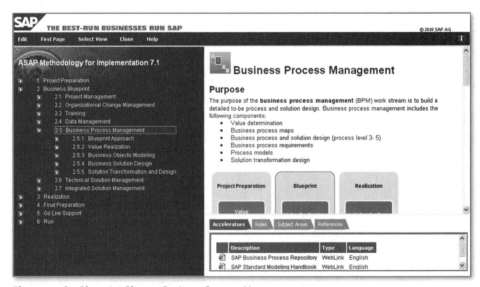

Figure 13.28 Blueprint Phase – Business Process Management

▶ **Blueprint approach**

Blueprinting is based on a show-and-tell approach that leverages SAP demo environments and visualization techniques wherever applicable. The purpose of the subdeliverable solution manager and business process management is to transfer designed business processes into SAP Solution Manager. The approach is determined by whether or not a modeling tool was used during earlier phases to set up a business process structure. If the modeling tool SAP Enterprise Modeling by IDS Scheer was used, the business add-on to ASAP that delivers solution manager integration with SAP Enterprise Modeling by IDS Scheer can be activated. The following seven business add-ons to ASAP delivery content for SAP Enterprise Modeling Applications by IDS Scheer are available:

▶ Redocumentation using SAP Solution Manager and SAP Enterprise Modeling by IDS Scheer

▶ SAP Solution Manager integration with SAP Enterprise Modeling by IDS Scheer

▶ Enterprise Services Repository integration for SAP Enterprise Modeling by IDS Scheer

▶ SAP Business Process Optimization by IDS Scheer

▶ Process intelligence for SAP Process Performance Management by IDS Scheer

▶ Process publishing for SAP Business Server and Publisher by IDS Scheer

▶ SAP Enterprise Modeling by IDS Scheer (consolidated add-on)

> **More Information**
>
> For more information on these seven business add-ons to ASAP delivery content for SAP Enterprise Modeling Applications by IDS Scheer, please go to SAP EcoHub at *http://ecohub.sdn.sap.com/*.

▶ **Value realization**

Covered in the previous subsection.

▶ **Business objects modeling**

In this deliverable you need to identify all of the business objects that are relevant for the scope of the implementation, such as organizational structures, master data, and so on. Business objects are associated with processes and reflected in applications. Understanding these relationships is essential for the overall integration and cross-process integrity. Business object modeling also builds the foundation for service modeling, because a service-oriented architecture is intended to be implemented.

To support the business objects modeling deliverable, the SAP Standard Modeling Handbook can be applied. The handbook is linked as an accelerator to business objects modeling. The purpose of this handbook is to have a standard approach for executing modeling.

> **More Information**
>
> The SAP Standard Modeling Handbook is available on the BPX Community as a wiki (*http://wiki.sdn.sap.com/wiki/display/ModHandbook/SAP+Modeling+Handbook+-+Modeling+Standards*).

▶ **Business solution design**
Business solution design provides a process-based solution design that includes business requirements, process descriptions, and a functional and technical solution design. The approach is iterative and driven by the process hierarchy structures, referencing SAP standards and leveraging agile techniques to create transparency.

▶ **Solution transformation and design**
Solution transformation and design provides a detailed solution mapping to define to-be business processes. Each of the four bullet points listed below represents a solution track.

  ▷ Core implementation: configuration settings

  ▷ SOA/composition: detailed service-oriented architecture and composition requirements

  ▷ Solution gaps and core enhancements: detailed enhancement requirements

  ▷ Third-party solutions: available third-party solutions and detailed requirements for them

The inputs required for the business process management work stream during the business blueprint phase are the completed deliverables from the project preparation phase. Any outstanding deliverables that were not completed and therefore did not complete the project preparation quality gate must be completed to be used as inputs to the business blueprint phase.

The SAP Solution Manager project should be created and project standards put in place prior to beginning blueprinting. Additionally, the project teams should be trained on how to use SAP Solution Manager to capture deliverables and process decompositions. Project team training for implementation project tools used during blueprinting, such as those used for modeling the processes, also should be completed prior to beginning the blueprinting process.

Now that we have taken a closer look at value delivery and business process management considerations, we will take a closer look at the service-oriented architecture considerations in the business blueprint phase.

SOA Considerations for Business Blueprint

The ASAP 7 core methodology introduces a set of service-oriented architecture (SOA) implications to be considered within the business blueprint phase. These build upon the deliverables of the preparation phase while introducing new SOA considerations related to solution design and technical solution management. Projects that have identified SOA as a component of their IT strategy must take a comprehensive approach to blueprinting.

The purpose of the SOA activities within the blueprint phase is to document the proper approach and technology set together with the needed business solution design and technical solution management plan. These two topics are equally critical for a clear blueprint of the proposed SOA-enabling solution landscape. If any of these are incomplete, the project team will not understand the SOA technical and integration process within the realization phase. The purpose of the SOA and composition deliverable in the business process management work stream is to generate all models and specifications required to start the actual development process for the composite application that will take place in the realization phase. This involves translating the business requirements into models that can be implemented.

The business blueprint phase starts by classifying business processes as use cases or technical processes. A high-level screen-flow model and a user interface mock-up are created for every use case. These models allow for aligning business and IT concerns. The corresponding departments can see how the composite works even before any code is implemented. As soon as stakeholders accept these models, they can be used as a basis for devising more technical models.

A technical screen-flow model shows how various screens work together and what kind of service requirements must be met. In addition, a mock-up template describes every user interface element in detail, which enables a steady flow of work during the implementation phase. SOA and composition also consolidate and document the detailed service requirements and those from composite application design and development. These service requirements must be compared with SAP standard enterprise services to identify gaps and fits, which means differentiating among services that can be reused, services that have to be newly implemented, and services that need to be enhanced.

If you are applying SAP Enterprise Modeling by IDS Scheer, you can use the business add-on to ASAP that delivers Enterprise Services Repository integration for SAP Enterprise Modeling by IDS Scheer as illustrated in Figure 13.29.

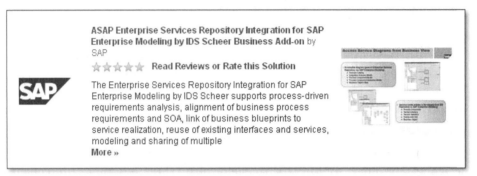

Figure 13.29 Business Add-On that Delivers Enterprise Services Repository Integration for SAP Enterprise Modeling by IDS Scheer

The Enterprise Services Repository Integration for SAP Enterprise Modeling by IDS Scheer add-on supports process-driven requirements analysis, alignment of business process requirements and SOA, linking of business blueprints to service realization, reuse of existing interfaces and services, and modeling and sharing of multiple planning scenarios in SAP enterprise modeling before implementation, and requirements analysis can define the need for new services.

> **More Information**
>
> For more details on the business add-on to ASAP that delivers Enterprise Services Repository integration for SAP Enterprise Modeling by IDS Scheer, please go to SAP EcoHub at *http://ecohub.sdn.sap.com/*.

The technical solution management work stream prescribes the installation of a viable, technical development environment that is available for use by the project teams to begin the realization phase. Once SOA requirements have been identified and the technical and integration SOA solution has been designed, you need to proceed with the planning and setup of the development environment (SAP

NetWeaver Composition Environment), work breakdown structure (WBS) 2.6.7, as illustrated in Figure 13.30.

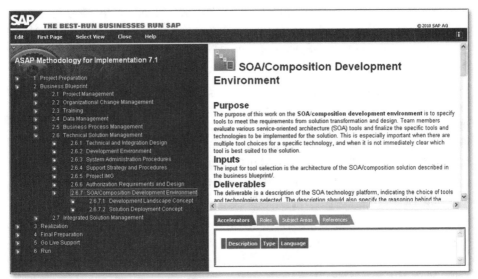

Figure 13.30 Technical Solution Management – SOA/Composition Development Environment

The purpose of the SOA/composition development environment (2.6.7) is to specify tools to meet the requirements from solution transformation and design. Team members evaluate various service-oriented architecture (SOA) tools and finalize the specific tools and technologies to be implemented for the solution. This is especially important when there are multiple tool choices for a specific technology and when it is not immediately clear which tool is best suited to the solution. The input for tool selection is the architecture of the SOA/composition solution described in the business blueprint. The deliverable is a description of the SOA technology platform, indicating the choice of tools and technologies selected. The description should also specify the reasoning behind the selection of the tools for the various layers. For more details please go to Chapter 14, Section 14.1.

In Chapter 14, Section 14.5, we will introduce the simple samples for enterprise services consumption, which are ready-to-run applications based on the most commonly used enterprise services and various SAP consumption technologies. The simple samples can be used for education and as a good starting point for working with SOA/composition.

The purpose of the development landscape concept (2.6.7.1) is to explain how an SOA-based solution introduces new infrastructure tools such as Enterprise Services Repository (ES Repository), a service registry, a process integration service bus, a composition environment, and so on, to a development landscape that may already contain other development infrastructure tools such as SAP Solution Manager or the system landscape directory and development infrastructure in the SAP NetWeaver technology platform.

The appropriate landscapes for these new tools need to be planned well in advance of solution implementation, because procurement, installation, and configuration of these systems may significantly affect the overall time line for the project. The development landscape concept identifies the software tools and systems needed for the development of the solution. Further, it specifies the roles of developers in terms of the tools and systems to be accessed. It serves as an input to the planning of the physical development landscape.

Next, we will take a look at the considerations in respect to skills that project team members need to have to practice the new ASAP methodology.

Consultants, Business Process Experts, Project Managers and Team Leads – Considerations for the Business Blueprint

The purpose of the business blueprint phase is to create the business blueprint, which is a detailed, process-oriented and technical documentation of the results gathered during requirements and design workshops. The business blueprint consists of multiple documents and is considered to be a body of work that illustrates how the company intends to run its business utilizing SAP solutions. To be able to do this, the process and application consultant must not only have knowledge of the capabilities of the applications, but also needs to have knowledge of the end-to-end business processes within his expertise area. The business process design needs to be detailed, including all of the different process objects and parameters, and it needs to have the end user in the center, including the need for a thorough understanding of the IT capabilities and flexibilities SOA/composition provide. After the details of the process design have been completed, the process and application consultant must be able to execute an equal mapping to the four solution transformation options, and he can only do this if he understands the four IT capability options:

► **Core implementation**
  Describe detailed configuration settings.

▶ **SOA/composition**
Describe detailed service-oriented architecture and composition requirements.

▶ **Solution gaps and core enhancements**
Describe detailed enhancement requirements.

▶ **Third-party solutions**
Describe available third-party solutions and detailed requirements for them.

This new set of requirements calls for the process and application consultant to obtain some new skills, which are provided via the business process expert role and skills set. You can find more details about this skill set in Chapter 16, Section 16.1.

We will now go to the third phase, realization, and describe how value delivery, business process management, and service-oriented architecture are reflected in this phase, including the skills enablement requirements for project team members.

13.3.3 Realization

The purpose of the realization phase, which has the same seven work streams as the two previous phases, is to implement the business scenarios and process requirements based on the business blueprint completed in the previous phase. Initially, the baseline configuration, which represents the core business process settings, is performed, tested, and confirmed. This is followed by a series of configuration and development cycles to implement the entire end-to-end solution. The solution is tested in several cycle tests and in focused end-to-end integration tests. Configuration is documented in SAP Solution Manager. All developments such as enterprise services, composite applications, interfaces, data conversion programs, reports, and any required enhancements are built and documented in SAP Solution Manager. Legacy data conversion programs are created and tested. The production system is installed during realization. In parallel with the configuration process, end-user documentation and end-user training documentation are created, according to the training analysis and strategy defined in the business blueprint phase. Table 13.9 shows the deliverables, milestones, and key decisions to work on during the realization phase. For each deliverable, the ASAP Roadmap explains in detail the purpose, inputs, and outputs and, where applicable, gives further details and information about the expected result.

Purpose	Deliverables	Milestones & Key Decisions
Build and test a complete business and system environment	Test data and configuration	Project team trained (realization)
Develop training material and end-user documentation	Business process procedures	Final design and configuration
Obtain business approval	Quality assurance system environment	Integration test
	Production system environment	End-user system infrastructure
	Develop and test interfaces, conversions and reports	User acceptance
	Evaluate and enhance security and controls	Phase quality assessment
	End-user training material and plan	Readiness review
	End-user training system environment	
	Data conversion plan	
	User acceptance test	

Table 13.9 Realization Phase – Deliverables

After this short intro to the realization phase, we will now take a closer look at the value delivery and business process management considerations in the realization phase.

Value Delivery and BPM Considerations for Realization

The purpose of the business process management work stream during the realization phase is to build the solution based upon the process and solution design created during the business blueprint phase and "realize" the solution design by building functional business processes during baseline and final configuration, complete SOA and composition development, complete workflow, reports, interfaces, conversion, enhancement, forms (WRICEF) developments, and create testing to ensure consistency and continuity in the productive solution. Business process procedures and end-user training are also created during this phase, including definition of requirements and set-up for business process monitoring, which both need to cover IT and business process monitoring.

Realization of the solution design includes the development of technical specifications, data design, baseline and final IMG configuration resulting in functioning business processes, and successful completion of both unit and integration testing (cycles 1 to 3) for each of the business scenarios and business processes as designed during the blueprint phase.

Testing of the realized solution is completed during the realization phase to validate that the solution built matches the solution as it was designed. The realization phase includes activities and deliverables that close the cycle of design and build. Deliverables created during realization include the following:

▶ Configured general settings and organizational structures

▶ Configured scenarios and business processes

▶ Complete and approved configuration reference documents

▶ Development objects documentation

▶ Implementation of development objects – WRICEF

▶ Development of enterprise services

▶ Development of composition applications

▶ Enterprise services and composition technical documentation

▶ Manual and automated test cases

▶ Completed test cycles

▶ Business process procedures (BPPs)

▶ Implemented business process monitoring capabilities

By completing the deliverables of the realization phase correctly, the project completes the build of the designed solution, documents the build activities, and creates and executes test scripts that confirm that the solution built meets the requirements and design documented in the blueprint deliverables. The realization phase confirms that the solution is built as defined in the design documentation and works as expected.

The achievement of the goals of the implementation project are essential to the successful delivery of the SAP solution. Completion of the build and test phase provides the inputs to the final prep and go-live phase, which will implement the solution into the productive landscape and turn it over to the end users.

The primary changes for business process management during the realization phase are included in the following work packages:

▸ **3.5.1 Value audits**

Value audits assist with the tracking, monitoring, and controlling of the value drivers and key process changes during each phase of the project. Value audits ensure that the project lives up to the initial value expectations as defined in the initial business case. Value audits enhance the capabilities of the project team to manage expectations and focus on key deliverables. They support the transparency of value delivery during the project and assist in tracking key process changes during the project. The key deliverable for a value audit includes the value status (value and cost actuals versus targets and issues) and identifies measures to achieve the value targets and is updated regularly throughout the project phase.

▸ **3.5.9 Business process monitoring**

As shown in Figure 13.31, business process monitoring describes the considerations that are required to define business process monitoring requirements in respect to business process stabilization, business process improvement, and business process optimization and innovation from both an IT and a business perspective. This deliverable also needs to select and set up the business process monitoring tools.

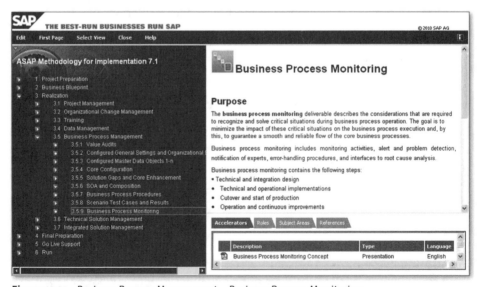

Figure 13.31 Business Process Management – Business Process Monitoring

Let's take a closer look at business process monitoring.

The term *business process monitoring* is widely used in the SAP community, and everybody has a different understanding of business process monitoring. This is not really surprising because monitoring capabilities have to serve different target groups and different purposes. There cannot be one business process monitoring tool that serves all. If there were one, you could be sure that (like all other tools that try to serve each and every purpose) this tool would provide everything in a mediocre manner but nothing in excellent quality.

This is why SAP decided to follow a different path and provide different business process monitoring tools that can clearly focus on specific target groups and/or specific purposes. Before we look deeper into those tools we want to clarify another term. In public discussions you also hear the term *business process optimization* (in a broader sense) a lot, where again everybody has a different understanding of what *optimization* really means. SAP split this term into three different pieces: business process stabilization, business process improvement, and business process optimization (in a narrower sense). This split may look somewhat artificial at first, but it helps understand why different business process monitoring tools are provided and which tool should be used for which purposes (see Figure 13.32).

▶ **Business process stabilization**
You current business process is operated at a certain level. However, sometimes an exception occurs, as illustrated in Figure 13.32. This exception could be, for example, a failure in an interface communication or a failure during the background processing, so that certain business documents are not created or updated. The output level of your business process drops to a lower level. Business process stabilization means either avoiding the process exception in the first place or, if the exception occurred, resolving the problem as fast as possible to bring the process output back to the expected level.

▶ **Business process improvement**
Your business process is operated without exceptions or with a minimum of exceptions as described above and illustrated in Figure 13.32. By looking at the output level of the process you determine that the process does not achieve 100% of what it was initially planned to achieve when the business process was designed and implemented. This may be related to inefficiencies caused by end users who do not use the SAP system as intended. Or this may be caused by configuration issues within the process or old open business documents that are not properly closed and removed from the system. Business process

367

improvement means the current output level is increased in the future, ideally up to the optimum that can be achieved with the initial process design.

▶ **Business process optimization**
Your business process is operated stably, and all improvements mentioned above have been realized; that is, the output level of the process is 100 percent according to plan as illustrated in Figure 13.32. But by comparing your various business KPIs and PPIs with industry benchmarks or competitors, you find out that your process is still not good enough or that you are missing the competitive edge. Your process needs some further process innovation, or the process needs to be optimized to set the bar for the process output level even higher than the current 100 percent. The current process design has to be changed.

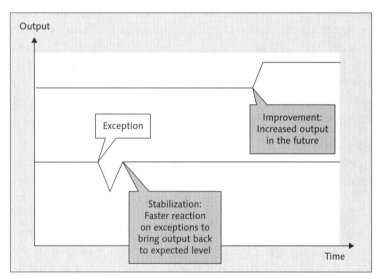

Figure 13.32 Business Process Stabilization and Improvement

The logical flow can be as follows. Company X implements an SAP solution with the target standardizing and improving the current business processes and thereby obtains a certain return on investment (ROI) within a certain time frame based on optimized and standardized processes. This initial plan can only be fulfilled if the newly implemented business processes are running smoothly and stably; that is, errors in interfaces and background processing should be minimized, and functional errors should be avoided. In this sense the business process stabilization phase protects the initial investment made by company X. To achieve the ROI as fast as possible the business processes should be operated at 100 percent output level. Here the business process improvement phase should help ensure that the business processes are operated at an optimum level according to plan. If company X then decides that their business processes should be operated at an even higher output level or even more efficiently, additional investment is required to reengineer or innovate the existing processes in a business process optimization phase.

From a target group perspective it can be generally stated that business process stabilization is mainly the task of the IT department, whereas business process optimization is clearly the task of the business department. Business process improvement is the grey zone where both IT and business have to collaborate, although more responsibility for this is normally found within business, which is illustrated in Figure 13.33.

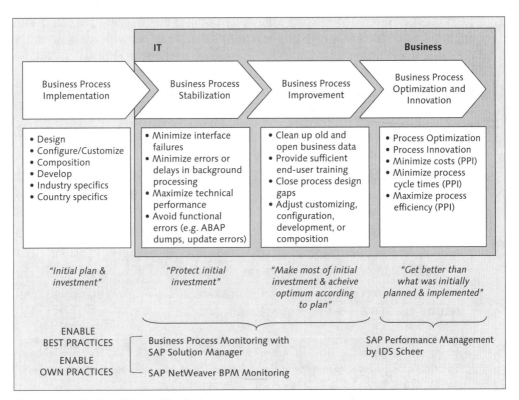

Figure 13.33 Business Process Monitoring

From a business process monitoring tool perspective, business process monitoring can support the two phases (business process stabilization and improvement) in

SAP Solution Manager. Here the focus is on SAP Business Suite's Best Practices that are mainly based on transaction codes and ABAP reports. Business process monitoring in SAP Solution Manager provides, on the one hand, more technical monitoring capabilities for background jobs (single jobs and BW process chains) for all common SAP interface technologies (IDoc, tRFC, qRFC, BDoc, batch input, flat file, SAP NetWeaver PI, ABAP dumps, update errors, etc.). On the other hand, about 300 preconfigured application-specific key figures are provided out of the box and currently cover SAP ERP, SAP Customer Relationship Management (CRM), SAP Supplier Relationship Management (SRM), SAP Advanced Planning & Optimization (APO), and industry specifics for SAP Apparel and Footwear, SAP for Automotive, SAP for Banking, SAP for Retail, and SAP for Utilities.

The business process monitoring tool also allows the monitoring of your own practice, also referred to as composite applications. You can build the composite applications on top of the SAP Business Suite's Best Practices with the application core processes and on arbitrary backend systems. Composite applications follow the SOA paradigm of "non-intrusiveness," which means these applications are bound to provide modification-free process extensions to the core business applications. Below, you will find examples that you can use for your own practice:

▶ With mobile workflow approval on the BlackBerry or iPhone you improve the cost efficiency of your workflow processes.

▶ You can leverage emerging social media channels such as Twitter within SAP CRM to reach out to a broader network of customers, run more effective marketing campaigns, and track them.

▶ You can leverage emerging social media channels such as Twitter within SAP CRM to receive open feedback from customers, provide superior customer service, and monitor customers' opinions about products or services

▶ The customer fact sheet solution offers customer service agents and sales representatives a 360-degree view of customer data.

More Information

You can find more information about these own practice processes and solutions at SAP EcoHub, *http://ecohub.sdn.sap.com/*, and in Chapter 15, Section 15.1.2.

The composite applications can be built on top of the SAP Business Suite's Best Practices with the application core processes and on arbitrary backend systems. SAP NetWeaver BPM provides the business process monitoring capabilities to monitor composite applications' own practices.

If you are looking at process efficiency analysis from a business perspective with dedicated process performance indicators (PPIs), you can use SAP Process Performance Management by IDS Scheer to identify where process reengineering is appropriate to optimize your business processes and reach even higher process efficiencies or higher output levels than initially planned. SAP Process Performance Management By IDS Scheer is available as a business add-ons to ASAP via SAP EcoHub, *http://ecohub.sdn.sap.com/*, as illustrated in Figure 13.34.

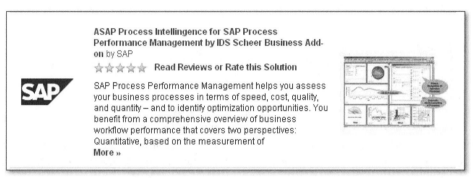

Figure 13.34 Business Add-On to ASAP that Delivers Process Performance Management by IDS Scheer

The input required for business process management during realization is the completed deliverables from the business blueprint phase. Any outstanding deliverables that were not completed and therefore did not complete the business blueprint quality gate must be completed to be used as inputs to the realization phase.

Now that we have taken a closer look at value delivery and business process management considerations, we will look at the service-oriented architecture considerations in the realization phase.

SOA Considerations for Realization

The SOA technical design and specifications developed within the business blueprint phase have a significant influence on how services ought to be realized in the best possible manner. Done properly, the SOA efforts within the blueprint phase consider all of the various design and implementation alternatives. The realization phase aims to formalize the final realization decision for each service and provides justification for the choice.

The purpose of the SOA work stream during the realization phase is to develop, implement, and document the enterprise services and composite applications as defined during the business blueprint phase. The approach to implementing SOA within the realization phase is segregated into two distinct technological paths:

▶ **Path 1**
Explains the inputs, technique and accelerators for enterprise services. These represent a standards-based way of encapsulating enterprise functionality and exposing it as a reusable business service that can be combined with other services to meet new requirements.

▶ **Path 2**
This path works through the aggregation of enterprise services to compose new applications and enable new business processes to take shape.

Each path has a very different starting point, input technique and accelerators. Enterprise services are sourced from a service provider such as the Enterprise Services Repository (ES Repository), whereas composite applications are often sought to aggregate these same system-centric services within human-centric scenarios.

By correctly completing the SOA/composite deliverables prescribed within the realization phase, you will not only ensure the completeness of your overall composite solution, but will also have documented the build activities and confirmed that your composite solution meets the requirements and design prescribed by the blueprint deliverables.

The new version of ASAP includes the following SOA deliverables that are included in the business process management work stream: The first is SOA/composition (3.5.6). The purpose of the SOA and composition deliverable is to implement and document the enterprise services, including developing and realizing the composite application. The business process, functional design, and specifications from the business blueprint phase serve as input. The work stream has two substreams:

▶ **3.5.6.1 Enterprise Services Development**
The purpose of the enterprise services development subdeliverable as illustrated in Figure 13.35 is to implement and document the enterprise services modeled in the business blueprint phase.

The enterprise services that are modeled can be exported in the Web Services Description Language (WSDL) format from the ES Repository. These can, in turn, be imported into the backend, and the corresponding implementation proxies (or stubs) can be generated. The necessary service logic must be coded in the generated implementation proxy to complete the service implementation.

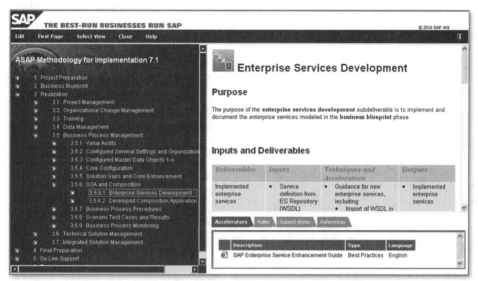

Figure 13.35 Business Process Management – SOA and Composition – Enterprise Services Development

Documentation of enterprise services is an important activity for SOA-based solutions. Because the reuse of enterprise services is one of the cornerstones of a successful service-oriented architecture, even services that are modeled in the best way possible need to be accompanied by thorough documentation to ensure widespread reusability.

Enterprise services documentation should describe the technical contract between the service provider and the consumer. This is required to understand the services' behavior in detail. Typically, these contracts group the service description documents and technical diagrams and may be supplemented by other, nontechnical documents.

The service models in ES Repository, which are created in the design activity, are a binding contract between the consumer and the service provider. These models therefore provide a very good starting point for documenting enterprise services. Ensure that the service models in the ES Repository include these components: process component models, integration scenario models, process component interaction models, and signature definition (contract).

Governance plays a central role in the implementation of services. Governance of an SOA implementation must include standardizing the general runtime behavior of enterprise services and their static models by establishing clear design and programming paradigms and guidelines. For example, the exception reporting and handling strategy should be similar across the various service implementations. This kind of governance is a prerequisite for ensuring easy-to-use, reusable services and achieving higher productivity during implementation. As mentioned earlier in the chapter, we recommend that the deliverable project standards (1.1.5) have an enterprise services design standard (1.1.5.11).

▶ **3.5.6.2 Developed Composition Application**

The purpose of the developed composition application subdeliverable as illustrated in Figure 13.36 is to develop and realize the composite application where the solution design, development specification, solution architecture, development process, guidelines, and so on serve as input.

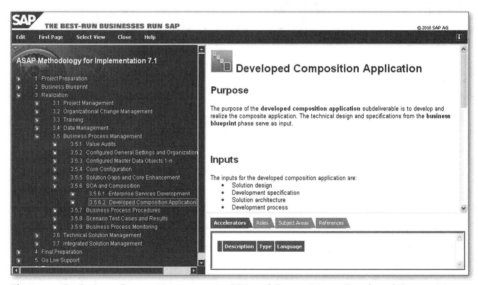

Figure 13.36 Business Process Management – SOA and Composition – Developed Composition Application

Composite applications are typical consumers within an enterprise SOA system landscape and are usually built on existing services and infrastructure. They combine these services into user-centric processes and views, supported by their own business logic and specific user interfaces. These typically span several application areas and may even cross enterprise boundaries. Composite applications are loosely coupled with the backend systems on which they are based, resulting in a new logical application tier, which can be deployed and upgraded independent of the backend infrastructure. In many cases, composite applications are combined with business integration scenarios to establish corresponding business network solutions.

A human-centric composite scenario typically consists of the following:

▶ **User interface**
This is typically created with a graphical modeling approach (SAP NetWeaver BPM, BRM, Visual Composer, the Web Dynpro development environment, Adobe Forms, and so on) and is therefore easily adjusted to specific needs.

▶ **Composite process**
Process flow is modeled with graphical tools, and workflows can be assembled from reusable blocks.

▶ **Business objects and local services**
Composite logic is implemented on modeled business objects, based on imported enterprise services.

In some cases, primarily human-centric composite scenarios are combined with system-centric integration scenarios, which means the overall composite process comprises both human-centric and system-centric parts. For more details see Chapter 14, Section 14.1.

The starting point for the implementation of enterprise services is the service model, which is the output of the business blueprint phase. After gathering the inputs prescribed within WBS 3.5.6.1 and reviewing that section's roadmap thoroughly, familiarize yourself with the accelerator called Building an End-to-End Enterprise SOA Scenario. This document will explain the SOA service provider and consumer models necessary for you to understand the concepts of the enterprise service lifecycle. The next step is to refer to the second accelerator, SAP Enterprise Service Enhancement Guide, which is required to modify the behavior of out-of-the-box services exported from the Enterprise Services Repository (ES Repository) to fit your project's requirements.

The detailed enterprise services implementation process outlined within the two accelerators together with the abbreviated explanation available within WBS 3.5.6.1 represent foundational knowledge for those overseeing the project activities. However, the enterprise services implementation within the realization phase should be delegated to an SOA engineer.

The enterprise services implementation would not be complete without proper detailed documentation of the technical contract between the service provider and the consumer services. Typically, these contracts group the service description documents and technical diagrams and may be supplemented by other, nontechnical documents.

To complete the service documentation, any other semantic or technical information that the service owner wants to publicize can be added. This documentation can also be enriched by service-level agreements (SLAs) for the specific enterprise services.

It is understood that composite applications that enable enterprise services need to reflect certain preferred business intents. That intent should be well described within the inputs of WBS 3.5.6.2, created during the blueprint phase. Reviewing and understanding the phase inputs should be the first step toward understanding the project perspectives of creating composite applications.

> **More Information**
>
> The detailed composite application implementation process outlined within the Building an End-to-End Enterprise SOA Scenario accelerator together with the abbreviated explanation available within WBS 3.5.6.2 represent foundational knowledge for those overseeing the project's SOA activities. For more details see Chapter 14, Section 14.1.

The composite application implementation would not be complete without proper documentation of the Implementation Guide (documentation about how to deploy the separate parts) and development documentation.

In Chapter 16, Section 16.4 we will introduce the SOA kit, an add-on to ASAP. The SOA kit empowers various roles within IT implementation projects. The kit provides hands-on documentation, that is, accelerators and samples of key topics such as governance and methodology and guidance about architecture patterns, business add-ons, consulting services, and educational offerings. For more information on the SOA kit, an add-on to ASAP, simply go to *http://www.sdn.sap.com/irj/sdn/soa-kit*.

The last topic we will cover is considerations for skills that project team members need to have to practice the new ASAP methodology.

Consultants, Business Process Experts, Project Managers, and Team Leads – Considerations for Realization

The purpose of the realization phase is to implement the business scenario and process requirements based on the business blueprint completed in the previous phase. As before, team members continue to carry out the following activities, but within the framework of value delivery: configure the system, continue to define system roles and authorizations, regardless of offshore or onshore locations, and go through third-level project team training and end-user training. The project team along with the project managers needs to ensure that the solution is ready for the customer.

During realization, consultants build on deliverables created in the business blueprint phase and work with the technical teams in an integrated fashion. Ultimately, teams that execute configuration, development, and composite applications need to ensure that the system meets all of the business requirements that were defined in the business blueprint document so that project managers and auditors can meet traceability requirements and user acceptance of the solution.

The project manager needs to run the project more as a continuum of deliverables, rather than as isolated deliverables. The deliverables are linked in a chain, and the project manager's role is to ensure that teams are ready at the proper time for the handovers.

We will now go to the last three phases: final preparation, go-live support, and the run phase and describe how business process management and service-oriented architecture are reflected in these phases, including the skills enablement requirements for the project team members.

13.3.4 Final Preparation, Go-Live Support, and Run

The purpose of the final preparation phase is to finalize readiness of the solution and its supporting tools and processes for production go-live. This includes, but is not limited to, system tests, end-user training, system management, and cutover activities (including data migration). The phase deliverables also enable the resolution of all crucial open issues. On successful completion of this phase, the business is ready to run the live SAP software system. During this phase, the following activities are also completed: ensuring the execution of organizational change management (OCM) plans and ensuring functional and technical support for the production system. The major work streams for final preparation are: project management, organizational change management, training, production support readiness, approved nonfunctional tests, and production cutover.

The support organization is put in place, and end-user training is completed. The phase deliverables also enable the resolution of all crucial open issues. At the end of this phase the production system is switched on, and business operations start in the new environment.

The purpose of the go-live support phase is to provide support for the solution during the period immediately following production cutover. Exceptional items such as additional production support, exceptional business monitoring processes, and extraordinary technical support are planned and executed in this phase. In addition, the disposition of all issues encountered in the transition to the new solution is determined and documented.

At the end of the designated extra-care period, sustaining production support processes planned in final preparation and executed as part of go-live support become the core support for continuous improvement in the ongoing solution. The major work streams for go-live support are project management, organizational change management, training, production support, and transfer to solution.

Final preparation and go-live support have deliverables, milestones, and key decisions to be worked on during the phase as illustrated in Table 13.10 and Table 13.11. During the final preparation phase, the deliverables reflect the integrated nature of the solution — hence the reason for having the work streams of data management, business process management, technical solution management, and integration solution management merge into the following:

▶ Production support readiness

▶ Approved technical and operational tests

▶ Production cutover

In go-live support these work streams become:

▶ Production support

▶ Transfer to solution

Purpose	Deliverables	Milestones & Key Decisions
Prepare system for production release	Data converted	Organizational changes implemented
Prepare the internal and external organization for go-live	Cutover plan	Go/no-go decision
	End users trained	
	End-user system IDs created	
	System support organization in place ▸ Help desk ▸ Technical support	
	Operational production system environment	

Table 13.10 Deliverables for the Final Preparation Phase

Purpose	Deliverables	Milestones & Key Decisions
Business owns and executes new business processes and systems	Live production environment	Go-live
Monitor business process results	Operational help desk	Project close
Monitor production environment	Cutover and conversion activities completed	
Establish center of excellence for support and enhancements	Post go-live end-user training	
	Updated business case	
	Lessons learned	

Table 13.11 Deliverables for the Go-Live Support Phase

For each deliverable, the ASAP Roadmap explains in detail the purpose, inputs, and outputs and, where applicable, gives further details and information about the expected result.

Let's now take a closer look at the business process management considerations in the final preparation and go-live support phases.

BPM Considerations for Final Preparation and Go-Live Support

The final preparation and go-live support phases of the project, as they relate to business process management, include the final readiness of the business and support processes for cutover and production go-live and the completion of all project documentation so the content of the project can be moved into the solution in SAP Solution Manager. At this point in the methodology, many of the work streams begin to integrate as the design and build of the solution is completed, testing is being finalized, and cutover preparations are underway.

There is no formal business process management work stream during the final prep and go-live support phases, but rather the finalization and preparation for operations take place as part of the production support readiness (4.4) and production support (5.4) work packages.

The final preparation phase deliverables reflect the integrated nature of the solution, and the work streams of data management, business process management, technical solution management, and integration solution management merge into the following work streams:

▶ **4.4 Production Support Readiness**
Ensures that the resources and processes are in place to support the solution after cutover. This includes the sub–work stream business process operations (4.4.1.5). This work stream contains the deliverables associated with business process management and is designed to ensure that processes are in place to monitor and manage business-critical operations and core business processes.

▶ **4.5 Approved Technical and Operational Tests**
Includes the confirmation that the solution is ready for use in production.

▶ **4.6 Production Cutover**
Includes the cutover to production and go-live. All organizational business, functional, technical, and system aspects of the project are production-ready.

The go-live support phase deliverables further integrate the previous work streams and become simply:

▶ Production support

▶ Transfer to solution

The business process management activities are integrated into the work stream of transfer to solution (5.5). The purpose of this stream is to prepare to transfer the business process hierarchy and all associated deliverables into the productive solutions in SAP Solution Manager. It has two substreams:

▶ **5.5.1 Solution Manager Update**
All deliverables, open issues from cutover and final prep, lessons learned, and project management plans are finalized. The SAP Solution Manager project is reviewed for completeness including deliverable status reports to ensure that all deliverables have the Released status value assigned and are locked for changes.

▶ **5.5.2 Solution Documentation**
The purpose of this work package is to provide the framework for monitoring business processes, KPIs, and PPIs through the lifecycle of the productive solution. SAP Solution Manager provides the central management platform, and the content moved into the solution becomes the primary documentation for this support.

From a functional project team member perspective, the focus of both phases is to finalize the documentation of the solution and test results, prepare for production support of the business processes, and implement production support operation processes. The project teams need to ensure that the core business process documentation including configuration, development, and testing documentation is completed.

Completion of documents means that all documentation has the status "Released." This must be done prior to moving the project contents into the productive solution, in SAP Solution Manager, because once a productive business process (in a solution) is "checked out" for maintenance, the entire process cannot be checked back in unless all documents have a Released status. Therefore, if the documentation was not finalized prior to go-live, the documentation would need to be finalized prior to moving the adapted productive business process back into the productive solution.

This is of primary importance, and anyone working with the processes and preparing them for transfer to the solution during this phase of the project needs to ensure that all documentation is complete, with the Released status (or a similar status that indicates the document is complete). For most team members this will be their primary activity during these phases — ensuring the completeness of the documentation. Business processes are moved into the solution individually, so as the validation is done, the solution can be built using the content from the SAP Solution Manager project.

Once the business processes are transferred into the solution, the content of the solution is used for operations, maintenance, and optimization of the business processes from both an IT and business perspective. Business process monitoring (3.5.9), as described earlier in the chapter, can now be activated to start the monitoring to support business process stabilization, business process optimization, and business process improvement. It is also in this phase that you can prepare to publish your business processes to the various audiences.

More Information

To support this activity you can apply the business add-ons to ASAP that implement SAP Business Server and Publisher by IDS Scheer as illustrated in Figure 13.37. For more details please go to SAP EcoHub: *http://ecohub.sdn.sap.com/*.

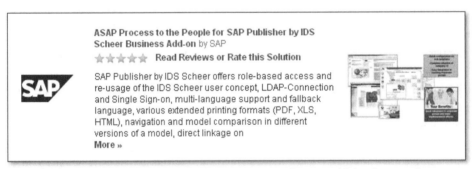

Figure 13.37 Business Add-On to ASAP Delivering Content for SAP Publisher by IDS Scheer

You can run reports which can be run from Transaction SOLAR_EVAL to verify that all documents in the project have the Released status assigned and are ready to be transferred. Project management completes their project closing activities, and all outstanding issues are resolved or have a plan for resolution. The solution is set up and ready to receive the business process hierarchy (BPH), and the content of the project is transferred over and the project is closed.

Keep in mind that all deliverables from each of the previous phases have to be complete by this stage, and incomplete deliverables will adversely impact the project's ability to go-live and/or deliver business process operations support.

Now that we have had a closer look at the business process management considerations, we will take a closer look at the service-oriented architecture considerations for final preparation and go-live support.

SOA Considerations for Final Preparation and Go-Live Support

The ASAP methodology introduces a set of service-oriented architecture (SOA) efforts to consider within the final preparation and go-live support phases. These build upon the deliverables of the prior phase while introducing new SOA considerations related to the governance model for operations.

SAP projects with identified SOA as a component of the IT strategy must take a comprehensive approach to the following considerations within the final preparation and go-live support phases: The governance model for operations extended business flexibility, facilitated through new technologies and SOA, increases the complexity of individual application management tasks. A governance model for end-to-end operations encompasses the organizational model, operational processes, the collaboration platform, quality management, and continual improvement, each tying into the customers' SOA strategies. The creation of a customer CoE to oversee the governance model requires an organization with specialized roles for an integrated approach to quality management for solution operations, end-to-end enabled operational processes, and a technology platform capable of matching the solution complexity.

In the final preparation phase and go-live support, you become productive — packaging and deploying SOA applications, configuring applications for runtime (adapted to the IT landscape), testing and validating applications, and executing deployed SOA applications. To make enterprise SOA deliver on this promise, this ASAP promotes the creation of a holistic approach to good governance for your SOA initiatives. The governance model for operations seeks to describe governance applied to the runtime aspects of SOA. It typically includes service monitoring, security, and management with a runtime governance policy system.

A governance model for SOA operations becomes even more important as volumes scale and when multiple application service servers are required to support the workloads. Your starting point should be in the governance model for operations section in WBS 4.4.1.4 of the final preparation phase. Note that you will encounter the same content in the go-live support phase WBS 5.4.1.4. In each of these WBS areas, the ASAP methodology promotes the creation of a governance model for operations set along with the procedure described in the SOA Readiness link within each WBS.

Subdeliverables prescribed in WBS 4.4.1.5 and 5.4.1.4 are shared among other aspects of the governance model for operations and may not necessarily be aimed directly at SOA. Nonetheless, you should consider these in your approach to SOA governance to include:

▶ Determined maturity level

▶ Defined vision and strategy

▶ Defined implementation roadmap

▶ Defined governance fundamentals (e.g., boards, organizational model, sourcing model)

▶ Defined process model and relevant processes

▶ Defined essential architecture standards

These factors are part of a work package ensemble of deliverables that together form the governance model for operations. Under the Topics section of each WBS, you will find details of each subdeliverable together with links to supporting documentation. For more details please go to Chapter 14, Section 14.1.

> **More Information**
>
> For the SOA governance model you can also apply the business add-on to ASAP that implements SOA governance and strategy. You can find more information about this add-on in Section 13.4.3. Included is the SOA kit, an add-on to ASAP, *http://www.sdn.sap.com/irj/sdn/soa-kit*, described in Chapter 16, Section 16.4.

The last thing we will look at is the considerations for skills that project team members need to have to practice the new ASAP methodology.

Consultants, Business Process Experts, Project Managers, and Team Leads – Considerations for Final Preparation and Go-Live Support

All work stream leads involved in the final preparation phase assist the project managers in making certain that KPIs and PPIs that were established within the value delivery framework during the project prep phase are documented, complete, and signed off; work with the technical teams to ensure that production support processes are established, that is, volume and stress tests are performed; assist in refining and validating cutover plans; and assist with knowledge transfer and documentation.

Consultants should also keep in mind that comprehensive end-user training is an essential part of this phase, and the leads may be asked to work with the education team and assist in end-user training and documentation.

During the go-live support phase, teams should have a basic understanding of the various services that SAP offers such as customer program optimization and SAP Security Optimization. For example, a key service is SAP EarlyWatch, where experts from SAP analyze the system's technical infrastructure. The aim is to ensure that the system functions as smoothly as possible. The purpose of the SAP EarlyWatch service is to improve the performance of the live system by preventing system bottlenecks. The underlying concept of SAP EarlyWatch is prevention: taking appropriate action before a problem situation develops.

The production support work stream and Basis team leads play a key role in this phase. Along with services, many SAP customers need help with managing complex IT solutions, and the new ASAP methodology guides the customer through setting up a center of excellence (CoE) or a help desk. The customer COE is a facilitating organization that implements the methodologies for end-to-end operations and reports and enforces them. Therefore, an appropriate governance model is the core for establishing an effectively empowered customer CoE. Note that in small organizations, though less formal, the leadership team should still come up with a strategy for how to transition their resources going forward.

Last, the information and the business processes can be taken over to a productive solution in SAP Solution Manager and provide the platform for follow-up scenarios in Run SAP such as business process monitoring, change request management, upgrade projects, and releases.

While the OCM and training teams are concentrating on end-user education needs and support, the production team plays a key role during this phase.

There are two critical periods during the going live process. The production support plan must be executed within the first few days, the results checked, and any issues or problems quickly resolved. Following these first few days, the long-term monitoring of issues must be addressed, particularly system performance, capacity, and functions.

It is important that whenever a problem arises, end users know who to contact and how. The help desk is particularly important in the first weeks after going live, but you require help desk support throughout the production life of your SAP system. A CoE helps customers develop and hone the skills of their resources who transition from a project environment to production support. A help desk is a single point of contact with access to internal first-level support for hardware, network, operating system, database, training, and application system problems. First-level support personnel must not only possess special knowledge in these areas, but must also have company-specific knowledge concerning organization and processes.

KPI/PPI management does not finish after going live; activities to improve the business processes continue as mentioned earlier in the chapter. The measurement results should be compared with the target values. If they are not satisfactory, appropriate activities to improve the business processes should be defined and realized. After this, subsequent measurement can be initiated. This cycle of measurement and activities should be repeated until the defined objectives have been reached. During go-live support and later, the success of improvement or optimization activities should be measured regularly.

Resolution and closure for all outstanding problems in the issue management system must take place for the formal signoff of project team members. The value drivers and the business measurements, both of which were defined at the start of the project in phase 1, are reviewed to check project results against the goals set at its outset. This review is then presented to executive management. An ongoing evaluation procedure is established to monitor the benefits of the SAP implementation over time.

To ensure the operability of the SAP solution you have implemented, we recommend that you use the *SAP standards for solution operations* by running the SAP methodology. You need to ensure that daily operations perform properly and that the originally designed operations processes are optimized and adapted to new challenges. The Run SAP methodology will support in scoping, design, setup, and optimization of the solution operations standards. The Run SAP methodology is the last phase in the ASAP methodology.

In Table 13.12 you can see the key deliverables, milestones, and key decisions of the run phase.

Purpose	Deliverables	Milestones & Key Decisions
Run implemented SAP solution	Assessment of operation standards for optimized solution operation ▸ Identify scope ▸ Set up project schedule for implementing	Identification of operation standards for optimized solution operation

Table 13.12 Run Phase Summary

Purpose	Deliverables	Milestones & Key Decisions
Optimize solution operation by implementing SAP operation standards	For each relevant operation standard: ▸ Design of processes, organization, and roles; blueprint for tool usage ▸ Setup of processes, organization; and roles; tool setup ▸ Transition into production including training and rollout ▸ Operating the solution	Design, setup, and operation of SAP operations standards
		Tool implementation (mostly SAP Solution Manager scenarios for operation)

Table 13.12 Run Phase Summary (Cont.)

We have now completed the description of each of the six phases in the new ASAP core 7 methodology, including how value delivery, business process management, and service-oriented architecture are reflected in the six phases, and including the skills enablement requirements for the project team members. The next step is to go into the details of the second visible components of the ASAP methodology: The business add-ons to ASAP that extend the ASAP Roadmap with modular business implementation content.

13.4   Business Add-Ons to ASAP

The business add-ons to ASAP extend the ASAP methodology with modular business implementation content and additional methodology and governance frameworks. The business add-ons provide proven implementation content for implementation of various industry solutions, solutions packages, and other related areas such as agile methodology, BPM, SOA, Value Management, EA governance, and strategy frameworks. The business add-on concept is the gateway to executing process-based and easier-to-consume solutions including enabling simpler, shorter, and less disruptive implementations. The first business add-ons to ASAP were released to the SAP community on June 7, 2010.

In the following sections we will introduce the business add-on to the ASAP concept, the way in which the content flavoring occurs, the toolsets used, the direct link between the business add-ons and business process management, and what value can be gained from such an approach including how to view and activate business add-ons in an SAP implementation project.

13.4.1 Business Add-Ons to ASAP – a New Flavored Approach

One of the fundamental steps in the redesign of the ASAP implementation methodology was the removal of all industry solution and other related content. This process helped to significantly streamline the ASAP implementation methodology and at the same time made the ASAP implementation methodology flavorless.

To cater to the diverse solutions and industry solutions plus other types of scope that would be possible in an SAP implementation project, we have introduced the concept of the business add-ons to ASAP. The business add-on is what provides the flavor to the scope of an SAP implementation project. For example, if the scope of the implementation project is defined as requiring a point of sales (POS) solution for a retail customer, then SAP has provided a business add-on to ASAP that delivers POS implementation content that comes prepackaged with all of the relevant POS content for such an implementation.

This concept of adding the relevant flavor of a business add-on to ASAP is extended if the scope of the implementation contains an industry solution, a solution if you choose more than one business add-on, and another SAP-related component. In such an instance multiple business add-ons to ASAP would be used in combination to create the right flavor to meet the scope of the implementation. Figure 13.38 describes the concept of the business add-ons to ASAP in more detail.

The key message from this figure is that combination of the ASAP implementation roadmap with the business add-on to ASAP provides for a detailed WBS for each individual project based on its scope.

The main ingredients when working with a business add-on include the following characteristics:

▶ Can be switched on/off based on project needs
▶ Uses ASAP Roadmap content as basis

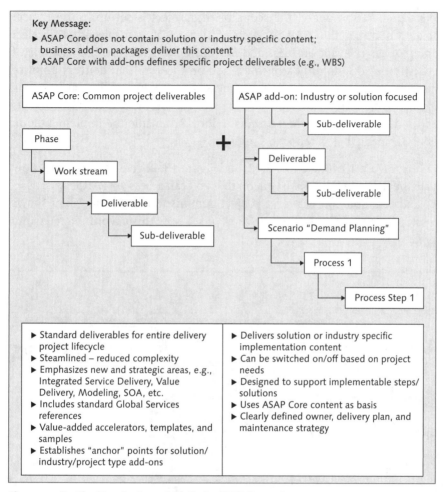

Figure 13.38 The New Business Add-On to ASAP Concept

Can Be Switched On/Off Based on Project Needs

Project flexibility is key in our fast-changing economic, political, and social environment. The scope of a project can increase or decrease during different phase of the project. Therefore, the business add-ons have the ability to adapt to the various levels of flexibility required.

Each of the business add-ons is fitted with a specific flavor that matches the name of the add-on. The business add-on flavor is added to the roadmap flavor in the SAP Solution Manager system or the HTML extract that you can view or download from SAP Service Marketplace via *https://service.sap.com/asap-business-add-ons*. During

389

the project preparation phase, the scope of the project is set up in the Project Administration area within SAP Solution Manager. You can select and deselect the scoping of the relevant business add-ons during this process. For example, if a project is initiated with only a business add-on to ASAP that delivers point of sales implementation content, and the business later requires additional reporting development using SAP BusinessObjects reporting, then the SAP BusinessObjects reporting add-on can be switched on to support and enable the implementation of the SAP BusinessObjects reporting solution.

Figure 13.39, Figure 13.40, Figure 13.41, and Figure 13.42 give an example of how to activate the flavor in the HTML version that you can access via SAP Service Marketplace and SAP Solution Manager project administration. Figure 13.39 shows how to select a flavor. In Figure 13.40 you can see how this flavor integrates into the general roadmap.

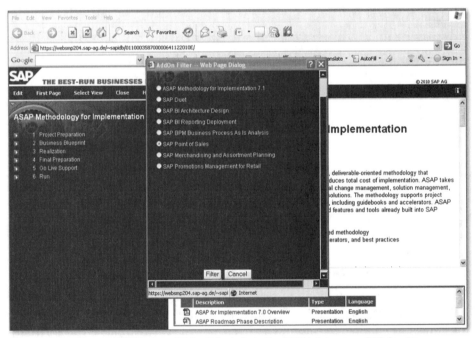

Figure 13.39 Flavor of SAP Point of Sales Selected via the HTML Extract on SAP Service Marketplace

Figure 13.41 shows how the flavor of SAP Merchandise and Assortment Planning and SAP Promotion Management for Retail is selected via the ROADMAP SELECT tab in SAP Solution Manager project administration.

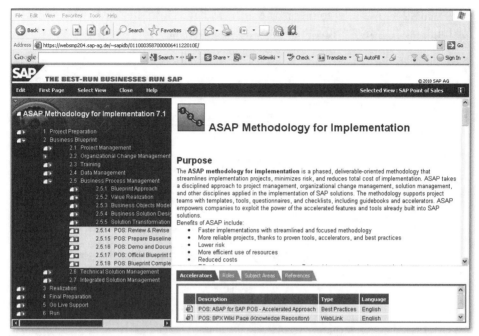

Figure 13.40 Flavor Content from SAP Point of Sales Merged into the ASAP Methodology for Implementation 7.1

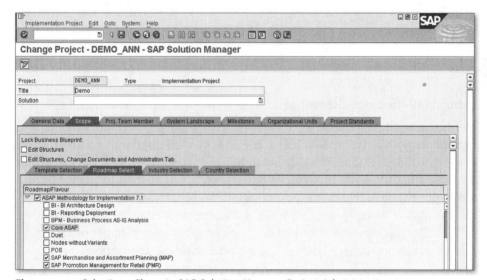

Figure 13.41 Selecting a Flavor in SAP Solution Manager Project Administration

Figure 13.42 shows how to merge the selected flavor into the ASAP Methodology for Implementation 7.1 Roadmap in SAP Solution Manager.

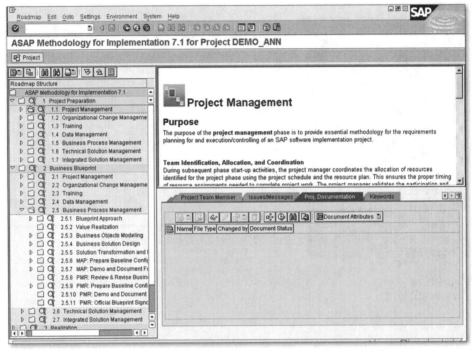

Figure 13.42 The Flavor in the ASAP Methodology for Implementation 7.1 Roadmap in SAP Solution Manager

Using ASAP Roadmap Content as a Basis

The business add-on concepts exploits the use of SAP's generic implementation methodology foundation — ASAP. The ASAP Methodology for Implementation is a phased, deliverable-oriented methodology that streamlines implementation projects, minimizes risk, and reduces the total cost of implementation. ASAP takes a disciplined approach to project management, organizational change management, solution management, and other disciplines applied in the implementation of SAP solutions. The methodology supports project teams with templates, tools, questionnaires, and checklists, including guidebooks and accelerators.

The business add-ons are not aimed at duplicating the ASAP methodology but serve as flavored enhancements to it.

Categories of Business Add-Ons and Their Content

The business add-ons to ASAP are grouped into three categories of add-ons that each can include content as described below:

1. Business add-ons to ASAP that deliver methodology, governance frameworks, and implementation technology content

   ► Methodology and governance (roadmaps, accelerators, handbooks, examples, etc.)

   ► Enablement content (education, literature, white papers, service offerings, starter kits, etc.)

2. Business add-ons to ASAP that deliver implementation content

   ► Flavor methodology (project scope statement, configuration guide, etc.)

   ► Business content (business process structure, process descriptions, value drivers, KPIs/ PPIs)

   ► Implementation content (solution descriptions, links to IMG objects, transactions, SOA services, test cases, etc.)

   ► Enablement content (education, literature, white papers, service offerings, starter kits, etc.)

3. Business add-ons to ASAP that deliver small innovative BPM- and SOA-based implementation content

   ► Flavor methodology (project scope statement, composite guide, etc.)

   ► Business content (business process structure, process descriptions, value drivers, KPIs/ PPIs)

   ► Implementation content (solution descriptions, SOA services, test cases, etc.)

   ► Enablement content (education, literature, white papers, service offerings, starter kits, etc.)

13.4.2 Tools for Applying Business Add-Ons to ASAP

The tools that are used to view, activate, and consume business add-ons are aligned with the current architecture governing SAP implementations. You can view the business add-ons via:

▶ SAP EcoHub (*http://ecohub.sdn.sap.com/*)
On SAP EcoHub the business add-ons can be sorted by industry, line of business, solution type, and hot topics.

▶ SAP Service Marketplace (*https://service.sap.com/asap-business-add-ons*)
On the ASAP business add-ons landing page on SAP Service Marketplace, the business add-ons can be sorted by industry, solution type, platform and technology, and cross-solution.

For each business add-on the available information is split into:

▶ Learn about the business add-on

▶ Learn from others

▶ Download area

▶ Feedback

You can activate and consume the business add-ons via:

▶ SAP Solution Manager

▶ SAP Enterprise Modeling by IDS Scheer via a database

▶ SAP Service Marketplace and SAP EcoHub, where you can download the HTML Extract

Each of these tools has a unique role and function in presenting and delivering business add-ons, which we will discuss in detail in the following sections, starting with SAP Solution Manager.

SAP Solution Manager

SAP Solution Manager is an integrated toolset encompassing content, tools, and methodologies for the implementation and operation of SAP solutions. The business content is complemented with flexible functionality that helps project teams during the entire lifecycle of the SAP solution. The business add-ons to ASAP are included in the SAP Solution Manager content support implementation packages (ST-ICO).

The business add-ons are delivered via two steps in SAP Solution Manger. You need to activate these two steps in SAP Solution Manager project administration. First, the business add-ons are delivered through SAP Solution Manager roadmap selection (see Figure 13.43) and, second, through template selection (see Figure 13.44). In these figures, you will see how to activate the business add-on via the two steps. We are using the business add-ons Assortment Planning and Promotion Management for Retail as examples.

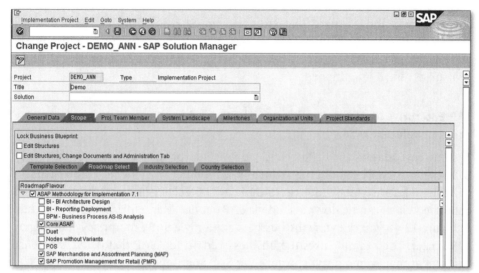

Figure 13.43 Step 1: Activate Business Add-Ons in Roadmap Selection in Project Administration

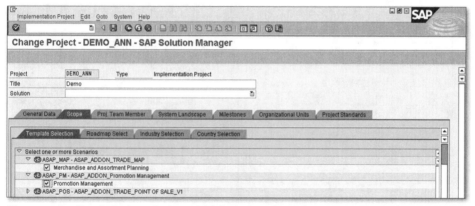

Figure 13.44 Step 2: Activate Business Add-On in Template Selection in Project Administration

The business add-on content that is included in a template project covers all of the relevant business process content required for that specific scope of SAP implementation. The template contains the business process content that enhances the development and execution of the business blueprint (SOLAR01) and realization (SOLAR02) phase deliverables.

This process of providing both methodology (business add-on roadmap) and business process content (business add-on template package) within SAP Solution Manager greatly enhances the overall delivery of SAP implementation projects.

For customers and partners who are not using SAP Solution Manager for their project implementation, an HTML extract of each of the business add-ons has been made. This HTML extract is available in the SAP Service Marketplace and SAP EcoHub as already mentioned.

SAP Enterprise Modeling Applications by IDS Scheer and SAP Solution Manager

The business add-ons can be linked to the SAP enterprise modeling applications by IDS Scheer through the inherited synchronization between SAP Solution Manager and SAP enterprise modeling applications by IDS Scheer or by restoring the ARIS database, which can be downloaded via SAP Service Marketplace or SAP EcoHub. In Figure 13.45 you can view the business add-on via SAP Enterprise Modeling by IDS Scheer. The example uses the business add-on to ASAP that delivers defense equipment management, synchronized to SAP Solution Manager.

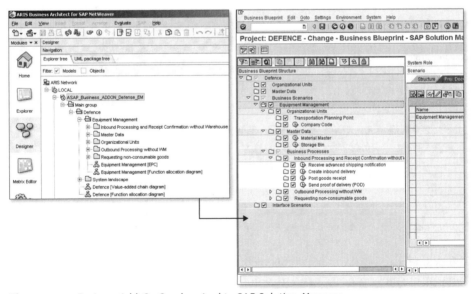

Figure 13.45 Business Add-On Synchronized to SAP Solution Manager

The business add-on in SAP Enterprise Modeling by IDS Sheer includes the models value add-chain diagram, EPC column display diagram, and a function allocation diagram as shown in Figure 13.46.

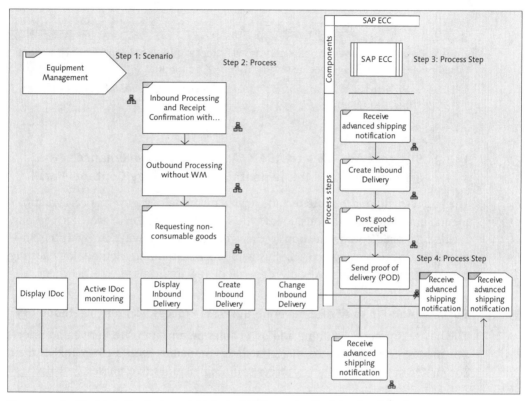

Figure 13.46 Models in the Business Add-On in SAP Enterprise Modeling by IDS Scheer

SAP Service Marketplace and SAP EcoHub

In the development of business add-ons it is clear that the content in the form of accelerators (guidebooks, white papers, templates, etc.) needs to be stored in a location that is accessible to SAP customers, partners, and internal staff. The SAP Service Marketplace and SDN/BPX Community has been selected as the repository for all business add-on content that related to the accelerators. The SAP Service Marketplace and SAP EcoHub are also where you can get an HTML version of the business add-ons. Each business add-on that is delivered for consumption has a single page describing the business add-on and provides a link to an online and offline HTML version.

In the following sections we will give more detailed information about the three categories of business add-ons (Section 13.4.3). In Chapter 15, Section 15.1 we will provide details and corresponding examples. We will start with the methodology, governance frameworks, and implementation technology content category.

More Information

You can learn more about business add-ons via "Real World BPM in an SAP Environment Webinar Series" that runs weekly on the SDN/BPX Community.

Please go to: *http://www.sdn.sap.com/irj/sdn/index?rid=/webcontent/uuid/40b722af-7e30-2d10-d296-a29ecd1c8fda*

13.4.3 Business Add-Ons to ASAP Methodology, Governance Frameworks, and Implementation Technology Content: Part I

The business add-ons to ASAP include several methodology, governance, and implementation technology add-ons. Below you will find a selection of available add-ons, including a detailed introduction to the agile add-on. We will start with the Business Add-Ons to ASAP delivering Business Process Scanning Methodology, testing content, and content for SAP enterprise modeling applications by IDS Scheer.

Business Add-On to ASAP Delivering Business Process Scanning Methodology

The business process scanning add-on enables organizations to derive and prioritize process improvement projects in their companies with a clear link to their corporate strategies. Business process scanning includes two phases:

1. **Calibration**
   The objective of the calibration phase is to reach agreement on a list of processes that are to be analyzed and optimized.

2. **As-is analysis**
   The objective of this phase is to understand the as-is situation of the selected processes and the IT landscape and to identify weaknesses, pain points, and as-is process performance measurements (PPIs) in respect to cost, cycle time, and cost.

Business Add-Ons to ASAP that Deliver Content for Testing

▶ Testing Strategy

▶ SAP Quality Center by HP

- ▸ TAO for SAP

- ▸ TDMS

Business add-ons to ASAP deliver content for SAP enterprise modeling applications by IDS Scheer:

- ▸ Redocumentation using SAP Solution Manager and SAP Enterprise Modeling by IDS Scheer

- ▸ SAP Solution Manager integration with SAP Enterprise Modeling by IDS Scheer

- ▸ Enterprise Services Repository integration for SAP Enterprise Modeling by IDS Scheer

- ▸ SAP Business Process Optimization by IDS Scheer

- ▸ Process intelligence for SAP Process Performance Management by IDS Scheer

- ▸ Process publishing for SAP Business Server and Publisher by IDS Scheer

- ▸ SAP enterprise modeling applications by IDS Scheer (consolidated add-on)

> **More Information**
>
> For more details about the add-ons described in this section, please go SAP EcoHub, *http://ecohub.sdn.sap.com/*, SAP Service Marketplace, *https://service.sap.com/asap-business-add-ons*, or SAP Solution Manager, where you can view and activate each of the add-ons.

Now we will go into the details of the business add-on to ASAP delivering agile methodology.

Business Add-On to ASAP delivering Agile Methodology

The current economic climate demands a fast return on investment and lower total cost of implementation. It is fairly common to see project requirements evolve or outright change during the project lifecycle due to changes in the business environment or business priorities.

One of the ways the new ASAP Methodology for Implementation addresses this uncertainty is through the adoption of selected acceleration techniques and practices geared to build a common understanding of requirements and their validation. With these techniques, project teams can rapidly respond to changing or evolving business requirements as described in earlier chapters. To complement the acceleration techniques that are built into ASAP core, the new business add-on concept enables project teams to activate the business add-on to ASAP for agile implementations that reshapes the traditional ASAP implementation approach into a more streamlined iterative model that leverages proven principles of agile methods. The business add-on for agile is based on a Scrum-like approach that utilizes proven techniques suited for SAP implementation projects. This chapter discusses the acceleration techniques of core ASAP and agile business add-ons in more detail.

Agile software development methods have been gaining popularity in software development projects over the past several decades. The first major evolution of these techniques happened in the mid-1990s when methods such as Scrum and Extreme Programming were popularized for software development projects.

The key characteristics of these methods are:

- An adaptive approach with less focus on planning and documentation
- Short time-boxed delivery cycles
- Close cooperation between business users and developers
- Face-to-face communication
- Frequent team meetings to keep alignment
- Simplicity/leanness
- Frequent validation of requirements with business users

Agile project teams utilize shorter iterative cycles of planning, design, and realization to deliver work product increments on a regular basis. They also frequently validate their understanding of requirements to minimize the chance of rework. This enables them to respond to changes in requirements quickly and to frequently deliver work products or work product increments. This attention to changes also enables the project teams to adopt and learn about the evolving nature of requirements (which may not be fully understood in early stages of the project) and the ability to slice large projects or software products into smaller, easier to digest and deliver releases of business functionality.

Whereas many software development teams have been successfully deploying methods like Scrum and Extreme Programming, deployment of these methods in enterprise implementation projects has been limited. Only in the past few years has the trend of using agile methods and principles in implementation projects, beyond the areas of software development and standard product enhancements, been taking hold.

As discussed in Section 13.3, SAP has redesigned the ASAP Methodology for Implementation to enable creation of industry, solution, and other types of business add-on content. With the business add-ons the standard ASAP methodology for implementation can be extended to provide implementation content and methodology guidance not only for a specific industry or solution, but also to adjust the traditional implementation approach to enable the use of selected, proven agile methodology principles that work in SAP implementation projects.

Although this approach is not suitable for every implementation project, there is a large body of SAP projects that can benefit from all or selected techniques using short time-boxed cycles (sprints) to deliver working solutions in frequent cycles. Note that SAP extracted a set of acceleration techniques into the core ASAP methodology.

Let's take a look at how the agile methods and techniques are implemented in business add-ons and how they extend or modify the ASAP Methodology for Implementation. The business add-on for agile is overlaid on top of the core ASAP methodology; it preserves key components and deliverables from ASAP while extending it with new concepts.

The project starts with a standard project preparation phase in which the project team completes the standard set of deliverables, for example, high-level project WBS, high-level project schedule, project scope statement, and so on. The key driver for the project scope is the initial project scope statement that is determined in early stages of project preparation phase.

This is the key deliverable that drives subsequent activities in the business blueprint phase during which the team completes the project backlog. The project backlog is built following acceleration techniques for blueprinting and the ASAP blueprint approach. These standard techniques are extended to support a clear way to prioritize the requirements and validate them with the business process owners.

The project backlog in turn forms the basis for determining the scope of individual sprints that implement the iterative process of building working a solution in short time-boxed cycles. Each sprint scope is then represented in a sprint backlog.

During each sprint the project team works on functionality, feature sets, or configuration outlined in the sprint backlog. Each sprint is a cycle of detailed design, development, composition, configuration, and testing. Before completing the sprint, the project team conducts validation of the functionality specified in the sprint backlog with the end users through demo or presentation of results and formal sign-off.

After the completion of the sprint, the sprint backlog is revised; for example, completed items are closed and any new scope items are added and prioritized. This revised and prioritized project backlog sets the scope for next sprint.

Sprints are not the only new technique in the agile approach to implementation. The second key concept is the schedule for release of incremental work products to the business. The releases can be planned after an individual sprint or multiple sprints are completed. Typically, in SAP implementations release occurs after multiple sprints. You can think of release as a smaller version of cutover for specific functionality to production. Once the project team completes the work on final sprint before a release, work increments of this last sprint and all preceding sprints are released to the end users in a structured way. This procedure is graphically shown in Figure 13.47.

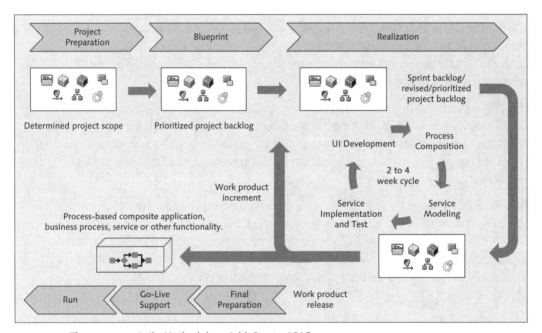

Figure 13.47 Agile Methodology Add-Ons to ASAP

After the release the project team continues with next sprint until next release milestone is reached. This process continues until the project backlog is eliminated or until the project objectives are met.

The business add-on for agile not only contains the agile approaches discussed above (such as the iterative approach, frequent validation of requirements, etc.), but also leverages proven acceleration techniques that help project teams reach a better understanding of requirements and business objectives to be achieved in the project.

These acceleration techniques are built into the core ASAP Methodology for Implementation because they benefit not only project teams using the business add-on for agile, but also teams following a traditional ASAP cycle approach.

The following list outlines the key acceleration techniques built into the ASAP methodology:

▶ **IP reuse**
SAP delivers different assets, which enable acceleration of specific activities in a project. One example is the use of business add-ons to ASAP that deliver implementation content that enables project teams to leverage prepackaged content as a starting point for implementation. Another example is the use of SAP Best Practices that play key role in building preconfigured solutions. The Best Practices are based on business configuration sets (BC sets) and solution documentation that enable project teams to gain early access to fully functional business process scenarios to build a common understanding of requirements and needs.

▶ **Elimination of rework through solution visualization**
Early visualization of solutions in the blueprint phase leads to a better understanding of requirements and solution capabilities. Iterative development paired with conference room pilots is often leveraged to validate the solution design before full-scale implementation commences in the realization phase. This eliminates costly rework in later stages of the project that is often caused by misunderstandings between the project team, the business process owner, and the IT team.

▶ **Use of services**
SAP offers many services that can be used to address specific challenging areas of the project. For example, value prototyping services are often utilized to assist in development or configuration of more complex environments; the scope is based on customers' areas of interest and pain points. Generally, this approach is used in the discovery stage or early in the blueprint phase. The value prototyping team goes through n time-boxed implementation periods (four weeks) and uses a lab environment to configure the preferred solution or part of the solution that is typically brought back to the project. An example of the use of this service is large transaction volumes that need to be processed in a predefined time or the building of interfaces to high-risk legacy systems

and others. You can find more information about value prototyping for BPM in Chapter 16, Section 16.6.

We outlined the key concepts of the principles built into the business add-on to ASAP that delivers agile methodology and the acceleration techniques that are included in the core ASAP Methodology for Implementation. This section attempts to summarize the key benefits of the above outlined techniques for project teams and organizations:

- Faster results through step-by-step delivery of software via sprints and frequent releases
- Delivery of software based on the priorities of the business process owner
- Clear visibility of costs and value of each sprint
- Higher level of transparency through continuous monitoring of the project backlog and sprint backlog
- Frequent meetings and sync points keep the project team engaged and aligned
- Permanent and close involvement of business users in shaping the solution
- Increased flexibility — project team is able to respond to changes in prioritization or business needs per sprint.

Agile in SAP Implementation at LM Wind Power

Let's explore how LM Wind Power, an SAP customer, used an agile implementation approach to successfully deploy a solution in their environment. LM Wind Power is the world's leading supplier in fiberglass blades, which are used in wind turbines. The company's main office is located in Kolding, Denmark, and they employ approximately 5,000 employees in 9 countries. LM Wind Power first began their agile implementation in 2009, with a go-live date of January of 2010.

The LM Wind Power Group had been running best-of-breed applications in the business prior to implementing their integrated solution from SAP.

The company has a strong focus on green energy. An aggressive global growth strategy that was executed at the same time the financial crisis hit required a corporate HR system to optimize the organization. For Norbert Stein, HR director at LM Wind Power, SAP was the natural choice. LM Wind Power decided to go for a full HR implementation, divided into several phases.

This customer case only covers phase 1, which included:

- Organizational management (OM)
- Personnel administration (PA)
- Performance management (PRM)
- Employee self-service (ESS)
- Manager self-service (MSS)

During the selection process for the best methodology approach, the LM Wind Power team highlighted the following needs:

- The cost of implementation must be low.
- The implementation time must be short.
- The resulting solution should be as close to the SAP standard as possible.

In addition, the LM Wind Power team stated that they did not want to see all of the different configuration possibilities within SAP. LM Wind Power wanted SAP to choose what would be the "best fit" for them and their business.

For these reasons it was obvious to SAP that the traditional implementation approach would not be good fit, and the team had to become more agile. The proposed implementation approach was inspired by both the ASAP methodology and the Scrum methodology. A new hybrid agile implementation methodology was designed for this project.

The methodology is divided into multiple phases, and the applicable content from the ASAP Roadmap was reused as needed. The inspiration from Scrum came into play in the scoping, design, and build phases. The phase naming was kept as close to ASAP as possible, but business blueprint phase and realization phase were changed to scoping, design, and build and transition phase because they were using and developing a new hybrid approach.

Just as in the ASAP methodology the project preparation phase of the agile approach sets the scene for the project. The activities and deliverables were to a large degree adopted from ASAP. It was very important to provide agile methodology training to the project team at this early stage. Because this case was an accelerated implementation, and "time to value" needed to be reduced, the team was forced to move some of the deliverables from scoping, design, and build to the project preparation phase.

It is important to emphasize that areas like organizational change management, support strategy and procedures, and data management strategy must be considered during project preparation. Activities within these areas must commence right after the project kickoff. SAP Solution Manager configuration for an implementation project is also done during this phase.

Because LM Wind Power was new to SAP software, proper management attention was the key driver in putting the necessary focus on these areas at such an early stage.

During the scoping phase the scope for the project was outlined in the project scope statement. To complete this deliverable the team conducted a detailed scoping workshop to document the scope of the required level of detail. The workshop was conducted as a fit/gap analysis workshop containing a walkthrough of all of the business processes. Because this workshop formed the basis for what was going to be built later, the table content had to be decided as well.

The outcome of this activity was the requirements document captured as a product backlog. The requirements in the product backlog must be prioritized, outlining which of the requirements should be realized first.

At LM Wind Power the scope was not too large, and the team realized the complete scope in one sprint. The detailed scoping workshop was a two-day workshop, and the scoping phase was set for two weeks. Consolidating the outcome of the workshop included producing the clarified issues and additional customer deliverables of the final product backlog. The LM Wind Power team then signed off on the backlog. The final product backlog is to be considered as the business blueprint guiding the planning and execution of the solution.

On the technical side, the system landscape document was finalized, and the development system was installed.

In the design and build phase, the SAP team planned the sprints, completed the final design, and implemented the solution. Planning the sprints consists of taking the final product backlog and defining what to build in the different sprints, for example, producing the sprint schedule. Because the scope at LM Wind Power was limited, it was fairly straightforward to define the release schedule because the scope could be realized in one sprint. Based on lessons learned, sprints should be from two to four weeks.

The final design was done as the team detailed each task for building the solution. Each task was estimated down to hours, and the task duration was reflected in the sprint schedule. This was one of the most difficult and one of the most important tasks in the project, because the sprint schedule sets the baseline for the project manager to measure the progress of the building of the solution. Because the consultants were new to the agile implementation approach, the project manager spent extra time educating the team. Before initiating the sprint the team performed a "readiness check" to confirm that all required elements are in place and the team was ready to go.

The sprint was kicked off, progress was measured on the burn-down chart, and the project status was discussed in the daily Scrum meetings.

The project team decided to use a demo during the sprint, not only to present the project progress, but also to get the initial approval for the solution from the business process owners.

Then the sprint the team presented the built solution to LM Wind Power's global HR management team in a workshop. This activity identified six additional requirements that were realized shortly after presenting the build solution, and the solution was signed off by the customer team.

Other deliverables completed during this phase were the traditional ASAP deliverables such as test plans, test cases, the training plan, training materials, the end-user role concept, the role map, the detailed data management plan, and so on.

During the transition phase the project team performed quality assurance on the solution, prepared the productive system, trained the end users, and formed the support organization for ongoing operations and support of the solution. Both functional and integration tests were planned and executed with the help of SAP Solution Manager testing functionality. The customer signed off on the solution before the cutover activities commenced.

During the cutover the team benefited from the numerous simulation test migrations, and the production data load ran smoothly. The new end users of the system were trained, and after LM Wind Power performed a short user acceptance test the productive system was approved for go-live as planned. Initially the businesses in Denmark and Poland went live; the remaining businesses followed one month later.

The initial days and weeks of using the new system in the pilot countries went as intended during the go-live and support phase. The project team received useful feedback from the end-user community that helped fine-tune go-live activities in the remaining countries. The rest of the business went live in early January 2010. The project team supported the solution for another month after go-live, before handing over the operations to the customer team.

Both LM Wind Power and SAP agree that the implementation has been successful and use of hybrid methodology based on traditional ASAP combined with a Scrum approach is promising to open new ground for successful projects. LM Wind Power has decided to use the same implementation methodology for the remaining parts of the scope. SAP has leveraged the lessons from this and other agile projects and reflected them in both core ASAP methodology and the business add-on to ASAP delivery of agile methodology. For more details about this case refer to the customer success story on SAP's corporate website (*http://www.sap.com*).

13.4.4 Business Add-Ons that Deliver Methodology, Governance Frameworks, and Implementation Content: Part II

We will now look at a selection of the available governance add-ons, which include business add-ons to ASAP that deliver value management organization, program management office, customer center of expertise, and business process management office, SOA strategy and governance, etc., as illustrated in Figure 13.48.

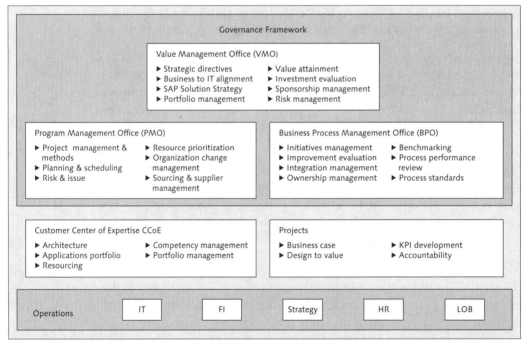

Figure 13.48 Governance Framework Add-Ons Included in the SAP ValuePartnerShip Framework

The governance add-ons are also included into the ValuePartnerShip (VPS) framework, which includes customized SAP services to address your specific business and IT transformation needs. The SAP VPS framework is presented in Section 16.7.

Let us now take a detailed look at the details of the business add-ons to ASAP that delivers SOA strategy and governance and BPM strategy and governance frameworks.

> **More Information**
>
> For more details about these add-ons please go SAP EcoHub, *http://ecohub.sdn.sap.com/*, SAP Service Marketplace, *http://service.sap.com/asap-business-add-ons*, or SAP Solution Manager, where you can view and activate each of the add-ons.

Business Add-On to ASAP Delivering SOA Strategy and Governance Framework

Earlier in this chapter we mentioned that effective service-oriented architecture (SOA) governance is important to ensure the success of your SOA-based SAP implementation projects. Effective SOA governance calls for a holistic management approach that integrates and aligns the corporate business strategy, the IT strategy, and the planning and operational activities associated with service-oriented solutions. This approach encompasses people, processes, and technologies. In most companies, some elements of SOA governance already exist. For instance, you can leverage IT governance as part of the foundation for SOA governance. But SOA governance includes additional capabilities within the organizational structures, skills, and procedures that have an even closer alignment with the business.

Effective SOA governance is built upon four elements. The first element is the governance management, which includes the organizational structures, skill sets, and procedures that are aligned with the specific needs of the company. The second element is toolsets and lifecycle management, which include all of the tools required to support good governance and to achieve the ultimate goal of automated governance. The third element is a design and modeling methodology that includes a methodology that spans all phases of service design, harmonization, and implementation. The last element is community building, which includes continually sharing ideas and Best Practices, inside and outside of the company, for a faster time to value and sustained success. To build or improve your existing service-oriented architecture governance you can apply the business add-on to ASAP that delivers SOA strategy and governance framework. The add-on is a roadmap that you can access via SAP EcoHub, SAP Service Marketplace, and SAP Solution Manager.

The service-oriented architecture framework within the add-on (as seen in Figure 13.49) is composed of three phases: SOA analyze, SOA design, and SOA transform. Each of the phases includes a description of the steps necessary to achieve the preferred SOA strategy and governance state.

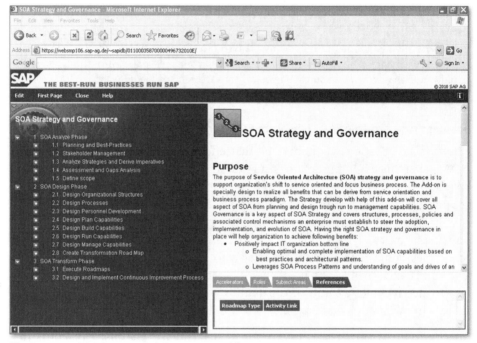

Figure 13.49 SOA Strategy and Governance Add-On

Let's take a look at the phases:

1. **SOA Analyze Phase**

   The purpose of the analyze phase of the SOA strategy and governance roadmap is threefold:

   ▶ Articulate what needs to change to achieve the SOA goals.

   ▶ Understand the focus and goal of the corporate strategy (includes understanding all relevant parties and linking SOA strategy and governance activities to the strategy of the organization).

▸ Document the organization's specific coverage of the reference model's (SOA reference architecture and governance and organization framework) elements as a basis for the definition and prioritization of action areas and scope of the future state.

Important functions of this phase include interpreting needs and influencing both the external and internal environments. To do this, the analyze phase helps initiate the creation of positive relationships with stakeholders through the appropriate management of their expectations and agreed objectives. Toward the completion of this phase, the project team scopes SOA strategy and governance activities and prioritizes a list of activities that must be realized to reach the goal state as part of the analyze phase.

2. **SOA Design Phase**

The goal for the SOA design phase is to design the organization of the process, process fundamentals, and define a transformation roadmap and measurable success criteria. The team describes necessary personnel development measures and develops a high-level training concept including various training methods. They seek to design the SOA plan; build, run, and manage capabilities; and define a transformation roadmap and measurable success criteria. During this phase the overall SOA strategy and governance transformation are synchronized, described, and visualized. The major work streams of this phase cover the design of organizational structures, processes, and personnel development and the planning, building, running, and managing of SOA architecture capabilities. The final step of this phase is to create a transformation roadmap.

3. **SOA Transform Phase**

In the transform phase of the SOA strategy and governance roadmap, the project team develops missing SOA capabilities and modifies existing ones as discovered and outlined in the design phase. Activities in this phase transform the organization according to roadmaps developed in the design phases. The transform phase is an ongoing effort to improve SOA strategy and governance. These efforts seek incremental improvement over time. SOA strategy and governance is constantly evaluated and improved in light of efficiency, effectiveness, and flexibility. The major work streams of the transform phase are to execute roadmaps and design and implement continuous improvement process.

More Information

For more details on the business add-on to ASAP that delivers service-oriented architecture strategy and governance framework, please go to SAP EcoHub, *http://ecohub. sdn.sap.com/*, SAP Service Marketplace, *http://service.sap.com/asap-business-add-ons*, or SAP Solution Manager, where you can view and activate the add-on.

Business Add-On to ASAP Delivering BPM Strategy and Governance Framework

The add-on BPM Governance and Strategy enables organizations to shift to process-centric thinking, and to manage the complete improvement cycles of their business processes, from process design to monitoring and optimization, and to be able to change business processes more frequently to adjust to changing circumstances. The add-on BPM Governance and Strategy is a governances framework that includes the following phases: BPM strategy, BPM setup, BPM transition, and BPM supporting. The purpose of the BPM Governance and Strategy add-on is to provide organizations with a strategy and governance framework for developing a BPM Strategy and BPM goals and roadmap linked to overall corporate mission; setting up an organizational and governance structure with clear role and task definitions for efficient BPM (process owners, BPXs, process-centric IT, etc.); setting up a framework for process modeling, simulation, optimization, and measurement including process maturity assessments; setting up methods and a BPM tool landscape to run and manage business process lifecycle projects; transitioning the company to become process-centric; and creating structures for continuous business improvement.

More Information

The business add-on to ASAP that delivers BPM strategy and governance is based on the BPM roadmap described in detail in Part II of *Business Process Management — the SAP Roadmap*, which is available at *http://www.sap-press.com*.

"It isn't sufficient just to want — you've got to ask yourself what you are going to do to get the things you want."
– Franklin D. Roosevelt

14   BPM Tools — From Modeling to Execution

Ann Rosenberg, Ulf Fildebrandt, Andrey Hoursanov, Bernhard Drabant, Bogdan Vatkov, Emil Simeonov, Erik Dick, Jens Ittel, Kesavaprakash Vasudevan, Matthias Steiner, Nikolay Kabadzhov, Penka Tatarova, Ulrich Keil, Volker Stiehl, Wolfgang Hilpert, Thomas Volmering, James Taylor, Carsten Ziegler, Christoph Gollmick

In this chapter we will explore some of the key modeling to execution tools that we recommend you use in your SAP-centric business and IT environment. In Section 14.1 we will go into the details of the composite development architecture guidelines for SAP NetWeaver Composition Environment (CE), which targets two distinct areas. First, SAP NetWeaver CE enables model-driven development of "own practices," also referred to as composite applications. The composite applications can be built on top of SAP Business Suite Best practices with the application core processes and on arbitrary backend systems. Composite applications follow the SOA paradigm of "nonintrusiveness," which means these applications are bound to provide modification-free process extensions to the core business applications. Additionally, customers are enabled to design, deploy, and run Java applications with SAP NetWeaver Composition Environment following the JEE standards.

In Section 14.2 we provide the highlights of the innovation provided by SAP NetWeaver BPM and SAP NetWeaver BRM. Then we will go into the details of business rules management in respect to both handling decisions and business rules in a BPM approach (Section 14.3) and business rules management systems from SAP, where we will take a detailed look at the business rules framework plus and SAP NetWeaver Business Rules Management (Section 14.4). Finally, we will explore the simple samples for enterprise services consumption (Section 14.5), which are ready-to-run applications based on the most commonly used enterprise services and various SAP consumption technologies.

14.1   Composite Development Architecture Guidelines

The Composition Development Architecture Guidelines have been created based on feedback and experience from the first customers using SAP NetWeaver Composition Environment. The guidelines include recommendations that will help you in implementing applications following the SOA principles.

14.1.1   Value Proposition of SAP NetWeaver CE

SAP NetWeaver Composition Environment (CE) targets two distinct areas. First, SAP NetWeaver CE enables model-driven development of own practices, also referred to as composite applications. Secondly, customers are enabled to design, deploy, and run Java applications with SAP NetWeaver Composition Environment following the JEE standards.

14.1.2   Platform Overview

SAP NetWeaver Composition Environment is designed and implemented as a usage type of the SAP NetWeaver Java stack that integrates with different components of the full SAP NetWeaver stack on various levels (see Figure 14.1). Therefore, SAP NetWeaver Composition Environment, once it is installed in the customer landscape, leverages already existing components:

- ▶ **SAP NetWeaver Portal**
  Composite applications can be incorporated into a customer portal via a federated portal network (FPN).
- ▶ **Knowledge management (KM)**
  SAP NetWeaver CE frameworks can connect to a remote KM and its content.
- ▶ **SAP NetWeaver Business Warehouse (BW)**
  Data can be retrieved from remote servers and used in composite applications.
- ▶ **SAP NetWeaver Development Infrastructure (NWDI)**
  SAP NetWeaver CE could host its own NWDI, but it is also possible to configure SAP NetWeaver CE to use a remote NWDI.

Besides a lean runtime, SAP NetWeaver CE offers a standards-based design time, the Eclipse-based SAP NetWeaver Developer Studio (NWDS). The goal of SAP NetWeaver CE's design time is to reduce the total cost of understanding and expedite time to value by:

▶ Embracing community standards and Best Practices

▶ Providing good tool support for leveraging the SAP application through Web services

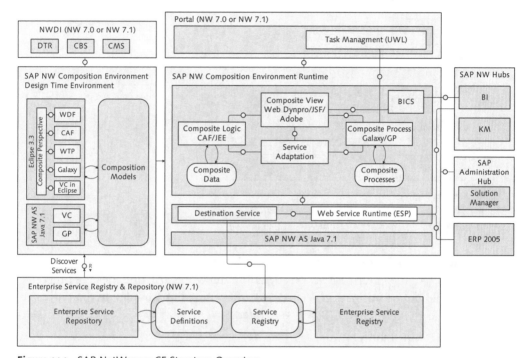

Figure 14.1 SAP NetWeaver CE Structure Overview

Overview of Layers

A composite application is structured in such a way that it contains content for specific purposes. Some parts are UI related, whereas some parts define the process flow, and other parts are specific to the business logic. The common functionality that all frameworks provide is the consumption of enterprise services.

The main SAP NetWeaver Composition Environment frameworks (see Figure 14.2) are:

▶ **Java EE frameworks (EJB, JSP/JSF)**
This is the basic framework for Java Enterprise Edition (Java EE) applications. SAP NetWeaver CE supports all applications that are Java EE 5 compliant.

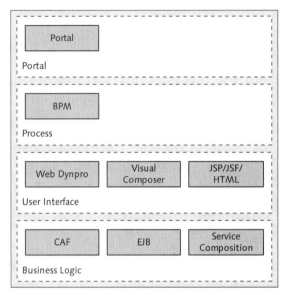

Figure 14.2   Layering of SAP NetWeaver CE Frameworks

▶ **SAP Composite Application Framework (CAF)**
On top of the Enterprise JavaBean (EJB) framework, SAP provides the function-ality to define business objects (BOs) and services in a model-driven way. The logic is modeled, and EJBs are generated.

▶ **Web Dynpro foundation**
Most SAP UI applications run with the Web Dynpro runtime. The Web Dynpro runtime is a framework that runs inside the Java EE web container. It provides its own programming model including components, controllers, views, and so on. It follows the model-view-controller (MVC) pattern.

▶ **SAP NetWeaver Visual Composer**
Model-driven UI-applications can be developed efficiently with SAP NetWeaver Visual Composer in a completely model-driven way. The design time is avail-able as a browser-based application running on the server or as a tool in SAP NetWeaver Developer Studio (NWDS).

▶ **SAP NetWeaver BPM**
Model-driven process definitions and execution are supported via SAP NetWeaver BPM, a component that uses Business Process Modeling Notation (BPMN) as the standard notation from model directly to execution.

▶ **SAP NetWeaver BRM**
SAP NetWeaver BRM supports model-driven rule definition and execution.

Server Architecture

Though it seems obvious at first sight, SAP NetWeaver CE cannot simply be divided into a runtime stack running on a server and a design time running in Eclipse. The Eclipse parts are all related to design-time purposes; however, not all components on the server are relevant just for runtime. Complete design time solutions run on the server, mainly with SAP NetWeaver Visual Composer.

The applications still run on the Java EE 5 stack and utilize the standards, which means the runtimes on top of the Java EE 5 standard use the concepts of the Java server. The most important frameworks running on top of the Java EE runtime are:

▶ The Web Dynpro runtime is integrated with the web container, and every Web Dynpro application runs in the Web Dynpro servlet.

▶ The BPM runtime runs on the Java EE infrastructure. Especially for execution of a process, the cluster capabilities of the server are used to scale execution of many process instances.

Design-Time Architecture in SAP NetWeaver Developer Studio

Composite applications are mainly developed in the Eclipse environment. Guided procedure and SAP NetWeaver Visual Composer models are developed on the server. The specific SAP NetWeaver Composition Environment frameworks have tools that are best suited for their use cases to reduce the development time of an application.

As explained before, there are several design times on the server, but the goal is to bring these toolsets to Eclipse. Lately, there have been some improvements in SAP NetWeaver Visual Composer in Eclipse. SAP NetWeaver Visual Composer runs locally in Eclipse, and it is no longer necessary to connect to a server to model a UI or portal content.

The toolset for the domain-specific models are bundled within the composite designer. This tool provides a consistent overview of a composite application, showing the dependencies and checking if the contracts between the various objects in the various domains are violated.

SAP NetWeaver CE Programming Model

SAP NetWeaver CE provides a programming model like all platforms do. There are specific frameworks for the domains (user interface, process, business logic, etc.), but the entities of the domains are connected in defined ways. Figure 14.3 shows how they are connected.

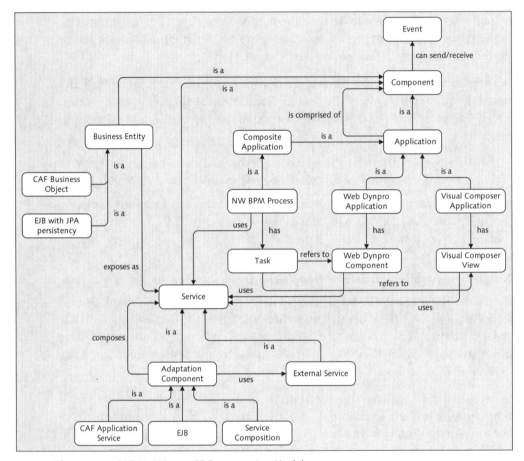

Figure 14.3 SAP NetWeaver CE Programming Model

The domains contribute the following entities to the overall programming model:

▸ **BPM**
Provides the process and task definition. A process can use services and tasks. The task itself can use user interfaces.

▸ **Web Dynpro**
Provides a Web Dynpro application that can run stand-alone and provides the

Web Dynpro component as reusable entity. Web Dynpro components can use services.

▸ **SAP NetWeaver Visual Composer**
Provides the application and the views in SAP NetWeaver Visual Composer models. SAP NetWeaver Visual Composer models can use services.

▸ **SAP CAF**
Provides the SAP CAF application service as an adaptation component to adapt data and the SAP CAF business object to locally store data. The SAP CAF application services are exposed as Web services and can compose other services.

▸ **Service composition**
Provides service composition models that are exposed as services and can compose other services.

▸ **Java EE**
Provides EJB technology to implement business logic and the Java Persistence API (JPA) to persist data locally. Every EJB can be exposed as a service.

The service notion is very important in the composition environment. In the local case, for example, SAP CAF application services and service composition, are exposed as Web services or EJBs. In the remote case, SAP NetWeaver CE can consume services that are available as Web services or remote function calls (RFCs).

14.1.3   Structure of Composites

A composite application usually contains a lot of components (see definition of the programming model above), assembled in development components and software components. The power of the frameworks allows powerful application, but unfortunately the composite application can be structured such that developer productivity, performance, or maintainability is not achieved. The following guidelines therefore explain basic principles for structuring a composite application.

Business Data

A composite application contains a lot of artifacts from different domains. Many of these artifacts can be used to store information. We describe the appropriate type of storage in the following.

The programming model of SAP NetWeaver CE provides various domain frameworks for specific purposes:

- Definition and execution of business processes: SAP NetWeaver BPM
- Definition and execution of user interfaces: SAP NetWeaver Portal, Web Dynpro Java, Java EE (JSP, JSF), and SAP NetWeaver Visual Composer
- Definition and usage of business entities: SAP CAF, Service Composer, and Java EE (EJB, JPA)

A business entity is not (yet) a concrete modeling artifact in the CE landscape but abstracts (from a consumption perspective) a certain business concern. In SAP NetWeaver CE, we perceive the business entities mainly as data-centric artifacts and as mediators when accessing services that operate on the associated business data.

> **Alternate Approach**
>
> If you opted for the loosely coupled approach, utilize the business entity concept to transform business data from the type system of the service providers (e.g. SAP backend BO) to your canonical data type system in the composite context and vice versa.

Depending on the chosen implementation technique, business entities have various characteristics. Very prominent implementation/usage patterns are:

- Provide intermediate data storage for the local execution context (SAP CAF, Java EE); see Figure 14.4.

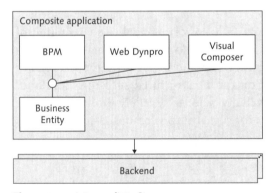

Figure 14.4 Intermediate Storage

- Provide facades to access a single or multiple more complex entities in a simplified manner, such as enterprise services or business objects (Service Composer); see Figure 14.5.

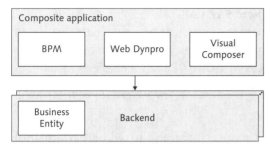

Figure 14.5 Storage in the Backend

A design decision is made at the beginning of the composite application development concerning where to store the data. Both options are possible, and which one is appropriate depends on the business logic. The local persistency of data is the preferred option if it is acceptable to have a copy of the data in the composite application. Keeping the data in the composite would mean the data in the composite application has to be synchronized later with the remote systems later. If the data in the backend systems always has to be consistent, and a local copy is not acceptable, then the data can only be persisted in the remote systems.

SAP NetWeaver BPM and the UI technologies also provide their own method for managing data in their context, which can be used to store/transport data from the business context. There are therefore various options for dealing with the data and the characteristics of the storage concept:

▶ **Storing data in the BPM process context**
A data object in the workflow holds the data that has to be available for all human activities and automated activities. The data is only transferred to the activities in a mapping step. After an activity is executed, the data object is updated.

Scope: Data in a process context is persistent and available during the lifetime of the workflow, that is, only in the scope of the process instance.

▶ **Storing data in the UI component context**
If the composite is a UI application without a process surrounding it, it is a valid option to store the data in the context of the Web Dynpro application. This option is only possible if the data should not be persisted on the server side, that is, to survive a server shut down.

Scope: Data in a Web Dynpro context is transient — available during the lifetime of the UI component, that is, a user session.

▶ **Storing data in a business entity (here SAP CAF)**
Business objects in SAP CAF can be used as persistent storage of data that has to be available in processes and UI applications. Here, the lifecycle of the content is not bound to a UI session or process instance. It has a lifecycle of its own.

Scope: Data in an SAP CAF business object has its own lifetime, is persistable, and is not coupled to anything else.

Based on the concept of separation of concerns, but also based on performance considerations, we recommend that you keep the amount of business-related information stored in the process context small. Try isolating the business data and maintaining it in a business entity instead.

Leading Artifact

A composite application contains a lot of artifacts from various domains. Many of these artifacts can be used to store information.

During the definition process of the composite, it is important to think about the leading artifacts of the composites. A leading artifact is an entity in a composite application that is accessible during the whole lifecycle of a composite and can hold the data so that other entities can access the data and do not have to replicate all content.

Therefore, the composite application designer has to decide which would be the leading artifact of the particular composite or part of it. This is essentially a question of the scope of the data and the lifecycle. There are different options based on some criteria:

▶ If the process definition is the most important entity, the natural choice is for the data to follow. As a consequence there would be no local persistency (after execution of the process instance).

▶ If the data is important and should have its own lifecycle, an SAP CAF business object is a good choice.

▶ If the data is only relevant in one UI task, the data can be stored in the Web Dynpro context.

As usual in application development there could be a mixture of these approaches, and this is not a contradiction. The only decision to make is how important a specific part of the application is, for example if the data simply follows the process definition, if the data should only be available in a user interface, or if the data should be persisted in the database.

Nevertheless, there are some possible overlaps. It would be possible, for example, for the data to be persisted in an SAP CAF business object or the process context. Both solutions therefore have advantages and disadvantages (see Table 14.1).

Arguments for Storing Data in the Process Context	Arguments for Storing Data in the SAP CAF BO and Referencing It in the Process via ID
Data that is required in the whole process is connected with the process itself by defining it in the process.	▶ The data can be accessed independently of the process instance. Data has its own lifecycle. ▶ A large amount of data is not transferred between activities. Only the ID is passed between the process steps.

Table 14.1 Storage of Data

Complexity

Complexity is one of the key problems in designing a composite application. It can exist at different places:

▶ In the control flow
▶ In the data flow

Avoid Complexity in Control Flow

SAP NetWeaver BPM offers a graphical design tool. The process graph shows control flow and data objects and their usage in process steps. This allows for a quick overview of the process flow in general *if* the size of the process remains manageable. *Manageable* means the process designer does not have to look at and simultaneously understand the interaction between more than 25 to 50 graphical objects at a time. Our first recommendation is therefore:

Recommendation: Keep process model complexity at 25 to 50 process steps.
If your model grows beyond 50 steps, there will be clear candidates for reuse, that is, portions of your process that encapsulate a meaningful (set of) feature(s) worth putting into a separate process. Use subprocesses in SAP NetWeaver CE 7.20 in the form of *referenced subprocesses* wherever possible to encapsulate reusable functionality. In SAP NetWeaver CE 7.11, use an automated activity to invoke another process. You can also leverage *embedded subprocesses* in SAP NetWeaver CE 7.20 to manage the complexity of your process model even if your subprocess is not intended for reuse.

Be aware that there is also a runtime aspect to this recommendation. The process visualization (graphical log) will look as complicated as your design time model but in addition has instance data attributed to it. The business log (textual representation of your process instances) needs to convey this information in textual form; there it will be even harder to see complex relationships between steps.

Closely related to the model complexity in terms of size (number of steps) is the shape of the model in terms of its graph. A nice compact graph attracts a second look, whereas a large, chaotic graph easily distracts from what it wants to convey: The idea of your business process could be in a single picture. BPMN is a very powerful graphical notation that you should use with care. One feature in particular tends to let people lose the overview of a diagram if used too excessively — hence our next recommendation:

Recommendation: Model block-oriented wherever possible.
Taking advantage of BPMN means you utilize the *flow-oriented* modeling technique, which is well suited to describing real business processes. Nevertheless, the *block-oriented* modeling concepts can come in handy sometimes: A block is a piece of a diagram with one entry line and one exit line. This makes it a portion of a diagram that easily lends itself to refactoring and that can, for example, be easily converted into a subprocess and be easily copied from one part of the diagram to another. Block-oriented diagrams, with their typical nesting and lack of overcrossing lines, tend to look simpler and convey the existing structure more easily. BPMN allows you to connect any step in your diagram to any other step: this feature tends to clutter the diagram and, if the source and target are not on the same screen, easily lets you lose track of the control flow. It should therefore be used with care.

Avoid Complexity in Data Flow
The BPMN diagram clearly shows the control flow for your process. The data flow is only visualized for top-level data elements, however. To find out where a certain attribute of a large structured data object is populated, where it is manipulated, and which steps it is actually consumed in requires navigation to each step and inspection of the input and output mappings.

Therefore, it wise to carefully plan the data context of the process (*global data*) and the data context of each step. A process designer must consider which data is actually required to "drive" the process (e.g., status variables that are needed to make decisions in the process, deadlines that need to be monitored, relevant user information): We call this *primary data*. In contrast to this is secondary data, which is only "carried" by the process because the process acts as a data mediator between steps (e.g., details read via a service call that is then passed to a UI) or as a convenient generic persistence layer.

Recommendation: Name your primary data as such.
Use meaningful names, comments, or your own conventions to achieve this. Primary data, in particular status variables, must be understood by anybody who attempts to use, manipulate, or refactor the process. Overlooking or misinterpreting primary data results in difficult-to-catch application errors and misuse of the process.

Recommendation: Minimize the amount of secondary data in your process.
If you reuse services or UIs, you have to work with the given set of interfaces that you have to populate or interpret, meaning your choice of data you have to provide or accept is limited. You should, however, be able to use reduced (thinned out) data structures within your process that only store the attributes you actually need. In SAP NetWeaver Composition Environment [7.20], you can use CE service adaptation to thin out vast interfaces to the data you really require. See the performance and data volume sections to fully appreciate the meaning of this recommendation. See the concept/notion of business entities as well.

If you determine the interfaces of services and UIs yourself, for example, because you design them as part of your project, you should do everything you can to adhere to this guideline. In particular:

Recommendation: Design new interfaces with small signatures.
Let these interfaces expose less than 25 parameters and favor copy-by-reference to copy-by-value. Whereas the first part of the recommendation is self-explanatory (smaller interfaces = fewer dependencies, less complexity, and less data overhead), the second part merits an example because it is valid both for services and for UIs. Passing references (e.g., to business objects) typically works well if the receiving application can interpret the references and can access the referenced object's data effectively. Passing references typically means you transport only the ID/key of a business entity between different participants in the flow. For example, if you pass the reference to a service contract, the contract number, for example, to a UI, and the UI application can use this key to read the required details of the contract, such as the issue date, the contract value, and so on without a performance penalty. As a consequence, the UI's interface contains only the contract number instead of the 75 attributes that a fully fledged contract business object might have.

Copying data (as opposed to referencing it) has several other unwanted implications, such as:

▶ The copied data in your process can run out of sync with the original object's data. This can cause the process to make incorrect decisions, because it is based on outdated information.

▶ The copied data can pose a security risk if it is sensitive. In releases 7.11 to 7.20, SAP NetWeaver BPM does not offer fine granular access rights to process data. If you are allowed to see the process instance, you are allowed to see all of its data. Not every contract value or every business decision is suitable for viewing by an administrator. A service or a UI always implements dedicated security policies that are more finely granular (because they are specific to the object at hand) than a generic business process infrastructure.

▶ The amount of data that is generically stored with your process grows with the size of your data context. See the performance section for further impact.

Recommendation: Keep the number of attributes to be mapped at any one interface below 50.
Finally, a large data context or a large activity interface requires large data-mapping definitions. BPM supports a graphical mapping tool that can visualize even complex mappings efficiently. In practice, however, there are limits to the efficiency of any graphical tool.

If you find that more than 50 attributes are to be mapped, apply the recommendation "Design new interfaces with small signatures" guidelines above. A mapping designer will easily lose track if the entire mapping does not fit onto one screen. Refactoring and maintenance of mappings like this are problematic: Did I really need attribute X? How does the underlying UI interpret attribute Y? What is the correct mapping function for attribute Z? In some BPM projects, the mapping consumes up to 50 percent of the time needed to design a process. This is a clear indicator that simplifying the data structure will reduce project costs in at least the mid to long term.

Another aspect must also be mentioned here. SAP NetWeaver CE allows you to design a composite application very easily using BPM. One reason for this is that the BPM tool provides a generic persistence; at no extra design cost, all attributes of a business process are saved automatically whenever the corresponding process instance reaches an automatic save point. The process engine takes care of rollbacks, transaction handling, and so on. As with any automatism, there are limits.

Performance Considerations

Performance must be considered in two aspects:

- Design time
- Runtime

Design Time

In many ways, design-time performance is directly related to the size of your models. If you use all features of SAP NetWeaver CE at once, meaning the process editor, UI designers, composite designer, and so on, many elaborate components will be competing for CPU and memory resources. Significant improvements in terms of memory consumption in SAP NWDS have been implemented in version 7.20. Focusing on BPM, it is worth mentioning a few simple hints that can help you significantly reduce the footprint of the process composer.

Recommendation: Use "move-corresponding" wherever possible.
This is especially true for large structures. A mapping definition is represented as a model in the design-time repository. The complexity of this mapping model can be quite significant when many individual attributes are mapped from one BPMN artifact to another, for example from data objects to activities or from events to data objects. MOVE-CORRESPONDING is a convenient way to move data between structurally equivalent (or similar) deep data structures, based on (sub)attribute names and relative positions. In version 7.20, MOVE-CORRESPONDING has been condensed to one mapping command, regardless of the size of the structure to be mapped. In addition, if you design a canonical type of system for your composite and you either deal with high load or have many mapping definitions, make this feature part of your considerations.

In version 7.11, MOVE-CORRESPONDING is expanded at design time, meaning a set of mapping statements is recursively generated to map the entire structure. The memory footprint of mapping a larger structure (>50 attributes) in the input and output mapping of a human activity when using MOVE-CORRESPONDING can go down by a factor of 10 when using the version 7.20 design time. Memory consumption improves accordingly.

Recommendation: Reuse human tasks wherever appropriate.
To achieve good performance, the number of tasks should be reduced. A task in BPM is a reusable object. Because BPM implements the full web service human task compliant status model, a task should be imagined as a rather complex object (which it is). Reusing tasks as opposed to copying them has a significant (positive) impact on memory consumption in a BPM project.

Recommendation: Housekeeping at the IDE

It is advisable to constantly clean up your projects in the SAP NetWeaver Developer Studio to keep the performance of SAP NWDS on a good level. Close or remove artifacts in the IDE that active processes no longer reference in your runtime systems. Such artifacts could be:

▸ WD/VC UIs

▸ Service endpoint definition

▸ Individual task definition

▸ Rules

Please note that removing artifacts from a processes model (or referenced development component (DC) is an operation that you should execute carefully. If you deploy such reworked artifacts to a server that has still active instances based on the preceding definitions, it is likely that the deployment will invalidate these instances. This is considered to be an incompatible change. Be especially careful with the service endpoint (e.g., event trigger).

For Web Dynpro Java UI components a re-import feature is provided that allows the user to reread its definition for UI to update the metadata. Again, ensure that you do not perform incompatible changes (e.g., remove a parameter at the I/O of the UI); otherwise, running instances on a server might break when you deploy the new definition. If only compatible changes are made to the UI component, the system will preserve the existing mapping at the I/O interfaces from task to task UI.

There is currently no support from the system to detect incompatible changes automatically.

Runtime

Runtime performance here means factors that influence the CPU and main memory consumption of the process engine that runs on your Java server and executes the instances of your process model. There are several factors like this that you can influence with the design of your process model. A few theoretical remarks about the BPM process engine are required to elucidate the following guidelines.

The BPM engine uses an in-memory algorithm to efficiently share resources (memory and CPU) between all process instances currently in execution. On a clustered installation, one engine instance will run per node. Elaborate load balancing, communication, and fail-over mechanisms are in place to ensure efficient use of the full cluster resource.

The engine executes process instances in a transactional and fail-safe manner. This means the state of a process is stored in the database (DB) at *save points* whenever the process logic, technical constraints, or general monitoring requirements demand it. Because the engine executes an arbitrary number of different process models, all with different data context definitions, it cannot use dedicated (transparent) DB tables to store this data. Instead, at every save point, the data context of a process is serialized to XML and stored as one "blob." When the data needs to be read back, it is fetched from the DB and parsed to re-instantiate the data objects in the memory. This engine-persistent storage is required to enable fail-over of process instances in case of a Java engine — or a hardware failure. If this occurs, the engine will simply reload its previous state and continue process execution from the previous save point.

Whenever a context switch occurs for a process instance, the entire instance must be serialized on the node where it is currently executed and later de-serialized on the node where execution is to continue. A context switch like this can occur when an incoming request is issued on a node in the cluster where the process instance is not currently running. Requests of this kind are service requests, a BPMN event (via correlation), or a human interaction leading to a status change of a task.

For auditing reasons, note that there are at least two save points for every activity in your process: one after creation when the input data is available and another one after completion, when the output data is available. Human tasks can have significantly more save points than automated activities, typically one after each status change (e.g., task created, task started, task claimed, task failed, task completed, etc.). Also note that all major changes to a process instance and its activities (including changed process data) are written to the business log, where they are the basis for providing information about the history and the current state of the process (in graphical or textual form).

In memory, data objects are represented using a standard compliant Service Data Objects (SDO) implementation.

The size and complexity of the data context of a process therefore directly impact engine performance in three ways:

▶ The data context of every process instance currently in execution must be kept in the main memory. Very large data contexts (>1MB) can significantly impact the number of process instances that can be simultaneously executed.

- When a save point is reached, the process instance must be serialized and written to the database. Serialization consumes application server CPU time, and the serialized data stream consumes DB server CPU time and DB space.

- When a process instance is reloaded from the database, its data is de-serialized, and the Java runtime objects are reconstructed.

Please consider that each attribute in the global data context is serialized and stored in the business log whenever it is changed. Each activity in the process has at least two save points, where the full input and output data, respectively, are serialized and stored.

Sizing

Note that a dedicated sizing procedure document for SAP NetWeaver BPM starting with release 7.20 is available on SAP Service Marketplace.

Structure

The artifacts of a composite application can be structured in many different ways according to the SAP component model. This is an explanation of how to structure a composite application.

During development of a composite application, one of the most important questions is how the application will be structured in projects, in particular, how many software components (SCs) and development components (DCs) will be used. Also, considering build-time procedures and the possibility of clustering content will help resolve structuring issues.

Software Component Granularity
An SC is usually created if the parts of the composite applications should be executed on different servers because an SC is defining the deployment granularity or if the parts of a composite application can be deployed independently, for example, if some of the functionality is optional.

Every software component archive (SCA) defines a distribution archive. The argument for SC granularity is therefore deployment. We definitely do not recommend creating different SCs only to bundle the business-relevant parts together (or separate them). If the parts of a composite application should be executed on one server, and there is absolutely no intention of deploying them on different servers, the content should be put into the same SC.

If the application design is done in such a way that different parts can be distributed independently, we recommend putting the parts of the application in different SCs, because the smallest distribution granularity in software logistics is the software component. The SC is also the entity that is versioned, so the SC is the entity that is meant to structure the deployment.

There are other reasons to define SCs, such as project organization and semantic reasons.

Development Component Granularity

The different domains provide separate DC types. It is therefore a good choice (and sometimes the only option) to put the content for different domains in separate DCs. Therefore, all process content is located in a process composer DC, all Web Dynpro content is part of a Web Dynpro DC, and so on.

A DC is the atom of reuse, that is, the smallest undividable functional piece. The composite application developer therefore has to plan for reuse and proper segregation of reusable pieces into a minimal number of DCs. For generic functions, individual DCs should be created to facilitate their reusability and to collect all required elements of the function in this DC.

As a result, parts that are meant for reuse should be put into separate DCs including sufficient definition time for planning the API and separate API and implementation. You can add the API to a public part of your DC in these ways:

▶ Choose the DC structure according to its function and not according to the organizational structure of the responsible developers.

▶ Choose the DCs in such a way that the involved developers work in the same team and at the same location. Only if these conditions are met can you use the inactive state of objects, which is mandatory for distributed responsibilities.

These two guidelines seem contradictory, but you should use both guidelines together, so that together they define the minimal structure of DCs.

After a change, you must rebuild the entire DC. You should therefore choose the size carefully so that it does not contain too many objects. This is a very broad statement, so some more details are required.

Build Time

This section provides more details regarding the general recommendations about how to structure content and what these recommendations look like in the light

431

of build times. To illustrate how the structure influences the build times, we chose Web Dynpro as an example.

Web Dynpro recommendations to structure the content are as follows:

Recommendation: Optimize the development performance with the best deployment granularity.
Web Dynpro development components (Web Dynpro DCs) should be as slim as possible to accelerate build/deploy/run turnaround cycles. If the Web Dynpro DCs become bigger, the build time will increase, so a small change in coding will result in builds that take a very long time.

Recommendation: Optimize the application architecture with the best Web Dynpro component granularity.
One business task should be implemented in one Web Dynpro component, but the Web Dynpro components should not be too large. If the components become too large, then it is not as easy to distribute the work, because the team of developers works on the same component. This would lead to blocking operations, and reuse potential is low. On the other hand, if the component granularity is too small, the application might not perform very well, because every component comes with a system management overhead. All of the components have to be handled by the system.

Recommendation: Apply Web Dynpro component separation principles.
Web Dynpro components have to be defined for a specific purpose, and a component should not be defined for two purposes at the same time. If a component is responsible for displaying the UI, then it should not do model import. So there are at least visual Web Dynpro components for the UI and faceless components for the model handling (connectivity). Generally, the components are designed for one purpose.

This last sentence in particular indicates that there is more behind the separation than just the theoretical guidelines. A very interesting point in this area is that the build times are to some degree related to the number of DCs. Table 14.2 summarizes the situation for the same functionality, located either in one DC or in four DCs. The measurement is performed on one PC, so the numbers are comparable to each other, but the numbers are not a guarantee that every PC with the same performance will achieve the same performance.

Merged Web Dynpro DC	Separate DCs
\all (a WD DC consisting of four WD components)	31.609 seconds
\change	7 seconds
\create	6.328 seconds
\result	11.141 seconds
\search	25.578 seconds
Sum	50.47 seconds

Table 14.2 Comparison of Build Times

What becomes very obvious is the fact that the build of a DC has some overhead. Opting for too many DCs will therefore create problems during build time.

The structure of the DCs of a composite application is therefore always a compromise between the guidelines for business separation of logic in DCs (as small as possible according to the business needs) and the overhead of the infrastructure for each DC. There is normally a conflict between optimizing either the number of DCs for the fastest overall build (as few DCs as possible) or the fastest build for developers (as many DCs as possible). The numbers in the table should provide some guidance about how much the additional overhead for development would be. If the decision is to use the more coarse-grained DC design, the build times for developers will increase. If the decision is to use fine-grained DCs, the overhead of the infrastructure (build time and maintenance of DC dependencies between the DCs) will increase. It is therefore important to make a balanced decision.

The actual guidelines are highly dependent on the application use case, but you still have to take into account the build time and infrastructure aspects during the decision process of the composite application structure.

Clustering of Content

Usually a composite application contains a lot of entities of one programming model, such as Web Dynpro components and EJBs. The recommendation is to put entities that are highly related into one DC. This does not mean all components are put into one DC. In principle, it is a question of how to cluster the components in DCs. A cluster belongs in one DC. If the connection between two potential clusters is very weak (only one or two dependencies), the components are put into two DCs. This recommendation can be defined as follows:

▶ If a set of components uses the same set of external components, the set of components should be put into one DC (see Figure 14.6). They belong to a cluster of components.

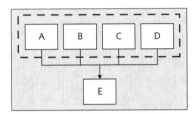

Figure 14.6   Bundling of Consumers

▶ If a set of components is grouped together and only one component is accessible externally (defining a public API), the components should be put into one DC (see Figure 14.7). They belong to a cluster of components.

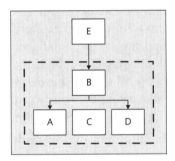

Figure 14.7   Bundling of Used Components

At the start of the composite application design process, you therefore need to think about the components and how they are connected.

Using Services

A composite application usually uses services from various other systems. This section describes how you can use these services.

Usually when the application design is done for the business functionality and the user interfaces that are required, the next question is how the services that are needed can be consumed. Sometimes the available services are not sufficient to fulfill the business requirements of the composite application, and therefore services have to be defined and implemented in a remote system. This design step is not described here and neither is the definition and implementation of these services. After this is clarified, and the set of services to be used by the composite is identified, the obvious next question is where the data of the service calls is used. And here the first architecture decisions will be made, because SAP NetWeaver CE frameworks such as Web Dynpro, BPM, and SAP CAF provide the capability to consume services directly. The first decision now is whether a service should be used directly or not. This section will focus on this question and provide some guidance about how this can be done and what the advantages and disadvantages are.

The term *loosely coupling* gives you an indication of the design principle for an application regarding service consumption.

Very often the discussion is reduced to the question of whether an application talks synchronously or asynchronously with its peers. Although this is certainly one aspect, it doesn't cover all relevant dimensions of loose coupling. The goal of loose coupling is to reduce dependencies between systems. Therefore, to provide a definite answer about how tightly an application is coupled to other systems, you can be guided by a second simple question: What are the consequences for system A (the calling system) if you make changes in system B (the called system)? Probably, this question reveals a large number of dependencies between your application and others that go beyond a classification of the communication style between them. There are a few more assumptions about application design. Which assumptions can be made for coupling systems?

▶ **Assumption 1: location of the called system (its physical address)**
Does your application use direct URLs for accessing systems, or is your application decoupled via an abstraction layer that is responsible for maintaining connections between systems? The service group paradigm used in SAP NetWeaver CE is a perfect example of what such an abstraction might look like. Using an Enterprise Service Bus is another example.

▶ **Assumption 2: number of receivers**
Does your application take care of the receivers of a service call? Or does it simply drop a message "somewhere," and other mechanisms take care of transporting the message to the receiving systems? Don't underestimate the important of this assumption. If you take the loosely coupled approach, it means that you are not making any assumptions about the systems you are talking to. This implies a completely different architecture compared to tightly coupled applications. You never know when or if a service call returns due to the number of involved systems, and your application must be prepared for that.

▶ **Assumption 3: availability of systems**
Does your application require that all of the systems you are connecting to

are up and running all of the time? This is obviously a very hard requirement, especially if you want to connect to external systems that are not under your control. If your answer is "Yes, all of the systems must be running all of the time," you are obviously tightly coupled in this regard.

▶ **Assumption 4: data format**
Does your application reuse data formats as they are provided by the back end systems, or do you use a canonical data type system that is independent from the types of systems used in the called applications? If you reuse the data types from the backends, you probably have to struggle with data-type conversions in your application. This is not a very loosely coupled approach.

▶ **Assumption 5: response time**
Does your application require the called systems to respond within a certain (acceptable) time frame, or is it acceptable for your application to receive an answer minutes, hours, or even days later?

There are even more dependencies, but the message should be clear: loose coupling is not one-dimensional. For each of the aforementioned aspects of loose coupling, you have to make decisions. And they are not easy, because moving toward loose coupling has serious implications for the architecture of your application. So loose coupling comes at a price, especially in terms of complexity, and you have to decide whether you want to pay the price for it.

The benefit of loose coupling is flexibility and agility. If you are aiming for a loosely coupled approach, you will get unparalleled flexibility for adaptations to changing landscapes. Because you aren't making any assumptions about the landscape your application is running against, you can easily adapt it as needed (provided your frameworks and tools support you like SAP NetWeaver Composition Environment does). This is especially important for partners and independent software vendors (ISVs) who can develop applications once and easily install and configure them at their customers' side. The application itself stays untouched.

It isn't just partners and ISVs who will benefit from this approach. It is useful within companies as well: Once you've established a successful new application, you will most likely want to reuse it within your company in other locations or regions. Very often, the IT landscape in the new locations differs from the one the application was originally designed for. If you take the loosely coupled approach right from the beginning, this undertaking will not frighten you. Another aspect you should consider is the probability of landscape changes during the lifetime of your new application. Due to mergers and acquisitions, or due to system consolidations, the landscape underneath your application is constantly changing. If you are not prepared for loose coupling, you'll be forced to adapt your application again and again.

Concrete Implementation of Loose Coupling in Service Consumption

The concrete implementation of the loose coupling principle in a composite application can be performed as follows:

▸ Enterprise services are used only via WS proxies in EJBs or SAP CAF external services.

▸ There is an intermediate layer that abstracts from the underlying enterprise service so that only the used data is exposed to the composite application. The intermediate layer defines a service contract to the upper layers, and the implementation of these interfaces is called a service contract implementation layer.

▸ The upper layers of a composite application (Web Dynpro, SAP NetWeaver Visual Composer, or SAP NetWeaver BPM) only use the service contracts.

Figure 14.8 shows the architecture of a concrete implementation of the loose coupling principle.

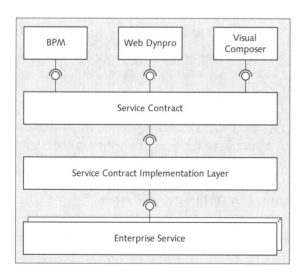

Figure 14.8 Loose Coupling Architecture

With the service contract layer, it is possible to achieve decoupling from a concrete landscape, data-type structure, communication protocol, and so on. The service contract implementation layer can be implemented in different ways. First, the composite application design has to be clear if a complete decoupling has to be achieved. In that case SAP provides the following solutions:

▶ **SAP NetWeaver BPM**

The service contract implementation layer implements an interface by using BPM modeling capabilities to allow execution of service calls asynchronously (see Asynchronous Write in Section 14.1.5). If an error happens during invocation of the Enterprise Service, a full error handling including user steps can be implemented.

▶ **SAP NetWeaver Process Integration (PI)**

The implementation of the service contract implementation layer is not done via SAP NetWeaver CE; it is done via the process integration hub of SAP. The benefit is the same as the case of SAP NetWeaver CE; the only difference is that the capabilities of SAP NetWeaver Process Integration can be used (e.g., routing, ccBPM, etc.).

▶ **Java Message Service (JMS)**

The service contract implementation layer contains a very small implementation of the service contract, and only an event via JMS is raised that is processed on the Java server itself, so the message queue is used to decouple the functionality. The benefit is that only Java EE technologies are used.

The above options decouple the execution of the enterprise service call from the basic composite application. If the asynchronous behavior is not a requirement, then the other technologies of SAP NetWeaver CE (SAP CAF, service composition, EJB) that transform the delivered data of the enterprise services to the composite can be used. This solution has the drawback that a complete decoupling of the UI parts of the composite application is not achieved; it goes in the direction of tight coupling with all of the disadvantages.

Structure of the Service Contract Layer in a Composite Application
The service contract and the service contract implementation layer have to be structured in a way that real decoupling is achieved. Figure 14.9 shows the structure of a decoupled composite application.

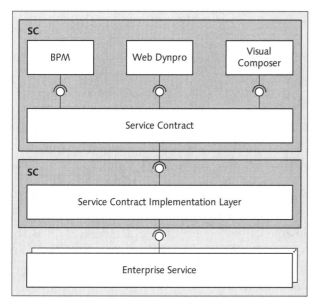

Figure 14.9 Structure of a Decoupled Composite Application

The entities of the composite application and the service contract definition are contained in one software component (SC), and the service contract implementation is contained in another SC. The contract and the implementation are in different SCs, because this allows switching of the implementations. These software components do not have any dependency, because they are loosely coupled and the communication between the composite application and the service contract implementation is only done via interfaces and configuration of the used services in the composite application.

Concrete Implementation of Tight Coupling in Terms of Service Consumption

Loose coupling is not always the best architecture. If you don't require flexibility, performance indicates that an intermediate layer is not allowed, or dependencies to the backend systems are not an issue, SAP NetWeaver CE allows all frameworks (Web Dynpro, SAP NetWeaver BPM, SAP NetWeaver Visual Composer, etc.) to call services directly. Figure 14.10 shows the architecture.

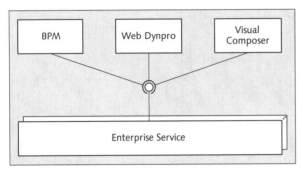

Figure 14.10 Tight Coupling

Example

The most commonly used implementation pattern in SAP NetWeaver CE is to implement an application service in SAP CAF that consumes one or many external services. The Java coding inside the application service is then responsible for mapping the data to the correct output data.

The intermediate SAP CAF application service is used if one of the following abstractions is required for the composite application:

▶ **Concrete landscape**
The application services that are exposed by SAP CAF can be deployed with the composite application. If the landscape changes at the customer's side, however, other application services can be implemented using the same signature. Their implementation differs in such a way that the data is now retrieved from another system (or systems) within the customer landscape. Only a small configuration step is needed to activate the new application service for the composite.

▶ **Data type structure**
The enterprise services provide a specific data type structure and require these data structures. If the application is not interested in all data, it is all right to implement an SAP CAF application service, define your own data types in SAP CAF, and only expose the data structures of CAF.

▶ **Communication protocol**
SAP CAF provides the functionality to call Web services and RFCs. If the application is loosely coupled in the sense that it should be able to run with Web services and get the data via similar RFCs later on, the recommended way is to implement an SAP CAF application service and implement the switch inside the

application service. Whether the data comes from an RFC or a Web service is transparent for the upper layers of the application.

Web Dynpro and SAP NetWeaver Visual Composer can follow either loose coupling or tight coupling architecture styles depending on the specific requirements defined in the general considerations to use tight coupling or loose coupling.

Task Handling in a Process

A composite application usually contains process definitions and corresponding tasks. This section describes how to define the tasks.

As of Release 7, enhancement package 1 and enhancement package 2, the lifecycle of a task instance is bound to a surrounding process in SAP NetWeaver BPM, even though it is possible to define a task as a stand-alone artifact in its own DC.

Under very specific conditions, you can reduce the number of DCs. Imagine the following situation:

- Multiple SAP NetWeaver BPM processes are modeled that contain a human activity as their single artifact (ignoring start/end events).
- The tasks that back the human activity all point to the same task UI and differ only in the occurrence of the process context.
- The task description can be constructed by using/interpreting the process context.

In a situation like this, implement only a single, generic process, and create tasks and their work item description based on the process context, which needs to be fed accordingly by the start event message.

We therefore also recommend investigating whether existing processes, tasks, and task UIs can be refactored to make use of this approach.

As an example for a generic approach, you have a set of different processes running in the backend (say process A and process B). For each of the processes, at a certain point a confirmation should be requested from responsible users. Instead of modeling the processes "confirmation for step x (process A)" and "confirmation for step x (process B)," model a single process, "generic confirmation." Your start event message should carry all data that you require to make the necessary recipient determination and fill your fields in the confirmation UI. Add a human activity to the process. Implement your notification UI in Web Dynpro, and fill all task-specific information from the context. Connect your Web Dynpro UI as the task UI to the activity in your process. Pass all your task-specific details from the start message to the human activity/task (thus the Web Dynpro context) via data mapping.

Alternatively, if the confirmation task is still trivial and based on the same attributes of the different processes but requests different UIs, think of a gateway in the process to select the different task and thus the target UIs.

Extensibility

The extensibility configuration framework was introduced in SAP NetWeaver Composition Environment 7.2, and the technology requires a specific structure. This section describes how the composite application has to be structured.

Extensibility is an important issue during the development of a composite application. Extensibility is normally understood as the ability of SAP NetWeaver CE to change an application behavior without design modification (only certain implementations are replaced). The support of the composite application therefore stays, but new functionality can be plugged in.

There are many ways to design an application for extensibility purposes, but SAP NetWeaver CE provides a specific framework for extensibility. The extensibility configuration framework demonstrates an innovative conceptual approach, which allows different interface implementations of the application parts to be exchanged during the runtime of an application.

To do this, you first need to define extension points in your application. An extension point is a reference to a development object interface of a redirectable technology. The extension point allows exchanging or actually redirecting to different interface implementations during the runtime of an application.

You can create extension points for the interfaces of the following development objects:

- ▶ Enterprise JavaBeans (EJBs)
- ▶ SAP Composite Application Framework (CAF)
- ▶ Web Dynpro. In the (individual) Adobe Interactive Forms (AIF) use case, the extension point is not an interface, but a single form marked as extensible.

To create an extension point, there must be at least two development objects from one of the above types, because there needs to be a relation between them.

The extensibility configuration framework requires a specific structure of the application. The application has to be prepared to be extensible.

SAP CAF and EJBs have to follow the same principle. Even if the EJB is only a place holder, the redirect from an existing implementation in an EJB can only happen in an EJB container. Therefore, an EJB that has to be redirected has to be invoked from another EJB.

The consequence of this limitation is that an EJB that is consumed by a web application (Web Dynpro, servlet, etc.) has to be wrapped by another EJB, because invocation of the first EJB is performed by the web container, not the EJB container of the Java EE engine.

The extension components (components that replace the functionality of the composite application) have to be put in a customer *product*. The original product does not contain the extensions; the extensions are put in the customer product that has a dependency to the original product.

14.1.4 Separation of Functionality

SAP NetWeaver CE provides frameworks for different purposes. There are frameworks for business logic implementation, user interface modeling, and process modeling. The functionality of these frameworks sometimes overlaps, and you need to decide when to use which framework. The following explanations will provide some guidance.

UI Flow (SAP NetWeaver BPM and Web Dynpro)

The issue: The various steps of a user interface can be implemented in different ways. In particular, Web Dynpro and SAP NetWeaver BPM can be used to model the user interface steps. This section describes how to decide how to model the steps.

In general, both Web Dynpro and SAP NetWeaver BPM work well together for the realization of business processes or composites. How to wire them together or to use them exclusively depends on the concrete requirements of a business process. As already described, business processes can come in a plethora of occurrences. In this chapter, we will focus just on human interaction, because this is where SAP NetWeaver BPM and Web Dynpro are complementary.

The two technical offerings are best described by the domains that they belong to. SAP NetWeaver BPM allows you to model and execute workflows (generally it is a process orchestration engine), whereas Web Dynpro (for Java) is a UI technology with screen-flow capabilities. As indicated by the word *flow,* both technologies can deliver *one-to-many* business activities to human users. Whereas Web Dynpro screen flows concern the interaction with a single user, SAP NetWeaver BPM focuses on a more global approach where a single flow model can involve multiple users on multiple activities.

The following discussion assumes that you leverage BPMN as the language to describe your business process (and discuss it with the line of business [LOB]).

When implementing a business process with concrete technology, it is important to understand the difference between human activities in a pure descriptive BPMN model and their realization in a system. At present, SAP NetWeaver only allows implementation of human activities as tasks. A task is a very explicit means. It creates a work item in an inbox (here UWL) that has to be picked up by the corresponding user to be executed. There is currently no option to use BPMN models in SAP NetWeaver BPM to express that individual human activities will be grouped and executed as a screen flow for a certain task. This provides a hint about the typical division of labor between the technologies. Whereas SAP NetWeaver BPM executes an overall business process flow to instantiate tasks, Web Dynpro is leveraged when interacting with a user on an individual task.

As a result, some of your human activities in the descriptive model will not make it to the executable BPMN model in SAP NetWeaver BPM. Others will not show up because you implement them as views in Web Dynpro.

When transforming a descriptive BPMN model into an executable model, you might end up with the situation that all activities have to be executed by a sole user. Here, the only remaining question is how the user will execute this process: as a task or as a self-initiated activity? If it will be a task, a process with a single human activity has to be modeled in SAP NetWeaver BPM, and all of the logic goes into Web Dynpro and is linked to the SAP NetWeaver BPM activity as a task UI. If the latter applies, you implement a Web Dynpro application only and share the link with your users (via portal technologies, for example).

At present, the processes in SAP NetWeaver start with an event message. There are three options for this:

1. Call the process directly via Web service technology

2. Connect to the process indirectly via the event (message) infrastructure

3. Use the SAP NetWeaver Administrator functionality

If you want your processes to start with a user-initiated UI activity, there is currently no way to model this in SAP NetWeaver BPM. The proposal is to implement a Web Dynpro application and call the Web service endpoint of the process directly when required. In your modeled SAP NetWeaver BPM process, add a comment referring to the Web Dynpro UI that is intended to initiate this process.

UI Modeling (Web Dynpro and SAP NetWeaver Visual Composer)

SAP NetWeaver CE contains different UI programming models. This section describes when to use which.

SAP NetWeaver CE contains several UI programming models that usually require a clear separation. The frameworks explained here are Web Dynpro Java with SAP NWDS tools and SAP NetWeaver Visual Composer with Web Dynpro Java runtime (WD4VC).

First, we will explain the frameworks and how they are related from a technical point of view. Web Dynpro is a UI framework that runs in the web container of the Java EE server. It provides an own component model for reuse, which means the Web Dynpro component is a very crucial entity in the whole programming model. The Web Dynpro runtime, running in the web container, can instantiate and execute an arbitrary number of components. The connection to SAP NetWeaver Visual Composer is that the runtime to execute SAP NetWeaver Visual Composer models is implemented as Web Dynpro components. In principle, all of the features that SAP NetWeaver Visual Composer models can use at runtime are therefore available in Web Dynpro at the same time, but if something is available in Web Dynpro, this does not mean it is automatically available in SAP NetWeaver Visual Composer; it has to be implemented in the components.

The Web Dynpro development environment is Eclipse based, and many tools for the different entities of the programming model are available. For SAP NetWeaver Visual Composer, there is a browser-based modeling environment, implemented in JavaScript, HTML, and the SVG (scalable vector graphics) plug-in from Adobe. As a result of implementations in two different environments, they do not reuse common frameworks. The SAP NetWeaver Visual Composer development environment might therefore provide more features in the area of developer productivity than Web Dynpro itself. The SAP NetWeaver Visual Composer development environment is integrated in Eclipse using the HTML editor integration in Eclipse, meaning the SAP NetWeaver Visual Composer models can be edited in SAP NetWeaver Developer Studio, too. Using this integration therefore makes it possible to navigate and edit SAP NetWeaver Visual Composer models, and some basic frameworks that are available in SAP NetWeaver Developer Studio only can be used by SAP NetWeaver Visual Composer. The most prominent example of a framework that is only available in SAP NetWeaver Visual Composer in Eclipse is the mass configuration support via service groups. These entities cannot be created in the browser-only environment, only by SAP NetWeaver Visual Composer in Eclipse.

Having said this, the easiest way to explain the differences is to summarize them in a table (see Table 14.3) and provide more details afterward.

Feature	Web Dynpro	SAP NetWeaver Visual Composer
Adobe Interactive Form support	Basic support of forms by providing a UI element that can host an interactive form	No support of Adobe Interactive Forms
Stateless applications and asynchronous UI part	Available	Only stateful applications
Analytics	Implementation-dependent, no direct integration	SAP NetWeaver Visual Composer BI kit to access different data sources
Extensibility support	Redirection of Web Dynpro components	No change of the application without modification
Expressions	Implementation-specific, no declarative tool support	Properties can take expressions as values, similar to expression language in Excel
Implementation by native language	Web Dynpro provides a Java API to allow Java coding for development	Implementation in SAP NetWeaver Visual Composer models is not supported
Developer productivity	Model-driven tools integrated with implementation tools	SAP NetWeaver Visual Composer is designed to allow fast development of modeled UIs, so the whole design time is tailored for a small learning curve

Table 14.3 UI Technology Comparison

▶ **Adobe Interactive Forms**
With Web Dynpro, a UI element can be put to a Web Dynpro view and the data transferred from the Web Dynpro context to the Adobe Interactive Form, thus allowing direct context binding. The form is persisted in a specific folder of the Web Dynpro project and can be edited by the dedicated Adobe Template Designer.

▶ **Stateless applications and asynchronous UI part**
Stateless Web Dynpro Java applications keep all information needed to approve a user's request on the client. This information is passed to the server on each round-trip. This allows the server to release resources during the user think times and fits perfectly with scenarios where many users have either long think times (one round-trip in half an hour, say) or where the application they use only needs a small amount of information for the interaction step (so startup is inexpensive). Stateless applications do not suit applications that need a lot of information to work properly.

▶ **Web Dynpro Java applications embedding other Web Dynpro Java applications**
The user sees a seamless UI and can interact with both applications. However, the embedded application can run asynchronously to the embedding application, meaning a response can be sent to the client while the embedded application is still running. The embedded application can fill its screen area with an intermediate result, and the client is instructed to look for content updates after a certain amount of time has elapsed. Once the embedded application has finished processing a user round-trip and the update has been transported to the client, the corresponding UI area is unlocked, allowing user interaction.

▶ **Analytics**
The business intelligence (BI) capabilities of SAP NetWeaver can be accessed in SAP NetWeaver Visual Composer by a specific extension of SAP NetWeaver Visual Composer. This is the BI kit. This kit allows the connection to BI systems to display data. It is a very natural integration of data, because the handling of data is completely integrated in the SAP NetWeaver Visual Composer modeling environment. BI functionality is only available in the browser-based solution of SAP NetWeaver Visual Composer.

▶ **Extensibility**
In Web Dynpro it is possible to mark components that can be replaced by other component implementations, fulfilling the same interface. The replacement

of the original components does not require any modification of the existing application.

▶ **Expressions**

In SAP NetWeaver Visual Composer, expressions can be used as values for nearly all properties. By doing this, SAP NetWeaver Visual Composer provides an easy way to make a lot of changes without detailed knowledge of a programming language. The expression language is similar to the expression language available in Excel for formulas and the like. To achieve similar behavior in Web Dynpro, Java coding is required.

▶ **Implementation by native language**

Web Dynpro is based on the web container implementation and provides Java API so that nearly all entities can be edited by Java calls. This gives the user complete freedom to implement all UI applications.

▶ **Developer productivity**

The area of developer productivity is very broad. To explain the difference between Web Dynpro tools and SAP NetWeaver Visual Composer, it helps to explain the starting points of the frameworks. Web Dynpro was started as a complete programming model to enable easy development of UIs for enterprise applications. SAP NetWeaver Visual Composer started as a composition tool for business users to create small UIs for reporting. Based on the different user groups — Web Dynpro for developers and SAP NetWeaver Visual Composer for business users — the focus was on different areas.

Web Dynpro provides all entities and APIs to implement a powerful application and support the developer in implementing complex applications. Over the years, Web Dynpro improved in the area of development tools but so far has not achieved the same level of simplicity as SAP NetWeaver Visual Composer for simple UIs. Nevertheless, Web Dynpro provides developers with excellent support when developing complex UIs.

Unfortunately, SAP NetWeaver Visual Composer models cannot be transferred to Web Dynpro components. This makes it impossible to start with the better developer productivity and go to Web Dynpro later. During application design, the developer has to decide which user interfaces are simple enough to be modeled in SAP NetWeaver Visual Composer and which are too complex. We already listed and described the additional features above.

The two user interface programming models are not completely isolated. Simple UIs can be modeled in SAP NetWeaver Visual Composer, whereas the complex parts are developed in Web Dynpro and integrated via black box integration in SAP NetWeaver Visual Composer.

Data Transformation (SAP CAF, SAP NetWeaver BPM, Service Adaption)

SAP NetWeaver CE contains different programming models for data transformation. This section describes when to use which.

If a composite application developer has to design the application, he first has to think about tight or loose coupling. In this area, there are a number of recommendations for the specific frameworks available for data transformation.

Tight coupling is recommended when:

▶ *Single place consumption* of a particular service is needed in the scope of a composite application. In cases like this, we recommend importing and transforming (adapted/simplified/mapped) services or using them directly in Web Dynpro/ SAP NetWeaver VC/SAP NetWeaver BPM.

▶ *High performance* is needed when service is being consumed. Mediation steps with SAP CAF or Service Composer are considered as overhead compared to direct service consumption.

Loose coupling is recommended when:

▶ *Service adaptation reuse* is needed in multiple places (screens, processes, etc.) in a composite application. We then recommend mediating/wrapping this service in SAP CAF or Service Composer. The service is consumed, transformed (adapted/ simplified/mapped), and then exposed using SAP CAF or Service Composer, thus making the transformation logic reusable. We recommend using Service Composer when the transformation logic complexity is low to moderate and can be modeled with a simple flow diagram and structure mapping. We do not recommend implementing business logic with Service Composer, because conditional and error-handling behavior modeling is not supported yet. We recommend using SAP CAF when the transformation logic is too complex and implementation is easier with Java coding (or if high performance is a prerequisite; current performance measurements indicate that Service Composer is slower than SAP CAF). We also recommend SAP CAF when consumption of a backend service alone is not sufficient and additional data (specific to the composite) has to be managed, in a local database, for example.

▶ *Service composition reuse* is needed in multiple places in a composite. We recommend importing, transforming (adapted/simplified/mapped), or using the set of consumed services as is and then composing it (the result is exposed as a single service) in SAP CAF or Service Composer, thus making the composition logic reusable.

▶ *A backend abstraction layer* pattern is needed to allow for backend system decoupling at runtime. We recommend implementing the platform-independent service interface, backend service adaptations, and switching configuration mechanism with SAP CAF.

SAP CAF and Service Composer both provide data transformation capabilities. The differences are in the specific details of the frameworks (see Table 14.4). The following section provides a basic description of the developer of a composite application and supports him in the decision process.

Capability/Tool	CAF	Service Composer	Java EE
Service consumption (WS, RFC)	Modeled and generated to leverage Java API for XML Web services (JAX-WS) and SAP Java Connector (JCo) static proxies for optimum performance, no service mocking, no service interface reimport	Modeled and interpreted; service mocking, service interface reimport with delta detection, flexible protocol switching	JAX-WS, Java Architecture for XML Binding (JAXB), SAP JCo
Type reuse and collision handling	Conflicting type definitions cannot be imported (first wins)	Conflicting type definitions are interactively imported	n/a
Service simplification	n/a (modeled manually)	Modeled (simplification wizard SI) and automatically derived mappings and service consumption)	n/a (coded manually)
Flow	Coded	Modeled and interpreted	Coded

Table 14.4 Data Transformation Technology Comparison

Capability/Tool	CAF	Service Composer	Java EE
Data transformation mapping	Modeled and generated to static code, one-to-one, constant mapping	Modeled and interpreted, emulation, expression language, one-to-one, one-to-many, many-to-many, constant mapping, mapping functions, iterations (730), collection handling, type conversion, type casting (730), built-in functions, custom functions, function nesting	Coded
Service provisioning	Modeled and generated to leverage JAX-WS and EJB	Modeled and generated to leverage JAX-WS and EJB	JAX-WS
Persistency	Remote persistence, entity-level permissions, instance-level permissions, language-dependent attributes, generated JPA entities, multiple (bulk) operations over BO nodes, SAP NetWeaver BW integration, business data transport, modeling of custom findBy operations, ServiceBrowser for runtime testing, graphical modeler (7.11)	n/a	JPA

Table 14.4 Data Transformation Technology Comparison (Cont.)

Capability/Tool	CAF	Service Composer	Java EE
Custom coding in Java	Controlled	Limited to mapping functions	Unlimited
Write operations	Logic is implemented, and therefore the execution of many service calls in a chain can be implemented such that errors can be handled	If there are many write operations in a model, then it is difficult to do good enough error handling, because there is no way to trigger user interaction. Only if the error is exposed and some implementation outside of the model reacts to it	Logic is implemented, and therefore error handling is possible to every degree

Table 14.4 Data Transformation Technology Comparison (Cont.)

SAP CAF and Service Composer are both model-driven architecture (MDA) tools for service development, but they provide different design-time and runtime capabilities, resulting in corresponding benefits. Depending on the particular use case, it might be better to use one or the other technology.

▸ **Service consumption**
In SAP CAF, WSDL artifacts can be imported to consume Web services and SAP JCo models to consume RFCs and business application programming interfaces (BAPIs). From the consumed services models, it then generates JAX-WS and RFC static proxies, resulting in improved consumption performance. Because communication–technology-specific proxies are used, it is not possible to switch the type (WS/RFC) of the consumed service once the service interface has been imported. Service Composer uses WSDL artifacts to describe imported services for both WS and RFC types. Instead of generating static proxies (as in SAP CAF), WSDL description is interpreted at runtime by SCA runtime and corresponding SDO data access services (for WS or RFC), which leads to lower performance compared to static proxies, but makes it possible to switch between WS and RFC types of consumed services. Easy service mocking can also be applied. Service Composer provides service interface reimport with delta detection

capability, thus preserving the existing service flow and data transformation mapping models.

▶ **Type reuse and collision handling**
Both SAP CAF and Service Composer provide type reuse functionality, but they offer different conflict resolution approaches. In SAP CAF, conflicting type definitions cannot be imported, and the first type definition wins. In Service Composer, conflicting type definitions can be imported. Users are prompted to pick one of the conflicting type versions, and — if the newly imported version is selected — all of the occurrences of the conflicting version in the existing (previously imported) WSDL and XSD documents are replaced with the new one.

▶ **Service simplification**
Service Composer offers a wizard to create new (simplified) service from the existing service interface. The new service interface definition starts by taking the service interface of a service to be consumed and simplified and then selectively removing parts of the input and output data types. This results in a completely implemented simplified service delegate to the original service. It contains a new (simplified) service interface, import of the original service, and corresponding data transformation mappings. In SAP CAF, all steps have to be performed manually: modeling the new (simplified) service interface, importing the original service, defining mappings.

▶ **Service execution flow**
Service Composer offers a graphical modeling tool to define service execution flows using a minimal subset of BPMN, where only unconditional transitions are supported. In SAP CAF, execution flows cannot be modeled but are coded in Java using dedicated custom code sections, thus allowing more sophisticated flows — conditions, error handling, and so on.

▶ **Data transformation mappings**
SAP CAF provides a graphical tool for modeling data transformation mappings, which leads to the generation of Java code that implements the actual transformation. This allows for higher runtime performance. Only one-to-one and constant mappings are supported in SAP CAF. Service Composer offers easy graphical modeling for much more sophisticated mapping definitions. In addition to the one-to-one, one-to-many, many-to-many, and constant mapping styles there are capabilities such as mapping functions, built-in function libraries, custom functions, function nesting, iterations, collection addressing, type

453

conversion, type casting (SAP NetWeaver CE 7.30), and evaluation at design time. Service Composer mappings are dynamically interpreted at runtime, offering poorer performance than static mappings in SAP CAF.

- ▶ **Service provisioning**
  SAP CAF services are generated in both Web service and EJB form using JAX-WS and JAXB. In addition to JAX-WS and JAXB service implementations, Service Composer generates SDO-based EJBs that are exposed as Web services through the SCA runtime.

- ▶ **Data persistency**
  Service Composer does not offer data persistency capabilities, because it is focused on service adaptation (such as simplification) and composition only. In SAP CAF, graphical and form-based modeling can be used to define models of the persisted data types, which are then used to generate JPA entities. There are also services on top of the JPA entities, such as data type and data instance level permissions, language-dependent attributes, bulk operations (only in SAP NetWeaver 7.3), SAP NetWeaver BW integration (SAP NetWeaver BW pulls data from SAP CAF BO nodes), and business data transport. SAP CAF also provides modeling of findBy operations, which are less powerful than Java Persistence Query Language (JPAQL) but much easier to define. There is also the Service-Browser web tool for runtime testing of services developed with SAP CAF.

- ▶ **Custom coding**
  The custom coding in Service Composer is limited to the area of custom data mapping functions, where functions can be implemented with EJBs, whereas SAP CAF provides much more controlled opportunities for custom code. In SAP CAF, you can create custom coding for declared application service operations and can override any operation in BO node and external Services. You can also add any code that is not covered by any of the models in the EJBMODULE folder.

- ▶ **Write operations**
  The Service Composer is a model-driven tool, so all functionality has to be modeled. Unfortunately, this would even be true for the error handling, so there are definitely some limitations to the error handling in comparison to SAP NetWeaver BPM (where human activities can do error handling and error states to start compensating for successful service calls (see Error Resolution: Compensation in Section 14.1.5). These limitations make it difficult to handle many service calls in a chain in the Service Composer, so it is usually better

to handle write operations in the frameworks that allow custom coding and handling of all cases (SAP CAF, Java EE).

SAP CAF provides better overall performance at runtime, whereas Service Composer provides improved usability. Below, you can find some example scenario measurements comparing Service Composer and SAP CAF in terms of runtime performance.

To illustrate this fact, Table 14.5 and Table 14.6 list performance indicators. The measurement was made on one PC, so the indicators are comparable to the each other, although there is no guarantee that every PC with the same performance will achieve the same performance.

Technology	Test Duration	Number of Transactions	Average Response Time	Java AS CPU	Memory per Transaction
SC	~2 hours	126,296	113 ms	60%	14.2 MB
CAF	~2 hours	127,062	45 ms	39%	5.9 MB
Technical scenario definition: average payload size of composed service: 12 KB, local Java services, protocol HTTP					

Table 14.5 Performance Comparison of Service Composer and CAP CAF for Local Services

Technology	Test Duration	Number of Transactions	Average Response Time	Java AS CPU	Memory per Transaction
SC	~2 hours	125,845	117 ms	57%	12.5 MB
CAF	~2 hours	126,503	70 ms	35%	5.2 MB
Technical scenario definition: average payload size of composed service: 12 KB, remote Java services, protocol HTTP					

Table 14.6 Performance Comparison of Service Composer and SAP CAF for Remote Services

Types are used in service consumption in SAP NetWeaver CE. All frameworks are able to consume Web services and XSD data type definitions, but there are some limitations if SAP enterprise services are consumed.

According to the XML Schema specification, any kind of a XSD entity with global scope (type definition, element declaration, attribute declaration, etc.) is uniquely defined by its QName, that is, the ordered pair of target namespace and entity name. Entities can be distinguished by comparing their QNames. In other words, in respect to the schema specification, two entities of the same kind (e.g., type definitions) are considered equal if their target namespaces and names are equal.

With SAP enterprise services there are situations when a given entity — usually a type definition — is defined one way within one service interface and a different way (structurally) in another service interface. According to the schema specification, they should equal to each other, because their QNames are the same. In reality, the structural definitions of the entities differ, which usually leads to unpredictable behavior at runtime during service consumption execution.

Data Persistency (SAP CAF, JPA)

SAP NetWeaver Composition Environment contains various programming models for persisting data. This section explains when to use which.

In SAP NetWeaver CE, SAP Composite Application Framework (CAF) is based on standard Java EE 5 features and consequently uses Java Persistence API (JPA) for object-relational mapping (ORM) and data storage.

JPA provides an object-relational mapping functionality that allows Java developers to concentrate on Java objects without needing to worry about how to store them in the database and so on. JPA shields all of the low-level details dealing with Java Database Connectivity (JDBC) drivers and (Open-)SQL. The objects that are persisted are pure Java beans (plain old Java objects [POJOs]).

SAP Composite Application Framework provides a design-time modeling environment as a distinct Eclipse perspective within SAP NetWeaver Developer Studio (NWDS). Here, you can graphically model your business objects (BOs). During generation, the necessary database tables (in the dictionary DC) and the corresponding Java classes (within the EJB module DC) are generated automatically. This frees the developer from repetitive and tedious programming of CRUD operations (create, read, update, and delete) and the like. Put briefly, SAP CAF generates a stateless session bean, which acts as a facade and provides the CRUD operations.

Model-driven development tools like SAP CAF are bound to define a common set of assumptions and standard use cases, which they support best, because otherwise the tools would become just as complex to handle as the underlying technologies.

SAP CAF supports limited configuration options of the JPA Persistence Manager:

1. SAP CAF users cannot control "lazy/eager" loading policy mechanisms. If the default value (lazy loading) needs to be changed, this can only be done by defining the value in JPA XML descriptors.

2. The JPA `EntityManager` is capable of caching several database operations without directly performing these operations to the database immediately. The corresponding database operations (SQL statements) are performed once the EntityManager is flushed. This is normally done in alignment with the transactional context in which the operation runs.

3. SAP CAF flushes the cache after each operation. There is a partial improvement in SAP NWDS 7.30 in terms of operations, which work on many instances of the same type at once, but the flush is still called after every operation. This behavior may cause performance issues, but it has been introduced to guarantee correct error handling if exceptions occur. A plain JPA application can choose when this use case would be most important and would flush the cache accordingly — probably not often. As a consequence, SAP CAF is not meant as a tool for mass database operations.

The following guidelines can be applied as a concrete recommendation for when using plain JPA is preferable to using SAP CAF persistence:

1. If the usage of complex arbitrary queries would be necessary, choose JPA.

2. If flushing the entity manager cache after every operation is not preferable and/or DB modification performance is critical, choose JPA.

3. If the application database design would require the use of relationships, which are not supported by SAP CAF, choose JPA.

Nevertheless, there are ways to bring SAP CAF and JPA together, because SAP CAF uses the Java EE standards. The interaction between the frameworks is based on the concept that JPA can reference the generated entities of SAP CAF.

Failure Handling

Failure can appear in all areas of a composite application. This section explains how to react in the different situations.

Failure handling can be required in both read-intensive and write-intensive scenarios, such as reading from a second service if the original fails for some reason in read-intensive scenarios or a repeat service call in write-intensive scenarios.

Based on the cause of the failure, we can identify three flavors of failures and recommend different approaches for handling them:

1. **Data validation failure**

   This is when the (user) input data is not valid according to the system, and there is no way for the system to automatically handle (fix) this kind of failure. It is expected that the user can fix the failure easily, for example, by fixing the input data and trying again. Handling the failure then means informing the user about the failure and maybe (if this is not intuitive) providing hints on how to (manually) fix the problem. We recommend formalizing these types of failures first by specific Java exceptions or Web service faults. Exceptions and faults can then be represented in a proper way by the UI part of the composite.

2. **Process logic failure**

   This is when there are certain known exceptions to the normal process flow, where a corresponding action may already have been taken by the system according to the specific business process logic. The action itself could be an automated task (service call or trigger of another process, for example) or even a user (manual) task, but the activation of the user task is triggered automatically based on the failure condition. We recommend modeling process exceptions via BPMN intermediate events/exception flows in BPM if the business logic is already modeled as a business process. If the business logic is implemented in SAP CAF or Java EE, we recommend handling exceptions by using the try-catch-finally clause accompanied by proper Java exception definitions. Service Composer (as of enhancement package 2) does not offer this.

3. **System failure**

   This is when the normal (expected) work of the system is not possible due to a technical issue. An issue is technical when the end user cannot directly fix the main cause (meaning it is not a matter of business data validity or business process conditions). This could be anything from misconfiguration of a system to hardware failure. It is not expected that the user can fix the problem directly, and it is likely that only users with special system authorizations (system administrator or account administrator, for example) or system support providers can fix it. We recommend informing the user (via proper UI) about the problem and the immediate steps needed to fix the issue (configure system, call support center, file a bug report, etc.).

External Libraries

External libraries are usually important in Java development in SAP NetWeaver Composition Environment. This section describes how to use external libraries.

Using external libraries in the SAP component world is a quite complex task. This section explains the steps required to use an external library DC in your Java application using SAP NetWeaver CE 7.1.

You can deploy external libraries on the AS Java in two ways.

▶ **As a stand-alone library**
   In this case, the application is deployed as an enterprise archive (EAR) archive, and other applications on the AS Java can use this external library too.

▶ **As a bundled library**
   The external library is packaged and deployed with your own application.

Stand-Alone Case

In the stand-alone scenario, you have your own application consisting of three DCs. These are a web module DC (web DC), an EJB module (EJB DC), and the EAR project (EAR 1 DC). Your external library is packed in the extLib DC, which is packaged in the corresponding EAR 2 DC. You can now deploy your external library (EAR 2 DC) like any other application. To use the external library from your application, you have to set a runtime dependency from your EAR 1 DC to the EAR 2 DC.

If you want to deploy your external library stand-alone, you have to create an external library DC and a new EAR 2 DC, which references the assembly public part of your external library DC. After you have defined this dependency, the external library files (jar files) are automatically added to the EAR 2 archive. The EAR 2 DC can now be deployed like a normal application.

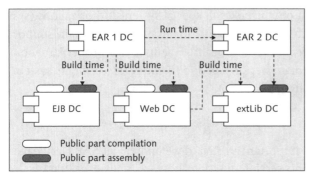

Figure 14.11 Stand-Alone Libraries

If you want to use the external library in your own application (EAR 1 DC), you need to add a runtime dependency between your EAR 1 DC and the EAR 2 DC. To be able to use the library classes, for example, in your web DC, you also have to add a dependency from your web DC to the compilation public part of your external library DC.

Bundled Case

In the bundled scenario, you have your own application consisting of three DCs. These are a web module DC (web DC), an EJB module (EJB DC), and the EAR project (EAR 1 DC). Your external library is packed in the extLib DC, which is packaged into the EAR 1 DC and also deployed with the EAR 1 DC.

The EAR 1 DC must have dependencies (build time) to the assembly public part of the EJB DC and the assembly public part of the web DC. These dependencies are created automatically when you assign your web and EJB modules to your EAR project. Public parts of the type assembly can be packaged into the build result of the EAR file for deployment reasons, which means the WAR archive (from the web module), the EJB.jar archive (from the EJB module), and the external library jar file are added to the EAR 1 DC.

If you want to bundle an external library with your EAR 1 DC, you first need to create a DC of the type external library and create a dependency from your EAR 1 DC to the assembly public part of your external library DC. After you have defined this dependency, the external library files are automatically added to the EAR 1 archive and finally deployed with the application.

To use the external library classes, in your web DC for example, you also need to add a dependency from your web DC to the compilation public part of your external library DC.

Logging

There are various methods of logging in a composite application. This section explains how to perform logging.

A composite application often implements one or more business processes. A commonly raised requirement is to provide information about the process execution from the business perspective. SAP NetWeaver CE is an assembly of several components, where no common facility (out of the box) exists to perform business activity logging. The business log is intended to provide relevant information about the process execution to the business user (in some cases, it can indicate where technical issues have occurred). To drill down to the technical aspects of the process execution, you need to inspect the trace facilities of the involved components.

If the whole business process is driven by or executed as an SAP NetWeaver BPM model, the business log for this engine can be leveraged to provide the requested information about the process. Using lean analytics, it is possible to provide better visualization of the business data in different reporting styles. You can use SAP NetWeaver Visual Composer to provide a reporting UI for logged business data. The BI tool kit available with SAP NetWeaver Visual Composer can use locally persisted business data as a data source. The BI tool kit uses BI Consumer Services (BICS), which abstracts data sources from consuming clients (see Figure 14.12).

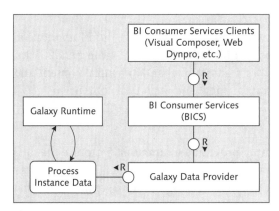

Figure 14.12 Process Logging

IF BPM is not used, this type of business data logging functionality can be built using SAP CAF BOs (see Figure 14.13). SAP CAF and BI integration enables extraction of SAP CAF services data and loading of it into a BI system. The extraction of SAP CAF applications data is provided by SAP CAF runtime automatically. If you want to make custom data source and extraction logic, you should use application service BI extractor methods. SAP CAF runtime automatically provides a data source for each method and calls it when extraction is initiated. With this integration, it is possible to generate the required reporting supported by SAP BI. The SAP NetWeaver Visual Composer BI tool kit can also be used to generate reports.

There are different levels of integration regarding logging. All of the scenarios use a BI system to log the data.

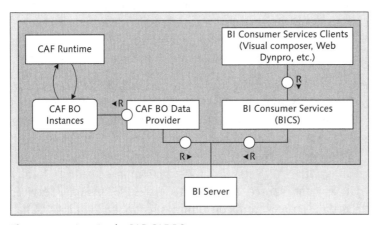

Figure 14.13   Logging by SAP CAF BOs

Tight coupling is a typical scenario with composition, where the BI application is embedded seamlessly in a composite application. This has some benefits, for example, one integrated design time for transactional and analytical content and one integrated UI runtime to cover transactional and analytical content.

Loose Coupling

The logging is loosely coupled by simply providing a functionality to use the data in separate applications. So data is available in the BI system but is not in any way integrated in a composite application. Examples of stand-alone BI applications that can be loosely coupled are:

- Formatted reporting (Crystal Reports)
- Excel-based analytics (SAP Business Explorer [BEx] Excel analyzer tool)
- Multidimensional analysis (Pioneer)
- Dashboards (Xcelcius)

14.1.5 SOA Pattern

Development in SOA requires specific application design patterns. This section describes the most common ones.

Service-oriented architecture is based on services and the assembly of services. There are therefore numerous ways to structure the services in the process area and the user interface area. The following concepts provide guidelines for how to structure the assembly and how the services are connected. The principles are structured in the usual architecture pattern method in computer science, focused on SOA.

ID Cross-Referencing

Composite applications work with data from different backend systems. The data is retrieved or persisted using services (in this case it does not matter if Web service technology or RFC is used). But holding data in different backend systems and bringing it together with a composite application means the origin of the data is not really changed; data about a customer is still stored in one backend system, but data in other systems refers to it.

The composite application therefore brings together and tries to correlate data from various systems. Unfortunately, there is always the problem of a data set in one system being related to the data in another system. A very common problem is that the different identifiers for the data sets have to be mapped between the systems.

To solve the problem of ID mapping in a composite application, we recommend that there be an SAP CAF BO that holds the mapping information. The data structure is then always the same:

- Unique identifier in the composite application — key field
- Identifier of data in System A
- Identifier of data in System B

If the composite application design follows the decoupling principles and has introduced a service contract and service contract implementation layer, then the mapping functionality of IDs is part of the service contract implementation layer, because all functionality that has to deal with different remote systems has to be part of the service contract layer implementation.

If the composite application is not implemented in the loosely coupled way, then the data in different remote systems has to be accessed from the composite application itself. Here the ID referencing problems are similar, and therefore the following section explains how to implement the pattern in the tight coupling case. Nevertheless, the recommendation is to decouple a composite application as much as possible from the backend systems to be as flexible as possible (SOA principle).

If the composite application has to create new data in one system that is transferred or used in another system, an entry in the mapping SAP CAF BO has to be created. Usually, entering and requesting a new object in a remote system is done from a user interface component, meaning the mapping SAP CAF BO has to provide the access operations (at least the CRUD operations) in a way that the user interface layer can consume. It does not mean the handling of the SAP CAF BO for ID storage is done in the UI; the persistency of the IDs and their mapping is an own entity in the composite application.

Later, when the process wants to work with the data, the mapping information should be retrieved, allowing the data retrieved from System A to be correlated with the data in System B (and vice versa).

Usually the ID referencing pattern is used in the service contract implementation layer (see *Loose Coupling*), because it is responsible for the abstraction from a concrete remote system, but it is not mandatory to couple both architecture patterns.

The pattern would look like the representation in Figure 14.14.

The pattern provides the following characteristics:

▶ Synchronously call service for local persistency.
  ▶ Fast
  ▶ End user immediately gets feedback
  ▶ Internal ID for request generation
▶ Process correlates the different IDs for the same data in different systems.

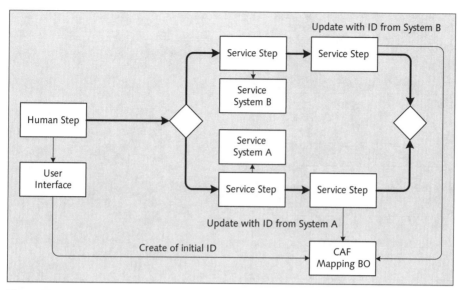

Figure 14.14 Cross-Referencing

In process modeling, the initial creation of the IDs looks like the representation in Figure 14.15.

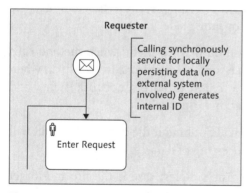

Figure 14.15 Initial Creation of ID

The human activity is calling the SAP CAF BO directly, so the relation to the SAP CAF BO is not visible in the process modeling.

The parallel service calls with subsequent correlation ID persistency look like Figure 14.16.

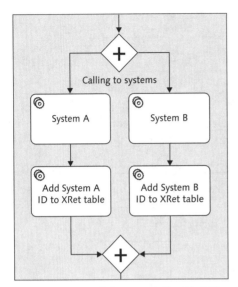

Figure 14.16   Parallel Service Calls with Different IDs

Asynchronous Write

This pattern generally describes how to establish remote write operations on services asynchronously. This decouples the frequently time-consuming write operation from the process flow on the consumer side.

Asynchronous operations and communication may be useful when method calls are invoked across process boundaries via remote mechanisms. In particular, when calling Web services using HTTP or similar remote protocols, network latency and bandwidth restrictions create communication bottlenecks.

Asynchronous communication therefore will not hinder the process flow, but will just initiate the remote operation and processing of data.

There are various flavors of the pattern. The simplest case is the fire-and-forget sort of operation. On the other hand, the consumer might want to get confirmation of the termination status of the operation either through active polling or notification. To phase the call and the possible downstream reply, an asynchronous operation needs to be supplied with a message ID. For a notification, the ID is part of the notification. For polling, the ID has to be part of the poll request. The consumer always has to keep track of the ID, for instance, through a call handle, an in-memory map, or the like.

Figure 14.17 depicts the polling version of the asynchronous write. Figure 14.18 shows the notification version.

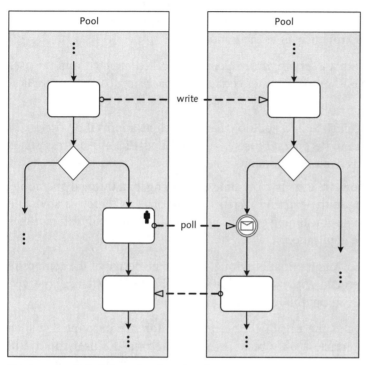

Figure 14.17 Poll of Operation Complete Status

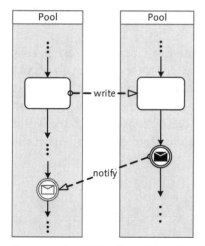

Figure 14.18 Notification of Operation Complete Status

Delayed Write

Composite applications are created based on a variety of technologies. There are process layers and UI layers in the SAP NetWeaver CE programming model. All technologies have the potential to use services, so all layers can make calls to any backend, either synchronously or asynchronously.

The problem now is that a service write operation is called directly from the user interface. This kind of direct call creates certain drawbacks in a composite application:

▶ There is no possibility to add additional steps such as approval or checks by other users. If the write operation succeeds, and updating the process status fails, the process is in an inconsistent state.

▶ The write operations are usually more time-consuming than the read operations because of locking in the backend systems and so on. It is therefore advisable to decouple the time-consuming operations from the UI to avoid waiting times for the user of the application.

As always, there is no definite right or wrong as far as the design of the composite application is concerned. With write operations to backend systems, however, there are guidelines you can follow.

The user interface and the call of the write operation are decoupled, which means the user interface is only responsible for getting the user input and for storing it in the process context. The write operation is performed as a subsequent step, meaning the write operation is delayed in comparison to the solution if the user interface makes the call directly. This would look similar to Figure 14.19.

Decoupling the specific service calls does not come free. Separating service calls into dedicated process steps causes additional effort, for error handling, for example. Only modifying service calls should be separated into a subsequent process step, because these service calls change the backend data state. Further separation is not required. Check services can be called by the UI component directly, for example, because a check service is stateless and therefore does not impact the data consistency of the backend system.

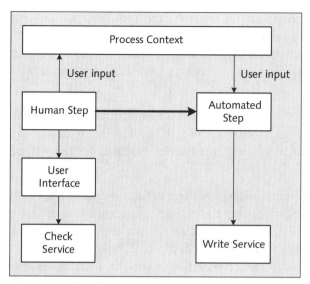

Figure 14.19 Asynchronous Write

Error Resolution: Compensation

Composite applications are the applications in the SOA landscape that have the task of calling services in different backend systems. A requirement that arises immediately is how to deal with operations that have to happen consistently in the different backend systems. A collection of operations like this is usually called a transaction, and all characteristics of a transaction are expected in an SOA landscape.

Even handing transactions in one system is not easy. SAP NetWeaver Composition Environment provides support for consistent handling of resources by a transaction manager such as database and JMS messaging. Unfortunately, this becomes nearly impossible in distributed and decoupled landscapes as we are facing it in SOA environments. One of the SOA principles is to decouple the business logic as much as possible — so, bundling services that are not really meant to work together (because they are implemented and defined as different services) must be avoided. This is a conflict with the basic principles of SOA, because bundling of services violates the decoupling principle.

The general problem is therefore how the consistency of different systems can be achieved.

The solution for achieving consistency in an SOA landscape with subsequent service calls is to introduce a compensation service. A compensation service is designed to roll back all changes (even partial changes) made by a service call in the corresponding system. This means the service and the compensation service always form a pair.

In real process modeling, this would mean error handling always calls the compensation service if the original service call fails. So far, this is not a very complex infrastructure, because it only involves manual modeling for the process designer.

It becomes a little bit more difficult, however, if there are subsequent service calls that belong together to achieve a consistent state in the connected systems. If one of the calls fails, all changes have to be rolled back. As a result, service call A, which happened before service call B and which failed, has to be rolled back too. In this case, the compensation services for B and A therefore have to be invoked, because otherwise the state in System A is not consistent with the state in System B. The modeling for a pattern of this kind looks like Figure 14.20.

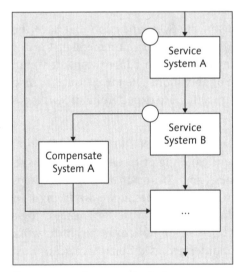

Figure 14.20 Compensation in Process

Error Resolution: Retry

Because composite applications are applications that call services at different back-end systems in a probably loosely coupled way, a requirement is that service calls may need to be re-launched if the initial call fails. Usually in SOA, HTTP is used as the protocol, and within this protocol the failure can occur at the delivery of the information packages. The retry of a service is accompanied by a retry policy. If the condition of the policy evaluates true, a retry is triggered; otherwise other measures such as compensation patterns may take effect.

There are two kinds of failures for which the service consumer cannot be sure that the request has been processed properly:

1. **Undelivered request**

   The message is sent but does not reach the provider (see Figure 14.21).

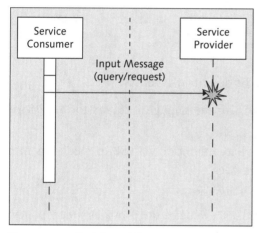

Figure 14.21 Undelivered Request

2. **Undelivered response**

   The message is sent and the response is sent, but the response does not reach the consumer (see Figure 14.22).

The retry pattern describes the infrastructure rather than a particular behavior of one of the involved components. Thus, it is not a matter of how customers using services can resolve the issue, but rather the solution of the issue affects all communicating and mediating components.

Nonetheless, evaluation of the conditions of retry policies can be handled in a process model; no particular requirements of the infrastructure need to be taken into account. At the end of this chapter a process model we depict a sample that demonstrates the usage of retry policies.

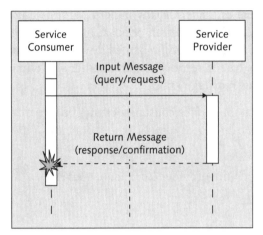

Figure 14.22 Undelivered Response

In general, the infrastructure issue can be described as follows:

1. The service call is routed over an ESB or messaging mediators to the service provider or an alternative provider.

2. The consumers and service providers communicate via ESB or mediators that intercede between consumer and provider.

3. An ESB acts as an intermediate service requestor.

4. The ESB intercepts the request messages, evaluates the provider's retry policy, and may even determine alternative providers.

Reliable messaging, as specified for instance by the WS-RM standard, is an example of such mediated communication:

1. The service is idempotent, and another call with the same payload and ID will not cause additional state changes in the corresponding backend system.

2. A service call/message will be identified by a unique ID (e.g., UUID) attached to the message.

There are two fault scenarios:

▶ The service provider receives the message and caches or persists the ID and sends the response the first time the request arrives at the provider. However, the consumer does not obtain the message, due to transmission errors.

▸ The service provider does not receive the message, due to transmission errors.

The fault situations can be handled in this way:

1. If the consumer does not receive the response, it will retry the request with the same message ID.

2. The consumer evaluates the retry policy and retries its response accordingly.

3. The service provider provides the response message for the given ID. The payload for the response is evaluated from scratch, or it may be retrieved from cached data if the provider successfully received the request in a previous call.

4. The service is not idempotent but will provide an operation by which the service consumer may poll or request again the response for the initially sent request.

This pattern is very similar to the one for idempotent calls. The only difference is that a service provider has to keep track of already obtained messages/IDs, and the cache has to be in sync. This pattern is similar to the previous pattern, but instead of the request being sent again, a lightweight repetition request is sent.

The lightweight request contains the previous message ID. The provider sends either the response or a notification that the request for the message ID has not arrived at the service provider. In the latter case the consumer needs to send another request containing the initial payload.

As in the previous pattern, additional infrastructure on both the provider and consumer side is required.

Apart from these infrastructure considerations, a retry policy may be evaluated in a dedicated evaluation activity in a process model. The activity precedes the service consumption. If the policy condition evaluates true and the service will be consumed successfully, the normal flow will be followed. Otherwise a compensation flow will be chosen, for instance. Figure 14.23 depicts an example of this pattern where a timer determines the timeout for the request-response time.

There are more variants of the pattern. For instance, it might be crucial that both the consumer and provider need to commit their state changes. In this case some sort of two-phase commit patterns may be additionally applied.

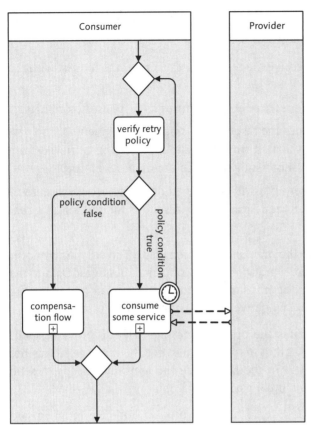

Figure 14.23 Error Resolution – Retry. Example Using Timeout and Retry Policy

14.1.6 Conclusion

Many guidelines make sense in the BPM area when you are implementing applications. The most important topics concern structuring the application in the right way, so the performance is good in SAP NetWeaver Composition Environment. Besides that, some important SOA principles have to be fulfilled to allow flexible application development. This section offered some guidelines for how to implement the application according to these principles.

14.2 Highlights of the Innovation Provided by SAP NetWeaver BPM and BRM

The second released version of SAP NetWeaver Business Process Management provides several innovations to customers and partners who want to extend the value of their SAP applications.

These innovations address the needs of business process analysts and experts, process developers, and process participants. Additionally, interoperability with SAP applications and other task user interfaces has been improved.

SAP NetWeaver BPM provides a comprehensive business process management system, unifying human and system automation processing steps, where a business process is more than just several orchestrated services. This BPM system supports the composition of event-driven processes through a seamless combination of service, event, and human task with business rules through a tight integration with SAP NetWeaver Business Rules Management (BRM). SAP NetWeaver BPM includes a business-friendly graphical modeler based on the standard Business Process Modeling Notation (BPMN) that is used to define and drive the business process execution by the process server. People starting or participating within processes interact with SAP NetWeaver BPM via the process desk.

SAP NetWeaver BPM benefits from the fact that it ships as part of an integrated composition environment, SAP NetWeaver Composition Environment, which supports model-driven development via an integrated toolset including out-of-the-box Enterprise Service Repository (ESR) integration and consistent lifecycle management for all composite design artifacts. Next we will present some of the highlights of the innovation provided by SAP NetWeaver BPM and BRM 7.2.

14.2.1 Business Analyst Experience

In SAP NetWeaver BPM 7.2, the business-friendly modeling has been enabled through various capabilities. A new, dedicated process modeling perspective for process sketching has been introduced (see Figure 14.24).

This business-friendly perspective focuses on the nontechnical aspects of the process model and the hand-over to the process development perspective that developers use to complete an initial process model resulting from that process sketching effort with implementation details.

475

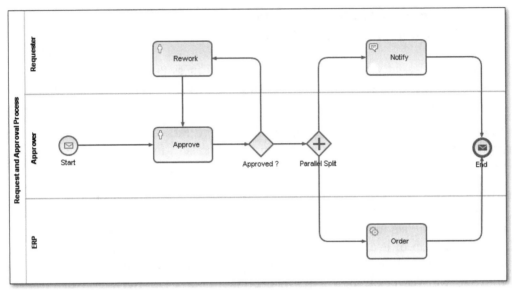

Figure 14.24 New Business Analyst Perspective

Process performance reporting and monitoring has been introduced as model arti-facts to support gaining better process performance insight and thus help improve process quality.

A browser-based rules manager has been introduced to enable process analysts to directly modify business rules without the need to use the full developer experi-ence. In addition, the expressiveness of rules has been enhanced by the addition of common definitions, effective dates for rules, and overrides.

14.2.2 Process Developer Experience

In SAP NetWeaver BPM 7.2 the various stages of composite process design are more effectively supported, starting from rapid prototyping with the ability to build and deploy incomplete process models by inclusion of default tasks and mock services targeted at increasing developer productivity. As illustrated in Figure 14.25 and Figure 14.26, the following improvements have been included:

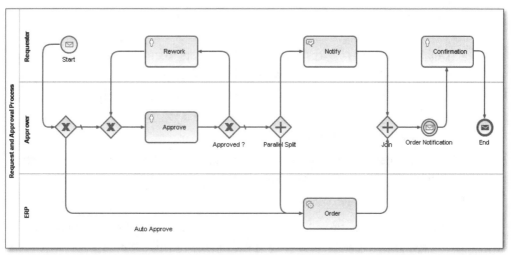

Figure 14.25 Process Development Perspective

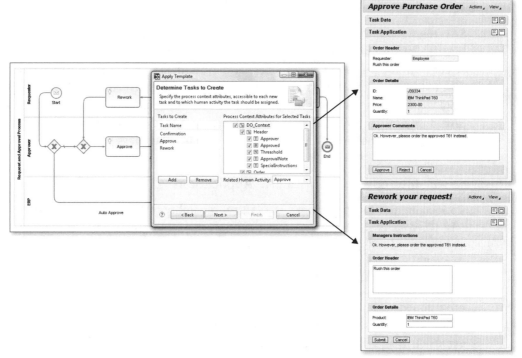

Figure 14.26 Auto-Generation of User Interfaces out of the Process Context for SAP NetWeaver Visual Composer and Web Dynpro Java

▸ Automated user interface generation to significantly accelerate the creation of human task UIs

▸ Default tasks and services that allow developers to quickly sketch and run processes even with incomplete tasks and services designs

▸ Improved consumption of Web services, including SAP enterprise services, by simplifying configuration via service groups

▸ Rule flow modeling for complex decision processes

▸ New rule development tools (rules editing within Microsoft Excel, reporting, differencing, consistency checking, service generation)

▸ Code-free, automated, bulk rule testing

It should also be mentioned that the shared tasks in SAP NetWeaver BPM 7.2 also provide a simple means for process participants to collaborate on a task that has been assigned to them with other process participants.

14.2.3 Improved Business Insight

SAP NetWeaver BPM 7.2 extends the process model to include a new type of business process activity, the reporting activity, which allows developers to easily select from the process data context the relevant data items to submit as custom data to SAP NetWeaver BPM's business-oriented tracking stream, the business log. Data written to the business log can then be consumed using SAP NetWeaver and SAP BusinessObjects' rich business intelligence portfolio, giving business users unprecedented insight into the performance of their business processes.

14.2.4 Interoperability with SAP Applications

Connecting to SAP applications is a critical capability for composite applications. SAP NetWeaver BPM 7.2 introduces support for SAP proprietary protocols such as RFCs and BAPIs and continues to support Web services.

With this second version, the end-to-end event mechanism of SAP NetWeaver BPM has been integrated with SAP and non-SAP applications via events that have been provisioned within the applications, for example SAP applications' local business events (event provisioning based on the BusinessObjects Repository). Business events such as a change to a sales order are correlated with the process directly and expressed as intermediate message events within the BPMN-based process model (see Figure 14.27).

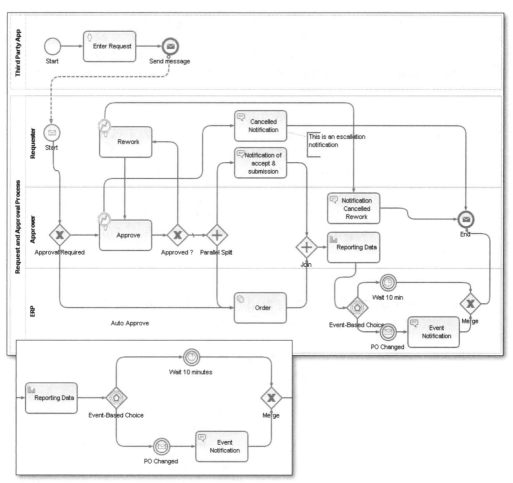

Figure 14.27 Intermediate Message Events Support Correlation of Event Messages to Running Process Instances

14.2.5 Interoperability with Other Task User Interfaces

Developers create specialized UIs for human tasks defined as part of an SAP NetWeaver BPM process. In the first version of SAP NetWeaver BPM, these UIs were developed using SAP's model-driven Java UI technology, Web Dynpro for Java. In SAP NetWeaver BPM 7.2, task UIs created with SAP NetWeaver Visual Composer are also supported. SAP NetWeaver Visual Composer is a powerful design tool that supports graphical, model-driven definition of UIs rather than coding. Although simple enough to use for some power business users, SAP NetWeaver

Visual Composer provides rich connections to SAP applications. Both UI technologies can be used directly from the process context of the BPM model, and with the help of a wizard the UIs can be generated automatically, which increases developer productivity considerably, particularly when complex data structures are included in the process context.

SAP NetWeaver BPM 7.2 also offers support for Adobe offline forms, allowing task participants to interact with business processes offline via email. Tightly integrated support for offline forms extends the reach of SAP NetWeaver BPM to a new class of task workers, including sales professionals who spend much of their workday in the field.

SAP NetWeaver BPM is part of SAP NetWeaver Composition Environment (CE). For more details about how to leverage the capabilities of SAP NetWeaver CE, please go to Section 14.1.

14.3 Handling Decisions and Business Rules in a BPM Approach

In this chapter we explore how managing decisions and business processes as peers creates simpler and more agile processes and more flexible business applications. Externalizing operational decisions from process designs and applying SAP's business rules offerings to effectively manage the logic behind those decisions improves visibility, gives the business the power to maintain policies themselves, builds in a capacity for change, and helps ensure business-IT alignment. The key is to apply focus on the decisions within processes in addition to the processes themselves. This makes these decisions and the business rules within them explicit and provides a basis for line-of-business owners to assert control over these decisions.

Many business processes are about arriving at decisions. They define the collaboration and collection of information and documentation required to make a decision. Decisions are also at the heart of many operational business processes. To execute an enrollment process, we must know if someone is eligible for the product. To sell a complex, highly configured product to a company, we must know if the product configuration is valid and what the price would be for that customer. To process a claim or a tax return, we must be able to decide if it should be fast-tracked, reviewed, or investigated for fraud. We must make these potentially complex decisions every time we execute the process. Other operational processes involve less critical, but still valuable, decisions such as the decision to make a cross-sell offer and what offer to make.

This chapter describes the kinds of decisions that should be managed, shows how decisions and business rules relate, and outlines some Best Practices. For technical specifics on SAP's business rules offerings — SAP NetWeaver Business Rules Management (BRM) and Business Rule Framework plus (BRFplus) — see Section 14.4.

14.3.1 The Power of Decisioning

The increasingly real-time, distributed nature of most businesses means that no organization can be more effective than its systems. These systems must be aligned with the organization, its goals, and its people. A business process management approach allows organizations to focus on end-to-end business processes rather than functional silos and applications to achieve this alignment. When a business process orientation is paired with a focus on decisions, an organization can develop simpler processes, eliminate rigidity in business applications, increase their capacity for change, and deliver business control and alignment.

Simpler and More Agile Processes

Most, if not all, business processes require decisions to be made: Claims must be approved or rejected, cross-sell offers must be selected, and product discounts must be calculated. Explicitly modeling the decisions that happen in your business process ensures that the as-is model is closer to reality. Even if a complete as-is process is not modeled, the identification of the critical decision-making activities within the as-is process is essential for a complete enough understanding of the current state.

When decisions are not identified and automated, the resulting business processes have either many manual steps or unnecessary complexity. When decision-making remains manual, processes constantly stop and wait for human intervention, reducing improvements in efficiency and cycle time and having a negative impact on quality and consistency. When process automation is used to manage decision-making, the result is often large numbers of process constructs such as branches and steps. Replacing manual decisioning or such a nest of branches and steps with a single, explicit decision point clarifies the behavior of the process, makes it easier to see if the process or the decision must change, and allows for changes in the decision-making approach to be independent from process change.

Take the process shown in Figure 14.28, for instance. In this case the process has been designed without an explicit decision, and a series of branches has been used to select from the various options — the activities that process an applicant differently according to the risk of the applicant. One can easily see how the process might have started with a single gateway, perhaps one based on age, and gradually become more complex as more specificity was added over time. Even with a few simple checks this process is already becoming messy and hard to follow.

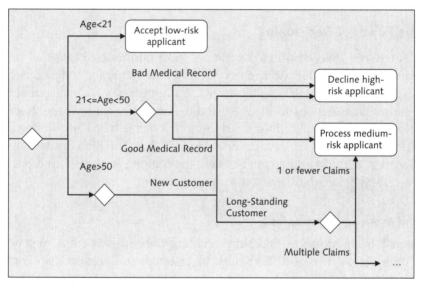

Figure 14.28 Complexity Resulting from an Implicit Decision

Contrast this with Figure 14.29. In this case the process has an explicit decision identified — an activity for deciding how risky an applicant is. The process is simpler, with a single gateway, and it will not need changing unless we decide to add a fourth risk category with associated risk-specific processing. Any changes we decide to make regarding how we determine the riskiness of the applicant take place within the decision-making activity and do not impact the process design. If a government were to release new rules forbidding age to be used, for example, the process would not have to change, because we could simply update the decision-making activity to reflect this new regulation. We have separated these concerns, allowing us to change them independently, and we have simplified the process dramatically.

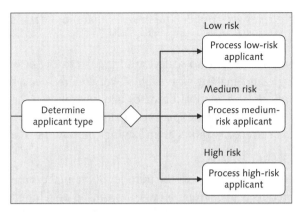

Figure 14.29 Externalizing a Decision to Simplify a Process

Clearly, we still have to manage the logic behind this decision — how we decide on the riskiness of the applicant — and for this we use business rules as described below.

Another potential consequence of explicit decision-making in process designs is reducing the number of explicit processes required. When an organization has several similar transactions to process — various subtypes — it's typical for multiple processes to grow organically to meet the different requirements. Instead, a single, common process could be defined with a decision used to encapsulate variations in requirements. For instance, Ericsson (see Chapter 7, Section 7.2) uses a single process design for supplier onboarding in every country. There are many country-specific variations in required data, allowed values, and formats for suppliers. By externalizing the validate-supplier decision, Ericsson was able to use a single process and reduce the time to onboard a supplier by 50 percent while still supporting local variations.

Explicit decision handling also increases the rate of straight-through processing (STP) and reduces the number of process instances that wait while items are put on worklists or in queues. This marriage of explicit decisions and process management keeps transactions moving, with only exceptions ending up on worklists or in an inbox. For instance, SAP uses automated decision handling in its data migration process (see Chapter 7, Section 7.3). Rather than having a manual process for resolving overlaps and incompleteness, an automated decision applies a standard and consistent set of business rules for approvals and survivorship. By automating the decision about which data survives in the case of overlaps in the data migration process, SAP ensures that the right rules are applied and ensures that more data is migrated automatically for significant time and cost savings.

With human experts being expensive and hard to scale, capturing the know-how of experts in explicit decision logic and making it available everywhere focuses scarce expert resources on exceptions and high-value cases and customers. The value of experts is increased by applying their expertise to rules that are used to process hundreds or thousands of records rather than having them work one process occurrence at a time.

Once an automated decision has been implemented, the number of manual exceptions can also be systematically reduced over time. New rules can be developed that extend the decision-making power of an activity as process execution is observed. Organizations can observe process performance, identify new rules to handle particular cases, and automate those rules so that future cases will not need manual referral. This results in continuous improvement while ensuring process stability; the changes are localized within a decision, allowing improvement without constant process changes.

More Flexible Business Applications

Business applications are rich sources of functionality and Best Practices for new and extended processes. Modern business applications such as the SAP Business Suite come service-enabled, exposing critical functionality as reusable services. A business process-oriented approach integrates this functionality into new and existing processes. Although including these services within an explicit and easy-to-change process increases agility and flexibility, this can be undermined if the exposed functionality cannot also be easily changed.

The agility and flexibility of the processes that use these services are going to be constrained by the flexibility of the components being shared. Yet the components of a business application that are most useful to business processes are often decision-making components such as pricing engines, product configurators, or eligibility determinations. And these decision-making components must change often; they are among the most dynamic parts of the application.

For example, a core business application for customer management such as SAP CRM might handle a loyalty program. For an organization with lots of products or services, loyalty programs can be very complex. If the loyalty component is coded or even managed using database tables, the degree of flexibility and the ability of the business users to define new loyalty rewards, or new ways to calculate loyalty bonuses, will be limited. Externalizing the loyalty reward decisions as an explicit component and using business rules to manage its behavior (in this case as a BRF-plus function in SAP CRM Loyalty Management) will address this.

Increased Capacity for Change

Hard-coded decisions and manual decision-making both reduce your capacity for change. Hard-to-change systems, those requiring significant IT resources to be devoted to changing programmed logic, cannot be changed quickly, and many IT organizations are so backlogged that only business-critical changes can be considered. If you rely on manual decision-making, you are not dependent on bottlenecked IT resources. However, updating policy manuals and retraining staff are time-consuming and expensive. Ensuring that changes to decision-making are promulgated throughout the organization and that the decisions are made consistently can be a massive and expensive undertaking. Inconsistent decisions resulting from partially implemented changes to manual decision-making can lead to fines, bad customer service, and unnecessary losses.

To be responsive to change, you need to keep key business decision-making visible, understandable, and changeable. Critical decisions cannot be buried in software code or company manuals where the business has zero visibility into the behavior they represent. Explicitly identifying decisions and describing the logic behind them allows this logic to be managed separately from processes and systems, increasing your capacity for change.

Business users like business process management software because it allows them to change their workflow easily; it increases the capacity for change of the process. Managing decisions further increases this capacity because business changes often involve updates to business decisions — to pricing, eligibility, or risk assessment decisions, for example. These decisions are often the most dynamic part of a process, the part that changes most often.

For instance, a company's pricing rules are likely to change far more often than its order-to-cash process. Adding an explicit pricing decision that business users can control allows them to make pricing changes without impacting the process. They can manage the process and the decision separately.

Improved Alignment

Given the importance of systems and processes to today's organization, business and IT professionals must be aligned. The IT department plays a critical role in developing, managing, and assuring the systems an organization requires. Yet it cannot specify the behavior of those systems. The behavior is, after all, *business* behavior. Expecting the IT department to be able to specify this behavior accurately is unreasonable.

Most organizations rely on some kind of requirements-gathering process to allow business owners to specify the behavior they need. This process is almost always slower and more prone to errors and omissions than anyone likes. Yet most tools that allow business owners to build their own systems and specify their own behavior rarely work as replacements, because they lack the robustness and scalability required for operational processes and create significant governance issues.

To get alignment, business owners must be able to effectively collaborate with their IT department to define and manage the behavior of their systems and processes. Explicitly managing decisions and processes allows for this alignment because the flow of work in the systems and processes is explicit and so are the points at which logic must be applied — the decision points.

14.3.2 Identifying Operational Decisions

Managing decisions and processes results in simpler, smarter, and more agile business processes. The first step is to identify the operational decisions that matter to the processes being managed. When you are analyzing an existing process, many decisions will be clear. Any time work is put on someone's worklist, especially when that worklist is for "review" or "approval," a decision is being made. Most analysts can, once they realize they should, find the majority of the decisions in their process fairly easily. There are many different types of decisions, and an understanding of these different types of decisions can help in their identification and description.

One of the most critical steps when managing decisions, especially when managing decisions in the context of business process management, is correctly identifying operational decisions. These decisions are part of operational business processes and transactional systems. Managing and automating these decisions is essential if processes are to be simplified and made more agile.

Defining Decisions

The basic decision-making process is simple. Data is gathered on which to base the decision. Some analysis of this data is performed, and rules derived from company policy, regulations, Best Practices, and experience are applied. A course of action, a selection from the possible options, is then made so that it can be acted on. When considering decisions in operational business processes, the way the decision is made is often constrained such that it can be described and automated effectively in many, even most, cases.

One of the easiest mistakes to make when identifying decisions is to focus on information or knowledge and not on action. Knowing that a claim has a high risk of being fraudulent, for instance, is not a decision: acting on that knowledge to route the claim to the fraud investigation unit is. Decisions do not just add to what is known about a customer or a transaction; decisions specify what should be done next.

> **Tip**
>
> Deciding to do nothing is a decision. Taking no action is a perfectly valid outcome of a decision, and even if a step in a process does not always result in an action, it may still be a decision.

When an operational decision is well defined and automatable, the possible outcomes can be defined in advance. The list of possible outcomes may vary over time, but the approach to making the choice is likely to change more often than the choices. These outcomes or choices can be quite varied. A decision might select from the available offers or treatments for a customer, it might approve or decline an application, or it might involve the selection of a discount from a range of allowed discounts

Defining Operational Decisions

An operational decision is simply a decision made in the context of day to day operational execution. It is typically made in the context of a single transaction or a single customer interaction. Deciding what to do about a specific claim, for instance, or establishing which government services a particular individual is eligible for are operational decisions. Each decision relates to a single claim of a single citizen. As a result, operational decisions are high-volume decisions: Companies and other organizations make these decisions often and make lots of them.

Operational decisions are repeatable. A decision-making approach can be defined for operational decisions and executed again and again to successfully make a series of decisions. The decisions themselves, the outcomes, may be different in each case, but a repeatable approach can be defined. The options available for an operational decision, and the possible ways an operational decision can be made, are often quite limited; the decisions are not very complex. The repeatability of operational decisions and their generally straightforward nature is what makes the management of those decisions both possible and desirable.

A more or less direct corollary of this repeatability is that an operational decision is high volume. Because these repeatable decisions are about how to act on a transaction or how to treat a customer at a particular interaction point, they must be made often. Because customers are often waiting at these interaction points and because processes are on hold while the decision is being made, operational decisions are often low latency and must be made quickly.

The value of a single operational decision is often quite low. Making a single good or bad operational decision is unlikely to make or break an organization. Because operational decisions are made in high volume, however, the cumulative effect of good decisions (or bad ones) is significant.

Because operational decisions often relate to customers, consumers, or citizens, many are covered by regulations. Taxes must be calculated correctly, for instance, and countries impose regulations and procedures on how taxes should be calculated and in what circumstances. The degree of regulation varies by industry, with financial services, healthcare, and utilities being among the most regulated. In addition, companies make policies about operational decisions to ensure that they are made consistently and appropriately. Operational decisions must comply with these policies just as they must comply with the regulations involved.

Once managed, operational decisions can personalize the response of an organization to a specific customer. What was a generic decision applied to all customers can be replaced with one tailored to a customer segment or even to a single customer. The effective management of operational decisions also allows straight-through processing and fully automated processes that no longer need to wait for human intervention but can continue to execute using the decision as soon as it is made.

Finding Operational Decisions

When defining and modeling an operational business process, many operational decisions will be obvious. When activities use words like choose, select, calculate, determine, assess, validate, or decide, then they are almost certain to be decisions. Defining these decisions involves finding the question that the activity should answer. "Is this invoice valid?" (see the Braskem case study in Chapter 9) or "What failure do these symptoms imply?" (see the KAESER KOMPRESSOREN case study in Chapter 9).

When decisions are less obvious, as they may be especially when an as-is process is being documented, there are a number of quick and easy ways to find decisions:

- When something is put on a worklist, it is often because someone must make a decision. When a process stops to ask a human to do something, it is generally either because of a need to interact with the real world (talk to a customer, visit a location, or similar activity) or because the process needs a decision to be made.

- Steps that have procedures or cheat sheets, especially when they follow data-gathering steps, are often decision-making. BPM is often used to improve the process of collecting and presenting information required for a decision. It is important not to underestimate the potential for automating the decision completely or for providing intelligent recommendations or guidance to the decision-maker.

- Any time someone must ask for an approval or escalate to level 2, then there is potential for a decision to improve things. If, instead of having to wait while someone more experienced or senior makes a decision, the original process executor could get a decision from the system, then the process would move along faster and more smoothly. Thresholds for escalation can often be increased using automated decisions, reducing the number that must be escalated.

- Points in the process where transaction or customer information is used to change data or drive routing: Price this order or cross-sell this customer, for instance.

- Branches that lead to other branches or gateways connected to other gateways, all designed to route a transaction through the process a certain way. This kind of complex branching logic can almost always be eliminated and replaced with a decision.

One of the most common ways to miss operational decisions is to focus too much on a strategic or management decision that impacts many customers as though this is a single decision. It is more useful to consider any decision that impacts all your customers as a collection of many *micro decisions* that each impacts a single customer. A concept first introduced in Smart (Enough) Systems, micro decisions focus on customers one at a time, decomposing a high-level decision (how to retain high-value customers) into many customer-specific ones (how do we retain this particular high-value customer).

For instance, consider how many decisions are involved in sending a marketing letter to 10,000 customers. It could be argued that just a few design decisions are involved — what kind of letter to send, what offer to make in the letter, and so on. However, 10,000 micro decisions have been made — one per customer. The company has decided to send each customer a specific letter — one decision each. Even if it chose to make all 10,000 decisions the same way, it has still made 10,000 decisions. After all, each customer will react to the letter as though it was sent just to them. They don't know the other customers who received it, and they are not aware of them.

The recipients will regard the sending of the letter, and the choice of its content, to be a deliberate decision on the part of the company. By focusing on these micro decisions, the company can ensure that each letter is the result of a deliberate decision. Breaking the process down and considering each of these decisions separately allows them to be customized and targeted to each customer.

Any time a process treats all instances of the process (all customers, all orders, all claims, or all tax returns) the same, there is the potential to introduce differentiation if the treatment decision is broken down into its constituent micro decisions. For instance, a company might use the same price for every customer. Yet each customer regards this as the price the company is willing to offer them personally. If the company considered these micro decisions and considered varying the price for each customer, it might find that different customers put different values on the product.

Many strategic decisions can only be implemented if many supporting micro decisions are also made. For instance, a strategic decision to increase customer retention requires that many individual micro decisions — how to retain this specific customer — are improved. The strategic decision will have no impact unless the micro decisions are also improved.

When reviewing processes for operational decisions, it can also be helpful to consider the various types of operational decisions that typically exist in an organization. The most common types are eligibility decisions, calculations, risk-based decisions, and opportunity-based decisions:

▶ **Eligibility decisions**
Eligibility decisions like "Is this customer eligible for this product?" are one of the most basic and common operational decision types. Eligibility decisions must be made repeatedly and consistently so that every customer or citizen has the same rules applied to determine if they are eligible. The policies and regulations driving these decisions can be extensive, and the critical challenge

will be managing the many rules involved so that changes can be made quickly and easily when policies and regulations change.

▶ **Calculations**
Calculation decisions call for questions like "What is the correct price for this product for this customer?" Calculations are often embedded in code because programmers do not see them as business decisions, whereas business users see them as just part of the system. However, being able to treat them as business decisions and being able to change them in certain circumstances or differentiate them for different kinds of customers is a potential source of differentiation.

▶ **Risk-based decisions**
Risk is acquired one customer, one transaction at a time. Risk-based operational decisions ask questions like "How risky is this loan customer and how should we price the loan as a result?" These decisions are much higher value that many operational decisions because there is generally a big gap between the value of a good decision and the value of a bad one. If risk is assessed poorly, then the potential for a damaging loss is real.

▶ **Opportunity-based decisions**
Customer-centric decisions include cross-sell and up-sell decisions where the right choice of action is the one that maximizes opportunity. These decisions must often change rapidly to take advantage of competitive and market circumstances, so agility in decision-making is highly valuable.

Becoming decision-centric means building a more explicit and more complete understanding of the decisions that are part of your business processes. Without such an understanding of the decisions in your processes, you will not be able to become truly process-centric. Managing both decisions and processes helps ensure an effective separation of concerns, which is increasingly important in many regulated industries.

Which Decisions to Prioritize

When an organization finds that it has many decisions across many processes, it may need to prioritize them in terms of which decisions to automate first. The most effective way to do this is to take the KPIs being used for value determination and then find the decisions that make a difference to these KPIs. In addition, a significant difference in the value of a good decision and a bad one is a sign that a decision should be prioritized. Decisions that affect the customer experience are also likely to be worth prioritizing, as are those that are used across multiple systems, events, and processes.

The characteristics of the decisions themselves can also help in prioritization. Decisions where large numbers of policies or regulations must be applied, where those policies or regulations change often, or where the policies and regulations are complex and require real domain expertise to understand, should be prioritized. These decision points will benefit the most from using business rules because they allow business users a more direct role in the definition, management, and evolution of the rules that implement these policies and regulations. Compliance and audit requirements such as strict governance over the logic applied or separation of responsibilities required for Sarbanes-Oxley can also be good drivers because business rules offer much better support for explicit tracing of outcomes and much more accessible descriptions of behavior than traditional code. As a result, business rules-based functions or decisions are easier to audit and demonstrate compliance.

14.3.3 Implementing Decisions with Business Rules

Making decisions explicit in process and application design offers many benefits regardless of how decision-making logic is managed. Decision-making logic can come from many sources. Regulations and legislation, internal policies and procedures, expert know-how, and the logic of legacy applications can all drive how a decision is made. Organizations can manage this logic in several ways.

The logic can be explicitly coded within application components or database Stored Procedures. This is familiar territory for IT departments and simplifies both development and testing processes. However, this means the IT department must be involved in any change to decision-making, largely eliminating the opportunity to improve agility and making it harder for the business to be involved in managing this logic and thus the decisions. Reuse of logic across multiple decisions can also be complex, because IT approaches to code modularization may not map to the internal structure of a decision.

Sometimes simple logic can be parameterized, and the parameters stored in database tables or configuration files. This decreases the cost of change by making it possible to make changes without deploying new code. This does not necessarily improve the engagement of the business, however. Whereas they might understand the parameters, they still cannot read and understand the code that uses the parameters. In addition, the use of parameters can even decrease the readability of the code to programmers, further complicating the situation. System testing and the need to version the code and parameters simultaneously can also increase complexity. Finally, parameterized logic also assumes that the kinds of changes that might be required can be exhaustively specified in advance. As a result, any change that was not planned for will require coding changes, eliminating the value of parameterization.

There are a number of circumstances in which neither approach is going to be successful. If a decision is based on many policies or regulations, then the management of the resulting logic — being able to find what you need to change — is critical, and huge parameter tables or long programs are poor tools for this. Similarly, if the logic involved changes often, then the time required to find, change, and deploy a change is critical. Parameterization can work for this scenario, but code works particularly poorly. Neither approach is effective if the logic is complex and has complex interactions. Code becomes increasingly complex, with deeply nested IF/THEN logic, for instance. It is unrealistic to parameterize this kind of logic due to the need to consider the impact of a change to one parameter on others in a complex relationship.

Finally, neither approach allows business users to truly participate and collaborate, so if the logic requires business domain know-how to understand (e.g., drug interaction checks that require medical know-how or heavy equipment maintenance rules that require experience using the vehicles), then neither approach is suitable. It is also true that sometimes business users insist on being able to change the logic in a system. As business users develop more small applications themselves, they become used to being able to make their own changes. When these systems are replaced with a more corporate version of the same functionality, the need for business user ownership will be explicit.

In each of these cases, and any time business logic needs to be reused across multiple decisions, the most effective way to manage decisions is to define those decisions in terms of business rules. Business rules are individual statements or fragments of business logic consisting of a set of conditions and an action to take if those conditions are met. Defining logic in terms of business rules and grouping those rules into rulesets allows logic to be understood and controlled.

The use of business rules to manage decision-making logic represents the next natural step in the separation of business logic from other aspects of a system — the last step in the decomposition of the monolithic system. This has long been understood as a Best Practice in software development, and developers have increasingly broken up applications into separate architectural elements for data access, user experience, business process, and so on. Separating out the business logic as decision-making components makes perfect sense architecturally while also allowing the IT department to remove themselves as much as possible from the ongoing maintenance of this business logic.

Managing business rules and rulesets using a business rules management system (BRMS) and deploying the right rules for a given decision as a decision service combines effective management with a deployment approach compatible with BPM and SOA. These are the four key concepts to managing decisions — business rules, rulesets, decision services, and business rules management systems. SAP has two business rules management systems — SAP NetWeaver BRM and BRFplus — that can be used to manage business rules and develop decision services, and these are described in Section 14.4.

Business Rules

Business rules are the rules by which you conduct business. More formally, a business rule is a statement of business logic that specifies performing one or more actions if its conditions are satisfied.

Each business rule should be atomic in that it should stand alone. Each business rule can be read and understood individually, and it should be possible to identify a finite set of business rules that represent a particular policy or a clause in a regulation. Because business rules are the lowest-level component in a business rules approach, it is business rules that should be versioned, and it is changes to business rules that should be logged and captured in an audit trail. Tracing policies to the business rules that implement them, analyzing the impact of a business rule change and more all depend on the effective management of individual business rules. That said, business rules are rarely used individually. They are used in rulesets.

Rulesets

The reality of managing business rules is that a grouping structure is required to organize and control them. It is not enough to simply have a list of rules managed individually. There will be too many of them to navigate easily, and the overhead of defining access control, ownership, and so on at the level of individual rules will be too high. Similarly, whereas decisions and decision services (defined below) represent an effective integration point for other systems and an effective deployment aggregation of business rules, they are often a poor management structure. Decisions are often based on rules that are owned by different groups within an organization and so require a collaborative approach. This makes it hard to be definitive about who owns the rules in a decision.

To relate a decision and a decision service to business rules, an additional layer is required — rulesets. Rulesets are coherent groupings of business rules that can and should be used together. Generally, individual business rules are not that helpful for anything in business systems and a ruleset is required. For instance, a business rule might describe a set of conditions that indicate fraud. In reality, however, there are likely to be many such rules. The more useful unit is a ruleset consisting of all of the rules that indicate, say, first-party fraud. Other rulesets might be defined that manage different kinds of rules for fraud so that different groups can own and manage their own rules. When new regulations or new policies drive changes to decision-making, they will require multiple rules to be changed. Most changes will be to a set of rules within a ruleset, so versioning and release management should be applied at the ruleset level.

Rulesets can be represented in a variety of formats in SAP's business rule offerings. They can be represented as a simple list of rules, as a decision table, or as a decision tree. These representations are described in Section 14.4.3. The best representation depends somewhat on the particular business rules. Regardless of representation, the business rules in a ruleset execute as a set and get reused as a set.

Multiple decisions often use a common ruleset. A single ruleset decision might also be part of a more complex decision, whereas complex decisions often use multiple rulesets. This reuse allows, for instance, multiple decisions to use customer segmentation logic without forcing a call to a service for customer segmentation; each decision uses the shared ruleset. This allows decisions to use business rules owned by multiple parts of the business. This is important because legal, customer service, marketing, and production could all easily have business rules that contribute to a single decision.

Because rulesets are coherent sets of business rules on a single topic, they typically have an obvious business owner — an individual or a group. This allows a clear separation of rule management (by ruleset) from rule execution (by decision). Not only is it easier to define ownership and edit privileges for a ruleset, but managing rules this way allows different rule maintenance environments for each set of business rules and each group of users.

As shown in Figure 14.30, each decision service uses several different rulesets. Each ruleset contains a coherent and related set of rules that can be considered as a single unit for these purposes.

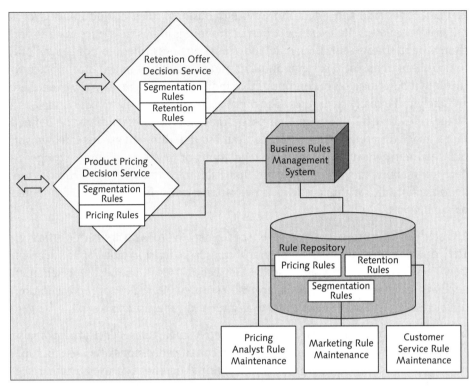

Figure 14.30 How Decision Services and Rulesets Relate

The product pricing decision service uses both segmentation and pricing rules to answer the question, "What price does this customer get for this product?" The retention offer decision service uses the same segmentation rules and adds a ruleset to determine the relevant retention offer for each segment. These rulesets are managed by different groups. Pricing analysts own the pricing rules, whereas marketing owns the segmentation rules. Each group can and should have slightly different environments to manage these rulesets, environments that maximize their ability to manage these rules effectively.

Decision Services

Some decisions require a single ruleset, and some require many. A single ruleset decision might determine the price of a product or identify the segment into which to put a customer, for instance. A multiple ruleset decision might underwrite a policy using a ruleset to check for a complete application, another to segment customers into different risk tiers, a third to rate and price, and so on. A multiple-ruleset decision lays out the steps involved in a decision, any branches or loops, and maps the steps to specific rulesets. With SAP NetWeaver BRM, for example, use a flow ruleset to define these steps (see Section 14.4.4).

Decisions are separate from the rulesets and business rules from which they are constructed. Changes to decisions can be made independently to changes to the rules, and these are more structural in nature — changing the sequence of the steps in a decision or adding rulesets to handle new cases, for instance.

In the same way that rulesets are the basic rule management component, decision services are the basic implementation component. Decision services execute on the same platform that supports the business process management system being used. In an ABAP environment, decision services are implemented as BRFplus functions (see Section 14.4.3), whereas in a Java environment, they are implemented as Web services using SAP NetWeaver BRM (see Section 14.4.4).

Decision services are services with a single purpose — making decisions. They can be thought of as services that answer business questions (make business decisions) for other services and processes. As such, they take a set of information as input, execute the necessary decision-making logic, and return the action to be taken or the selection made. This might be as simple as an approve/decline decision or as complex as an ordered list of products for which a customer is eligible.

The complexity of the decision is encapsulated in the decision service, allowing any other service or process to access the decision as long as it has the minimum data required — this data being defined as part of the standard service contract for the decision service.

Decision services have some critical characteristics:

▶ Their behavior is defined in a way that is understandable to non-technical business users using business rules and a business rules management system.

▶ They support rapid change without disruption, allowing rules representing new policies or regulations to be implemented without downtime and without introducing instability.

▶ They are designed to expect multichannel and multiprocess use so that decisions can be made consistently across channels and processes. Decisions may be required by everything from an ATM or a smart phone to call center applications and bill printing.

▶ They manage exceptions well so that they can be integrated with manual decision-making processes when an automated decision cannot be made. Few decision services handle 100 percent of all transactions. Most refer some for manual review.

- ▶ They explain their execution, logging the business rules that were executed each time a decision is made. This allows each decision made by the service to be reviewed for compliance and to see if the decision-making logic can be improved.

- ▶ They do not change the state of the business. They have no side effects, so they can be used in different circumstances — to see what the decision would be and to actually make the decision, for instance.

Decision services are an essential component in successful implementations because they give the IT environment, and the systems and processes within it, a standard way to access decision-making logic. Effective implementation of decision services requires a business rules management system such as those developed by SAP.

Business Rules Management Systems

A business rules management system (BRMS) is a set of software components that support the creation, testing, management, deployment, and ongoing maintenance of business rules in a production environment. At the core of a BRMS is a business rules engine that determines which business rules need to be executed in what order at runtime. A BRMS supports the development and testing of business rules, linking business rules to data sources, measuring and reporting on business rules, and deployment of business rules into production. A BRMS also gives business users and analysts the ability to make routine changes and updates to critical business systems while freeing IT resources to concentrate on higher-value initiatives. SAP has two business rules management systems — BRFplus for use in ABAP environments and SAP NetWeaver BRM for use in Java or composite application environments — and these products are described below in Section 14.4.

Several advantages can be gained by expressing business logic in business rules and using the processing and management facilities included with SAP's business rules offerings to work with them:

- ▶ Business rules are more understandable to business people, leading to better business-technical cooperation and alignment, reduced implementation times, and fewer opportunities for interpretation errors.

- ▶ Business rules are easily segmented into rulesets, providing clear ownership, management, and control.

▸ Rules can be updated, and new rules can be deployed to a decision service without taking the decision service offline, allowing live updates to running systems.

▸ Business rules can have explicit times and dates when they should go into and out of effect, making it easier to implement policies and regulations.

14.3.4 Best Practices in Decision Management

Business rules and business rules management systems are well established and have been used in many projects around the world and in every industry. Rising from this body of experience are Best Practices around rule writing, business rule discovery, decision service design, and business rules maintenance that also apply to SAP's business rules offerings.

Business Rule Writing

The most important aspect of writing business rules is to keep them simple. Having a single definition of the rules that is directly executable and understandable by both the business and IT teams reduces confusion, increases accuracy, and increases alignment.

Ensuring that business rules are atomic (one rule, one concept) keeps each rule as simple as possible. Limit rule conditions to simple conjunctions and limit rule consequences to one action or a closely related set of actions. If the same conditions result in more than one consequence, it is typically better to write two rules, one for each consequence. This has no real performance implications and makes both for simpler rules and easier maintenance because the two rules can be edited independently. Break OR statements into multiple rules to make for easier-to-understand business rules. More, simpler rules are always better. SAP's business rules offerings are more than capable of handling large numbers of rules at scale, and more, simpler rules will be easier to manage and maintain over time.

> **Tip**
>
> Both SAP business rules offerings support ELSE clauses. If a design intention is for business rules to be maintained by business users, we recommend not using ELSE clauses because this will add complexity and limit readability, making these rules difficult to understand for business users. Write a second rule instead.

Each business rule should also be written so that it has no implicit sequencing relative to other business rules — so that it is declarative. If necessary, re-factor the rules into multiple rulesets and then orchestrate the sequence, with an SAP NetWeaver BRM flow ruleset, for example (see Section 14.4.4). Business rules may be executed sequentially, but they should make sense individually.

Rules can be written in terms of what conditions are included to make an action happen (defining what is "good") or, conversely, what should not happen (defining what is "bad"). Business users think of rules in terms of inclusion, so this approach is preferred. For instance, if the business acts differently when a customer is female, then the business rule should be written to check that gender is equal to female rather than that gender is not equal to male.

Rules should be as verbose and semantically rich as possible so that everyone, programmers and non-programmers, can have a common understanding. Business rules should also use names for business objects that will be familiar to business users. If the objects being manipulated are not recognizable, then the rule will appear complex no matter how it is written. SAP NetWeaver BRM has a feature that allows aliasing of technical objects precisely to allow more business-friendly names to be used (see Section 14.4.4).

> **Tip**
>
> Do not use programming style guides for business rules. Programmers tend to write code that is very terse, using short variable names, programming shortcuts such as ++, and technical abbreviations. This makes for hard-to-read business rules that look like code to business users. If business rules look like code, then business people will "check out" and refuse to participate.

Always consider the golden rule:

When considering alternative ways to write a rule, always pick the approach that makes most sense to the business.

Decision Service Design

In most organizations, many decision services are used by multiple processes and multiple services. Because consistency of decision making is important, the ability to safely and effectively reuse a decision service is critical. To this end, it is important to develop decision services with two particular characteristics: they should be stateless and they should not have any side effects.

A stateless decision service can be called at any point in a process execution, and the process can be sure that it will get an answer, or a prompt time out, so that it can continue to execute. Ensuring that the decision service does not call stateful services or access data that may not be readily available is essential. If a decision service is stateful, because it depends on a stateful service, for instance, then its usefulness and reuse will be compromised.

This is not to say that stateful decision services are never a good idea, only that making a decision service stateless should be the preferred approach, and that organizations should think hard before building stateful decision services. When a decision service needs data from many different sources, an organization may decide it's appropriate to violate this guideline for performance considerations as discussed later in this chapter.

Similarly, ensure that a decision service does not have any side effects. It should not update customer records, send emails, or otherwise take actions. It should return the recommended or appropriate action so that the calling process or service can act, but it should not change the state of the business itself. It can be helpful to think of decision services as advisers to other services — always available to answer questions but not having any direct impact on execution.

Take, for example, a decision service that calculates the correct cost of a construction permit based on many different aspects of a construction project. A stateless decision service with no side effects could be used by the process for issuing a permit and by a website that allows construction companies to estimate how much a permit would cost them (allowing them to see if changes to the project would make a big difference to the cost) and allowing an amendment process to use the same calculation. If the decision service were built to take the action — if it updates the cost of the permit in the database — then it will only be usable in the initial permit creation process, and this will limit its value.

Decision services should also have a simple interface. It should be easy to call a decision service, pass in a coherent set of information, and get a coherent set of information back. Both BRFplus functions and SAP NetWeaver BRM services support the definition of this information explicitly as discussed in Section 14.4.3. In addition to the data passed in, decision services vary in the extent to which they gather their own data once they have been invoked. Many decision services require only a small amount of data as the basis for the decision. This can be passed in as part of the invocation of the decision service when the amount of data is small and when the various calling systems are all likely to have the data required. It becomes more complex for decisions that might require large amounts of data or where the calling context varies a great deal.

Four broad options for data in decision services exist. At one extreme are decision services that must be passed all the data they require. At the other extreme are decision services in which even long-running requests for data, say those involving a human, can be accommodated:

1. Pass all of the data available into a decision service and design it to either decide or to pass back some reason why it could not do so. This approach is synchronous, simple, and fast. It can result in multiple attempts to get a decision and can result in calling applications investing time in collecting data that may or may not be relevant to a specific decision, and this can be a problem when some data is only required occasionally. Given the power of a BPMS to assemble the data required, these limitations are lessened when the decision service is being deployed only within business processes.

2. Pass the data available to the decision service but allow it to make synchronous calls to gather the rest of the data it needs to complete the decision. This approach allows costly or time-consuming requests for information to be deferred until they are required — to execute the rules in a particular ruleset for example. It does make the decision service dependent on other components, however. Both SAP business rules offerings support this kind of rules-based gathering of additional data, using the option to execute other services as the consequence of a rule.

3. Pass the data available to the decision service and allow it to gather the data it needs in any way, but allow the decision service to wait or suspend until the data has been gathered. The decision service can no longer be used in a synchronous way because it cannot be relied upon to make a decision in a reasonable time. It should be invoked asynchronously, gather the data it needs and then transmit its result, typically across an enterprise service bus. This approach is common in event-based architectures.

4. Pass the data available to the decision service and allow it to request additional data from a user interface. The decision is invoked as data is entered and continues to run until the data provided through the user interface is validated or some other decision is made. For instance, the Ericsson use case (see Chapter 7, Section 7.2) illustrates a validate supplier decision that is used as data is being entered about a new supplier. Once the supplier definition is complete, the decision validates the supplier, and the process continues. Other business

rules may handle the interaction, display different questions, and adapt the user interface to gather the required data.

Good decision service design requires a clear understanding of what is needed from a requirements perspective and what is plausible from an architectural and technical perspective. Option 1 is the cleanest and most common but can be limiting when large amounts of optional data are involved. Options 2 to 4 provide more flexibility but increase the challenges: The number of failure points increases, which can be crippling if not managed well; the complexity can rapidly increase because of maintenance, monitoring, and error-handling needs; and more resources must be dedicated to manage the additional integration points in the infrastructure.

Business Rules Management

Most organizations adopting business rules find that different rulesets require different types of business rules management. Sometimes business people change the business rules in production, sometimes business people make changes to business rules in a development environment, sometimes business analysts or IT staff make changes, and so on. SAP's business rules offerings support a variety of editing approaches designed for both business and IT users and the necessary access controls as described in Section 14.4.4.

Whereas there are pros and cons for each approach, it is important to remember that, fundamentally, the value of business rules and of business rules management system lies in collaboration. It matters less who makes the changes than who can collaborate to ensure that the right change is made at the right time.

SAP's business rules syntax allows for flexibility and power not available in traditional programming languages. This lets business policymakers work side by side with the implementation team, reading and discussing the business rules directly. This is true regardless of the approach taken to business rules management.

Several distinct choices must be made for each ruleset:

▶ Who should be able to make changes to the rules?

▶ How quickly do those changes need to get into production?

▶ How rigorous does checking and testing need to be before the changes go into production?

Each ruleset can have different answers, though many rulesets have the same set of answers and can be treated the same way. You should not, however, assume that a new ruleset can just be treated like an existing one but should go through the exercise of determining what is right for that ruleset.

Three main options exist for editing rulesets: business users, business analysts, or programmers make changes. It is quite rare for business users to make changes directly. It is more common that business analysts or programmers make the changes while business users participate as collaborators and reviewers. Most organizations initially find that programmers make all of the changes but that gradually more and more rulesets are edited by business analysts.

Programmers can and will use the standard design environment to make most business rule changes. Working within the SAP NetWeaver Composition Environment, for instance, they have access to a full palette of business rules functionality using SAP NetWeaver Business Rules Management (see Section 14.4.4). Some business analysts are also comfortable making business rule changes in this environment. It is not uncommon to find that business analysts are comfortable and competent writing business rules once they have been taught the syntax. Many find the degree of technical information presented alongside the rules overwhelming, however, and a more streamlined environment such as the Rules Manager web interface will be more appropriate. Using the built-in capabilities of the SAP business rules offerings to focus on the business rules without exposing the technical details, and using metaphors such as decision tables and decision trees, empowers business analysts to manage rules themselves.

If business users are to make rule changes directly, they need an interface that allows business rule changes to be presented such that the business user sees them as part of running their business, not as part of changing a system. For instance, rules about product eligibility should be edited alongside the definition of the product so that specifying these rules is just part of defining a new product.

Some decision services contain rulesets where agility is so important that rule changes are made directly in a production system. These are, however, rare. What is more common is a need to make a change in production in an emergency while generally making changes in a preproduction environment of some kind. Business rules that can be affected by legal rulings or by the behavior of competitors often fall into this category. It is generally acceptable to make a change and have it go into effect the next day, but once in a while it will be necessary to make a change immediately.

Most rulesets, however, go through a relatively standard develop-test-release sequence. Changes are made in a development environment, and impact analysis is conducted to ensure that the change does what is expected and has no unacceptable business implications. These changes are moved to a QA or acceptance testing environment where a standard set of regression tests are performed to catch any unexpected consequences of the change. Once these tests are complete, a regularly scheduled update pulls the rule changes into the production environment.

> **Tip**
>
> Although this sounds very similar to the approach used for code, it is important that it is managed separately. Business rule changes are more common, more timely, and more limited in scope, and the update process should reflect this. An independent update process for business rules should be created. Do not just use the standard IT process for updates.

The most important things to remember about business rules management are that it varies by ruleset and that lots of different approaches are potentially valid. Think through the business value of each approach for each ruleset to maximize the value of business rules.

Business Rule Discovery

Although most of this chapter is concerned with how business rules should be realized, it is important to note that the business rules and decisions must be discovered and captured too. Several approaches are currently in use for discovering and capturing business rules.

Business rules and decisions are identified during the development of a business blueprint (see Chapter 13, Section 13.3.2). The techniques used in a business blueprint workshop to identify business processes and business requirements also identify business rules and process activities that are focused on decision-making. It is important to note, however, that business rules are not the same as business requirements. Business rules often change independently of requirements and are reused across multiple decisions, which are themselves reused across multiple processes. They should therefore be documented alongside the processes and requirements identified in the blueprint.

Candidate business rules can be captured in a variety of ways. The simplest is to document a natural language business rule in a rule catalog. Each rule can be described, its source (regulation, policy, best practice) documented, and it can be linked to the system artifacts that implement it. It is typically very helpful to define a vocabulary — a set of terms — as part of creating these business rules. This helps ensure that everyone is talking about the same things in their rules, improving alignment and collaboration. This business vocabulary can be used elsewhere in the blueprint and be used as the basis for the vocabulary used in SAP NetWeaver BRM. Some organizations find it helpful to use a more formal language for documenting business rules such as RuleSpeak or the language based on the Semantics of Business Vocabulary and Business Rules SBVR standard. These approaches formalize the underlying vocabulary and the way in which business rules are written against that vocabulary without considering the technical implementation of the business rules.

Decisions can also be modeled as a decision hierarchy. This approach decomposes a decision into subdecisions and then models the data and knowledge required for each decision or subdecision. Decisions and subdecisions are often reused, so decisions are modeled in an acyclic network rather than a strict hierarchy. Mapping in data sources and categories of knowledge (regulations, policies, analytic models) helps scope each decision and identify sources for rule discovery. The properties of a decision can be captured for each decision and subdecision as they are decomposed and modeled.

> **Tip**
>
> It is essential that business rules be managed only once. Therefore, every element of the business blueprint needs to reference the decisions and business rules involved rather than repeat them. Generally, decisions are the most useful cross-reference point.

Impact Analysis

IT departments' developing decision services need to be aware that business users, when they change how a decision is being made, are less interested in testing the change and more interested in assessing its impact. For instance, if the business wishes to loosen the eligibility rules for a product (changing the decision service that returns the eligible product list), then they will want to understand how that might have impacted last month's, or last year's, customers. They will want to understand that a certain number of customers who had been ruled ineligible would, under the new rules, be eligible. They will want to see what happened to the customers who were ineligible — what they did after the product list was presented. They will want to estimate the number of additional product sales that this new approach to eligibility will produce and so on.

Making this kind of analysis possible, even easy, is critical for effective management of the decision because business owners will be reluctant to make changes to the decision unless they can conduct this kind of analysis. This requires making it easy to select historical or sample data, easy to compare two versions of a decision service in terms of its impact on those data, and easy to ripple the results of the decisions through subsequent processing. A change to a fraud detection decision, for instance, has an impact in terms of the number of transactions that must be investigated by the fraud investigation unit. This determines staffing and workload and impacts time to completion metrics.

Because impact analysis is very specific to a business problem, it requires development effort to build a suitable environment on top of the features provided by the SAP business rules offerings. The simulation capabilities of BRFplus (see Section 14.4.3) provide an ideal platform for impact analysis, allowing the impact of a rule change to be assessed before the rules are put into production. The testing facilities of the SAP business rules offerings can also be used to provide impact analysis if historical data is made available as test cases and some reporting infrastructure is created.

Where rule changes are both regular and significant, an investment in extending prebuilt testing and simulation functionality to show the impact of a change on key performance indicators that the business tracks should be considered. Standard reporting of averages and totals can be used because these can give good indications of the overall impact. Reporting that shows which customers or customer segments will be treated differently when the rules are changed is also powerful because it shows business users who will be impacted.

Decision Analysis

Decision-making should be included in performance management and reporting environments. For instance, if a dashboard displays information about customer retention, it might be very useful to be able to drill down into customer records and see those who were made offers but not retained, see what offers were made to them, and see what alternatives were presented to the customer by the decision service. This would allow comparisons and analysis to see how offers might be improved in the future.

Many decisions also require experimentation to improve the quality of decision-making. You constantly learn more about your customers and gather more information about their behavior. New insights and market trends come from you, your competitors, and third parties. A process for continual review and improvement of how you make a decision allows you to detect and respond to changes in the behavior of your customers without having to start a special project and helps you show an ROI for the data you collect and analyze.

Whereas impact analysis can compare the results of a change to see if it would have been better in the past, it does not allow live comparison of two approaches. Whereas reporting shows that an approach has been working less and less effectively, it does not automatically allow comparison of this approach to an alternative. For both of these important activities it is necessary to build in experimentation to the decision service.

The basic approach to support experimentation and adaptive control is to allow a decision service to pick between one of several distinct decision-making approaches for each transaction. Each transaction is randomly assigned to an approach, that approach is used to decide, and the results are returned — both the selected action and information about which approach was used. Over time, the results of applying different approaches can be compared. Because operational decisions repeat in large numbers, it is possible to find similar transactions that have been run through each approach. This allows the more effective approach to be identified.

Both SAP business rules offerings can be used to build this kind of random assignment to one of several approaches. Within a single BRFplus function or SAP NetWeaver BRM flow ruleset, different rulesets can be created for each approach, and additional rules can be used to randomly assign each transaction to a test group so that the relevant rules can be applied. The rules executed in each case are logged as usual, and the rules that assign transactions should add this assignment to the log for future analysis. Decision services that involve predictive analytics or judgment calls on the part of an organization should generally be designed to support this kind of experimentation from the beginning. In contrast, decision services that implement a tightly regulated decision, such as a government benefit eligibility decision, do not need this capability.

14.3.5 Governance

Business rules and the use of a business rules management system help promote agility and clarity while facilitating change and alignment. Using these tools in a fairly ad hoc and uncontrolled way is typically fine for a first project. The boundaries and decisions are clear, ownership of business rules is straightforward, and so on. As organizations move past the first project and when business rules begin to be reused, a more formal approach is required. At this point multiple groups clearly own different rulesets, and rulesets owned by different groups need to be combined so that they can contribute to a specific decision. Understanding the impact of changes to business rules on the various decisions of which they are part and providing a mechanism to review and agree on changes before they are made becomes critical.

Issues are likely to arise around the various stakeholders, their roles and responsibilities, and the governance processes required. Most organizations decide they need an organization to manage all of this. It is important to remember, however, that it is just as dangerous to do this too early (when the organization lacks experience with using a BRMS, for example, and has no real examples of rule reuse) as too late (when overlapping projects are arguing about change control). Organizations should not attempt to define all of this before they have some experience and examples, but they should not delay until it becomes a problem. Refactoring some rulesets already developed is to be expected and is acceptable. Chaos is not.

Stakeholders, Roles, and Responsibilities

Organizations working extensively with business rules find they need to include multiple stakeholders — from business executives to programmers — and it is important to clearly define who is involved in making changes, who is responsible for reviewing changes, and who is on the governance committee.

In particular, it is important to define who owns which business rules, typically ruleset by ruleset. Owners might have the right to create, modify, and delete business rules or might be involved only in review and impact analysis. In general, at least one business expert is among these owners, if only as a reviewer. In addition to those with ownership or edit rights, a second group is allowed to access a ruleset. These are business and technical people who might need to understand what a ruleset does and how it works, but who have no right to modify the ruleset. Generally, this group should be as broad as possible, with restrictions based only on security or policy needs (only allowing those working in the fraud group to see the rules used to detect fraud, for instance). Most rulesets can be widely readable, even if only a few people can make changes. SAP's business rules offerings are integrated with standard SAP access control and security capabilities, making it easy to use existing groups and roles to control access to business rules.

Rule Lifecycle

Part of managing business rules effectively is preparing for inevitable changes. After all, business rules are valuable to an organization in part because such change is more easily managed. All information systems are changed during their life, and decision services are likely to see much more rapid and extensive changes than other components. Different rulesets have different rule lifecycles that reflect the different drivers for change.

Each organization needs to define its own rule lifecycles for the various kinds of rules it must manage. It is often helpful, however, to consider the lifecycle in various phases. First, there are the stages or states through which a rule passes before it is ready to be put into production. These involve discovery and documentation, authoring, and review both in terms of validating that the rule does what is needed and verification that the rule is consistent and complete. Some sequence of testing and deployment to different environments such as user acceptance test follows before the rule is deployed.

Once deployed, business rules move into a maintenance or evolution phase. In this phase changes to the business or regulatory environment, changing competitive needs, or changing customer expectations might push an organization to consider a change to the rule. In this phase the new version of the rule is described and the change made, impact analysis is conducted, and if the change seems to be beneficial, the rule is updated in the production environment (typically passing through various test and QA systems).

Ultimately, some rules are retired, and this too needs to be considered.

This process describes the lifecycle of rules driven by regulation or policy. However, many organizations also have rules that are extremely transitory. These rules conform to a structure or style. There are always rules of a particular type in the system, but the specific rules in force at any moment are highly variable. Examples are marketing or promotion rules, customer preference rules, and (in very dynamic markets) pricing rules. With these kinds of rules the predeployment phase is quite different because there is no value in having the rules that could be discovered when analysis begins be the first ones implemented. They will be completely out of date by the time they go live.

Instead, the early stages of the lifecycle should focus on the structure of the rules and the kinds of rules involved, using the rules in place at the time as examples. What is deployed is the template or structure of the rules — an empty decision table, for instance. Only once this is available are rules actually edited and updated. These production rules may even be changed directly in the production system, though this is not common. They will certainly go through a much more truncated and automated verification and testing process because a rule that takes too long to implement will automatically be wrong in such a dynamic situation. Rapid identification of issues and rollback are more important than testing in such a case.

Governance Processes

As organizations broaden and deepen their use of business rules and of a business rules management system, they need to develop various governance processes. In particular they need to develop a change management process, a release management process, and an overall governance process. These processes have much in common with similar processes developed for other technologies. The release management process for business rules, for instance, has much in common with a standard IT release management process.

Even though they will be based on and derived from existing processes, business rules require distinct processes of their own. The release management process should be adapted to reflect more regular updates with a more localized scope. It should also be changed to bring business users and business analysts inside the process early rather than having them act as mostly passive approvers. The use of business rules makes it much easier for business users to understand and collaborate on the logic involved, and the release management process should take advantage of this.

Business rules represent a new approach for many organizations, and they need to create a process that supports their increasing understanding over time. Ensuring that a group of stakeholders participate in discussing the governance approach being taken and how it can and should evolve is important in maximizing the value of business rules.

14.3.6 Managing the Organizational Implications

A decisioning approach and a business rules management system enable and require IT and business users to come together more closely than ever before, to dramatically change the alignment of these two groups. Business decisions are intensely important to business management. They are central to how the business operates. Yet they must be embedded into high-volume transactional systems and processes. Although products like SAP's business rules offerings help business and IT people collaborate, there is also a cultural aspect to aligning the two groups. Some business departments simply don't trust their IT departments, and some IT departments return this suspicion.

Decisioning can also cause organizational change. Roles can change. For example, some people will go from making many simple decisions to considering the overall patterns of decisions. Underwriters might stop spending their days manually approving individual policies and spend far more time analyzing the overall book of business. This change will benefit some, who will perform better in the new role, but not all. Someone who was adept at handling the transactions rapidly could find this skill less in demand. Successful adoption must manage the implications of this kind of change. Decisioning can also be used to drive staff reductions, with the attendant organizational change issues. Even when this is not the plan, staff may be concerned that the computer will replace them when previously manual decisions are automated.

Organizational issues also come up when decisioning is used in a customer-facing environment. Staff may be reluctant to trust the system when dealing with their customers, especially if commissions or bonuses are on the line. Giving small groups the opportunity to test a system, and showing everyone how much better they did as a result, can be very effective in changing this mindset. Nothing succeeds like success. Good tools for analyzing and reporting on the improvements are critical in driving adoption.

When customers are impacted by decisions, they may appreciate the improved response time or increased self-service that is possible, but they may feel aggrieved if they don't get what they want because "the computer said so." Ensuring that the system can explain its decisions, to staff and potentially to customers, is critical. This is greatly enabled by the ability to record exactly which business rules fired in each decision. It is also easier to get customers to accept decisions that try to say "No, but..." rather than just "No." A system that says "You are not eligible for this product, but we can offer you this other one instead" will get less resistance than one that simply declines an application.

Finally, beware of counterproductive incentives. Sometimes decisioning systems overwhelm performance and reward structures. For example, a marketing department might be rewarded for the number of leads generated. Using decisioning to find which leads would be more useful, and excluding those that are not, might improve business results while penalizing the marketing department by reducing their lead totals. To be adopted, decisioning cannot be good only for the company; it must also be good for those who use it.

14.4 Business Rules Management from SAP

This section introduces SAP's products in the area of business rules management. It explains SAP's strategy around the Business Rule Framework plus and SAP NetWeaver Business Rules Management and gives usage recommendations for different scenarios.

14.4.1 Roots of Business Rule Framework Plus

In the year 2005, SAP investigated the usage of business rules in the new technology platform for SAP Business ByDesign. There was consensus about the importance of business rules and the advantage of highly flexible and code-free configuration. However, existing products did not seem to be powerful enough to make a general purpose BRMS. Consequently, development started for what is known today as Business Rule Framework plus (BRFplus). Although there were limitations and problems with the existing tools and engines, it was always very clear that these tools had an impressive wealth of experience and expertise that had to be preserved in the architecture of BRFplus. BRFplus is a new code line, but its name indicates the big architectural influence from BRF that is apparent.

14.4.2 Roots of SAP NetWeaver BRM

In October, 2007, SAP announced the acquisition of Yasu Technologies with its flagship product Yasu QuickRules, a leading BRMS especially for the Java stack. The product was renamed SAP NetWeaver Business Rules Management (BRM). Since then, it has been adapted and integrated into SAP NetWeaver Composition Environment (CE). It can be used on its own, and it can be leveraged in conjunction with SAP NetWeaver Business Process Management (BPM) to compose and integrate rules within the context of a modeled business process.

Today, with BRFplus and SAP NetWeaver BRM, SAP offers a pair of business rules management systems to embed business rules and decisioning power into business applications.

14.4.3 Business Rule Framework Plus

BRFplus supports business analysts and IT experts with tools to find, understand, change, test, and organize business rules in an integrated user interface. BRFplus facilitates seamless collaboration between business analysts and IT experts.

BRFplus perfectly integrates with SAP NetWeaver Application Server and the ABAP-based applications in the SAP Business Suite and SAP Business ByDesign. Best performance, high flexibility, and lowest total cost of ownership (TCO) achieved by optimal integration with existing concepts and approaches are the design principles that influence BRFplus.

BRFplus functions act as decision service definitions. Functions are interfaces between orchestrated or hard-coded processes and the flexible decisioning logic incorporated into the business rules. Business rules are organized in rulesets that are attached to the functions, as depicted in Figure 14.31.

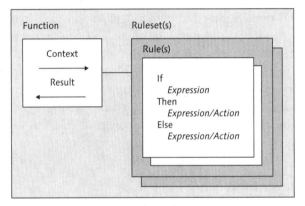

Figure 14.31 Architecture of BRFplus

BRFplus is part of the SAP Basis software component, which is included in SAP NetWeaver and therefore available in all ABAP-based applications.

BRFplus Components

BRFplus consists of three components:

► Rules workbench
► Rules engine
► Rules repository

In BRFplus, *rules authorization* is done with help of the BRFplus *workbench*. The workbench comprises all of the tools needed to manage the business rule assets in one place through a collaborative web-based user interface developed in Web Dynpro for ABAP that can be started via the ABAP transaction BRFplus. The workbench supports modeling, editing, and managing business rules and related artifacts such as rulesets, rules, and data objects, which form the vocabulary on which the rules are written. The complete workbench or selected parts can be embedded into other application UIs. Because the workbench runs completely in the browser and the backend is part of the SAP NetWeaver Application Server ABAP, no additional installations are needed, either on the client or on the server side.

The workbench includes capabilities such as configuration and various catalogs that act like folders to organize all of the rule artifacts for easier access and to allow users to focus on their particular responsibilities.

The building blocks for the modeling of business logic are called rules, expressions, and actions. They have their own user interface and provide business user-friendly rich rule formats. This approach has two advantages:

- Best visualization and approach for a specific problem
- Easily possible extensions with custom UIs

The most popular rule formats are:

- Decision tables
- Decision trees
- `IF-THEN` rules
- Formulas

The workbench provides logs and views for change and execution tracking of rules supporting audits and regulatory compliance. The workbench also provides access to several tools such as object catalogs, simulation, consistency checks, dependency analysis, XML, and Microsoft Excel data exchange, as well as a Web service creation wizard. In particular, the simulation capabilities being part of the integrated environment helps directly test the changes before releasing.

The workbench was developed according to the model-view-controller paradigm (MVC). Nearly all of the backend methods are published. Therefore, it is possible to create and activate rules in background or even to create a custom UI.

BRFplus allows business users to find the rules that matter to their business, explore and understand the rules, change and simulate/test them, and ultimately manage the rules with the BRFplus workbench.

The BRFplus *rules engine* provides several ways for invocation of the rules:

- ABAP objects API
- RFC-enabled function modules (generated)
- Web services (generated)

In standard scenarios the ABAP objects API is usually used for rules processing. However, it is also possible to invoke the processing by RFC or a Web service when access from outside the ABAP environment is required.

BRFplus has built-in code-generation capabilities that create executable code on the fly for the highest performance. Sometimes evaluation of rules in BRFplus is even faster than a buffered single select in the data base. Usually, data retrieval and preparation or remote communication is much more critical to the overall performance than actual rules processing in BRFplus. Output of the code generation is a class with a method containing all of the definitions and execution instructions. The generated code can further support runtime traces for rules execution logging and decision justification in business-user-friendly format. This helps users understand when the rules have been executed and why results have been found. The BRFplus rules engine can also use the fully versioned repository providing the capabilities of time travel — allowing a user to execute the rules that were in effect for a particular moment in time.

The *rules repository* is the place where all artifacts and related information such as documentation are saved. It is possible to store the business rules and related entities such as rulesets, catalogs, and data objects in the database as local or transportable objects using SAP's Change and Transport System (CTS). Further, the repository can save the artifacts in client-dependent or -independent database tables to influence changeability and visibility in different clients and support the widely adopted three-system approach. This approach consists of a system for development, a system for tests, and a productive system and CTS being used to manage the updates of source code, data dictionary, and customizing objects. All repository services are accessible through the BRFplus workbench. The repository provides further versioning capabilities and access control.

BRFplus allows for great deployment flexibility. There are two main scenarios:

- Distributed
- Centralized

In the distributed scenario rules are managed in one instance and transported to connected instances with the CTS or per XML data exchange allowing for local rules processing. The connection is done with an RFC function module call or a

Web service. In the centralized scenario a central instance is used for the management of the BRFplus content. Other instances connect to the central instance for processing of the rules. BRFplus can also support mixed scenarios. The many capabilities of the BRFplus repository give the advantages of a very deep integration into the applications. BRFplus can support virtually any application data lifecycle, minimizing costs for embedding it into applications and administration.

Authoring Business Rules with BRFplus

It is very simple to work with BRFplus. There are only a few mandatory and optional steps to follow:

1. Create a function.
2. Create and assign context data objects (optional).
3. Create and assign result data objects (optional).
4. Create and assign one or many rulesets.
5. Create and assign rules.
6. Create and assign one or many expressions (optional).
7. Create and assign one or many actions (optional).
8. Activate all objects.
9. Simulate rules evaluation (optional).
10. Organize the rules in a catalog (optional).

The steps are described in the following text with help of an example of a price calculation.

Function

The starting point of writing business rules in BRFplus is the creation of a function. A function is the glue between code and business rules. It has a specific purpose such as validate request, calculation of risk profile, or check for exceptions. Usually, the name gives an idea about the piece of logic to be defined with business rules. A function as any other object in BRFplus has a technical ID (name), business user-friendly description, and documentation capabilities.

Additionally, a function describes the input for the evaluation, called the context. In BRFplus data objects exist for this purpose. A data object is a description of a variable. Data objects can be elementary (e.g., Name or Age) structured (e.g., Address including the components Name, Street, and Post Code), or tabular (e.g., a list of addresses). Data objects are also used to define result parameters of the function. Context and result define the vocabulary with which the rules are written. Both are optional. Data objects can be created with reference to the data dictionary (DDIC), from which type definitions, documentation, and value help can be retrieved, which automates the creation of business vocabulary and saves a lot of work.

Figure 14.32 shows the function PRICE CALCULATION. It has four elementary context data objects as input and a result data object called FINAL PRICE.

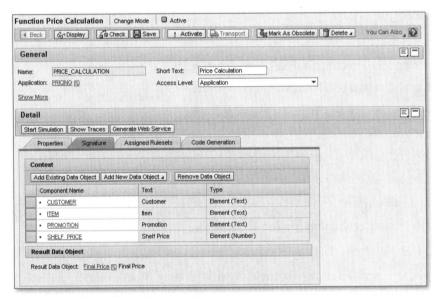

Figure 14.32 "Price Calculation" Function

Rulesets

The function is not a carrier of any business logic. All logic is contained in business rules that are grouped into rulesets. Several rulesets can be assigned to one function, allowing separation of the tasks into different rulesets or to organize the rules in a better way such as having one ruleset per customer classification, country, and so on. Rulesets provide the possibility to define preconditions to ensure that the rules inside the rulesets are only called for the purpose for which they were built. Whenever there is a precondition that does not evaluate to true, the processing of all rules in the ruleset is skipped, and processing continues with the next ruleset. With priorities defined at the ruleset level, it is possible to influence the processing sequence if more than one ruleset is assigned to a function.

Figure 14.33 shows the ruleset PRICE CALC. RULES, that is assigned to the function PRICE CALCULATION. It contains three rules, which are all active, indicated by the green icon in front of the rule description.

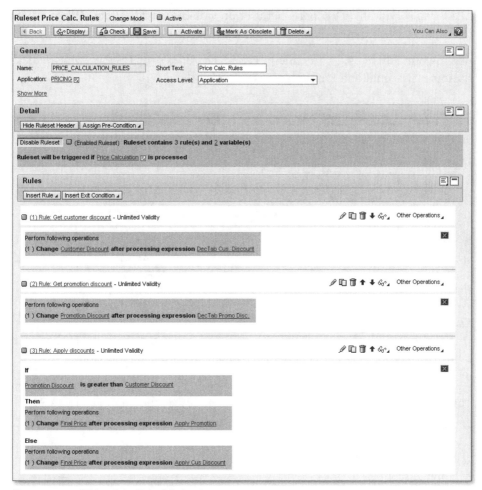

Figure 14.33 "Price Calc. Rules" Ruleset

The ruleset contains two ruleset variables. Ruleset variables can be used to extend the context of a function, which means adding to the business vocabulary available for the rule definitions. This is very helpful for intermediate values in a sequence of rule steps or when the data provided in the context is not sufficient for the definition of all business rules. In this case ruleset variables contain the missing data so that business experts can work with it as if it would be part of the context, for example, a context that contains customer data but misses the customer group. A ruleset variable for the customer group can be defined, and in a second step an initialization expression can be assigned for reading the customer group into it. Initialization expressions may look up the missing data in the database or use ABAP code. Typically, IT experts help set up variable initializations. When done, the variables can be used like any other context data object.

As shown in Figure 14.34, the ruleset Price Calc. Rules contains the two variables: Customer Discount and Promotion Discount.

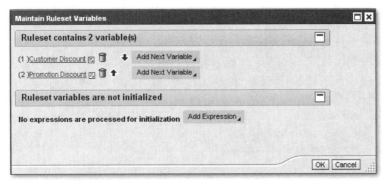

Figure 14.34 Variables in the "Price Calc. Rules" Ruleset

Rules

One ruleset can contain many rules. The rules are evaluated according to the order in the rulesets. Rules can be constrained by their status (enabled/disabled), by time, or by dynamic preconditions so that they are excluded from the evaluation.

There are three rules in the ruleset Price Calc. Rules, as shown in Figure 14.34:

1. Get customer discount

2. Get promotion discount

3. Apply discounts

The ruleset is expanded so that the content of the rules can be seen. In this view it is easy to understand how the business logic is captured in the business rules.

Whereas rulesets organize which rules are evaluated in what sequence, rules are the central entity of BRFplus. They contain several pieces of the business logic. Rules have a simple structure:

IF *condition*
THEN *operation(s)*
ELSE *operation(s)*

First, the condition is evaluated. The condition is optional. Conditions can be defined three ways:

▶ Elementary data object from the context with Boolean (true/false) type

▶ Built-in value range expressions (for simple conditions)

▶ Expression that returns a Boolean result (for complex conditions)

When the condition is left empty or the condition evaluates to true, the THEN block is executed. If the condition evaluates to false, the optional ELSE block is executed. Both blocks provide the same capabilities:

▶ Assigning values to data objects in the context

▶ Processing of expressions and updating context data objects from expression results

▶ Processing of other rules

▶ Execution of an action

A block can include many operations that are executed sequentially. Therefore, it is possible to, first, execute an expression to calculate the value of a ruleset variable and, second, to use it in another expression within in the same block of a rule. Rules are self-contained objects and may be reused across rulesets. Rules can be maintained embedded into a ruleset or stand-alone.

Expressions

Rules can call expressions, actions, and other rules. Several expression types are available. Expression types define the computational power of BRFplus. Each expression type is a self-contained computational unit with a well-defined logic. The data to be processed via an expression type is defined by expressions. Thus, an expression can be considered to be an instance of an expression type, behaving according to the expression type's logic.

In general, an expression uses some input to calculate or derive some output, called the result. The input sources may either be context data objects or the results of nested expressions. BRFplus comes with a set of common expression types and is regularly enhanced by improved or new expression types. Table 14.7 contains a list most popular expression types used in BRFplus.

Expression Type	Description
Boolean	Boolean arithmetic for any number of operands (all combinations with AND, OR, and NOT are possible)
BRMS connector	Connects to an external business rules management system (BRMS) such as SAP NetWeaver BRM
Case	Arbitrary number of results, depending on input value; works like the ABAP CASE statement
Constant	Returns a constant value
DB lookup	Retrieves values from the database or performs an existence check
Decision table	Sequentially processes a table of conditions and results; returns either the first or all rows where the condition matches
Decision tree	Traverses a binary tree with nodes carrying conditions and leafs carrying results
Formula	Allows the definition of complex formulas to be evaluated at runtime
Loop	Repeats a sequence of operations on an array of data
Procedure call	Calls an ABAP procedure (method or function module)
Random number	Returns a random value or indicates whether a specified probability was met
Search tree	Traverses a nonbinary tree with nodes carrying conditions and leafs carrying results
Table operation	Operates on entire tables to carry out aggregations, existence checks, and line counts
Value range	Checks if a given value lies within a certain range

Table 14.7 Expression Types

The rules in the ruleset Price Calc. Rules use four expressions, of which two are decision tables and two are formulas:

▶ Decision table DecTab Cus. Discount

▶ Decision table DecTab Promo Discount

▶ Formula Apply Promotion

▶ Formula Apply Cus Discount

Figure 14.35 shows a decision table expression used to determine the numeric value Customer Discount based on the two inputs Item and Customer, which are contained in the context. There are two lines for customer SAP. Empty cells indicate that all values are accepted and no check is done. The table is processed top to bottom. When all cells in a row evaluate to true, the result is returned and processing is stopped. In this case you can read the decision table as "If Item is Ballpen or Pen and Customer is SAP, the Customer Discount is 0.12."

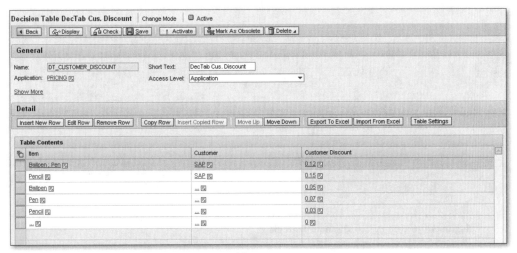

Figure 14.35 DecTab Cus. Discount Decision Table

Decision tables are used where the rules have a similar structure — the same condition elements and results being combined in different rules. The decision table allows many condition columns and result columns and still performs very efficiently, even with thousands of lines. It has features to handle completeness and consistency and exchange with Microsoft Excel.

Figure 14.36 shows a formula expression to calculate the final price based on shelf price and customer discount. This is the customer discount that was determined by the decision table DECTAB CUS. DISCOUNT in a previous rule. Formula expressions work like calculators, with the addition of using the context data objects as variables. There are also a variety of formula functions available to calculate durations, absolute values, square roots, and so on.

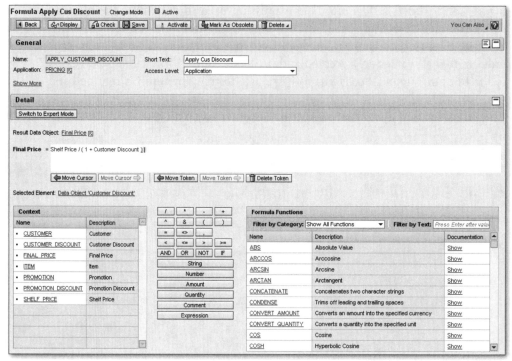

Figure 14.36 Apply Cus Discount Formula

Actions

Action types define the interactive part of BRFplus. Action types are special kinds of expressions types. An instance of an action type is called action. Actions do not have a result, but they can carry out activities that leave the borders of BRFplus (side effect). Similar to expressions, actions can use nested expressions and context data as input to accomplish their work. Usually, action types are more application-dependent than expression types. Hence, only a few generic action types are shipped with BRFplus. These are listed in Table 14.8.

Action and expression types can be also created by partners and customers to implement specific logic to the customer use case. Many more action and expression types have been added by SAP applications using BRFplus.

Action Type	Description
Call procedure	Calls an ABAP procedure (method or function module)
Log message	Writes a message into a message log
Raise event	Raises a business event
Send email	Sends an email to a specified list of recipients
Start workflow	Triggers the SAP business workflow

Table 14.8 Action Types

Simulation

The business logic modeled in the business rules can become very complex. When this happens, it is very helpful to use the simulation capabilities of BRFplus to test the rules against sample data. The tool generates a dialog to define the inputs for the various data objects in the context of the function. Figure 14.37 shows the dialog to simulate the price calculation function. It is also possible to upload data from a Microsoft Excel file.

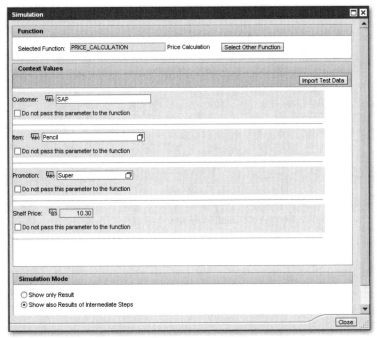

Figure 14.37 Simulation Dialog for Price Calculation Function

The simulation tool allows function testing with test data in two modes:

▶ Show only Result

▶ Show also Results of Intermediate Steps

The second mode with the intermediate steps, in particular, can help find the source of a problem when the processing output does not meet the expectations. Figure 14.38 shows a result protocol of the simulation. The root node represents the function. In Figure 14.38 you can see the context values and rulesets that are assigned to the function. In the rulesets there are the rules and calls to expressions (and actions if available). Each value change is highlighted in the value column. At the very top the result is shown.

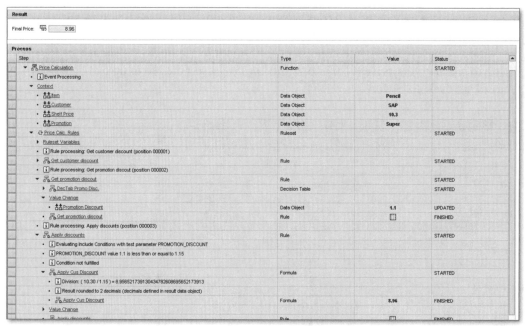

Figure 14.38 Simulation Result for the Price Calculation Function

Catalog

A catalog simplifies the rules maintenance process for the business user by hiding the repository and displaying only the relevant objects that are necessary for the maintenance of business rules in a given business scenario. A catalog comprises three node types:

- ▸ Structure nodes
- ▸ Object nodes
- ▸ Link nodes

Structure nodes provide the option to organize the catalog content in folders; object nodes have references to BRFplus objects such as expressions, rulesets, or functions; and link nodes have references to nodes from other catalogs and allow you to embed one catalog or nodes from one catalog into another catalog. Working with and organizing BRFplus objects in catalogs can be compared with working in Microsoft Explorer, which also allows you to create folders and organize files.

Figure 14.39 shows a catalog containing all of the objects of the price calculation example. On the left-hand side the catalog structure shows how the folders and BRFplus artifacts are organized. The right-hand side is used to display or change a specific object from the catalog. In combination with configuration and authorizations, a catalog can be an effective way to simplify the user interface and manage the visibility of objects and features for different user groups.

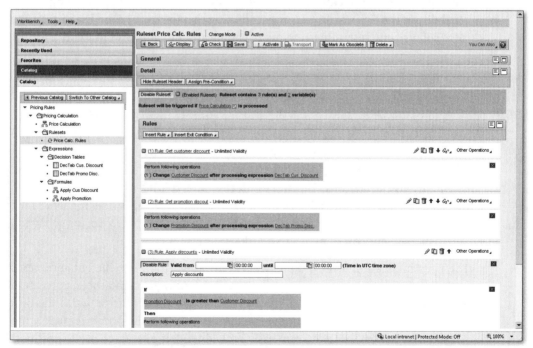

Figure 14.39 Pricing Rules Catalog

BRFplus thus allows business users to find the rules that matter to their business, explore and understand the rules, change and simulate/test them, and ultimately manage the rules.

BRFplus Adoption

BRFplus is included in many SAP standard applications in SAP ERP and SAP Business ByDesign such as SAP CRM Loyalty Management, SAP CRM Territory Management, SAP Transportation Management, SAP Advanced Metering Infrastructure, SAP BusinessObjects Governance, Risk, and Compliance Solutions, risk management and SAP Master Data Governance. The range of usages spans from very simple decision scenarios to highly complex rules processing. A simple case is, for example, in the SAP Business ByDesign HR module the determination of a provision variant in the expense report that is based on a simple decision table.

In contrast to that there is the usage of BRFplus in Grantor Management as of SAP ERP 6.0, enhancement package 5. Grantor Management is an SAP solution in the public sector domain that contains the processes needed for managing grants, from the application to the closing of the grant. Business rules are such an important capability of the Grantor Management solution that the quality and usability of the rules component determines the overall application quality and usability.

SAP Social Services Management for Public Sector is a similar case. BRFplus is used to manage monetary social benefits. Rules are managed in BRFplus for benefit determination and deduction calculations. This decision-making takes place early in the process, allowing the rest of the process to be executed directly from net calculations to billing documents, accounting, invoicing and payment, and account management follow-up when necessary. BRFplus rules handle validation of applications for benefits, case assignment, entitlement determination, and all of the various calculations. The end result combines a front-office decision-making processes with an automated back-office solution that leverages functionality in the social case management component in SAP CRM and the public sector collection and disbursement component in SAP ERP.

The tight integration with BRFplus allows for application-specific enhancements in the form of action and expression types and automatic data objects creation and bundling of forms with BRFplus functions. Only BRFplus provides the best possible performance and seamless integration. Out-of-the-box integration, no additional installations, and seamlessly embedded UIs guarantee the lowest possible total cost of ownership.

Since 2008 several new SAP applications have included BRFplus. Also since then several SAP applications have migrated from various tools and engines to BRFplus to power the application with state of the art business rules. First, the focus was on pilots for migration from BRF and Derivation Tool to BRFplus. An important pilot application was SAP Tax and Revenue Management for Public Sector that migrated from BRF to BRFplus with SAP ERP 6, enhancement package 5. Switching in SAP Tax and Revenue Management for Public Sector from BRF to BRFplus significantly reduces the TCO, improves performances by 70 to 80 percent, and reduces the effort for changes because of changes legislation by 60 to 70 percent. Only after migration to BRFplus are business experts able to understand the business logic and directly implement the required changes in BRFplus.

Today, any SAP application using business rules technology in the ABAP stack other than BRFplus is a migration candidate because BRFplus has been defined as the must-use BRMS for all ABAP-based applications. However, in some cases more investment in BRFplus is needed for smooth migration that will make migration a continuous effort over the following years.

14.4.4 SAP NetWeaver Business Rules Management

SAP NetWeaver Business Rules Management (BRM) is a set of pure Java components that provides rules modeling, management, and execution; versioning; and governance capabilities. SAP NetWeaver BRM ships as part of SAP NetWeaver Composition Environment (CE).

SAP NetWeaver BRM Components

SAP NetWeaver BRM has the following components:

▶ Rules composer

▶ Rules manager

▶ Rules repository

▶ Rules engine

The *rules composer* is the modeling and implementation environment for business rules. It provides a set of tools for rules modeling and implementation. The rules composer also allows generation of an HTML document with all artifacts such as rulesets, flow rulesets, definitions, decision tables, and so on.

It is optimized for business rules developers but may also be used by business analysts. The rules composer supports a variety of data model definitions and an environment to validate and regression-test business rules.

These functionalities are available in two flavors: from within SAP NetWeaver Business Process Management (SAP NetWeaver BPM) process composer to model rules in a business process context and as a separate perspective in SAP NetWeaver CE to model rules to be used by non-BPM composite applications. The rules composer is based on the open Eclipse platform.

The *rules manager* is a rules runtime authoring tool for business analysts and business rules owners. It provides a Web-based interface for maintenance and administration of business rules. Further, it contains Web-based collaborative functionality for modeling, editing, and managing business rules by business analysts.

SAP NetWeaver BRM provides complete lifecycle change management capabilities for securing, governing, and managing business rules. The *rules repository* is the environment that provides rules versioning and other repository services that enable the auditable change history of rules.

SAP NetWeaver BRM provides both design-time and runtime rules repository services. Business users can completely coordinate management and review and change approval activities in a collaborative fashion using a secure and protected Web-based business user interface.

Access management, reporting services, traceability, and change approval mechanisms enable organizations to perform rules asset management, having the security of managing their business rules as concisely as any other organizational asset.

The *rules engine* is the runtime component that serves as a decision delivery vehicle. It represents the runtime for rules execution.

The rules engine has different algorithm implementations for Rete inferencing, decision table execution, and sequential rules. A connector to BRFplus is available for ABAP-based business applications and out-of-the-box integration for rules-enabled composite applications, services, or business processes.

Integrated rule engine execution, logging, and decision justification capabilities provide organizations with the ability to revise conditions and reasons why certain decisions were made for fulfilling auditing and compliance requirements.

Business rules must be available for consumption across the entire application stack. Business rules are a concept that is ubiquitous. They are used by business applications of all varieties:

▶ Composite applications

▶ Modeled business processes

▶ Backend applications

Therefore, the following possibilities to use the rule engine are provided:

▶ A JEE application can look up and invoke the rule engine as a stateless session bean.

▶ A Web service (decision or rules service) can be created that will look up and invoke the rule engine as a stateless session bean internally. This Web service can be exposed as a reusable Web service.

Authoring Business Rules with SAP NetWeaver BRM

It is very easy to model rules using SAP NetWeaver BRM. The following are a set of steps to create rules as required:

1. Create business rules vocabulary.

2. Create definitions.

3. Create enumerations.

4. Create aliases.

5. Create a ruleset.

6. Create rules.

7. Create decision tables.

8. Create a flow ruleset.

9. Create a rule script.

10. Create a rule flow.

11. Test rules.

The steps are described in the following text with help of a simplified example of student fee calculation.

Business Rules Vocabulary

The business rules vocabulary defines the link to underlying program objects and the terminology on which the business rules are written. It consists of three concepts: definitions, enumerations and aliases.

A definition in the rules composer, shown in Figure 14.40, represents a business term or a local computational variable required in a business rules model. A common definition is a definition that can be used across many rulesets. Common definitions can be fixed or variable. During the processing of a list of order items, a definition can be created called `CurrentOrderItem` to identify the current item being processed.

Figure 14.40   Definitions in Rules Composer

An enumeration type allows you to define an abstract type that holds a list of values that are logically related in a given context. For example, you can define an enumeration type `Customer Status` with the values `Basic`, `Silver`, `Gold`, and `Platinum`. When creating rules or decision table rows, it is not necessary to type in values, but instead a dropdown menu is dynamically created.

Aliases allow you to express a rule in a manner that is easy to understand. Functional users can manage rules without knowing the underlying code. An alias hides the underlying technical data definitions such as XML schemas and its elements or Java classes with attributes and methods. The rules are presented to the user in a simple and natural language. For example, there may be a class `Buyer` and a method `getName` that has the alias `the buyer's name`. The alias can then be used in rules such as `If the buyer's name is Joe`.

Ruleset

A ruleset is a logical collection of rules. A ruleset helps you group business rules that govern a specific function. A simple If-Then ruleset consists of If-Then rules and decision tables. Figure 14.41 shows a ruleset in the rules composer. It contains several rules and two decision tables.

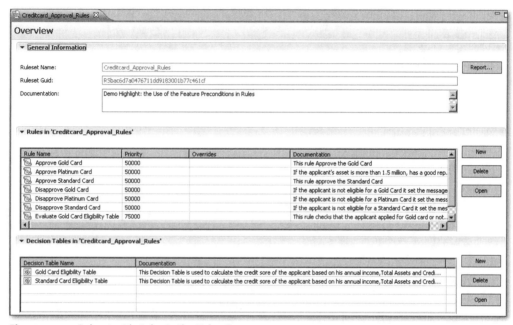

Figure 14.41 Ruleset with Rules in the Rules Composer

Rules

A rule is a set of conditions and associated actions that are performed when the conditions are satisfied. Rules can be written in two forms:

▶ If-Then statements

▶ Decision tables

A simple if-then rule contains the condition and the action parts, where the condition is the "If" part of a rule, with the LHS (left-hand side) value, the comparator, and the RHS (right-hand side) value. A condition is said to evaluate as true if the LHS value and RHS value satisfy the comparison relationship.

The action is the "Then" part of a rule. These are the steps to be taken when a rule is satisfied. There are six types of actions: assert, assign, execute, reevaluate, retract, and evaluate decision table. Whereas execute and assign relate to the application, assert, retract, and reevaluate affect the way other rules are evaluated. Figure 14.42 shows the rule Approve Platinum Card with a condition (If) and action (Then).

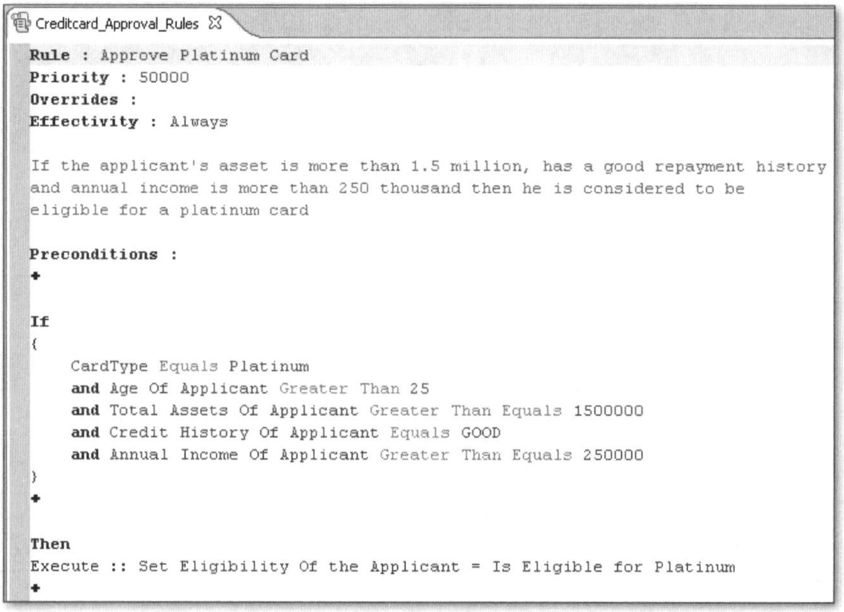

```
Creditcard_Approval_Rules ⊠

Rule : Approve Platinum Card
Priority : 50000
Overrides :
Effectivity : Always

If the applicant's asset is more than 1.5 million, has a good repayment history
and annual income is more than 250 thousand then he is considered to be
eligible for a platinum card

Preconditions :
✦

If
{
    CardType Equals Platinum
    and Age Of Applicant Greater Than 25
    and Total Assets Of Applicant Greater Than Equals 1500000
    and Credit History Of Applicant Equals GOOD
    and Annual Income Of Applicant Greater Than Equals 250000
}
✦

Then
Execute :: Set Eligibility Of the Applicant = Is Eligible for Platinum
✦
```

Figure 14.42 A Rule in the Rule Composer

Decision Tables

A decision table is a tabular representation of related rules. Instead of maintaining a list of rules with conditions and actions operating on the same definitions, the rules are better converted into a decision table. Figure 14.43 shows a decision table with many eligibility rules. Instead of the well-organized tabular format, the rules could also be written with the condition and action pattern such as:

▶ "If Credit History of Application is GOOD and Annual Income of Applicant <50000 and Total Assets of Applicant <100000 Then Credit Score = 42"

▸ "If Credit History of Application is MODERATE and Annual Income of Applicant < 50000 and Total Assets of Applicant <100000 Then Credit Score = 37"

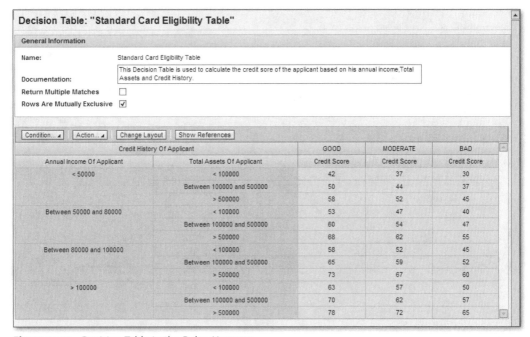

Figure 14.43 Decision Table in the Rules Manager

Flow Rulesets

A flow ruleset is a ruleset providing capabilities to group business rules that need to be executed as in a flow chart. It always has one flow, designated as main flow, and possibly many other rule flows. The execution of the flow ruleset starts with the main flow. A flow ruleset uses aliases and definitions. It also consists of:

▸ If-Then rules

▸ Decision tables

▸ Rule flows

▸ Rule scripts

Figure 14.44 shows a flow ruleset for credit card eligibility checks. It contains a main flow, three rule scripts, two decision tables, and several rules.

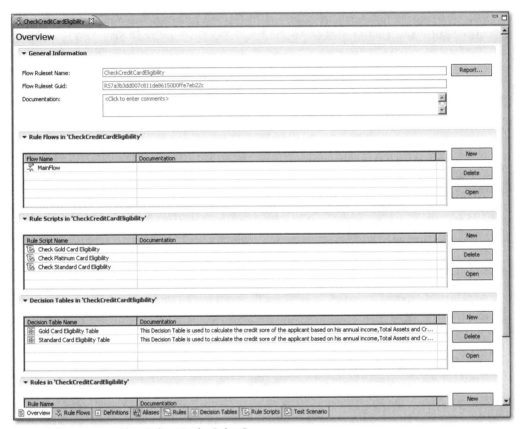

Figure 14.44   Flow Ruleset in the Rules Composer

Rule Scripts

A rule script is a reusable artifact within a flow ruleset and is a sequence of actions. It is associated with other activities in a flow ruleset and is triggered when the conditions listed in the preceding activities are satisfied. A rule script can contain any of the following action types: assign, assert, evaluate decision table, execute, execute ruleset, execute rule, for each, if-else-if, while, retract, break, and continue. Figure 14.45 shows a rule script for a platinum card eligibility check as a reusable artifact.

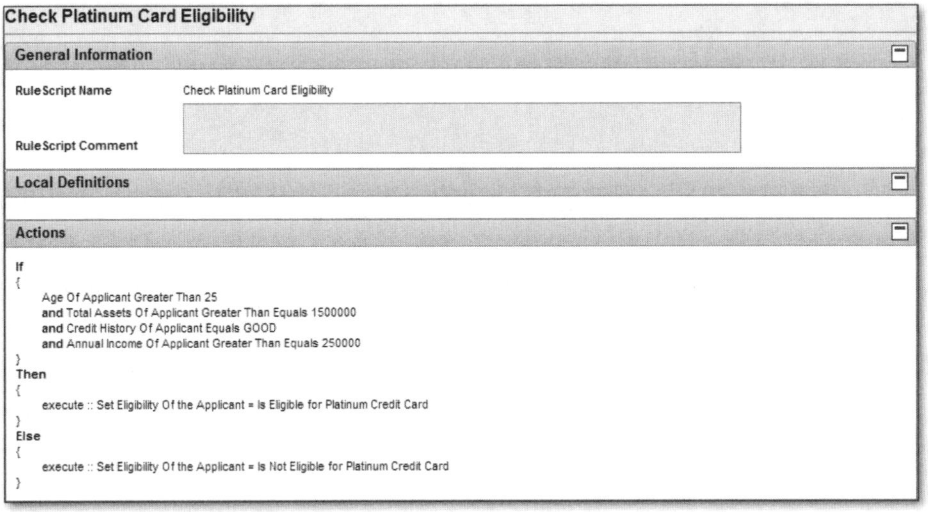

Check Platinum Card Eligibility

General Information

RuleScript Name   Check Platinum Card Eligibility

RuleScript Comment

Local Definitions

Actions

```
If
{
    Age Of Applicant Greater Than 25
    and Total Assets Of Applicant Greater Than Equals 1500000
    and Credit History Of Applicant Equals GOOD
    and Annual Income Of Applicant Greater Than Equals 250000
}
Then
{
    execute :: Set Eligibility Of the Applicant = Is Eligible for Platinum Credit Card
}
Else
{
    execute :: Set Eligibility Of the Applicant = Is Not Eligible for Platinum Credit Card
}
```

Figure 14.45 Rule Script in the Rules Manager

Rule Flows

A rule flow is a sequence of activities for evaluating business rules. The order of the execution of the rules is diagrammatically represented in the form of a flow chart. It is a reusable entity within a flow ruleset and is based on activities associated with artifacts such as rule scripts, rule flows, rulesets, flow rulesets, rules, and decision tables. The artifacts and their activities are summarized in Table 14.9.

Artifact	Activity
Rule script	Execute rule script
Exclusive choice	Execute exclusive choice
Gateway	Gateway
Ruleset	Execute ruleset
If-Then rule	Execute If-Then rule
Decision table	Execute decision table
Rule flow	Execute rule flow

Table 14.9 Artifacts and Activities in Rule Flows

Figure 14.46 shows a rule flow for credit card eligibility checks. The rule flow consists of a gateway and three possible paths for the three card types: standard, gold, and platinum.

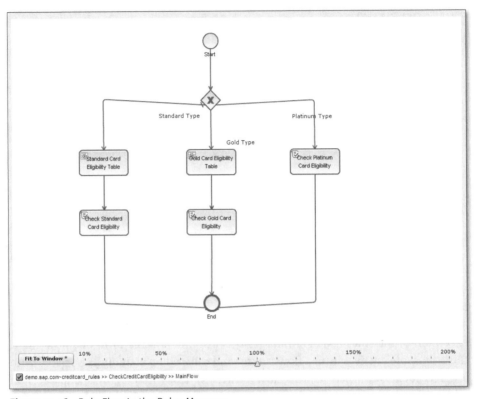

Figure 14.46 Rule Flow in the Rules Manager

A flow ruleset always has one rule flow, designated as the main flow, and possibly many other rule flows. The execution of the ruleset starts with the main flow.

Rules Testing

The rules testing feature allows business rules developers and analysts to test and validate the correctness of the rules before they go into the production stage. The tests are based on an XML schema and consist of a test target and test data.

Because the executable unit of any business rules project is a ruleset, the test target is an if-then ruleset or a flow ruleset that contain the rules that need to be tested given a set of input data and expected output data. Figure 14.47 shows the definition of a test case in the rules composer. Test data is the input and expected output data required for testing rules. The input data can be historical data or simulated data that is captured in a CSV file. The test target is invoked for each test data row.

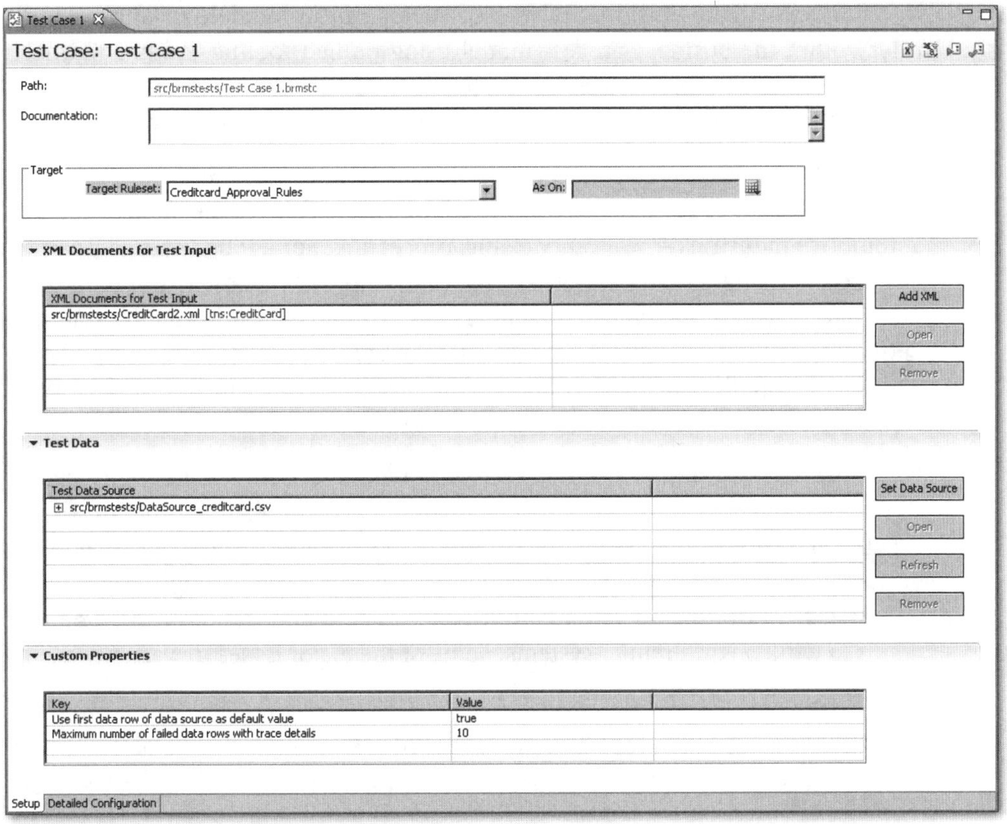

Figure 14.47 Test Case Editor in the Rules Composer

Integration into SAP NetWeaver BPM

Whereas application core processes represent business process Best Practices, composite business processes are Best Practices, differentiating processes that can over time also evolve into application core processes. Composite business processes are either human-centric (collaborative processes) or system-centric (integration processes). Many organizations recognize the need for composite applications at the edge of the application core for a specific functional area. SAP NetWeaver Business Process Management (BPM), offered as part of SAP NetWeaver Composition Environment supports model-driven development of business processes by business process experts.

SAP NetWeaver BRM compliments the SAP NetWeaver Business Process Management (BPM) by automating decisioning activities within a business process.

Decisioning activities inside a business process can be modeled using business rules within the business process model using unified tooling. Automated decisioning through business rules eliminates the need for human intervention in a business process, thus improving automation levels in business processes up to 80 to 90 percent.

In this context, let's review a common business process in the manufacturing and automotive industries — warranty claims processing. For a long time, company X has been working with a network of dealers to get their products to the market. They have partnered with many suppliers, and contracts have varied by supplier. Different dealers have different contract agreements with manufacturers, and contracts with suppliers or dealers have been changing over time. New dealers or suppliers have been joining the business ecosystem.

For company X, products normally vary by type and number; warranty claims can flow from customer to dealer to manufacturer to supplier, and the inventory cost is usually high when warranty claims are managed incorrectly. Also, multiple departments are usually involved in the whole process including IT, inventory, purchasing, recovery, and so on, and it is not uncommon for all of these departments to work on different IT systems. Some of the major issues in warranty claims processing are as follows:

▶ Warranty claims processing, validation, and review are all manual and prone to error activities. In some cases, the whole process can take up to six to eight weeks.

▶ Warranty policies and contracts are typically not strictly enforced. This can lead to fraudulent claims, incorrect billing, and excessive payments.

▶ When a supplier's contract changes, these changes may not flow back into the system immediately, leading to incorrect billing.

▶ The multiple departments (IT, inventory, purchasing, recovery) involved may not have the same visibility into the system, or may even use different systems. This can cause delays in payments for approved claims.

▶ Mistakes in separating the company's warranty responsibilities from those of suppliers or distributors result in covering costs that are the responsibility of others.

The implications of not improving process efficiency are summarized below:

▶ Time spent and resources engaged in manual processing increase go-to-market costs.

▶ The same resources cannot be channeled to perform other important activities, which adds to opportunity losses costs.

▶ The unrealized claim value can be about 20 percent, which could add up to tens of thousands of claims a year.

▶ Inefficient claims management means that inventory has to remain stocked. The consequences, as financial balances show, may be huge.

Communication gaps lead to poor data sharing about defects. Inefficient claims management may influence relationships with dealers and suppliers and may even affect customer satisfaction adversely.

It is clear that these policies and contracts can change, and hence the business process model should accommodate these changes. Also, such decisions can't be handled through human intervention in the process. Business rules and SAP NetWeaver BRM can address these problems.

SAP NetWeaver BRM enables the automation of operational policy decisions in an agile, precise, consistent, compliant, and auditable fashion while giving business users the control to influence business rules. SAP NetWeaver BRM stands out as an effective solution for similar business scenarios where a large scale of human and automated activities have to be performed in a concise, consistent, and timely manner, because it enables automation of critical guidelines and policy-driven decisions in a transparent and agile fashion.

14.4.5 Usage Recommendations

SAP business rules offerings — both BRFplus and SAP NetWeaver BRM — provide optimal support for applications in terms of flexibility, performance, and total cost of ownership. BRFplus and SAP NetWeaver BRM provide an integrated and holistic solution for different use cases such as:

▶ Business rules in SAP Business Suite applications and extensions

▶ Stand-alone business rules management

▶ Distributed business rules execution in a heterogeneous landscape across SAP and non-SAP solutions

The decision of which rules offering to use for a particular use case is often non-trivial and based on the specific challenges to be solved. Often, the choice of rule engine broadly depends on a combination of the following factors:

▶ Technology stack (execution environment) of the application

▶ The stack in which application data resides

▶ Features (such as Rete and flow rules or the ability to extend the BRMS)

As a rule of thumb, for best performance and integrated rule-editing experiences, we recommend using a rule engine that integrates deeply into the execution stack of business applications. Consequently, SAP provides two rule engines that seamlessly integrate with ABAP and Java stacks, respectively. For pure ABAP stack use cases, BRFplus shipped with SAP Business Suite is the best suited, whereas SAP NetWeaver BRM is best suited for pure Java use cases. For example, when a customer wants to leverage business rules in an SAP Business Suite application or add flexibility to an SAP Business Suite process, BRFplus would be the ideal choice. For customers creating composite applications and business processes using SAP NetWeaver CE, SAP NetWeaver BRM would be the ideal choice. The decision of which rules engine to use may go beyond technology stack considerations and hinge on the requirements of a particular use case.

In Figure 14.48, five usage recommendations are presented that can help in deciding which rule offering to use. On the horizontal axis there are the rule engines, SAP NetWeaver BRM and BRFplus, and on the vertical axis there are the SAP Business Suite core processes and composite applications (modeled processes).

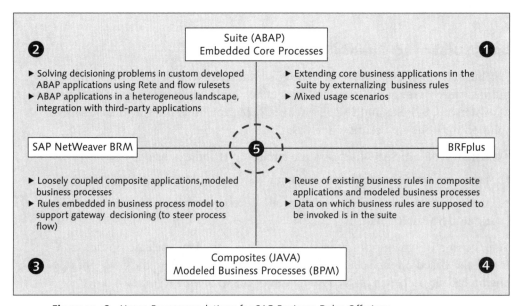

Figure 14.48 Usage Recommendations for SAP Business Rules Offerings

▶ **Quadrant ❶: custom developed SAP Business Suite applications using BRFplus**
Quadrant 1 characterizes standard use cases where BRFplus is used to solve business rules requirements for custom developed applications, which extend the business suite functionality. Custom developed applications can externalize business logic using BRFplus and improve the flexibility greatly. Because the execution environment and the application data reside on the ABAP stack, BRFplus is the natural technology fit in such cases, providing deep integration and best performance.

▶ **Quadrant ❷: custom developed SAP Business Suite applications using SAP NetWeaver BRM**
Quadrant 2 characterizes use cases where custom developed applications in the suite (ABAP stack) use SAP NetWeaver BRM for managing business rules. In such use cases applications may need Rete rules capabilities that are not available in BRFplus. Or applications may interact with non-SAP systems in a heterogeneous landscape, and the data needed for the business rule processing is mostly spread across this landscape. When applications in the ABAP stack use SAP NetWeaver BRM, it is possible to make the usage transparent by natively connecting to SAP NetWeaver BRM by using a BRFplus BRMS connector expression that is optimized for SAP NetWeaver BRM.

▶ **Quadrant ❸: composite applications using SAP NetWeaver BRM**
Quadrant 3 characterizes use cases where composites developed with SAP NetWeaver Composition Environment (CE) use SAP NetWeaver BRM natively. SAP NetWeaver BRM is closely integrated with SAP NetWeaver Business Process Management, so modeled business processes use SAP NetWeaver BRM to solve decisioning problems.

▶ **Quadrant ❹: composite applications using BRFplus**
Quadrant 4 characterizes use cases where composite applications developed using SAP NetWeaver CE and modeled business processes in SAP NetWeaver BPM use existing business rules in the core suite applications designed using BRFplus. In these use cases, composites leverage existing rules in BRFplus by calling them as Web services.

▶ **Circle ❺: mixed-usage scenarios with BRFplus and SAP NetWeaver BRM**
In addition to BRFplus-only and SAP NetWeaver BRM-only usage scenarios in the four quadrants, there is an increasing need for mixed usage scenarios in which BRFplus and SAP NetWeaver BRM are used together in heterogeneous environments involving both SAP and non-SAP systems. Several use cases require business rules to be modeled in a single place and executed in both BRFplus and SAP NetWeaver BRM within the same scenario.

The five usage recommendations presented here are for the specific use case characteristics described above. Most customer use cases fit in these quadrants. Hence, the five usage recommendations could serve as a reference plan for making a decision about which SAP business rule offering to use.

BRFplus and SAP NetWeaver BRM independently support several business rules use cases in a heterogeneous customer landscape. Increasingly, there are cases where both BRFplus and SAP NetWeaver BRM are used to solve decisioning problems.

There are several mixed-usage scenarios where out-of-the-box core business processes in the suite are enhanced or customized in composites using SAP NetWeaver Composition Environment (CE). Business rules that underlie core business suite processes and applications have to be either reused or enhanced for the composites leading to mixed usage.

In order to support mixed usage scenarios and support close integrations between SAP's BRMS offerings (BRFplus and SAP NetWeaver BRM), alignment activities have been defined. These are centered on five themes discussed below.

▶ **Vocabulary alignment for modeling business rules**
It is important to have a common business vocabulary — a set of terms and definitions — to model business rules. The goal is to support common vocabulary across BRFplus and SAP NetWeaver BRM for definition of business rules. Business vocabulary shall be specified using ABAP Data Dictionary objects (DDIC), SAP Global Data Types (GDTs) and native XSD schemas and be used for defining business rules in both BRM and BRFplus.

▶ **Harmonized user-experience for business users**
Business users prefer easy-to-use, intuitive user interfaces to modify and maintain business rules. The goal is to support a harmonized user-experience for business users across SAP NetWeaver BRM and BRFplus, especially for business-user relevant artifacts such as decision tables.

▶ **Unified search for rule artifacts**
Capabilities to search and navigate to business rules spread across several systems and repositories is of foremost importance in complex and heterogeneous IT environments. Such a capability will ultimately lead to a higher degree of control, automation, and better decisions. We will support a unified search interface for business rules artifacts such as rules, rulesets, expressions, actions, and vocabulary objects from both BRFplus as well as SAP NetWeaver BRM repositories.

▶ **Exchange and cross-invocation of rules artifacts**
Currently it is possible to invoke SAP NetWeaver BRM rules from BRFplus. The next step is to support invocation for BRFplus rules from SAP NetWeaver BRM using an optimized infrastructure using a simple FIND-INVOKE model. Also, support of exchange of business rules artifacts such as decision tables from SAP NetWeaver BRM to BRFplus, and vice-versa, is planned.

▶ **Rules management, analytics, and pre-shipped content**
Provisioning of central management capabilities in the form of a management console for managing the lifecycle of rule artifacts across SAP NetWeaver BRM and BRFplus is rounding off the alignment capabilities. The business rules management console shall support central authorization, exchange of rules, and support monitoring of rule execution, including rule analytics. Also, support for pre-shipped rules content, which can be turned on and off using simple switches, is planned.

We believe that these five alignment themes outlined above will bring the two SAP Business Rules offerings together and support mixed usage scenarios more seamlessly in customer environments. However, these themes are still intended strategies to bring BRFplus and SAP NetWeaver BRM together at the time of writing this book, some of which may change based on feedback and newer requirements, both internally from SAP products as well as externally from customer response.

14.5 Simple Sample Application for Enterprise Service Consumption

With service-oriented architecture and SAP NetWeaver's SOA platform, it is possible to encapsulate business logic and expose it as enterprise services — smaller functionality components enabling the rapid composition of business solutions that meet changing business requirements.

SAP has provided a high number of enterprise services, which addresses a wide variety of business tasks. Most enterprise services have complex interfaces with many parameters; each parameter requires a specific data type and has its own business semantic. Hence, it is quite difficult to understand and consume enterprise services without the right information, examples, and test data.

In the following sections we will introduce simple sample applications for enterprise service consumption and SAP's Enterprise Services Workplace site. In more detail we will then describe how to utilize the different resources come with simple samples and are offered free of charge.

To help consumers of enterprise services, SAP offers simple sample applications. Simple samples are ready-to-run composite applications for the most commonly used enterprise services and various SAP consumption technologies. As of September 2010, SAP offers more than 60 simple samples demonstrating more than 150 enterprise services. The samples cover business processes from the topics:

- Sales and CRM
- Customer service
- Procurement
- Quality management
- Real estate management
- Inventory management
- Enterprise asset management
- Human capital management
- Manufacturing and supply chain management (SCM)

They utilize the following consumption technologies:

- SAP NetWeaver Visual Composer
- Web Dynpro for Java
- Web Dynpro for ABAP
- SAP NetWeaver Business Process Management with Web Dynpro for Java

Focusing on SAP NetWeaver BPM, we will describe the available simple sample use cases for this consumption technology in more detail. The offering includes the following six BPM simple samples (as of September 2010):

- **Approve Purchase Requisition and Create Purchase Order (Procurement)**
  This simple sample demonstrates how a requester can create a purchase requisition that then is forwarded to the approver. If the request is approved according to the defined release strategy in the backend, it is forwarded to the purchaser, who triggers creation of the purchase order. In case of rejection, the requester is notified and the process ends.

- **Approve Sales Order Change Request (Sales and CRM)**
  In this simple sample an account executive requests a price change (discount) for an existing sales order. The sales manager must then approve the request if it exceeds a defined limit. In case of approval (or if the limit holds), the sales

order is updated in background. A notification about the outcome is sent back to the account executive.

▶ **External Quality Inspection (Quality Management)**
The external quality inspection process refers to the creation of a material inspection and sending the same to an external laboratory for inspection. This simple sample demonstrates how enterprise services and SAP NetWeaver BPM can be used to quickly and easily perform the following parts of the external quality inspection: create material inspection, record results, record defects, and create usage decision. After starting the process, the quality inspector creates the material inspection for the material to inspect and a work item for the external laboratory technician. Next, the laboratory technician reviews the inspection lot and records the results of the assigned inspection plan. If necessary, the laboratory technician records any defects in the results. The work item is then sent back to the quality inspector for a final usage decision.

▶ **Manage Leave Request (Human Capital Management)**
This simple sample demonstrates how to process a leave request. Two roles are involved: an employee and the corresponding manager. In the first process step, the employee creates a leave request that is forwarded to the manager for approval. In the second process step, the manager approves or rejects the employee's leave request.

▶ **Phase In Equipment (Enterprise Asset Management)**
The equipment phase in a process generally refers to the creation of the equipment master data (installation). This BPM simple sample demonstrates how this could be done easily using enterprise services. The process starts with the process initiator, who requests the phase-in of particular equipment. The maintenance engineer is then guided through a roadmap for creating the equipment master data. Subsequently, the maintenance planner is guided through a roadmap for creating the measuring device and maintenance plan.

▶ **Unexpected Returns Handling (Sales and CRM)**
If a warehouse clerk receives an unexpected return from a customer, the return has to be approved by an account executive and checked by a quality clerk to decide on further usage. This BPM simple sample demonstrates how this process can be simplified and automated. A warehouse clerk prepares an unexpected customer return by identifying the material and customer. The information is forwarded to an account executive for approval. If the return is approved, a customer return, a customer return delivery, and posts of the goods receipt are created in the background. In the next step the quality clerk has to check the condition of the returned goods and decides if they can be used for unrestricted

shipment or if they have to be scraped. Based on this decision, an automatic step creates a goods movement accordingly.

Simple sample applications demonstrate end-to-end what it takes to build a small composite application for typical but nonstandard use cases, using enterprise services and consumption technologies that SAP delivers. You can take them as starting points for your own SOA projects to lower the hurdle to deal with new technology. Nevertheless, simple samples are for educational purposes only and are not intended for productive usage. Therefore, no maintenance obligation from SAP is associated with them.

The simple sample offering is part of SAP's Enterprise Services Workplace site (ES Workplace). The ES Workplace site (*http://esworkplace.sap.com/*) is the central place to view consolidated information about all available enterprise services delivered by SAP (see Figure 14.49). It provides various entry points for different roles, from developers to process experts. ES Workplace is the starting point for SOA adoption, from discovery of services to evaluation of services and test driving simple sample applications.

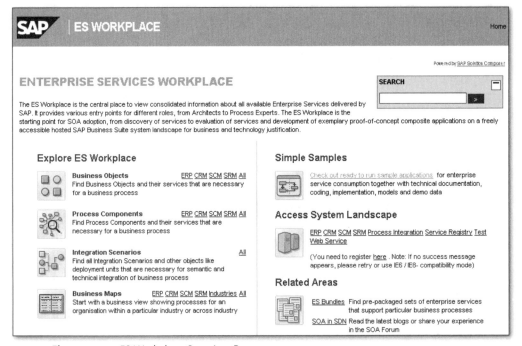

Figure 14.49 ES Workplace Overview Page

To be able to access the hosted environment free of charge, you need to register only once for ES Workplace systems via SDN.

For each simple sample application, the following assets are available:

▶ **Online demo version**
A demo on a hosted sandbox environment that is available for all SAP Business Suite solutions with IDES sample data to test-drive sample applications and services.

▶ **Documentation**
Includes comprehensive technical and nontechnical information about the business process, details of the implementation, and how the services are called (e.g., which fields and sample data are used).

▶ **Source code file (SCA)**
Source code ready to be imported into your local SAP NetWeaver Developer Studio.

▶ **List of enterprise services**
Consumed within the simple sample with links to the service documentation.

▶ **Test data**
Test your application (for all consumed enterprise services) with data that is ready to download and includes links to execute the simple samples within SAP's sandbox environment.

The sandbox environment provided by ES Workplace offers SAP Business Suite systems with recent enhancement packages of SAP ERP, SAP CRM, SAP SCM, SAP SRM, and SAP NetWeaver Process Integration (PI) together with preinstalled IDES data. After you have registered for ES Workplace, you can freely access and use these systems to:

▶ Test-drive all available enterprise services using hosted Web Service Navigator (WS Navigator) or any other consumption tool.

▶ Run simple sample applications on the also hosted SAP NetWeaver Composition Environment (CE).

▶ Call enterprise services out of locally installed test applications (e.g., downloaded simple samples).

▶ Log on directly via WebGUI to check IDES data and results from service executions.

On each simple sample page you will find a RUN THIS SAMPLE button that, after logon with the ES Workplace account, starts the sample on SAP's hosted SAP NetWeaver CE. For an SAP NetWeaver BPM-based simple sample you will be redirected to the integrated SAP Portal, where you have access to your Universal Worklist (UWL) and other BPM simple samples (see Figure 14.50). All other simple samples start directly with the first screen in a new window because they don't require the Universal Worklist in the portal.

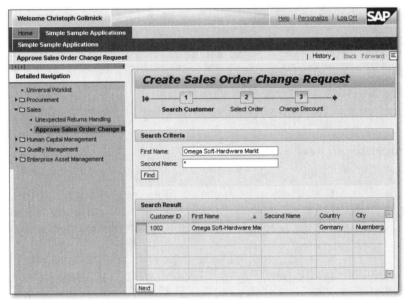

Figure 14.50 Run a BPM Simple Sample

To be able to demonstrate BPM processes with different roles using only one ES Workplace account, BPM samples map their activities to the logon user. In a productive system you would not do that, but for educational purposes this special configuration fits best.

Also, most of the required input fields in screens are prefilled with known-to-work test data. Sometimes you have to enter a custom name or description text, but in general you can run through simple samples by just clicking the Next buttons and selecting new items from the UWL. This gives you a quick start that doesn't require reading through the documentation first. However, the documentation describes the process and steps in detail and contains additional information for developers regarding the service fields and test data used within the simple sample.

Besides the online demo, each Java-based simple sample can be downloaded as source code (software component archive). The SCA can then be imported to a locally installed SAP NetWeaver Developer Studio (NWDS) system where you can explore and modify process models and screens (see Figure 14.51). If you do so, please keep in mind that simple samples are for educational purposes only and that no maintenance obligation from SAP is associated with them. For simple samples based on ABAP technology you can directly view the sources using the Web Application Builder via WebGUI.

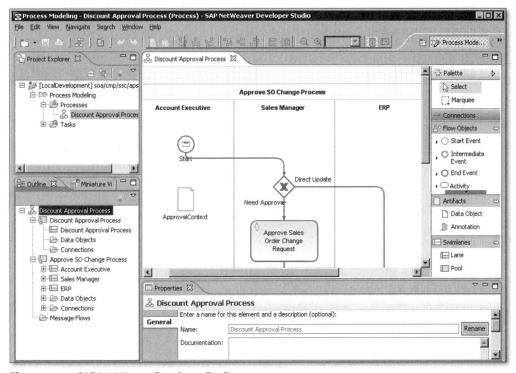

Figure 14.51 SAP NetWeaver Developer Studio

To run simple samples locally SAP NetWeaver CE 7.1 enhancement package 1 is sufficient and can be obtained together with SAP NWDS free of charge as a preview from SDN. An installation and configuration guide will lead you through the additional steps to take to run simple samples, especially how to configure a local SAP NetWeaver CE system to use SAP's sandbox systems for service execution. You can download the guide from each simple sample's individual web page.

Each service documentation and simple sample page offers to invoke a test of enterprise services with SAP's Web Services (WS) Navigator tool (see Figure 14.52). When you click on the link, you need to log on twice, first to the SAP NetWeaver CE Server (to start the WS Navigator) and then to the backend (to authorize the upcoming service calls) using your ES Workplace account. After successful logon the screen presents the parameter input tree, where you can specify the input values for the service execution. If you followed the link from a simple sample test data page, the tree will be prefilled with test data originating from the business context of the simple sample. Clicking the NEXT button executes the service against the respective ES Workplace backend, and the result is presented on the right side in tree format and as downloadable XML.

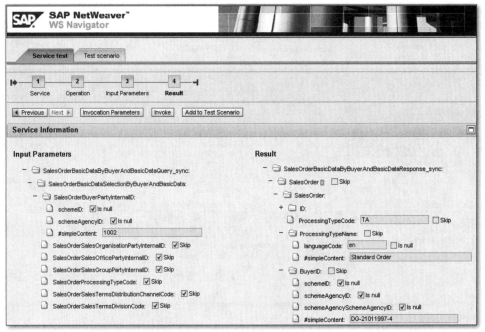

Figure 14.52 WS Navigator

The ES Workplace team will further extend the portfolio of simple samples. Please join the discussions about simple samples on SDN. To help SAP improve their simple sample offering, we encourage you to fill out the simple sample feedback form on the ES Workplace site.

"The secret of getting ahead is getting started."
– Mark Twain

15 Process-Based Implementation Content

Ann Rosenberg, Oleg Figlin, Rogan Morrison, Steve Rittinghaus

In this chapter we will explore prepackaged implementation content that is based on SAP Business Suite best practices, best insight, and own practices, also referred to as composite applications. The composite applications can be built on top of the SAP Business Suite best practices with the application core processes and on arbitrary backend systems. Composite applications follow the SOA paradigm of non-intrusiveness, which means these applications are bound to provide modification-free process extensions to the core business applications. This prepackaged content enables the building of process-based and easier to consume solutions within your SAP-centric business and IT environment. The prepackaged content also enables simpler, shorter, and less disruptive implementations.

If we have a closer look at the automobile platform and learn from its success over the past decades, we can see that one of the main success factors is its structure built of predefined modular pieces that enable easier, faster, and high-quality assembly. This model brings huge benefits both to customers and companies, so why not adopt and transform this approach into an SAP implementation?

In an SAP implementation these predefined modular pieces are process-based implementation content and services that project managers and consultants can access and assemble just like they do in the automotive industry. SAP uses different implementation content concepts (illustrated in Figure 15.1) that can be used in different consumption scenarios. In this chapter we will introduce some of these concepts: business add-ons to ASAP that deliver implementation content (see Section 15.1) and rapid deployment solutions (see Section 15.2). We will start with the business add-ons to ASAP.

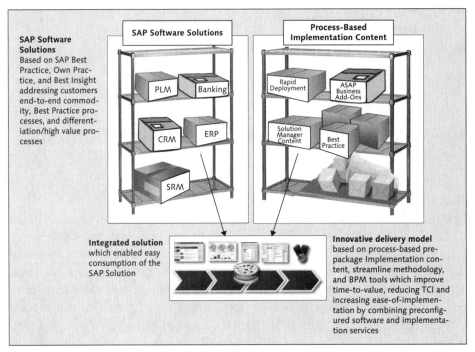

Figure 15.1 Implementation Content

15.1 Business Add-Ons to ASAP that Deliver Implementation Content

As introduced in Chapter 13, Section 13.4, in June 2010 SAP released the first wave of business add-ons to ASAP, which consist of three categories. The first category of add-on was introduced in Section 13.4.4. In this chapter we will go into details of the last two categories: implementation content packages and small, innovative BPM/SOA-based content packages. The add-ons can include content such as flavor methodology (project scope statement, configuration guide, etc.), business content (business process structure, process descriptions, value drivers, KPIs/PPIs), implementation content (solution descriptions, links to IMG objects, transactions, SOA services, test cases, etc.), and enablement content (education, literature, white papers, service offerings, starter kits, etc.).

Let's start with an example of the implementation content package category, where we will introduce the business add-ons to ASAP that deliver SAP point of sales implementation content within trade. The purpose of the example in Section 15.1.1 is to illustrate how process-based implementation content can be consumed in a SAP implementation, including configuration, SOA Composite, etc. Then we will look at the last category, small, innovative BPM/SOA-based content packages, where we will introduce business add-ons to ASAP that deliver implementation content for social media (Twitter customer service and marketing campaign), workflows on the BlackBerry, and the Supply Network Planning (SNP) Master Data Cockpit.

> **More Information**
>
> For more details on the available add-ons please go SAP EcoHub, *http://ecohub.sdn.sap.com/*, SAP Service Marketplace, *http://service.sap.com/asap-business-add-ons*, or SAP Solution Manager, where you can view and activate each of the add-ons.

15.1.1 Business Add-On to ASAP Delivering Point of Sales Implementation Content

We will now take a detailed look at the business add-on to ASAP that delivers point of sales implementation content where the activation of the add-on starts in the project preparation phase. The high-level scope of the project has normally been defined by this stage, and the project initiation has begun. To access this business add-on, there are two access points: SAP Solution Manager, where the business add-ons to ASAP are included in the Solution Manager content support packages (ST-ICO) and an HTML extract from SAP Service Marketplace, as mentioned in Chapter 13, Section 13.4.2. In this example we will use SAP Solution Manager, which is an integrated toolset encompassing content, tools, and methodologies for the implementation and operation of SAP solutions. The business add-on to ASAP that delivers point of sales implementation content needs to be activated via two steps within SAP Solution Manger project administration. First, select POS and Core ASAP on the ROADMAP SELECTION tab as shown in Figure 15.2.

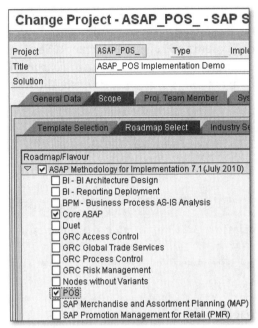

Figure 15.2 Roadmap Selection Tab – Solution Manager Project Administration

Next go to the TEMPLATE SELECTION tab and select the POINT OF SALES template scenario as illustrated in Figure 15.3.

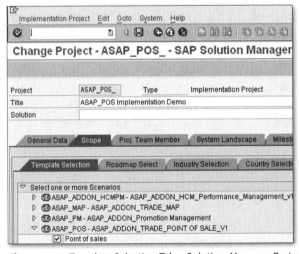

Figure 15.3 Template Selection Tab – Solution Manager Project Administration

After you select the template scenario, the system landscape logical component, product instance, and product version are automatically set up for the point of sales solution as shown in Figure 15.4.

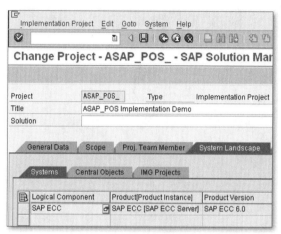

Figure 15.4 Logical Component, Product Instance, and Product Version Setup

Now when you access the ASAP methodology roadmap in Transaction RMMAIN, you can see that the POS-specific implementation methodology content has been merged into the ASAP core. In Figure 15.5 you can see the additional methodology content for the project charter, scope statement, and schedule for project planning within project initiation (1.1.2).

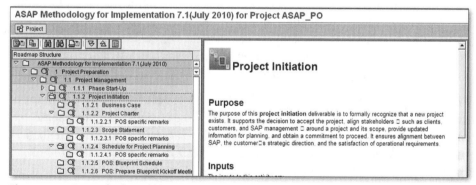

Figure 15.5 Point of Sales Additional Methodology Content

In Figure 15.6 you can also see how there is specific point of sales content for the business process map (1.5.2) and business scenario design (1.5.3).

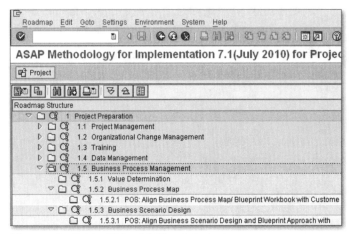

Figure 15.6 Point of Sales Additional Content

This additional POS-specific implementation content is available throughout the phases of the ASAP Roadmap. You can find information such as the POS sizing guide, POS project team skills requirements, POS process descriptions, POS configuration and core enhancement guidelines, POS sample integration test cases, and so on.

Now when you access business blueprint Transaction SOLAR01, you will already have a suggested process structure for the point of sales implementation including process descriptions, transactions, and so on. This is available in the GEN. DOCUMENTATION tab, TRANSACTION tab as illustrated in Figure 15.7. This information comes from your activation of the POS template scenario in SAP Solution Manager project administration template selection.

This is a good starting point for creating the business blueprint for your point of sales implementation. When you have completed the business blueprint phase and move into the realization phase, you will be able to access configuration, enhancement, test, and end-user training material information for POS, which are links to the Configuration, Development, Test Cases, and Training Materials tabs and the associated process step.

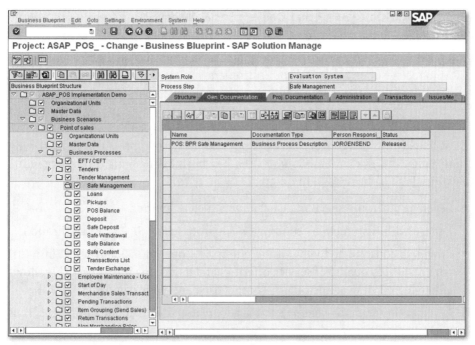

Figure 15.7 Business Blueprint SOLAR01 Suggested Process structure

---

More Information

For further details on the add-on described in this section and other business add-ons to ASAP that deliver implementation content, please go to SAP EcoHub, *http://ecohub. sdn.sap.com/*, SAP Service Marketplace, *https://service.sap.com/asap-business-add-ons*, or SAP Solution Manager, where you can view and display the implementation content for each of the add-ons.

15.1.2 Business Add-Ons to ASAP that Deliver Small SOA/BPM-Based Implementation Content Packages

In this section we will introduce the last category of add-on to ASAP, which delivers small SOA/BPM-based implementation content packages.

The following selection is a small fragment of the SOA/BPM implementation content packages, which are growing rapidly.

Business Add-On to ASAP that Delivers Social Media Prepackaged Implementation Content

It is possible to leverage emerging social media channels such as Twitter within SAP CRM to receive open feedback from customers, provide superior customer service, and monitor the customers' sentiments about products or services. These implementation packages include SOA and BPM content. Furthermore, they support marketing campaigns that run on social media channels such as Twitter within SAP CRM to reach out to a broader network of customers, run more effective marketing campaigns, and track them. Some of the key business benefits of implementing this social media business add-on are:

▶ Leverage emerging social media channels such as Twitter.

▶ Engage with customers by sending tweets from inside SAP CRM applications.

▶ Provide a consolidated view of the enterprise (operational and social insights) with respect to quality of service offerings and marketing initiatives. This allows a 360 degree view of customers, competitors, and your company.

▶ Leverage social media channels to execute planned and ad hoc campaigns, thus widening message reach to your customers.

The two add-ons are illustrated in Figure 15.8 on SAP EcoHub, where you can view and display all of the content.

Figure 15.8 Business Add-On to ASAP Delivering Social Media (Twitter Customer Service + Marketing Campaign) Implementation Content

Business Add-On to ASAP that Delivers Workflows on BlackBerry or iPhone

With mobile workflow approval on the BlackBerry or iPhone you improve the cost efficiency of your workflow processes. Workflows are pushed to the mobile device, where approval is possible anytime, even if no network connectivity exists at the moment. A simple approval contains a comment field and two buttons to accept or reject. More complex approvals can contain radio buttons, drop-down lists, or more input fields, for example, to rate a supplier.

Some of the key business benefits of implementing this business add-on for workflows on the BlackBerry or iPhone are that it:

▸ Enables the approval workflow on your BlackBerry or iPhone device.

▸ Enhances the cost efficiency of workflows by shortening their execution time.

▸ Shortens the invoicing cycle by faster access to your decision makers and directly pushing workflow information onto BlackBerry or iPhone devices.

▸ Allows mobilization of all workflows processes and items such as leave requests, supplier evaluation, invoices, shopping carts, opportunities, and more.

Figure 15.9 shows the add-on on SAP EcoHub, where you can view and display all of the content.

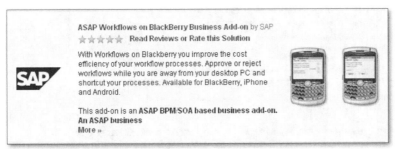

Figure 15.9 Business Add-On to ASAP that Delivers Workflows on BlackBerry Business Implementation Content

Business Add-On to ASAP that Delivers SCM Master Data Cockpit Prepackaged Implementation Content

Master data maintenance is a crucial and time-intensive task. With heterogeneous system landscapes the complexity involved in maintaining master data increases. At the object level the master data can be stored in central repositories such as SAP NetWeaver Master Data Management (MDM). Despite using a central data repository, each system may need master data in a slightly different way.

With the SCM Master Data Cockpit you can maintain all relevant master data of a vendor-managed inventory process in a simplified and user-friendly way. The goal is to improve usability and simplify the master data creation and maintenance process for the end user, leading to fewer errors and less time spent on master data maintenance. With the SCM Master Data Cockpit end users can free up time to spend on more important supply planning activities.

Some of the key business benefits of implementing this business add-on are:

▸ Improved master data leads to more accurate planning results in the context of the vendor-managed inventory process.

▸ It provides an easy-to-learn user interface.

▸ Each step in the vendor-managed inventory process can be started separately.

▸ You can create multiple location products in one step.

▸ Replenishment parameters can be maintained for products.

▸ You can create and maintain transportation lanes.

Figure 15.10 shows the add-on on SAP EcoHub, where you can view and display all of the content.

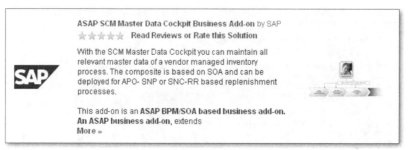

Figure 15.10   Business Add-On to ASAP Delivering SCM Master Data Cockpit Business Implementation Content

More Information

For further details on these add-ons and other business add-ons to ASAP that deliver BPM/SOA-based implementation content, please go to SAP EcoHub, *http://ecohub. sdn.sap.com/*, SAP Service Marketplace, *https://service.sap.com/asap-business-add-ons*, or SAP Solution Manager, where you can view and display the implementation content for each of the add-ons.

15.2   SAP Rapid Deployment Solutions

The second implementation content concept we will introduce is the SAP Rapid Deployment solutions. SAP announced in 2010 the availability of the first SAP Rapid Deployment solutions. The strategy behind these solutions aims to make it easy, fast, and affordable for the SAP community to consume SAP solutions. SAP Rapid Deployment solutions, a new key offering as part of an on-premise strategy, combines preconfigured software and predefined services, accelerators to speed implementation, and SAP Best Practices content to deliver immediate and tangible value at a predictable price — with flexibility for future extensions. This innovative delivery concept can enable lower the total cost of implementation (TCI) and faster time to value while retaining the flexibility to extend the solution wherever needed.

This also means that every SAP Rapid Deployment solution will by default have a predefined service component that is based on ready-to-use content and service components for end-to-end processes with clearly defined scope, time line, and effort — ensuring that assembly is easier and quicker, with better quality and lower risk of implementation.

To ensure the best results, SAP Rapid Deployment solutions are delivered based on the SAP Rapid Deployment solutions implementation methodology. This methodology is based on ASAP methodology (follows the same terminology and standards and reuses elements from the ASAP work breakdown structure–WBS) and tailored specifically for SAP Rapid Deployment solutions. It is a phased, deliverable-oriented methodology that streamlines implementation projects for SAP Rapid Deployment solutions.

The methodology supports project teams with templates, tools, questionnaires, and checklists as well as guidebooks and accelerators to ensure the step-by-step and pragmatic implementation of the new SAP solution packages. The methodology follows four phases:

1. Discovery: Select the scope.
2. Project preparation: Project is formally initiated and kicked off.
3. Realization: Solution is implemented and tested. Includes key user training.
4. Go-live and closing: End users are trained. Final tests and technical go-live, closing of the project, and post go-live activities are executed.

Unless you are using ASAP methodology core you can't see business blueprint phase here, and one of the reasons for this is that all SAP Rapid Deployment solutions have a predefined scope, meaning there is no need to conduct requirements and design workshops, but customers can choose to implement the full SAP Rapid Deployment solution or different variants to suit their situations.

More Information

The following SAP Rapid Deployment solutions are available: SAP Customer Relationship Management (CRM), SAP Business Communications Management, and SAP Supplier Relationship Management (SRM). More solutions will follow.

For more details on these solutions and others, please go to the SAP Rapid Deployment homepage at SAP Service Marketplace:
https://websmp207.sap-ag.de/solutionpackages

"An investment in knowledge always pays the best interest."
– Benjamin Franklin

16   Enablement and Communities

Ann Rosenberg, Frank Klees, Mark von Rosing, Arno Onnen, Steven
Rittinghaus, Roman Hayer, Hosin Min, Alexander Friedrich Holzmann,
Owen Pettiford, Gregor Müller, Marilyn Pratt

The correct enablement is needed to obtained and work with the new mind-set, skills, methodology, governance frameworks, BPM tooling, and prepackaged implementation content. This enablement is provided via different sources; in Section 16.1, SAP's new and comprehensive BPX associate, professional, and project management associate curriculum is introduced together with other key skills, which enables organizations to enhance the key roles, skills, and capabilities of their staff. This enhancement is essential for successfully rolling out BPM practices across the organization including running process-based SAP implementation, via the SAP University Alliances program, an academic business process management curriculum (see Section 16.2). The BPM curriculum is being rolled out to universities all over the world.

Another enablement source is the Starter Kit for Business Process Management, an add-on to ASAP, and the SOA kit, an add-on to ASAP that provides a structured approach to assimilating SAP's extensive BPM and SOA content and offers a channel for easy consumption. It is a one-stop shop for all BPM- and SOA-related information, providing both vision and guidance. We'll explain the Starter Kit for BPM and the SOA Kit in Sections 16.3 and 16.4 of this chapter. As part of the SOA kit, you will also find the *SOA CIO Guide*, which introduces a reference architecture for various scenario classes in service-oriented architecture and business process management based on SAP products. The document addresses multiple reader groups with slightly varying targets: chief information officers (CIOs) will be supported to translate business requirements into IT strategic decisions, and enterprise architects will be supported to plan the overall system architecture and derive/ optimize project-specific variations. In Section 16.5, we'll give you an abstract of the contents of this document which — at the time of writing this book — is still under development.

The next three enablement sources we'll mention are value prototyping, the SAP ValuePartnerShip service, and Composite in a Day workshop. Value prototyping (Section 16.6) provides the best possible high-level solution design and custom-tailored prototype system, combining business, industry, solution, and technology into one. SAP ValuePartnerShip (VPS) (Section 16.7) includes customized SAP services to address your specific business and IT transformation. The SAP VPS framework comes with a set of standard engagement elements, such as the establishment of a value management office, a business process management office, and so on. The Composite in a Day workshop (Section 16.8) enables business process owners and IT to quickly evaluate SAP's BPM capabilities by modeling and executing their organization's specific business processes on the SAP platform. The last enablement source (Section 16.9), includes several communities that we recommend you join for additional enablement. Let's take a closer look at these enablement options.

16.1 Enablement: People as Key Success Factor

Linking business and IT strategies is one of the top strategies of the world's leading companies. In a complex and continuously changing economic environment, it is important to improve the relationship between business and IT to realize business priorities such as cutting operating costs or increasing revenues.

Organizations must be able to sense and respond rapidly to customer and market-place changes. Cost structures and business processes must be adapted in a flexible manner to maintain productivity and reduce risk. Technology is vitally important to support the business. Its value varies with a company's core business priorities, such as whether it aims for an organizational transformation or operational excellence. Technology becomes an enabler for innovation, change, and economic success.

The implementation of new processes and business functions based on technology for improvement of economic performance requires a new skill set for the employees who work in the interface area between IT and business. New knowledge and new capabilities are needed to obtain the adaptability for the required transformations and change processes. People enablement is therefore a key success factor for transformation processes and organizational change.

16.1.1 The Link Between IT and Business

Executing an integrated and harmonized IT and business planning process is a critical business competence that will help companies define how they will move from their current state toward the strategy. In this manner the role of IT in many organizations has to evolve from supporting the business to enabling the business.

Business and technology change continues to increase at accelerating rates. This requires an adaptable workforce and raises the expectation that IT staff has, besides technology, business and communications skills. Companies have to make clear to their staff what is important for the future and will secure success. A lack of qualified resources leads to the following challenges:

- Quality problems
- Increasing cost
- Longer projects
- Slowdown in the growth of incremental revenue

Many projects fail due to a lack of skilled resources and management commitment. Companies that successfully build a labor force that possesses both technical skills and business skills will be more competitive and profitable than those that do not.

Roles and responsibilities of IT and business become more blurred to meet these new requirements. But also, new roles are required to operate in an interface area between business and IT. According to this development, skill requirements in IT and especially in the SAP environment are changing.

We can already see a shift in demand for expert and commodity services. Whereas the demand is increasing for expert services that require professional roles such as business process experts or architects increases, commodity services will be outsourced to offshore service providers.

Software- or technology-specific roles such as developers or application consultants are encouraged to broaden their existing skills and to acquire new skills. In parallel, new roles will represent the link between pure business and pure IT roles and translate business requirements into technology architecture.

The area of responsibility will extend to:

- Business/IT strategy alignment
- Process/application strategy definition

- ▸ Business case development
- ▸ Performance management
- ▸ Change management
- ▸ Relationship management
- ▸ Business process management
- ▸ Enterprise architecture definition
- ▸ Value and project management
- ▸ Risk management

These skills are combined with soft skills such as communication, leadership, and conflict management. IT professionals have to understand the business priorities and define and measure value in business terms. They have to proactively propose business-IT initiatives.

Among these new roles we can find enterprise architects, business process experts, technology architects, and change management experts.

The roles have, especially in the area of soft skills, a lot in common and share the same responsibilities. But there are also role-specific tasks and skills such as specific methodologies and technical knowledge, which were introduced in the introduction and Chapters 14 and 15.

Critical to the success of the project is, in addition to the availability of relevant knowledge the interplay of the different roles and the utilization of individual knowledge and harnessing collective wisdom.

16.1.2 Role-Based Education for Organizational Performance

A training program that can build a bridge from the traditional roles to new business-oriented roles is a key element for successful transition phases. Such a program supports the development of further business architecture know-how, methodology, and soft skills based on the existing skill set and know-how. It offers role-specific learning maps to obtain the necessary knowledge and to enable continuous learning.

Knowledge today has only a limited and sometimes very short validity. A learning program for continuous learning ensures that employees are up to date with their knowledge and always fully operational.

SAP offers a program for training and continuing education that supports both a transition from an existing role to a business-oriented role and advanced knowledge for professionals, as illustrated in Figure 16.1.

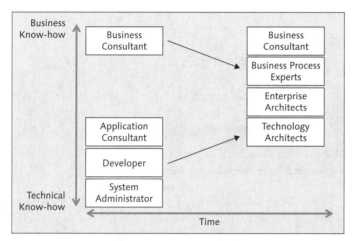

Figure 16.1 Shift to Business and Architecture Roles

As part of the SAP's education and training program, technology consultants and project managers can obtain the necessary knowledge to cope with new challenges, and experienced architects can specialize and refresh their knowledge.

In collaboration with partners and customers, a blended training program has been developed, which offers courses for beginners and professionals. Duration, content, and delivery channel are thereby adapted to the needs of the market and the requirements of learners.

Many training programs end with a prestigious SAP certification, which represents a high value on the market for consulting services. The certification ensures that the participant has the necessary knowledge and that this knowledge has been tested. Companies that want to perform a transformation project are faced with the choice of which consulting services vendor they want to engage. The certification program supports companies in finding suitable consultants for their projects who have the required skills. Even an objective comparison of different consultant profiles is simplified.

SAP offers a multi-tier certification program. This gives the consultant the opportunity to validate his skills on the appropriate level within a given subject area. Employers can assign resources based on clearly defined benchmarks, which are mapped and validated on the basis of job tasks, and benefit from a predefined career path for their employees.

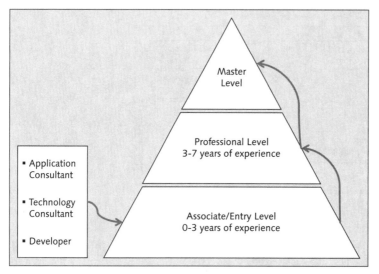

Figure 16.2 SAP's Certification Program

The multi-tiered certification program, as illustrated in Figure 16.2, consists of three levels:

1. **Associate certification on the entry level**

   This certification and training program covers the fundamental knowledge requirements for a specific role. It ensures the successful acquisition of broad solution, technology, and business knowledge and skills. The associate certification is the appropriate training program for SAP application or technology consultants to move into a new architecture role.

2. **Professional certification**

   This is the advanced certification and training program that requires proven project experience, business process knowledge, and a more detailed understanding of SAP solutions or technology. With professional-level certification, consultants demonstrate experience and expertise. During three to five years of real-life experience in an architecture or business process expert role combined with continuous learning and education, employees can prepare for the advanced professional certification.

3. **Master certification**

This final level involves demonstrating expert-level understanding of a specific area of SAP software and the ability to drive innovation and solution optimization through in-depth knowledge and vision. Holding a master certificate demonstrates broad project experience; comprehensive knowledge in the area of business, architecture, or technology; and the ability to create a future IT vision within complex project environments. The master-level certification is the entrance to a selected community of well-known experts and thought leaders.

16.1.3 Roles and Required Skills

Project Manager

Today's project management requires the ability to develop concepts and roadmaps to mobilize, deliver, and measure business results to meet the project goals on time, in budget, with quality, and with value. Project managers must have advanced business skills and the ability to apply methodologies and tools. Besides advanced communication and presentation skills, the project manager needs skills to manage internal and external stakeholders.

Project managers have a basic knowledge of change management processes and their communication. They manage the end-to-end transition of the project from project preparation to run. Project managers develop roadmaps for project execution and for testing and quality management. For SAP projects in particular, the project manager applies SAP-specific methodology roadmaps and tools such as ASAP and SAP Solution Manager. Finally, they are responsible for risk and quality management.

SAP offers the following courses specifically for project management:

► ASA380: Managing SAP Projects

► BPM/SOA: BPM and SOA for Project Managers and the SAP Certified Associate Project Manager Certification

---

More Information

For more details please go to the SAP Education Portal: *http://www.sap.com/services/education/index.epx.*

Business Process Expert

The business process expert analyzes business processes and aligns business functions with technologies. The business process expert applies methodologies and BPM tools to analyze and improve the as-is status and to determine the to-be design and to transform the business. The business process expert understands how business process management will change the way companies operate and implements governance frameworks such as business and process governance.

The business process expert outlines and applies concepts such as the business model framework and the process mapping framework and process-based methodologies such as ASAP, Six Sigma, and Lean including process maturity assessment, process performance measurement, process ownership, and so on. He understands from both a business and an IT perspective how to move between the different stages within the lifecycle of a business process and how to execute business-to-model and modeling-to-execution to support SOA-related activities to create business value via the creation of easily consumable automated business processes.

For this advanced role SAP offers training programs on the associate and professional levels. The following course prepare for the certification:

▶ TBPM10 – Business Process Management

▶ SAP Certified BPX Associate Certification

▶ TBPM20 – Business Process Management Level II

▶ SAP Certified BPX Professional Certification

More Information

For more details please go to the SAP Education Portal: *http://www.sap.com/services/education/index.epx.*

Enterprise Architect

Enterprise architects work with stakeholders to align IT strategies with business goals. Enterprise architects drive flexible adoption of enterprise architectures and have a broad organizational perspective that involves both technical and strategic activities. In addition, enterprise architects are responsible for mapping the current enterprise IT landscape, planning the target architecture, and managing the transition from the current architecture to target architecture tied to business goals and objectives. Enterprise architects conduct workshops with internal and external stakeholders and present results at a senior management level. Therefore, the enterprise architect needs strong communication and presentation skills and a solid IT background.

SAP offers two levels of certification for enterprise architects:

▶ The associate level certification for application consultants who want to transition into this new role

▶ The professional certification for experienced architects

> **More Information**
>
> For both certifications SAP offers a tailored training program. For more details please go to the SAP Education Portal: *http://www.sap.com/services/education/index.epx.*

Technology Architect

The technology architect is an expert on the latest development technologies, platform technologies, tools, and standards and their implications for the industries, such as enterprise SOA. The technology architect reviews existing landscapes and aligns target IT landscapes to customer roadmaps. He drives technology and infrastructure change within the customer environment and roll-in for generic solutions and enterprise services. The technology architect is responsible for defining industry-related technology projects at the customer site. He drives prototypes or early adapter projects in SAP and with partners and customers and supports customer evaluations and proof-of-concept projects. He reviews strategic customer projects and supports enterprise SOA projects with partners and customers.

The technology architect needs general knowledge and experience in the current SAP technology, development tools, and development methodology. He needs broad knowledge across multiple information technologies, standards, methodologies, and BPM concepts and services and expertise in SAP architecture and the enterprise architecture frameworks.

> **More Information**
>
> For preparation for the technology architect certification on the associate level, SAP offers a unique training academy. For more details please go to the SAP Education Portal: *http://www.sap.com/services/education/index.epx.*

Organizational Change Management Expert

The organizational change management expert is responsible for identifying stakeholders of the transformation and identifying the right level of communication to these stakeholders. The OCM expert manages the communication and information activities and analyzes the feedback and acceptance from these activities. He conducts surveys and training needs analysis and defines the required role-based training program. He defines escalation concepts and conducts readiness and health checks.

> **More Information**
>
> SAP offers several courses for organizational change management. For more details please go to the SAP Education Portal: *http://www.sap.com/services/education/index. epx.*

16.1.4 Summary

Roles and responsibilities between IT and business become more blurred based on the evolution within process management and IT, and changes to existing roles and the creation of new roles are required to operate in an interface area between business and IT. According to this development, skill requirements in IT and especially in the SAP environment are changing. The new training offerings support this evolution and enable organizations to enhance the key roles, skills, and capabilities of their staff, which is essential for successfully rolling out BPM practices across the organization including running process-based SAP implementations.

16.2 Enablement: SAP University Alliances BPM Curriculum

Since the company's founding in 1972, SAP has valued the essential role of higher education in advancing the future of information technology and business strategy. Today, the SAP University Alliances program provides software licenses for SAP products and services for academic use to more than 1,000 leading institutions of higher education worldwide.

SAP also provides free workshops and conferences to thousands of professors, supplying them with course materials and other instructional resources. Every year, hundreds of thousands of students at participating campuses experience firsthand how the fully integrated SAP enterprise information software systems operate.

They learn how these solutions support their future employers' organizations in becoming more productive, profitable, and sustainable.

The University Alliances Community site, *www.uac.sap.com*, an online environment utilizing the latest social media tools and technologies, provides academic resources to professors and students worldwide, facilitating professional opportunities. SAP customers and partners are invited to build relationships with participating universities for recruiting interns and graduates, enhancing the learning environment and project opportunities for students, and furthering professors' research and publication efforts.

Through these initiatives, SAP University Alliances enhances the key academic and professional outcomes of higher-education degree and diploma programs worldwide, combining business process knowledge with enterprise software expertise to develop one of the most valuable skills portfolios on the market.

Via SAP University Alliances a BPM curriculum has been developed and is in the process of being rolled-out globally to leading institutions of higher education. The core team that developed this innovative curriculum joined their forces from four universities (both IT universities and business schools) in three countries, with interest in business process management, business modeling, value management, performance management, and enterprise architecture. They brought together a rich blend of both academic and industry experience to contribute to a maturing field in business and IT. The team consisted of Siavash Moshiri (Sheffield Business School, United Kingdom), Ann Rosenberg (SAP, Copenhagen Business School and IT University, Denmark), Karin Gräslund (Wiesbaden Business School, Germany), and Mark von Rosing (Copenhagen Business School and IT University, Denmark).

The development team adopted an agile collaboration approach to the development of the curriculum to be able to deliver the output in a very short time. The curriculum incorporates 14 sessions covering the following topics: business process management as a management tool, processes and the process evolution, technology evolution, BPM framework – method and models, BPM and business model management, BPM governance in detail (strategy, setup, transition, and continued improvement), BPM governance link to IT and business governance, BPM and sustainability, the new approach for implementing process-based IT solutions, and BPM technology (business-to-model and model-to-execution).

This BPM curriculum will give students the possibility in addition to their BPM university exam to take the TOGAF Business Architecture Certification, which will be available in 2011 from the Open Group, and SAP Business Process Expert (BPX) Associate Certification. This is truly an innovative approach; it is one university BPM curriculum that enables three certifications.

16.3 Enablement: Starter Kit for Business Process Management, an Add-On to ASAP

To help customers drive their business process transformation, SAP has introduced the Starter Kit for Business Process Management, an add-on to ASAP. The kit provides easy access to the most relevant data needed to start off a BPM journey. The Starter Kit for Business Process Management provides a structured approach to assimilating SAP's extensive BPM offerings. The goal of the starter kit is not just to help the SAP community in getting started with BPM but also to act as a ready reference that can guide them throughout their BPM journey. The starter kit is available online at SAP's BPX community area, and it will be continuously updated to reflect newly available BPM content.

> **More Information**
>
> You can access the Starter Kit for Business Process Management, an add-on to ASAP, at the following location: *https://www.sdn.sap.com/irj/bpx/starterkit-for-bpm*.

16.3.1 Benefits and Target Audience

The main purpose of the Starter Kit for BPM is to provide a one-stop shop experience to members of the SAP community who are either interested in better understanding the overall BPM discipline or in learning in detail about how to best apply SAP's capabilities to support their own business transformation.

Within the starter kit, you will find detailed information about the concepts according to different use cases, methodologies, relive use cases, step-by-step approaches, and supporting enablement offerings from both SAP and system implementation partners.

Implementing targeted business process management and applying all related IT activities will change the way you implement SAP projects. Although SAP already provides significant information about how to best implement its software products, there is a need for a more holistic approach considering the entire business process management discipline but at the same time highlighting only the relevant parts of the implementation activities. The starter kit contains several assets for easy access and fast deployment, but beyond just compiling available assets, it knits together a BPM information network by providing the right links at the right place to existing information in published information sources. It is therefore a collaborative information framework that — based on customer and partner feedback — will grow and improve over time.

This approach allows not only easy access within the SAP community, but also ensures the inclusion of the latest available information.

Available through SAP's BPX network, the starter kit is a good starting point for organizations embarking on a BPM journey. Generic BPM information presented in the kit is applicable even for organizations not running an SAP solution. However, companies running at least some of their core processes on SAP systems and considering extending the best practices provided with the SAP Business Suite can benefit the most from this starter kit.

The Starter Kit for BPM, an add-on to ASAP, addresses key decision-makers within an organization who drive process improvements and process excellence. Such decision-makers are commonly known as business process experts and/or enterprise architects and often take ownership of process definitions and transform them into IT requirements.

16.3.2 Navigating Through the Starter Kit for BPM, an Add-On to ASAP

The landing page of the starter kit provides a choice between the four BPM use cases as a starting point to drill down into the kit content. The landing page provides a brief overview of each of the use cases to help you decide which of them best fits your company's BPM strategy, as shown in Figure 16.3.

It is important to understand that these use cases are not mutually exclusive. They serve only as entry points, and an organization can start more than one use case in parallel and move from one use case to another depending on how far the organization has proceeded in its BPM journey. Relationships between the use cases, where they may make sense, are suggested throughout the starter kit. For example, an organization may start with the use case to execute a continuous process improvement program, which in turn may spawn one or more projects to build process-based applications.

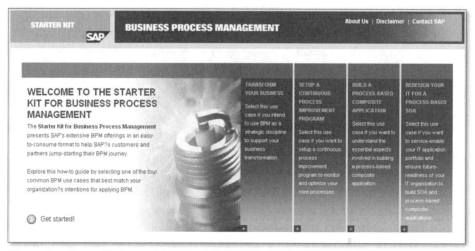

Figure 16.3 Starter Kit for BPM Overview of Use Cases

Each use case provides relevant content that helps users better understand and execute it (see Figure 16.4).

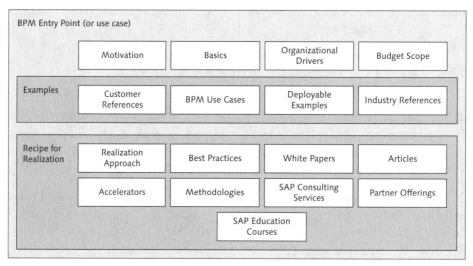

Figure 16.4 Content Provided in the Starter Kit for BPM

To begin with, an introduction to the use case indicates the benefits of implementing it, the main drivers (business or IT) behind the use case, and the typical scope of the budget within which the use case is realized.

Reference stories from other organizations who have realized this use case and their detailed approach are also available in the starter kit. Where applicable, implementation examples from SAP are also presented, allowing you to immediately see the positive results of an implemented use case.

Finally, a handy recipe helps organizations get started with implementing the use case within their own business environment. The main steps involved in executing the use case are listed, and direct references to relevant white papers, guidelines, and methodologies are provided to ease the realization of the use case.

Consulting services offered by SAP and relevant to the use case are also listed. A similar approach is taken for the educational offerings. All relevant material is presented as an easy-to-process, consumable package.

16.4   Enablement: SOA KIT, an Add-On to ASAP

In its infancy, service-oriented architecture (SOA) was only used by companies with sufficient strategic IT budgets. It is now part of day-to-day business. It enables the connecting of innovation, new applications, processes, and functionalities to your systems, for example, enabling processes on mobile devices, while keeping your legacy business running. Service-oriented architecture gives companies the necessary flexibility to pave the way for innovations while not affecting day-to-day business operations.

SOA enables companies to implement and adapt business processes with unprecedented speed and ease for sustainable transformation. It supports a decomposition of processes into smaller process steps for reusable enterprise services that can easily be adapted to changing business needs.

The SOA KIT, an add-on to ASAP, is a "one-stop shop" of integrated accelerators complementing the new ASAP 7 methodology framework. The SOA KIT offers the SAP Community a wide range of accelerators complementing ASAP 7, which are aligned along the strategy, plan, build, and run phases of your SOA journey, as illustrated in Figure 16.5.

Figure 16.5 SOA KIT, an Add-On to ASAP

The following topics respectively demonstrate their relevance within the particular areas:

▶ **Experience**
Challenged by the increasing speed and scope of business change, companies need to evolve their existing IT infrastructure into a more flexible environment that reduces complexity and supports business agility across their business network. See how others have done it and share your experience within the SOA community in SCN and beyond.

▶ **SAP Consulting Offerings**
SAP Consulting offers professional services to support a company's SOA projects. Benefit from SAP Packaged Composite Implementations and jumpstart your SOA project.

▶ **Value and Benefits**
Before embarking on SOA projects, a company needs to know what tangible

benefits it will bring and how to support the value achievement, measurement, and monitoring.

▶ **Methodology, Governance, and Solution Architecture**
In order to exploit the benefits SOA promises to deliver (reduce operational costs, accelerate profitable growth, support business agility, etc.) a company needs to have good governance practices. Access information about how to plan your IT landscape, implement SOA-related services and composites, and optimally run and manage it all. The reference architecture for SOA describes a broad range of SOA-related concepts.

▶ **Enablement**
Explore how to best leverage existing courses supporting workshop and materials.

▶ **Composition and Integration**
Explore what tools and approach you need to model, build, and integrate SOA-based applications.

▶ **Operations**
Explore what tools and assets are available to keep your business running fast and efficiently.

▶ **Partner Offerings**
Find out how you can benefit from the valuable partner community of SAP in regards to service-oriented architecture, based on the business process platform.

The SOA kit offers a phase- and role-based structure, which is needed to efficiently guide, enable, and leverage SOA within a company's implementation projects. This SOA kit empowers the SAP community with the end-to-end SOA knowledge to support the construction of user-centric applications on top of the business suite and to reach simpler, shorter, and less disruptive SOA-based implementations.

More Information

For more information on the SOA kit, an add-on to ASAP, simply go to *http://www.sdn. sap.com/irj/sdn/soa-kit*.

The content offered provides the possibility of collaboration via content wiki pages to ensure constant improvement and helps you keep the right focus to best support your implementation project needs.

16.5   Enablement: SOA CIO Guide — Abstract

SOA promises to change the way software is going to be developed in the future, with a value proposition that is more than attractive, at least on the paper. In reality, however, many attempts to adapt SOA fail for various reasons. This section discusses a document called *SOA CIO Guide*, which is going to be published at the end of 2010 within the SOA kit, an add-on to ASAP. This guide will be part of a series of CIO guides for various areas such as business intelligence, master data management, user interfaces, and so on. The *SOA CIO Guide* addresses multiple reader groups with slightly varying targets:

▶ CIOs will be supported to translate business requirements into IT strategic decisions.

▶ Enterprise architects will be supported to plan the overall system architecture and derive/optimize project-specific variations.

The goal of SOA is to change the approach to software projects to increase business values, but it is important to incrementally incorporate small pieces of business value on the long and strategic way to SOA, even if this requires small deviations from the strategic path. The *SOA CIO Guide* aims to assist CIOs and enterprise architects in finding the right balance to combine increasing SOA maturity with incremental business value benefits. In this section, we'll discuss how the guide — once completed — will help CIOs with this task.

16.5.1 Solution Space and Key Capabilities

SOA calls for more than implementing a piece of software that is executed in an IT landscape. An enterprise must plan the efforts and approach to achieve a sustainable and manageable IT department comprising enterprise architecture, organizational planning, governance, methodologies, and portfolio planning. This enables the enterprise to build iteratively the software artifacts that support employees in delivering the required business value. IT infrastructure provides the required capabilities to efficiently run the deployed software artifacts. A set of tools and procedures to manage the automated processes closes the set of SOA-related capabilities.

The segmentation depicted in Figure 16.6 is used throughout this chapter to present SOA-related capabilities.

PLAN	BUILD	RUN	MANAGE
Comprises capabilities, tools, and methodologies to document, analyze, plan, and optimize the enterprise's business process evolution, including manual and automated processes and governance over time.	Provides the environment to model and develop the automated process support based on the planning in iterative steps.	Enumerates the capabilities that are required to run the planned and built automated process support by IT infrastructure.	Comprises all tools and procedures to manage the running automated business processes.

Figure 16.6   SOA Capability Segmentation

▶ **Plan**

Planning the enterprise's journey through the SOA transition is an integral part of successful SOA implementation. Enterprise modeling is a tangible approach to understanding and analyzing the current situation, with the goal to optimize manual and automated processes. As SOA introduces a new paradigm, enterprises have to adapt their organization, namely, the processes, structures, and people development. These changes should be based on accepted and approved methodologies such as the Open Group Architecture Framework (TOGAF) or SAP's enhancement called SAP Enterprise Architecture Framework. Lastly, portfolio planning is vital to a successful path to SOA with constantly increasing maturity and incremental business value benefits.

▶ **Build**

Executing a plan means creating software artifacts that efficiently support the business processes. Depending on the skills and available technologies, it is important to provide productive and quality-oriented development environments and repositories to minimize the total cost of development (TCD). An integrated test environment supports the requirements for high-quality software development processes.

▶ **Run**

Following the OASIS SOA Reference Model, a consumer has needs, which can be met by capabilities, which are provided by services. The relationship is not one-to-one, so a given need may require the combining of numerous capabilities, whereas any single capability may address more than one need. The expectation of SOA is the provisioning of a powerful framework for matching and combining capabilities to address existing and upcoming needs. This leads us to a three-layer-architecture view of the execution capabilities.

▶ **Service consumption**

Functionality to consume services to address the consumer's needs. Service consumption can be utilized either by human beings in terms of user

583

interface-centric service consumption or by systems in terms of system integration.

▶ **Service integration**
Functionality to mediate between the provided services and the required consumption.

▶ **Service provisioning**
Functionality to provide the capabilities in terms of services.

▶ **Manage**
Keeping a software stack up and running requires additional configuration, administration, and monitoring capabilities. These comprise software logistics, lifecycle management, monitoring, technical/business configuration, system landscape management, process analytics, and many other management tasks.

Figure 16.7 gives a high-level overview of all of the described capabilities.

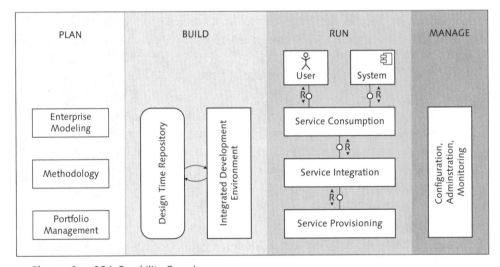

Figure 16.7 SOA Capability Overview

We will use this overview map and a more detailed one to outline SAP product mapping and roadmap planning in the final *SOA CIO Guide*.

16.5.2 Reference Architectures and Maturity Model

Planning and implementing an SOA-based solution calls for some architectural planning. Starting without an appropriate architecture foundation can be the first step into problems. To avoid this, we need to identify, understand, and negotiate the requirements and constraints that drive the architecture. It is also essential to transform this input into appropriate architecture decisions.

Architecture Definition Framework

The quality of the architecture decision depends heavily on the experience and analytical skills of the architect. To support this process we developed a framework of a typical SOA pattern, which is segmented into the three runtime layers: service consumption, service integration, and service provisioning.

For each of the layers, we introduce architecture variants and architecture options and provide quality- and constraint-based assessment. This supports the architect's decision-making and leverages him on a higher experience level by reusing the broad experience of the enterprise architect community. Figure 16.8 provides an overview of the framework.

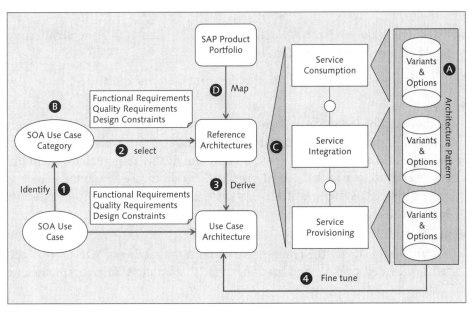

Figure 16.8 Architecture Definition Framework

SAP has already completed some tasks that are necessary to apply this framework, and customers can use the results. SAP delivers:

1. Descriptions of a set of typical architecture patterns and assessments of key qualities and drawbacks

2. Categorization of typical SOA use cases into a manageable number of SOA process patterns

3. Creation of architecture blueprints/reference architectures for a typical set of process patterns under typical constraints

4. Mapping of SAP product portfolio to the reference architectures

Based on the results of SAP's applications, the customer is then able to:

1. Analyze the use case to be implemented and identify the best-matching SOA process pattern

2. Select the best-fitting reference architecture by using his quality requirements and design constraints as a filter criterion

3. Derive the use-case-specific architecture from the selected reference architecture

4. Finish the major architecture definition work by fine-tuning the architecture based on the underlying pattern framework

Let's go through a simple example to understand the principles:

▶ **Step 1**
Within our portfolio management we decide to create a new vacation request application. We know the attitudes of our users, and thus we explicitly formulate high-end user performance as an important quality requirement. Additionally, we know our backend landscape and decide to use the functionality of our existing R/3 system, which is not on the newest version and thus not yet service-enabled.

▶ **Step 2**
The architect matches the requirements against the catalog of SOA process patterns, provided by SAP, and identifies the UI simplification as best-matching pattern.

▶ **Step 3**
Based on the additional constraints and quality requirements, he chooses the appropriate reference architecture for this SOA process pattern.

▶ **Step 4**
The reference architecture proposes encapsulation of the backend by a dedicated frontend server and an enterprise service bus to transform remote function

calls to enterprise services. SAP NetWeaver Composition Environment and SAP NetWeaver Process Integration seem to be good offerings for this purpose.

▸ **Step 5**
To optimize the performance of the solution, the architect explores the pattern catalog and identifies backend service adaptation as an additional architecture option to fine-tune the solution.

SOA Process Pattern

Identifying most typical process pattern is an ongoing exercise. Analysis of more than 100 customer projects, interviews with consultants, regional implementation group surveys, development product owner expertise, and other inputs are constantly reviewed to keep the pattern up to date.

Figure 16.9 provides an overview of the currently identified SOA process pattern.

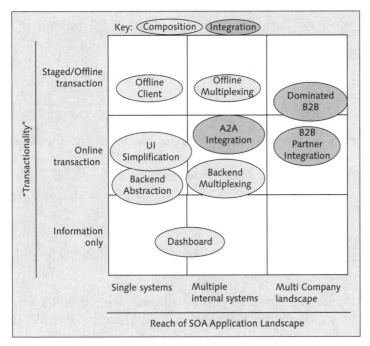

Figure 16.9 SOA Process Pattern

We distinguish primarily composition process patterns and integration process patterns. We know that the boundaries are not sharp, but at least it helps to structure our thoughts on use cases. A key differentiator between these process patterns is the consumer type. Human end users are assumed to be consumers of composition implementations, and systems are the consumers of integrations.

The composition process patterns are:

▸ **Backend abstraction**
Service enabling of backend systems

▸ **Dashboard**
Information access to single or multiple systems

▸ **UI simplification**
Role-based UI simplification on a single system

▸ **Backend multiplexing**
Role-based UI simplification on multiple systems

▸ **Offline client**
Occasionally offline role-based UI simplification on a single system

▸ **Offline multiplexing**
Occasionally offline role-based UI simplification on multiple systems

The integration process pattern are:

▸ **A2A integration**
Integration of internal systems to connect business activities and exchange information

▸ **B2B partner integration**
Integration of systems across company boundaries based on common standards

▸ **Dominated B2B integration**
Integration of systems across company boundaries with one dominating partner, for example, manufacturer – supplier integration

To find appropriate architectures for these process patterns, we start to identify bigger building blocks, which deliver dedicated qualities. These building blocks are provided for each of the layers: service consumption, service integration, and service provisioning. They are then composed into reference architectures per SOA process pattern and assessed against typical qualities.

Variants and Options

The pattern catalog provides a set of architecture building blocks, which are aggregated from smaller structural elements. These aggregated building blocks are assessed for their respective architecture qualities and drawbacks to assist the architect in deciding whether a certain building block should be included in a specific use case architecture or not. We distinguish two types of architecture building blocks: architecture variants and architecture options.

An *architecture variant* represents the basic architecture topology of a layer. Variants are typically mutually exclusive for a single use case but can coexist in a system landscape.

> **Example**
>
> For your specific use case you must decide whether you want to have:
>
> ▶ Frontend UI server or use the UI technology within a backend
> ▶ Peer-to-peer or enterprise service bus (ESB) hub or distributed ESB as the integration topology
> ▶ Service-enabled backend or legacy API usage

These alternatives can be treated as the architecture variants of the three layers: service consumption, service integration, and service provisioning.

An *architecture option* is an additional architecture building block, which can be added to an architecture variant. Options are additive. One option might be dependent on another option.

> **Example**
>
> An option is independent if you do service integration peer to peer. With an ESB hub or a distributed ESB you can add the following options to add additional qualities:
>
> ▶ Service registry
> ▶ Service virtualization

The creation of an architecture pattern catalog is an ongoing task, and we'll introduce an early example from the consumption layer to show the way forward.

The quality assessment for each architecture pattern (variants and options) is structured as follows:

▶ *Preconditions* describe necessary constraints to apply the building block.

▶ The *description* explains the building block verbally.

▶ The *quality assessment* explains the pros and cons of the building block.

▶ A high-level *architecture block diagram* completes the assessment.

The notation used for architecture diagrams follows the SAP technical architecture modeling standard TAM. Figure 16.10 shows the major elements and their interpretation.

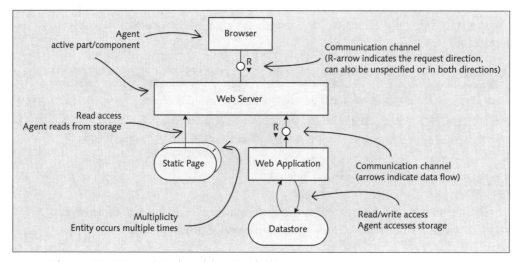

Figure 16.10 SAP Technical Modeling Standard TAM

Example from the Service Consumption Layer

Within the service consumption layer, we now introduce the architecture option of replication as an example.

Before we discuss the situations in which we recommend this option, we need to clarify the preconditions that must be met in order to apply replication. The first requirement is of local storage capabilities on the consumption system.

The information from various service providers is replicated to the consumption system via the system integration capabilities, and the consumption logic operates on the local store. A dedicated replication mechanism synchronizes the service providers with the consumption system. Figure 16.11 shows the basic topology of this building block.

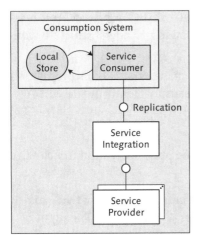

Figure 16.11   Service Consumption – Architecture Option – Replication

If we compare a replicated solution with a solution that directly acts on the service provider's data, we can find the following advantages for the replication:

▶ End-user performance is optimized, because the consumption logic operates with local storage and does not suffer from additional network latencies.

▶ Users are decoupled from the service providers, because they access only the consumption server. Potential consolidation of service provider systems can be hidden from the user. If, for example, a service provider system is exchanged by another system with a different application programming interface but the same functionality, the adaptations can be done in the system integration and consumption logic without changing the user interface.

▶ Modern consumption servers typically offer state-of-the-art UI technologies, which allows high usability and integration into user productivity tools.

▶ The pattern is mandatory for occasional offline scenarios, such as mobile usage.

Unfortunately, there is a price to pay for these advantages. The major drawbacks of a replicated solution are described below:

▶ The user operates on replicated data and thus might encounter some latency in shared data with other users, because the replication typically follows a regular schedule, e.g., once per night.

▶ Developing replicated solutions adds additional effort to a project. You need mapping of a local data structure to the information providers' structure, conflict management, replication scheduling, and so on.

▶ Replication data (mapping, scheduling) must be maintained. Conflict resolution might even cause manual resolutions. This all leads to slightly increased TCO.

Reference Architectures

How can the framework above be used in a specific project situation to help find an appropriate architecture?

The described framework delivers powerful but numerous alternatives, and it is not trivial to find an appropriate architecture for a given input. The input of a planned project can be separated in several groups:

▶ Functional requirements

▶ Nonfunctional requirements, also called quality attribute requirements (security, scalability, etc.) following Software Engineering Institute methodology

▶ Design constraints, also called external forces and boundary conditions, which are given by laws, corporate rules, or technical limitations

Besides the approach to use this input, explore the pattern catalog, and compose an architecture blueprint based on the architecture variants and options, we want to analyze typical project situations and create an architecture blueprint for these typical situations upfront. We call such a preassessed architecture blueprint the reference architecture. This would be a very mature starting point for further enhancements.

A weak but self-explanatory analogy can be found in car purchasing: You can either select your favorite model, start a car configurator, and define your major requirements such as engine, color, interior color, multimedia equipment, security features, and much more, or the manufacturer can offer you preselected compositions (such as the models business, family, or sports), which all are optimized combinations of basic features for typical usage situations.

To outline the idea, we introduce a more detailed assessment of the example referenced in Section 16.5.2.

Reference Architecture Example – UI Simplification on Single Legacy Backend

In our example we assume the typical project situation: We have a backend system with business functionality and local/remote programming interface technology, but it is not service-enabled in the sense of SOA. Let's assume we need a simplified user interface for a given business process, which is supported by this backend system. Based on the pattern catalog, we can sketch many architectural drafts to fulfill these requirements. The most typical solutions for this category of use cases look like the following.

Either use the backend UI technology to provide an additional user interface, which is a subset of the fields or functionality of the given user interface (see Figure 16.12) or enrich the landscape with a dedicated consumption frontend with dedicated state-of-the-art user interface technology and connect this frontend to the backend system, which must be service-enabled first (see Figure 16.13). Alternatively, we can replace the service enabling by an additional enterprise service bus, which offers an adapter to translate the legacy programming interface of the backend system (see Figure 16.14).

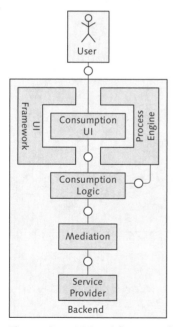

Figure 16.12 UI Simplification Reference Architecture – Simple System

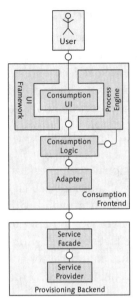

Figure 16.13   UI Simplification Reference Architecture – Consumption Server P2P

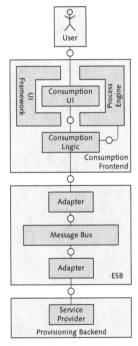

Figure 16.14   UI Simplification Reference Architecture – Consumption Server on ESB

How can we decide which of the alternatives fits our project best? Table 16.1 summarizes the planned assessments that will be detailed in the final *SOA CIO Guide*.

Quality	Single System	Consumption Server P2P	Consumption Server ESB
End-user performance	+	–	–
UI flexibility	–	+	+
UI integration backend	+	–	0
TCO	+	+	0
TCD/required skills	+	–	0
System landscape flexibility	–	+	+

Table 16.1 Quality Assessment of Reference Architectures

The first column contains qualities, which can be mapped against the requirements of the project. The heading row contains the architecture alternatives, and the cells show a simplified assessment of each quality for each of the architectures. With this preassessment, the enterprise architect can easily find the best-fitting reference architecture as a starting point for architecture fine-tuning.

SOA Maturity Model

In addition to single project support, we also want to support the strategic planning of the path to SOA. This chapter will introduce a helpful instrument, the SOA maturity model. An SOA maturity model describes the maturity of an enterprise regarding SOA in multiple dimensions. As we have seen earlier, SOA is not only a question of architecture, but also of governance aspects, organizational aspects, and more. The model will reflect this.

You can use the model to determine the enterprise's maturity level and plan the next steps based on the model and strategic goals of the enterprise.

The final *SOA CIO Guide* will contain strategic guidance throughout. Here is an example of the SOA strategy.

Example
Customers should plan their SOA adoption along a maturity model:
▶ Determine your current maturity level.
▶ Make small steps along all dimensions.

▶ Use frontrunner projects to evolve single dimensions.

▶ Balance project portfolio decisions between business value and SOA evolution steps: no big bang service enablement, no ultra pragmatic proprietary integration solutions.

16.5.3 SAP Product Implementation Guidance

SAP product implementation guidance will map the SAP products to the reference architectures and outline some prominent positioning questions about SAP products. For example, we compare the SAP products that deliver process flow capabilities:

1. SAP NetWeaver BPM is designed to orchestrate automated processes across multiple systems. Both human interaction and service orchestration are focused activity types.

2. SAP Business Workflow has significant strength for tight integration into a single ABAB-based system. It is best used when an ABAP-only application is developed that operates on a single system.

3. Guided Procedures was primarily designed to guide users to subsequent interactive processing steps across multiple systems. SAP aims to substitute this product with SAP NetWeaver BPM.

4. ccBPM is optimized to orchestrate services, especially for integration processes. It is a built-in part of SAP NetWeaver Process Integration.

Figure 16.15 illustrates this assessment.

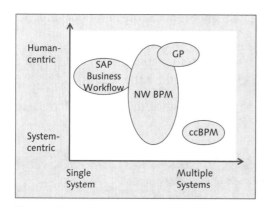

Figure 16.15 SAP NetWeaver BPM Products

16.5.4 Trends and Roadmap

The final chapter in the SOA CIO guide discusses current business and technology trends and their implications for SAP product planning and strategic alignment with customers.

Important examples of technology trends are:

▶ Decentralized execution of enterprise service bus (a.k.a. distributed ESB) to combine the benefits of central administration and monitoring with decentral, high-performance execution.

▶ Further impact can be derived from the growing rich internet application (RIA) technologies such as Adobe Flex, Microsoft Silverlight, and HTML5 with Ajax.

▶ A very prominent technology trend is the on-demand space, which explicitly leverages the SOA style and enables fully virtualized services with automatic self-configuration of service networks in the cloud.

▶ We will see a growing impact of representational state transfer (RESTful) protocols, which will influence the SOAP-based Web service world dramatically.

The dominating business trends that drive SOA are:

▶ Growing empowerment of lines of business. Totally IT-centric software provisioning in an enterprise will slowly be enriched by LOB-specific services, which might be created and/or provided by the LOBs themselves.

▶ Cost pressure will definitely continue and require consolidation projects, which are very prominent in the value proposition of SOA.

▶ The further best-of-breed consolidation of vendors leads to additional needs for interoperability of software and thus will be leveraged by SOA principles.

16.5.5 Conclusion

The overall goal of this section is the support of enterprise architects and CIOs to improve their results. The architecture definition framework discloses some analytical steps that happen in the decision-making process of experienced architects and leverages all architects' decisions to a higher maturity level. The SAP product mapping helps improve the SAP portfolio adoption and the maturity model together with enterprise SOA governance assists CIOs in the strategic planning of their path to SOA. Lastly, the business trends and roadmap help protect investments by aligning IT investments with SAP product roadmaps. This chapter gives an overview of the *SOA CIO Guide*, which will be published at the end of 2010 within the SOA kit, an add-on to ASAP.

16.6 Enablement: Value Prototyping

Value prototyping provides the best possible high-level solution design and custom-tailored prototype system, combining business, industry, solution, and technology into one. Comprising this holistic approach and focusing on fast tangible results, it provides in-depth insight and confidence before committing to the real world. Both business and IT can explore and address such uncertainties as ambiguous and changing requirements, technical complexity and unexpected errors, and even skepticism from business users. This helps reduce guesswork and solve critical problems early, before the project goes too far. In other words, we scaffold opinion leaders and power users to design, build together based on their live testimony, and prove it by their experience rather than by analysis with logical assumptions.

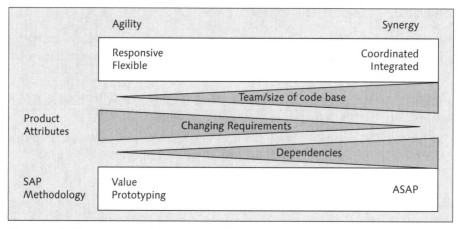

Figure 16.16 Characteristics of the Business Add-On to ASAP that Delivers Value Prototyping Methodology

The prototype system can also be utilized as either a reference system or a development template (with limitations). This brings a complex project up to speed, resulting in reducing approximately one-third of design and implementation efforts. In addition, the early experience of power users and thought leaders (opinion leaders) stimulates constructive and precise feedback and sets up a viable change environment; power users are intensively educated and actively participate in the changes throughout the two weeks of prototyping iterations, and they often are core team members to drive the project success. Value prototyping is a methodology business add-on to ASAP. Figure 16.16 shows the characteristics of the add-on.

Value prototyping starts with and envision workshop, which is designed to critically and systematically review customer's needs and confirm what they really want to envision through the dynamic and iterative methodology. Then the prototype system is dynamically implemented in an SAP intensive lab environment in a way that brings all of the expertise, hardware, software, and iterative prototyping methodology into one place to answer the proof points identified in the envision workshop. Checkpoint sessions/workshops take place in every two weeks to confirm and refocus and build exactly what customers want in the end. Figure 16.17 illustrates the process.

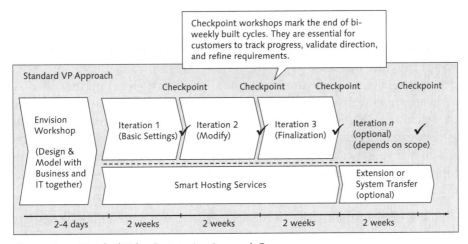

Figure 16.17 Standard Value Prototyping Approach Process

Deliverables in general are:

▶ Prototype systems

▶ Demo system environment (accessible through Internet)

▶ Documents: high-level solution document, configuration guide, development guide (if any), and demo script (optional)

After the value prototyping is executed, a prototype system including a demo system environment is established that includes high-level solution documentation.

To see a practical case using value prototyping you can read the use case regarding SAP's implementation in Chapter 7, Section 7.3.

16.7 Enablement: SAP Value Partnership

SAP ValuePartnerShip Service (VPS) is an exclusive commercial offering designed to tailor a strategic engagement model between customers and SAP. VPS includes customized SAP services to address the customer's specific business and IT transformation. The VPS framework comes with a set of standard engagement elements such as the establishment of a value management office, the design of a strategic roadmap, and an onsite business architect. It also includes customizable SAP Consulting Business Transformation Services to maximize the investments in SAP software. The key pillars are long-term roles, mutually agreed objectives, and intensive collaboration between the customer and SAP along the value lifecycle from the discovery to the realization to the optimization phase.

A value partnership with SAP helps remove roadblocks that can keep your firm from realizing the full value of its IT investments, such as inefficient processes and process governance in core and support functions; global business and IT transformations involving various subsidiaries or regions, with ineffective local engagement models, multiple systems integrators or partners; incomplete models that fail to consider the full engagement lifecycle (planning, implementing, and optimizing processes and IT landscapes); engagements lacking a value management focus, methodologies, tools, and experience; and IT-focused implementations that disregard the impact on business value.

To find more information about the SAP value partnership please go to *www.sap.com/services/bts*.

16.8 Enablement: Composite in a Day Workshop

The Composite in a Day workshop enables business process owners and IT to quickly evaluate SAP's BPM capabilities by modeling and executing their organization's specific business processes on the SAP platform. By the end of the day you will have a small prototype composite running including obtaining experience on model-driven development using a combination of classroom training, development workshops, and show-and-tell sessions and hands-on development.

Composite in a Day is divided into three steps. The first step is preparation, where the evaluation criteria for the process are discussed; ideally, the customer has a sample process that leverages BPM capabilities. Furthermore, options for runtime systems are presented, and needed infrastructure requirements are clarified.

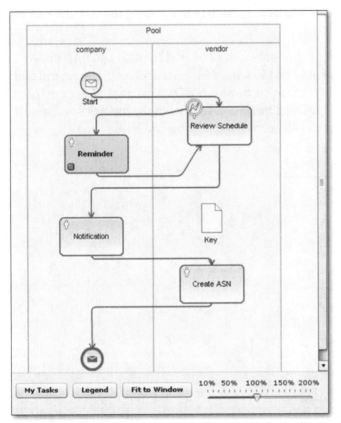

Figure 16.18 BPMN Example Process to Create ASNs for Smaller Vendors

The second step is a one-day workshop with two SAP consultants: one business process expert and a solution architect with a strong programming background. The workshop starts with a presentation of SAP NetWeaver BPM capabilities and typical usage scenarios and the Business Process Modeling Notation (BPMN). Next the customer process and involved roles are discussed along with the means of agile development approaches. Therefore, SAP NetWeaver Developer Studio (NWDS) is used in the process modeling perspective. All findings are simultaneously trans-ferred into BPMN as shown in Figure 16.18. A basic understanding of the notation is gained quickly and is the basis of lively discussions because a common language is established. Ideally, the customer has attendees from both technical and business departments. This leads to many fruitful talks, and the process model grows step by step. Typically, several iterations are undertaken by going through the process model repeatedly.

As soon as the process model is stable, the underlying data model is analyzed. What business entities are used and in what their relationships are is determined. Then relevant attributes are modeled in SAP NWDS as shown in Figure 16.19. This is then used to start enriching the process model in the process development perspective with technical details such as the information flow.

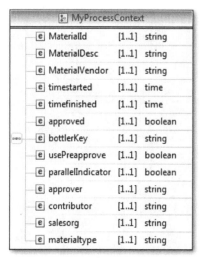

Figure 16.19 Attributes Modeled in SAP NWDS

Furthermore, the data model allows the automatic generation of needed user inter-faces by choosing which information has to be displayed in which part of the process. The user interfaces typically need some fine-tuning. Sometimes discus-sions restart when the user interfaces are visible to every participant as illustrated in Figure 16.20. This may lead to changes in the process flow and data model.

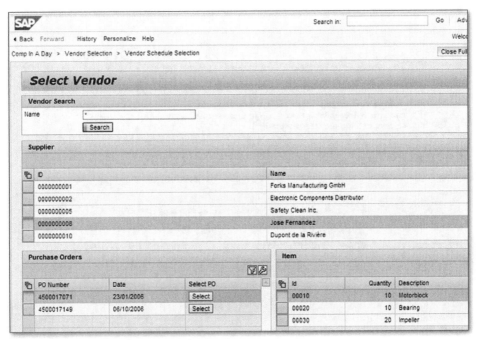

Figure 16.20 Example of a User Interface

Besides the user interfaces, another important aspect is backend services. There-fore, the candidates are identified from BPMN and user interfaces. With the data model and needed attributes, the discovery of existing enterprise services in the Enterprise Services Workplace is possible as shown in Figure 16.21. Besides lever-aging existing services, the Enterprise Services Builder in the Enterprise Services (ES) Repository is used to demonstrate the modeling and design of services. This allows for building custom enterprise services according to SAP's design-time gov-ernance (the same approach SAP used to publish their enterprise services). These allow integrating SAP and non-SAP applications in the BPM process.

With a stable process and data model and user interfaces and services, the solu-tion architect finishes the technical enrichments in the process with the goal of it being executable. Parallel to technical completion, the business process expert and customer discussions related to value realization, process lifecycle, and process governance.

The third and final step is the presentation of the process to the audience and hand-over either via Screencam or deployment on a local engine. Many customers use this jumpstart to invest in making the process productive afterward.

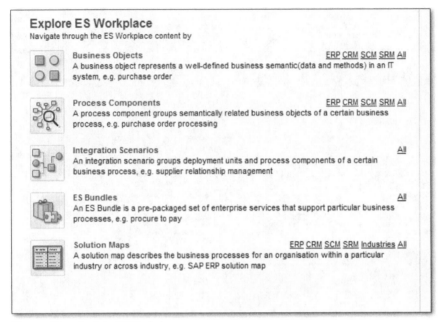

Figure 16.21 Explore ES Workplace

16.9   Enablement: Communities

Communities such as SAP Developer Network (SDN), Business Process Expert (BPX), University Alliances Community (UAC), and SAP EcoHub, which all are part of the SAP Community Network (SCN), provide you with information, guidelines, and training resources to enable you to apply BPM in all of its aspect in your SAP-centric business and IT environment, and they give you access to the power of true co-innovation. The SAP Community Network (SCN) is SAP's professional social network. It provides trusted connections to our dynamic community of SAP customers, partners, employees, and experts. It delivers an unparalleled depth and breadth of knowledge, insight, and rich content about SAP solutions and services in a collaborative environment that encourages innovation and sharing of best-run business practices.

When you join SCN, you'll connect directly with a diverse member base that engages in an unparalleled level of knowledge sharing. You'll participate in orchestrated collaboration that enables innovation, and you'll access marketplaces of solutions, services, ideas, and jobs. As a member, the more you participate and contribute, the more you get in return through the Contributor Recognition Program.

There are communities for technical and business audiences, helping individuals and companies gain more value from their SAP implementations:

- ▶ SAP Developer Network (SDN) offers deep technical content and expertise for IT pros, developers, and enterprise architects who configure, install, run, optimize, and innovate on the SAP NetWeaver platform.

- ▶ Business Process Expert (BPX) Community is your trusted community for business solution collaboration, knowledge, and insight on implementation and business process, connecting functional application consultants, business analysts, product and solution managers, customers in various roles, and opinion leaders/topic experts.

- ▶ University Alliances Community (UAC) is an open academic-oriented community for professors, lecturers, and students at universities worldwide, providing connections and access for them to engage and collaborate with SAP customers and partners.

- ▶ SAP EcoHub is a community-driven online enterprise solution marketplace that delivers a holistic view of solutions and services offered by SAP and its ecosystem of partners. For customers, it delivers a streamlined approach to discover, evaluate, and buy the right solution for their business needs.

"It is common sense to take a method and try it. If it fails, admit it frankly and try another. But above all, try something."
– Franklin D. Roosevelt

17   Conclusion

You have just received a comprehensive guide on how to apply BPM in all of its aspects in your SAP-centric business and IT environment. The guide has introduced a new methodology and governance framework in detail. You first explored a framework for connecting your strategy to your business model and your business model to your operational business processes, including how to identify, create, and realize value through this connection that is the starting point for any business process change or creation of new business processes you execute within your operational business process environment.

You also learned about the new ASAP 7 methodology and governance framework, which brings together the previous ASAP methodology, Business Intelligence Solution Accelerator (BISA) methodology, value delivery principles, business process management methodology, and service-oriented architecture methodology. You explored the two highly visible components of the new ASAP 7 methodology framework: First, the ASAP Roadmap 7 core methodology, which covers four life-cycles: business process, application, project, and value. Each of the ASAP phases (project preparation, business blueprint, realization, final preparation, go-live support and run) in the ASAP Roadmap 7 core was explained in detail in respect to how value delivery, business process management, and service-oriented architecture are reflected in each of the phases. You were also introduced to the additional skills that are required for the project team members to use the new ASAP methodology.

The second visible component you were introduced to was the business add-ons to ASAP that extend the ASAP Roadmap with modular business implementation content providing proven implementation content for various industries, cross-industry solutions packages, and other related areas such as agile methodology,

BPM, SOA, value management, and EA governance and strategy frameworks. You explored the three different categories of add-ons: business add-ons that deliver methodology and governance frameworks, business add-ons that deliver implementation content, and business add-ons that deliver small BPM/SOA-based implementation content packages. We went into the details of the methodology and governance add-ons, where we introduce the following add-ons to ASAP: business process scanning methodology, agile methodology, content for testing, content for SAP enterprise modeling applications by IDS Scheer, service-oriented architecture strategy and governance framework, and BPM strategy and governance framework.

As part of the guide that will enable you to apply BPM in all of its aspects, we also introduced in detail some of the key modeling to the execution tools that we recommend you apply in your SAP implementation projects. We first went into the details of the composite development architecture guidelines for SAP NetWeaver Composite Environment (CE), which targets two distinct areas: composite applications and Java applications. First, SAP NetWeaver CE enables model-driven development of own practices, also referred to as composite applications. The composite applications can be built on top of the SAP Business Suite Best Practices with the application core processes and on arbitrary backend systems. Composite applications follow the SOA paradigm of nonintrusiveness, which means these applications are bound to provide modification-free process extensions to the core business applications. Second, customers are enabled to design, deploy, and run Java applications with SAP NetWeaver Composition Environment following the JEE standards. This new set of composite development guidelines were created based on feedback and experience from the first customers using the SAP NetWeaver Composite Environment. The guidelines include recommendations that will help you implement applications following the SOA principles: you received a detailed introduction to layers, the server architecture, the design-time architecture in SAP NetWeaver Developer Studio, and the programming model of SAP NetWeaver Composition Environment including the structure of composition and separation of functionality. You also explored the details of SOA pattterns.

Secondly, you were provided with highlights of the innovation provided by SAP NetWeaver BPM and BRM, to which additional innovation capabilities have been added to business-friendly modeling from a business analyst experience such as a new, dedicated process modeling perspective for process sketching. This modeling perspective focuses on the nontechnical aspects of the process model and the hand-over to the process development perspective that developers use to complete an initial process model resulting from the process sketching effort with implementation details.

We introduced process performance reporting and monitoring as model artifacts to support gaining better process performance insight and thus help improve process quality. We also introduced a browser-based rules manager to enable business analysts to directly modify business rules without the need to use the full developer experience. In addition, the expressiveness of rules has been enhanced by the addition of common definitions, effective dates for rules, and overrides. From a process developer perspective, innovation capabilities have been added such as automated user interface generation to significantly accelerate the creation of human task UIs; default tasks and services that allow developers to quickly sketch and run processes even with incomplete tasks and services designs; improved consumption of Web services, including SAP enterprise services, by simplifying configuration via service groups; rule flow modeling for complex decision processes; new rule development tools (rules editing within Microsoft Excel, reporting, differencing, consistency checking, service generation); and code-free, automated, bulk rule testing.

The third area of modeling execution tools that we provided went into the details of business rules management, where we looked at handling decisions and business rules in a BPM approach where you explore how managing decisions and business processes as peers creates simpler and more agile processes and more flexible business applications. We also learned details about business rules management systems from SAP where we looked at Business Rules Framework Plus and SAP NetWeaver Business Rules Management and learned about the different usage scenarios.

Finally, we explored the simple samples for enterprise services consumption that demonstrate end-to-end what it takes to build a small composite application using enterprise services and the different consumption technologies that SAP delivers today. You can take the simple samples as starting points for your own SOA projects to lower the hurdle to deal with new technology. Simple samples are for educational purposes only and are not intended for productive usage.

Another key component of the guide that will enable you to apply BPM in all of its aspects and that we introduced is the process-based prepackaged implementation content. This content is based on SAP Business Suite best practices, best insight, and own practices, also referred to as composite applications. The composites applications, as mentioned earlier, can be built on top of SAP Business Suite Best Practices with the application core processes and on arbitrary backend systems. This prepackaged content enables you to build process-based and easier-to-consume solutions within your SAP-centric business and IT environment. The prepackaged content also enables simpler, shorter, and less disruptive implementations.

You were introduced to SAP's various implementation content concepts, which can be used in different consumptions scenarios. You explored in detail the business add-ons to ASAP that deliver the two categories of implementation content: The first category was small SOA/BPM-based implementation content packages where you were introduced to social media (Twitter customer service + marketing campaign) and workflows on BlackBerry or iPhone prepackaged implementation content. The second category was pre-packaged implementation content, including industry or cross-industry content, where we described the add-on for trade: Point of sales. We also introduced the rapid deployment solutions, which include preconfigured software and predefined services, accelerators, and SAP Best Practice content.

The last key component (enablement and communities) introduced nine sources for good enablement, which is needed to obtain and work with the new mindset, skills, methodology, governance frameworks, service-oriented architecture, SAP NetWeaver Composition Environment, and prepackaged implementation content. The first source we introduced was SAP's new and comprehensive BPX associate, professional, and project management associate curriculums that enable organizations to enhance the key roles, skills, and capabilities of their staff, which is essential for successfully rolling out BPM practices across the organization, including running process-based SAP implementation. The second education enablement source we introduced was SAP University Alliances, an academic business process management curriculum that is being rolled out to universities globally. The third and fourth enablement sources were the Starter Kit for Business Process Management, an add-on to ASAP and the SOA kit, add-on to ASAP that provides a structured approach to assimilating SAP's extensive BPM and SOA content and offers a channel for easy consumption. They complement the new ASAP 7 implementation and governance framework, with a one-stop shop for BPM- and SOA-related information, providing both vision and guidance.

Enablement source five was an overview of a document called the *SOA CIO Guide*, which is going to be published at the end of 2010 within the SOA kit, an add-on to ASAP. This SOA CIO Guide aims to assist CIOs and enterprise architects in finding the right balance to combine increasing SOA maturity with incremental business value benefits. Source six was SAP Value Partnership (VPS), which includes customized SAP services to address your business and IT transformation. Source seven was value prototyping, which provides the best possible high-level solution design and custom-tailored prototype system, combining business, industry, solution, and technology. Source eight was the Composite in a Day workshop, which enables business process owners and IT to quickly evaluate SAP's BPM capabilities by modeling and executing their organization's business processes on the SAP platform. The last enablement source (nine) was several communities that we recommend you join for additional enablement.

We will now move on to Part IV, which will focus on the future outlook of BPM.

PART IV
Future Outlook

In our world, it is more important than ever to bring business and IT together in a functional and productive way to optimize our businesses. This book has illustrated how to apply BPM within an SAP-centric business IT environment. In Part I, we described how business models should be the prime targets for the innovation and transformation of an organization's core competitive and differentiated competencies. We addressed the fact that vital aspects are missing from many BPM projects today: the concepts of value drivers to ensure value identification, creation and realization, and how to identify the essential processes and activities that provide competitive differentiation. Beyond the issue of missing components in BPM, it is important to approach implementation with a holistic approach, a fact that was mentioned throughout the book. To successfully use a holistic approach, one must combine BPM with value and performance management, enterprise architecture, governance, and SOA. With this basis, we defined the importance of business models to identify and create value for a company, and suggested a method for innovating and transforming business models and business processes to achieve further business value. We hope that by reading Part I, everyone can understand the critical role competencies play to identify the few essential processes and activities that set your company apart — and find innovative ways to create and realize value.

Part II provided real-world use cases of SAP customers implementing BPM within different industries. We illustrated the true value that BPM can bring to a company, as well as SAP's contribution and worth. We understand that it is sometimes difficult to read about a product or idea and imagine how it is applied. Therefore, we approached these companies in order to provide in-depth insight into each company's business challenges, BPM enabled solutions, the lessons they learned, and the benefits realized. We also explored the commonalities across BPM implementations to help you identify and qualify potential BPM projects.

In Part III we provided essential guidance to enable you in applying BPM in all of its aspects in your SAP-centric business IT environments. As the most methodology- and technology-specific part of the book, this part introduced new methodology and governance frameworks and delved in detail into the new ASAP 7 framework, which also includes agile methodology, BPM, SOA, value management, and enterprise architecture governance and strategy frameworks. We also spent some time recommending key modeling execution tools to use in your own SAP implementation projects, which include areas in NetWeaver BPM/BRM and SAP NetWeaver CE. After we provided you with these tools, we provided guidance by highlighting SAP's various process-based implementation content concepts. We ended this comprehensive part by walking you through nine sources of good enablement.

We will now conclude this book by discussing several areas where we, as well as other BPM experts, foresee trends and growth in BPM's future. We also include information on the topics of business trends and their technology and development. These topics are dealt with in more detail in several bonus articles available for download on the catalog pages for this book at *www.sap-press.com* and *www. sap-press.de*.

"The best thing about the future is that it comes only one day at a time."
– Abraham Lincoln

18   Future Trends for BPM

Ann Rosenberg, Rukhshaan Omar, Mark von Rosing, Greg Chase, Sandy Kemsley, Gregory Prickril

In this last part of the book, we will give you some suggestions about the outlook and the future for BPM, including current trends. We will start with Sandy Kemsley's six ideas, which can be the heart of the future of BPM. In Section 18.2, we will explain how the potential of knowledge workers, which are they key contributors to a company's development, can be maximized by these future BPM trends. Section 18.3 gives an overview of some further areas of BPM technology development and thereby the business trends they support.

18.1   BPM Future Outlook: Six Ideas

Business process management is reaching a state of mainstream acceptance: few organizations today are not engaged in some form of process improvement, whether through purely manual means or the application of technology. That mainstream acceptance doesn't mean stagnation, however: BPM is still evolving in response to new business drivers. We will now take a closer look at some of the ideas that can be the heart of the future of BPM:

1. Supporting the knowledge worker

2. Fostering collaboration

3. Responding to rapidly changing situations

4. Working anytime, anywhere

5. Developing process skills

6. Giving control to the business

18.1.1 Supporting the Knowledge Worker

In today's business, routine work is increasingly being replaced with knowledge work as many simple routine tasks become fully automated or even performed by customers through self-service portals. This leaves the more complex situations that require the skills of more knowledgeable workers, not just to perform the individual tasks, but even to decide which tasks to perform to accomplish a goal.

BPM methodology and technology are changing to support this knowledge worker environment, with less up-front process modeling and design required and more autonomy given to the workers while they are processing work. This requires more agile and dynamic BPM systems that allow processes to be modified on the fly by participants or even have no structured process defined in advance. More importantly, this requires that management put control over the processes — requiring a high degree of trust — into the hands of the knowledge workers rather than requiring that everyone follow a predefined process.

Dynamic processes managed by a knowledge worker have the potential to greatly improve customer satisfaction, because the worker is empowered to do what's right for the customer, not just what the system was designed to do.

18.1.2 Fostering Collaboration

Businesses today are placing an increased value on workplace collaboration, precipitated in part by consumer social software and the new forms of interaction that have developed in the world of social networking. Concepts of social production — using collaboration to create a work product — and social interaction — using social networks to locate skills — are being seen in organizations' use of enterprise social software such as wikis.

Collaboration between business and IT during process discovery and design can create fundamentally better processes, using the "wisdom of the crowd" to ensure that all stakeholders' concerns are addressed and that knowledge that may exist only in a few people's heads is captured as part of the process. To facilitate this, BPM systems may include collaborative process discovery tools, allowing multiple stakeholders in business and IT — and even outside the organization — to contribute to a shared view of a process.

A second emerging trend in collaborative BPM is the ability to collaborate during runtime, that is, while a process is executing. Related to the dynamic BPM discussed above, runtime collaboration exploits the weak ties between people within organizations by allowing a worker to invite someone to collaborate on a process because of their personal knowledge of that person's capabilities. In this way, the collaborative process can take advantage of the enterprise social network of the process participants.

18.1.3 Responding to Rapidly Changing Situations

Today's business changes at a breakneck pace, and business processes must be able to sense those changes and respond to them. To do this in a timely manner, processes need to become event-driven, such that events can effect changes to the process.

Events may be external to the process, or even to the organization that owns the process, such as an order cancellation received from a customer. Events may also be generated by analysis of the executing process itself, such as escalating the priority of a process if the projected completion date will not meet required deadlines.

As processes become more intelligent — both to their own executing environment and to external events — it is possible to make them highly responsive to those conditions without human intervention, significantly improving the response time and quality of decision-making in the process.

This level of process intelligence and event responsiveness requires the technology to analyze the processes and respond to events, but also requires that the organization cede control of some process decisions to the process itself, rather than relying on human intervention.

18.1.4 Working Any Time, Anywhere

Business no longer happens at a single location: Many organizations operate in multiple locations, even multiple countries, and may have customers and trading partners all over the world. There is increasing pressure on organizations to allow their employees and other stakeholders to participate in business processes from anywhere, at any time.

One method to support geographically dispersed process participants is to host the processes in the cloud, and cloud-based BPM is starting to become a reality. There are many privacy and security hurdles to hosting in the public cloud, but the benefits in terms of reduced infrastructure costs and increased reach can be significant.

As acceptance of the cloud as a business platform increases, more business processes will move to cloud-based BPM systems.

18.1.5 Developing Process Skills

New methodologies and technologies require new workforce skills, from business to IT. Business users and managers need to gain a level of process awareness to fully participate in process modeling and dynamic BPM: It's necessary for them to see where their tasks fit in the larger process context and be able to generate and execute ideas for process improvement. Business analysts need to understand the complexities of process analysis and how it differs from other forms of business analysis through the availability of simulation and optimization techniques and tools. Even in the IT groups involved with developing and supporting a BPM system, new skills specific to process management are required.

A focal point for much of this skills development is a BPM center of excellence, and forward-thinking organizations are establishing BPM CoEs to act both as repositories of process-related information and skills development materials and as homes for core teams of process specialists that can assist business users, business analysts, and developers to gain proficiency.

18.1.6 Giving Control to the Business

A key thread running through many of these BPM trends is to give greater control over processes to the business users and managers. Collaborative BPM allows users to be involved in process modeling and design, and dynamic BPM allows them to modify processes on the fly to suit current conditions. Cloud-based BPM solutions make it possible for business areas to provision their own BPM systems with minimal involvement from IT, providing further independence in how they manage their business. And developing the necessary process-related skills creates a process-aware workforce that is ready to assume their role in making their business processes better.

This requires changes to the business culture to become more collaborative and allow a greater degree of control to some classes of business users and managers, rather than requiring that IT implement all changes to business processes.

In turn, this requires that the tools used for the business-led activities be optimized for business use, rather than use by technologists.

18.1.7   Summary

These ideas, then, are at the heart of the future of BPM:

▸ Dynamic BPM to support agile processes

▸ Social BPM to allow design-time and runtime collaboration

▸ Event-driven intelligent processes

▸ BPM in the cloud for geographic distribution

▸ Business-led BPM

From collaboration to dynamic BPM to smarter processes to the cloud, new technologies are evolving to handle new business challenges, yet many organizations are not yet taking advantage of them. The future of BPM depends on the adoption of these new methods and technologies where appropriate, without discarding the tried and true structured BPM methods where they can provide the most benefit. For those implementing BPM systems, the challenge will lie in deciding what parts of that BPM future to distribute to which people for the maximum benefit.

18.2   BPM for Knowledge Workers

The term *knowledge worker* was coined by management guru Peter Drucker to describe people who are valued for using their knowledge and expertise to solve problems, as opposed to task workers, who are primarily measured on the efficient execution of predefined activities. Because knowledge workers are responsible for much of the differentiation in many organizations, unblocking their potential is one of the key challenges facing organizations of all sizes attempting to grow in a highly competitive global business environment. SAP believes that BPM should play a major role in maximizing the potential of knowledge workers but that existing approaches and technology will likely need to be extended to best meet their needs.

18.2.1   What Is a Business Process?

Simply put, a *process* turns inputs into outputs. A *business process* is a process that is described from a business perspective. Because of the nature of existing business process management software, it is common for people to equate BPM with traditional workflow approaches, in which a flow of activities, both human and automated, is represented as boxes (activities) connected by arrows indicating the direction of the flow. Business Process Management Notation (BPMN) is a standard notation based on this approach. Figure 18.1 shows a traditional workflow model expressed with BPMN.

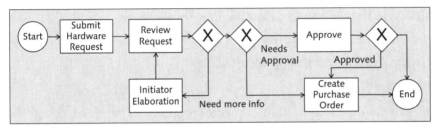

Figure 18.1 Traditional Graphical Representation of a Business Process' Control Flow

These models are appropriate for many scenarios but often have difficulty expressing the variability common in many processes that are executed collaboratively by knowledge workers, processes such as creating a product vision or executing a corporate merger. These processes are repeated but typically adjusted based on the business context by leveraging the collective experience of the team executing them; that is, they are executed based on *practices* rather than traditional formal business processes.

To underscore the distinction between traditional processes and practices, we can classify processes based on the degree to which they can be repeated based on an a priori definition. Figure 18.2 depicts the business process structure continuum.

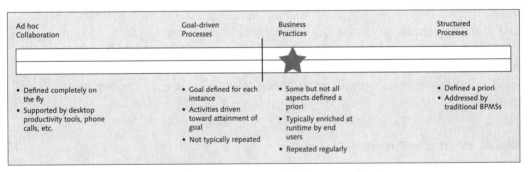

Figure 18.2 Continuum of Business Processes with Respect to Structure

On the far left, business processes are supported by ad hoc collaboration, an approach often used by knowledge workers to execute many, if not most, of the processes in which they are involved. Execution of these processes often relies opportunistically on email and productivity software such as spreadsheets. Although these processes are not predefined and are not supported by customer software, they should not be misinterpreted as being trivial or unimportant. Many critical business processes are approached in an essentially ad hoc manner.

On the far right of the continuum lie traditional scenarios that can be modeled a priori, using notations such as BPMN. This is the type of process that is supported by SAP NetWeaver Business Process Management. Historically, scenarios on this end of the continuum have received the most focus from customers and software vendors because their high a priori descriptions lend them well to software support, and their repeatability makes associated business cases more straightforward.

Toward the center of the spectrum are classes of scenarios that share attributes from both the extremes. As their name implies, goal-driven processes are executed in the context of an explicit goal, often expressed declaratively by a business rule, for example. Between goal-oriented processes and full structured processes lie practices referred to formally as business practices.

The tendency of software vendors in the market today is to marginalize the BPM problem at the extremes of the structure continuum. Both the general collaboration and business process management markets are mature, boasting a variety of offerings from companies of all sizes. "Power vendors" such as SAP, IBM, and Microsoft have also made significant investments in these areas, including significant acquisitions. However, software platforms to support scenarios closer to the business practice point on the structure continuum are relatively rare, although related approaches such as case management seem to be gaining traction in the market. Although collaboration software gives knowledge workers the freedom they expect, it does little to provide guidance and the appropriate constraints to teams of knowledge workers, nor does it typically facilitate learning from previous collaborations. Support for structured processes is critical but typically fails to provide the adaptability required by business practices and typically requires that modelers understand sophisticated business process metamodels to describe business processes. A few of the key limitations of traditional approaches to BPM and workflow are:

▸ Requires knowledge of all activities and the paths between them a priori

▸ Requires knowledge of control flow and other concepts that are too sophisticated for many knowledge workers

▸ Optimized for individual task work rather than collaborative groups

18.2.2   What Is a Business Practice?

First, business practices are business processes; that is, they turn inputs into outputs and are described from a business perspective. However, business practices differ from traditional structured business processes in that they typically place much more emphasis on providing guidance than enforcing consistency. Business practices share the following key characteristics:

▶ **They cannot be completely described a priori**
Business practices lie between highly structured business processes that must be described in detail a priori and ad hoc collaboration, which is typically executed with no a priori description or planning. Most tasks executed by knowledge workers are repeated, so something is known about how the process could be executed, although not everything regarding process execution can be described ahead of time.

▶ **They are driven by knowledge workers**
Because they can't be described completely a priori, business practices are often driven by knowledge workers, who must use their discretion and experience to fill in the gaps as the process executes.

▶ **They are collaborative**
Most work done by knowledge workers is collaborative, leveraging collective experience, knowledge, and judgment. Although collaboration can contribute to almost any business process, business practices are assumed to be collaborative and therefore surface user interaction in a collaboration tool by default.

▶ **They are described with simple concepts**
To simplify the capture of business knowledge about business practices, they are described using a very simple set of concepts that are approachable to knowledge workers. Traditional notations such as BPMN are aimed at a specialized type of business user called business analysts, so they are simply too complex for many knowledge workers.

How Are Business Practices Described?

Business practices are described using a very simple set of concepts that is designed to be intuitive to knowledge workers. First, business practices are described as a fairly high-level set of activities called stages. Stages are sequential and do not represent specific work items, but instead are containers for a set of related artifacts and activities necessary to move the process forward. Figure 18.3 depicts the stages of executing a corporate acquisition.

Figure 18.3 Typical High-Level Representation of the Corporate Acquisition Process

To those with even basic awareness of the acquisition process, it is fairly obvious that each of these stages can be decomposed into multiple activities that accomplish the higher-level goal implied by the name of the stage. For example, the due diligence stage might contain an activity or set of activities for performing financial due diligence and another for technical due diligence. This simple graphical representation provides an overview of the process that is approachable to almost any business user. Experience with customers has demonstrated that many business processes are described at this high level of abstraction before more detailed descriptions are generated. For example, although SAP NetWeaver BPM is capable of describing complex workflows, customers have requested the ability to provide a simplified representation of business processes much like the one in Figure 18.3.

To further refine the business practice, a set of *stage items* can be associated with each stage. A stage item represents a user-centric entity such as a task, checklist, document, or even application UI that is associated with the completion of that stage. For example, the *make offer* stage might contain a task called *legal review* and a link to a word processing template for formal offers.

Generally, stage items are designed to provide guidance to the business practice participants, not constrain them to a predetermined sequence of activities. Stage items can also be added by users at runtime.

What Type of Software Is Needed to Manage Business Practices?

To better manage business practices, software must evolve beyond the BPM and workflow offerings available in the market today. Furthermore, the key enabling capabilities must be tightly integrated in a coherent and holistic offering. A software platform to provide rich support for the lifecycle of a business practice must provide the following key capabilities:

1. **Collaboration platform**

    Because it is assumed that most practices are collaborative, it is important to surface the user interaction within a collaboration environment like SAP's 12sprints. Business practices benefit greatly from this type of platform's user management, document management, threaded discussions, and other collaborative facilities. Workspaces also provide an intuitive entry point for users participating in the practice. Although a workspace can be considered the default entry point for a practice, various information such as the business practice's status, active tasks, or key documents could be surfaced in other user experiences such as business applications.

2. **Business process enactments**

   Although some business practices are managed manually, requiring no sophisticated BPM execution capability, others require rich task management and constraints on execution, such as a maximum available time to complete a stage.

3. **Integration services**

   Just like more traditional executable business processes, some business practices require integration with existing business systems. For example, after a collaborative practice is designed to fulfill a custom sales order, a corresponding business object in a business application could be created.

4. **Templates**

   For business practices to become Best Practices, knowledge workers must be able to easily create templates available for use by teams in their organizations. Users should also be able to convert an instance of a business practice into a template.

5. **Simple modeling**

   Knowledge workers need a very simple experience for describing business practices in a way that they can be executed. This modeling experience may not be graphical, but could leverage simple UI paradigms such as bulleted lists, with indenting and out-denting of list items representing stages and stage items. Because it is assumed that business practices are typically adapted at runtime, the business practice modeling experience should blur the line between an explicit design time and run time.

6. **Analytics**

   As with any business process, knowledge workers are interested in the performance of their Best Practices such as the duration of entire practices or the duration of individual tasks. Because practices are typically adapted as they are used, analytics capability should also allow business users to reason over these changes in the composition or structure of the business practice. For example, a simply query could show which tasks were added to the business practice at runtime and assigned to users in the accounting department. Commonality or patterns within these tasks might drive insight that would allow the template to be refined.

18.2.3 Business Practice Example: Part Replacement

This section describes a business scenario that highlights some of the key value drivers for a dedicated software platform to support the lifecycle of business practices.

Background

Imagine a manufacturer of commercial refrigeration equipment that regularly receives notifications from suppliers regarding significant changes to the delivery of supplied parts. For example, a vendor might decide to stop providing a bracket used in an industrial water chiller. Various product teams at the manufacturer have developed their own way (practices) of dealing with these "part replacement" cases. They tend to use a combination of email, collaboration in SAP StreamWork, and access to the SAP Supply Chain Management (SCM) to assess the situation and determine how to proceed, including finding replacement parts and suppliers as necessary.

Describing the Business Practice

Ellen, an experienced product manager, has been asked by the management team to describe her Best Practice for handling part replacements to provide guidance to other teams. She uses a very simple outline-like experience to define the key stages in the process and the relevant stage items, such as a checklist to help prepare for the part replacement. After capturing her knowledge as a description of a business practice, she saves the practice as a template for others in the company to use.

Interacting with a Business Practice

Jann, a new employee, has been asked to lead a part replacement for a precision bolt. A coworker refers him to a page on the company's portal where he can search for a best practice template. He searches for "part replacement" and finds the business practice template that Ellen created. He clicks the START button next to the part replacement template in the search results, and a new business practice workspace is provisioned and displayed in a browser window. Jann takes the following steps to start the collaboration on this part replacement:

1. He invites the appropriate coworkers to the workspace.

2. He assigns the "complete preparation checklist" to Bob, the group's operations manager.

3. He attaches a scanned copy of the letter received from the manufacturer to the site for the participants' reference.

As the business practice evolves, Jann can get a history of the activity from the workspace itself or from visualizations created in traditional knowledge worker artifacts like a mind map (see Figure 18.4). In the artifacts you can see the contributors, input, and phases to the Best Practice.

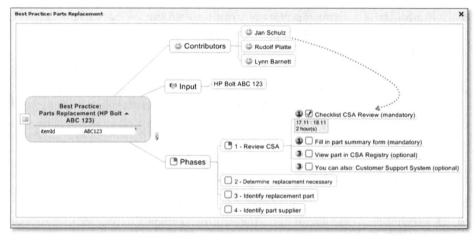

Figure 18.4 Business-Consumable Business Practice Monitoring Dashboard (Mind Map)

Monitoring Business Practices

Peter, director for product development, opens the Part Replacement Monitoring page form the corporate portal (see Figure 18.5). He can see all of the ongoing part replacements throughout the organization, including their status. He notices that a part replacement involving a screw for a compressor has been in progress for weeks and is in red status because the team is unable to get the appropriate approval to onboard a new supplier. He opens the associated workspace to get more context before sending an email to the CFO to help unblock the practice.

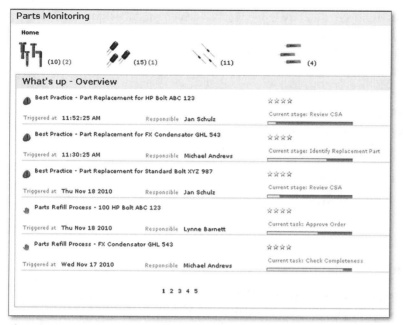

Figure 18.5 Monitoring View of Active Business Practices

Learning from Completed Business Practices

To drive learning from the execution of business practices, Ellen can leverage rich analytics related to the changes that knowledge workers have made to practice workspaces and templates. For example, she can easily query for all documents that have been added to practice workspaces, categorized by the role of the person that created them. Such a query might give her insight into contributions from participants or roles that she wasn't aware of. For example, she might see that the role "product specialist" often adds a technical specification document to part replacement workspaces. She could then easily update the template with a new role and task, providing valuable guidance to future teams that might otherwise remain unaware of the value that a technical specification can add to the execution of the business practice.

18.2.4 SAP ASAP Methodology

It's not often acknowledged, but defining a process is itself a process. The SAP ASAP Methodology helps customers get the most out of their BPM-related efforts and is a perfect example of a knowledge worker-driven practice that would benefit from rich collaboration capabilities and guidance and enforcement. This section describes other basic process patterns that could be effectively approached as business practices.

Problem-Solving

There are numerous approaches or methodologies for generic problem-solving. A related practice might guide workers through the following stages:

1. Articulating the problem statement

2. Defining the solution state

3. Brainstorming on alternatives

4. Picking an alternative

5. Implementing the selected alternative

This type of methodical approach can result in much better solutions than less structured approaches not based on process-centric concepts.

Event Resolution

Applications (such as SAP Business Suite) can end up in a state that requires human intervention to resume normal operations. For example, a product or material that is very difficult to obtain may be depleted in inventory stock without a replenishment order being placed within 10 business days. Often there is not an obvious, predefined response to this type of event. However, this type of event could be consumed by a platform that provisions a generic problem-solving business practice workspace or a specific business practice that evolves to handle specific types of event.

Business Practices as Composite Applications

In many scenarios, knowledge workers need information in enterprise systems to provide context and drive decisions. Once decisions are made, the ability to appropriately update information in enterprise systems such as SAP Business Suite is also critical. For years SAP NetWeaver Composition Environment (CE) has provided SAP customers with the ability to leverage the data and behavior in enterprise applications by creating their own differentiating composite applications.

Many business practices require interaction with an enterprise system, such as retrieving information to drive decisions or create information in backend systems.

18.2.5 Summary

Knowledge workers generate much of the differentiation in many organizations but have a flexible style of working that isn't always well supported by traditional BPM approaches. SAP is thinking deeply about how traditional BPM approaches can be extended and blended with social computing and collaboration to help organizations turn implicit practices into explicit Best Practices. By allowing organizations to quickly capture descriptions of business practices, adapt them as they execute them, and systematically learn from them, SAP can help its customers maximize the impact of their knowledge workers.

18.3 Exploring Additional Future BPM and SOA Trends

To increase your understanding and knowledge of future BPM trends, we will highlight a few articles written by authors who are passionate about BPM and SOA. Readers of this book can download this bonus material free of charge from this book's catalog pages on *www.sap-press.com* and *www.sap-press.de*. In the following subsections, you will find a short summary of each of the articles:

- "Business Process Management and Semantic Interoperability," by Alexander Dreiling
- "SOA for Business Networks – Service Delivery Framework," by Alistair Barros
- "A Requirements Framework for Semantic Business Process Modeling," by Alistair Barros and Ingo M. Weber
- "Process-Centric Decision Support," by Mathias Fritzsche, Wasif Gilani, and Michael Picht
- "Semantic Technologies: An Enabler of Intelligent Business Processes," by Ivan Markovic
- "Customer and Partner Views on the Future of BPM: A View from Two SAP Mentors," by Twan van den Broek and Richard Hirsch

18.3.1 "Business Process Management and Semantic Interoperability" by Alexander Dreiling

Business process management and semantic interoperability (BPM&SI) research has its roots in three distinct areas: business process management, semantics, and interoperability. Today, we have a sophisticated understanding of various aspects within these areas. Whereas the term *business process management* is rather established, semantic interoperability, despite past inflated expectations, is a concept that has only recently emerged. In a recent research roadmap provided by the European Union, the concept has been tangibly described within the domain of healthcare: All efforts at creating electronic health records are pointless unless all relevant stakeholders can access these health records securely and meaning is transmitted correctly and without alteration between different systems, despite changing formats and languages, using different protocols, and so on.

Business or end users hold the expertise in procedures and operations in organizations. Systematically including them in BPM initiatives must go beyond involving them in interviews about how processes are executed. Understanding and supporting the needs of business or end users directly leads to a second research theme, that of communities. Human beings have been forming communities for a long time, but it is an undeniable societal trend, enforced through technological progress, that many of these communities become virtual. Examples within the consumer space show us that people see value in joining technology-enabled networks and building communities there. So far, there is no reason to believe that the mechanisms that work for Facebook, MySpace, and others, cannot work in an organizational setting for the sake of collaboration and for supporting business processes within and across organizations.

The article "Business Process Management and Semantic Interoperability" expresses the belief that research in Business Process Management and Semantic Interoperability needs to stretch beyond the directions currently taken. It is of paramount importance to focus on business user enablement as well as community enablement. That means that we need to build up an understanding of which BPM aspects business users are capable of understanding and expressing. In a similar way, we need to understand how to build technology and tools in order to support their close involvement within BPM initiatives. It also means that we need to understand how to effectively promote collaboration between business users in BPM initiatives with regards to technology. Given an increasing degree of geographical dispersion in contemporary organizations, cloud architectures may lend themselves from a technological perspective to achieve effective community enablement. In order to benefit from cloud architectures for BPM solutions, we need to understand how to move BPM into the cloud (beyond its mere deployment) and effectively leverage the fact that other companies are there, too.

18.3.2 "SOA for Business Networks – Service Delivery Framework" by Alistair Barros

The next generation of SOA needs to scale for flexible service consumption, beyond organizational boundaries and current B2B applications, into communities, ecosystems, and business networks. In the wider and, ultimately, global settings, new capabilities are needed so that business partners can efficiently and reliably enable, adapt, and expose services where they can be discovered, ordered, consumed, metered, and paid for, through new applications and opportunities, driven by third parties in the global "village." This trend is already underway, in different ways, through various early adopter market segments. For the small medium enterprises segment, Google, Intuit-Microsoft, and others have launched *appstores*, through which an open-ended array of hosted applications are sourced from the development community and procured as marketplace commodities. In the corporate sector, the marketplace model and business network hubs are being put in place on top of connectivity and network orchestration investments for capitalizing services as tradable assets, seen in banking/finance (e.g., American Express Intelligent Marketplace), logistics (e.g., the E2open hub), and the public sector (e.g., UK DirectGov whole-of-government citizen services delivery).

To complement current developments in on-demand applications and business network orchestration and to accelerate their future effectiveness, a common integration platform is needed for the provisioning and delivery of services in communities, ecosystems, and business networks — a service delivery framework (SDF). The SDF is intended to support multiple industries and deployments where an SOA delivery platform is needed for collaborating partners and diverse consumers. Specifically, the SDF allows providers to publish their services into network directories so they can be repurposed, traded, and consumed. Unlike current platforms used to enable today's appstores and service marketplaces, the SDF aims at brokering more complex enterprise and business services and allowing utilities in the business network to be leveraged, opening up service hosting to a choice of clouds and adapting services through a choice of B2B gateway services. Beyond present-day "walled gardens," the SDF allows third-parties such as aggregators and channel partners to extend and target services to new monetization points. The article "SOA for Business Networks – Service Delivery Framework," by Alistair Barros, addresses the need for the next generation of SOA to scale for flexible service consumption, beyond organizational boundaries and current B2B applications, into communities, ecosystems, and business networks. The author then proposes a service delivery framework to support the need of a common integration platform to support provisioning and delivery of services in communities, ecosystems, and business networks to complement developments that are ongoing as of today.

18.3.3 "A Requirements Framework for Semantic Business Process Modeling" by Alistair Barros and Ingo M. Weber

The emergence of semantic technologies to deal with the underlying meaning of things, instead of a purely syntactical representation, has led to new developments in various fields, including business process modeling. Inspired by artificial intelligence research, technologies for semantic Web services have been proposed and extended to process modeling. However, the applicability of semantic Web services for semantic business processes is limited because business processes encompass wider requirements of businesses than Web services. In particular, processes are concerned with the composition of tasks, that is, in which order activities are carried out, regardless of their implementation details; resources assigned to carry out tasks, such as machinery, people, and goods; data exchange; and security and compliance concerns.

Semantics can be used to support designers of business processes who are more concerned with business requirements than the technical prowess of modeling. Drawing on insights of business process language constructs, we can identify several requirements for semantic extensions to business process modeling. This list of requirements can be perceived as a wish list of features that endow classical business process modeling with semantic contexts, such as semantically correct sequencing of tasks, binding correct implementation-level artifacts (e.g., service operations) for process activities, and model correspondence to the corporate context, for example, taking policies and regulations into account when searching for the artifacts required in business process models.

The list of requirements presented in this article is not exhaustive but is based on anecdotal evidence and notations, standards, and Best Practices in the BPM field.

Thus, the list contains a mix of feasible and preferred features in the practice of BPM. The authors present some of their work to implement requirements from this list in a business-user-friendly way and discuss the feasibility of implementing more of the requirements.

18.3.4 "Process-Centric Decision Support" by Mathias Fritzsche, Wasif Gilani, and Michael Picht

To stay competitive companies need to continuously monitor and improve their business processes. The target is to implement the so-called closed loop of continuous business process improvement. This closed loop is a highly innovative paradigm that will drive the continuous adaptation of business processes to rapidly evolving market contexts, user requirements, and business imperatives.

In the configuration phase processes are designed and business systems are configured to be able to execute the desired business processes accordingly.

During the process execution phase, data that is relevant to evaluate process efficiency is collected. Based on this data, different types of analysis can be done: quantitative process analysis, process efficiency analysis, benchmarking, and business continuity analysis.

Finally, in the decide phase, decisions about the resolution of the inefficiencies are made and then implemented in the configuration phase.

This article focuses on the "analyze" and the "decide" phases of the loop, and explains the advantages, specific challenges, and approaches.

Additionally, the authors propose an architecture, which provides a highly generic Process-centric Decision Support that solves the limitations of the currently existing approaches. The contribution of this framework to the state of the art is twofold. First, it encapsulates process-centric decision support in a way that it can be employ for processes which are spanning cross-systems, including BPM Suites as well as classical Enterprise Resource Planning (ERP) systems. Second, the support is sophisticated as it is based on a Decision Support Model which allows calculating different kinds of process-centric KFs based on historical information, predicted information, optimization and sensitivity information.

18.3.5 "Semantic Technologies: An Enabler of Intelligent Business Processes" by Ivan Markovic

Business process management as an approach to manage the execution of IT-supported business operations has gained significant attention from the industry in recent years. However, two important problems in BPM have emerged:

► The degree of automation in BPM is very limited.

► BPM does not provide a unified view of the process space of an organization.

By increasing the level of automation in BPM, the tasks such as discovery and composition of services into processes could be performed by machines, and a more intelligent BPM tooling support would be possible. Through providing a unified view on process space, we would allow managers to pose intelligent queries over the business process space to better support their decision-making.

To achieve a higher degree of automation in BPM and provide a uniform representation of process space, an organization's business processes need to be described on a semantic level. Semantic technologies stand for methods and tools that represent meanings and knowledge separately from data, content, and application code. A semantic technology-based application uses the semantic models as a basis for its operation. In this context, the use of a semantic model is often referred to as "reasoning over the model."

The fact that semantic models represent the domain knowledge separately from data, content, and application code significantly increases the flexibility of applications. When using standard information technologies, the domain knowledge needs to be predefined and hard-wired into data formats and application code at design time. If something needs to be changed, humans need to get involved. Data structures and application logic need to be recoded, and then the changes need to be applied to the database and the application. When using semantic models, changing and implementing new relationships or interconnecting applications in a different way requires only changing the semantic model that the applications share. This external semantic model is then consulted by the applications at execution time.

By enabling the possibility to intelligently reason over the domain models, semantic technologies allow for building applications that can learn and adapt their behavior based on experience. In contrast, with standard information technologies, the reasoning algorithms are hard-wired in the application code. If anything new is learned, and hence the algorithm must be changed, humans must reprogram its logic offline.

The benefits that semantic technologies offer have been demonstrated in areas such as information integration, information retrieval, knowledge management, and software engineering. In recent years, semantic technologies have been used in business process management (BPM) to address the limited degree of automation in BPM and to provide a unified view on the process space of an organization, yielding a new area of research called semantic business process management.

This article focuses on the early stages of the BPM lifecycle and shows how semantic technologies can facilitate business process modeling in particular.

18.3.6 "Customer and Partner Views on the Future of BPM: A View from Two SAP Mentors" by Twan van den Broek and Richard Hirsch

BPM refers to more than the technology involved. It also includes the methodology on which such work is based and "organizational" factors that influence process-related work. BPM-related requirements for partners and customers may not be identical. Not only do these two groups have different relationships to SAP as a corporation or to its technology, but they also have a relationship to one another that influences how they view this topic. For example, customers may be interested in increased the usability of process environments. Partners, on the other hand, may be interested in the ability to provide BPM-related projects on time and on budget that still meet end-user requirements. These interests may conflict with one another and must thus not be ignored. A unified view on these distinct perspectives is necessary.

If you examine each group in question — customers and partners — you will also see that these are not homogeneous groups but are composed of distinct perspectives, each of which has particular requirements. For example, "customers" could include managers whose employees use BPM technology and end users who use this technology on a daily basis. These two different groups may have conflicting goals as well. Managers might focus on achieving their KPIs or greater efficiency in process-related work, whereas end users might demand process-related user interfaces that are more enjoyable to work with. Other distinctions might be between power users who use a tool on a regular basis and other knowledge workers who use a process environment infrequently. For "partners," there are also different possible perspectives. These distinctions might be associated with the size of the partner firm in question or the technological focus of the company.

This article explains how these distinct perspectives can be brought together in a unified view. Two topics in particular that have recently received a great deal of attention and will, in the authors' opinion, have the greatest impact in the next five years — agile process methodologies and social BPM — will be dealt with in detail.

Appendices

A   IT Performance and Value Management Research 639

B   Value Driver Processes Sorted After Strategic, Tactical,
     and Operational Levels 641

C   Bibliography 657

D   The Authors 673

A   IT Performance and Value Management Research

This table provides sources for performance and value management research and discussion that has taken place over the past 30 years.

Level	Cross-Sector	Manufacturing	Services
Aggregate-level studies	Jonscher [1983, 1994]	Morrison and Berndt [1991]	Brand and Duke [1982]
Economy-wide and industry-level	▶ Baily [1986b], Baily & Chakrabarti [1988], Baily and Gordon [1988] ▶ Roach [1987, 1988, 1989b] ▶ Brooke [1992] ▶ Lau and Tokutsu [1992] ▶ Oliner and Sichel [1994] ▶ Jorgenson and Stiroh [1995] ▶ Brynjolfsson [1995] ▶ Peppard and Ward [2003] ▶ Brynjolfsson [2005] ▶ Butler Group [2005] ▶ IBM CEO study [2006, 2008, 2009, 2010] ▶ von Rosing [2010]	▶ Berndt et al. [1992], Berndt and Morrison [1995] ▶ Siegel and Griliches [1992] ▶ Siegel [2004] ▶ Dahl, Jensen, and von Rosing [2010]	▶ Baily [1986] ▶ Roach [1987, 1991, 2001]

Level	Cross-Sector	Manufacturing	Services
Micro-level studies	▶ Osterman [1986] ▶ Dos Santos [1993] ▶ Krueger [1993] ▶ Pfeffer and Sutton [2000] ▶ Brynjolfsson [2005] ▶ Butler Group [2005] ▶ Cook [2007]	▶ Loveman [1994] ▶ Weill [1988, 1992] ▶ Dudley and Lasserre [1989]	▶ Cron and Sobol [1983] ▶ Pulley and Braunstein [1984] ▶ Bender [1986]
Firms and workers	▶ Brynjolfsson and Hitt [1994] ▶ Lichtenberg [1995] ▶ Pfeffer and Sutton [2000] ▶ Peppard and Ward [2003] ▶ von Rosing [2009, 2010]	▶ Barua, Kriebel, and Mukhopad-hyay [1991] ▶ Brynjolfsson and Hitt [1993, 1995] ▶ Brynjolfsson [2005]	▶ Bresnahan [1986] ▶ Franke [1987] ▶ Strassmann [1985, 1990] ▶ Harris and Katz [1999] ▶ Parsons et al. [2007] ▶ Diewert and Smith [2008]

B   Value Driver Processes Sorted After Strategic, Tactical, and Operational Levels

This table shows how processes should be sorted after strategic, tactical, and operational activities. Then all levels are linked to the key performance indicators, critical success factors, and strategic business objectives, including the business owner who would receive the value.

Business Model Level	BPM Key Focus	Process	Activity	Key Performance Indicator	Critical Success Factors	Strategies & Objectives
1. Strategic	1. Strategy process	Evaluate performance of existing products/services against market opportunities	—	Improve platform and portfolio strategies for products and services	Strengthen innovation – CMO, CRDO	Improve competitiveness – CEO
		Manage sales partners and alliances	Evaluate partner/alliance results	Increase focus on partnership, merger, and acquisition opportunities	Improve partner and relationship collaboration – CFO, COO	
		Develop production and materials strategies	Define production network and supply constraints	Develop low-inventory business models	Improve logistics, material and services – COO	Improve operational efficiency – CEO
		Develop and manage media	Define target audience	Enter new segments and markets	Increase revenue through volume optimization – CFO, CMO	Increase shareholder value – CEO
		Develop the IT development strategy	Establish sourcing strategy for IT development	Consolidate or outsource IT design and development functions	Reduce sales and administration costs – CFO, COO	

Business Model Level	BPM Key Focus	Process	Activity	Key Performance Indicator	Critical Success Factors	Strategies & Objectives
				Consolidate or outsource IT design, development, and deployment services		
		Establish marketing budgets	Confirm marketing alignment to business strategy	Align advertising with pricing strategies	Increase revenue through price optimization – CFO, CMO	
		Coordinate and align functional and process strategies	–	Improve alignment of customer, product, sales, service, support, and fulfillment strategies	Improve risk management – CFO, CRSO	Lower risk – CEO
		Develop and perform preventive law programs	–	Improve anticipation and understanding of current and potential regulation/legislation	Optimize regulation compliance – CFO	
	2. Customer process	Establish goals, objectives, and metrics for products by channels/segments	Define media objectives	Target new geographies	Increase revenue through volume optimization – CFO, CMO	Increase shareholder value – CEO
	2. Internal company process	Develop sales forecast	Analyze historical and planned promotions and events	Increase emphasis on operational integration with partners	Improve partner and relationship collaboration – CFO, COO	Improve competitiveness – CEO

Business Model Level	BPM Key Focus	Process	Activity	Key Performance Indicator	Critical Success Factors	Strategies & Objectives
		Develop sales partner/alliance relationships	Design alliance programs and methods for selecting and managing relationships	Improve ability to identify and assess partnering opportunities		
		Establish goals, objectives, and metrics for products by channels/segments	–	Improve marketing and advertising performance management methods and tools	Improve brand awareness – CMO	
			–	Rationalize and/or refocus channel/media usage		
		Design, build, and evaluate products and services	Collaborate on design with suppliers and contract manufacturers	Increase emphasis on modular, extensible, scalable designs	Reduce cost of goods sold – CFO, COO	Increase shareholder value – CEO
		Develop and manage business resiliency	Develop the business resilience strategy	More effective damage handling roadmaps	Improve business recovery – CRSO, CIO	Lower risk – CEO
				Improve incorporation of risk analysis in business planning	Improve risk planning – CFO, CRSO	
			Maintain continuous business operations	Effective business continuity roadmaps	Improve business recovery – CRSO, CIO	
		Develop IT services and solution delivery strategy	Select delivery methodologies and tools	Establish recovery and maintenance plans		

Business Model Level	BPM Key Focus	Process	Activity	Key Performance Indicator	Critical Success Factors	Strategies & Objectives
		Develop overall mission statement	Define current business	Improve integration of short- and long-term business planning	Improve risk planning – CFO, CRSO	
		Ensure compliance	Plan and initiate compliance program	Compliance with environmental standards	Optimize regulation compliance – CFO	
				Compliance with industry standards		
				Compliance with health standards		
				Data and privacy protection compliance		
		Evaluate strategic options to achieve the objectives	Develop lean/continuous improvement strategy	Improve business continuity planning	Improve business recovery – CRSO, CIO	
		Perform customer and market intelligence analysis	Analyze market and industry trends	Provide greater predictability in performance	Optimize intelligence – CFO, COO	
		Plan for change	Conduct risk analysis	Increase emphasis on risk-informed, scenario-based planning	Improve risk planning – CFO, CRSO	

Business Model Level	BPM Key Focus	Process	Activity	Key Performance Indicator	Critical Success Factors	Strategies & Objectives
	2. Products and services processes	Design and launch knowledge management (KM) projects	Design process for knowledge sharing, capture, and use	Better settings for innovation to flourish	Strengthen innovation – CMO, CRDO	Improve competitiveness – CEO
		Perform discovery research	Identify new technologies	Increase focus on R&D, product innovation, and product leadership		
1. Strategic	2. Product and service processes	Define product/service development requirements	Identify potential improvements to existing products and services	Design product for ease-of-use/self-service	Reduce sales and administration costs – CFO, COO	Increase shareholder value CEO
		Measure customer satisfaction with customer requests/inquiries handling	Analyze product and service satisfaction data and identify improvement opportunities	Rationalize and/or refocus product and service portfolios	Reduce cost of goods sold – CFO, COO	
2. Tactical	2. Customer process	Assess the external environment	Analyze and evaluate competition	Improve competitive research	Strengthen innovation – CMO, CRDO	Improve competitiveness – CEO
		Manage relations with quasi-government bodies	–	Optimal collaboration across the value chain	Speed up time-to-market – CMO, CRDO	
		Survey market and determine customer needs and wants	Conduct qualitative/quantitative assessments	Improve market intelligence		

Business Model Level	BPM Key Focus	Process	Activity	Key Performance Indicator	Critical Success Factors	Strategies & Objectives
		Perform customer and market intelligence analysis	Conduct customer and market research	Improve focus on higher-value customer segments	Reduce cost of goods sold – CFO, COO	Increase shareholder value – CEO
				Rationalize targeted markets and customer segments	Reduce sales and administration costs – CFO, COO	
				Reduce business risk by aligning with changing market needs	Optimize intelligence – CFO, COO	Lower risk – CEO
	2. Internal company process	Design, build, and evaluate products and services	Prepare high-level business case and technical assessment	Improve project management	Fasten time-to-market – CMO, CRDO	Improve competitiveness – CEO
		Develop sales partner/alliance relationships	Develop partner and alliance management strategies	Improve quality of information provided to stakeholders	Improve partner and relationship collaboration – CFO, COO	
		Manage sales orders	Collect and maintain customer account information	Improve sales forecasting and campaign execution processes and tools	Improve customer interaction – COO, CMO	
		Perform customer and market intelligence analysis	Analyze market and industry trends	Increase focus on business insight and forward-looking information	Reduce sales and administration costs – CFO, COO	Increase shareholder value – CEO

Business Model Level	BPM Key Focus	Process	Activity	Key Performance Indicator	Critical Success Factors	Strategies & Objectives
		Create enterprise measurement systems model	Establish performance measures	Improve determination of key performance metrics and targets	Optimize intelligence – CFO, COO	Lower risk – CEO
	2. Internal company process	Create organizational design (structure, governance, reporting, etc.)	Design the relationships between organizational units	Strengthen corporate governance structures	Improve risk management – CFO, CRSO	
		Develop and manage business resiliency	Develop the business resilience strategy	► Improve company-wide monitoring and management of risks ► Increase emphasis on risk identification and management		
		Develop information and content management strategies	Assess the information and content management implications of new technologies	Improve identification and prediction of industry and market trends	Optimize intelligence – CFO, COO	
		Develop KM strategy	Develop core KM methodologies	Improve analysis of managerial information		

Business Model Level	BPM Key Focus	Process	Activity	Key Performance Indicator	Critical Success Factors	Strategies & Objectives
		Develop overall mission statement	Define current business	Improve effectiveness of program/ project governance models	Improve risk planning – CFO, CRSO	
		Develop tax strategy and plan	Monitor tax compliance	Ensure that tax planning activities and tax filings comply with regulatory environment	Optimize regulation compliance – CFO	
		Develop the IT development strategy	Establish sourcing strategy for IT development	Improve monitoring and management of regulatory compliance		
		Establish internal controls, policies, and procedures	Define and communicate code of ethics	Improve focus on internal controls and regulatory compliance		
			Define business process objectives and risks	Align internal audit practices with business and risk objectives	Improve risk management – CFO, CRSO	
			Establish board of directors and audit committee	Improve/ implement internal control frameworks and policies	Improve risk planning – CFO, CRSO	
		Perform cost management	Determine critical activities	Improve focus of company resources on high-priority initiatives	Improve risk management – CFO, CRSO	

Business Model Level	BPM Key Focus	Process	Activity	Key Performance Indicator	Critical Success Factors	Strategies & Objectives
		Perform customer and market intelligence analysis	Analyze competing organizations, competitive/substitute products	Improve identification of opportunities and threats	Optimize intelligence – CFO, COO	
2. Tactical	2. Internal company process	Perform customer and market intelligence analysis	Analyze market and industry trends	Secure use of information that is accurate and real-time	Optimize intelligence – CFO, COO	Lower risk – CEO
	2. Products and services processes	Design, build, and evaluate products and services	Conduct in-house product/service testing and evaluate feasibility	Increase number and quality of product and service launches	Speed up time-to-market – CMO, CRDO	Improve competitiveness – CEO
		Develop and manage reward, recognition, and motivation programs	Develop salary/compensation structure and plan	Improve incentives for product development and innovation	Improve human capital management – CHRO	Improve operational efficiency – CEO
		Define product/service development requirements	Identify potential improvements to existing products and services	Improve emphasis on product quality and ease of service	Reduce sales and administration costs – CFO, COO	Increase shareholder value – CEO
		Develop production and materials strategies	Define manufacturing goals	Improve quality assurance programs	Improve risk management – CFO, CRSO	Lower risk – CEO
	4. Organizational focused process	Conduct gap analysis to understand need for change and degree needed	—	Identify organization's limits and weakness	Optimize intelligence – CFO, COO	

Business Model Level	BPM Key Focus	Process	Activity	Key Performance Indicator	Critical Success Factors	Strategies & Objectives
3. Operational	1. Strategy process	Evaluate and prioritize market opportunities	Quantify market opportunities	Develop, spin-off, and sell new business	Improve capital management – CFO	Improve operational efficiency – CEO
		Establish goals, objectives, and metrics for products by channels/segments	—	Penetrate new markets better and faster	Increase revenue through volume optimization – CFO, CMO	Increase shareholder value – CEO
		Evaluate and prioritize market opportunities	Quantify market opportunities	Gain market share while others recover from external shocks		
		Survey market and determine customer needs and wants	Conduct qualitative/quantitative assessments	Improve ability to develop and spin off new businesses	Capital optimization – CFO	
	2. Customer process	Define offering and customer value proposition	Develop value proposition including brand positioning for target segments	Tailor marketing approaches to customer segments	Improve brand awareness – CMO	Improve competitiveness – CEO
		Define product/service development requirements	Identify potential new products and services	Better match of trends and buying patterns	Strengthen innovation – CMO, CRDO	
		Design, build, and evaluate products and services	Collaborate on design with suppliers and contract manufacturers	Reduce research and development time through collaboration	Speed up time-to-market – CMO, CRDO	

Business Model Level	BPM Key Focus	Process	Activity	Key Performance Indicator	Critical Success Factors	Strategies & Objectives
		Manage sales orders	Enter orders into system and identify/perform cross-sell/up-sell activity	Improve effectiveness of cross-sell and up-sell approaches/models	Improve customer interaction – COO, CMO	
		Manage sales partners and alliances	Agree on partner and alliance commissions	Improve terms with advertising channels		
		Perform customer and market intelligence analysis	Conduct customer and market research	Improve accuracy of consumer analysis	Strengthen innovation – CMO, CRDO	
		Establish overall sales budgets	Determine variable costs	Differentiate treatment of customers/segments	Improve logistics, material and services – COO	Improve operational efficiency – CEO
		Establish goals, objectives, and metrics for products by channels/segments	—	Improve cross-sell and up-sell campaigns	Increase revenue through volume optimization – CFO, CMO	Increase shareholder value – CEO
		Generate leads	Identify potential customers	▶ Tailor sales approaches to customer segments ▶ Target new segments within current geographies		
		Perform customer and market intelligence analysis	Conduct customer and market research	Rationalize targeted customer segments	Reduce sales and administration costs – CFO, COO	

Business Model Level	BPM Key Focus	Process	Activity	Key Performance Indicator	Critical Success Factors	Strategies & Objectives
	2. Internal company process	Design, build, and evaluate products and services	Develop product/service design specifications	Improve design and development approaches	Strengthen innovation – CMO, CRDO	Improve competitiveness – CEO
			Identify design/development performance indicators	Improve methods and tools for managing innovation performance		
			Prepare high-level business case and technical assessment	Improve integration of research and development		
		Develop sales partner/alliance relationships	Develop partner and alliance management strategies	Improve ability to turn strong relationships into competitive advantage	Improve partner and relationship collaboration – CFO, COO	
		Design, build, and evaluate products and services	Collaborate on design with suppliers and contract manufacturers	Increase emphasis on designing for efficient materials management	Improve logistics, material, and services – COO	Improve operational efficiency – CEO
3. Operational	2. Internal company process	Develop and train employees	Develop, conduct, and manage employee and/or management training programs	Develop and maintain better competencies	Improve human capital management – CHRO	Improve operational efficiency CEO
		Develop human resources strategy	Identify strategic HR needs	Establish process improvement and innovation as key competencies		

Business Model Level	BPM Key Focus	Process	Activity	Key Performance Indicator	Critical Success Factors	Strategies & Objectives
		Develop production and materials strategies	Define production network and supply constraints	Route low-value transactions to lower-cost service channels	Improve logistics, material, and services – COO	
		Evaluate and manage financial performance	Assess customer and product profitability	Improve business case development and analysis processes	Improve corporate services – CFO, COO	Improve operational efficiency – CEO
		Manage human resource information systems (HRIS)	—	Improve knowledge sharing	Improve human caital maagee – CHRO	
		Perform planning, budgeting, and forecasting	Prepare periodic budgets and plans	Reduce capital requirements through partnering	Improve capital management – CFO	
		Define and manage channel strategy	Evaluate channel attributes and partners	Improve focus on higher-value advertising channels/media	Reduce sales and administration costs – CFO, COO	Increase shareholder value – CEO
		Manage treasury policies and procedures	Revise treasury procedures	Exploit variable cost opportunities	Capital optimization – CFO	
		Design, build, and evaluate products and services	Develop product/service design specifications	Improve development and analysis of business cases	Improve risk management – CFO, CRSO	Lower risk – CEO
		Develop and manage business resiliency	Develop business resilience strategy	Effective and efficient risk management procedures		

Business Model Level	BPM Key Focus	Process	Activity	Key Performance Indicator	Critical Success Factors	Strategies & Objectives
		Develop and manage business resiliency	Develop business resilience strategy	Improve identification and assessment of risk	Improve risk management – CFO, CRSO	Lower risk – CEO
				Improve understanding of regulatory requirements	Optimize regulation compliance – CFO	
		Develop human resources strategy	Identify strategic HR needs	Minimize risk by increasing expertise in selected activities and markets	Improve risk planning – CFO, CRSO	Lower risk – CEO
		Develop information and content management strategies	Assess information and content management implications of new technologies	Improve analytical processes and tools	Optimize intelligence – CFO, COO	
		Develop overall mission statement	Communicate mission	Strengthen and communicate mission, vision, values, and ethics	Improve risk management – CFO, CRSO	
				Improve communication between board, management, shareholders, and public		
			Define current business	Improve effectiveness of governance models	Improve risk planning – CFO, CRSO	

Business Model Level	BPM Key Focus	Process	Activity	Key Performance Indicator	Critical Success Factors	Strategies & Objectives
		Manage lobbying activities	—	Improve effectiveness of legislative/lobbying efforts	Improve risk management – CFO, CRSO	
	2. Products and services processes	Define product/service development requirements	Identify potential new products and services	Tailor products and services to new customer segments	Increase revenue through volume optimization – CFO, CMO	Increase shareholder value – CEO
		Design, build, and evaluate products and services	Identify design/development performance indicators	Rationalize and/or realign product development efforts	Reduce cost of goods sold – CFO, COO	
		Develop and manage packaging strategy	Execute promotional activities	Improve execution of market- and supply-driven promotions	Increase revenue through price optimization – CFO, CMO	
			Refine promotional performance metrics	Improve structuring and pricing of promotions		
		Develop customer service segmentation/ prioritization (e.g., tiers)	Analyze feedback of customer needs	Consolidate service and support operations	Reduce sales and administration costs – CFO, COO	
		Evaluate strategic options to achieve objectives	Develop risk mitigation and management strategy	Risk management across product and services	Improve risk management –CFO, CRSO	Lower risk – CEO
	3. Technology-focused process	Perform capital planning and project approval	Conduct financial justification for project approval	Avoid expensive recovery investments	Improve corporate services – CFO, COO	Improve operational efficiency – CEO

Business Model Level	BPM Key Focus	Process	Activity	Key Performance Indicator	Critical Success Factors	Strategies & Objectives
		Develop IT services and solution delivery strategy	Select delivery methodologies and tools	▶ Effective and efficient backup systems ▶ Efficient fall-back systems ▶ Efficient recovery solutions	Improve business recovery – CRSO, CIO	Lower risk – CEO
3. Operational	4. Organization-focused process	Create and develop employee requisitions	Align staffing plan to work force plan and business unit strategies/resource needs	Improve executive development, recruiting, and succession planning	Improve human capital management – CHRO	Improve operational efficiency – CEO
		Develop and implement human resources plans	Develop other HR programs	Improve talent management models and programs		
		Create ethics policies	—	Build values and ethics into corporate culture	Improve risk planning – CFO, CRSO	Lower risk – CEO
		Define customer service policies and procedures	—	Improve management of organizational change in support of initiatives	Improve risk management – CFO, CRSO	
		Develop overall mission statement	Communicate mission	Improve communication of strategic directions and priorities		

C   Bibliography

Part I

Afuah, A. 2003. *Business Models: A Strategic Management Approach.* McGraw-Hill/Irwin.

Aiken, L. S. and S. G. West. 1991. *Multiple Regression: Testing and Interpreting Interactions.* Sage: Thousand Oaks, CA.

Aldrich, H. E. 1979. *Organizations and Environments.* Prentice Hall: Englewood Cliffs, NJ.

Aldrich, H. E. 1999. *Organizations Evolving.* Sage: Thousand Oaks, CA.

Amit, R. and C. Zott. 2001. "Value creation in e-business." *Strategic Management Journal* 22, 493–520.

ARC. 2005. *Operational Excellence in the LSP Industry: A Strategy for Profitable Growth and Differentiation. http://www.sap.com/uk/images/bankinginsight/ARCReport.pdf.*

Arvato. 2010. Arvato – At Your Service. Retrieved March 11, 2010, from *http://www.arvato.de/wms/arvato/Home.html?language=2.*

Ashton, H. and D. Kelly. *The Business Impact of BPM with SOA: Building a Case for BPM with SOA ROI.* pp. 9–10. *http://www-01.ibm.com/software/info/bpmsoa/pdf/UR-IBM-BPM_Business_Case-Final-1.pdf.*

Bhide, A. 2000. *The Origin and Evolution of New Businesses.* Oxford University Press: New York.

Brandenburger, A. and B. Nalebuff. 1996. *Co-Opetition: A Revolution Mindset that Combines Competition and Cooperation.* Doubleday: New York.

Brandenburger, A. M. and H. Stuart. 1996. "Value-based business strategy." *Journal of Economics & Management Strategy* 5, 5–25.

Bresnahan, T., E. Brynjolfsson, and L. Hitt. 2002. "Information technology, workplace organization, and the demand for skilled labor: Firm-level evidence." *Quarterly Journal of Economics* 117, 339–376.

Brynjolfsson, E. 2010. "The 4 ways IT is driving innovation: An interview with Eric Brynjolfsson." *MIT Sloan Management Review*, February.

Brynjolfsson, E., L. Hitt, and S. Yang. 2004. "Intangible assets and the economic impact of computers." In W. Dutton, B. Kahin, R. O'Callaghan, and A. Wyckoff (eds.), *Transforming Enterprise*. MIT Press: Boston, pp. 27–48.

Business Process Management Survey. 2009. *http://www.global360.com/xres/uploads/resource-center-documents/BPM_Survey_final_1.pdf.*

Butler Group. "Measuring IT Costs and Value." East Yorkshire: England, Butler Group Press, September 2005.

Campa, J. M. and S. Keida. 2002. Explaining the diversification discount. *Journal of Finance* LVII:1731–1762.

Cantara, M. 2008–2010. *Market Trends: Impact of Business Process Management on Consulting and Development & Integration Services, Worldwide.* Gartner, *http://www.gartner.com/DisplayDocument?doc_cd=163729&ref=g_rss.*

Chesbrough, H.W. 2003. *Open Innovation: The New Imperative for Creating and Profiting from Technology*. Harvard Business Press: Boston.

Chesbrough, H. and R. Rosenbloom. 2002. "The role of the business model in capturing value from innovation: Evidence from Xerox Corporation's technology spinoff companies." *Industrial and Corporate Change* 11, 529–555.

Christensen, C.M. 2001. "The past and future of competitive advantage." *MIT Sloan Management Review* 42, 105–109.

Clemons, E.K. and M.C. Row. 1992. "Information technology and industrial cooperation: The changing economics of coordination and ownership." *Journal of Management Information Systems* 9, 9–28.

Cluetrain. 2000. The Cluetrain Manifesto: People on Earth. Retrieved March 16, 2000, from *http://www.cluetrain.com/.*

Cook, R. "How to Spot a Failing IT Project." *CIO Magazine*, 17 July 2007.

Coff, R. L. 1999. "When competitive advantage doesn't lead to performance: The resource-based view and stakeholder bargaining power." *Organization Science* 10, 119–133.

Cohen, J. and P. Cohen. 1983. *Applied Multiple Regression: Correlation Analysis for the Behavioral Sciences*, 2nd ed. Lawrence Erlbaum: Hillsdale, NJ.

Daft, R..L. and A.Y. Lewin. 1993. "Where are the theories for the 'new' organizational forms? An editorial essay." *Organization Science* 4, i – vi.

Daft, R.L. 2004. *Organization Theory and Design.* 8th ed. Thomson South-Western: Mason, OH.

Davidow, W. H. and M. S. Malone. 1992. *The Virtual Corporation: Structuring and Revitalizing the Corporation for the 21st Century.* HarperBusiness: New York.

Deephouse, D. L. 1999. "To be different, or to be the same? It's a question [and theory] of strategic balance." *Strategic Management J.* 20, 147–166.

Deloitte. 2004. *Driving Enterprise Value.* Deloite Press: New York.

Dess, G. and D.W. Beard. 1984. "Dimensions of organizational task environments." *Administrative Science Quarterly* 29, 52–74.

Dess, G. G. and R. Robinson. 1984. "Measuring organizational performance in the absence of objective measures." *Strategic Management J.* 5, 265–273.

Dibrell, R.M. and C. Clay. 1999. "Conceptual and Empirical Evidence of International Macro and Micro Congruent Generic Strategies: A Study of Japan and the U.S." *Advances in Competitive Research.* *http://www.allbusiness.com/government/398366–1.html*

Dowling, M. J. and J. E. McGee. 1994. "Business and technology strategies and new venture performance: A study of the telecommunications equipment industry." *Management Science* 40, 1663–1677.

Drucker, P. 1985. *Innovation and Entrepreneurship.* Harper & Row: New York.

Eijpe, R.A., C. Laar, and M. Gerritsen. 2010. *Het ICASIO patroon,* internal paper (Dutch only), NL for Business, Retrieved July 31, 2010.

Filson, D. 2004. "The impact of e-commerce strategies on firm value: Lessons from Amazon.com and its early competitors." *Journal of Business* 77, 135–154.

Finegar P. 2009. *Dot Cloud: The 21st Century Business Platform.* Meghan-Kiffer Press: Tampa, FL.

Fornell, C. and D. F. Larcker. 1981. "Evaluating structural equation models with unobservable variables and management error." *Journal of Marketing Research* 18, 39–50.

Foss, N. J. 2002. "Introduction: New organizational forms – critical perspectives." *International Journal of the Economics of Business* 9, 1–8.

Gartner EXP Worldwide CIO Survey, 2009. *http://www.gartner.com/it/page. jsp?id=855612.*

Gatignon, H. 2003. *Statistical Analysis of Management Data.* Kluwer Academic: Boston.

Gatignon, H., M. Tushman, W. Smith, and P. Anderson. 2002. "A structural approach to assessing innovation: Construct development of innovation locus, type and characteristics." *Management Science* 48, 1103–1122.

Gold-Bernstein, B. 2009. "Service-driven enterprises: Aptly named." Retrieved September 23, 2009, from *http://www.ebizq.net/topics/bpm/features/4596.html?rss.*

Greene, W. 2003. *Econometric Analysis.* Prentice-Hall: Upper Saddle River, NJ.

Hargadorn, A. B. and Y. Douglas. 2001. "When innovations meet institutions: Edison and the design of the electric light." *Administrative Science Quarterly* 46, 476–501.

Hawawini, G., V. Subramanian, and P. Verdin. 2003. "Is performance driven by industry- or firm-specific factors? A new look at the evidence." *Strategic Management Journal* 24, 1–16.

Hill, C.W.L. and S.A. Snell. 1988. "External Control, Corporate Strategy, and Firm Performance in Research-Intensive Industries." *Strategic Management Journal* 9, 577–590.

Hill, J. 2008. Making the Case for BPM in a Time of Crisis. Gartner Keynote, London.

Hite, J. M. and W. S. Hesterly. 2001. "The evolution of firm networks: From emergence to early growth of the firm." *Strategic Management Journal 22,* 275–286.

Hitt, M. A., R. D. Ireland, S. M. Camp, and D. L. Sexton. 2001. "Strategic entrepreneurship: Entrepreneurial strategies for wealth creation." *Strategic Management Journal 22,* 479–491.

HP. 2010. *Hit Print Intelligently: The HP Printing Payback Guarantee.* Retrieved March 14, 2010, from *http://www.hp.com/large/campaign/guarantee/index.html?jumpid=re_ r11400_us/en/large/IPG/ipg20_ppg_int_staticimage.*

HP. 2006. *HP Energizes Enterprise Imaging and Printing Growth with Revitalized Sales Approach, Expanded Portfolio.* Retrieved September 25, 2006, from *http://h30261. www3.hp.com/phoenix.zhtml?c=71087&p=irol-newsArticle&ID=911663&highlight.*

Hulland, J. 1999. "Use of partial least squares [PLS] in strategic management research: A review of four recent studies." *Strategic Management Journal* 20, 195–204.

IBM Global CEO Study. 2006, 2007, 2008, 2009 and 2010. IBM Value Institute Press: New York.

Iansiti, M. and K. B. Clark. 1994. "Integration and dynamic capability: Evidence from product development in automobiles and mainframe computers." *Industrial and Corporate Change* 3, 557–605.

Ichniowski, C., T. A. Kochan, D. Levine, C. Olson, and G. Strauss. 1996. "What works at work: Overview and assessment." *Industrial Relations* 35, 299–333.

IDC. 2010. Managed Print Services – Global Market & Provider Analysis. Framingham, MA.

Ilinitch, A. Y., R. A. D'Aveni, and A. Y. Lewin. 1996. "New organizational forms and strategies for managing in hypercompetitive environments." *Organization Science* 7, 211–220.

Ireland, R. D., M. A. Hitt, M. Camp, and D. L. Sexton. 2001. "Integrating entrepreneurship and strategic management actions to create firm wealth." *Academy of Management Executive* 15, 49–63.

Johnson, M. W., C. M. Christensen, and H. Kagermann. "Reinventing your business model." *Harvard Business Review* December, 2008.

Kaplan, S. N., B. A. Sensoy, and P. Stromberg. 2005. What Are Organizations? Evolution from Birth to Public Companies. Working Paper, University of Chicago: Chicago.

Kim, E.N., Dae-il Stimpert, J.L. 2004. "Testing the applicability of Porter's generic strategies in the digital age." *Journal of Business Strategies*.

Kleinbaum, D. G., L. L. Kupper, K. E. Muller, and A. Nizam. 1998. *Applied Regression Analysis and Other Multivariable Methods,* 3rd ed. Duxberry Press: Pacific Grove, CA.

Kogut, B. 2000. "The network as knowledge: Generative rules and the emergence of structure." *Strategic Management Journal* 21, 405–425.

Kotha, S., S. Rajgopal, and M. Venkatchalam. 2004. "The role of online buying experience as a competitive advantage: Evidence from third party ratings from e-commerce organizations." *Journal of Business* 77, 109–133.

Kotha, S., V. Rindova, and F. Rothaermel. 2001. "Assets and actions: Firm-specific factors in the internationalization of US Internet organizations." *Journal of International Business Studies* 32, 769–791.

Kuhlmann, S. and M. von Rosing. 2010. "Achieving Performance and Value with BPM and EA Together: Applying BPM Principles to SAP EAF." BPM and Enterprise Architecture Foundation: SAP whitepaper.

Kuhlmann, S. and M. von Rosing. 2010. "Applying BPM Principles to SAP EAF." SAP whitepaper.

Kuhlmann, S. and M. von Rosing. 2010. "Applying Continuous Improvement and Governance Principles to the SAP EAF." BPM and Enterprise Architecture Foundation: SAP whitepaper.

Levitt, T. 1972. "Production-line approach to service." *Harvard Business Review.* September, 41–52.

Lee, H., K. G. Smith, and C. G. Grimm. 2003. "The effect of new product radicality and scope on the extent and speed of innovation diffusion." *Journal of Management* 29, 753–768.

Lewin, A. Y. and H. Volbverda. 1999. "Prolegomena on coevolution: A framework for research on strategy and new organizational forms." *Organization Science* 10, 519–534.

Lieberman, M. 2005. "Did First-Mover Advantage Survive the Dot-Com Crash?" Working paper, UCLA, Los Angeles.

Linz, C. 2010. "From Product Vendor Towards Solution Provider," Working paper CeTIM, München.

Linz, C. 2009c. "SOA – from buzz to business: An interview with Carsten Linz," *SAP News,* September.

Linz, C. 2009b. *Nothing Could Be Further from Customer Disorientation.* Retrieved August 28, 2009, from *http://www.computerwoche.de/software/soa-bpm/1904316/.*

Linz, C. 2009a. "From product towards solution: service orientation and solution selling." *International Journal of Interoperability in Business Information Systems* 3(2), 31–35.

Linz, C. 2001. *Corporate Group as Entrepreneurial Enterprise: Revolutionary Innovation Management in Accelerated Markets*. Gabler: Wiesbaden, Germany.

MacCormack, A., R. Verganti, and M. Iansiti. 2001. "Developing products on 'Internet time': The anatomy of a flexible development process." *Management Science* 47, 133–150.

Maddala, G. S. 1986. *Limited-Dependent and Qualitative Variables in Econometrics*. Cambridge University Press: Cambridge, UK.

Marquis, C. 2003. "The pressure of the past: Network imprinting in intercorporate communities." *Administrative Science Quarterly* 48, 655–689.

McArthur, A. W. and P. C. Nystrom. 1991. "Environmental dynamism, complexity and munificence as moderators of strategy-performance relationships." *Journal of Business Research* 23, 349–361.

McGahan, A. and M. Porter. 2002. "What do we know about variance in accounting profitability?" *Management Science* 48, 834–851.

McGrath, R. and I. MacMillan. 2000. *The Entrepreneurial Mindset*. Harvard Business School Press: Boston.

Mendelson, H. 2000. "Organizational architecture and success in the information technology industry." *Management Science* 46, 513–529.

Meyer, A. D., A. S. Tsui, and C. R. Hinings. 1993. "Guest co-editors' introduction: Configurational approaches to organizational analysis." *Academy of Management Journal* 36, 1175–1195.

Miles, R. E. and C. C. Snow. 1978. *Organization Structure, Strategy, and Process*. McGraw-Hill: New York.

Miles, R. E. and C. C. Snow. 1986. "Organizations: New concepts for new forms." *California Management Review* 28, 62–73.

Milgrom, P. R. and J. Roberts. 1992. *Economics, Organization, and Management*. Prentice-Hall: Upper Saddle River, NJ.

Miller, D. 1996. "Configurations revisited." *Strategic Management Journal* 17, 505–512.

Mirow, M. and C. Linz. 2000. "Planning and organization of innovations from a system-theoretic perspective." G. E. Häfliger and J. D. Meier (eds.). *Current Tendencies in Innovation Management*. 249–268. Physica: Heidelberg, Germany.

Mizik, N. and R. Jacobson. 2003. "Trading off between value creation and value appropriation: The financial implications of shifts in strategic emphasis." *J. Marketing* 67, 63–76.

Mullins, J. and R. Komisar. 2009. *Getting to Plan B: Breaking Through to a Better Business Model*. Harvard Business Press: Boston, MA.

Neumann, J. and O. Morgenstern. 1928: *Theory of Games and Economic Behavior*. Princeton University Press: Princeton, NJ.

Nonaka, I. and H. Takeuchi. 1995. *The Knowledge-Creating Company.* Oxford University Press: New York.

Nunnally, J. C. 1978. *Psychometric Theory.* McGraw-Hill: New York.

Nystrom, P. C. and W. H. Starbuck. 1981. *Handbook of Organizational Design.* Oxford University Press: London.

Prajogo, D.I. and M. Goh. 2007. "Operations Management activities and operational performance in service firms." *IJSTM* 8, 478–490.

Park, N. K. and J. Mezias. 2005. "Before and after the technology sector crash: Stock market response to alliances of e-commerce organizations." *Strategic Management Journal* 26, 987–1007.

Pastor, L. and P. Veronesi. 2004. "Was there a NASDAQ Bubble in the Late 1990s?" Working paper, University of Chicago: Chicago.

Peloquin, J. 2007. Next Generation ERP and the Rise of the Agile Organization. *http://www.itjungle.com/tfh/tfh011507-story03.html.*

Peppard, J. and J. Ward. 2003. *Unlocking Sustained Business Value From IT Investments*. Cranfield School of Management: UK.

Pfeffer, J. and G. R. Salancik. 1978. *The External Control of Organizations*. Harper & Row: New York.

Pine, B. J. 1992. *Mass Customization: The New Frontier in Business Competition*. Harvard Business Press: Boston, MA.

Poppo, L. and T. Zenger. 1998. "Testing alternative theories of the firm: Transaction cost, knowledge based, and measurement explanations for make-or-buy decisions in information services." *Strategic Management Journal* 19, 853–877.

Porter, M. E. 1980. *Competitive Strategy: Techniques for Analyzing Industries and Competitors*. Free Press/Macmillan: New York.

Rajgopal, S., M. Venkatachalam, and S. Kohta. 2002. "Managerial actions, stock returns, and earnings: The case of business-to-business Internet organizations." *Journal of Accounting Research* 40, 529–556.

Rajgopal, S., M. Venkatachalam, and S. Kotha. 2003. "The value relevance of network advantages: The case of e-commerce organizations." *Journal of Accounting Research* 41, 135–162.

Randolph, W. A. and G. G. Dess. 1984. "The congruence perspective of organization design: A conceptual model and multivariate research approach." *Academy of Management Reviev* 9, 114–128.

Reinartz, W., M. Krafft, and W. Hoyer. 2004. "The CRM process: Its measurement and performance." *Journal of Marketing Research* 41, 293–305.

Rindova, V. and S. Kotha. 2001. "Continuous 'morphing': Competing through dynamic competencies/capabilities, form, and function." *Academy of Management Journal* 44, 1263–1280.

Rolls Royce. 2010. Corporate Presentation. Retrieved January 11, 2010, from *http://www.rolls-royce.com/Images/2009_h1_presentation_appendices_tcm92-13336.pdf*.

Romanelli, E. 1991. "The evolution of new organizational forms." *Annual Review of Sociology* 17, 79–103.

Romme, A. G. L. 2003. "Making a difference: Organization as design." *Organization Science* 14, 558–573.

Ross, J. 2005. "Forget strategy." CISR V(3), *http://web.mit.edu/cisr/resbrfgs/2005_12_3C_OperatingModels.pdf*.

Ross J., C. Curran, and J. Chapman. 2008. "Reuse and SOA: Recalibrating Expectations." *MIT Sloan Management*. VIII, Article 3A. Retrieved from *http://web.mit.edu/cisr/resbrfgs/2008_12_3A_SOA_RossCurranChapman.pdf*.

Rumelt, R. 1987. "Theory, strategy, and entrepreneurship." In D. J. Teece (ed.), *The Competitive Challenge*, pp. 137–158. Ballinger: Cambridge, MA.

Rumelt, R. 1991. "How much does industry matter?" *Strategic Management Journal* 12, 167–185.

Scheel, H., A. Rosenberg, M. von Rosing. 2009. "The Evolution of Processes." Copenhagen Business School Press.

Schoemaker, P.J.H. and Amit, R. 1994. "Investment in Strategic Assets: Industry and Firm-Level Perspectives." *Strategic Management Journal*.

Schumpeter, J. A. 1934. *The Theory of Economic Development: An Inquiry into Profits, Capital, Credit, Interest, and the Business Cycle*. Harvard University Press: Cambridge, MA.

Shleifer, A. and R. W. Vishny. 1991. "Takeovers in the 60s and the 80s: Evidence and implications." *Strategic Management Journal* 12, 51–61.

Siemens. 2010. Next Generation Enterprise. Retrieved February 18, 2010, from *http://www.medical.siemens.com/webapp/wcs/stores/servlet/ ProductDisplay~q_catalogId~e_-1~a_catTree~e_100010,1008631,1025982,1025984 ~a_langId~e_-1~a_productId~e_191004~a_storeId~e_10001.htm*.

Silverman, B. 2001. "Organizational economics." In J. A. C. Baum (ed.), pp. 465–493. *Blackwell Companion to Organizations*. Blackwell: London.

Sorensen, J. 2002. "The strength of corporate culture and the reliability of firm performance." *Administrative Science Quarterly* 47, 70–91.

Sorenson, O. and J. Sorensen. 2001. "Finding the right mix: Franchising, organizational learning, and chain performance." *Strategic Management Journal* 22, 713–724.

Stinchcombe, A. 1965. "Social structure and organizations." J. G. March (ed.). *Handbook of Organizations*, 142–193. Rand McNally: Chicago.

Stuart, T. E., H. Hoang, and R. C. Hybels. 1999. "Interorganizational endorsements and the performance of entrepreneurial ventures." *Administrative Science Quarterly* 44, 315–349.

Surowiecki, J. 2004. *The Wisdom of Crowds: Why the Many Are Smarter Than the Few and How Collective Wisdom Shapes Business*. Doubleday: New York.

Teubner, C. 2007. *The Forrester Wave: Human-Centric BPM For Java Platforms, Q3 2009*. Forrester Research. *http://www.forrester.com/rb/Research/wave%26trade%3B_ human-centric_bpm_for_java_platforms%2C_q3/q/id/38886/t/2*.

Thompson, J. D. 1967. *Organizations in Action*. McGraw-Hill: New York.

Toffler, A.1980. *The Third Wave*. Collins: New York.

Turban, E. and L. Volonino. 2009. *Information Technology for Management*. Wiley Press.

Tushman, M. L. and P. Anderson. 1986. "Technological discontinuities and organizational environments." *Administrative Science Quarterly* 31, 439–465.

Unhelkar, B., A. Ghanbary, and H. Younessi. 2010. *Collaborative Business Process Engineering and Global Organizations: Frameworks for Service Integration*. Business Science Reference Book News, Inc.: Portland, OR.

Van de Ven, A., D. Hudson, and M. Schroeder. 1984. "Designing new business startups: Entrepreneurial, organizational, and ecological considerations." *Journal of Management* 10, 87–107.

von Hippel, E. 2006. *Democratizing Innovation*. MIT Press: Boston, MA.

Von Hippel, E. and R. Katz. 2002. "Shifting innovation to users via toolkits." *Management Science* 48, 821–833.

von Rosing, M. 2009. "Business Value Management: A Way To Plan, Create and Realize Value." IT University: Denmark. *http://www.valueteam.biz/downloads/article_value_management.pdf.* (Danish only).

von Rosing, M. 2010. "Building new levels of excellence with the right Business Performance Management framework." Copenhagen Business School Press.

von Rosing, M. and H. von Scheel. 2010. "How to Identify, Plan, Create and Realize Value." Copenhagen Business School Press: Denmark.

Wernerfelt, B. 1984. "The Resource-Based View of the Firm." *Strategic Management Journal*. 5 (2), 171–180.

Williamson, O. E. 1975. *Markets and Hierarchies: Analysis and Antitrust Implications*. The Free Press: New York.

Williamson, O. E. 1983. "Organizational innovation: The transaction cost approach." J. Ronen (ed.). *Entrepreneurship*, 101–133. Lexington Books: Lanham, MD.

Winkler, M. 2010. "Full steam ahead." *SAP Spectrum*, January, 38–40.

Zimmerman, M. A. and G. J. Zeitz. 2002. "Beyond survival: Achieving new venture growth by building legitimacy." *Academy of Management Review* 27, 414–431.

Zott, C. 2003. "Dynamic competencies/capabilities and the emergence of intra-industry differential firm performance: Insights from a simulation study." *Strategic Management Journal* 24, 97–125.

Zott, C. and R. Amit. 2005. "Business Strategy and Business Model: Extending the Strategy-Structure Performance Paradigm." Working paper, INSEAD: Fontainebleau, France.

Zott, C. and Q. Huy. 2005. "Symbolic Emphasizing: How Entrepreneurs Use Symbolism to Acquire Resources." Working paper, INSEAD: Fontainebleau, France.

Part III

APQC. 2009. APQC Process Classification Framework (PCF) – Cross Industry – PDF Version 5.1.0. Retrieved June 29, 2010, from *http://www.apqc.org/knowledge-base/documents/apqc-process-classification-framework-pcf-cross-industry-pdf-version-510*.

Austin, R. D. 1996. *Measuring and Managing Performance in Organizations.* Dorset House: New York.

Bate, R., S. Garcia, J. Armitage, K. Cusick, R. Jones, D. Kuhn, I. Minnich, H. Pierson, T. Powell, and A. Reichner. 1994. *A Systems Engineering Capability Maturity Model version 1.0.* CMU/SEI-94-HB-04. Carnegie Mellon University, Software Engineering Institute: Pittsburgh, PA.

Beer, M., R. A. Eisenstat, and B. Spector. 1990. "Why change programs don't produce change." *Harvard Business Review* November/December: 158–166.

Besselman, J. J. 1992. "A collection of software capability evaluation (SCE) findings: Many lessons learned." In *Proceedings of the Eighth Annual National Joint Conference on Software Quality and Productivity,* Arlington, VA, pp. 196–215.

Besselman, J. J., P. Byrnes, C. J. Lin, M. C. Paulk, and R. Puranik. 1993. "Software capability evaluations: Experiences from the field." *SEI Technical Review '93.*

Besselman, J. J. and S. Rifkin. 1995. "Exploiting the synergism between product line focus and software maturity." In *Proceedings of the 1995 Acquisition Research Symposium,* pp. 95–107. Washington, DC.

Boehm, B. W., C. Abts, A. W. Brown, S. Chulani, B. K. Clark, E. Horowitz, R. J. Madachy, D. Reifer, and B. Steece. 2000. *Software Cost Estimation with COCOMO II.* Prentice Hall: Upper Saddle River, NJ.

Britz, G., D. Emerling, L. Hare, R. Hoerl, and J. Shade. 1996. "Statistical Thinking." A Special Publication of the ASQC Statistics Division (spring).

Chrissis, M. B., M. D. Konrad, and S. Shrum. 2006. *CMMI: Guidelines for Process Integration and Product Improvement,* 2nd ed. Addison-Wesley: Boston, MA.

Clark, B. K. 2000. "Quantifying the effects of process improvement on effort." *IEEE Software* 17(6):65–70.

Crosby, P. B. 1979. *Quality Is Free.* McGraw-Hill: New York.

Curtis, B., W. E. Hefley, and S. Miller. 1995. *People Capability Maturity Model.* CMU/SEI-95-MM-02. Carnegie Mellon University, Software Engineering Institute: Pittsburgh, PA.

Deming, W. E. 1986. *Out of the Crisis.* MIT Center for Advanced Engineering Study: Cambridge, MA.

DOD. 1988. "Excerpts from fall 1987 Report of the defense science board task force on military software." *ACM Ada Letters* July/August:35–46.

Eijpe, R. A., C. Laar, and M. Gerritsen. 2010. Het ICASIO patroon, internal paper (Dutch only), NL for Business, Retrieved July 31, 2010, *http://master.nl4b.com:50000/irj/go/km/docs/portaldrive/het%20ICASIO%20patroon.doc.*

Emam, K. and D. R. Goldenson. 1999. An Empirical Review of Software Process Assessments. NRC/ERB-1065 (NRC 43610). National Research Council Canada, Institute for Information Tech.

Gallagher, B. P., M. Phillips, K. J. Richter, and S. Shrum. 2009. *CMMIACQ: Guidelines for Improving the Acquisition of Products and Services.* Addison-Wesley Professional: Boston.

Harter, D. E., M. S. Krishnan, and S. A. Slaughter. 2000. "Effects of process maturity on quality, cycle time, and effort in software product development." *Management Science* 46(4):451–466.

Hays, D. W. 1994. "Quality improvement and its origin in scientific management." *Quality Progress* 27(6):89–90.

Hefner, R. 1997. "Lessons learned with the systems security engineering capability maturity model." *Proceedings of the 19th International Conference on Software Engineering,* Boston, pp. 566–567.

Humphrey, W. S. 1987. *Characterizing the Software Process: A Maturity Framework.* CMU/SEI-87-TR-11. Carnegie Mellon University, Software Engineering Institute: Pittsburgh, PA.

Humphrey, W. S. and W. L. Sweet. 1987. *A Method for Assessing the Software Engineering Capability of Contractors.* CMU/SEI-87-TR-23. Carnegie Mellon University, Software Engineering Institute: Pittsburgh, PA.

Humphrey, W. S. 1988. "Characterizing the software process." *IEEE Software* 5(2):73–79.

Humphrey, W. S. 1989. *Managing the software Process.* Addison-Wesley: Reading, MA.

Humphrey, W. S. 2002. "Three process perspectives: Organizations, teams, and people." *Annals of Software Engineering* 4:39–72.

IBM Institute for Business Value Analysis. 2009. IBM Press: New York.

ISO. 2008. ISO/IEC 15504–7. *Technology: Process Assessment.* Part 7. *Assessment of Organizational Maturity.* International Organization for Standardization and International Electrotechnical Commission: Geneva, Switzerland.

Juran, J. M. 1988. *Juran on Planning for Quality.* Macmillan: New York.

Krasner, H. 2001. "Accumulating the body of evidence for the payoff of software process improvement – 1997." In *Software Process Improvement,* R. B. Hunter and R. H. Thayer (eds.), pp. 519–539. IEEE Computer Society Press: New York.

Paulk, M. C., B. Curtis, M. B. Chrissis, E. L. Averill, J. Bamberger, T. C. Kasse, M. D. Konrad, J. R. Perdue, C. V. Weber, and J. V. Withey. 1991. *Capability Maturity Model for Software.* CMU/SEI-91-TR-24. Carnegie Mellon University, Software Engineering Institute: Pittsburgh, PA.

Paulk, M. C., W. S. Humphrey, and G. J. Pandelios. 1992. "Software process assessments: Issues and lessons learned." In *Proceedings of ISQE92,* Juran Institute, March, 4B/41–58.

Paulk, M. C., B. Curtis, M. B. Chrissis, and C. V. Weber. 1993a. *Capability Maturity Model for Software, Version 1.1.* CMU/SEI-93-TR-24. Carnegie Mellon University, Software Engineering Institute: Pittsburgh, PA.

Paulk, M. C., C. V. Weber, S. M. Garcia, M. B. Chrissis, and M. W. Bush. 1993b. *Key Practices of the Capability Maturity Model, Version 1.1.* CMU/SEI-93-TR-25. Carnegie Mellon University, Software Engineering Institute: Pittsburgh, PA.

Paulk, M. C., C. V. Weber, B. Curtis, and M. B. Chrissis. 1995a. *The Capability Maturity Model: Guidelines for Improving the Software Process.* Addison-Wesley: Boston, MA.

Paulk, M. C., M. D. Konrad, and S. M. Garcia. 1995b. "CMM versus SPICE architectures." *Software Process Newsletter Spring.* IEEE Technical Committee on Software Engineering.

Paulk, M. C. 2008. *A Taxonomy for Improvement Frameworks.* 15–18. World Congress for Software Quality: Bethesda, MD.

Pfeffer, J. and R. I. Sutton. 2006. *Hard Facts, Dangerous Half-Truths, & Total Nonsense: Profiting from Evidence-Based Management.* Harvard Business School Press: Boston, MA.

Pohle, G., P. Korsten, and S. Ramamurthy. 2005. "The specialized enterprise: A fundamental redesign of firms and industries." IBM Institute for Business Value. *http://www-1.ibm.com/services/us/index.wss/ibvstudy/imc/a1009224?cntxt=a1005266.*

Porter, M. E. 1996. "What is strategy?" *Harvard Business Review.* November-December: 61–78.

Ramamurthy, S. and M. S. Robinson. 2005. "Simplify to succeed: Optimise the customer franchise and achieve operational scale: Retail financial institutions in 2005." *IBM Business Consulting Services. http://www- 8.ibm.com/services/pdf/gw510-9108-00_fs_exec.pdf.*

SAP. 2010. SAP Business Maps. Retrieved August 8, 2010, from *http://www.sap.com/solutions/businessmaps/index.epx.*

SCOR. 2008. SCOR 90 Overview Brochure. Retrieved June 29, 2010, from *http://supply-chain.org/f/SCOR%2090%20Overview%20Booklet.pdf.*

SEI. 2006. *Process Maturity Profile: Software CMM 2005 End-Year Update,* Carnegie Mellon University, Software Engineering Institute: Pittsburgh, PA.

SEI. 2007. *CMMI for Acquisition, Version 1.2.* CMU/SEI-2007-TR-017. Carnegie Mellon University, Software Engineering Institute: Pittsburgh, PA.

SEI. 2009. *CMMI for Services, Version 1.2.* CMU/SEI-2009-TR-001. Carnegie Mellon University, Software Engineering Institute: Pittsburgh, PA.

SpecJ. 2010. SPECjEnterprise2010. *http://www.spec.org/jEnterprise2010/.*

Steiner, M. 2009. *Building Extensible Composite Applications with SAP.* SAP Press: Braintree, MA.

Steiner, M. "Dynamic Duo: CAF and JPA Interplay." *http://www.sdn.sap.com/irj/scn/ weblogs?blog=/pub/wlg/16879.*

Opgenorth J., S. Volker, and P. Zimmer. 2008. TS-5748 "Composite Application Design Patterns," pp. 21-24. *http://developers.sun.com/learning/javaoneonline/j1sessn. jsp?sessn=TS-5748&yr=2008&track=soa*

Volker, S. "SAP Guideline for Best-Built Applications: One Short Sentence with Huge Implications." *http://www.sdn.sap.com/irj/scn/weblogs?blog=/pub/wlg/16224.*

Volker, S. "Take a Serious Look at the 'A' in SOA and Gain Flexible, Adaptable Architecture." *http://www.sappro.com/article.cfm?session=&id=5081.*

Volker, S. "SAP NetWeaver Composition Environment 7.2 New Feature Improves Development of Loosely Coupled SOA-Based Applications."

Walker, B. "The Guts of a New Machine." *New York Times.* November 30, 2003.

D   The Authors

Chase, Greg

▶ Director of Solution Marketing for BPM at SAP

Greg Chase is an SAP mentor and is director of solution marketing for business process management (BPM) at SAP. Greg's areas of expertise include customer use cases and solution development using a BPM approach, value engineering in a BPM context, and BPM for enterprise information management (EIM). He is responsible for working with SAP partners to create and position service offerings utilizing SAP developer technologies. Greg has been in the software industry for over 20 years at various startup companies and global leaders, including SAP and Oracle. He holds a bachelor's degree from the University of California at Davis.

Omar, Rukhshaan

▶ BPM Product Marketing Specialist

Rukhshaan (Ruks) Omar is an independent global marketing specialist responsible for industry positioning for SAP NetWeaver BPM. Ruks has compiled a comprehensive collection of industry-relevant BPM use cases based on analyzing early projects from adopters and market research. She has more than 20 years of IT experience working with leading global software vendors. She holds degrees in computer science and mathematics from the University of Durban-Westville and the University of South Africa.

Rosenberg, Ann

▶ Global Business Process Management Lead, GPMO

▶ Business Support Principal Business Add-Ons to ASAP

▶ Global KM Champion SOA Practice

▶ SAP Field Services

▶ External Lecturer, IT University of Copenhagen

▶ Leading the BPM RoundTable SAP University Alliances

▶ Vice Chairman of the Open Group Business Architect Group

As a global business process management lead at SAP and business support principal for business add-ons to ASAP in global project management organization, field services, Ann Rosenberg is responsible for the business process management, business architecture and SOA methodology, and governance frameworks that are offered and used in the SAP community globally including the ASAP business add-ons factory.

She has designed the SAP BPX certification program for associates and professionals, which is being taught globally to the SAP community, and she is the head and co-founder of the SAP Global University Alliance BPM curriculum, which is being rolled-out to 900 universities globally. Ann is also global KM champion for the SOA practice.

She is vice chair of the Open Group Business Architect Group, external lecturer in business process management at the IT University of Copenhagen, and teaching assistant at Copenhagen Business School.

Ann Rosenberg has authored the book *Business Process Management — the SAP Roadmap*.

Taylor, James

▶ CEO and Principal Consultant, Decision Management Solutions

As CEO and principal consultant at Decision Management Solutions, James works with clients to develop action-oriented, flexible, forward-looking systems that learn and adapt. With over 20 years of experience developing software, James is one of the leading experts in decision management and in the effective use of business rules and analytic technology. James founded Decision Management Solutions in 2008 and is an active consultant, trainer, keynote speaker, and blogger. The best-known proponent of the decision management approach, James has been helping create the emerging decision management market for the past eight years. James has experience at FICO, PeopleSoft R&D, and as a strategic business consultant with Ernst and Young.

James is the lead author of *Smart (Enough) Systems: How to Deliver Competitive Advantage by Automating Hidden Decisions* (Prentice Hall, 2007) with Neil Raden and has contributed chapters to *The Decision Model, The Business Rules Revolution: Doing Business the Right Way,* and *Business Intelligence Implementation: Issues and Perspectives (2006)*.

von Rosing, Mark

- ▶ Senior Lecturer, Copenhagen Business School
- ▶ Senior Lecturer, IT University, Denmark
- ▶ Managing Director, Value Team ApS

As a professor for business model management, business process management, business sustainability management, and value management, Mark lectures on both the bachelor and master's levels. Mark von Rosing is also managing director for Value Team ApS and is furthermore:

- ▶ Chair and founder of the SAP Global University Alliance Enterprise Architecture curriculum program
- ▶ Co-founder of the SAP Global University Alliance BPM curriculum program
- ▶ Member and co-developer of the Global TOGAF Business Architecture development group
- ▶ Designer and co-developer of the new SAP BPX certification program for associate and professional level
- ▶ Co-developer of the SAP LEAD Enterprise Architecture program
- ▶ Developer of the competency maturity model, developed for The Open Group (TOGAF)
- ▶ Developer of the value management approach (including the value tree)
- ▶ Author of numerous publications in the area of business model management, business process management, value management, and sustainability
- ▶ Founder of the European BPM User Group, which consists of over 200 companies (*www.openroundtable.org*)
- ▶ Recipient of IBM's prestigious Growth Award 2009/2010 for contributing as the strongest growth enabler across EMEA.

Andersen, Bettina Haven

- ▶ Student Help
- ▶ SAP Denmark

Argarwal, Manish (Chapter 8.1)

- ▶ Head of SAP Practice
- ▶ Nagarro, Inc.

Barros, Alistair (Online Articles, *SOA for Business Networks — Service Delivery Frameworks* and *A Requirements Framework for Semantic Business Process Modeling*)

▸ Global Research Leader and Entrepreneur

▸ SAP Research/ SAP Australia Pty Ltd

Betadpur, Girish (Chapter 13.1)

▸ Senior Business Processes Consultant, Business Transformation Services

▸ SAP AG

Bogaards, Ferry (Chapter 3)

▸ Consulting Director

▸ IDS Scheer

Broetzmann, Jens (Chapter 13.1)

▸ Methods and Tools Specialist

▸ SAP Netherlands

Carrera, Alberto (Chapter 9.2)

▸ BPM Project Manager

▸ Braskem S.A.

Dahl, Torben Claus (Chapter 11.2)

▸ Commander s.g., ERP Planning Branch

▸ Defense Command Denmark

Datsichin, Peter (Chapter 13.1)

▸ Principal Enterprise Architect

▸ SAP AG

Deano, Darwin (Chapter 7.1)

▸ Senior Manager

▸ Deloitte Consulting LLP

Dick, Erik (Chapter 14.1)

▸ Development Architect, SOA Infrastructure Foundation

▸ **SAP AG**

Drabant, Bernhard (Chapter 14.1)

▸ Development Architect, SOA Infrastructure

▸ SAP AG

Dreiling, Alexander (Online Article, *Business Process Management and Semantic Interoperability*)

▸ Research Program Manager, Business Process Management

▸ SAP Research/SAP Australia Pty Ltd

Drinan, Stacey (Chapter 7.2)

▸ IT Platform Area Manager

▸ Ericsson AB

Eijpe, Robert (Chapters 4, 13.2)

▸ General Manager and Cofounder of NL for Business

▸ Senior Business Process Management Consultant, Value Team Consulting

Fiegl, Patrik (Chapter 2)

▸ Chief Solution Architect; SAP Architecture and Innovation Services, SAP AG

▸ Professional Advisor, Applied Professional Studies, DePaul University

Figlin, Oleg (Chapter 15.1)

▸ Director, Global Project Management Office, SAP Field Services

▸ **SAP AG**

Fildebrandt, Ulf (Chapter 14.1)

▸ Chief Development Architect, SOA Infrastructure

▸ SAP AG

Fritzsche, Mathias (Online Article, *Process-Centric Decision Support*)

▸ Researcher, Process-centric Decision Support for BPM; Analytics, Simulation, and Optimization

▸ SAP Research, SAP AG

Gilani, Wasif (Online Article, *Process-Centric Decision Support*)

▸ Senior Researcher, Process-Centric Decision Support for BPM; Analytics, Simulation, and Optimization

▸ SAP Research, SAP UK

Gollmick, Christoph (Chapter 14.5)

▸ Development Architect/Product Owner

▸ SAP AG

Grobe, Alexander (Chapter 8.2)

▸ Manager, Enterprise Architecture and Innovation

▸ Coca-Cola Erfrischungsgetränke AG

Harezlak, Michal (Chapter 13.4.3)

▸ Principal Enterprise Architect, Business Transformation Services

▸ SAP America

Hayer, Roman (Chapter 16.5)

▸ Senior Development Architect, Technology and Innovation Platform

▸ SAP America

Heuer, Christian (Chapter 8.4)

▸ Global Head of Smart Grid

▸ Siemens IT Solutions and Services

Hilpert, Wolfgang (Chapter 14.2)

- ► Senior Vice President/Head of Product Management, Process Orchestration (BPM & ESB)
- ► Chief Product Owner, Process Orchestration
- ► SAP AG

Hirsch, Richard (Online Article, *Customer and Partner Views on the Future of BPM: A View from Two SAP Mentors*)

- ► Senior Consultant, Enterprise Portal Solutions
- ► Siemens IT Solutions and Services

Hoeliner, Raimar G. (Chapter 13.4.3)

- ► Program Delivery Manager, North American Program Delivery Enablement Office
- ► SAP Field Services

Holzmann, Alexander Friedrich (Chapter 16.7)

- ► ValuePartnerShip, Business Transformation Services
- ► SAP AG

Hoursanov, Andrey (Chapter 14.1)

- ► Development Architect, Office of CTO
- ► SAP AG

Hvass, Jan (Chapter 7.2)

- ► Manager
- ► Ecenta AG

Ittel, Jens (Chapter 14.1)

- ► Development Architect
- ► SAP AG

Jennrich, Fin (Chapter 8.4)

- ▸ Management Consultant for Smart Grid
- ▸ Siemens IT Solutions and Services

Johansen, Patrick Arendal

- ▸ Student Help
- ▸ SAP Field Services, Denmark

Jørgensen, Kim Peiter (Chapter 11.2)

- ▸ Senior Partner, Value Team ApS
- ▸ External Lecturer, IT University Copenhagen
- ▸ Assistant Lecturer, Copenhagen Business School

Kabadzhov, Nikolay (Chapter 14.1)

- ▸ Senior Developer, SOA Infrastructure
- ▸ SAP Labs Bulgaria

Keil, Ulrich (Chapter 14.1)

- ▸ Development Architect, SOA Infrastructure Foundation
- ▸ SAP AG

Kemsley, Sandy (Chapter 18.1)

- ▸ Independent Analyst
- ▸ Kemsley Design Ltd.

Klees, Frank (Chapter 16.3)

- ▸ Head of Program Management Office
- ▸ Program Director, Center for BPM-/SOA-Based Practices
- ▸ SAP AG

Kravets, Jewgeni (Chapter 9.1)

- ▶ Program Manager
- ▶ Enterprise SOA Field Services Deutschland, Österreich, Schweiz
- ▶ SAP Deutschland AG & Co. KG

Kristensen, Klaus Skov (Chapter 13.4.3)

- ▶ Senior Project Manager
- ▶ SAP Denmark

Kuhlmann, Sascha (Chapter 4)

- ▶ Director of Enterprise Architecture, Business Transformation Services
- ▶ SAP America

Laar, Caspar (Chapters 4, 13.2)

- ▶ Enterprise Architect
- ▶ NL for Business and Value Team Consulting

Linz, Carsten (Chapter 2)

- ▶ Global Head, Center for BPM-/SOA-Based Practices
- ▶ Senior Vice President
- ▶ SAP AG
- ▶ Senior Lecturer, University of St. Gallen

Markovic, Ivan (Online Article, *Semantic Technologies: An Enabler of Intelligent Business Processes*)

- ▶ Senior Researcher
- ▶ SAP Research, SAP AG

Min, Hosin (Chapter 16.6)

▸ Lead Business Architect (Business Consultant), Project Coach

▸ Value Prototyping, Center of Excellence

▸ SAP Field Services Delivery America

Morales, Gerardo (Chapter 8.1)

▸ Senior Project Manager

▸ Patrimonio Hipotecaria

Morales, Marco-Antonio (Chapter 13.3)

▸ Senior Project Manager, SAP Field Services

▸ SAP Sweden

Morris, Wayne (Chapters 7.3, 10.2)

▸ Program Director

▸ SAP America

Morrison, Rogan (Chapters 13.4, 15.1)

▸ Global Project Management Knowledge Management, GPMO

▸ Senior Project Manager, Business Add-Ons to ASAP

▸ SAP Field Services, SAP South Africa

Mørup, Ida Martinsen

▸ Student Help

▸ SAP Denmark

Müller, Gregor (Chapters 6.3, 8.2, 10.2, 16.8)

▸ Business Development Manager

▸ SAP Consulting Germany

Muno, Andreas (Chapter 10.1)

► Solution Management, Strategic IT in Public Sector

► SAP Labs LLC

Musil, Jan (Chapters 13.3, 13.4.3)

► Director, Global Project Management Office

► SAP Field Services

► SAP America

Nielsen, Jens Theodor (Chapter 11.2)

► Chief Adviser, ERP Planning Branch

► Defense Command Denmark

Onnen, Arno (Chapter 16.1)

► Global Education Portfolio Manager

► SAP Field Services, SAP AG

► External Lecturer, DHBW Mosbach

Pettiford, Owen (Chapters 8.5, 16.8)

► Co-CEO

► CompriseIT

Picht, Michael (Online Article, *Process-Centric Decision Support*)

► Development Project Manager

► SAP On-Premise Manufacturing Industries Platform

► SAP AG

Pfeiffer, Ingo (Chapter 13.3)

► Senior Business Transformation Consultant and Project Manager

► SAP Field Services Sweden

Pratt, Marilyn (Chapter 16.9)

▸ Community Advocate, SAP Community Network

▸ Global Ecosystem and Partner Group

▸ SAP AG

Prickril, Greg (Chapter 18.2)

▸ Lead Product Designer, SAP NetWeaver Composition Environment

▸ SAP NetWeaver SOA & BPM

▸ SAP AG

Reinecke, Hans Ludwig (Chapter 8.3)

▸ SAP Manager

▸ GISA GmbH

Rittinghaus, Steve (Chapters 15.1.2, 16.4)

▸ Senior Project Manager, Business Transformation Services

▸ SAP AG

Roeleven, Sven (Chapters 13.3, 13.4.3)

▸ Head of BPM Solutions, The Netherlands

▸ IDS Scheer

Santa Rita, Marcelo (Chapter 9.2)

▸ Director de Soluções SAP NW

▸ FirsTeam Consulting

Simeonov, Emil (Chapter 14.1)

▸ Development Architect, SOA Infrastructure Foundation

▸ SAP Labs Bulgaria

Steiner, Matthias (Chapter 14.1)

▶ Principal Solution Architect, Custom Development

▶ SAP AG

Stiehl, Volker (Chapter 14.1)

▶ Product Management SAP NetWeaver Process Integration

▶ SAP AG

Subbarao, Raghavendra (Rao) (Chapter 11.1)

▶ Global Head, SAP Platform Architecture, Hospira

▶ Chair, Business Process Architecture SIG, ASUG

Tatarova, Penka (Chapter 14.1)

▶ Development Architect, SOA Infrastructure Foundation

▶ SAP Labs Bulgaria

van den Broek, Twan (Online Article, *Customer and Partner Views on the Future of BPM: A View from Two SAP Mentors*)

▶ Principal Consultant

▶ CIBER NL

Vasudevan, Kesavaprakash (Chapter 14.1)

▶ Development Architect, SOA Integration and Orchestration

▶ SAP AG

Vatkov, Bogdan (Chapter 14.1)

▶ Development Architect, SOA Infrastructure Foundation

▶ SAP Labs Bulgaria

Volmering, Thomas (Chapter 14.2)

▶ Vice President

▶ Product Management SOA Composition

▶ SAP AG

von Gloeden, Volker (Chapter 13.3)

▶ Platinum Support Consultant

▶ SAP AG

von Scheel, Henrik (Chapter 13.2)

▶ Vice President

▶ IBM Software Group, North East Europe

Wagner, Oktavian (Chapter 7.3)

▶ M&A Business Process and Application Migration Lead

▶ SAP Global IT, SAP AG

Weber, Ingo (Online Article, *A Requirements Framework for Semantic Business Process Modeling*)

▶ Senior Research Associate, School of Computer Science & Engineering

▶ The University of New South Wales

Wiffen, Graham (Chapter 8.5)

▶ SAP Practice Manager

▶ RS Components

Ziegler, Carsten (Chapter 14.4)

▶ Chief Product Owner, Development Manager BRFplus

▶ Business Rules Evangelist

▶ SAP AG

Index

A

A2A, 307
ABAP, 304, 370, 514, 529, 546
 objects API, 516
 technology, 551
ABAP-based business applications, 530
Abbreviations, 240
Accelerated transformation, 300
Account executive, 546, 547
Accurate communication, 71
ACR form, 191
Ad hoc collaboration, 620, 622
Adobe Document Services, 305
Adobe Forms, 170
Advanced planning, 237
Agile companies, 86
Agile methodology, 341
Agile techniques and practices, 399
Air compressors, 197
Aliases, 532, 535
Allied Electronics, 190
Annual business planning process, 172
Apple Computer's business model, 309
Application management tasks, 383
Application Migration Team, 151
Approver, 546
Appstores, 631
A priori, 622
Architectural blueprint, 302
Architecture, 570
 lifecycle, 110
ARIS, 242, 286
 house, 244
 license management process, 243
 methods and conventions for process design, 243
 SAP Solution Manager integration standards, 243
 Release Cycle Management, 243
 training, 242
Artificial intelligence research, 632

Arvato AG, 65
 Lead Logistics Services, 64, 65, 67
ASAP, 100, 119, 306
 ASAP 7, 105
 BPM/SOA-based business add-ons, 393
 business add-on concept, 387, 400
 business add-on for agile, 306, 400, 401, 403
 business add-ons, 387, 389
 core methodology, 359
 cycle approach, 403
 implementation content business add-ons, 554
 implementation methodology, 339
 implementation roadmap, 388
 methodology, 202, 212, 301, 387, 399, 401
 methodology and governance business add-ons, 393
 Methodology for Implementation, 392
 Roadmap, 344, 363, 379
 Roadmap 7.0, 339
As-is process, 143, 151, 153, 165, 191, 199
Assortment planning, 395

B

B2B, 195, 307
 applications, 631
Backend application, 201, 531
Background, 142, 150, 164, 190, 198
Balancing, 282
Banking solution, 164
Basis group, 307
Batch input, 370
BDoc, 370
Bertelsmann Group, 65
Best Practices, 370
BISA (Business Intelligence Solution Accelerator) methodology, 339

BPM, 21, 73, 96, 106, 233, 619
  adoption, 123
  based orchestration, 133
  Center of Expertise (CoE), 246, 274
  competency, 125
  field, 632
  Future Outlook, 615
  implementation, 123
  initiatives, 112
  journey, 236
  method approach, 114
  methodology, 205
  methods and tools, 199
  principles and disciplines, 110
  process flows, 203
  (process lifecycle) principles, 111
  project, 176, 427
  Roadmap, 248
  solution, 143, 154, 174, 191
  suites (BPMS), 271
  task force, 274
  technologies, 297
  tool, 171, 426
  tooling, 565
Business Process Modeling Notation (BPMN),
176, 186, 194, 203, 226, 335, 620
  artifact, 427
  compliant process modeler, 138
  diagram, 424
  modeling, 115
  process, 234
  process models, 175
BPMS, 286
  task force, 287
BPX, 565, 574
Braskem S.A., 205
  BPM payment process, 211
  process transformation program, 214
Brazilian petrochemical industry, 206
BRFplus, 201, 203, 513, 514, 515, 524, 527,
528, 529, 543, 545
BRM, 145, 147, 158
  decision tables, 211
BRMS, 498, 529
Build, 300
Business add-on to ASAP agile methodology,
399

Business analysts, 530
Business architecture, 105, 108, 110, 117, 236
Business blueprint, 115, 353
Business blueprint phase, 359, 362
Business case, 142, 145, 164, 190, 198
Business competencies, 46, 243
Business competency development vision/
roadmap, 50
Business configuration sets (BC sets), 403
Business governance, 251, 262
Business innovation and transformation, 46,
55
Business intelligence reports, 257
Business intelligence systems, 131
Business-IT alignment, 52, 74, 80, 108
Business logic implementation, 443
Business model, 28, 35, 252, 308, 327
  analysis, 319
  approach, 38
  design, 40
  improvement and optimization, 314
  innovation, 31, 33
  innovation and transformation, 26, 55
Business modeling, 49, 251, 316, 319
Business model management (BMM), 257,
337
Business networks, 58
BusinessObjects, 151
Business performance indicator (BPI), 271
Business practices, 622
Business process, 114, 151, 321, 619
  expert, 249, 568, 570, 572
  hierarchy, 322, 382
  improvement, 367, 368, 369
  management, 185, 198, 206, 235, 249,
  250, 257, 266, 356, 634, 635
Business Process Management
  The SAP Roadmap, 57
Business process management (BPM), 21, 74,
105, 106, 117
  principles, 311
Business process map, 348
Business process modeling, 632
Business process monitoring, 367
Business process operations support, 382
Business process optimization, 367
Business process requirements, 112

Business process stabilization, 367
Business process stabilization and improvement, 369
Business process structure continuum, 620
Business process transformation, 253
Business Rule Framework plus, 513
Business rules, 141, 143, 147, 530, 531
   maintenance, 499
   management, 198
   management system, 494, 498, 503, 511
   system artifact(s), 506
Business scenario design, 348
Business services, 202
   networks, 57
Business-to-IT linchpin, 71
Business transformation project, 138
Business value identification, 206

C

CAF BO, 463
Canonical data models, 241
CBM approach, 40
CCE AG, 172, 174
CE landscape, 420
Center of excellence (CoE), 385
CFO, 626
Change management, 110
   experts, 568
   process, 511
CIO, 597
Cloud computing, 76
CMDB, 250
Coca-Cola GmbH, 172
CoE model, 246
CoE organization, 246
Cohesion, 49
Coke One, 172, 178
   template, 175
Combine, 76
Commoditization of products, 86
Communities, 604
Competency of the business model, 47
Competitive advantage, 318
Compliance solutions, 528
Component Business Model (CBM), 40

Components development, 40
Components of a business model, 36
Composite application, 433, 463, 470, 531
Composite designer, 417, 427
Composite in a Day workshop, 600
CompriseIT, 189, 191, 194
Consumer products, 162
Continuous improvement, 117
Co-opetition, 59
Core business, 266
   competency innovation and transformation, 56
Core competitiveness, 53
Core differentiation, 53
Corporate management, 292
Corporate merger, 620
Corrective maintenance process, 231
Create a flow ruleset, 531
Create aliases, 531
Create a rule flow, 531
Create a rule script, 531
Create a ruleset, 531
Create business rules vocabulary, 531
Create decision tables, 531
Create definitions, 531
Create enumerations, 531
Create rules, 531
Critical core competencies (CCCs), 31
Critical success factor (CSF), 52, 89, 100, 271, 321
CTS, 516
Cultivating Communities of Practice, 249
Customer-centric business networks, 79
Customer-facing environment, 512
Customer-focused business competency innovation and transformation, 56
Customer satisfaction, 199
Customer service, 546

D

Danish Armed Forces, 253
Danish Defense, 251
Danish Defense value driver model, 262
Data Dictionary, 518
Data governance, 135

Decisioning, 512
Decisioning approach, 511
Decisions, 480, 492
    service, 494
    service design, 499
Defense industry, 251
Defense organizations, 252
Define value drivers, 243
Definitions, 532, 535
Deloitte, 138
Designers of business processes, 632
Development components (DC), 430
Development group, 307
Development infrastructure (NWDI), 189
Documentation, 549
Dot com era, 33
Due diligence stage, 623
Dunn & Bradstreet, 155

E

EA, 107, 247
    governance and strategy frameworks, 341
    metamodel, 112
    vision, 108
EAI, 195
Ecenta AG, 146
Eclipse environment, 417
Economical negotiation, 199
EDI, 191, 195
Efficiency, 199
Electrical engineering and electronics, 184
Electrocomponents plc, 190
Emergency maintenance, 199, 200
End-result-orientated solution paradigm, 59
End-to-end, 142, 163
    operations, 206
    processes, 131
    process integration, 178
End user, 146, 167, 635
eNOVI, 210
Enterprise application integration layer, 195
Enterprise architects, 568, 572, 597
Enterprise-architectural methodologies, 107

Enterprise architecture, 73, 105, 106, 107,
117, 235, 236, 240
    CoE, 248
    framework, 110, 111, 573
    practice, 246
Enterprise asset management, 546
Enterprise business model, 26
    innovation and transformation, 26
Enterprise information management (EIM),
128
Enterprise IT architecture, 146
Enterprise JavaBeans (EJBs), 442
Enterprise portal, 147
Enterprise primary processes, 324
Enterprise resource planning, 70
Enterprise resource planning (ERP) solution,
266
Enterprise service bus, 586
Enterprise service orientation, 55
Enterprise services, 198, 415, 545, 546, 547,
549
Enterprise Services Repository, 175, 234, 302,
303, 304
Enterprise SOA Experience Workshop, 305
Enterprise SOA governance, 597
Enumerations, 532
EPC, 202
Ericsson, 141
ERP, 148, 175, 203, 209, 229
    landscape, 223
    paradigm, 75
    system, 211, 228, 233
ES Repository, 171
ES Workplace, 548
ES Workplace systems, 549
Execution, 74

F

Facebook, 58
Fast translation, 71
Federal Enterprise Architecture Framework
(FEAF), 108
Final preparation phase, 377
Final Price, 518
Financial processes, 163, 164

Financial services, 161
Flat file, 370
Flexible IT solutions, 114
Flexible skeleton, 74
Flow-oriented modeling technique, 424
Flow ruleset, 529, 535
FOVISSSTE, 165, 167, 169, 170, 171
    process, 164
Framework for organizing competencies, 49
Full structured processes, 621
Function-oriented enterprise, 56, 60

G

Gartner EA method, 247
Gartner (formerly the Meta Framework), 108
Generic acute-care, 236
GIS, 180
    systems, 182
GISA GmbH, 179
Globalization, 141
Global master data management, 144, 150
Goal-oriented processes, 621
Go-live support phase, 378
Governance, 106
    model for operations, 383
    processes, 511
Governance, risk, and compliance (GRC)
    management, 253
Governmental-thinking organization, 255
Grid Asset Management Suite (GAMS), 186
Grid assets, 184
Grid operators, 184

H

Hewlett Packard, 66
Hewlett Packard Managed Printing Solutions, 64, 67
High tech, 163
Holistic approach, 337, 383
Holistic business model approach, 39
Holistic solution, 64
Hospira, 235

Hospira Information Technology, 237
HR, 229
    system, 228, 233
Human capital management, 546

I

IBM, 146, 621
ICASIO pattern, 328, 332
Identification of value opportunities, 319
Identify performance parameters, 243
IDES, 222
ID mapping, 463
IDoc, 370
IDS Scheer, 199, 371
Industry model innovation, 26
Industry-specific IT solutions, 184
Information architecture, 105, 236
Information technology, 56, 108
Information technology systems, 108
Integrated change control, 342
Integrated infusion therapy, 236
Integrated payment process, 214
Intellectual capital (IC), 88
Internet-enabled networked markets, 59
Inventory management, 546
Inventory planning, 189
INVISTA, 136
IO structure-conduct-performance framework, 23
IS-Banking, 169
IT, 146, 150, 151, 194, 204
    alignment, 108
    backend systems, 336
    department, 135
    domain, 107
    enablement, 118
    environment, 498
    flexibility, 108
    infrastructure, 55
    landscape, 398, 572
    market, 21
    process, and outsourcing supplier, 179
    IT-related consulting services, 179
    solution, 111, 112, 335
    strategy, 359

J

Java, 546
 coding, 440
 EE frameworks (EJB, JSP/JSF), 415
 EE standards, 457
 Persistence API, 175
 Web Dynpro, 175
JEE application, 531
JMS messaging, 469
JMS queue, 195
JPA Persistence Manager, 457
Just-in-time, 199

K

KAESER KOMPRESSOREN, 197
Key performance indicators (KPIs), 52, 89,
100, 143, 166, 167, 185, 204, 272, 368, 635
Knowledge management (KM), 414
Knowledge workers, 622, 624
KPI tracking, 211

L

Leading artifact, 422
Lead times, 190
Learning program, 568
Legacy systems, 237
Legal review, 623
Less end-user training, 178
Lightweight portal, 175
List of enterprise services, 549
LM Wind Power, 404
Logistics planning, 199
Lombardi, 621
Long-term competitive advantage, 21
Loose coupling, 48
Lotus, 171, 621
Lotus Notes, 165

M

M&A, 158
Maintenance department, 218
Maintenance engineer, 547
Maintenance manager dashboard, 219
Maintenance planer, 231
Maintenance system, 232
Make offer stage, 623
Management discipline, 251, 270
Management of issues, 342
Management processes, 324
Managing business rules, 494
Manufacturing, 546
Mass customization, 63
Master data, 142, 201
Master data maintenance, 561
Master data management, 136, 148
Master data processes, 141
Mayne Pharma, 237
MDM, 144, 146, 148
 governance process, 135
 solution, 140
Measurement of process cycle times, 208
Medication management systems, 236
Metamodel, 111
Microsoft, 621
Microsoft Navision, 266
Microsoft .NET, 171
MIRO transaction, 211
Mobile communication, 142
Mobile workflow approval, 370, 561
Model-driven architecture (MDA) tools, 452
Model-driven development, 414
Model-driven process tools, 204
Modeled business processes, 531
Modeling, 74
Modern governmental organization, 255
Mortgage bank, 163

N

Nagarro, 166
NetWeaver, 628

Networked economy, 59
Networked markets, 59
New ASAP Methodology for Implementation, 339
Nimble IT, 76
Non-core competencies (NNCs), 52
Non-SAP applications, 163
Non-SAP system, 148
NW BRM, 545

O

Object Management group, 247
OCM expert, 574
OCR process, 214
Open Group Architecture Framework (TOGAF), 107
Operational business processes, 135
Operational model, 106
OPEX, 187
Optimization, 237
Organizational roles, 243
Organization business model, 25
Outline-like experience, 625
Overall governance process, 511

P

Parameterization, 493
Part replacement, 625
  monitoring, 626
  template, 625
Patrimonio Hipotecaria, 163
Payment process, 214
Performance and real sustainable value, 86
Performance and value management, 87
Performance heterogeneity, 23
Performance improvement, 101
Performance management, 110, 251
Petrochemical, 206
Plan, 300
Planned maintenance, 199
Portfolio management, 292
Postmerger data, 150

Postmerger data migration, 150
Postmerger integration, 150
Power users, 635
Power vendors, 621
PPM, 173, 174
Practices, 620
Price calculation, 518
PRINCE2, 292
Private sector solutions, 221
Problem classification, 199
Process, 619
  alignment, 117
  architecture, 236
  automation, 141, 164
  choices, 309
  composer DC, 431
  deployment, 258
  flow, 198
  governance, 327
  governance framework, 243
  harmonization, 339
  implementation, 258
  initiator, 547
  integration content, 302
  management, 235, 252, 258
  mapping framework, 572
  maturity assessment, 572
  modeling, 465
  optimization, harmonization, and standardization, 310
  owner, 284
  ownership, 572
  parameters, 243
  performance, 90
  redesign, 209
Process-centric IT lifecycle management, 77, 84
Process-centric organization, 236
Process management lifecycle (PML), 111
Process performance indicator (PPI), 100, 101, 274, 371
Process performance measurement, 572
Procurement, 546
Procurement Excellence Project (PEP), 136
Productive solution, 381
Program management, 292
Project flexibility, 389

Project management plan, 342
Project managers, 571
Project preparation phase, 401
Promotion management for retail, 395
Promotion project manager, 173
Prosumerism, 59
Public administration, 217
Public sector, 217
Purchase orders, 175
Purchaser, 546

Q

qRFC, 370
Quality management, 546
Quality of service, 241

R

RACI, 329
  model, 331
Radiospares, 190
Ramp-up, 203
Real estate development sector, 164
Real estate management, 546
Realization phase, 360
Release management process, 511
Requester, 546
Resource-based view, 24
Return on investment, 368
RFC, 516
RFC-enabled function modules, 516
Risk, 528
Risk management, 528
ROI measurement, 241
Rolls Royce Total Care, 64, 67
RS Components, 189, 194
Rule lifecycle, 510
Rule management, 495
Rules composer, 529
Rules composition, 514
Rules engine, 514
Rulesets, 495, 529, 533
Rules repository, 514

S

SAP, 150, 199, 201
SAP 12sprints, 625
SAP Advanced Metering Infrastructure, 528
SAP APO, 370
SAP Basis software, 514
SAP best insight, 322
SAP Best Practices, 341
SAP Best Practices, Own Practice, and Best
Insight, 342
SAP BPM, 236, 248
SAP BRM, 168
SAP business applications, 182
SAP Business ByDesign, 513, 514, 528
SAP Business ByDesign HR module, 528
SAP BusinessObjects, 390
  Data Services, 158
  Governance, 528
SAP business process platform, 300
SAP Business Rules, 545
SAP Business Suite, 166, 179, 514, 577, 628
  applications, 161
  Best Practices, 553
SAP business warehouse, 142
SAP CAF, 450
  application, 440
  business object, 423
SAP-centric business and IT environment, 20,
297, 413, 553
SAP certification, 569
SAP Composite Application Framework (CAF),
416, 442
SAP Consulting, 576
SAP core applications, 125
SAP CRM, 370, 528, 549
  Loyalty Management, 528
  Territory Management, 528
SAP customer base, 123
SAP Customer Relationship Management, 157
SAP ECC, 171, 237
SAP EcoHub, 394, 399, 559, 562
SAP enterprise modeling applications, 396
SAP enterprise modeling applications by IDS
Scheer, 398, 399
SAP enterprise services, 221, 456

SAP ERP, 137, 148, 157, 175, 180, 194, 202, 370, 528, 549
SAP ERP system, 221, 285
SAP for Automotive, 370
SAP for Banking, 162, 163, 370
SAP for Oil and Gas, 212
SAP for Retail, 370
SAP for Utilities, 181, 370
SAP HR, 265
SAP implementation project, 388
SAP implementations, 339
SAP IS-Banking, 163
SAP BPX community, 576
SAP BRMS offerings, 544
SAP Change and Transport System, 516
SAP Enterprise Services Workplace site, 545, 548
SAP ASAP Implementation Methodology, 105
SAP IT, 125, 158
SAP IT Business Process and Application Migration team, 158
SAP landscape, 126, 158, 170, 195
SAP Master Data Governance, 528
SAP NetWeaver, 163, 166, 171, 178, 205, 514, 549
    Administrator, 302
    Application Server, 514
SAP NetWeaver BI, 414
SAP NetWeaver BPM, 125, 140, 148, 161, 162, 168, 201, 221, 234, 421, 438
SAP NetWeaver BPM and SAP NetWeaver BRM 7.2, 411
SAP NetWeaver BPM approach, 244
SAP NetWeaver BPM model, 461
SAP NetWeaver BPM processes, 221, 441
SAP NetWeaver BRM, 147, 148, 149, 179, 202, 413, 513, 529
SAP NetWeaver Business Process Management, 125, 144, 158, 163, 175, 202, 207, 305, 530, 621
SAP NetWeaver Business Warehouse, 175, 194, 237
SAP NetWeaver CE, 126, 158, 413, 426, 445, 461, 468, 550
SAP NetWeaver CE 7.1, 203
SAP NetWeaver CE 7.11, 423
SAP NetWeaver CE 7.20, 423

SAP NetWeaver CE frameworks, 435
SAP NetWeaver Composition Environment, 158, 166, 179, 181, 202, 237, 361, 413, 414, 513, 529, 543, 544
SAP NetWeaver Developer Studio (NWDS), 188, 551
SAP NetWeaver Development Infrastructure, 302, 414
SAP NetWeaver SOA, 545
SAP NetWeaver Java stack, 414
SAP NetWeaver Master Data Management (MDM), 128, 146
SAP NetWeaver PI, 148, 214, 237
SAP NetWeaver Portal, 144, 226, 237, 414
SAP NetWeaver Process Integration, 147, 304, 370, 438
SAP NetWeaver Technologies, 250
SAP NetWeaver Technology Platform, 185
SAP NetWeaver Visual Composer, 546
SAP own practices, 323
SAP point of sale, 555
SAP Portals, 170
SAP processes and process framework (APQC) alignment, 243
SAP PS module, 291
SAP Rapid Deployment solutions, 562
SAP Records Management, 180
SAP SCM, 549
SAP Service Marketplace, 389, 399, 430, 559, 562
SAP SOA Implementation Roadmap, 212
SAP Social Services Management for Public Sector, 528
SAP solution, 341
SAP Solution Composer, 188
SAP Solution Manager, 237, 286, 353, 363, 381, 389, 559, 562
SAP SRM, 370, 549
SAP Supply Chain Management, 625
SAP systems, 136, 209
SAP Trade Promotion Management, 178
SAP Transportation Management, 528
SAP University Alliances, 565, 574
SAP Value Academy program, 207
SAP ValuePartnerShip Service (VPS), 600
SAP Web Dynpro, 226
SCM, 546

SCM system, 228, 229
Scrum, 126, 400
   agile methodology, 194
SDN, 549
Security and access management standards,
243
Semantically correct sequencing, 632
Semantic business processes, 632
Semantics of Business Vocabulary and
Business Rules, 506
Semantic technologies, 632
Service and process automation, 68
Service Composer, 450, 455
Service consumption, 304
Service delivery, 199
Service delivery framework (SDF), 631
Service-driven enterprises, 59
Service interfaces, 302
Service-level agreement (SLA), 60, 376
Service-oriented architecture (SOA), 55, 105,
117, 168, 185, 206, 300, 336, 383, 463, 545,
579
Service-oriented architecture methodology,
339
Service-oriented architecture (SOA)
implications, 359
Service-oriented enterprise, 55, 56, 59, 67, 70
Service-oriented enterprise paradigm, 79
Service provisioning, 304
Service Registry, 171, 302
Service technician, 200
Shared services center, 209
Shareholder activism, 86
Siemens IT Solutions and Services, 184
Simple sample, 545, 552
Simple sample applications, 546
SLA, 60, 62, 68, 69
SLA commitment, 63
SME segment, 631
SNP Master Data Cockpit, 562
SOA, 232, 308, 572
SOA-based, 302
SOA-based applications, 162
SOA-based processes, 84
SOA capabilities, 115
SOA CIO Guide, 582, 598

SOA considerations, 351
SOA design time governance, 234
SOA-enabled business services, 57
SOA environments, 469
SOA implementation, 350
SOA implementation projects, 301
SOA kit, 579, 598
SOA landscape, 469
SOA methodology, 301
SOA paradigm, 553
SOA perspective, 115
SOA principle, 464
SOA process pattern, 586, 588
SOA strategy and governance, 409, 555
SOA work packages, 372
Social BPM, 636
Soft skills, 568
Software AG, 242
Software component archive, 551
Software component (SC), 430
Software lifecycle management, 189
Solar_Eval, 382
Solution architecture, 158, 170, 195
Solution Manager, 399
Solution transformation, 111, 201
Solution transformation design, 347
Source code file (SCA), 549
Sourcing Workbench, 148
Spreadsheets, 621
SRM system, 233
Stage items, 623
Standard application, 201
Standard attribute change request, 191
Standard & Poor, 163
Starter Kit for Business Process Management,
576
Strategic alignment of business and IT, 119
Strategic asset management, 184
Strategic business objectives (SBOs), 52, 271
Strategic competitiveness, 29
Strategic differentiators, 319
Strategic Grid Management, 185, 186
Strategic link
   business model, 243
Supplier-focused competency process
innovation and transformation, 56

Supplier master data, 146
Supplier master data governance, 141
Supplier performance management, 189
Suppliers, 190
Supply chain, 189, 191
Supply chain collaboration, 189
Supporting processes, 324
SWB, 148

T

Tangible business benefits, 326
TCCC, 171, 172
TCO, 178, 201
T&D companies, 185
Technical governance, 303
Technical solution management, 359
Technology architects, 568
Technology architecture, 105
Technology platform, 164
Telecommunications equipment, 142
Test data, 549
Testing SAP NetWeaver Business Process
Management, 145
Test rules, 531
Thermoplastic resins, 206
The SAP Roadmap, 236, 248
Time to market, 164
To-be process, 199
TOGAF, 111
    architectural domains, 244
    Framework Enterprise Architecture
    methods, 247
Total cost of ownership, 204
Train-the-trainer, 169
Transactional data migration, 158
Transformation design, 114
Transformation roadmap, 328
Transition process, 114
Translation framework, 69
Transparency, 199
tRFC, 370
Twitter, 58, 560

U

UI Paradigms, 624
UI technologies, 421
Universal Worklist, 170
Up-front shipment, 199
Upstream-downstream processes, 238
User-centric entity, 623
User interface mock ups, 175
User interface screens, 302
Utilities, 127, 162
Utilities sector, 179
UWL, 550

V

Value-added chain diagrams, 324
Value-based approach, 346
Value-based management, 271
Value-based solution design, 346
Value chain, 199
Value creating processes and performance, 88
Value creation, 101, 117
Value creation coordination, 61
Value delivery, 346
    principles, 339
Value determination, 347
Value driver field, 267
Value driver model, 292
Value drivers, 88
Value engineering, 199
Value engineering approach, 197
Value lifecycle, 87
    inputs, 100
    manager tool, 207
Value management, 105, 106, 110, 117, 251
    disciplines, 107
    organization, 408
    perspective, 114
Value planning, 100
Value prototyping, 150, 598
Value Prototyping team, 158
Value realization gaps, 320
Vendor, 625

Vendor and bank data migration, 158
Vertically focused entities, 60

W

Web Dynpro, 157, 158, 166, 167, 169, 170,
302, 305, 417, 441, 514, 546
Web Dynpro programming, 212
WebGUI, 549, 551

Web service, 516, 531
Workflow, 147, 165
Writing business rules, 499

Z

Zachman Framework for Enterprise
Architectures, 107

Explains the support offering, including concepts, services, and tools

Details SAP standards for solution operations, Run SAP, and Customer COE

New coverage of measurement platform and customer experience reports

Gerhard Oswald, Uwe Hommel

SAP Enterprise Support

ASAP to Run SAP

This book provides IT managers and decision makers with a detailed guide to SAP Enterprise Support. The book begins by explaining why Enterprise Support was introduced, and then details the concrete benefits and concept of Enterprise Support. It teaches you how and why to use Enterprise Support and covers the new services that have been included in the portfolio. This is the one book you need to really understand what SAP Enterprise Support can do for your organization. This 2nd edition has been updated and significantly extended. New topics include the KPI measurement platform, the updated SAP Solution Manager strategy, and everything you need to know about choosing between different support models.

371 pp., 2010, 59,95 Euro / US$ 59.95
ISBN 978-1-59229-349-0

>> www.sap-press.com

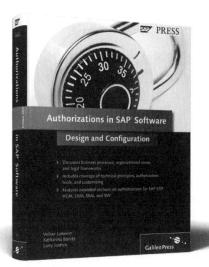

Explains the business, organizational, and legal framework requirements for authorizations

Provides an overview of the technical fundamentals and customization of authorizations in SAP

Includes chapters on authorizations in Web UIs and SAP BusinessObjects Access Control

Volker Lehnert, Katharina Bonitz, Larry Justice

Authorizations in SAP Software: Design and Configuration

This book gives you a practical and comprehensive overview of the design and management of authorizations in SAP. You'll learn how to develop a meaningful authorization concept that meets statutory requirements and is tailored to your business processes and how those processes are implemented as authorizations in your SAP system. In addition you'll gain insight into which tools and functions of the change management process in SAP play a role in designing and implementing an authorizations concept, and learn about SAP NetWeaver IdM, CUA, SAP Business Objects Access Control, and the UME. Finally, you'll discover how to implement an authorizations concept in various other SAP applications and components (SAP ERP, HCM, CRM, SRM, and BW).

684 pp., 2010, 79,95 Euro / US$ 79.95
ISBN 978-1-59229-342-1

>> www.sap-press.com

Setting up and performing functional and stress tests

Detailed description of eCATT, SAP Solution Manager, SAP TDMS, SAP Quality Center by HP, and more

Including extensive real-life examples from well-known SAP customers

Markus Helfen, Hans Martin Trauthwein

Testing SAP Solutions

This complete guide to test planning and test execution answers all of your questions. Not only will you learn the basics for a test strategy and a test methodology that fits the requirements of your solution, you will also understand functionality and usage of all the tools SAP and their partners provide for testing: Extensive, practical chapters on the most important tools, SAP Solution Manager and eCATT, as well as substantial introductions to TDMS, HP Quality Center, and SAP LoadRunner show exactly how to perform functional and performance tests. In addition, for each tool you'll find a real-life project report from a renowned SAP customer. For this second edition, the book has been thoroughly revised and extended by more than 350 pages. New topics include SAP TAO, HP Quality Center, RunSAP, and SOA testing.

approx. 728 pp., 2. edition, 79,95 Euro / US$ 79.95
ISBN 978-1-59229-366-7, Dec 2010

>> www.sap-press.com